ENTANGLEMENTS

SUNY series in American Philosophy and Cultural Thought

Randall E. Auxier and John R. Shook, editors

ENTANGLEMENTS

A System of Philosophy

CRISPIN SARTWELL

SUNY PRESS

Published by
STATE UNIVERSITY OF NEW YORK PRESS, ALBANY

© 2017 State University of New York

All rights reserved

Printed in the United States of America

No part of this book may be used or reproduced in any manner whatsoever without written permission. No part of this book may be stored in a retrieval system or transmitted in any form or by any means including electronic, electrostatic, magnetic tape, mechanical, photocopying, recording, or otherwise without the prior permission in writing of the publisher.

For information, contact
STATE UNIVERSITY OF NEW YORK PRESS, ALBANY, NY
www.sunypress.edu

Production, Laurie D. Searl
Marketing, Anne M. Valentine

Library of Congress Cataloging-in-Publication Data

Names: Sartwell, Crispin, 1958– author.
Title: Entanglements : a system of philosophy / Crispin Sartwell.
Description: Albany, NY : State University of New York, 2017. | Series: SUNY series in American philosophy and cultural thought | Includes bibliographical references and index.
Identifiers: LCCN 2016031446 (print) | LCCN 2017000564 (ebook) | ISBN 9781438463872 (hardcover : alk. paper) | ISBN 9781438463889 (pbk. : alk. paper) | ISBN 9781438463896 (e-book)
Subjects: LCSH: Philosophy, American. | Philosophy, Modern.
Classification: LCC B851 .S27 2017 (print) | LCC B851 (ebook) | DDC 191—dc23
LC record available at https://lccn.loc.gov/2016031446

10 9 8 7 6 5 4 3 2 1

What we know is a point to what we do not know. The first questions are still to be asked. Let any man bestow a thought on himself, how he came hither, and whither he tends, and he will find that all literature, all the philosophy that is on record, have done little to dull the edge of inquiry.

—Ralph Waldo Emerson

No ideas but in things.

—William Carlos Williams

Contents

I. First Philosophy: Reality, Truth, and Knowledge

Introduction: The Universe in Brief	3
1. Ontology	29
2. Theory of Truth	81
3. Epistemology	121

II. Axiology: Goodness, Beauty, and Liberty

Introduction: Values as Situations	193
4. Ethics	203
5. Aesthetics	291
6. Political Philosophy	337
Conclusion	389
Notes	391
Index	405

PART I

First Philosophy: Reality, Truth, and Knowledge

Introduction

The Universe in Brief

Here's how to think about the universe. It's a skein, fabric, or—better—tangle, like rough twine tied and twisted together back and forth in snarls. It's a mess, not a grid. There are many strings, or perhaps there is a single string, forming something like a fabric at a distance, consisting of myriad knots closer up. Each knot is an individual and each individual a knot; it has a distinct form and location and physical composition. Each knot consists, without remainder, of string connecting it to other nodes of the skein; each individual is itself only as and in relation. Different points of view on the skein produce different perspectives, so that at a wider angle larger structures emerge; nevertheless, the skein itself does not depend from any point of view, interpretation, or description, though such things as these are actually themselves part of the skein. The tangle is continually being deformed, as though one person were holding it on each side and each was performing a random set of up-and-down and side-to-side motions, so knots keep coming undone, new tangles emerge, and so on. And the whole thing is fraying and disintegrating.

It's true that "the fabric of reality" is an old saw or the merest cliché; you keep running into it everywhere, from Confucius to the Greeks to the latest popularization of string theory or what I am calling knot theory: the theory of entanglements; universe as macramé or crochet. From one point of view, the fact that I am harping on a cliché is a drawback. From another, it suggests that we've latched on to some fundamental insight. It would not be surprising if the true nature of the universe were surprising. But it would not be surprising if the true nature of the universe were not surprising; maybe it's something we're fundamentally acquainted with every day. On the other hand, a lot of metaphors might be worth playing with, and you're always trying to decide what is and what is not a mere metaphor.

With regard to the science or everyday experience of the knotscape, we could pick out indefinitely many structures or introduce various ontological ordering principles for various purposes: taxonomies of knots or of subknot elements that show the structure of particular knots (precisely the function of skein analysis in knot theory) or a table of elements. In some sense, what counts as a knot has to be fixed and is a question: the question of whether that tangle is a single knot or a stack of knots or not even a knot always implicates a particular standpoint that is being taken up, or the rough conventional ontology. You could pick out indefinitely many structures or introduce various ontological ordering principles for various purposes. But for a given claim to be true, the skein has really to be as the claim says it is. There are multiple correct systems of representation of the skein, but there are also incorrect ones. And though the system by which knots are individuated can yield to convention and circumstance, there are often perfectly definite answers to questions within such a system: no, that one can't be part of that one.

The way we order the array into individuals is not whimsical or merely conventional, however. Indeed, if we did not order our experience of the world more or less the way the world actually is, we would long ago have been extinguished. We order the world from within the world, as part of the world. If we didn't distinguish lions from various portions of their and our shared environment, we'd merely be prey. Nevertheless, of course, the body of the lion or the human being is not fully distinct from its surroundings, and as the lion is breathing, seeing, smelling, eating, excreting, growing, aging, it is in interchange. We are actual creatures functioning in an actual environment; we are, of necessity, continuously responsive to actual features of it in their emergence through us. We have to "mirror" reality, we might say, but I see attention and perception as much more intimate than that, as an actual taking-in of external objects: perception and description are entanglements, in which the knot that is oneself gets snagged on something or snarled up in a different order.

2.

Though I hope that many of the positions advocated in this book are radical or at least provocative, I take a classical approach to the matter of what philosophy is. As I understand it, philosophy is concerned with questions about ultimate values, each of which stands at the apex of a dimension of value: truth, knowledge, goodness, justice, and beauty. And as the above passage suggests, I take philosophy also to be concerned with characterizing or describing the world at the most general or fundamental level (the traditional task of "metaphysics" or "the question of truth"). I talk about these matters directly here, or at least I intend to. The goal is not a factual characterization of the world's ultimate constituents or figuring out what are the basic subatomic particles, for instance (though a true metaphysics must be consistent with accurate scientific theories), but the aesthetic project of creating a picture of what there is and how it all hangs together, in all senses of "hang."

That is, I regard philosophy as, among other things, the collection of its subdisciplines, including metaphysics, logic, epistemology, ethics, aesthetics, and political philosophy. Mine, we might say—or you might say—is a painfully reactionary conception of the field; I love the traditional philosophical questions, actually. Now the idea of philosophy as the attempt to characterize the ultimate nature of reality, truth, goodness, beauty, and so on sounds both woolly and grandiose, and it is. Many people, including many philosophers, would reject or have actually rejected such a project as ill-defined, impossible, or without use or results and any particular realization of it as unjustifiable, rationally arbitrary, and purposeless. These are serious objections.

But though I am not necessarily compelled to write books, I am compelled to address myself to philosophy as a project, whether it is a defensible or wholesome project or not. One might call this impulse morbid abstraction: I have a tendency to try to draw the most general conclusions from any set of data; I always gravitate to the widest possible generalization. This might be problematic or even pathological. But it is my problem and pathology, and of course I am not completely alone in having that impulse. I suppose I could say that the question of whether it is a profitable enterprise can only be answered by examining the upshot of actual attempts. But I could also merely say that whatever the profit to be derived or costs undertaken, it is not a project I have ever felt I could actually avoid. One could think of it as an inquiry, with whatever results an inquiry might have—increased knowledge, control of the environment, personal prestige, wisdom, and so on—or not. One could think of it more as an art project or as a form of play, an amusement or distraction. In fact, I think it is all of those.

It is occasionally held that philosophy is a fundamental human need or impulse. We are creatures that reflect, it is said, and we want to know why we are what we are and where we are. But though philosophy is my profession, or my hobby, or my derangement, I don't think it's everybody's. This seems evident from the fact that sales of philosophy books are miniscule or the fact that most folks cannot name a single living philosopher. I don't necessarily decry this situation, any more than I think most people have to collect stamps or skateboard. I've hung around with many people who seemed to get on quite well without philosophy—or who found the whole way of thinking profoundly alien—including many of the people to whom I've tried to teach it and many people whose intellects I respect. No doubt in more or less all human lives questions arise that edge into philosophical territory, questions like whether it's ok to do things like x, or whether they should expect anything to answer their prayers. But for most folks, a quick rationalization is as good as a well-worked theory, or better, or what most people say is a good enough guide to what it is reasonable to believe. I've known many such people who seemed happy and also some deeply reflective people who seemed miserable. But some people are drawn inexorably toward joyful, or compulsive, or morbid reflection on what the whole world is and what they are within it. Some people find in such reflection a source of pleasure, possibly perverse, as well as a source of puzzlement or a job. I am such a person, and I suppose I am directing this book at such people, though I welcome sales to any demographic segment, including stamp collectors and skateboarders.

My characterization of philosophy makes it the pursuit of answers to "the eternal questions." Even the possibility of questions or values that persist in the same form across ages or cultures would be widely rejected today, or perhaps we have reached the point where it doesn't have to be rejected, so obvious to everyone is it that the whole approach is baldly ridiculous. You can't come out of Hegel, Marx, Nietzsche, Dewey, Wittgenstein, cultural anthropology, Freud, and Foucault talking about ultimate objective eternal values with a good conscience, and if we know anything, we know that conceptions of truth, or of the good life, or of God, emerge only within practices, cultures, languages, forms of life, relations of power, and so on.

Indeed, Nietzsche and Foucault, among others, make us see that the claim of access to such values—the claim to know what they are—is often an assertion of power. An old girlfriend of mine used to say, "When I hear the word 'truth,' I reach for my pistol." That is, if people were telling her what the truth was, they were disqualifying her, seeking to oppress her. She actually had a pistol in her underwear drawer. Priests tell you what the truth is, and the truth enriches and empowers the Church. The people who write the standardized tests tell you what the truth is, and your life will be circumscribed if you don't all fill in the same little circles.

It is not only a political suspicion. The ultimate values have been exploded—exploded thoroughly and repeatedly—intraphilosophically, as we might say. Starting at latest with Hume, arguments were put forward to the effect that insofar as such values were conceived to transcend ordinary sensible experience, the words by which we try to refer to them are meaningless; Hume retrenched to practice, custom, and rules commonly agreed on. Indeed, the critique is ancient: in the first century B.C., Lucretius was busy setting in dactylic hexameter a raw materialism admitting no overarching purpose and trying to give ethics a feet-on-the-ground origin in actual pleasures and pains. On such grounds the logical positivists proclaimed all the so-called eternal questions either trivial or meaningless and sentences expressing or explaining them mere grunts of pleasure or displeasure. Justice doesn't change the color of that solution in your beaker, and though our telescopes have peered deeply into the universe, they haven't suddenly come across Truth out there glowing like a nebula.

Not only that, but many philosophers have argued that we get on quite well day to day without eternal truths or a universal conception of flawless Beauty, and it is a fact that thousands of years of inquiry into these ideas has not produced a consensus of opinion on such matters or even very widely held standards by which good answers could be distinguished from bad ones. The pragmatists asked what "goodness" or "knowledge" or "God" actually do to guide us in our experience; that, they held, was the entire content of these concepts. The values shift with the needs we are trying to address and the projects we are trying to bring to completion. They are our values, developed in relation to our purposes. William James said that truth was what worked in our experience and that an assertion or theory was true for as long as it worked, or true to the extent that it worked; every assertion or theory that was true was true provisionally, locally, and true in relation to specific people's actual problems, situations, or conventions.

Now probably ultimately my position on these matters is indeed reactionary, and with a slight dose of irony or self-consciousness I do hold that there is something we are trying to grasp in these basic questions, some substance or subject matter that they actually do indicate, and some tasks to which they are indispensable even in their apparently transcultural or transhistorical forms. Different cultures and different eras and different individuals might approach these matters from different angles or reveal them from different perspectives, but the questions are real questions, in my view.

3.

Many of these strands of critique have concluded from the alleged fact that the ultimate values are illusions that philosophy is over. Indeed, there is no matter on which a greater proportion of important philosophers of the last 150 years have agreed than that philosophy is finished, or just about to be. Nietzsche thought so. Heidegger thought so. Perhaps James and Dewey thought so, at least in the sense in which philosophy was going to yield generally or cross-temporally viable answers to its big questions. Carnap thought so. Wittgenstein. Derrida. Rorty. Now this represents something of a back-handed concession to, though also a slap at, the sort of characterization of philosophy I have been urging. These figures do, in fact, regard philosophy as being, or as having been, engaged in the attempt to elucidate the Big Questions, even if they thought that they had shown that there were no answers to such questions or even any questions. More significantly, perhaps, and more relevantly to the present project, the critiques that attack or dismiss the questions are, of course, also attempts to address them. The question of what truth is might be answered by saying it's like an eternal sun glowing in an infinite sky. Or it might be answered by saying that there's no such thing as truth, or that the concept of truth is trivial, or even that we should cease asking the question of truth. Each of those is, equally, philosophy.

I am willing, in other words, to count any engagement with these questions—including giving reasons why they should be abandoned or why they never actually arose in the first place—as philosophy, and as a matter of fact, the rejection of philosophy has historically been part of philosophy. Now, the rejection of science cannot, itself, be part of science, and the rejection of religion cannot be part of religion, exactly. Art, however, has included the rejection of art at least since early in the twentieth century, which is perhaps a kind of analogy here. It is strictly possible that philosophy or metaphysics could cease to exist, as philosophers from Carnap to Heidegger to Wittgenstein to Rorty have proclaimed that it has or will. But it certainly does not cease to exist in the works of these figures themselves, as they brutalize previous conceptions of truth or goodness or throw doubt on the legitimacy of such concepts altogether. Honestly, I don't think they can do without at least some of these notions even in their attack on them, but whether they can or not, they are just as engaged in the philosophical questions as were the rank metaphysicians they historicize or deconstruct. To end philosophy, you'd have to leave it, cease doing it, go do something else, shut up and play badminton. Rejecting it, with arguments, for the length of a book or career, *is* it.

I have my own ways of trying to brutalize various moments, movements, figures in the philosophical tradition, my own set of objections to values as glittering eternal abstract objects, and so on. But I would like my objections to be direct: I think Plato was wrong about what justice is. I have a more or less materialist ontology, for example, and when I assert that everything that exists is a physical object, I realize that there are many difficulties with or obscurities in my position, and there are many cultural resonances and local reasons that I have the position I do. I would like to be reflective about these to whatever extent that is possible. But I also want to be taken as flatly asserting that the only things that exist are physical objects. When Aristotle, for example, said to Plato that his ontology of Forms was wrong, he was raising related objections to the same position. Well, that would take some care, and whatever modern materialism is, it is not precisely the same as, for example, ancient atomism. But that, too, is still subject to elucidation, and we have not lost the ability to ask and to try to answer some of the very same questions raised by the Greeks.

It is easy to regard this in a hypersimplistic and entirely dehistoricized way, to think you can be in a direct dialogue with Plato and ignore the innumerable, extremely complex developments of understanding and vocabulary—the long series of translations—that come between ourselves and Plato and account for both the illusion of our proximity to him and for the real distance between us. One has to engage in these complexities as responsibly as possible or, at any rate, as best one can. But I would be lying if I said that I don't regard the project of this book as being the same project assayed by Plato, by Descartes, by Hume, by Kant, by Hegel. My understanding of these problems, and the solutions I affirm, are different than theirs for many reasons, among others that they come from a different time and place. But they are also located in the same history. That there is continuity in the questions through all the innumerable transformations is something I will also insist on. Well, there is continuity in the human organism, and in its environment, and in social systems, and in texts, even as there are also profound transformations. I hope that readers who are inclined to regard the project as reactionary or misguided will be relieved at the radicalness or weirdness of some of the answers and at my suspicion of my own foundations—or of any foundations.

And if—and I will argue for this—the truth of the claims I make, or the truth of metaphysical (or ethical, or aesthetic) claims in general, is not subject to scientific test, or even ultimately to any clear or specific form of empirical confirmation or refutation, I do not think it would follow that the question of their truth or falsity does not arise or that we have no equipment to assess it. Even if the answers to questions like this do not transform one's life or one's world, it would not follow, I believe, that they are not real questions or that any answer is just as good as any other. After all, we share this world in which we live. We are embedded in it utterly; we are some of its parts or regions or processes. We have some sense of where and what we are, though of course we often disagree about such matters. The truth, for me, about such claims begins with their truth to my person and my situation. Or, I might say that I am seeking answers that feel right or feel true. That is not a merely subjective test—vague though it is—insofar as I am not merely a subject but also an object and also a portion of a whole to which I am more than connected, which constitutes me and is partly constituted by me. The results of such a procedure cannot have the certainty of a mathematical demonstration or of a series of carefully performed experiments. But they can have the sort of certainty and the degree of certainty of ordinary claims we make in ordinary life: that I love you, for example; that that's the Conewago Creek. And those are truths that are certain enough for ordinary purposes. They are things about which it is possible to be right or wrong.

I regard philosophy with tremendous affection, and I would hate to see it be over. As I say, I don't think that more philosophers saying it's over will particularly threaten its continued existence, so I'm not necessarily that worried. And I could never see the urgency of ending it; surely, it is relatively harmless. Really, I don't ask for culture-wide sway—though I think sciencey types and literary people could use more philosophy than they have, often—but I do ask for continued tolerance of our existence in some little corner of the culture and the academy.

4.

Philosophy has, at least since Hegel, and ultimately as a strategy for self-destruction, been historicized. That is, it has been held that philosophical terms, concepts, styles, and arguments emerge only in particular contexts and are sensible only within those contexts. This is an "anti-Platonic" move, among other things. We do wrong, according to it, to think of the Greek term *dike* as picking out, in Platonic heaven, our concept of justice (if we have a shared concept of justice). We can translate the *Analects of Confucius* into modern English; that does not mean we understand it. Concepts have histories: look at the meanings through the centuries or across cultures of various terms that might be translated as "beauty," for instance. Translation, famously, is indeterminate, and the full-fledged conceptuality of, say, the medieval period is inaccessible or always only seen through the lenses we actually do have. And if you don't worry about "beauty" or "justice" in this regard, well surely you ought to worry about "race" or "democracy." A famous case is Foucault on taxonomies of what we term *sexual orientation*: he holds that there were no homosexuals and also no heterosexuals before (if I'm recalling this correctly) 1878, and he shows in detail that the basic conception of sexuality as a dyadic selection between identities is something that developed at a certain time for certain purposes. He shows the same about "punishment," "guilt," "responsibility," and even "truth."

I think we need to take such claims seriously. But even if the basic concepts of philosophy develop or even reverse valence historically, even if the ways that analogous concepts developed historically are to some extent inaccessible, it does not follow that there's nothing we're doing when we try to elucidate these concepts. First of all, of course, there is a way, or there are ways, that the present emerges from the past. And, to some extent, these ways can be traced through careful translation, etymologies, immersive reading, and examination of as many features of historical context as possible. Even if such procedures are limited, they are also not entirely futile. Thomas Kuhn famously argued that science proceeds by shifts between "incommensurable" paradigms, though he ended up denying—as well he should have—that this lands you in total relativism, or that previous paradigms are entirely inaccessible, or that truth is only a feature of sentences or observations or theories within a paradigm. But also, the paradigms of science emerge out of one another, by elaboration, rejection, development, and reversal. There are continuities as well as discontinuities. We can't assure ourselves that we can think outside our own paradigms, and every claim to truth takes place within a certain moment, a certain set of conceptual structures, a certain linguistic situation. But our moments, structures, and languages emerge in an incredibly complex history out of others and in dialogue with others and with the world.

And even if some things that might be evident to the Greeks, or to the Hopi, are impossible to see from our perspective, certain things are also available to us that weren't to them. "Standpoint epistemology" argues that, for example, there are things that women can know that men can't, or that black people can know that white people can't. This, and vice versa, may well be true. But that itself presupposes that there is something that can be known about the world and about our social practices in the world. Seeing across standpoints is not fully possible. Seeing as broadly as possible from our own standpoint is important, and in fact every person occupies myriad standpoints over time. And putting various standpoints into dialogue is important as well. The standpoints, after all, are constituted in relation to one another. These relations are fraught with complexity, with powers and projects, prejudices and blinders, communications and failures of communication. It does not follow that there is nothing we can do, only that we'd better do it with as much self-awareness as we can muster. And we ought to try, to whatever extent this is possible, to achieve awareness of the limitations and humility before them. We have to acknowledge that our point of view is our point of view. And then we have to try to see what we can see.

Some of these possibilities might include rather insouciant appropriations or crossings, or grabbing what we can use from here or there, or enriching our concepts with other concepts (though, of course, not merely dumping out our concepts and grabbing somebody else's, which is, I am admitting, a mere delusion). Even if we need care and humility and scholarship, we also need curiosity and courage and even carelessness. You can't know what works until you try. And one thing about treating philosophy in what we might term a nonpragmatic way, or about admitting that it does not necessarily have a lot of consequences and that most people couldn't care less, is that it is liberating. Truly, even if I am wrong about absolutely everything, that won't make millions of people starve or contribute significantly to climate change. More or less, philosophy is action without consequence (unless you get extremely lucky or unfortunate, like Locke or Confucius or Marx), and that is liberating. There is no point in being frozen by historicism or in other ways into inaction. Let's plow ahead and see what happens. Not much, I suspect, of any serious consequence (and I am provisionally grateful for that) but maybe much of intrinsic and fundamental interest to folks like us.

5.

If my conception of the subject matter of philosophy is untoward in its conservative rigidity, my conception of philosophical methodology is rather flexible. Philosophy is often enough associated with "reason," which ironically is one the most elastic concepts in the pantheon of concepts. Philosophy is sometimes said to have emerged in the Greeks with reason and to be characterized, at minimum, as the rational exploration of questions such as the nature of goodness, truth, beauty, and reality. Though "reason" and "rationality" are often deployed without a clear sense of the complexity and richness of those terms, I regard them as only part of the range of philosophical techniques. Various forms of emotional expression and persuasion, various dimensions of artistic construction or inspiration, and the asseveration of various forms of faith have also been employed, and when they are employed well, in my opinion, they are potentially just as legitimate as reason—whatever exactly that may be—as philosophical methods.

One might date philosophy from Plato's rational dialectic or from Aristotle's codification of the principles of logic. But one might also date it from the poetry of

Heraclitus or Parmenides: elusive, suggestive, aesthetic, though also argumentative and intended to be persuasive. Or one might associate it with Plato's myths. One might associate it with Descartes' method of systematic skepticism, but one might also associate it with the scholasticism Descartes rejected or a crisis of unbelief in the man himself: the attempt to reconcile reason and faith or dogma and argumentation. One might associate it with the attempt of Kant to put all the ultimate philosophical questions on a purely rational basis, or one might associate it with Kierkegaard's ecstatic and ironic affirmation of faith and the limits of knowledge and his creation of fictional scenarios and fictional authors. One might associate it with Hume's bold but meticulous reasoning or with Emerson's ecstatic essays constructed out of a series of ringing, unjustified aphorisms. One might associate it with the magnificent universal scope of the logic of Frege and Russell; or with the humble investigation of ordinary language of J. L. Austin; or with the oracular profundities of Heidegger; the grand speculative systems of Schelling, Fichte, Hegel; or the detailed archival examinations of Foucault. It can be sermon, poem, novel, painting, pudding. I think we should associate philosophy with all these things, all these texts, all these strategies, all these styles of prose and poetry, all these objects, and many others.

I started with the universe as a tangle of string. It's a metaphor, of course, though perhaps not only a metaphor, even if the string isn't actually hardware store twine. It is intended to have various effects. It was an attempt by me to clarify for myself what I actually did believe or could say about the way I see the universe at the most general level; I felt (somewhat) clearer about what I believed after I developed it than before. It is intended to persuade you, or rather to make you more sympathetic to, a certain (still quite obscure, of course) way of seeing the world; it is a rhetorical strategy or flourish. It is something I felt I could play with, like a kitten with a ball of twine, something that got and kept me writing for a while with some pleasure. And underneath it all, it was also an attempt to state the truth. These are not separable in the actual process of coming up with and setting out the figure.

As a matter of fact, philosophy as its history is actually told—to students, for example—does encompass all these styles, all these strategies, all these dimensions of formulation, and I would think that we should note that many of them might, in some sense, be expressed and exploited from the beginning, for example, in the dialogues of Plato: full of fictions, metaphors, myths, and mystical faiths as well as bulging with arguments and precise definitions. That is, I think philosophy has a coherent subject matter, elusive and beset with complexities as it is, but I do not think it has a single method or style or voice. I will not usually abandon reason (unless I can develop reasons to do so) or celebrate sheer irrationality for its own sake. But I do intend to broaden our sense of how philosophy has been done and how it might continue to be done.

I do not intend to conflate philosophy with poetry, or comedy, or science, and I do not intend to dismiss its claims to have a distinctive subject matter or to be concerned with arriving at the truth. Only I think that there are many ways of arriving at the truth. Science can be a way—or many ways—of arriving at the truth, but so can certain forms of play, or certain forms of art, or sudden unaccountable flashes of intuition, or sudden direct illuminations from God, if there is a God (which I do not think there is). And if you ask me, any way of arriving at the truth is a good way, and we should try—at least provisionally—to open up as many as possible. There is no telling in advance what might shed light, or be persuasive, or clarify ourselves to ourselves, or what might hook on how to reality.

6.

Now if "philosophy" gives some people (especially some philosophers) the willies, the idea of "system" gives them to me. It is true, I think, that the great systems of philosophy—above all those of the German idealists: Kant, Hegel, Schelling, Fichte, and Schopenhauer, for instance—are among the most impressive achievements in the history of the human intellect. If my project were to do what Hegel did, or thought he did—explain all of the universe and the human relation to it from the ground up in a way that led to perfect self-consciousness—then I would have regarded the project as too intimidating to set out on. The project is intimidating enough, conceived as I conceive it.

Impressive as these systems are, they are, I believe, fantastic. Even if each hangs together within itself (which seems unlikely), it has abandoned what I might term *the weirdness of the real:* its recalcitrance to our categories; its unpredictability; its contingency; its arbitrariness; its excess to human experience. And each such system, to the extent it is successful in achieving its own goals, leaves behind also our strangeness to ourselves, our excess to ourselves, the ways we elude our own grasp. Fortunately and necessarily, there is deep obscurity at their heart: the unplumbed mystery that comes from trying to parse the syntax.

I will construct a system in the sense that I will try to take up the outstanding issues—many of them, at any rate—in the history of philosophy and formulate a set of answers that will, I hope, hang together fairly well with one another. But I will not seek certainty at the foundations, or I will deny that it is forthcoming. I will argue that at the heart of any picture of the universe is a faith, a commitment, that is ultimately personal: any philosophical system must rest on an inchoate and ultimately unjustified sense of where and what one is. There is no escaping this situation, I believe, and it is not entirely unsatisfactory. So the status of the claims I put forward is to try to capture and make compelling my own fundamental commitments and my own fundamental sense of where and what I am. Whether the stuff is true or not is, I believe, a genuine question. But for me it is of equal importance—and connected to the question of truth—that it is an honest representation of my real experience and thinking.

So if what follows is a system of philosophy, it is an antisystematic system: the goal is to open up to a world around and outside and running through us, not to constrain the world to the conditions of human reason or even consciousness. It is not a system that could give you the assurance that you now understand all that was before concealed in shadow. Even with these qualifications, however, I must remark that the idea of system remains problematic, and one is constantly in danger of being seduced away from the world by the niftiness of some notion or of the way a whole bunch of stuff hangs together. That is a danger to which philosophy has succumbed again and again, and though I cannot claim to have avoided it, I can at least say that I have been alert to the problem.

I am not sure there has ever been a more ponderous, less human, or more humorless discourse than systematic philosophy, though the first great systematizer—Plato, of course—had various semicomic and ironic moves at his disposal. Now humorlessness is, I believe, a problem. It's a failure of character. But it is also a symptom of the real problems of systematic philosophy: its lack of a sense of the limitations of the mind of the thinker. Even a Kant or Schelling made mistakes, harbored prejudices, had to start where he actually was, however he portrayed himself or whatever authorial voice he took up. The groping, confusion, and doubt are erased. There is not a hint of the actual comedy continually being enacted: a finite, merely human intellect, suffering as it may be from a head cold, speaking in a voice and with a knowledge the model of which is God, slipping continuously on banana peels that it is itself strewing around itself. We might call it Satanic. It is an infinite ambition carried on by a finite creature. In its incredible ambition, systematic philosophy is touching, noble, and redolent of tragic, excessive pride and the comical inability to pay off on the promises made in the preface.

My teacher Richard Rorty famously argued that philosophy is merely a genre of literature, and whether that's exactly true or not, philosophy is surely a way, or several ways, of writing, along with whatever else it is (an attempt to generate truths at the highest level of generality, for example). One of these modes or styles of writing is the style of the German system makers: huge, immensely complex sentences chock full of clauses; a new jargon of technical terms for each system; passive voice; absence of the first person. And where the problems become intractable or transhuman, obscurity fills the gap between the knowledge that can be possessed by an actual human subject and omniscience; you feel that if you could fully grasp the vocabulary, you'd see that the problem was solved or the darkness illuminated after all, even as you continue to sit there in the dark. That, indeed, is the seductive power of system: the very idea that someone has seen everything, that there are answers, even if you could spend a lifetime trying to figure out what the author actually meant. This leads philosophers toward the temptation to become acolytes: of Plato, Hegel, Nietzsche, Heidegger, Wittgenstein.

In part, the material demands a very elaborate and difficult expression. And, in part, the elaborate and difficult expression is a rhetorical strategy. One thing it certainly accomplishes: it makes it a badge of extreme cultivation and intelligence to have read these books; the prestige of the books varies with their difficulty. To have read and understood Hegel's *Phenomenology of Spirit* or Heidegger's *Being and Time* (or to be able plausibly to claim to have read and understood them) shows that you are a very smart person. To have written them, of course, is to show an intelligence (and an industry) that is apparently more than human, which is why reading them confers this prestige.

But there are, in fact, many styles in philosophy. The great contrast to the German system is the sort of extreme clarity first assayed by Aristotle and shown in different forms, for example, in Hume or Quine. The differences between Hume and Kant on the issues of philosophy have been formulated many times, but the difference is as easily captured in their ways of writing as in their actual positions. And the ways of writing also reflect this: Hume was satisfied with, or even gloried in, the limitations of the intellect that he identified and experienced; Hegel, for example, was dedicated to overcoming such limitations, and he advanced a discourse that eventually took no limitations seriously. So Hume wants you to understand what he's saying as precisely as possible. Hegel needs to give you a sense that he's not quite saying absolutely everything, but he just might.

At any rate, if we think of philosophy as a literary genre—which I would not, exactly—we need to think of some of its eccentrics, poets, ironists, comedians. Pascal, for example, with his humility and seemingly infinite irony; Nietzsche with his whip-like aphorisms; Diderot with his forays of wit and refusal of system; James, showing the extent to which interminable difficult arguments can be cast into everyday language; Austin happily wandering about in the funny ways people actually talk; Wittgenstein with his artful deflection of philosophical questions; and so on.

Looking at the table of contents for this book, it will seem pretty ponderous: a good doorstop; a brick of human thought suitable for use as a weapon if still shrink-wrapped. But I hope I can inscribe in this writing not only a sense of ambition but an awareness of limitation, not only solutions but a sense of the provisionality of all solutions, and the sense of a limited and eccentric voice even amidst the resolution to tackle the whole damn thing from top to bottom.

7.

So I hope that this book does not represent a system in quite the traditional sense. Indeed, if I can proceed by paradox, my system rests on the thought that reality is bristling with complexities or is infinitely rich and largely uncontrollable, or as H. L. Mencken put it: *Truth shifts and changes like a cataract of diamonds.*[1] It's precisely the reality of the real or the volatility and hardness of truth that I want to emphasize and embrace, in the face of all systems that make the world our fantasy or our construction or our narrative. We do not make reality. Reality makes us. And here I turn from metaphilosophy to a bit of actual philosophy and history of philosophy by trying to say what I will be rejecting, or objecting to, in this book.

As Berkeley argued, some form of idealism is a gravitational result of empiricism, but it is also the pull of rationalism as historically constituted. The view that Descartes and Locke have in common is that we are immediately acquainted not with objects external to the mind but with ideas or sense impressions or, at any rate, representations. In my opinion, this is where Western philosophy went extremely, radically wrong; it is the place where philosophers—empiricists, rationalists, transcendental and absolute idealists, positivists, narrativists, and postmodernists—lost faith with the experience of which they were trying to give an account and with the world in which they were embedded. The idea that we are directly acquainted not with a world or with each other but with ideas or impressions or vocabularies or stories immediately suggests that one could dispense with the world that is represented entirely; the world appears to do no work. Berkeley shows the result as clearly as anyone: he simply razors the physical universe off and makes do with "ideas."

> The table I write on I say exists; that is, I see and feel it: and if I were out of my study I should say it existed; meaning thereby that if I was in my study I might perceive it, or that some other spirit actually does. . . . For as to what is said of the absolute existence of unthinking things, without any relation to their being perceived, that is to me perfectly unintelligible. Their *esse* is *percipi*; nor is it possible they should have any existence out of the minds or thinking things which perceive them.[2]

Here is a typical presentation of this most fundamental error in Western philosophy, from Schopenhauer:

> The world is my representation: this is a truth valid with reference to every living and knowing being, although man alone can bring it into reflective, abstract consciousness. If he really does so, philosophical discernment has dawned on him. It then becomes clear and certain to him that he does not know a sun and an earth, but only an eye that sees a sun, a hand that feels an earth; that the world around him is there only as a representation, in other words, only in reference to another thing, namely that which represents, and this is himself. If any truth can be expressed a priori, it is this; for it is a statement of the form of all possible and conceivable experience . . . Therefore no truth is more certain, more independent of

all others, and less in need of proof than this, namely that everything that exists for knowledge, and hence the whole of this world, is only an object in relation to the subject, perception of a perceiver, in a word, representation.[3]

The idealists began with human consciousness, from which they created or inferred a universe: the Kantian "Copernican revolution" is precisely to turn from outward inward. In the famous preface to the second edition of the *Critique of Pure Reason*, Kant writes,

> Hitherto it has been assumed that all our knowledge must conform to objects. But all attempts to extend our knowledge of objects by establishing something in regard to them a priori, by means of concepts, have, on this assumption, ended in failure. We must therefore make trial of whether we may not have more success in the tasks of metaphysics, if we suppose that objects must conform to our knowledge.[4]

For my money, it's precisely at that foundational moment that Western philosophy becomes entirely fictional, more or less intentionally: it yields an invented rather than a discovered and explored universe.

If nothing else, Darwinism should have been the downfall of this movement: it must surely follow from natural selection that we, by and large, respond to, rather than make or manufacture, an environment. Kant held that space, time, and causation were (merely) necessary forms of consciousness or transcendental conditions of any possible experience. On a Darwinian conception, our perceptual apparatus and attendant representational systems are as they are because of their power to help the organism adapt to an external world, and that means, among other things, their ability to experience what is actually there. Perception is not the essence of being; it's a responsive process of an organism in a physical world. I hold that space, time, and causation are forms of our consciousness precisely because they are external aspects of the real world. This is not something that I feel can be demonstrated, but even on Kant's view, we must all more or less act as though it were true.

Near the beginning of Hume's *Treatise*, he says that "all our simple ideas in their first appearance are deriv'd from simple impressions, which are correspondent to them, and which they exactly represent."[5] Here we have multiplying layers of representation without a physical thing or a worldly situation making any sort of appearance: there's the flow of sensory experience—impressions, pictures—and then a faculty for copying or representing those pictures in turn in memory, and so on. Or through the surface grammar we express the deep grammar, through which we express. . . . We enter layers of subjectivity, trying to tease real objects out of impressions, impressions of impressions, impressions of those, words for words, and so on.

It is worth pausing, I believe, to meditate on the strangeness of a Carnap, who proposed to build the universe from "auto-psychological objects," just as though this were the most natural idea in the world.[6] It is certainly one of the most familiar moves in philosophy (e.g., Jerry Fodor calls it "methodological solipsism"), and Carnap himself invokes Husserl's "bracketing." He starts by constructing objects from the immediate contents of consciousness and then goes on from there. Indeed, he proposes that talk of auto-psychological objects and talk of physical objects are interchangeable, and he says that he could have started the other way round. However, he also calls the sense impressions or whatever they may be "the given." He insists that the whole exercise is "scientific," and on the empiricist side, thinkers were always presenting one or another version of phenomenalism as an elucidation of, or foundation of, or propaedeutic to science. But the idea of retreating completely to interior states has to do with absolutely anything but science, which is hardly ever concerned with anyone's mental imagery.

As late as the arch-antipositivist Quine, we are building worlds out of mental phenomena: "Our talk of external things, our very notion of things, is just a conceptual apparatus that helps us foresee and control the triggering of our sensory receptors in the light of previous triggering of our sensory receptors. The triggering, first and last, is all we have to go on."[7] Berkeley almost word for word, mutatis mutandis. Now Quine's formulation is carefully agnostic about whether "the triggering of receptors" is a physical world process of actual cones and rods, or whatever it may be, or an array of images in one's sensorium, and Quine's view is preferable to that extent.

But I suggest that *we help ourselves to the world*. Belly up to the smorgasbord. At any rate, no scientist worth her salt is investigating the triggering of her own sensory receptors; she is investigating some portion of the world. If we were trying to get down to the foundational epistemological level, and trying to produce "observation sentences," they would be actual observations—what we actually saw happen out there. And of course, for the most part, they are. Or perhaps you should add a layer to the double-blind placebo procedure: one in which the researchers reduce the data to the immediate contents of their own consciousnesses, or describe the series of sense impressions they are having before they describe what actually happened, or eliminate problems such as that they might have only dreamed they were performing the study. No scientist would describe the observations on which his paper is based in terms of his auto-psychological states, for extremely good reasons.

Making representational or syntactic/semantic systems into worlds is the characteristic derangement of modern philosophy. We could start with Descartes's ideas, or further back than that (I will explore this history), and continue with the empiricists and their sense impressions, and the idealists and their categories and forms of perception. The pragmatists, positivists, phenomenologists, poststructuralists, and narrativists emerged in a rejection of idealism and reinscribed it. In various ways, they overcame idealist individualism of the sort that has Schopenhauer locating the world in each person's head, whatever in the world that could possibly mean, and brought out the social element of semantic systems. Heidegger, Derrida, Husserl; Ayer, Quine; Dewey, Mead, Rorty; vastly different, emerging out of idealism in various ways to various effects, extending Hegel or rejecting him; all anti-Cartesians, and so on. But the fundamental idealist or representationalist derangement runs ever at the flood.

Idealism is antinaturalistic, of course, and its rise with modern science, its attempts to make peace or provide phenomenalistic underpinnings for it and so on is a wild story, a battle between science and philosophy and between philosophy and experience that is wondrous in its extreme tensions and provisional reconciliations. One might compare it to the tensions between dogma and logic in Aquinas, for example. It is shocking how far apart from each other, how completely incompatible with one another, Enlightenment science and Enlightenment philosophy are. The logical positivists held that the purpose of philosophy was to describe the underpinnings of science, and they were phenomenalists; they held that all meaningful discourse must eventually reduce to "sensible contents," by which they meant representations in someone's mind. But you never seem to find actual scientists actually working from sense impressions; they report events: illnesses or chemical reactions, supernovas or the behavior of microparticles. The idea that one looks at the beaker as or through one's own impressions would be at best a completely otiose doctrine even if it were true in every case: that much wouldn't distinguish any experiment from any other, or any of them from any experience of any kind, even if the positivists were right in their phenomenalism. The idea that in scientific inquiry I'm really investigating my own sensations would be useless even if it were true. Also, it's not true. And if such an approach of breaking down objects into sensible experiences or representations ever actually pushed forward any particular investigation into some empirical subject matter, that would surprise me.

All kinds of uncanny mysteries arise with regard to auto-psychological objects, whether in my sensorium or my idiolect. Withdrawing to the level of representation, or explaining perception as representation, does not make us as lucid to ourselves as we would like; it just raises a host of new problems. In its positivist form, I think the doctrine was deftly destroyed by Austin in *Sense and Sensibilia*, which is one of the great artillery bombardments in the history of military philosophy. But Thomas Reid made the same point in relation to Hume's skepticism, which, said Reid, "leans with its whole weight upon a hypothesis which is ancient indeed, and hath been very generally received by philosophers, but of which I could find no solid proof," namely that there is a screen of ideas interposed between person and object.[8] We face, in idealism, positivism, phenomenology, linguistic constructivism, not only questions about the world externally to representation but about the representational system itself, which collapses into a system of differences, a pure syntax. Pretty soon you can unleash the deconstructionists and let them undermine the pillars on which the whole world appears to stand.

8.

I might adduce an ally in Emerson:

> Along with the civil and metaphysical history of man, another history goes daily forward,—that of the external world,—in which he is not less strictly implicated. He is the compend of time; he is also the correlative of nature. His power consists in the multitude of his affinities, in the fact that his life is intertwined with the whole chain of organic and inorganic being. . . . A man is a bundle of relations, a knot of roots, whose flower and fruitage is the world. His faculties refer to natures out of him, and predict the world he is to inhabit, as the fins of the fish foreshow that water exists, or the wings of an eagle in the egg presuppose air. He cannot live without a world. . . . Does not the eye of the human embryo predict the light? the ear of Handel predict the witchcraft of harmonic sound? Do not the constructive fingers of Watt, Fulton, Whittemore, Arkwright, predict the fusible, hard, and temperable textures of metals, the properties of stone, water, and wood? Do not the lovely attributes of the maiden child predict the refinements and decorations of civil society? Here also we are reminded of the actions of man on man. A mind might ponder its thought for ages, and not gain so much self-knowledge as the passion of love shall teach it in a day. Who knows himself before he has been thrilled with indignation at an outrage, or has heard an eloquent tongue, or has shared the throb of thousands in a national exultation or alarm? No man can antedate his experience, or guess what faculty or feeling a new object shall unlock, any more than he can draw today the face of a person that he shall see tomorrow for the first time.[9]

Emerson's idea is that we are constituted as unique individuals by our real-world relations. In other moods and moments, Emerson is an idealist; in this one he characteristically reverses valence. And this might suggest, in turn, that we go right ahead and avail ourselves of the real word in explanation, both as something to be explained and a means for doing the explaining. That idea might stand as a summary of the philosophy of Emerson's protégé Thoreau.

And consider this, from Pascal:

> The parts of the world are all so related and so linked to one another, that I believe it impossible to know one without the other and without the whole.

> Man, for example, is related to everything he knows. He needs place to hold him, time to endure, motion to live, elements to constitute him, warmth and food to nourish him, air to breathe. He sees light; he feels bodies. In short he is in a dependent alliance with everything. To know man, then, we must know why he needs air to live, and to understand air, we must know that it is related to man's life, etc.
>
> Flame cannot exist without air; therefore to understand the one, one must understand the other.
>
> All things, then, are caused and causing, supporting and dependent, mediate and immediate; and all support one another in a natural, though imperceptible chain linking things most distant and different.[10]

For Pascal, this was part of a battery of arguments to the effect that knowledge was more or less impossible for creatures such as we are except through a miracle. But the right conclusion is that knowledge is always rummaging in connections, focusing in on something in its situations: muddling through with objects and their contexts. That's the dilemma of a little mind in a replete universe. The point to be going on with is that everything is related to everything in infinitely many ways, and everything is what it is in virtue of its relations, or is what it is in its situations.

You have to start somewhere, as I will be arguing. I don't think it helps to start with our own consciousnesses, which are little embedded bits of a big old world. If you need a given, then start with things in the world. Some of these things could be vague as things, or problematic postulates, and so on. Mostly they're just exactly what we're acquainted with all the time, what we are actually trying to explore or investigate. Surely the natural direction of explanation is quite the reverse: the funny thing is not that our sense experience leads us right or is us in contact with a world but that it sometimes goes strange or wrong and produces illusions. Surely we are better acquainted with persons, trees, and roller-coasters than with the immediate contents of our own consciousness, and surely consciousness arises in the world, not the world in consciousness, and consciousness responds to the world continuously.

The same is true after the transposition from impressions to words, though this at least seems to presuppose the reality of other people, with whom we enter into linguistic practices or conventions. But the idea that in gazing through a telescope at a supernova, or in gazing through bifocals at a sparrow, I am gazing at words, or living out a narrative, is a very strange idea. Indeed, it's not even in keeping with the linguistic practices it celebrates or privileges as the source and nature of reality. These are cases, I think, of an endemic problem in philosophy. Philosophers often try to find the one thing that explains everything, the key that unlocks it all simultaneously. The idea that one has found such a an item has tremendous seductive or addictive power: the power to make smart people continue until they have lost everything, including the thing they were trying to realize or explain. The move toward "ideas" or "language"—the move to see all experience by analogy to pictures, for example (or stories, for another)—is an optional move, one of many possibilities. Once made it could well lead by its seductive pseudoexplanatory power, and the power of the intellect and writing of the great figures who take it up, to hundreds of years of ever-more elaborate or bewildering mistakes. The idea of "Form" in Plato, Platonism, and Neoplatonism is another example. It doesn't actually explain anything. But it feels profound; at a certain moment or in a certain region it feels inevitable. Plotinus starts there; he no longer has to try to argue for Forms at all.

A person of a sort now forgotten, Hans Vaihinger, solved all problems with the phrase "als ob": as if.[11] We live in a world of fictions or objects of our own construction and systems for their distribution. But we must behave as if we were living in a world of external objects, hard facts, and so on. It's as if there are red things, as if it's raining, as if I see a truck bearing down on me. It's just as if, almost as though, we're sitting on this couch, watching *American Idol*. This appears to me overly cautious.

There are signs of something else trying to get out of the idealist straitjacket: Austin's ordinary language philosophy, moments in Merleau-Ponty's ambiguous phenomenology. In Dewey, one gets the fundamental conception of experience as the organism moving through the environment as the environment moves through the organism, a basic metaphysics and epistemology of the situation as opposed to the subject or syntactic engine:

> The first great consideration is that life goes on in an environment; not merely in it but because of it, through interaction with it. No creature lives merely under its skin; its subcutaneous organs are means of connection with what lies beyond its bodily frame, and to which, in order to live, it must adjust itself, by accommodation and defense, but also by conquest. At every moment, the living creature is exposed to dangers from its surroundings, and at every moment, it must draw upon something in its surroundings to satisfy its needs. The career and destiny of a living being are bound up with its interchanges with its environment, not externally but in the most intimate way.[12]

Nevertheless, Dewey, like the phenomenologists, seems to waffle on the world outside consciousness. He should have maintained his thought that the "creature" is continuously constituted out of the world as the bedrock principle. Many figures, like Dewey or the whole of phenomenology, give a slippery or overly refined flavor to this question, while also yielding resources for a realist reading. In Heidegger, being might be de-concealed in language, but in his mystical moments language really is a route to the unknowable heart: language contains it or is contained by it, rather than serving as a sign of it. The same might be said of the Wittgenstein of the *Tractatus*. Foucault gets that you can't do political theory without bodies. Deleuze's rhizomes and nomads show real sources of philosophy in landscapes and the bodies traversing them together.

If in Rorty or in Derrida one feels trapped, perhaps that's because textualism of that stripe is a dead end, idealism's last moment. Language is not, any more than pictorial representation, the mode of our being-in-the-world; it is massively embedded in the world, not a field of force à la Quine, the inner bits remote from sense irritations, but in a constant interchange with, among other things, cultural practices, which in turn implicate technologies, which employ and respond massively to the physical surround. The vocabulary as a whole is always a register of the environment, and the social practices are a register of the environment and contributions to it, every inscription and utterance a thing, every one emerging from and into other things. Language has an origin, even: it is a piece of superstitious mumbo jumbo that makes it the always-already à la Gadamer, and it constantly alters that out of which it emerges, actually grinds up trees and so on.

9.

Consider a shadow as an object. It is best conceived as a situation, or an aspect, feature, or portion of a situation. We might say that the shadow is caused by the light source, object, and so on, but in truth it is a mercurial chunk of that situation: the shadow is not called into being by the light, and so on: it is the light in its differential flow, implicating an environment and certain sorts of sensory apparatus. The "modern" account of human consciousness as a "sensorium" or an arena of "ideas" reifies the shadow, isolates it, severs its connections, or actually deletes the situation that makes it possible and the material of which it consists.

We ought to think of human perception as a penetration of the body by the world: a strand going in and helping to compose the knot and then emerging again and on to the next. Perception makes use of holes in our bodies. When I see something, light literally enters my body and works its way through it in a series of transformations: my act of perception encompasses an external world situation or is itself an external/internal world situation. My consciousness is composed of stuff appropriated from the environment; it is not distinct from the environment. My consciousness is a trace or shadow in—or better, a knot of—physical reality.

The same is true of the social both ways round. So first of all, all these individual events/situations of perception are parts of the social. My consciousness is a portion of the social—or rather, of many social contexts and connections—as a knot is part of a larger section of a skein or indefinitely many larger sections. But social vocabularies, narratives, descriptions, and so on are massively constrained by a physical universe. That social systems in some sense emerge from physical environments is a commonplace, though no doubt controversial in the sense that a linguistic idealist such as Rorty would not even give me the term *physical environment* or would regard it as itself an artifact of social practices, language games, and the like. Well, it is an artifact of social practice, but no more than social practices are artifacts of it. Bruno Latour's work is exemplary here, and he shows minute by minute, detail by detail, how social practices are continuously embedded and reembedded in physical objects, as they transform those objects around their recalcitrances, are transformed by those objects around our own recalcitrances, and so on.

The inheritors of German idealism in this regard are various forms of "linguistic idealism," which have a relativist undertow. The Sapir-Whorf hypothesis, for example, has been interpreted in anthropology as declaring that we construct our worlds linguistically. But even here, anthropology has also most often held to the thought that the culture embodied in languages and practices is a response to the environment: the differences in environing conditions are used to explain some, at any rate, of the differences in cultural systems. My view is that there is much insight in linguistic idealism, though in another moment you may find me ridiculing the whole idea: there are various ways to structure experience through the use of language and other cultural/syntactical systems such as pictures. But I assert also that the differences take place against massive commonalities. The cultural systems in question have an external world context and act under massive external world constraints. We are in touch not only with our own representational or linguistic systems but with the material that they are used to represent and which they, in turn, alter. The representational system is always breaking on the real.

That is, I favor some sort of "direct realism," though that phrase has been used to stand for a number of different positions. Roughly, I will use the term to pick out two linked positions: in ontology, that there is a world in excess to (though in my version also encompassing) consciousness and in epistemology, the position that there is in normal experience no semantic screen interposed between the experiencing human being and the world she experiences.

10.

Among the Big Ones, I listed truth, beauty, goodness, justice; I'm not necessarily trying to set out an exhaustive list. The book is divided between ontological and axiological, or between fact and value, and I go on from ontology, alethiology, and epistemology to ethics, aesthetics, and political theory. This is not, as you'll see, because I think there is a hard and fast distinction between facts and values—though the distinction is important in certain contexts. In particular, I take aesthetics as providing a relatively revealing way into a conception of values as entanglements, as things that emerge in a human individual and a human community participating in a more than human world. Arts require physical media. The universe might be replete with all sorts of values that could be detected rather than invented or partly invented and partly detected.

I urge that we rethink conceptions of agency and responsibility in response to seeing more clearly the reality of ourselves. One result might be that we should think of responsibility as distributed through the elements of a situation, as we often already do. An individual's decision may or may not be a causal or other factor in a given case; responsibility is a matter of taking certain sorts of roles in an array or unfolding fact. Or, it is the mode of embeddedness or participation in a world of real persons and creatures and things that articulates responsible agents: not merely the subjective experience of the agent, not merely the conventions or customs of a people (though those, too) but the objectual context and the context of that context. I would like to be able to indicate that this will be clarified; it will be elaborated, anyway.

The political philosophy of the final chapter is a version of anarchism, which will surprise no one who is familiar with my work. This, in an instantiation of the overall conceptual structure, does not follow directly from the metaphysics or the aesthetics or even the ethics, but they are connected by many strands. In particular I'll say this: the idea that we are here to seize control of and transform and improve the world reflects from and onto the idea that we are here to seize control of and improve each other. This is not only a false and dangerous doctrine, it is a formula for the sort of statist misery we inflicted on one another throughout the twentieth century. Many actual monsters took up this point of view, and even the decent ones created oppression, whereas the indecent ones tried to kill everybody in the service of their inspiring vision. My political utopia goes like this: let people go and see what happens. And that, in a nutshell, is the beating heart of this whole project: I'm trying to let go, affirm, and I'm trying to work my way out of the self-enclosure of my pitiful little self and experience the genuine externality of the world and other people to me. Perhaps I'm doing that as a treatment for my own disease, my own moments of megalomania, certainty, my own impulse to oppress, foreclose, vitiate, destroy, or even to create what I think ought to be created. It's hard to doubt the sincerity of a Mussolini or a Mao: what I'd criticize is their extremely flawed self-reflection, their amazing idiotic disastrous attempts to realize their own vision. I'm trying to figure out how to let each thing and person realize itself or herself.

11.

One thing that stitches together the various pieces of this book (though I hope and expect not perfectly) is the heroes I keep returning to, the figures in the tradition with whom for one reason or another I feel a deep affiliation. Here are some figures who have articulated or overturned my thinking over the decades, who might appear here as relevant to almost any issue and are frequently lurking somewhere in the background: Søren Kierkegaard, J. L. Austin, Blaise Pascal, Ralph Waldo Emerson and Henry David Thoreau, Epictetus, Michel Foucault, Diogenes of Sinope, Bruno Latour (a later addition to my canon), Heinrich Wölfflin, G. E. Moore, Chuang Tzu, and Rembrandt. I will let you contemplate what these figures have in common as I try to figure that out myself. There are, at any rate, strands that run through them: individualism, affirmation of reality in various respects, intense self-reflection, and a suspicion of science and even of reason. I will express such suspicions too, while also providing heaping helpings of what I hope is rational argumentation.

And I might likewise, in a semiautobiographical vein, say that the positions in the book arose in response to the postmodern reality crisis. I was a graduate student in the 1980s, and I studied with Stanley Fish and Richard Rorty. I tried to defend a hard-nosed realism against the extraordinarily sophisticated critique of my teachers, who annexed many resources to their position that talk of reality or truth was exhausted, useless, over: Heidegger, Wittgenstein, Sellars, Davidson, Derrida. I was obliged to try to find a constructive project in the face of philosophy that said that philosophy was over. Back then, I was probably defending varieties of essentialism and representative realism against the Rortyan onslaught; if he was against it, I must be for it.

What I've come out with all these decades later tries to take the postmodern critique—including postmodern feminism, critical race theory, queer theory, genealogy, and so on—seriously. I accept a great deal of it. I'm insisting on a real world external to our consciousness and languages, but I am ditching the representational theory of mind. I ditch objectivity but retain truth. I ditch reductionism but hold on to materialism. I abandon scientism but keep naturalism. I pay respects to social constructionism, but I keep on pointing at nonhuman things. I am advocating a careful or gentle antiessentialism: like Rorty, I think of the universe as a web of relations (unlike him, I do not make us or our purposes or our languages central to that web) rather than as an array of fully discrete objects. But I also want to emphasize the way individual things and persons and persistent objects emerge in the welter. One thing I'm doing is trying to display many ways in which Rorty, and more generally postmodernism, were terribly wrong and, at the same time, take on board many of the fundamental insights.

12.

(1) The world is a system of physical things constituted in relation. Individuals are constituted by their relations to other things, in an accumulation over time. But each such set of accumulated relations (each individual) is massively unique precisely by virtue of its relations.

(2) The world is not a product of the human mind; the human mind is a product of the world.

(3) Direct realism: perception is not representation; it is a process in which human bodies are penetrated by the world, by which we ingest or inhale the world or are impaled on it.

(4) But there are representations, such as pictures, some sentences, or maps. With regard to such systems ("science," for example), it is false to say that there is a single privileged or "objective" representational system. There are bad ones, however.

(5) Truth = the world. "True" and "real" are, more or less, synonymous. True propositions, sentences, and pictures emerge from a reality-preserving relationship between world and consciousness, mediated by public language and pictorial systems and private character.

(6) Propositional knowledge is true belief: you know it just in case you believe it and it's true.

(7) Content-externalism or "extended mind": the mind actually encompasses external situations. The content of human mental states is not merely in the head.

(8) Attributions of value are true only under conditions which implicate "the natural," "the social," and "the subjective" in every case.

(9) Ethics concerns relations among persons, animals, and things that compromise their distinctness from one another or is a form of perception/communication understood as mutual permeation. This is captured in basic experiences/principles such as empathy and the golden rule: extensions of the self into the other and of the other into the self.

(10) The moral agent is not to be conceived as a rational deliberator, and a plausible conception of freedom would not connect it to such notions at all. Moral responsibility does not require free will and is distributed through the elements of a situation.

(11) Pleasure and happiness are not central to accounting for ethical, aesthetic, or political values. In general, teleological conceptions of values or human life are extremely impoverished or empty.

(12) Beauty ("the object of longing") is neither in the eye of the beholder nor (merely) a feature in the things beheld; it is a feature of the situation in which object is juxtaposed with perceiver, in which the integrity of each is cherished and compromised. In this it is exemplary of the ontological status of values.

(13) Art is characterized by intensities of relation between persons, materials, and audiences. Arts are to be broadly construed to include styles of movement, dress, self-ornamentation and transformation, distribution of elements in an environment, music, scent, writing, and so on.

(14) Social identities such as race, gender, and sexual orientation are profitably conceived as aesthetic repertoires expressed in all these ways, and they are always in volatile ways shifting as configurations of persons and materials.

(15) I refer to the emerging system of government in various parts of the world as "squishy totalitarianism." The left-right political spectrum must die, as shown by the great American reformers of the early 19th century, such as Lucretia Mott and William Lloyd Garrison. Anarchist non-utopia beckons: let people go and see what happens.

I

Ontology

1.

It has been proposed that physical objects, or whatever sorts of items may feature in everyday talk about things, are pragmatic postulates, that their reality, such as it is, consists in the fact that talking about them, or making them the value of bound variables and whatnot, helps us effectively organize our experience or adapt to a world, if any. But I propose to take the question of what sorts of things there actually are perfectly straightforwardly: I want to know what sorts of things actually exist, and I do not regard "exists" as a purely pragmatic category, or real objects as theoretical or pragmatic postulates, though the question of what is real has value valences as well. Or, reality has power, we might say—a compelling quality. Indeed, if we are real animals in a real world, then in the long run we must know this real world and respond to bits of it as they actually are, or be extinguished.

Here, in a series of quotations from Kant's *Prolegomena to Any Future Metaphsyics*,[1] is one sort of view I would like to be understood as completely rejecting: "The highest legislation of nature must lie in ourselves." "The understanding does not derive its laws from, but rather prescribes them to, nature." We must elucidate our basic concepts "not by deriving them from experience, but rather by deriving experience from them." "The principles of experience are the very laws of nature." "The unity of objects is entirely determined by the understanding." I think this position is, strictly speaking, psychotic; one might rather diagnose than argue with a nonphilosopher who asserted that he made up the world from the structure of his own sensibility.

Our orderings of things into kinds, species, individuals, and events result fundamentally from the actual state of those things externally to us; these things also embed us: our sensory experiences and the intellectual orderings of them are the result of processes of adaptation to an environment. Creatures who operated with a fundamentally imposed or constructed ontology could not survive in an actual universe. Indeed, worldly things actually physically produce the human body: the human body—and hence, mind—is a product of the environment it negotiates. We are made, as it were, to know the truth, and we are the truth, in one sort of manifestation. That is, we are physical things in a physical environment, like rocks or stars. Of course, this is not to say that we can't go wrong, even fundamentally, and I guess that, for example, spiritualist ontologies that enumerate supernatural beings are false, though the persistence of such ontologies should give one pause. On the other hand, the person who spends all day communing with angels steps out of his cell or spa and eats a meal and takes a leak, or else the communing doesn't last very long.

Not only are individual objects real and our individuation of them, by and large, a result of their character rather than ours, but they are distributed into facts, that is, situations and environments. That is to say, they not only appear to us—and, I am saying, actually exist—qua individuals but qua combinations of individuals, which are as fundamental to our true ontologies as are the individuals themselves. I might initially summarize my ontology, then, as a world of physical individuals in situations, or as a world of material situations consisting of individuals. Furthermore, these situations are fundamentally temporal; they unfold, and the objects embedded in them are in transformation, slow or rapid, at all times. And insofar as the objects are embedded in a situation, their unfolding is collaborative: they transform together as a situation as well as individuals. Individuals enter into and exit entanglements and come to exist and cease to exist within them. And finally, the whole of the universe may be considered in its aspect as a single unfolding situation of individuals in which we are all embedded.

I regard the world as perfectly real and as containing actual individuals, the entanglements of those individuals, and real events that occur in them and among them. But I admit that different systems of representation may be deployed with regard to them, for different purposes or highlighting different aspects. The world is infinitely rich, inexhaustible, and not fully comprehensible by any representational system. For a certain purpose, we may order a situation into trees and squirrels; for another, we may regard trees and squirrels as parts of the same ecosystem or even the same organism. Higgs bosons, air conditioners, hurricanes, and universes are notions or ways of bringing order to experience, even if they are also actual things. There are many—infinitely many, I want to say—possible correct orderings of the world, in that the world is infinitely profuse. And there are infinitely many possible incorrect orderings of the world, including some that might be useful or coherent. But there is exactly one world that is being ordered or disordered. There are accurate systems for representing the world that are classical or baroque, scientific or poetic. And there are also hybrid systems or compromises, poetic science and scientific poetry (e.g., Lucretius's).

Or, we might consider a table to be a swarm of atoms or a surface for holding cups; these are fundamentally compatible with one another. It's not the case that a swarm of atoms, which consists mostly of empty space, cannot be solid, for example, though a demonstration that a table is a cloud or swarm might be surprising. Science cannot discover that the average table isn't solid, after all; it can only tell us a bit more about what we meant all along by "solid." We could order snow into twenty-seven different kinds or consider it all as one kind with various differentiations, but then we can translate one of these vernaculars into the other, or incorporate one into the other, without changing the stuff that is actually falling from the clouds. Think about the limits of the ability of the Inuit and ourselves to rearticulate reality linguistically if it is boulders rather than snowflakes falling from the sky. You can call them pillows if you like; you get squashed all the same. Such things happen. A system of representation may make things apparent that aren't made apparent in another system, and any such system necessarily occludes as well as, in the best case, reveals. But if there are two images of the world that are genuinely incompatible with one another, I want to say, at least one of them has at least one element that is false.

In a notorious passage, Thomas Kuhn says that "as a result of discovering oxygen, Lavoisier saw nature differently. And in the absence of some recourse to that hypothetical fixed nature that he 'saw differently,' the principle of economy will urge us to say that after discovering oxygen Lavoisier lived in a different world."[2] But not, for example, in a world in which he started breathing for the first time after that discovery, or at a moment in which the pervasive phlogiston was replaced by a different substance, or the universe dephlogisticated, or in which the atmosphere around Lavoisier or the composition of his body was suddenly transformed. For whatever motive, you might try to obscure this or fudge it. But you know it very well. Either "phlogiston" is an unclear word for stuff like oxygen, or "oxygen" is a clearer representation of some phlogiston, or neither one picks out anything, or one of them picks out something and the other does not, even if they each come with a constellation of related concepts. But Lavoisier's discovery either showed us something about what we were already breathing, or it didn't show anything or was a mere change in terminology (which, of course, is a material change in all sorts of ways; it leads to changes in the way ink stains are distributed on paper, for example, or changes in the sound waves coming out of people's mouths).

One thing that has always struck me as bizarre: the notion that "the principle of economy" urges us to multiply worlds, indeed more or less to stipulate a different world for each new widely accepted scientific theory. "Economy" is a slippery term, of course, but whatever William of Ockham might have had in mind, I don't think it was worlds upon worlds upon worlds, under no detectable explanatory pressure. If the principle of economy teaches us anything, it ought to be not to go around multiplying whole worlds willy-nilly: that way lies real ontological madness. Methodologically, we shouldn't do that until there really is no alternative, for example, no way to describe the transition from a "phlogiston"-based representational scheme to an "oxygen"-based one. Well, this transition has been told in a number of books. And phenomenologically we shouldn't do it at all: we know very well that we share a world, that there is something that includes ourselves that we are struggling to know and transform. The discontinuities are interesting or conspicuous; the continuities are massive.

2.

But that is not ontology proper; it is the theory of representation or the philosophy of language. Or it is, indeed, ontology proper, but only insofar as representational systems or languages are themselves massive concatenations of objects and events: texts, experiments, pictures, brain states, postures of attention or turnings-away. Now we are ourselves parts of various situations: we are not separate from a world we perceive. We are facts and portions of facts. And, for example, social situations or juxtapositions of persons are facts, and social conventions are facts, and languages are immensely complicated physical situations. So it is not entirely out of place to speak of such things as "the social construction of reality": our languages and practices are central features of our environment. Of course, to say that clouds are produced socially is fundamentally confused: clouds are things we perceive, things we denote, and so on, and they are also real things, not dependent for their existence on what anyone or everyone says. "Look at that big cloud" is not something that creates a cloud as though by incantation; it is a marker of a situation in which human bodies are actually juxtaposed with water vapor and also embedded in linguistic situations, simultaneously. In such a case, both the linguistic practices and the water vapor are actually internalized in the human body: light reflects from the cloud and penetrates and alters the body, as do features of the social surround, which have produced a language user. We breathe the clouds.

Of course, some entities are more socially constructed than others. Consider sexual identities, race, money, or whatever notions or things you may think are most clearly "mere" social constructions. The taxonomies that these things represent are historical: they enter into our practices at certain times for certain reasons and then depart. They appear optional in this sense. But they not only articulate, they massively reflect, physical situations: they are vernaculars in relation to environments. If "blackness" is a conventional idea or not a feature of DNA, it responds massively to physical facts bound up, for example, with the institution of slavery: crops, technologies, oceans, reproduction of laborers, manacles, and so on. These also are part of the complementary construction of "whiteness," of course. If what is meant by calling them "social constructions" is that they could simply be dumped overboard by an act of will or a censorship regime that would alter the terms, that seems false. They are stubborn realities because they are massively complex situations involving millions of human bodies negotiating a physical environment over time as well as a set of linguistic practices. Indeed, these linguistic practices themselves consist of massively elaborate physical facts, and though we may work to alter a particular taxonomy, we would have to work also to alter the physical environments that produce it and that it produces. Race both makes and reflects a situation of segregation; hooks on to physical realities such as skin tones, ancestry, and continent of origin in an excruciatingly complex and problematic way; reflects economic interests and practices; tracks regions and is altered by region; is reflected in aesthetic transformations of the environment; and so on, and treating it as a linguistic structure only takes a tiny slice of the massive facts. Race reflects all these facts, but it also manufactures them: ingests facts and spits them out again, emerges from and alters the physical situation massively.

The United States, let's say, is a hell of an object. It is not a stable physical region, and its borders have changed dramatically over its history. It consists of persons, artifacts, landscapes, and a government. It contains myriad internal political or economic or geographical articulations: regions and states and counties, for instance, which are no more easy to delineate than nations. Who counts as an "American" shifts radically over time and is subject to human decision making of many sorts from individual to collective. And "American identity" is an immensely complex thing that stands in relation to all these other things. But the United States isn't a mental object, or a vocabulary, or a set of conventions. It isn't an imaginary object, and it isn't a linguistic object, though it encompasses such objects. If the United States is a massively conventional object, and "the United States" a massively vague term ("How far into the earth does the United States extend?" we might ask), it also bristles with particularities. We could consider it, at least in part, as a massive concrete situation; a juxtaposition of persons, animals, plants, objects, institutions, geological formations; and so on. It might be hard to say in some cases whether a particular person is an American, for example, and there are all sorts of intermediate cases. And the United States is also an immensely volatile object, even within a provisional or regional or momentary stability: its constituents shift over time; the set of constituents changes over time, but also each constituent changes over time. If we thought of the United States as an abstract object or merely a conventional object, we would have to ignore its massed physical particularities and the massive physical effects that such an object actually has. If the United States—now identified as a state or government—is bombing Libya, for example, actual things and people are actually blown to smithereens. Or to get more mundane: here I am writing a check to the IRS; these are real events. The United States is not—or at any rate is not only—some sort of Platonic Form or linguistic convention: it is a massive bristling concatenation of volatile things and events.

On the third hand, we've got to be in a position to criticize the entities to which we're apparently committed. Someone has to be able to throw into question the reality or the unity of the United States, or of the races. Entities evolve, and some entities that people believe in do not exist at all. Names are deployed in the service of power or ideology, of course, as well as in the service of responding to and taking up a place within reality. Then the critique can take up a place in a realist ontology: there are no reliable biological markers of race or the United States does not really hang together as a situation on the ground. We'd have to go out and show this: get inside the "subcultures" of the United States, or actually show the aspects of disunion, or the ideological origins of the idea or term. The ontology can bend or break, but the best way to break it is not merely to deploy some counter-ideology with counter-purposes, but to show the unreality of the purported entanglement, to get inside its complexities, show its connections and distances, demonstrate it to be a pile or region of knots rather than itself a knot, and so on.

3.

Perhaps, however, we're too quick to start enumerating hard cases. We might start, instead, with objects picked out by articles or indexicals. Does this exist (he says, holding up a blade of grass, a stone, a television remote)? Well, yes indeed. We are massively embedded in real things. Do television remotes exist? It would be silly to deny it, or only a philosopher is worried about a question like that. But a point would be not to confuse ontology with the philosophy of language, not to get immediately or exhaustively caught up in the meaning of "television remote," or the problem of reference or the problem of universals, which are different problems than the problem of what actually does exist. That we can't talk about what actually exists without talking, or write about it without writing, is a difficulty, but it's not the only difficulty, and posing it at the go immediately embroils you in the idea that we only have words, which tempts you to lop off other things as otiose.

One move, again, would be into demonstratives and indexicals, or better, into actual demonstrations: holding up this and that, or throwing it at someone: kicking the stone with Johnson to demonstrate the existence of the material world, walking across the room like Diogenes to show that motion is possible. Or we could try doing ontology in pictures, or in a comic-book style concatenation of words and images. Or we could try to shut up for a while and just appreciate the things around us, a Zen discipline of letting go of words perhaps, after which mountains will again be mountains. Or we could do some language after all, and then note that in doing that we are precisely making or rearranging real things: throwing out audible vibrations, running paper through a printer. The idea that all we have is language is an odd idea in that you can't have language without a host of (other) material things and events. There have to be questions that are not merely questions about language, and even questions about language that are not merely questions about language.

4.

There is only one level, plane, kind of existence, but there are infinitely many situations: as many as there are things, plus as many as there are relations between and among them. It could be quarks, leptons, and bosons, or a cow, a car, and a cop. The minimal condition required for something to be a situation is that it has the following elements (1) individuals (physical objects), (2) in mutual transformation or unfolding in relation over time, (3) in an environment, or under atmospheric conditions. "Situations are basic and ubiquitous," write Barwise and Perry. "We are always in some situation or other. Human cognitive activity categorizes these situations in terms of objects having attributes and standing in relation to one another at locations."[3]

Some situations are experiences of sentient and intelligent creatures. For something to be a situation of this kind, an experiential situation, at least two additional elements appear to be necessary: (4) perceptual sensitivity or permeability, and (5) a socially articulated vocabulary, or representational schema. I am very much not saying that all situations are human experiences, a claim which would be a betrayal, among other things, of human experience. Some situations have human or other sorts of perceivers in them: some are just juxtapositions of trees or planets, orbiting over time in a surround. When I'm looking at something, and I turn away, something in the situation changes, but not everything, and the other embedded objects maintain some—most—of their relations.

It appears in the above structure that "individuals" are taken as an unanalyzable foundation or that I'm doing atomism or monadology. But I prefer to say or speculate that *it's situations all the way down*. Buber: "In the beginning was the relation." He's thinking about us, in relation to one another; he's thinking about our languages; he's talking about everything.[4] Each individual in a situation is a situation, or is constituted by its relations. That goes for quarks, leptons, and bosons, as well as for a cow, a car, and a cop. It goes for experiences, of course, as well. Perhaps this yields some sort of regress, but I suppose that whether it's situations all the way down is a quasiempirical question, and if we produce the ultimate relationless monads with a particle-beam accelerator, then I was wrong. At any rate, a situation is a group of situations in spatio-temporal relation.

To be an element of a situation, or an object or individual within a situation, is to be a situation that is environed or engulfed. We reside within a nested structure of situations in which to be an individual within one is to be an environment in the next one inward, as the human body is an environment from one perspective and is an individual thing from another. So to entertain the notion that "it's situations all the way down" is to speculate that there are no entities that are not constituted by their relations; or that we can never isolate fundamental particles, only fundamental relations between particles, which are defined in terms of those relations. Be that as it may, the fact remains that we live in an infinitely rich context of nested situations.

A corollary of this is that everything that exists is on a single ontological plane. Or as I put it in the introduction: it's all string. No knot is definable in isolation: you have to specify how the string enters and leaves it; you have to figure out where it leaves off and the next knot begins, or whether they form a single tangle. If I tie a pile of half-hitches, is that a single knot or a number of distinct knots? That is something that needs to be fixed conventionally, or relative to certain histories and purposes and locations, though there are limits on true or plausible answers with regard to any given tangle: it depends on how tight I pull it. You've got knots with more or less determinate or vague borders. There will be clear cases of bits that fall inside or outside the knot, and in this sense there are internal as well as external relations: basically, what we might term *intrinsic properties*, though the internal properties are not, in principle, different from the external relations because, again, individuals are themselves situations. One bit of the knot is to the left of or is bigger than or consists in part of another, and so on.

Though only some situations are experiences, experiential situations are rife with reconfigurations or resituations; experiences throw things together at a node in a chaotic way and at an incredibly rapid rate and in a characteristic manner. This profusion of material, or the status of a subject as a continual factory of new situations, gives to metaphysics an overabundance of material and not a lot of structure. Now if I talked about "human subjects as factories of fact," I would usually be taken to be an idealist. But what I have in mind is that human bodies and the perceptual and intellectual apparatuses that go with them actually move through a world that is moving through them, and as they do, their experience produces and consists of facts kaleidoscopically, even as the profusion of unexperienced situations is hardly reduced from its infinity. However, it may be that everything that exists is in some sufficiently broad sense experienceable: we're built to be in environments; we're built as environments by environments. This is made possible by the materiality of us and things, our sharing of the same ontological space, or opening into the same time. One should be an egalitarian about things: they are all ontologically equal, or else they are nothing, or are inaccessible. There is, as Paul Levi Bryant says in the title of one of his books, a democracy of objects.

The hardest of (1) to (5) to put in ontological communion with the rest, or to drop onto the one and only ontological plain, is the vocabulary or representational system. As should be evident by now, I am going to wave in the direction of a nominalistic approach. Because language, as I will argue, has meaning only in utterances and inscriptions in physical contexts, possibly including internal auditory or visual events, I propose to treat the representational system—a language, vocabulary, taxonomy, or pictorial system, or something that combines various languages, pictorial systems, and so on—as a vast scatter of physical objects in connection, mutually unfolding in time: as a situation.

So first of all, we could say that the idiolects or relevant bits of the neurology of each language/pictorial system user is part of "the language," but so also are many other objects, such as books (i.e., particular physical bound volumes) and pictures that aren't in anyone's head but rather, for example, in a hard drive or hanging on a wall. This situation displays structure, to a certain degree: for example, the *Oxford English Dictionary* is part of the language that also has the function of serving to state rules or principles that are constitutive of the language. Also, English bleeds off along the edges and is always mutating into slangs, vernaculars, codes; always hybridizing with environing languages, and so on. We might think of representational systems along Wittgensteinian lines as practices or even games—conventions, rules of transformation, perspective renderings—but we also need to think about bodies and the movements of bodies, objects, the passions and recalcitrances of things. I just want to emphasize one more time that there is nothing ontologically fundamental about experiences and that the world is not primarily composed of experiences. Of course there is something epistemologically fundamental about them; knowledge is impossible without experience. But experiences are physical situations.

5.

To repeat, when I define an individual as a situation, I am saying that it is composed out of its relations. It cannot be individuated in terms of intrinsic properties, even if the notion that particular things have intrinsic properties isn't itself ultimately wrong or senseless. We might try to sketch some of the varieties of relation that are relevant to constituting an individual.

> (a) *composition*. The material that appears in and as a knot is a portion of the preexisting twine. A human body is composed without remainder of material that already existed (in different configurations) before that body emerged. The environment and the individuals that appear in it are nodes, connected in the same material fabric. And this process of composition continues as long as the individual does: the individual thing is throughout its persistence being composed out of the material environment; for example, animal bodies eat and drink and respire. Boulders accrete. There was a theological vision (Leibniz has a version) in which every moment was taken to be a miracle, in which God's creative force is needed to sustain/re-create the world at every

moment. But this is literally true of the material fabric or environing situation in relation to the individuals in it: they are built out of it and sustained moment by moment within it.

(b) of course, also *decomposition*, and individuals of all sorts continually shed or bleed or shit into their contexts. They shed molecules into the atmosphere and replenish molecules from it. They exhale and expire. Boulders disintegrate. In the long run every individual is lost imperceptibly into the environment, or ceases to exist.

(c) *causation*. The route my body walks each day is massively articulated by the density of the physical stuffs around me: I spend all day trying not bark my shin or drive into a wall. I live most of my life near the ground, being of a certain density in a certain atmosphere: by and large the stuff below me is more dense than I am and the stuff above me less. Other things push me around all the time: the action of my hands is given shape by the buttons and knobs. Viruses enter and bring down this internal system or that. My daughter cuddles in my lap and my legs get tingly. The sunlight cooks my skin. I yell at you and you yell back. I get bit by mosquitoes. The television sends me on an internet search. Like Elmer Fudd, I get crushed by an anvil. We think of causation primarily as the effect of individuals on one another, like billiard balls causing the motion of other billiard balls. Here we might contrast it with composition, for example, a diffuse gradual process of accretion out of all around. The environing situation cannot be said to cause the individual, exactly. But events within it have direct physical effects on the things it embeds; they knock up against one another all the time and are altered in the encounter. We are directly in physical contact with things in our immediate surround, from time to time. And we are in indirect causal connection with a much wider assortment of things (a combination shot), which are in turn connected causally, outward in ripples, through everything. It's not just us, of course: all these connections are typical of all sorts of things.

(d) *spatial and temporal location*. If time and space are infinitely divisible, then everything bears to every other thing an infinity of spatial and temporal relations. I live more than 1900 years after Lucretius, and more than 1899 years after Lucretius, and more than 1898 years, 364 days, 23 hours, 58 minutes, and 59 seconds after Lucretius, and so on: I am directly temporally related to Lucretius in an infinity of relations. The space between me and Mars is infinitely divisible, and for each possible location in space between us, there is a relation between us:

I am spatially related to Mars in an infinity of relations, even as its gravitation exerts a tiny tug on me. If an individual is a situation, and situations are items constituted out of their relations, then every individual has infinities of infinities of aspects. Now it might sound like I'm all too happy to count the time of clocks and the space of yardsticks as real, and indeed I am. There are different ways of representing time: even analog and digital displays that. But there is something real picked out by a clock too. Time is not a phenomenon; it's a real dimension; it doesn't slow up because you're bored and speed up when you're having fun. It contains you, not you it.

(e) *resemblance*. Each thing resembles each other thing to the extent, informally, that it shares properties with it, which we are obliged in turn to cash out in terms of situations/relations. There is, over all things, a web of resemblance that is their detailed ontological intertwinement. And each thing differs from each other thing with regard to each property they do not share. Now it is easy to see that each thing resembles each other things in infinitely many (but not in all!) respects, and that each thing differs from each other thing in infinitely many respects. Garbage and the good are both referred to in this sentence; they're both real-world situations, and so on. So then the problem from our point of view is how to narrow down the relevant or salient resemblances. But the question is not what our sentences indicate, the question is about real-world situations of real-world objects, though the thing we use to ask this question is language; and in that world, the respects of resemblance between any two items cannot be fixed in advance. To describe each thing that any thing resembles, and to say in what respects they resemble one another, is to describe that thing.

(f) *difference*. Each thing is constituted as a thing in a system of differences from what is not itself. Atoms are conceptually connected to void. Everything that exists is, at were, carved out of non-existence; or, difference itself is a constitutive relation: differences are as real as resemblances. Things are what they are in virtue of, for example, occupying this region of space or of having this history *and not another*, indeed, not any other. Each being occupies a space and hence carves out a "void" shaped in perfect contrast, through which it extends its connections.

(g) *physical forces*. Gravity acts on us all through the medium of the atmosphere, and so on, and not only all God's children, but every thing that exists, is operated on by this force, which is definable only in terms of the relations between things. Likewise the electro-magnetic force or whatever forces there may be. Gravity hurls junk at me from above, and I have to jump out of the way; it is a situation in which the junk and I are juxtaposed and connected, enveloped by strands of connection. But every object exerts a gravitational pull on every other. This is one reason to expect or hope for a single fabric, the whole taking form within gigantic situations occurring among or implicating everything. These have to be material if my ontology is right, but what precisely that means is, as we've already seen, a hornet's nest.

Points (a) to (g) are, we might say, ways to try to elucidate or systematize the fundamental elements of my metaphysics; not particles or monads or entelechies but relations in which things stand: forces, coalitions, arrays, cascades. They are the ways situations are constructed. These are the things we'll find when we get all the way down, or all the way back into the big bang, believe it or not.

6.

I am a physicalist or materialist of some sort, though it might be hard for me to tell you just why. I would wave toward a possible understanding of each thing and event as a set of physical relations, though I no more think that macro-objects can be "reduced" to micro-objects than vice versa. This positions my project within a certain historical development in ontology (so also as an outgrowth, if also something of a critique, of scientism or sciencey materialism). But the question of what is and what is not physical is a relatively difficult one in many cases. If you didn't count quarks or entire universes, clouds or piles of this or that as physical objects, exactly, I wouldn't necessarily quibble. I could say I feel myself to be a physical object in a physical situation; I feel that I am well-acquainted with actual physical things. I run up against stuff like that all the time. I am satisfied that such things exist; we do have access to this one realm of reality, and any multiplication of ontological levels beyond necessity should be avoided.

My basic commitment in ontology is to the one-plane principle: there is only one level of being. If it's situations all the way down, also all the way up: the whole is a single interconnected mesh or tangle. A representation and what it represents are different things, but they are on the same level of being, or they share an ontology: they are material situations: seal and wax, for example. Materialism is one strategy for collapsing all beings onto the same ontological plane.

Spinoza's ontology is somewhat obscure, for example, and he is certainly not simply a materialist and just as surely not an idealist. But he is committed to the one-plane principle; indeed, I would regard that as his fundamental ontological commitment. In a letter, he writes, "each part of nature agrees with the whole, and is associated with the remaining parts. . . . A given number of things are parts of a whole, in so far as the nature of each of them is adapted to the nature of the rest, so that they all, as far as possible, agree together."[5] This perhaps picks out the motive force of Spinoza's whole philosophical project. It is somewhat obscure what "agree together" might mean here; it does not seem to pick out some sort of logical consistency, but compresence in a network of relations. Spinoza's problem, like that of much of his century, is to try to work out of the difficulties caused by the interactions of items at different ontological levels, centralized as an issue by Descartes. "Occasionalism" à la Malebranche is a symptom of the desperation that this problem induces. Spinoza keeps emphasizing and collapsing the Cartesian or Christian pair: soul and body, spirit and matter. He is desperate to show that they are not different things, but the same things under different descriptions/construals/interpretations/points of view, and so on. This is both a real attempt to save a spiritual reality and its annihilation: an identification of God with Nature that was certainly construed in its own time as atheistic. Spinoza, one wants to say, sees how it really is; this makes him almost hysterical to save how it was previously conceived, which he accomplishes. But then there's a hard undertow of nature, devouring God into something recognizable as our real world, something in principle fully open to scientific scrutiny, for example. Plato's philosophy and Christian theology and a thousand other strands of Western intellectual history are bedeviled by these issues: how Forms interact with physical reality, how properties interact with substances, body with spirit. Materialism and idealism are attempts to construct ontologies that don't face this problem, though of course they face other problems.

The idea of levels or planes of being is notoriously obscure, but I would ask: Does this other plane of being have any spatial, temporal, or causal relations to this one? Is it accessible from this one? If so, it's like enough to and near enough to ours to be part of it. Does it or is it not? Then what work is it doing, or why would we suppose such a thing? If it's accessible from here, it is not a different plane. If it isn't then it can have no place in our philosophy.

7.

It is important to me that the universe be material, which I think has a magical quality. Thoreau writes:

> What is it to be admitted to a museum, to see a myriad of particular things, compared with being shown some star's surface, some hard matter in its home! I stand in awe of my body, this matter to which I am bound has become so strange to me. . . . Think of our life in nature,—daily to be shown matter, to come in contact with it,—rocks, trees, wind on our

cheeks! the solid earth! the actual world! Contact! Contact! Who are we? Where are we?[6]

Matter is mysterious and more or less adorable. And it's a bitch, too, of course; you keep stubbing your toe. But I would be happier to have everything spiritual than to have a material/spiritual ontological gap or divide. I insist on this: I will, because I do, have a universe in which it is possible to tie any two or more things into an assemblage, network, or knot: an imminent god, or no god at all. That is a universe that is always a challenge to the imagination, or in which it is possible to be creative.

The history of materialist thought is quite something, admirable among other things for its feet-on-the-ground skepticism of cant and mumbo-jumbo. Even though the ancients' atoms ended up sort of mysterious, the theory began in a resolution to take the physical world in which we live seriously. In classical Greece or Rome, in Christian Europe, in Vedic India, in ancient China: materialism and related one-plane ontologies have been extremely counterconsensus positions that often carried for their advocates the possibility of being summarily executed. The resolution is to go further in to the world with all its drawbacks—scientifically, aesthetically, even "spiritually"—rather than to seek a way out. Thoreau's ecstasy reminds us that materialism also has had a reverential or even epiphanic aspect, and that if it threatens to leave us in a world without meaning, it is yet always concerned to find meaning precisely in the world's and our own materiality. In Democritus, Lucretius, Spinoza, Walking Stewart, and Thoreau, for example, the material world is the occasion for poetry and reverie and adoration.

Now, materialism is also—or ought to be, at any rate—the ontology of modern science; even in its early deistic forms, science—as in Bacon, Descartes, Newton—tries, at least, to take the material realm perfectly seriously and to explain it internally or in its own terms. Materialism threatens and promises to demystify the world, to render it knowable in virtue of our interaction with it. At latest in Marx, materialism also becomes a strategy or ontology of social science, and here the demystifying impulse of materialism is fully manifest; Gassendi and a hundred others tried to render atomism compatible with Christianity; by Marx, it can ditch its accommodations. In short, it's a long and incredibly rich history. It would certainly be preferable to think in terms of materialisms, multiple interconnected ontological orientations. Materialism has been taken up at many moments for many purposes and with many effects, and possibly with many underlying notions of the "material," "physical," and so on. In Epicurus, for example, the reasons to take it up were primarily ethical: one could be "cheerful" if one could eliminate one's superstitious fears, including the fear of death, and enjoy the pleasures of the body with a good conscience, knowing there was nothing beyond or higher. You're not going to be around to experience your death, being yourself the material body in dissolution. The concatenation of atoms that is you at your death will reconfigure or recirculate in its endless or even cyclical transformation. No one is going to punish or reward you; the drama is not of the soul's progress, but of the body's individuation and de-individuation.

The cosmologies of many of the pre-Socratics could be thought of as fundamentally materialist, as when different figures try to account for all of reality as being produced out of or consisting of modifications of a single underlying element: water for Thales, fire for Heraclitus, and so on. Though these cosmologies are apparently simple one-plane principles, they do face devastating empirical problems. Ancient atomism is an attempt to preserve the commitment to the physical world of such figures, in part in the face of the Eleatic critique of their concept of being, or to try to answer the question of how such things as elements originate and circulate: how they arise and how they change. And it wants to explain diversity as well as unity: "everything is water" is a too-unified ontology. Ancient atomism did not necessarily account adequately for the diversity of physical things there are, but it tried to do so while also saying of the universe that it ultimately consists of one sort of thing.

It did that in terms of physical "minima"; beginning with the observation that material things can be divided or crushed, atomism projected such procedures down indefinitely and held that physical things consist of particles that are themselves indivisible and not accessible to sense. The nature and disposition of these particles explains the behavior of the larger objects which consist of them, in an environment which also consists of them. Because both atoms and the objects that consist of atoms can move, there must be something for them to move through: the complete ontology is "only atoms and the void." Atomism is the dominant materialist ontology in the West—though not the only one, as we've already seen—and it had a remarkably persistent set of revivals throughout Western intellectual history, from the Epicureans to medieval Islamic thinkers to Gassendi and modern particle physics. In each revival, of course, the view shifts even as the connections are explicit.

Here is how Aristotle, according to Simplicius, explains Democritus's atomism:

> These atoms, which are separate from one another in the unlimited void and differ in shape and position and arrangement, move in the void, and when they overtake one another they collide, and some rebound in whatever direction they may happen to, but others become entangled in virtue of the relation of their shapes, sizes, positions, and arrangements, and stay together, and this is how complex entities are produced.[7]

The picture of the universe as consisting of entanglements of physical particles in a void is one I endorse, more or less, or at least it is a reasonably good initial picture of the sort of reality I believe I exist within. Democritus makes the universe a system of differences, or a network of presence/absence, à la Saussure with language. Indeed, a favorite image of the differences among atoms in shape, arrangement, and position is alphabetical: AN differs from NA in arrangement, for example, N from Z in position. And the idea that "arrangement" (or perhaps better, "configuration") and "position" are individuating properties of particular atoms suggests the possibility that atoms in at least some moments of ancient atomism were themselves defined relationally. This would violate everything most Greek philosophers, in particular Aristotle, thought was true about "substances" by definition, which might in turn suggest that many of Aristotle's arguments against the atomists along these lines turned on an underlying disagreement—perhaps irresolvable—about the nature of substance. Aristotle took the term *ousia* to denote whatever exists fundamentally and independently or whatever underlies accidents or properties, precisely the idea that got Parmenides rolling on the Eleatic highway to absolute stasis, though of course Aristotle also treats the whole thing in a much more common-sense sort of way.

What is crucially missing in the ancient atomist standpoint, so far as we can recover it, is an account of the forces or factors by which atoms become entangled and constitute objects at a perceptible scale. Such concepts as "position" and "arrangement" are awfully vague, and the "swerve" which accounts for reality being differentiated at all is notoriously an arbitrary stipulation that does not itself emerge from the a priori–style arguments in ontology, although perhaps the idea was clarified to some extent in ancient atomist or Epicurean writings that have been lost. What is clear is that the atomists wanted to be understood as describing the physical properties and relations of atoms in space as in principle explaining the disposition of objects at larger scales, but many a philosopher has focused on atomic swerves and collisions and arrays as mysterious.

Aristotle attributes to Democritus the quite traditional metaphysical claim that it is impossible for two real substances to become or to be one. This reading suggests that Democritus developed analogues to what became known as the "manifest image" and the "scientific image";[8] you seem to live in a world of people and houses and trees, but all there really are are atoms and the void which are not at all like people, houses, and trees—for one thing, they cannot be perceived—but which compose those things and ultimately explain in the manifest world their behavior. But the struggles over "substance" in the metaphysics and of the ancients and right through the Medieval to the Modern period seem to me to be far too a priori; as Ludwig would say, don't think about it and then tell me what is and what is not a single thing, but *look and see* what is a single thing. A tree is certainly a single thing, the sort of thing that gives such a term its meaning; if you like, which I don't, it is a substance. But of course it is also many things and not even a single thing (part of a grove, let's say).

Aristotle in one way or another is the source of most of our knowledge of the early atomists (Leucippus, Democritus); he was pre-occupied with the position, found it compelling yet unsatisfactory. I think reading ancient atomism through Aristotle's lens is problematic, but whether Leucippus thought so or not, let me point out that it is perfectly possible for two real things to become one: for two drops of water to become one drop, two people to make a couple, many pieces of debris to make a solar system, and so on. But the dispute in some ways is merely verbal: of course Leucippus and Democritus thought that many atoms could make one table, and so on, and in declaring the atoms to be fundamental, they are (merely) engaging the apparent entailments of the Greek concept of *ousia*.

Epicurus's "Letter to Herodotus" gives as clear a statement as any of the view.

> And the atoms move continuously, at all times, some recoiling far apart from one another upon collision, and others, by contrast, maintaining a vibration when they are locked into a compound by the surrounding atoms. This is the result of the nature of the void which separates each of them and is not able to provide any resistance; and their actual solidity causes their rebound vibration to extend, during the collision, as far as the distance which the entanglement [that is, the composite object] permits after the collision.[9]

Rather than appeal to forces per se, this appeals to the action or vibration that atoms gain in collision with one another, or which they maintain when they come into proximity and constitute an entanglement or compound or object. Now what maintains their vibrations it is hard to say, but atoms in a compound vibrate, we might say, sympathetically or in harmony (and one would have to be reminded of various aspects of Pythagoreanism here, though certainly the ancient atomists, as also Gassendi, rejected the mathematicization of reality). Then the "rebound vibration" emanates a material image (as well as scents and so on) that makes the object available to the material sense organs of a sensitive organism.

> One must also believe that it is when something from the external objects enters into us that we see and think about their shapes. For external objects would not stamp into us the nature of their own colour and shape via the air which is between us and them, nor via the rays or any kind of flow which moves from us to them, as well as they would by means of certain outlines which share the colour and shape of the objects and enter into us from them, entering the vision or the intellect according to the size and fit and moving very quickly; then for this reason, they give the presentation of a single, continuous thing, and preserve the harmonious aspects generated by the external object, as a result of the coordinate impact from that object on us, which originates in the vibration of the atoms deep inside the solid object.[10]

That is, perception is, as I have been urging, a form of ingestion or inhalation; or it's like being stabbed: a physical internalization of the real external world object. The "immediate contents of sense," to use the vernacular I particularly reject, are externally existing material "images" or even "skins"—themselves consisting of atoms—or their correspondents in other sense modalities, not subjective states of the perceiver. Both Lucretius and Walking Stewart (of whom more below), for example, constantly recur to the example of smell: the fire or the perfume or the corpse emits a material stream which enters the body of the perceiver, and Lucretius develops this picture of objects emitting material "films" or "skins" systematically if obscurely in the astonishing Book 4 of *De Rerum Natura*.

8.

It is a potentially disruptive principle of ancient atomism that "truth is in the appearance."[11] This appears to be in tension with the ontology of physically indivisible particles in a void, since we do not experience these particles directly; they do not appear. And again one might think of this as introducing precisely an ontological category of appearances, intervening between the atoms and ourselves. Atomism needs to be placed in the context of Eleatic and also possibly Heraclitean metaphysics: the basic project of ancient atomism is to explain how both motion and rest, or flux and persistence, as well as unity and diversity, are possible in the face of philosophies that were always threatening to collapse into one or the other and thus lose faith with our experience of the world. It tries to explain how there can be both one and many in the face of philosophies that argued that there can be only one or only many, how there can be both change and things that persist through change. The project emerges, that is, as a defense of the "ordinary world," the world as it is actually experienced by human beings. It tries to answer the *a priori* arguments of Parmenides to the effect that motion and change are impossible by reversing the chain of reasoning: given that we are actually moving and changing things in a moving and changing universe, what must be the case at the level of fundamental ontology?

Atomism enacts the same reversal of momentum that we find in Diogenes of Sinope: look; I just walked across the room, so motion is possible. But then they ask, given that it is, *how* is it possible? That's certainly a question we'll never get to through the deductive/poetic Eleatic method. Well you need things and you need space in which they can move and processes or forces or relations by which they can be transformed. It is an empirical a priori that begins not by regarding the world as experienced with suspicion, but with an affirmation that is an ethical as well as an ontological criticism of Parmenides or Plato. We need to commit ourselves to the world; the world is what needs to be explained; it is what we need to reconcile ourselves to in order to find peace, not something to be exposed as an illusion. Aristotle in another register also expresses this basic orientation: the stance of the realist in my sense: Aristotle *starts with* a world that needs explaining.

Now even at this early date the question of what is and what is not material is obscure: the concept of "materiality" remains crucially undefined. Is "void" a material thing? That's quite the little tickler; "void" is perhaps defined precisely by contrast to the material, as where the atoms ain't. Then again, is nothing something, and so on? The atomists even debated whether, for example, light was a substance consisting of particles, or something else again (this debate was dramatically resuscitated in late-Renaissance humanistic science), and I wouldn't say we've managed to put this question to rest with our wavicles or whatever it may be. Is "energy" material? Some folks would say so, others not; at any rate you'd have to say it has material effects, or is defined by its material effects; it can't be promoted or demoted to a different ontological level than that of material things. What is light without material manifestations and effects? Or how about "forces" such as gravity (to say nothing of the wacky quantum things/events/forces of contemporary physics)? Well they certainly are, again, conceived and detected by physical effects, but whether they are themselves material in any sense or in what sense is a fully obscure problem. It is certainly one that bedeviled Newton: was his theory committed to causation at a distance? That is, was gravity supernatural? Then again, people have tried to think it through with "gravitrons": like the skins emitted by visible objects.

One might define materiality in terms of extension in or occupancy of space, for example, à la Descartes and many others. But whether or not the ancient void is conceived as space itself, this does recapitulate the atoms-and-void structure, at least until we relocate space as a form of perception rather than itself an external fact or pool in which we are all at swim. Descartes held that space must be real or external to the mind or however we may want to put this, because if it weren't, God would be a deceiver. Even without God, we could say that if we do not meet with things external to ourselves in space then we are globally deceived or at any rate entirely mistaken, and one might read Descartes's observation essentially as registering a resolution of faith that there really is an external world, a way to get himself to believe his own experience.

I will not be assaying the definition of "material." What I will resort to is demonstration, which admittedly is harder to accomplish across the writer-reader abyss. Well, physical stuff is stuff like this (smacks the wall). Here is a hand (upside your head). Like this (pinches your cheek). Every thing is *a thing like that*, though in precisely what respect it is hard to say without saying "physical," "material," and so on. But communication does not entirely consist of linguistic signifiers: one also uses physical gestures and objects in the world: see this here brick is part of what I am trying to communicate to you. Not a subject and a predicate, but a thing and the ways it is and what it does.

Really that is how I would like to read the ancient materialists: as systematizing a resolution to affirm the real, whatever in detail atoms and the void, or material objects and their medium, might be. The role of the materialist in a variety of cultures (in India, for example, in the form of Carvaka) is to roll his eyes at the mumbo-jumbo, the profusion of abstractions or entities no one can detect by ordinary means; in that sense materialism might be allied with empiricism, though empiricism, precisely in its defense of the ordinary sensible world, ended up making a disastrous idealist turn. Certainly you can picture Democritus rolling his eyes at Plato. Richard McKirahan writes of atomism that

> The crucial features of this cosmogony are that it results from atomic movements without purpose or divine agency, and that our KOSMOS is not special, only one of an infinite number of similar KOSMOI with similar histories. That our world is not unique or located at the center of the universe, and that we are insignificant from a cosmic point of view, are strikingly modern ideas and drastic departures from what sense experience would lead us to believe.[12]

Ancient materialism, that is, had a pretension-puncturing function, reintegrating human beings fully into the order of nature, as material chunks or swarms presenting only whatever significance chunks or swarms of atoms can have. But I would flatly reject the claim that such an idea is strikingly modern or that it isn't "what sense experience would lead us to believe." On the contrary, sense experience is constantly informing us of our puniness and vulnerability, our ignorance and error, and our embeddedness in a material world. That experience is registered all the time in all sorts of different philosophical and religious orientations, even if there are also many grandiose moments in which human consciousness is placed at the center of the world.

9.

The life of the materialist philosopher Walking Stewart—author of thirty unreadable books and friend of great poets—is a crystallization of his ontology and mine. John Stewart the Traveller was born on Bond Street in London in 1749; his father was a linen-draper from Scotland. After getting kicked out of a variety of schools, young John was sent to Madras as a secretary with the East India Company at age 15. He accompanied a warlike Company expedition into Tibet and Bhutan, which he portrays in a letter to the Royal Society in 1777 as one of the few Western contacts with these places and cultures since Marco Polo. Disgusted by the entire system of colonialism, particularly as expressed in the East India Company itself, beginning with the fact that the British stationed in India did not speak the local languages, he drafted a letter of protest addressed to the Court of Directors concerning the treatment of indigenous population. His second letter of protest to the Directors, a year later (circa 1765) "from its juvenile insolence and audacity, is preserved on their records to this day." Then,

> From accounts written within a year or so of Stewart's death, it appears that on leaving the Company's service he struck into the interior of India with the general purpose of learning the native dialects. According to the *Gentleman's Magazine*, he "prosecuted his route over Hindostan, and *walked to Delhi*"; "he traversed the greater part of the Indian Peninsula. [Bronson's note: "Apparently, though the fact has not been noted, he got as far east as the Malay peninsula."] Wandering of this sort must have consumed at least a couple of years, during which he acquired a considerable proficiency in the tongues. In an evil hour his adventurous disposition drew him to Seringapatam, the capital of the warlike and treacherous Hyder Ali.[13]

Possibly Hyder Ali (1720–1782) was regarded as warlike and treacherous because he was in the habit of launching rockets at the British, an innovative yet profoundly irritating anticolonial strategy. So Stewart's service to Hyder Ali itself had the scent of treason. Indeed "a relative" described Stewart as "a general" in the Dalwai of Mysore's (Hyder Ali's) service, where others merely describe him as an interpreter. At any rate a direct explanation of this interlude would be that Stewart was so disgusted by the behavior of the East India Company that he joined up with the other side. He was shot in Hyder Ali's service, and his relative Everard Brande reports in general that "his body bore the marks of several desperate wounds by sword and bullet, and the crown of his head was indented nearly an inch in depth with a blow from some warlike instrument."[14] Stewart escaped assassination by the Dalwai's men by swimming a river. Brande then places him in the service of the Nabob of Arcot in south-central India, as Prime Minister. He was greeted here and there as a heretic, though it is not clear whether as a young man striding around Asia he had already developed his frankly atheistic materialism.

> [While Stewart was] crossing the Persian Gulf, in a vessel manned exclusively by Mahometans, a violent storm arose, which misfortune the crew attributed to their having a Giaour on board [Brande makes it "infidel"]; a counsel was held, and it was determined that the new Jonah should be cast overboard. It was with much difficulty that Mr. Stewart persuaded them to modify their resolution; it was at length settled that he should be immured in a hen-coop and suspended from the main-yard until the storm abated. In this elevated station he remained for some hours, nor was he released till the storm had entirely subsided.[15]

Another source has him hanging from the mast in the chicken coop for two weeks, during which he "was arranging in his mind the opinions he had formed of mankind."[16] From the Persian Gulf and the Arabian Peninsula he walked through "Ethiopia and Abyssinia," where he saw naked people. Thence "he crossed the Desert of Arabia, and arrived in Marseilles," walked more or less the entirety of France, crossed the Pyrenees, "tramped through Spain and Portugal," and took ship for England around 1784.[17] After alighting briefly in London, he trudged Sweden, Lapland, and Russia, but reported that "he found no means to penetrate" into China.[18] "In the autumn, probably, of 1786, Michael Kelly, the operatic tenor and friend of Mozart, ran across him in Vienna. Stewart had just arrived (on foot) from Calais, having passed through Italy and the Tyrol, and was on his way to Constantinople."[19]

In 1792 he was, among other places, in Paris during the September Massacres, where he turned against political radicalism and befriended Wordsworth and Thomas Paine. According to Thomas De Quincey, Wordsworth thought that Stewart was "the most eloquent man" he'd ever heard discourse on Wordsworth's favorite subject, nature.[20] Kelly Grovier argues plausibly that Stewart is the model for the "phantom drifter who haunts the apocalyptic beginning of Book Five of *The Prelude*."[21] Always perfectly balancing the sublime and ridiculous, Stewart was also the subject in the same 1792 of an operatic farce by William Pearce titled *Hartford-bridge; or, the Skirts of a Camp*, where he was portrayed by the great comic actor Joseph Munden.

He took two extended tours of the United States in the 1790s. A newspaper in Albany printed the following notice "On Thursday last, arrived in this city from London, via New York, and the same evening setting off for Canada, Mr. Stewart, the noted pedestrian."[22] Though he was chronically broke all over the world (the Jacobins confiscated what little cash he'd built up in South Asia, for which he never forgave them), he was particularly so in North America, where he was reduced to begging for food between lectures, but managed to publish the epic Lucretian poem *The Revelation of Nature* in New York in 1796. De Quincey has him bestriding the continent: "the solitary forests of Canada . . . the swarming life of the torrid zone, . . . the great deserts."[23] After the turn of the century, he seems to have wandered mostly in the British Isles and was seen in Devonshire. He crossed to Ireland, and walked from London to Edinburgh to consult Dugald Stewart (no relation).

Now his reputation for sheer omnipresence or for multiple simultaneous manifestation narrowed to London, but was all the more striking for being localized. In 1822, a correspondent for *The London Magazine* observed that everyone had seen Walking Stewart sitting on a bench on the Westminster Bridge as though he'd never not been there. But then again, there he was in Hyde Park, with "as perfectly an eternal air." But there he was shuffling around the Strand, and Charing Cross, and Cockspur Street. "Where really was he?" asks our reporter. De Quincey quotes this passage, then writes:

In 1812 it was I think that I saw him for the last time; and by the way, on the day of my parting with him, had an amusing proof in my own experience of that sort of ubiquity ascribed to him by a witty writer in the London Magazine: I met him and shook hands with him under Somerset-house, telling him that I should leave town that evening for Westmoreland. Thence I went by the very shortest road (*i.e.*, through Moor-street, Soho—for I am learned in many quarters of London) towards a point which necessarily led me through Tottenham-court-road; I stopped nowhere, and walked fast; yet so it was that in Tottenham-court-road I was not overtaken by (*that* was comprehensible), but overtook Walking Stewart.[24]

That is, there is the vague suggestion that The Traveller possessed X-Men-like mutant superpowers (perhaps teleportation, time bending, or self-cloning, or maybe his thought was so heavy that it distorted the space surrounding him, like a black hole, lending him the illusion of omnipresence).

The Traveller held nightly gatherings in his threadbare apartment, and was befriended and indeed revered with a touch of condescension by the great British Romantics. De Quincey compares Stewart to Shelley, who no doubt—like everyone else—was acquainted with Stewart.

Like the late Mr. Shelley he had a fine vague enthusiasm and lofty aspirations in connexion with human nature generally and its hopes; and like him he strove to give steadiness, a uniform direction, and an intelligible purpose to those feelings, by fitting them into a scheme of philosophical opinions. But unfortunately the philosophic system of both was so far from supporting their own views and the cravings of their own enthusiasm, that, as in some points it was baseless, incoherent, or unintelligible, so in others it tended to moral results, from which, if they had foreseen them, they would have been themselves the first to shrink as contradictory to the very purposes in which their system had originated.[25]

De Quincey places Stewart on one occasion at a "small party" with William Godwin, Coleridge, Wordsworth, Southey, and Charles Lamb. What could be more romantic in the pre-1800 and also the post-1800 sense, than walking solo over the face of the world, gaining acquaintance with who knows what cultures and ideas and costumes and cuisines and stories? Indeed, as my friend Glen Mazis pointed out to me with the simplicity of a good insight: you know all those people were great walkers. Later on, so were Emerson and Thoreau. And all the Romantics were younger than Stewart. Even Godwin was seven years his junior, and he had twenty-one years on

Wordsworth. The myth of Walking Stewart must have been with these chappies from childhood, teaching them the exotic like a series of paintings by Delacroix.

One should think of Stewart as a figure both of fun and of veneration among the early British Romantics: not only for the constant appeals to "Nature"—Stewart typically represents himself as the *omoousiast*: "Nature's only child"—but also in the very idea of someone who experiences all the world's cultures. Now on the other hand, most of these figures—in part because of the influence of thinkers such as Kant and Schiller—were philosophical idealists of one sort or another, and I hope that Stewart at his dinners brought out many a material stick to beat them with.

If you ask me, of course, the idealism of the Romantics was rather unfortunate, or perhaps the word I am groping for is *preposterous*. Both the British and American romantics read way too much German philosophy: along with the opium, quite the downfall of Coleridge, I believe. What Stewart's position shows is that it is possible to be a materialist—or more widely to celebrate and immerse oneself in the real world—and still be plenty Romantic. Surely Wordsworth in particular might have had some sympathy with this stance, to say nothing of Thoreau. The Romantics celebrated art and attacked reason. But Stewart's strategy was to expand the sense of "reason" from its Enlightenment/scientistic sense. He described his preferred mode of reasoning as "analogy," but by that he meant the very widest drawing of associations and the freest rushing to conclusions; he meant intellectual improvisational art. For that reason among others it is an awfully interesting brew: he's a materialist but a skeptic about or even an enemy of experimental science, which he regards as arid and completely incapable of dealing with the richness and ambiguity of the real world. The fact that he had cultivated a serious hatred of the French, and associated experimentalism with the French encyclopedists, could not have helped. But his basic idea was to keep walking: there's no telling in advance where your thinking feet might take you; let yourself go and see.

Stewart wrote many books, in which he repeated his materialist philosophy incessantly in language that seemed ambivalent about being understood. Indeed, like many no doubt greater philosophers of that era and the two centuries that followed, Stewart's work bristles with coined technical terms and extremely complex sentences embedding myriad clauses, the syntax of which does not invariably work out. At his best, he writes like Hegel or Schelling at their worst, in translation. And reading his texts, or even just examining his books, does raise the issue of barminess. His books had titles like *The Sophiometer; or Regulator of Mental Power; Forming the Nucleus of the Moral World, to Convert Talent, Abilities, Literature, and Science into Thought, Sense, Wisdom, and Prudence, the God of Man; to Form those Intermodifications*. He restarted history with the publication of his *Apocalypse of Nature*, dating his other works accordingly. His books feature many prefaces, introductions, forewords, and so on, so that they never seem actually to begin. Or to end: sometimes they finish five times over a hundred pages with a definitive THE END. He certainly took himself seriously as a major figure, beginning his *Opus Maximum* as follows:

> I shall open this stupendous Essay of intellectual energy with the most important discovery of the moral laws of nature that was ever made by human intelligence, viz. That the word knowledge signifies no more than a capacity of mind to conform the relations of thought to the phenomena or appearances of things, whereby we conceive the course or order of nature's action independent of its essence or unknown causes.[26]

"Certainly," writes De Quincey, "when I consider everything, he must have been crazy when the wind was NNE."[27] No one read Stewart's books at the time—with the possible exception of De Quincey who, like me, skimmed; they have never been reprinted, and they sank into complete obscurity, despite the fact that Stewart asked everyone he knew to bury copies of his work, so that after the disaster (a Jacobin revolution, perhaps), the world could again be redeemed by his astounding insights.

But unlikely as it seems, it is an extraordinary philosophy. "In many things he shocked the religious sense, especially as it exists in unphilosophic minds.... And indeed there can be no stronger proof of the utter obscurity in which his works have slumbered than that they should all have escaped prosecution," writes De Quincey.[28] Stewart is a realist about the world and our experience of it; he's a materialist in a Lucretian mode, as well as a kind of pantheist or worshiper of the whole in a way that bespeaks the influence both of Spinoza and of various Eastern traditions. But he is also fundamentally an "outsider" in philosophy, as well as in whatever society he inhabited, including London's. This has its advantages and its disadvantages, and Stewart by hook or crook latched on to many a critical or constructive insight.

His philosophy as a whole is remarkably similar to the one I am trying to articulate, though I would stop short of Stewart's many expressions of pan-psychism. At any rate, he is a realist in my sense, or in the sense of the term developed by "speculative realists" such as Graham Harman and Paul Levi Bryant.

> It burst upon my intelligence with a blaze of light the following momentous and natural notion, That all facts, relations, or analogies of things, were totally independent of all human opinion, and its forms of logic or language. Fire, light, matter, motion, mind, exist now with all their qualities, as they existed at all times of antiquity; and no errors of language or opinion can give any alteration to their different qualities, or degrees of relations, or analogies in real existence.[29]

That is, we do not articulate or construct a world linguistically; we grapple with it linguistically, or defer or deflect or falsify it, or commit ourselves to it, and so on. But Stewart is also explicit that human language and consciousness are themselves material things and relations.

> No power can exist without matter to support it, or give it a substratum. The action or power of any substance is nothing but matter modified into that action or power. The action of thought, or consciousness, in a human body, is nothing but matter modified through its organism into the action of thought; and it is not the action that feels or thinks, but the body or matter itself that perceives its own action. Thought does not perceive matter, but it is matter that perceives thought; and personal identity or modality is but a succession of thoughts produced by transmuting matter, and has itself no possible being or identity, which belongs entirely to matter.[30]

These are rather remarkable formulations of materialism with regard to mind, and I would say are fundamentally innovative in the history of Western philosophy, or would have been if they had been read. He locates human identity and consciousness fully in the material body in connection to other material bodies.

Stewart's materialism is not exactly atomism as that is usually defined: he held with most atomists that matter was indestructible, but also against most that it was infinitely divisible, so that you can never get down to the fundamental speck. Stewart's matter is, we might say, essentially liquid rather than particulate: it flows. I like this picture, and it is connected to my notion that it is "situations all the way down," or that individuals are individuated by their relations, or that matter is infinitely divisible. The atomists gave us, as it were, a digital reality, or a reality assembled out of distinct points, like a comic book or television image, or like a Pointillist painting. Epicurus says:

> One must not believe that there can be an unlimited number of masses—no matter how small—in any finite body. Consequently, not only must one eliminate unlimited division into smaller pieces (to avoid making everything weak and being forced in our comprehensive grasp of compound things to exhaust the things which exist by reducing them to non-existence), but one must also not believe that within finite bodies there is an unlimited movement, not even by smaller and smaller stages.[31]

This is surely the atomists' attempt to deal with the Eleatic a priori arguments; Epicurus accepts the Parmenidean adage that something cannot come from nothing, nor nothing from something. And the answer to Zeno's paradoxes appears to be simply that space is not infinitely divisible. But Stewart, while he does not necessarily reject the notion of void, makes matter continuous, or more like a wad of goo than a pile of sand. The issue might be empirical in some sense, and in order to pay off on a notion like that we might have to clear the ground of many problems.

So fungible and mobile is Stewart's matter and ours that the problem is to explain persistence and identity. But he also held that persistence and identity had been fundamentally exaggerated in the history of thought, and that in a world so liquid, which is flowing through us as we ourselves flow, only the good of the whole really bears scrutiny as an ontologically supportable ethical purpose. That, for Stewart, follows from our nondistinctness from all that is. We spent centuries imaginatively isolating ourselves or eternalizing ourselves or disembodying ourselves within the relentless and gorgeous and infinitely varied ubiquitous everything: now the point is to re-connect or experience the oneness of ourselves with the whole material system: a secular or materialist or naturalist redemption/nirvana. What he taught, he said, was a single principle: "The identification of self with nature."

> Such an analysis into the nature of *being, thing, essence, matter,* or *nature,* which words are all synonymous, teaches man the most important principles of self-knowledge; viz.—that, as immortal and indestructible matter is incessantly changing from the single agency of man into the patiency of all sensitive life, it is the interest of matter to augment the good of all sensitive life; and as the personal modality has no sameness of entity, being nothing but the action of that quantity of matter that supports it, like the eddy in the current, which is nothing but a succession of action produced by the substance of matter of water, changing from agitation of one wave into the waves of the whole pool; just so, matter transmutes from the agency of half a pound of brain, in the mode of man, into the patiency of the brain of the whole sensitive system; and the personal modality of *I, he,* or *you,* in its incessant change of life or annihilation by death, can have no possible relation to matter itself, to augment or diminish the patiency of its good or evil agency; and its interest and identity with universal being, matter, or nature, belongs wholly to matter; for, personal modality has no real, but only relative entity, when considered as distinct from matter, which alone has eternal identity or positive existence.[32]

Personal identity is a mere eddy in the riverine material world, an illusion of separateness. The key to ethics would then be to overcome this illusion or to feel our material being in the material world from which we are not distinct, or with which we flow.

The contrast between liquid (wave?) and particulate materialisms is, in its way and of course, a contrast about everything. The two pictures yield and reflect different senses of the relation of self and world; in that way they reflect the personality of or the yearnings of the philosophers who develop or endorse them. They are also in their way political: they could correspond to different senses of the relation of the individual to the collectivity; perhaps a gritty materialism reflects a sense of the polity as consisting without remainder of its individual citizens, under their auspices, whereas a smooth materialism might take the group as the fundamental reality within which individuals are constituted. Or perhaps a smooth political materialism could even deny that individual human beings are fully real; the fundamental organism is the group. But then it would place the whole group into the material flow of nature. These ethical or political or psychological corollaries are not entailments of the metaphysical views; rather, they might precede and motivate the metaphysical theories. Nor is that an illegitimate procedure. In kind, it is the only procedure there is; your metaphysics is going to be an attempt to express your experience and your longings. Of course, these can be roads to the truth.

Now really the problem with Stewart's liquid materialism is precisely that it does not pay sufficient respect to individuals. He is always on the edge of saying that individuals are an illusion, which would be an immense betrayal of, for one thing, his own mobile yet also solitary existence (he calls himself "the solitary traveller"; no one accompanied him on his journeys). One way to conceive the problem is precisely in terms of void, for which there appears to be no place in Stewart's materialist plenum: what's missing are the gaps and discontinuities that make it possible to pick out distinct objects or make it possible to be a distinct thing. Through what does Walking Stewart move? For the atomists, the question was how individuals could come into contact at all, how they could have any effect on each other when they were separated by and hence defined by void. It's like you have infinitely many Parmenidean spheres bouncing about. Leibniz's monads, though they are anything but merely material, face the same or a worse problem of yearning to come into contact with other monads. But they are by definition alone.

If the project is to try to systematize or encompass the world, in a way true to our experiences of it and, hence, potentially true to it, we need to come down somewhere that gets you both all and each, both individuals and their connections, objects and the ways they are not fully distinct. Every ontological system wrestles with this; even that of Parmenides, which concludes that individuals are an illusion, acknowledges that there is something to be explained. That is why Epicurus has atoms "vibrating," or why they exert various forces on one another in modern physics; we are trying both to have distinct things and to bring them together. And that is why Stewart is always acknowledging, for example, the individual consciousness, even as he's always undercutting it as an ephemeral bubble in the stream of time. Well, I suppose my metaphor is string. Notice that there is room for empty space in a skein; the string at a macro level is neither liquid nor particulate.

It is true that I melt individuals into relations. But it is also true that I build up massively incomparable individuals out of the totality of their relations. I regard individuals as occupying distinct sections of space and as having massively distinct histories. But no individual is not constituted out of the skein or ever loses its connection entirely. By direct tie or unimaginably complex maze, every individual is connected to every other individual, and is defined as an individual within a system of differences. To say of all this that it is vague and that it is essentially unargued is to say the obvious.

As infelicitous as Stewart's prose undoubtedly is, it expresses, at once with passionate intensity and extreme abstraction, the experience of a man who was himself a flow, and who felt himself both disintegrating and being reconstituted in every encounter with another society, geography, situation. Indeed his own suicide by laudanum overdose in 1822 was conceived ahead of time as an illustration of this flow:

> The intense action of thought and sense carried to its climax, will make a man sympathize with brute matter, which, by his food and the absorption of his pores, he is constantly transforming into consciousness or sensate life; and the morbid patient may conceive it both his interest and his duty to abstain from a redundancy of food, and save even half a pound of matter from the anguish of disease; and should his body arrive at a state of incurable chronic anguish, thought and sense would generate that high degree of fortitude to amputate his mode from the system of sensitive life, as he would amputate a gangrened or mortified arm from the system of his body, to augment the good and diminish the evil of identified self and nature.[33]

Stewart's materialism, in other words, gave him comfort in the face of death, or caused him to affirm his own death. As Socrates thought that the idealist philosopher studies to die, Stewart thought the same of materialist, and comfort in the face of suffering, loss, and death has—reputation to the contrary—been the business of materialists since Epicurus.

What connects materialism to "science" or makes it "modern" even in its ancient forms, is that it foregoes Aristotelian final causes and a teleological conception of the history of the universe. It specifically denies that the universe has an agent, a perpetrator, a design; it is just one thing after another. Democritus even taught that there were myriad *kosmoi*, perhaps as many as there are possible configurations of atoms in a vast but finite space; the fact that this one is as it is, for example that it is such as can give rise to and support creatures such as ourselves, is not the product of design but of a crapshoot. The specific appeal of this insight is that it refuses everything that is not in the order of nature, that it repudiates the supernatural, whether Platonic Forms, gods, miracles, disembodied souls, or minds. It keeps on trying to pull everything onto a single plane: a ham-handed philistine simplification or else a beautiful joining of all things in a web of connection and mutual dependence, a reconciliation—already necessary in the time of Plato—between people and the world.

10.

Forms of naturalism and materialism have flourished, until repressed, in various traditions. A particularly interesting locus is Taoist-influenced naturalism in the China of the early centuries AD. Figures such as Wang Ch'ung denied that the world had any particular teleology; with some ambiguity (like the atomists, for that matter), they denied the existence of spiritual things such as souls or gods. The denial of teleology is probably the fundamental impulse of materialist ontology—the most corrosive skepticism or what is most liberating from the shackles of superstition. And even if the materialism of ancient China or India must be somewhat different as a descriptive ontology than the Greek version, they have that in common; Wang Ch'ung is constantly inveighing against divination, on the grounds that it would be a violation of the order of nature, which makes no exceptions for the likes of you; the position is also what we might term *anti-humanist*: it displaces us from the center of the cosmos. I think it's likely that wherever you have elaborate animistic beliefs or swirling levels of spiritual beings, you also have people who are going to say: Wait. What? Look here is the real world. What the hell are you talking about? As the great historian of atomism A. J. Pyle says,

> Leucippus and Democritus were, so far as we are aware, the first great antiteleologists, the first major thinkers to deny that the concept of intelligent design is central to natural philosophy. According to Democritus, all things are formed by chance (*tuche*) and "necessity" (*ananke*): there is no need for a Mind or Deity to guide the motion of atoms so as to form and sustain an orderly cosmos. Atoms move quite *randomly* in the void: when a sufficient number of atoms aggregate and begin to "jostle" one another, a "whirl" or vortex is formed, which in turn sorts the elements FAWE (Fire Air Water Earth) according to particle sizes and thus produces a world.[34]

The denial of teleology is an ancient idea, but it is central to the pivot into the "modern era": science's struggles to liberate itself from Aristotelianism in the seventeenth century—the rise of naturalism, deism, chemistry, the mechanical or clockwork universe—all depend on or emerge from the implications of this deletion. "Nature has no end set before it . . . All things proceed by a certain eternal necessity of nature," says Spinoza in the Appendix of the *Ethics*.[35] And of course, the human has on such views to be accounted for in naturalistic terms, or has to be regarded as part of the order of nature, with no supernatural faculties or ability to defy the chain of causation.

One form this takes in Greek atomism, in Chinese naturalism, and in Indian Carvaka is a reconnection human to animal life or an account of human beings as animals, a thought which is fully realized scientifically in Darwin, of course.

> Man and things are bound by nature and nature is the master of man and things. . . . Man living in the universe is like a flea or a louse inside a garment or a cricket or an ant in a hole. Can the flea, louse, cricket, or ant, by being obedient or disobedient, cause the material force inside the garment or hole to move or to change? The flea, louse, cricket, and ant cannot do so; to say that man alone can is to fail to understand the principle of the material force of things. As the wind comes, the branches sway. But the tree cannot cause the wind.[36]

I think one thing that is represented in any given metaphysics is the metaphysician's sense of what our or his own place is within the universe. This has the usual complex permutations, so that it might express your longings; precisely what you can't believe to be true, but need or want to be. But we'd have to say that as gigantic as the human looms in Confucianism, or Hegelianism, there is a constant parallel stream of pretentiousness-puncturing diatribe: pin-prick philosophy. Even the excruciating Christian humility of, let's say, Pascal, or the skepticism of Pyrrho, are expressions of this impulse; indeed some of these strands actually seem to eliminate the human entirely: if nothing else, an understandable overreaction.

Both Wang Ch'ung (1st century A.D.) and, in his great commentary on the *Chuang Tzu*, Kuo Hsiang (3rd century A.D.) grope for a characterization of a world without agency: even, really, human agency. They picture a universe that is, as it were, flowering: in which everything is locally caused, but the system considered as a whole emerges spontaneously and arbitrarily: literally inexplicably. The picture also involves a yin-yang balance of Tao and world, or non-being and being: things emerge in the nothingness; they emerge by "non-action" (*wu wei*), or by letting things, including themselves, become rather than making them become. Kuo Hsiang writes:

> The music of Nature is not an entity existing outside of things. The different holes in the pipes and flutes, together with all beings, together constitute Nature. Since non-being is non-being, it cannot produce being. Before being itself is produced, it cannot produce other beings. Then by whom are all things produced? They spontaneously produce themselves, that is all. By this is not meant that there is an "I" to produce. The "I" cannot produce things and things cannot produce the "I." The "I" is self-existent. Because it is so by itself, we call it natural.[37]

The idea that one's own identity is a sort of illusion to be overcome is also a fundamental teaching or longing of many spiritual traditions, as also of Lucretius, Walking Stewart, and Thoreau. Wang Ch'ung really has more or less the whole Walking Stewart structure, making you wonder whether the Traveller made it to China after all: an arising of the human self/body out of what is and a letting go of the self into what is, as a cosmology and as an antispiritual spiritual discipline. Kuo Hsiang's "argument" is strikingly Parmenidean, but he draws entirely different conclusions. There is no final or complete explanation of things, or when we try to say how there can be or why there is something rather than nothing we are at a loss for how to proceed. The point isn't to get more comprehensive: the point is let go into the world in its spontaneous procedure, of which you form a portion. Indeed human agency too is a delusion in such structures of thought; or, if not a delusion, then a disaster; the point is to act within the whole as part of the whole, to "go with the flow" or "do what comes naturally." Good advice in certain circumstances, though awfully vague, I admit.

The fourteenth-century Carvaka text *Sarvadarsanasamgraha*, after denying the existence of spiritual beings and of human immortality, says, "an opponent will say, if you thus do not allow *adrsta* [spiritual power], the various phenomena of the world become destitute of any cause. But we cannot accept this objection as valid, since these phenomena can all be produced spontaneously from the inherent nature of things."[38] It is interesting, I think, that all these traditions describe the universe as arising and proceeding both "spontaneously" and "by necessity." These appear in tension, of course, as in the human world spontaneity and freedom are informally associated (these are all themes we will return to in the chapter on ethics). However, when one acts spontaneously, agency is also compromised in some senses: spontaneous action does not occur through an Aristotelian deliberative syllogism: it just emerges out of your body in a world. It might also be associated with joy. It hints at an interpretation of the universe as a living thing, or recurs to the idea of life, arising we know not how, blooming in excess to explanation. That the universe arises spontaneously hints that it is inexplicable but buzzing with an excess of life-energy. But it would make sense to say that, at that party say, you acted spontaneously but also perfectly expressed an underlying necessity of character: your spontaneous action is the action in which you are most intensely yourself, in which you don't follow anything but your own necessity because you are released from the torture or the homogenizing effect of deliberation, with its rules and structures.

We might think of this as, in a way, a strong or surprising form of compatibilism, applied to the universe as a whole, but also as a guide to human action: the freer or more spontaneous is an action, the more obviously necessitated it is. Or: when you act spontaneously, you act under the necessity of your own nature, you reveal what you essentially are. What happens can only be explained by what is: things unfold according to their own natures, or each thing acts spontaneously and hence expresses itself intensely. The world has no ruler, in some sense no agents, only natures welling up from within themselves and spilling over. The universe, we might say, does what it is, creates and expresses itself in the same act in every event.

11.

Is there such a thing as autumn? Who asks a question like that? A philosopher or a small child, and they should be answered the same way: of course there is; wait and see! Clement Rosset—a nice extreme realist—points out in a common sense way that

> The charm of autumn, for example, is related less to the fact that it is autumn than to the fact that it modifies summer before, in turn, finding itself modified by winter. And its real "being" consists precisely in the modification that it brings about. But one can hardly imagine what would make up the charm of autumn "in its essence," as the disciple of Plato might want to imagine it. I would add that an autumn in its essence, no matter how one might represent it, primarily and especially would not be very "autumnal." This goes to show that the charm of existence, far from being appreciated in proportion to a problematic participation in eternity, is measured, on the contrary, in its proportion to its distance from being as it is conceived by ontologists and metaphysicians—like autumn, which exists if and only if there is no "being" of autumn.[39]

If we're trying to pull individuals, even autumns, out of this holistic welter—and we should be—we can perhaps do it at a given moment by specifying the material composition, or across time as a history; both, of course, if we are trying for completeness. Each thing, even each of us, is vague at the margins; nevertheless we pick out knots. But though each knot resembles each other knot massively, each is also a massively incomparable object, precisely because of its multiplicitous relations and exponentially massive history of relation. Each knot, indeed, has infinite relations to all of the other knots; many of these are completely unique to it. Only knot x has spatial relation P to y, R to z, and so on. Each knot is not only massively compromised in its integrity in virtue of its relations, it is massively unique in virtue of relations; only *it* stands in these relations. Multiply this by an unfolding history and you not only have an intertwined universe, but one consisting of a myriad of incomparably unique objects.

The relations in which each thing stands are continuously multiplying, even from their infinities of infinities. Each new thing that emerges, and each moment in a continuously unfolding time through which each thing persists, multiplies the relations in which each thing stands. A corollary of this is that at each moment, each thing that persists through that moment is increasingly individuated or rendered more unique. Other relations fall away, but they remain concreted in the object's history. We might call this the paradox of essence: the more pure a thing is, the more self-enclosed, the less fully is it something, or the less fully itself it is: the less individuated it is by its unique relations.

This is why individuals of the insanely rich sort we find in reality depend for their individuality precisely on the ways they are compromised as individuals. The richer and more interconnected the world, the more incomparable each thing is within that world. As soon as we regard each thing as individuated in relations, a limitless increase in the possibilities for appreciation of the uniqueness of each thing is opened up. I am similar to all other human beings in some respects, similar to all mammals, or all objects. But among them all, none has my history or is materially composed out of the portion of material out of which I am composed right now. At every moment during which I persist I diverge, or multiply uniquenesses. If we were looking for a universe to provide the greatest profusion of individuals with the most extreme uniqueness, it would be a universe in which individuals were constituted from their relations; that is, it would be our universe.

12.

In their book *Austere Realism*, Terry Horgan and Matjaz Potrc argue that "vague objects and vague property/relations are logically impossible."[40] Leaning hard on this idea, they conclude that there is only one thing, which they denominate "the blobject." Now I admire this on account of its perversity and for its ontological egalitarianism. But in my view, not only are there some vague objects, there are *only* vague objects and properties and relations, which are always bleeding out into their situations. The argument for the view that there are no ontologically vague entities relies on deriving paradoxes from sorites-style arguments, or on van Inwagen's strategy of imposing a principle of individuation in a systematic way. "There cannot, then, be a body of specific compositional facts that are collectively disconnected and unsystematic and are individually unexplainable."[41] These arguments are oddly a priori. Indeed, to the contrary, the problem is that the compositional facts are unimaginably profuse, and any selection or principle of individuation is provisional and insufficient. We discover how things hang together and merge into and emerge out of one another. There's no telling in advance what is and what is not a thing; our ontologies evolve to keep pace with the profusion of experience of the world, or to retard it. Whether the middle class or a Higgs Boson is a single thing is an ideological matter, a political matter, a philosophical matter, a matter for research, an open question.

But it is also a reasonably straightforward question that could have various real answers; well, the middle class is regionally or ideologically divided on this and that; its borders, or the income levels included, need to be redefined; we need a more complicated or nuanced system of counting classes. Well, are there Higgs Bosons? Are they fundamental, indeed, or composite? What are their relations to other particles? What is a thing is a conclusion to arrive at through experience, not a concept to bring to it: that is how the Greeks and medievals got into terrible trouble: stipulating a concept of substance and then wondering why nothing seemed to instantiate it. But answers to such questions also constitute a map, which embodies exploration of the actual surface. If you don't think a mountain can actually be a vague object, then let's go to Old Rag and you show me just where it leaves off. Something tells me that people as ingenious as Terry Horgan could work out the supposed logical contradictions inherent in this idea, given that it's true. Did we just paint the baby's room red or pink? Well, perhaps you'll just have to be satisfied with "sort of both" or "halfway between," or you'll have to produce a more refined taxonomy of colors according to which it's neither red nor pink. I'm not talking about how to apply a predicate; I'm talking about the color of the walls. Or, as William James has it,

> Only concepts are self-identical; only "reason" deals with closed equations; nature is but a name for excess; every point in her opens out and runs into the more; and the only question, with reference to any point we may be considering, is how far into the rest of nature we may have to go in order to get entirely beyond its overflow.[42]

Whatever the paradoxes, there are only vague objects in the real world insofar as they are all part of the same fabric.

But at any rate, the idea that there is only one thing is no less false to us as real experiencers of a real world than would be the Leibniz-monad idea that there are only noninteracting particulars. A decent description of the skein needs to map the knots as well as the cords that flow from knot to knot; there really are medium-sized things, and insanely small things, and bigger things that engulf littler things like a galaxy gobbling stars, and one big thing that is them all. If we don't know that, we don't know anything. Surely all science presupposes it roughly, as well it should. The debate about whether there is more than one thing seems rather arid: yes; but there is also one thing that is all things.

What situations we take as individuals and what we take, for example, as environments, is to some extent or under some circumstances optional, but it depends upon your location and many other physical facts or factors. In other words, we cannot change the ontology at will by changing the taxonomy; in many cases a taxonomy (such as animal/vegetable/mineral, earth/air/fire/water) has a history in terms of which the world has been traced for millennia. But of course a taxonomy like that is cut across by many taxonomies, or rather each thing is a place where taxonomies cross, and every taxonomy is contestable, or can be adumbrated or qualified or multiplied.

What we can count as a thing is a matter that is much more determinate given the way things actually are than many philosophers countenance. If we were much, much tinier than we are, we might have a different sense to some extent about what is an individual and what an extremely complex swarm of individuals. Or is a tornado, for example, a single thing or an immensely complex situation embedding many things? Well, both, really. For us, the question also runs through representational systems, both linguistic and pictorial (and various coordinations among them), by which we try to decide what counts enough to be considered an individual. What counts as an individual might depend, for example, to some extent on whether it is referred to by a mass or a count noun: a cat vs. sugar: you can't have a lot of cat, I hope, or 27,000 fluid ounces of cat; and you can't have one sugar, unless the sugar has been pressed into cubes or divided into bags. But then the real differences between these things might be the reason we have mass and count nouns in the first place.

There are as many objects as there are situations: that is, collocations of objects in relation in contexts. Any old collection of things is an object. In a famous passage in *On the Plurality of Worlds*, David Lewis takes a similar extremely permissive approach:

> Whenever there are some things, no matter how disparate and unrelated, there is something composed of just those things. . . . We have no name for the mereological sum of the right half of my left shoe plus the Moon plus the sum of all Her Majesty's ear-rings, except for the long and clumsy name I just gave it; we have no predicates under which such entities fall, except for technical terms like "physical object" (in a special sense known to some philosophers) or blanket terms like "entity" and maybe "thing"; we seldom admit it to our domains of restricted quantification. It is very sensible to ignore such a thing in our everyday thought and language. But ignoring it won't make it go away.[43]

I think a lot of contemporary analytic metaphysicians have an overly restrictive or stereotypical picture of what we count as an individual, and an even narrower conception of all the individuals there actually are. They like tables or persons, but even just restricting ourselves to the things we do "quantify over" in ordinary talk, we deal with a remarkably disparate and motley crew of things. "Her Majesty's ear-rings" is liable to be a pretty scattered object; there's that one that's still inside Her Majesty's Couch, and so on. But then we have "autumn," for example; not exactly a compact space-time region or bunch of particles, but also definitely not a non-physical entity. Or "my family": there are people scattered all about, some of whom I don't even know about: dogs, deceased people, and so on. Or "the groceries"; "the yard"; "residential housing"; "the manufacturing sector." As I say, there's no telling what we might count as an object in conversation or representation, because there are infinities of infinities of objects. One thing is for sure: we're not going to run out before we run out of nouns.

Van Inwagen inveighs against Lewis-style ontology as "Super-universalism": the thesis that "any objects whatever have a sum."

> According to Super-universalism, for example, if there are such things as the color blue and key of C-sharp and I, then there is an object that has the color blue and the key of C-sharp and me as parts. I do not understand Super-universalism because, though I think that the color blue and the key of C-sharp and I all exist, I am unable to form a sufficiently general conception of parthood to be able to conceive of an object that has these there rather diverse things as parts.[44]

Really the discomfort here has to do with mixing abstract and concrete elements in the same object, and I do myself have reservations about the "existence" of the color blue and key of C-sharp. But either way, these things could be parts of the same thing only as embedded in a specific context. So, in fact, the kind of the object van Inwagen cannot imagine is quite common even in our everyday talk: the color blue (of the stage set), the key of C-sharp (in which the concerto was performed), and van Inwagen (the performer) are all parts of *the performance*. Actually we are very eclectic in our process of picking out individuals: cavalier, almost. Likely that has to do with the sort of universe in which we find ourselves.

13.

We might think of a situationist ontology as the opposite of a substance ontology or "haecceism," of which—though of course the whole conceptuality originates in the pre-Socratics—in some ways the clearest and most extreme is Leibniz's. Leibniz resolves all relations into properties, whereas I want to resolve all properties into relations. In the *Discourse on Metaphysics*, he writes

> It is evident that all true predication has some basis in the nature of things and that, when a proposition is not an identity, that is, when the predicate is not explicitly contained in the subject, it must be contained in it virtually. That is what philosophers call in-esse, when they say that the predicate is in the subject. Thus the subject term must always contain the predicate term, so that one who understands perfectly the notion of the subject would also know that the predicate belongs to it.[45]

I so like the idea that true predication has some basis in the nature of things that I hesitate to quibble with the rest, and indeed in some ways the substance view collapses into mine anyway, or the two converge. As in so much with Leibniz, this is extremely bold in its counterintuitiveness: every real relation that a thing has to anything else is prefigured or contained in its intrinsic properties.

Leibniz, of course, proceeds directly to the conclusion that every genuine individual contains the entire universe in germ or microcosm and that every thing has an internal standpoint from which the rest become visible. Perhaps the original method appears analytic: breaking things down to their ultimate components. But the project is compositional: to build a world again from separate things, each burdened with an infinite weight of intrinsicness, and yet each containing in germ the whole. This idea ultimately rests on an incorrigible attempt to understand human consciousness in terms of the inside/outside distinction, or the subjective point of view, the dream or hallucination, and then to understand the universe by analogy to monadic consciousness, as if it were built out of consciousnesses.

> God, seeing Alexander's individual notion or haeccity, sees in it at the same time the basis and reason for all the predicates which can be said truly of him, for example, that he vanquished Darius and Porus; he even knows a priori (and not by experience) whether he died a natural death or whether he was poisoned, something we can know only through history. Thus when we carefully consider the connection of things, we can say that from all time in Alexander's soul there are vestiges of everything that has happened to him and marks of everything that will happen to him and even traces of everything that happens in the universe, even though God alone could recognize them all.[46]

Now this is truly perverse: one would think that in order to vanquish Darius, Alexander had to meet Darius on the field of battle; you can't be poisoned without having real-world poison introduced into your body. No man is an entelechy. I would like to say that either option appears to me to be open here, and I'm not sure why exactly Leibniz took the strategy of pressing everything together like a snowball and trying to get everything to fit into each thing. It seems more likely to have some basis in the nature of things if there are swarms of relational individuals in a web: or, the individuals can be individuated only by their relations; or, each individual is a unique bundle of relations. That is precisely what individuates us: we are each a different site or snarl in the tangle of relations.

But there's the bit where Leibniz takes the world away from you—leaves you as a monadic consciousness tumbling alone through the void—and then there's the bit where he gives it all back by giving each monad access to the whole in virtue of being that whole in microcosm or in representation. In some sense this would converge in the end with a radical situationism: it does precisely see each thing as composed by its relations: Alexander by whom he defeated, for example, his death by poison part of what he is or his very is-ness. Only the view suffers from a too-great influx of haeccity, as do so many of us: too much quiddity, enteleological excess, an overdose of inherence: it must find individuals at the bottom of reality; Leibniz and so many others take that to be logically demonstrable. But the more fundamental and distinct an atom, a monad, a consciousness, a lepton, is conceived to be, the more will it only be definable in terms of its relations, I predict: individuals are only realized as relationship; context is constitutive; delete the environment and you have deleted its embedded individuals. That is precisely why Leibniz incorporates all relations into each thing.

So there is a fundamental insight in Leibniz's fantastic ideology of entirely separate monads coordinated in the colossal mind of God. In the *Monadology*, he writes:

> The interconnection or accommodation of all created things to each other, and each to all the others, brings it about that each simple substance has relations that express all the others, and consequently, that each simple substance is a perpetual, living mirror of the universe.[47]

Well, that seems right, more or less, at least until we tug on the various threads, as for example that each simple substance is indestructible, or what Leibniz means by a "mirror." Indeed, Leibniz went all the way into pictorial representation as a model for everything, further even than Berkeley or Schopenhauer, for example. "The nature of the monad is representative," he goes on to write. Each monad has within it a representation of the whole from a particular point of view. So Leibniz resolves all relation into representation, and thus recapitulates the skeptical problem simply by asserting that no monad actually does interact with anything else; each one is locked up within, as it were, its own skull because it only has access to its own representations. The ultimate purpose of Leibniz's metaphysics is to explain the outbreak of subjectivity or consciousness in a physical world and to guarantee its persistence after death. The model of the monad is always himself, Gottfried Wilhelm Leibniz. On the other hand, he does actually see that all things are connected. It's just that he registers that as a problem. The desperation of the solution comes from his dedication to take an a priori concept of identity, which he derives from various illusions about himself, and apply it to the world as a strategy for individuating objects. It would be wiser to keep hold of how liquid our ordinary concept of identity is, and how liquid our own identities are, and to look and see what really turns out to be an entity.

14.

Graham Harman's "object-oriented ontology" (OOO) is in some respects a revival of the Aristotelian/scholastic substance-accident orientation. I am very much in agreement, of course, with the realist conclusions that Harman draws, and the realist and pro-metaphysics impulse that leads him in this direction. However, Harman specifically contrasts OOO with a relational approach of the sort I take.

> What I have tried to show is that if we define an object through its role in a system of interrelations, objects are thereby undermined, reduced to the caricatured image they present to all other things. The only way to do justice to objects is to consider that their reality is free of all relation, deeper than all reciprocity. The object is a dark crystal veiled in a private vacuum: irreducible to its own pieces, and equally irreducible to its outward relations with all other things.[48]

The object, in Harman's ontology, is "dusted" or "encrusted" with its accidental properties, and infested or inhabited by its essential properties, but it is itself something beyond all of that. Now if it appears that objects are sinking into a mystical netherworld, the mystery is intentional, and if someone is emphasizing the deep mystery of existence, they will find me sympathetic. But the point is really to make objects excessive to their relations *to us*. Harman is trying to *fend off* our arrogance: the idea that we construct or create our reality. As in Whitehead's "prehension" or Leibniz's monads, Harman proceeds in terms of representation: each relation of a to b is, it seems, a representation of a in b, a "caricature" in b of a. But objects, Harman argues, cannot be exhausted by representation: every representation is a distortion or a misinterpretation as well as the opposite. Hence, beings withdraw.

Now, I think that Harman's ontology is an overreaction to the dangerous or at any rate profoundly annoying human invasion of all being. I think we can preserve the basic realist insight without resorting to such a lush ancient-style ontology of hidden substances, essences, accidents, and moments (as well as "sensible objects" such as images or viewpoints, real fictional objects, and so on), which I would need quite a bit more motivation than Harman gives to regard sympathetically. Human experience is a relation like any other: real, but partial. And if we're dealing with a world that is relations all the way down and possibly up, and in which every object bristles with myriads upon myriads of relations, human consciousness or experience will never exhaust the mystery of being. On the other hand, I wouldn't assume that any dimension is strictly, in principle inaccessible to experience broadly construed. And things maintain all sorts of relations to each other. Some of these could be construed as representational, such as the relation of a picture of x to x. But others are just being bigger than something or being on its left relative to some third element. Some particular relation might be something we perceive or experience, or something we don't. In most cases, we don't. We don't have to defend objects from their misinterpretation by other objects; mostly, they're just routinely banging into one another.

I am concerned, however, to defend myself against a charge that the ontology I'm sketching does not permit enough integrity or autonomy to objects, that it does not take individuals seriously: this is what threatens a relational ontology, as the specter of propertyless substances haunts OOO. And it's true that I don't make objects ultimate in my ontology. But I would suggest, overall, getting rid of the notion of finding the ultimate constituents, whether tropes, particles, atoms, the apeiron, the logos, or whatever it may be. Each object is also a situation, each situation an object, all the way down and as far up as there is. Neither point of view is comprehensive, neither is fundamental; they are mutually compatible. Wildebeests are as real as atoms. Now wildebeests consist of atoms; at a given moment the wildebeest is identical to its atoms; its relations are their collective relations. You could describe the same causal event in terms of the behavior of the wildebeest or (in principle) in terms of the reconfiguration and resituation of an atomic swarm; neither explanation is more fundamental or exclusively true or objective or empirical. The wildebeest and the atoms are really real, fundamentally real, truly true, and external to (as well as potentially in various relations to) human experiences.

I don't, finally, know what could be more real than that or why I should accept *in principle* inaccessible entities if the ordinary sort will do the work of inhabiting this world we share. Think about what we can experience now in our universe that we couldn't have experienced in 1450, before the introduction of the telescope, the microscope, the particle accelerator, the Hubble. As a possible subject of knowledge, the wildebeest is inexhaustible, and in its relations it closely or at a distance implicates everything. But at any rate, the ontology could be formulated alternately taking objects or situations as fundamental; these will yield different but not mutually incompatible interpretations, unless "object" or "substance" is an a priori stipulation or withdraws of necessity into concealment.

The Eleatic/Aristotelian conception of substance has, I must say, never been particularly clear to me. A typical formulation is Spinoza's: "by substance, would be understood that which is in itself, and is conceived through itself."[49] Is a wildebeest in itself or conceived through itself (and are these the same thing)? Rather hard to say, I believe. Now, through the seventeenth century, this conception of substance was more or less taken as obvious, an intuition so strong that systems such as Spinoza's depended entirely on it without taking it to be necessary to establish it at all: it is an axiom, though I am puzzled as to why it has such a status. The sorts of conclusions Spinoza draws from this definition—for example, that there is only one substance, that nothing can cause it to exist, that a substance is eternal, and so on—ought to give one pause, as should the Eleatic origins of the concept. This is something of a cautionary tale; keep repeating a stipulated definition long enough with enough authority and people take it as empirically true or as showing something about the world, when evidently it cannot be or do that at all: everything that follows from it follows analytically, and it means nothing about the world except insofar as words are in the world. It was supposed to flow from grammar or the necessary structure of thought in such a way as to be indubitable. Physics and metaphysics, I believe, can tick along and has ticked along quite well since 1740 without the notion of substance, and certainly without the notion of substance as foundational. Indeed, the very idea of telling us what exists by an a priori deduction was understandably unfashionable until its recent revival in object-oriented ontology and blobjects.

Objects are constituted out of their relations, but relations are constituted out of their objects: situations are objects in juxtaposition. There can be no reason to choose one level as fundamental unless after a Magic School Bus adventure all the way down to the heart of the boson. Meanwhile, the constitution of real things out of real parts, and of those parts from parts, all occurring in a context or environment, is perfectly familiar from ordinary experience. "Objects are always *in excess* of their local manifestations, harboring hidden volcanic powers irreducible to their manifestations in the world," writes Paul Levi Bryant, more or less characterizing Harman's position.[50] But though it is a legitimate question what there is outside of human experience, there is still a question about what necessity or motivation we are under to accept any particular position that conceals things in principle from us. I admit that I find Bryant's "transcendental" argument for such a position as little convincing as Harman's route to hidden substances through Husserl and Heidegger.

Bryant conceives of objects in terms of powers or capacities. And because every object harbors powers and capacities in excess to its manifestations at a given moment, the object is always at least partly concealed. The basic characterizations of entities such as subatomic particles necessarily presupposes such entities, according to Bryant following Bhaksar, and the activity of experimentation involves unlocking certain powers of the object while leaving others in concealment. But I think it is odd to regard in particular counterfactually specified powers—if it were brought into contact with x, it would do y—as constituting the quiddity of an object. That any given object intrinsically harbors such powers is a way of speaking, or a kind of figurative quantification over possibilia. What is being characterized are the implications of the properties and relations of the object, which provides the factual underpinning of such an assertion.

On the other hand, I do admire the degree of externality that Harman and Bryant attribute to things and hence the world; it is quite extreme, as things themselves are inaccessible to our experience. But perhaps the views are not ultimately as opposed in effect as they are in principle.

We find substance neither in the really, really tiny things, nor in the really, really natural things, nor in the really, really divine things. Substances are *everywhere*. What we have is not a universe split between aristocratic natural kinds and miserable, pauper-like accidents. Instead we have a universe of objects wrapped in objects wrapped in objects wrapped in objects. . . . Every object is both a substance and a complex of relations.[51]

Only, for Harman, the substantiality and the relationality must be carefully distinguished; we must not confuse the relationality (in particular, relations to us) with the substantiality. But as to a world of nested objects/situations that stubbornly maintains its externality to ourselves: on this Harman, Bryant and I all agree. More deeply, Harman and Bryant's celebration of the real world bespeaks their own actual relation—which they meanwhile seem to deny—to being itself as it really is; it's constantly glittering from the most ordinary things in their philosophy, as well it should be; they are really in relation to it all the while. It is tempting to devalue or to try to ignore human experience and language for a spell, after centuries of self-mesmerism. But on the other hand: let's trust ourselves enough to acknowledge our own embeddedness in or participation in the things we experience or describe and in things we don't, as living among them in war and peace. Harman rhapsodizes in tribute to cigars, mangoes, hurricanes, whips, zebras, chemicals, weddings, copper wires, bicycles, wolves, volcanoes, souls, bags of Christmas candy, "an oilcan, the Dead Sea, a specific mallard duck." "Sharks and scorpions never dream of eating empires and moons."[52]

15.

The persistence of objects over time is as vague and permeable as their extension in space. Honestly, we don't know when "human life" starts, or even sometimes when it ends. At what point in a process of weathering does a rock cease to be the very rock it was? Now I take this to be a place where, as it were, we register the actual situation in the universe, in which tangles gather and unravel and really exist as a set of relations (of interior causal connections in connection to what is outside them, for one thing). There really are things that slide into and out of existence; this ought to be a trivial observation; it's obvious if anything is. In characterizing his account of identity over time, David Wiggins talks about attributions of identity (for example, a claim like "She's just not the same person she was twenty years ago") as putting into play "the reciprocities and mutual interdependencies of concept, custom, and thing-singled-out." He says that these three factors form "a seamless web."[53]

Now, I think some things persist over time that are never conceptualized or expressed in a vocabulary, or that identity over time is a real feature of the world outside our consciousness. But these are precisely the right dimensions of evaluation for a claim regarding identity: a taxonomy of objects ("concept"), a system of representation or vocabulary ("custom"), and the actual stuff/things in regard to which the claim is made. Probably, we could delete the concepts or bundle them into the vocabulary. The opposite idea—insisting that there is only one thing, with Spinoza or Terry Horgan—makes the opposite mistake and has the same strengths. Namely, it is only within the whole that anything is what it is, or a thing is composed from its relations, or only the whole has intrinsic qualities, and only the whole has haecceity, or is a thing, or constitutes a substance. But one has to separate the idea of intrinsic qualities or substances from the idea of being a thing in the actual world, and permit relations to be conceived as fundamental. It might be true that there is one thing, but it doesn't follow, of course, that there is only one thing, any more than we have to choose between the reality of trees and forests. Spinoza goes on to say that within the one thing that is, all other things are modes or modifications, that is, relations.

To some extent, it is understandable if people cannot tell whether anything turns on distinctions like this or, for example, what we should expect if Leibniz is right, or Spinoza, or me. The fact that you can't quite tell whether these positions—there is one thing, there are many things, there are many things and one thing, things change and persist or persist not—contradict one another, or amount to the same thing in the end, is a bad sign for their meaningfulness. Some of the distinctions appear to be aptly dismissed as matters of jargon, merely verbal questions. What I am urging substantively is that the "substance/accident" ontology has to yield to relational webs or networks or tangles. But whether anything really turns on whether the latter picture is true is another matter, and in some form you get the whole relational web on any of these conceptions anyway. The question is what, behind the realm in which things appear, is the really real level, the soul level, the God level, the final fundamental particle. My view is that we are not going to discover or uncover the really real fundamental reality underlying everything else, including appearances; the world of trees and tables is just as fundamentally real as anything can be, and is connected to any other levels there may be (subatomic, etc.) in a single ontological framework or plane of being.

16.

I have been sort of assiduously avoiding the use of the term *property*, as well as various cognates and synonyms (one conspicuous exception was when I was trying to characterize "resemblances"). For example, you can tell I'm queasy about talking about value properties or values as properties. Obviously, I am going to struggle with regard to any apparently abstract entity. It would be nice to avail ourselves of a David Lewis–type account of properties as sets of objects. I don't think we should countenance excessive departures from ordinary words and ordinary questions; properties are not sets of objects, or else, for example, you could drop a property on someone's head. The whiteness of a chair, or that the chair is white, is not that chair. Or perhaps I am not understanding what is meant by "set"; I think of a set as a collection of objects, if that helps, or as one sort of what I call a fact or situation. I have never quite gotten hold ontologically of the idea of an abstract object (a set) that would have concrete things as elements (the set of all bears, for example). Not only that, but then to construct our universals we're going to have to quantify over possible worlds or at any rate over various merely possible individuals; blue is for Lewis the set of all this-worldly blue things and the set of all the other possible blue things, where possibility is defined as actuality in a possible world. That this yields an overly profuse ontology is not necessarily a decisive objection, but it is a real one, and I am posing throughout as the defender and champion of the actual world against all comers: spiritual, abstract, and merely possible.

From one point of view, it is odd to think of properties as nonphysical or abstract objects. Now, the car is blue. Where is its blueness? Why, right there; can't you see nothin'? The blueness of the car has a precise location and is explained by the circumstances and history of that real thing; the properties of something are it, or inhere in it, or radiate from it, at a spatio-temporal location. The situation in Syria is morally intolerable; its intolerability isn't something that hovers over it like a gas or the stench of death, that might reappear in Chechnya, or whatever it may be: it is right there, in the events and people and things.

Alexander Bryan Johnson, an American philosopher (and banker) of the nineteenth century, was possibly even more obscure than Walking Stewart. But his philosophy of language would have also been a contribution to human thought had it been more widely read. It looks back to and elaborates the classical empiricists and common sense philosophers in one direction and strikingly anticipates logical positivism and pragmatism on the other. For Johnson, the meaning of a statement or theory is the means that would be used to prove or give evidence for it; a statement means the difference it would practically make in experience. He attacked language on grounds that might be termed radically nominalistic. Nature, he said, appeared only in particulars, whereas the words applied to these particulars were always general. That is, in every instance of a different thing to which a word refers or which falls into its extension, the same word is applied, but in each case the particular phenomenon is distinct. This leads philosophers and the rest of us into a massively fallacious interpretation of nature, in which it is viewed as a series of instantiations of universals. Rather, language should be adapted to the ever more precise delineation of particulars.

> Individuality is characteristic of nature. Language unites under one name, as identities, what is only partially identical. Individuality is no anomaly of nature. It is nature's regular production, and boundless riches. No two

parcels of calomel possess the perfect identity which the sameness of their name implies. No two men possess the perfect identity which the sameness of their manhood implies; nor possesses any one man, at all times, and under all circumstances, the complete identity with which language invests his individuality.[54]

Johnson was a phenomenalist: he believed that the fundamental data of experience were what Hume termed "sense impressions" (Johnson calls them sights, sounds, feels, smells, and tastes) and that individual objects were composed of or identical with such impressions.

Any term that could not be referred to a specific impression—someone's experience at some time—was asserted by Johnson to be without meaning: it was returned to nature as a pristine, blank sound. However, he did not follow this into a Berkeleyan idealism, but to a radical realism (which, to be fair, is one reading of Berkeley).

My hand is red, hair is often red, the moon is sometimes red, fire is red, and Indians are red. These objects possess a congruity of appearance that entitles them to the appellation of red; but the precise meaning of the word in each application is the sight itself which the object exhibits. Whether an object shall or not be called red is a question which relates to the propriety of phraseology, and with which nature has no concern; but the meaning of the word red in each application, is a question which relates solely to nature, and with which language has no concern:—at least, language possesses over it no control.[55]

This is a remarkable doctrine, taken by Johnson to be a direct result of his nominalism: it returns us to nature and, explicitly, to language as a mirror of nature, albeit a dark mirror. Language is serviceable and sensible insofar as it reflects nature in its massed specificities. A perfect language would have a different name for each phenomenon of nature, but such a thing is beyond our power to wield. We must keep speaking in generalities, but we must open ourselves to the specificities of reality: real knowledge or science would consist of a degeneralization or an ever-closer approximation to nature, which consists in nothing but unique particulars. And we might read from Johnson's view a version of the externalism with regard to meaning associated with Putnam: the meaning of "red" in any specific utterance (by which Johnson means its reference), depends on how the world actually is, not on any person's language or even experience.

It won't be surprising that in my ontology, properties turn out to be situations, and I suppose situations properties; every situation in which a thing is embedded is a property of that thing in the real world. To the extent that we could define every situation as a property, however, we might call this an ontology in which properties are fundamental. But to the extent that properties are distinguished fundamentally ontologically from objects, we might say that this is a world with no properties. Or if entities and properties are relations, then we might say that all real things, or the most real things—the ultimate entities of the ontology—are relations. Individual objects must be defined in relation; it is the relations that are primordial or constitutive.

Then "blueness," the abstract general concept, if any, is a situation of situations. Or, it's like counting the predicate as meaning its extension, except that we are focusing not on every feature of every individual (or simply defining the extension as ranging over individuals as wholes), but rather on those aspects or locations or circumstances of each situation at which it is blue. Sometimes we have to work out by a close examination whether it's blue or not. To come to understand these circumstances would be to come more and more to understand what we already meant by "blue." We have to go and find out what blue is or what sorts of circumstances it emerges from, for example, what persons and things and vocabularies and lenses. What we mean by "blue" depends in part on how this all works out in actual research, on how things really are in the world, as well as on the notion of "blue" that we all worked with before.

The insight that in any given manifestation or realization, a quality has a particular location, composition, or that we never experience blue but some particular blue—the blueness of this sky at this moment—has been adumbrated into a kind of modified nominalism under the auspices of the "trope theory" of Donald Cary Williams and Keith Campbell. (According to Campbell, Williams chose the term *trope* more or less arbitrarily, as a word with no established philosophical use. This was highly unfortunate, since it would appear to linguistify reality. So try to disassociate the term with whatever you took it to mean before, if anything.) Williams, according to Campbell, characterizes tropes as "abstract particulars":

> The colour of this pea, the temperature of that wire, the solidity of this bell, are *abstract* in this sense only: that they (ordinarily) occur in conjunction with many other instances of qualities (all the other features of the pea, the piece of wire or the bell), and that, therefore, they can be *brought before the mind* only by a process of selection, of systematic setting aside, of these other qualities of which we are aware. Such an act of selective ignoring is an act of abstraction. Its result is that we have before the mind an item which (as a matter of fact, in general) occurs in company with others.
>
> But the pea's colour, the wire's temperature, the bell's solidity, are *not* in any sense *products of* the discriminating mind. They exist out there, waiting to be recognized for the independent, individual items that they have been all along.

For Williams, and for us following his usage, *abstract* does not imply *indefinite*, or *purely theoretical*. Most importantly, it does not imply that what is abstract is *non-spatio-temporal*. The solidity of this bell, here and now, is a definite, experienceable and locatable reality. It is so definite, experiencable and locatable that it can knock your head off, if you are not careful.[56]

Both Campbell and Williams argue that trope theory is at least compatible with materialism: the solidity of the bell is a physical fact. Despite the use of "abstract" in a somewhat unusual or at least restricted sense, the impulse is surely nominalistic, and properties "themselves" get built out of resemblances between tropes: between the solidity of the bell and the solidity of a boulder, and so on: one promises a reduction of properties to tropes, rather than an explanation of tropes via properties, as in the idea that what accounts for the solidity of the bell and the boulder is the presence in both of the same thing. What is present in each is a different trope, and these tropes resemble one another in a salient respect.

Indeed, Campbell and Williams actually propose that tropes are the ultimate constituents of reality, a doctrine which sounds worse than it is, but is perhaps not that great even as they intend it. That the ultimate constituents of reality are things like the solidity of that bell: I am not quite sure how to evaluate a claim like that. Regarding the bell itself as composed out of things like its own solidity and reducible thereunto seems to me perversely wrong way around. Campbell and Williams appear to treat its solidity as *part of* the bell, which doesn't seem right, though it is hard to say just why. On the other hand, if in some sense properties are relations (well, relations have been treated as properties, I suppose)—perhaps "internal" relations—and if things are constituted by their relations, then on my own view one might say that things are constituted in part by their tropes. And trope theory captures the basic myth-puncturing function of both materialism and nominalism: it insists that we live in an unrelenting, an incessant, world of particulars. We can try to coordinate or sort out these particulars, but we can't transcend or abandon them.

17.

Facts too are sometimes read as abstract entities, working off of readings of Frege or Wittgenstein; here, I'm with the Austin of "Unfair to Facts": facts are just real-world things, nothing exotic. Austin is arguing against the notion that facts are merely artifacts of language, as he had it that Strawson had it: entities kind of stipulated to fulfill logical formulae or to provide something like reference to ordinary-language sentences, consisting at a minimum of an object and a property or concept. I want to read facts as scatters, perhaps vast, of material things and their connections: *that it is raining* qua utterance in a context picks out a situation: a place, a set of conversational conventions, the meteorological conditions: it is either a fact that it is raining or it is not, and that is what it means to say that the utterance is true or false.

Strawson argued, for one thing, and in an ordinary-language vein, that things or individuals are not facts; we wouldn't say "the fact that Fred"; there is, sadly, no fact that Fred. The fact that Fred is asleep shows the minimum structure: subject and predicate, individual and property, the latter pair created as mirrors of the former. From this Strawson concludes that facts are "not things in the world"; rather, they are abstract types or perhaps, in a later idiom, entities stipulated to serve as the truth makers of our sentences. Austin responds:

> For example, although we perhaps rarely, and perhaps only in strained senses, say that a "thing" (e.g., the German navy) is a fact, and perhaps never say that a person is a fact, still, things and persons are far from being all that the ordinary man, and even Strawson, would admit to be genuinely things-in-the-world whatever exactly that may mean. Phenomena, events, situations, states of affairs are commonly supposed to be genuinely-in-the-world, and even Strawson admits events are so. Yet surely of all of these we can say that they *are facts*. The collapse of the Germans is an event and is a fact—was an event and was a fact. . . . It seems to me . . . that to say that something is a fact *is* at least in part precisely to say that it is something in the world.[57]

Again I intend to regard facts as, if anything, constellations or juxtapositions of objects. It is true that when we are treating something in a conversational context as an individual, we do not commonly call it a "fact"—that has the wrong syntax—but, nevertheless, things are, from another perspective, facts in the requisite sense. Like Ramsey on truth, and influenced thereby no doubt, Strawson reads "the fact that p" as simply meaning "p." True, true, but then again "p" means the same as "the fact that p." You might let this elucidate the content of the proposition that p; it is the fact that p; it is a real-world situation or fails to be. Or if that is too much legislation, then I might try to withdraw "fact" talk altogether, foregoing also states of affairs and what-is-the-cases as being simply synonymous with fact talk. Whether anything is gained or lost by withdrawing to situations and entanglements is another matter. At any rate, one would not say of a situation that it has to take such a form as to mirror a proposition or sentence; everyone admits that there are all sorts of sticky situations. I am happy to call such things "facts," but I do not insist on it.

18.

Now whether you loved or hated the last few sections or were unable to pay attention at all, you have to admit that they were speculative metaphysics. It may be impossible to do speculative metaphysics with a clear conscience or unselfconsciously in these late days, but you can do it, still, if you want. What makes it sensible to engage in speculative metaphysics is precisely the one-plane principle: we are the sorts of situations we're trying to explain, and not only that, situations are always blossoming everywhere all around us. We have, and can develop further, a sense of our situation. Now perhaps the unilateral declarations of my sketchy ontology constitute dogmatism, an appeal to the irrational or ineffable, arbitrary or mystical intuitionism. They are certainly unjustifiable, or at any rate unjustifiable by many standards of justification. And as I've indicated, I don't think justification could ever be forthcoming for truths at this level of generality. This is philosophy, the place where justifications run out. On the other hand, there is no particular reason not to try to figure out what you believe about this sort of thing, or not to declare it once you've formed an opinion. There's no reason you shouldn't riff on it, or see where one sort of thought takes you. No expression of opinion in such areas is liable to have disastrous or even detectible practical consequences. The only reason not to write speculative metaphysics is that no one will read it. But, you know, Schopenhauer did it. Lotze did it. Even educated fleas did it, in 1860.

I would take whatever justifications I could find with regard to committing to a fundamental ontology, but I'm also comfortable proceeding without them. It's certainly possible to think you've demonstrated something about the way things are, when all the time you were committed to one view or another, which drove the arguments rather than the other way round. That is one of the reasons that arguments in metaphysics, as in politics, seem so often disappointing, or to be fudged just at the key moment, as in Plato. The argument is not at the center of the commitment. It has to come out the way it does. Committing yourself to a fundamental ontology is an act of faith, an act of belief to which any possible evidence is radically inadequate. It is a matter of identity and aspiration as well as a propositional attitude and a professional posture. The good part about this religion is that it comes with no institutions, just doctrines. Now it's a further mystery where intuitions on such matters come from: childhood traumas or a chaste love of truth; it is hard to focus on what features of personality would direct you to be a nominalist or a realist, a materialist or an idealist. Why did Heraclitus choose motion and Parmenides stasis? Were they expressing what they were, or what they lacked, and if either, what were they and what did they lack? What longings are answered by atoms? And yet people find themselves committed, sometimes committed to the death on such matters. We are an odd species, some of us odder than others.

An important standard for evaluating a theory—especially your own—is whether it keeps faith with your experience, whether it is true to that experience. Now, to say that my material "situationism" does keep faith with its author's experience isn't much of an argument. But the commitment to any account in matters like this also has a concupiscent aspect: what would I like or want the universe to be? That surely is the sort of thing that gives people a benevolent god or a beautiful order of nature (much less the perfect union or coincidence of these, as in Spinoza, say), whatever argumentative conniptions they may perform to justify that belief if they go pro as theologians or philosophers.

2

Theory of Truth

1.

Truth is the Great White Whale of philosophy. In my view, it's the very biggest mystery, the deepest, most intractable problem—and not only in philosophy, but more or less everywhere, all the time. One of the themes of this book is that truth is ubiquitous and indispensable. Many philosophers (perhaps working from F. P. Ramsey) have asserted, on the contrary, that truth is a trivial or redundant notion. These might ultimately be alternative ways of saying the same thing. If "it is true that snow is white" means the same as "snow is white," then "snow is white" means the same as "it is true that snow is white." In other words, even if it's everywhere and is hence redundant, it is presupposed in every assertion and is hence fundamental.

The range of the ways the question has been addressed is immense, and the answers are as multifarious and mutually incompatible as could readily be imagined. The question of truth has been held to be a bad question. Or its answer has required vast systems of speculative metaphysics. It has been held to be the merest linguistic puzzle, and it has been held to underpin and make possible much or all of our linguistic activity. One purpose of this book is to call for a revival of worry about the issue and make a plea to do something more with the question than Tarski, or most contemporary analytic work in truth, thinks ought to be done.

Defining "truth" or giving a theory of truth is a wickedly difficult project, and it may in principle constitute an impossible task. If a theory of truth were true, it would be true according to its own definition of truth, but of course a theory of truth could be true according to itself even if it were false. For example, it might work to believe that truth is what works (though, for the record, I doubt it). That wouldn't show that "truth is what works" is a good theory.

The problem that puts you right on the edge of the sayable is that truth consistently reveals itself to be a weirdly redundant idea because it is indispensable for making any kind of assertion or description, and hence is both implied (or strictly entailed) and unnecessary to express explicitly with regard to any particular assertion or description: it's presupposed in the basic practices of communication—baked in, we might say—and hence not something substantive to communicate with regard to any particular thing to be communicated. Every claim about truth is doubled; it is about truth in that it is an assertion or belief (to assert something is to assert that it is true; to believe something is to take it to be true), and it is about truth in the ordinary sense that sentences can be about your dog or the weather. This problem will not, as it turns out, be entirely avoided in what follows, but it is very severe in the most celebrated formulations, as in "to say of what is that it is, is true," or "'snow is white' is true iff snow is white." Truth is implicated in every other piece of meaning, so that a definition appears empty or always folds back in on itself. Because of this fold, or because truth is always present, it need not be spoken of at all; the truth goes without saying, making it both impossible and trivial to cognize.

Nevertheless, I might begin with a rough taxonomy of traditional approaches, sorted by what we might call the "location" of truth: (a) The coherence theory and a variety of possibly related approaches essentially make truth internal to a sensorium or representational system or syntactic engine—us, in one of our aspects. (b) The correspondence theory makes truth a matter of the representational relation of this sensorium or syntactic engine to reality. (c) If there were to be a third overall approach in this dimension, it would locate truth outside the mind (this will need to be carefully qualified) or the subject, or the language, and in the external world. More specifically, it would identify truth with the world, of which we who speak and what we say form portions.

If I could frame my view in Aristotelian terms, it would be as follows: *What is, is true; what is not, is false.* Rather a crisp formulation, as you must admit.

We might describe the traditional project as trying to answer the following questions: what sorts of things can be true or false—that is, what is a "truth-bearer"—and in virtue of what properties or relations are such things true when they are true, or false when they are false? I don't think that such questions are ill-formed, and I don't think that they are addressed or superseded by the recursive or deflationary theories.

To ask what *truth* means and to ask what truth is are, it seems to me, two ways of putting more or less the same question. (To ask what *quark* means and to ask what a quark is are, at least on some occasions, to ask the very same thing.) There is no use trying to insulate the question of the extension of the truth predicate (if "true" is, indeed, a predicate) from the metaphysical questions of what reality is and what our relation to it consists in. These are not separate questions. I will take up both in what follows, and in each case the one bears on the other or could even be cast in terms of the other. This is one reason why I will start with an ordinary-language approach: not because the question of truth is only a question about language, but because questions about language are, in cases like this, questions about the world. For example, when Austin casts the question of truth as the question of how we use the word *true*, he is not at all abandoning traditional philosophy: he is finding another route into the metaphysical quandaries that have always befuddled and delighted philosophers.

2.

One of the few ways I think one could plausibly arrive at fresh observations about truth is by an ordinary-language approach, by trying to pay attention to the occasions and ways the term is used in natural language, and to the term's etymology, its translations into other languages, and so on. Now as soon as one tries to do this in an even semiserious way, one quickly comes to realize that "truth" is one of the richest terms in the language: it's certainly one of the richest entries in the *Oxford English Dictionary*. And one cannot but be struck by the limited uses of the term *true* that have, for the most part, come under philosophical scrutiny. The notion of truth that is held to be elucidated by the correspondence theory, the coherence theory, the pragmatic theory, recursive theories and so on—the sense in which a proposition or a statement or a sentence is true "of the world" is only one of many uses of the word.

Let me start with a distinction between what I'll call semantic and nonsemantic uses of "true" and its cognates ("truth," "truly"). Semantic entities are things that refer to or represent something other than themselves; they are things such as (some) words and sentences and pictures. "Phil" is a semantic entity that refers to that guy over there. "Phil is funny" refers, we might say, to a fact or situation or to Phil and a property he possesses, or even to a truth value. A portrait or photograph of Phil represents him. Philosophical discussions of truth are almost always limited to truth as a property or aspect of semantic entities, of sentences or propositions, beliefs, statements, and the like, though the picture case has received some attention. So the question would be what makes the sentence (proposition, etc.) "Phil is funny" true? Or, in virtue of *what* is it true?

But the word *true* is often applied to nonsemantic entities, both as a straightforward singular predication and as a relation. Consider the following locution:

(1) It was true love.

True love is real love, or we might even say it is intense love, sincere love, and so on. And notice that—as in many other very normal cases—truth here is not attributed to any sort of expression or representation: the truth of love cannot be a matter of correspondence to some fact, for example, because there is nothing to do the corresponding, no item with a semantics. Whatever love may be, it is not a sentence and not a picture; it is an emotion, not a proposition. This sort of use of the term is remarkably common: consider "true courage" or "true stupidity" or even "true colors," a general phrase for the authentic as opposed to the ersatz in human personality. Showing your true colors is displaying, perhaps in spite of yourself, who or what you really are.

We could try to work back toward the semantic notion and perhaps say that the sentence "It was true love" means something like "It is true that it was love," or simply "It was love." But neither of these versions adequately paraphrases the original sentence. "True" love is, of course, to be distinguished from "false" love—love infested by lies or betrayals—but it is also to be distinguished from everyday, run of the mill love. One might also try to treat "true" in this case as a kind of intensifier, and we might, indeed, get somewhere with paraphrases like this: "it was amazing love," "intense love," and so on. Or we might assay the adverbial formulation "truly, it was love," which I think is very close to synonymous with (1). But here, "truly" could not be considered an operator over the sentence "It was love," even a redundant or empty one. It functions, in some ways, as a tone of voice, a stab at sincerity. In some ways, it pits itself against love as an everyday happenstance or a word to be swapped casually: it suggests the sincerity of the speaker or/and of the love, tries to mark some kind of essence or authenticity of love.

There is a related range of cases in which "truth" appears to have a sense similar to "faithful":

(2) I'll be true to you.

Or, in the immortal words of the Beach Boys, "be true to your school." Here "truth to" is a relation—x is true to y—but x is not or, at first glance anyway, doesn't seem to be party to this relation in virtue of referring to or representing something. On the other hand, "true to life" or "true to the facts" and so on are phrases that do seem to attribute or describe a semantic relation. The closeness of the two uses here is suggestive: true to life might be parsed to mean faithful to life, which might, in turn, more or less mean "true."

Indeed, the parallel between the apparently semantic and the apparently nonsemantic uses of "truth to" are worth dwelling on. Being true to someone means, perhaps, not being "unfaithful" to her, or it means "keeping faith." But a musician may, for example, be true to a score, or rather, a performance may be true to a score, or even to the intentions of the composer, insofar as these are known. Here we seem to have in mind a vague idea of isomorphism, for one thing. To be true to a score one would have to play all the notes, for example, as written: one creates in sound a thing that is, in some sense, isomorphic to the notational/spatial entity. Or, one's performance reflects the score; it is, as it were, an imprint of it, like a wax seal of it. It's not enough, of course, for the two things to resemble one another. It is not a matter of chance when a performer performs a score faithfully: the items resemble one another by virtue of an intentional act or resolution, as well as due to such things as the competence and understanding of the performer. Nor is a performance that is true to a score necessarily a good performance or the only sort of good performance. The idea of being true to a score could be a dimension of aesthetic evaluation, as can be seen by the fact that it would usually be a criticism to say that the performance distorted or ran roughshod over the score or, for that matter, that it was merely accurate. But, of course, there are a thousand other possible dimensions of aesthetic evaluation. For good and ill, truth to the world, or to its motif or subject matter, of a picture, is also a dimension of aesthetic evaluation of it, and to some extent aesthetic values are relevant to assessments of truth in a variety of ways and dimensions. Obviously, truth can also have moral dimensions, and a false lover is a bad person as well as a bearer of truth value.

In both the cases of love and performance, truth of the sort picked out in (2) is the result of resolution or entails resolution—a basic insight of Heidegger. We might entertain the idea that we could describe the truth-to-life of a picture, or the truth-to-the world of a theory, in similar terms: that a theory that is true to the world or a picture that is true to life emerges through a resolution or an openness, necessarily intentional. The relation is, we might say, mimetic, or hermeneutic, but it also uses the self as a zone of inscription or denotes a resolution to openness or fluidity, imprintability.

What I am trying to do is to see the real resonances and connections of the term *truth* in the language. If you like, you can view all these remarks as attempts to elucidate homonyms, or even merely play with poetic resonances, in search of something that might be useful. What such examples so treated begin to do is show both how fundamental in a variety of dimensions and activities and identities the notion of truth is, and also how narrow are the uses under consideration in the usual philosophical treatments of the matter. Not that a theory of truth is required to account for every metaphorical or fantastic use, but of course some argument would be required that particular uses are metaphorical or fantastic. Or indeed, that some use—"It is true that snow is white," say—is central or literal. "True love" is of course such a common usage as to be a mere cliché, whereas "it is true that snow is white" or " 'snow is white' is true" and its ilk are sentences produced only in special professional circumstances.

There are, as remarked, adverbial/adjectival uses as well that function to make an assertion more emphatic, as in "Truly, the cows are lovely" or

(3) She is a truly annoying person.

Sentence (3) is, I think, roughly synonymous with "she is a genuinely annoying person," or a very annoying person, or an authentically annoying person, or even a really annoying person. Notice that the adverbial use can function basically synonymously with the sort of uses pointed up in (2). "I love you truly; truly, truly dear." If, of course, I love you truly, then my love is true. Here, again, the function of emphasis or reiteration can also be at work. To say that *p*, and then say, "truly, *p*," is to try to gain attention for the assertion that *p* or pluck it out from the muttering for emphasis. It is worth thinking, too, about the fact that "truly" can function similarly as an operator over sentences or as modifying terms within the sentence. (3) is very closely equivalent to "Truly, she is an annoying person": alternately, the object of emphasis is a sentence or an annoyingness. These appear to be extremely distinct, for in the one, "truly" operates over a semantic entity or a linguistic object, in the other over a person or her qualities; one appears to work within an idiolect and a set of signifying practices, the other to reach out and touch an external-world person and her qualities. And yet they mean (close to) the same. One can construe many sentences that are apparently about the world as being about the language; for example, "Truly, she is an annoying person" can mean that the sentence "She is an annoying person," is true. But then it appears to mean the same as "She is an annoying person," that is, the claim that a person has a property or however we may cash that out. But "She is a truly annoying person" appears to express that her annoyingness is itself true, or perhaps we might say, actual. For that matter, we might even resort to "She truly is annoying." Here what is true is apparently the copula, or what is true is the act of predication itself, or what is true is being—the very isness of "is."

Again, of course, we cannot keep sentences and what they are about separate in this way, as a treatment of any of a thousand similar cases will show. And though it seems that if there were any use for a truth operator in logic it would have to take as arguments complete expressions or formulae of the logical language, we could also treat "true" as a predicate or part of a predicate. We could say (a) "T(She is annoying)" ["She is annoying" is true]; or we could say (b) "G(she)" where G is the unanalyzable predicate "truly annoying" [She is truly annoying]. Or we might try (c) "H(she) & T(she)," where H means "annoying" and T means "true" [She is annoying and she is true]. The latter makes truth one of *her* qualities. (Well, that is a bad paraphrase of the original, but "She is truly sweet" fares a bit better as "She is sweet and true.") Or we could assay (d) "TH(she)" [She is truly annoying], treating "truly" as a predicate ranging over predicates, as a kind of annoyingness or sweetness, and so on. Expression (d) seems the truest to the usage. But only (a) makes the notion of truth semantic. Expressions (b) to (d) are about which predicates are really instantiated by things in the world (e.g., true sweetness), or as I would prefer to put it, the way the world actually is; they are about the way the world is, not about sentences, statements, beliefs, or propositions. At any rate, (a) gets something interesting about (3), but it does not mean the same.

It is worth emphasizing, again, that "Truly, she is an annoying person" and "She is a truly annoying person" are, roughly, used synonymously, though their logical forms appear wildly divergent. (Really, what we're trying to say is that she is a thoroughly annoying person.) And while a theory of truth in the traditional sense might do something with the former, I am suggesting that we might focus instead on the latter as fundamental: then we would be focusing on her annoyingness as something true rather than sentences as something true. That is, we might see to what extent the semantic uses might fall fairly straightforwardly out of the nonsemantic uses. (If her annoyingness is true—if she is, indeed, truly annoying—it is a *particular situation*; annoyingness appears at that node of space-time [as a "trope"], in those particular manifestations, as a feature of that person in relation.)

Truth is transparent and liquid across the elements of the proposition: the subject, the predicate, the copula. The reality of the real-world correlate of any of these is the reality of them all, insofar as they constitute a situation.

There is also a nonsemantic sense of "true" that is virtually synonymous with "accurate," though it may also have the added flavor of "direct":

(4) My aim is true.

Here, we might think in terms of means and ends or even of rationality: a true aim hits what it aims at or is suited to achieve its goal. A true line is a straight line, the best way of getting where you are going, other things being equal. Something that departs from the correct orientation can be termed "out of true." It's interesting to note that accuracy can be a property of items that have no semantics, like arrows in their flights, and so on., as well as of items that do, such as maps or theories. "Accurate" is used as a synonym for "true" in semantic contexts: to say of a description that it is accurate is to say that it is true, and to say that it is true is to say that it is true of or to the thing it describes. And we might ask to what extent a true sentence or proposition is like a true line or aim and to what extent a false sentence is a sentence out of true. Of course, such strategies may simply appear to make the notion of truth even more obscure than it already is. But they do suggest that questing for truth in the thicket of language or semantic theories might be limiting, that we might need the vocabulary not of Tarski's logic—or not only of Tarski's logic—but of ethics or aesthetics, or of target shooting or carpentry. There is a nautical sense in which the wind can be true: consistent as to force and direction. Also bearings taken from true north are true bearings. Also, "true" can simply mean level, and "trueing" is the process of making straight or level.

"Truth" is also sometimes, and has been traditionally, used to pick out a virtue, as a dimension of ethical evaluation. I myself used it to mean the sum of virtues in one of my books, and of the several objections that I got, none asserted there was no such sense of "true." It has the sense of reliable, steady, consistent, sure, and right, as well as again the flavor of faithful, and also honest, sincere, genuine. The eleventh-century Laws of Ethelred refer to a "true witness" in somewhat this sense.

(5) A true man does not think what his hearers are feeling, but what he is saying. (Helps: OED)

The OED gives a variety of other senses, including the semantic sense, and also points to the phrase "true to type," as of a person who behaves as we would expect him to behave given a category of persons he falls into.

One thing that's remarkable about (1) to (5) and their ilk is the variety of "truth-bearers" or sorts of things it makes sense to call true: persons, lines, loves, aims, sweetnesses, girders, and so on. This may appear to draw us into a hopeless muddle, or perhaps worse, simply to change the subject: it's not what we were looking for when we went looking for a theory of truth. These are not the phenomena that the correspondence or coherence theory were trying to explain, not what William James or Donald Davidson took themselves to be writing about. On the other hand, perhaps this is precisely what they were writing about, only they considered an artificially narrow range of cases. Or perhaps the uses are metaphorically or narratively or polemically connected in a way that at least yields some funky feeling of insight.

3.

At any rate, the neglect of philosophers, with the occasional exception of a Heidegger, to the real range of uses is surprising, especially considering their centrality to our everyday linguistic practices. Usually the philosopher simply starts out by adducing a series of examples, all of which put propositions or sentences in play. Or occasionally there is an acknowledgment that truth is not always used with regard to semantic entities. Then there's the usual ground clearing when the philosopher says "I'm trying to elucidate propositional truth." Even Austin, who of all philosophers ought to be sensitive to the range of uses, begins by defining certain (semantic) uses as "primary." But without an argument—an argument that cannot, of course, be about ordinary use of the term—there is no reason to regard them as primary. For that matter, there is no reason until some argument is produced to regard the use of "true" as it applies to semantic entities as amounting to a different sense of the term than any other uses we have just identified. If propositional truth is truth in one of those uses, then a theory of truth as applied to propositions (and so on) could fall out of an elucidation of one or more of them.

One thing we might begin to notice about the five nonsemantic uses is that they have a lot in common. It strikes me that "true" is not a group of unconnected words that are spelled the same; all the uses grow out of a single etymology. And furthermore, they all have similarities to occasions wherein we ascribe truth to statements or other semantic entities. One interesting thing we might note is that there is a form of the ancient Greek verb *esti*—to be—on which it has to be translated as "is true," or an equivalent. Parmenides' "Way of Truth" is being itself: isness, we might say. And many of the senses of "true" play very closely to the ideas of being and reality. This is certainly the case with the ethical senses and of the senses illustrated by such phrases as "true grit," where "true" is very close to meaning "real" or "authentic." To say of a thing that it is true may be to say that it truly is.

However, it is obvious that "real" or "actual" (and so on) cannot be substituted for "true" in every expression, and "My aim is true" does not mean the same as "My aim is real"; "I'll be true to you" does not mean the same as "I'll be real to you." But that is the sort of thing one must expect of words like "real" and "true" in ordinary language: even if they are closely related, each comes, as it were, with its own syntax, or a nexus of contexts within which a competent speaker would regard it as non-weird. Then if the project of defining the term were conceived as trying to capture something common or at the heart of many uses, different aspects might be emphasized, and the concepts will bleed off in a rich way into their environments. It would be nice to capture truth once and for all in a formula (e.g., "what is, is true") but insofar as we are defining the notion that we use, or want to know what people mean when they say of something that it is true, we have to be prepared for messier and more volatile solutions. This is precisely what led Tarski into defining a very narrow concept with regard to limited or formal languages: led him, in short, to change the subject. That is why I try to make the frame in terms of rough synonymies, or overlapping usages, or the possibilities of rephrasing various sentences which employ "true" using "real" and its cognates, and vice versa. For your dreams to come true is for them to be realized or made actual.

Within these limitations, and framing these generalizations at their outermost, I suggest that the world is what is true, or that the primary sense of "true" is more or less synonymous with "real." What I am calling a "primary" sense here is an attempt to boil down what the central ordinary uses—including the semantic uses—have in common: this seems like the central way to try to give a definition of a word that is in actual use, when it has the richness and complexity of something like "truth": one tries to account for the widest range of uses in the simplest possible way: that is certainly one way to construe the project of defining a word. Of course, one might stipulate a sense of "truth"—in which case, of course, the definition is already given in the stipulation; but then what one has defined is not what we mean by "truth."

That is, I believe, precisely the approach of Tarski and his immense entourage. Or one might be interested in the notion of truth only insofar as it bears on technical questions in logic or semantics, and thus restrict the admissible uses a priori as bearing or not bearing on the domain of inquiry. But either of these moves is arbitrary or at any rate premature.

We think of a veridical experience as opposed to an hallucination, an experience of what is real as opposed to what is unreal, as an experience of the truth. That seems like a normal way of talking, more or less. To experience something real is to experience the truth. Now when we talk about "experiencing the truth," I don't think we are talking, or necessarily talking, about experiencing some sort of relation between a proposition and the world; we are talking about experiencing the world, about truly making contact with some portion or aspect of reality. There's an idea according to which coming to know the truth involves gathering up a bunch of sentences or whatever and trying to confirm them: an activity performed between semantic entities and the things they mean—facts perhaps. But even "coming to know the truth" can have a nonsemantic edge: when you catch your spouse in bed with someone else, you are confronted with the truth, and it seems to me that all the propositional attitudes and operations that go along with that are subsidiary to your confrontation with the actual situation before you. "Now I see the awful truth" might describe coming to have certain propositional attitudes, but it is also used to report directly witnessing some terrible event. For example, there is a sense in which to know the truth about, let us say, genocide, or addiction, you have to have experienced such things. A person without such experiences may come to have all the same propositional attitudes, for example, by believing what the witness says, but the nonwitness's access to the truth is nonetheless attenuated.

I don't pretend that the suggestion that we need to move away from propositions to situations, that we might more or less subsume the term *true* under *real*, is clear enough to solve any puzzles by itself or to serve as a theory of truth. I just want to make a few moves that put into play the suggestion that moving away from the notion of semantic truth-bearers might be a promising direction. Obviously, there are various puzzles that do not arise if a rock rather than a sentence is a truth-bearer, and I would of course urge that you not take preservation of the going puzzles to be a requirement for a decent view about truth. That a certain range of befuddlements does not arise would of course frustrate those who have taken on such befuddlements as a task, but all things equal it is a good thing.

"True," in "My aim is true," or "a true line," or "true north," or "true plumb," or "trueing up," for example, has essentially the sense of accuracy, and furthermore accuracy as a goal or purpose: an aim or line is true relative to some project or goal, but relative to that goal there is a fact of the matter about whether you hit the bullseye. This gets us much closer to the semantic uses, evidently, and to say that a sentence is true iff it is accurate appears to be a version of correspondence, if it is not merely tautologous. But a target, an arrow, and an eye is not a semantic entity, and one's aim is not true in virtue of the world really displaying the objects and qualities picked out by something that refers to or represents them, because there is no such thing. There is, however, beyond an intention, a set of practices—craft practices, we might say—in which truth arises in target shooting or carpentry. You wouldn't say that hitting the bullseye is a matter of a picture matching a reality; it's a matter of firing an arrow into the bit in the center. That is, any particular case of truth in target practice or carpentry is a real-world situation, encompassing a person, a practice, and a juxtaposition of physical objects.

A yet closer approach to the semantic cases might be the truth of a performance to a score. Here, to begin with, we have two entities and a relation between them. Yet I wonder whether the performance represents the score, exactly. We might say that it "refers" to the score, but I wonder whether a given passage of a performance refers to a score in anything like the sense that a name refers to what it names, for example. On the other hand it makes sense to think of the performance corresponding to the score, or being an accurate rendition of it. The relation appears to be "mimetic" and here it does seem to make sense to talk about some sort of isomorphism between score and performance, though they seem to be such different sorts of things—the one a text in a system of notation, the other an audible event. It's interesting, too, that the semantic relation appears to be reversed from what most semiotics might lead us to suspect: the sonic event is true to or accurate with regard to the text, as also the performance of a play to its script. But the question of the accuracy of the score itself is a difficult matter to fix: it's a matter of its provenance, or its historical relations to a variety of other notational items, such as the composer's autograph.

In all these cases, we see the idea of truth growing richer and more complex, but we also see it configuring again and again around notions of reality and accuracy to and among real things. We see the widest variety of truth bearers and makers and of items juxtaposed in truth relations and in the relation juxtaposing them: truth is a feature of an extraordinarily elaborate set of situations. But again and again, it is situations—real things in real relations—that are in question or that are explored from one angle or another. The only subject matter that tempts us away from such a characterization is the relatively narrow range of properly semantic truth-bearers: pictures or sentences. These are often characterized precisely by their distinction from the realities they represent. So deep is this distinction in the tradition that it yawns as an *ontological* gap, between works of art and mere real things, or between concepts and objects. The differences between semantic and nonsemantic objects looms since Plato as a distinction between levels of being, and the alleged fact that our intellects are syntactic engines motivates human exceptionalism and dualism: the soul screen on which our sensa are projected, and so on. In other words, the problem of semantics lurks at the heart of metaphysics. But I suggest that this thought stems from an artificially narrow understanding of the makers and bearers of truth, or a kind of vicious intellectualism.

4.

Frege attributes truth to propositions, Austin to statements, Tarski to sentences, and so on. This reflects in some way the ontologies lurking behind the epistemologies because these different entities apparently have different degrees of abstractness. But once we at least fend off the temptation to focus exclusively on the attribution of truth to semantic entities, we can notice that all sorts of things can be truth-bearers, from people to winds to floors to shots to qualities like sweetness or loveliness to commitments and so on. This may appear just to make the subject of truth a hopeless confusion, but what I'm suggesting is that the first move in getting some kind of new start on truth is exactly to let it get complex, or to cease making the first few ground-clearing assumptions that restrict you to a few bearers, a few puzzles, and a few theories. The immense complexity of truth—its immense profusion (truth is precisely as profuse as the universe; truth is a cataract of diamonds)—has been lost to the philosophical tradition and needs to be recovered.

A traditional view is, to repeat, that the bearer of truth value is the proposition. The proposition is conceived to be an abstract object, not appearing in any natural language but expressible in language. So, for example, "Tous les meilleurs gens regardent beaucoup la télévision" and "All the best people watch a lot of television" are different sentences, but they express the same proposition. One might say that "they mean the same thing." Well, this "thing" they mean is supposed to be a particular proposition. Of course, propositions seem to be rather occult entities, a bit ectoplasmic for modern tastes. This is true even of accounts of the proposition that I might in other ways find fairly congenial, such as the notion that a proposition is a function from possible worlds to truth values. I like the idea that we're talking about whole worlds, whole situations. But this still seems profligate, committing us as it seems to an infinity of nonactual objects even by the simplest claim. We'd like something a trifle less Platonic, something we can get our hands on and throttle properly. Thus some philosophers of a more nominalistic bent have rested content with sentences as the bearers of truth value, and then tried to finesse the problems by saying that certain sentences covary in truth value, so that there are more or less logical entailments between them. Thus, if "All the best people watch a lot of television" is true, then so is "Tous les meilleurs gens regardent beaucoup la télévision," and vice versa. The famous Tarski theory or account of truth seems to use sentences as the fundamental bearers of truth value.

Now there are various problems with this. One of them is that sentences are no less abstract as entities than are propositions. (Actually "abstract" is pretty bivalent: you is or you ain't.) For example, "the same" sentence appears on this sheet of paper and that sheet. Right now (let's say) I'm looking at a sentence (in fact, this very sentence) on the page, and I'm also speaking the same sentence aloud (lecturing, perhaps). And sentences themselves consist of things like words, letters, and punctuation marks, which are themselves no less abstract than sentences and propositions.

Perhaps we shouldn't be so dismayed by abstract entities. Maybe we need to have a lush ontology, or perhaps there's some way to produce a translation from abstract to concrete things, and we could regard talk of sentences or propositions as a kind of shorthand, substituting for much longer assertions about inscriptions and utterances: actual particular objects and events. Of course we don't want to go around multiplying levels of being like wanton Plotinuses if there are any alternatives. But there are other problems—devastating problems—for the idea that the proposition or the sentence is the fundamental bearer of truth value, and these are problems that arise precisely from the distinction of propositions and sentences from their concrete occurrences.

There's a famous paper on reference by Keith Donellan in which he shows the kind of problems I mean. His example runs roughly like this. Let's say we're gossiping at a party, and I say "He's embezzling money from his company." And you say, "Really? Who?" And I say, "Don't look now. It's the guy drinking champagne." And you say "Oh my Lord, it's Freddie!" Now the phrase "the guy drinking champagne" in this example refers to Freddie. But let's stipulate that Freddie is a teetotaler, and in fact what he's got there in his flute is sparkling cider, indistinguishable from champagne at this distance. Donellan's view is that even though the description "the guy drinking champagne" is not satisfied by Freddie, I have successfully referred to Freddie. I think that is right: we perfectly well understand each other. And if Freddie is indeed an embezzler, then it follows that my utterance "The guy drinking champagne is embezzling money from his company" is true.[1]

Now what's the point of this example? Just this: it's not the sentence that is true, because actually considered as an abstract entity, apart from the occasion of its utterance (if, indeed, it is possible or legitimate to consider it this way at all), it is false. The phrase "the guy drinking champagne" only refers to Freddie in this particular context of its utterance, in which it enables you to understand what I'm asserting. This makes it appear that what is true or false are not propositions, not sentences, but utterances or inscriptions: particular things that occur in particular situations. I think this is what we should expect given the whole momentum of twentieth-century analytic philosophy. If we think about the accounts of meaning and truth that we get in philosophers like Austin, Wittgenstein, Quine, or Rorty, we'd have to identify meaning with use (though of course what such philosophers mean by "use" differs somewhat from guy to guy). If meaning only emerges in a context of use, then of course sentences are true or false, if at all, only within that context, since it's fair to say that truth has something to do with meaning (I'm not sure at the moment just what).

There are many ways into the same insight. Many sentences, including the one we've been considering ("The guy over there . . ."), contain indexical expressions that only have reference relative to an occasion and context of utterance, so that the sentence considered in itself does not have a meaning or a truth value in isolation from a context of use: an environment, a gesture, an inflection, all of the above. "That guy over there" is about as well-formed and common a referring expression as we've got, but obviously you need to encompass an environment and a set of practices if you're going to say what, on any particular occasion, it refers to. Very common are terms we might call "quasi-indexicals": "thingummy," for instance, or "whatchamacallit," "whatsername." These can easily convey a definite reference, but only in a context of utterance or inscription.

In fact, every general term participates in this structure to some extent: "thing," but for that matter, "chair"—"the chair is on the floor." Both terms refer relative to the context of utterance or inscription, of course, because there are many chairs and many floors. Verb tenses have the same effect, and what moment or period the present tense (and hence, what periods past or future tenses) indicates is relative to the moment or period in which the verb is uttered or inscribed. Proper names are, in general, not unique and have a role in successful communication in the sense that the thing referred to is the thing understood to be referred to, that is, only in a given context of utterance or inscription. The Donellan examples show that apparently nonindexical uses of the language (as in the definite description "the guy drinking champagne") function as indexicals in real contexts of communication. That is, the expression in its context can be wielded to pick out items in that context even though those items don't satisfy the description that the phrase apparently expresses.

The usual structure is to develop a theory of meaning and then try to deal with indexical elements piecemeal, to eliminate them. But I suggest, instead, that, first, the indexical elements are ineliminable, and second, that they're fundamental. Quine argues that language faces the world not word by word, as though nouns were labels on things, and so on, but as a whole, as a "field of force." There is truth in that, but we have to include extralinguistic material in this field of force. We need to temporalize it, show it in constant process. We have to include gestures, flashes of the eyes, shrugs, postures. These things are constantly in play in utterances, and display them in their capacities as deriving from and proceeding back into the world. The reference of "the guy drinking champagne" to Fred, who's drinking sparkling cider, is secured by the sidelong glance, the turn of the head, the whispery tone which indexes how far away Fred is. These things themselves, of course, have conventional elements; they operate as they do within socially authorized systems. But they are also "natural": they are the real gestures of real organisms, called out by and feeding back into a more-than-social surround. Written language attenuates the gestural elements to some extent, and this is precisely why shifting from spoken to written language increases abstraction, generality, and so on, and also why writing is, more deeply and more thoroughly than speaking, a site of untruth.

On the other hand, the scope or comprehension of written language is greater, as is its permanence: written language hedges against time. But even so, it is chock full of indexicality: it must be referred to a writer, to a time, to a culture, and to an environment in order to be understood. It employs pronouns, verb tenses. Like spoken language it can mean the opposite of what it says through sarcasm. It can refer to things without giving them their conventional names. It plays within a particular situation, is aimed at particular readers, calls into play whole contingent histories of texts and their production and particular cultures that in turn massively presuppose particular situations of embodiment, and so on. Its alphabets and ideograms arise in certain situations, for certain purposes that respond to environmental demands. It carries with it technologies, always constrained by, responsive to, and introducing, alterations of, the environment.

Indeed, once one starts to focus on what people say and what they mean on real occasions, each utterance bristles with what we might call occasional peculiarities. People often "say" precisely the opposite of what they "mean" in a variety of ways for a variety of purposes. Sometimes they are understood and sometimes not. Davidson's treatment in the classic paper "A Nice Derangement of Epitaphs" is exemplary in many ways. He distinguishes in interpretation between the interpreter's "prior" theory and his "passing" theory: what he thinks "Fred" or "2" might refer to if uttered and what it actually means as it is being uttered. These do not resolve into literal and figurative uses, and are both in process. But what Davidson, remarkably I think, omits, is the nonlinguistic context in which this is all taking place: the actual physical surroundings. Now I don't know if we want to call the gestures and inflections linguistic or nonlinguistic (they are, certainly, central to linguistic communication) but obviously, for example, a mere inflection, a pattern of intonation, can suffice, more or less, to invert the meaning of a sentence into its negation, for example. And you can't have gestures or inflections in language conceived in terms of abstract idiolects: they are describable fully only as physical events, although of course there are conventions and practices surrounding their use (which in turn can be inflected or inverted in irony or hyperbole). Who your use of some proper name refers to may well depend on various physical situations: proximity, familiarity, frequency. Both my mother-in-law and my daughter are named Jane, which does lead to occasional confusion. But the default interpretation ought to be the daughter because I talk about her more; I reside in the same physical space, and so on. The interpretation needs to reflect the physical juxtapositions. I think it's fair to say that Davidson himself was moving late in life in this direction, wherein meaning (reference, for example) cannot be fixed except in relation to an external world, and thus truth.

Consider, let's say, the paradigmatic true sentence "snow is white." Notice that in most situations that's an odd thing to say, like "the cat is on the mat." Indeed, people who keep piping up with things like that are insane: there had better be a context, a puzzlement, something funny about the cat or something. Ripping true sentences from occasions of utterance and inscription—the artificial isolation of truths—is exactly what would make an assessment of meaning or truth conditions a great puzzle. Removing occasions eventually might lead us into actual gobbledygook, which is what we should expect. I suppose one had better acknowledge that it is true that snow is white. But, for example, let's say I'm a man from the pristine Canadian Rockies, ignorant of the ways of the rest of the world. You transport me to Chicago and show me some notably grey snow, with black passages. I can deal with this in a variety of ways in a Quinean web of belief: I can insist that snow is white, so this stuff ain't snow, for example. But I have to deal with the real situation, encompassing the stuff, its color, the "general truth" that snow is white, and so on. The most general truths are going to bend at the moment of utterance, the juxtaposition of you and me and blackish snow, or stuff that seems like snow in some respects (it fell, frozen, from the sky) but which I resolve to regard as something else. The proposition always bends in this way to occasion; there is no way to preserve the atemporal meaning of the proposition, but the proposition, if it is considered at all, has to be treated as what is expressed on the particular occasion. Snow is white. But this is snow.

Everyone who has worked with the Tarski machinery has had to acknowledge that it needs adjusting with regard to indexical elements: usually they have simply written a check and hoped that it could somehow be worked through. (Though Hartry Field, for one, takes indexical-type cases as showing directly that the primary truth-bearers are utterances and inscriptions.[2]) "It's raining here" is true iff it's raining here. Obviously, that may be false when the context of evaluation is different from the context of utterance. But the whole structure is hopelessly abstract. One can hardly deny that "'snow is white' is true iff snow is white," I suppose. But "snow is white" said with a sarcastic intonation, or with irony, or as it hails, or in a work of fiction, or in a world with pink snow—one just cannot specify its truth conditions without a detailed experience of the real nature and context of utterance. Perhaps the Tarski machinery is a theory of truth, perhaps not, but it is certainly not a theory of what makes anything that anyone says or writes actually true or false.

Then, of course, we have analytic propositions, truths of logic and mathematics, and so on. The point of such things is precisely to give us a realm to work in outside of time, subjectivity, occasion, stuff. Here Quine's treatment is exemplary, and though "all bachelors are unmarried" merely restates or follows from the definition of the term *bachelor*, it actually is qualified or rejected under the pressures of real utterance, and it makes sense to say that Clinton is a married bachelor. This depends upon the meaning of the term, understood in terms of a massive accretion of utterances and inscriptions, and it contradicts that meaning: the accretion really is massive, providing resources we don't know we possess until we are already employing them. The truth of "Clinton is a married bachelor" isn't just some kind of engagement with uses or extension of metaphors; it is a way the world is, a juxtaposition of bodies, let us say, in process over time. It's really the way the world is causing our vocabulary to bend on real occasions: a causal interaction between world, word, speaker.

It is, I suggest, going to end up being impossible to hold on to the meaning of any given linguistic unit without treating this meaning as emerging only with regard to the place, the moment, the speaker or writer, and the histories of each, as well as the massive histories of usage, or as it were a core sample of them. The primary bearers of meaning are particular utterances and inscriptions in relation to their contexts. Obviously, an assertion like that requires a system or an answer to a million possible programs and a million possible problems. There are many ways to try to save sentences or propositions as bearers or meaning or truth value. Only it would at least be worthwhile to take seriously for a moment the idea that inscriptions and utterances are the primary or the only bearers of truth value in the linguistic case, and to treat sentences or propositions, to the extent we treat them at all, nominalistically. I want to emphasize that the ontology I'm deploying here is not driven primarily by nominalist or Quinean ontological queasiness, though I share that queasiness, but by the attempt to theorize truth in a new or upside-down way.

5.

Though it is implicated in an ontology and an epistemology I reject, one way into this series of insights is Russell's view, expressed in the famous "Mont Blanc letter" to Frege and in *The Principles of Mathematics*, that objects such as numbers or mountains can be constituents of propositions, apparently in particular with regard to the propositions expressed in sentences using proper names and indexicals.

> I believe that in spite of all its snowfields Mont Blanc itself is a component part of what is actually asserted in "Mont Blanc is more than 4,000 meters high." We do not assert the thought, for this is a private psychological matter: we assert the object of the thought, and this is, to my mind, a certain complex (an objective proposition, one might say) in which Mont Blanc is itself a component part. If we do not admit this, then we get the conclusion that we know nothing at all about Mont Blanc. This is why for me the *Bedeutung* [reference] of a proposition is not the true, but a certain complex which (in the given case) is true.[3]

Here we begin to conceive of propositions not as Platonic abstractions but as real-world situations, though of course the ontological status of the constituents picked out by predicates and other sorts of expressions seems more problematic—or even more problematic—than that of, say, Mont Blanc. One might elaborate the Russellian approach and express a line of thought parallel to the present one by saying things like "propositions are facts." The correspondence theory of truth might say that true utterances are utterances of sentences that express propositions that map or are isomorphic with or correspond to facts. But we could try to cut back on the baroque ontology by saying that utterances express propositions, which are facts, that is, real-world situations.

This "situational" account of truth may be thought of as a version of what is sometimes called "the identity theory," which is really a radical strategy for foreshortening the question. According to the identity theory, propositions are identical to facts, or, what we believe or say is the fact itself or the situation that is usually thought of as "corresponding to" the proposition. Or, if a proposition is true, it is identical to the fact that makes it true. This would be a natural construal of Plato's declaration in the *Cratylus* that "a true proposition says that which is, and a false proposition says that which is not."[4] Marian David gives the identity theory a beautifully simple formulation:

(IT) For every proposition x, x is true iff x is a fact;

For every proposition x, x is false iff x is not a fact.[5]

This has interesting mystical overtones, which I like, actually. Explicitly endorsed by (the early) G. E. Moore, it eventuates because of its insufficiency—particularly in explaining falsehood—in the *Tractatus* view of an isomorphism of proposition and fact; if there is no fact with which the proposition is isomorphic, it is false. What we say truly discloses the logical structure of the universe.

Moore writes:

> It is commonly supposed that the truth of a proposition consists in some relation which it bears to reality; and falsehood in the absence of this relation. The relation in question is generally called a "correspondence" or "agreement," and it seems to be generally conceived as one of partial similarity; but it is to be noted . . . that it is essential to the theory that a truth should differ in some specific way from the reality, in relation to which its truth is to consist . . . It is the impossibility of finding any such difference between a truth and the reality to which it is supposed to correspond which refutes the theory. . . . Once it is definitely recognized that the proposition is to denote, not a belief or form of words, but an object

of belief, it seems plain that a truth differs in no respect from the reality with which it was supposed merely to correspond: e.g., the truth that I exist differs in no respect from the corresponding reality—my existence.[6]

Though Moore eventually repudiated this view as a holdover from idealism (it is, in essence, a version of Bradley's view), it is certainly on the right track by my lights. Now though I cannot have an ontology that includes propositions in the traditional sense, I have no problem with propositions if they are identical to facts, which I regard as juxtapositions of objects in an environment.

David's formulation, however, has it that some propositions (the true ones) are identical to facts, and some (the false ones) are not. This pushes us again toward ontologically difficult objects, for it seems that while true propositions are perfectly concrete objects, false propositions are not. Nor is it necessarily idealistic, and though Moore eventually thought he was saying that reality could only be understood through the concept of truth, there's no reason it doesn't go just as well the other way round. It also, interestingly, anticipates a view such as Ramsey's that apparently gets rid of truth as a predicate altogether, or shows its dispensability. The truth that I exist is . . . my existence. Or to generalize: the truth that x is x's reality. (To which we might add, the truth that x is the fact that x.) Now what I want to add to this is that such facts, realities, and situations are only indicated within language on particular occasions of utterance, that the whole of the situation must be taken into account. But that just makes it doubly clear that this is no idealism, that truth isn't (only) in the head or the language or the culture, but that all of these things are in the world. To say the least this is a sensible way of speaking, if we admit philosophy into ordinary language at all. But truth is no more dispensable than reality, in that they are the same, and we might read Moore's identity theory as the most hard-nosed realism imaginable; it is to truth what "here is a hand and here is another" is to the concept of knowledge.

The sort of view I am putting forward, like the identity theory—or like any theory, really, but in proximity to the identity theory—needs to be able to explain false propositions but also modal propositions, normative propositions, counterfactuals, and so on. Putting it mildly, this does present certain challenges. But one thing that's wrong with modal realism, for example, is that possible worlds are parasitic on the actual world; they are *merely* possible, we should say, and making them actual destroys the idea you were endeavoring to explain. At any rate, we might consider there to be three modal operators: the diamond (it is possible that), the box (it is necessary that), and none (it is actual that). The "actuality" operator functions like Frege's "assertion stroke," which is to be read "it is true that." But I am reading every assertion as though it asserted the reality of some situation. Plato, again: "a true proposition says that which is." A Ramsey-like insight is that an assertion stroke is eliminable because redundant. Looking at it the other way round, it is eliminable because it is always implied in any claim. But rather than as a truth operator, let us read the actuality operator, which needs no representation in any particular formula, as "In reality," and stipulate that it appears before the beginning of each well-formed formula.

One thing we might notice at this insane level of generality is that modal claims themselves appear within the scope of the operator. So we would interpret "It is possible that p" as "In reality it is possible that p." What is possible in a given situation, or what would be true if the situation were altered in certain respects, I want to say, is itself a feature of the world, or a fact about it; or it must be, if claims about possibility are true. Something is possible *in virtue of what is actual*, we might say. As Kripke points out, possible worlds are things we stipulate, not things we discover with big telescopes, and we stipulate them in relation to this world: it's like our world except the H_2O is replaced with XYZ, or the organisms are silicon based, or whatever it may be. Many problems arise here, let me acknowledge, and what could be meant by "In reality if I go to the store, I'll be late," is a difficult question. Still it is not an insane way to speak, for a philosopher.

So here would be the basic picture: different utterances or inscriptions could, more or less, express the same proposition, but this proposition is a real-world situation, or a range of related real-world situations (related, for example, by embedding some of the same objects and events). The utterance by a particular person that the cat is on the mat, and by another person in the same room that the mat is under the cat are different utterances, and it is sensible to say that they are utterances of different sentences. But they express the same proposition: that is, they pick out more or less the same real-world situation.

The phrase "a truth" is an interesting one. "It is a truth that x" is used close to synonymously with "it is a fact that x," though the former locution would normally be used to introduce a fact of particular scope or generality. "It is a truth that Gladys is obese" seems alright but rather absurdly grand, though we'd be happy to say "It is a truth that man is mortal." Then we're back to trying to analyze the "that" clause: posing some quasi- or protolinguistic arrangement for the clause to introduce. But the clause introduces a situation, as Moore and Ramsey and Austin all saw: Gladys's obesity, the mortality of human beings. Gladys's obesity is a fact (let's say), but it's not a quasilinguistic entity or a propositional element or something: it is Gladys's actual rolls of fat, the way she tips the scale, and so on.

6.

But the fundamental semantic truth bearers are utterances and inscriptions, and an utterance or inscription is not identical to the situation in which it emerges; it is a part or bit or segment of that situation. And what we believe when we believe something is not exactly, directly, a chunk of the world. We have to figure out how to preserve everyday assertions like "what I said, believed, and so on, is true."

What makes the identity theory compelling is that it seems to entirely eliminate semantic entities, which, after all, are extremely bothersome: there is no longer any issue of reference or of representation or even, in the most radical moments, isomorphism: what we believe is the world. Yet this seems simplistic or perhaps merely wrong, and to talk of believing a barn would be odd, even if it is possible to believe in a barn, or to believe your family doctor. The identity theory is basically true, if you will allow me to say so, for it basically identifies truth and reality. But what we must do is treat truth for semantic entities as a special case of this general thesis. What we need to focus on in the semantic case is not the fact external to the utterer (as in the identity theory), nor the realm of the utterer's intellect or idiolect (as in idealisms or hermeneutics), but on the situation in which the two are juxtaposed by means of various intermediaries as well as immediately, by linguistic conventions and interpenetrations of perception. *The situation that makes the utterance true includes the fact it picks out, if any, but includes also the utterance itself and the utterer.*

Ramsey points out that we can say that the judgment aRb "is true if there exists a corresponding fact that a has R to b, but this is essentially not an analysis but a periphrasis, for "The fact a has R to b exists" is no different from "a has R to b."[7] Now what is worthy of remark is that all these terms are, with proper adjustments, interchangeable or can be used to express the same thing: "It is a fact that p," "It is true that p," "The circumstance described by p is real," "The situation picked out by p exists." And, um, p. Existence, reality, truth, fact, and so on.: these are all expressible in terms of one another, or merely by the mood of serious assertion. They are all, in some broad sense, the very same notion. All of these are ways of saying the same thing, and what they say, I think, is not that a proposition has a certain quality, but that the world is a certain way. What they say is the world.

In some ways, the view I am articulating is related to the "new realist" view of truth articulated by William Pepperrell Montague early in the twentieth century. (The "new realists" were an ephemeral local outbreak, fighting the various tides of idealism and positivism on behalf of their own real.) Montague flatly identifies truth as reality, and then considers the following objection: "True and false, it will be said, are adjectives which apply to beliefs, that is, to the acts or states of an individual. We do not call objects true or false; we call them real or unreal—beliefs alone are susceptible of truth and falsity." Now we've already seen plenty of reasons, I think, not to take "beliefs" as our exclusive truth-value bearers. Objects can be true or false in some usages of those terms: persons can be, aims, winds, and so on. Nevertheless, Montague—a charming and forgotten figure—assays a bold solution:

> To which it may be replied that true or false only apply to beliefs in a metonymous or borrowed sense, i.e., in virtue of the relation of the act of believing to the object believed in. There would be no sense in calling an act of belief as such either true or false. It is always because of what is

believed that the belief is either true or false. Belief borrows its truth or falsity from its object or content. . . . I hold that the true and the false are respectively the real and the unreal, considered as objects of a possible belief or judgment.[8]

This, it strikes me, is a rather remarkable passage. And now, perhaps, we should turn directly to the question of truth for semantic entities.

7.

One place all of this gets taken up in the literature, for reasons which we have already assayed, is in the arguments about indexicals, for example in the work of David Kaplan and John Perry. Perry "solves" the problem of indexicality—roughly, the problem that utterances using indexical expressions have different truth conditions on different occasions of utterance—by embedding utterances in a hierarchy of abstract entities: sentences, the uses of sentences, the roles of sentences, the senses of sentences, propositions, thoughts, and so on. Actually, I think on its own terms Perry's theory, the details of which I won't enter into, does a pretty good job of working indexicals into some sort of modified Fregean framework, and thus potentially saving some sort of traditional semantics. And indeed, potentially we could deal with the layers of abstract entities on a situationist account, either by promising a nominalist reduction to particulars, or by incorporating layers of abstract objects into the situation. However, this works for only a small portion of the context of utterance–dependent aspects of meaning: for Perry, proper indexicals such as "I" and "now." We have seen that there are many other context-sensitive aspects of any utterance, and there are many aspects we haven't looked at. Such considerations have made a number of philosophers, for example François Recanati, into radical contextualists, and pushed them ever further into what is almost a kind of subjectivism: that my utterance means roughly whatever I take myself to mean by it; this puts them back in the frame of an intentionalist theory of meaning, and thus an intentionalist context for evaluating utterances for truth.

I am sympathetic with this sort of contextualism, obviously, only I have a number of caveats to enter. I would take sarcasm and the many varieties of irony to provide particularly illuminating examples. Sarcasm is a particularly clear example because it flips "the meaning of a sentence" into the meaning the negation of that sentence. (That is only one of its effects, but obviously one of particular semantic moment.) If the reference of a sentence is a truth value—a la Frege—then no sentence refers outside of a full-bore context of utterance/inscription: you have to know whether it was meant sarcastically. Now it might appear that what makes a sentence express its negation is that the speaker intended it to express the negation. But such an intention is nowhere near sufficient for sarcasm. There is a range of quasilinguistic conventions for expressing sarcasm, above all concerning inflection. These conventions are not internal to the intentions of the speaker; they are community linguistic practices. One can fail to bring off sarcasm. And the linguistic practices are only one aspect of the situations of sarcasm: the specific conversational context—to whom one is speaking and how—and the actual physical and intellectual environment are indispensable for uttering and interpreting sarcastic remarks (to begin with, inflections are physical aspects of utterances).

We might consider again the Donellan-type example: the man drinking champagne is an embezzler. Now it appears to Recanati and others that ultimately "the man drinking champagne" refers to whomever the speaker intends to refer to, and that account does fairly well as an explanation of how the description gains a reference in this case. But first of all, it's certainly not true that any description would do as well at communicating the content, and if I referred to the embezzler as "the biggest polar bear in Alaska" or "the highest prime number" you would doubt my sanity, not to speak of the truth or comprehensibility of what I said. If I gaze surreptitiously and shrug toward the punch bowl as I say it, you'll be merely puzzled. My intention is a factor in the success of the reference. But there are many elements and many are outside everyone's head. Indeed, what I can possibly or sanely intend is massively hedged around with real-world factors.

Practices surrounding irony and sarcasm are myriad, incredibly elaborate. There are semi-sarcastic remarks, remarks that are highly ambiguous as between seriousness and sarcasm; there are remarks that are made with a light touch of irony: seriously, perhaps, but with a slightly raised eyebrow. There are remarks offered seriously, but dully, followed by "blah blah blah." Each of these expresses some subtle relation to the sentence being uttered. There are sarcastic bastards, sarcastic groups, sarcastic subcultures. There are all sorts of distances placed between speaker and sentence by the intervention of ironies.

Now it might be said that the sort of view I'm articulating actually presupposes that sentences or some such thing are truth-bearers. For example, "yeah, right" can express assent or dissent, but it expresses assent or dissent precisely to the content of some sentence (or paragraph, description, theory, etc.). Indeed, I do not want simply to opt for extreme radical pragmatics or contextualism in the sense that anything means whatever we want it to mean or take it as meaning on an occasion. The conventions that fix the meaning of words are real things, aspects of real situations, or else we wouldn't be able to distinguish sarcasm from seriousness at all. I merely want to point out, first, that sarcasm shows that it is the utterance and no abstract entity that is the bearer of truth value on any particular occasion, and that this truth is a feature of the utterance in an incredibly elaborate context of linguistic practices, human interactions, and physical surroundings.

We might consider the sort of pragmatics famously delineated by David Lewis in his paper "Scorekeeping in a Language Game."[9] Here we note that paradigmatic referring expressions, such as definite and even indefinite descriptions, gain reference only within contexts of use, and that the very "same" referring expression ("the cat," say, or "a cat") may change referents in a mercurial way in the course of a conversation. No doubt "the cat is on the mat" is true iff the cat is on the mat. But what cat we're referring to depends on what cat is salient in our conversational context, and cats often stroll through a conversational context and hence stroll through the referring expressions that pick them out. Now "the other cat is on the mat," which of course is true iff the other cat is on the mat; but which cat is the same and which the other: that depends on which is doing what where, who's seeing what, as well as a series of conversational conventions, the meanings of the terms, and so on.

Early on in this discussion, I said "It's not the sentence that is true because actually considered as an abstract entity, apart from the occasion of its utterance (if indeed it is possible or legitimate to consider it this way at all), it is false." This appears to assume what I mean to deny, that the sentence itself has a meaning underneath the situation in which it is deployed. The reference of "I" or "the cat" varies, but within a rough set of rules, and throughout we have been considering sentences—such as (1) to (5)—that we are evaluating for truth or falsity outside a context of utterance or inscription. Then you get the picture of enduring abstract entities like the meaning of "cat" in interchange with particular situations. What I would suggest about this is that some situations are more enduring than others; some are bigger than others. What *cat* means really does transform over time, or clarify, or we come to know more about what we always meant, that is, more about cats. But it transforms much more slowly than a situation in which the cat is on the mat: or it has more durable identity conditions or internal cohesion. We should think of language as a distribution or nest of situations, in which the utterance is a mercurial event in an enduring skein of usage conventions (which are, however, themselves in flux, though at a slower pace), in a sociophysical surround. At any rate "The man drinking champagne is an embezzler" has no truth conditions as it appears on this printed page, or only insofar as it evokes a particular situation that you imagine along with the interpretation of the utterance, or in which you embed the utterance in imagination: it gains a determinate meaning only in a situation, and the sensation that it is true or false as printed in this book is only a bit of charity or pretend.

8.

If we make this particular move, truth with regard to semantic entities turns out to be a relation between two situated particular physical things: an utterance/inscription (henceforward u/i) and a situation, where "situation" merely refers to a juxtaposition of things, including the u/i. This "situation" is not identical to the "fact" to which the proposition was supposed to correspond or the state of affairs in virtue of which the given sentence is true on the traditional accounts, though it encompasses such facts. This shows the limitations of the identity theory. The truth that that guy is an embezzler, when evaluated in utterance on a particular occasion, is not identical only to the fact that he is an embezzler, but to a wider situation in which the embezzler and the utterance are embedded. The situation encompasses the speaker/writer of the u/i and the u/i itself. It encompasses a set of linguistic (i.e., u/i-directive) practices or conventions (including, as portions of u's and i's, gestures, intonations, etc.); this is itself a vast scattered object. It might include the guy being an embezzler, which of course itself indicates not an intrinsic property of him, but a situation in which he is embedded, but also features of the social situation and wider environment that in turn make that the case or make it possible for such things to be the case, and make it a sensible or comprehensible thing to say. The situation is a particular time, place, juxtaposition of objects, subjects, a context of practices, a social situation of conversation, and so on.

The trouble with such a suggestion is that I am not giving much in the way of a strategy for individuating the situation relevant for assessing a particular utterance. Indeed, it might seem that ultimately there is only one situation: everything, the world. Well, a true u/i is true of the world, and in the world. And I do not think that I can provide any mechanical procedure for narrowing down the situations relevant to all utterances, though I can state that it includes some of the physical properties of the u/i, some subset of linguistic practices, the fact or state of affairs in play, the body of the utterer/inscriber, and some environing conditions. That is what is true or false, a puzzling claim only if we forget all the ways that "truth" as a notion is connected to "reality." If one doesn't think this can be a theory on account of its vagueness, I turn to the Aristotelian dictum that one shouldn't demand more precision in theorizing a certain notion than that notion could possibly yield up. And truth is really in some sense our very wooliest notion: it might be analogous to defining "everything" or "God." One theoretical task in such cases would be to avoid or attack premature simplifications, to stop ourselves from making the first move that narrows the field into something with which we can deal, but also narrows the field down in a way that betrays the initial project: saying what truth is or what we mean by "truth."

9.

Meaning and truth are related in myriad ways, but we can at least say this: if we don't know what someone means, we don't know whether what she says is true or false. "What someone says," of course isn't just some string of noises: it is (sometimes) something that can be true or false. Now what someone means is not in her head. Austin in "The Meaning of a Word," again, points out that asking what the word *rat* means and asking what a rat is are two ways of asking the same question. What the word *rat* means, we might say, is what a rat is: what distinguishes it from other things, what sort of thing the word refers to. What a rat is forms part of the truth conditions of sentences about rats, and what a rat is isn't in anyone's head: it's what a *rat* is.

That what the word *rat* means and what a rat is are more or less the same has led many thinkers to the belief that the world is linguistically constructed, or the like. But what it should indicate is that the language is world constructed: massively constrained at every node and moment by the way the world is. Meanings come from the world, or are features of situations. We've seen many reasons to think that meanings are not in the head, or that what someone means on some occasion isn't only inside her: at a minimum we have to consider the whole communicative context, and someone's gestures or intonations are not in her head; the books she writes are certainly not in her head, even if she could memorize them. And of course we have the basic arguments for externalism about content: what a person means by "I want some water" here on earth is, among other things, that she wants some H_2O, even if she is completely unacquainted with chemistry, even if she was asking in 21 B.C.E., while what a person means on Putnam-earth by a syntactically similar item is that she wants some XYZ. The truth conditions are different and the meanings are different, even if we stick to these abstracted propositional-type entities. If we don't, of course, she could be expressing that she's already had way too much water, or that she wants whiskey, or that she wants enlightenment, or love, or money, or that she doesn't want anything; what she means and what she could possibly mean and whether we can tell what she means and what we think she means will put into play a whole context of which her head is a little piece.

"Do you want some water?" the bartender asks the jiltee, and she rolls her eyes, "Yeah, I want some water." Well isn't what she wants in her head? No, not at all. It depends on what, for example, the bar has available. She wants whiskey: the whiskey isn't in her head until she drinks it. Is her desire for whiskey in her head? Bits of it are, but it has to do, too, with what's been available in her environment, and so on. The meaning is not whatever she may intend and it is not whatever the bartender may interpret her as saying; it emerges in the full-blown situation, many aspects of which must be in play in order to assess the truth-value of the utterance. "If the river was whiskey, and I was a diving duck, I'd swim to the bottom and never would come up." "You're pouring water on a drowning man." "I'm going down three times, but Lord I'm only coming up twice." "You're pouring water on a drowning man" is true iff you're pouring water on a drowning man. That's not going to help you understand the blues or see the truth.

10.

Now, the basic idea that truth could, in some cases, be a juxtaposition of physical items is supported within certain of the nonsemantic uses of "true." For example, the idea that "true" means accurate, or that a true shot is one that hits the bull's eye, is interesting. That is simply a description of a physical event in which a number of objects (person, bow, arrow, air, target) are juxtaposed in a particular arrangement or undergo a particular process in relation to one another. In the bow and arrow and target case, truth is a "sheer" physical relation. This is suggestive: the utterance is the arrow, the fact the target, but the true aim is only to be characterized as or in the situation embedding these and the aimer. Or, truth is accuracy in the sense that an imprint might be true: it has the right causal relation to the original, along with some other conditions. Or, the relationship might be like the relationship between two persons who are keeping faith. In a complex transaction, the utterance keeps faith with the world, and *the utterer keeps faith in the utterance with the world.*

What I'm suggesting, of course, is that some puzzles might vanish if the semantic were collapsed into the nonsemantic uses of "true": there might be no problem of reference, for example. Of course, putting it mildly, other puzzles might erupt. But the case of demonstrative acts makes it evident how natural the destruction of semantics might be: the act of pointing and the act of firing at a target are remarkably analogous. Indeed, they're the same act, only the projectile is tethered in the one case and not the other. As Wittgenstein pointed out, ostending is a practice; what it means depends on the practices of interpretation that surround it. For that matter, target practice is also a practice and you also have to be inside the practice or be acclimated to it to interpret it successfully: to know what the participants including yourself are trying to do and whether they have succeeded. But they also depend on the physical interaction of subject and object. The semantic is a trace, that is, of the physical juxtapositions, infinitely complex, out of which we're composed and by which we're compromised. How these juxtapositions are channeled through and expressed by a person is partly a matter of the communicative practices or systems in which the person is embedded. Then to be true, the utterance must emerge in the correct way from these interlocked systems of physical surround and communicative practice.

Consider again the basic Tarski approach, giving a "definition" of truth in a certain language by enumerating its sentences and explicating them, or quoting them and then saying them, as in "snow is white" is true iff snow is white. What is interesting about such statements is that they say much more than "'snow is white' is true iff 'snow is white' is true," and though they retain an air of tautology, they are not tautologous. "Snow is white" is a sentence, but the whiteness of the snow is a situation, and the relation between an utterance of "snow is white" and the whiteness of the snow is, itself, also a situation. For that matter, we might point out that "snow is white" means that snow is white. What makes the sentence true is that snow is, actually, white. The t-schema is not about language: it is about what makes linguistic items true; it is about the world, on both sides of the iff, actually. The sentence means the fact, leaving aside various pointless mysteries about facts, and is true in virtue of its meaning a fact or equivalently of not failing to mean a fact. One is not going to do a theory of truth without getting out into the world, as it were.

Now on my view, strictly speaking, "snow is white" cannot by itself be a bearer of truth value: it is true only as embedded in a particular situation. In fact, only in a particular situation does it make sense to say that "snow is white" means that snow is white. "Snow is white," in the absence of a particular situation, is only a particular concatenation of shapes: a sort of pure abstract painting, in reproduction. "Snow is white" means that snow is white only as inscribed or uttered in a world, only in a particular causal or, more widely, constitutive, chain. "General truths" like this mark situations of incredible elaborateness, proceeding from many snows and many people struggling through the snows, and histories of many people making many utterances in conventionalized practices. Even in such cases, however, the truth issues from and in the world, not in some kind of pure linguistic frame or sheer syntactic system.

This is true also of false generalizations, and of course, "snow is orange" means that snow is orange and is true iff snow is orange. But it isn't, we want to say. So what makes such a sentence false? Well, if anyone said it or uttered it sincerely, it would proceed from fact to idiolect in some warped or damaged way: the perceptual apparatus would be deranged, or the conditions abnormal, or the linguistic community messed up in some way, or the individual linguistically messed up by the standards of that community. Of course, in some circumstances it makes sense to say the snow is orange and in some cases an utterance of "snow is orange" might be true: we're on a glacier at sunset, and I say "Look, snow is orange!" You understand me, and we have access to the same physical situation, the same conventionalized color schemata, and so on.

11.

If I could, again, formulate this view about truth in a way parallel to Aristotle: *what is, is true; what is not, is false*. This is all very well and does indeed capture some of the ways the terms are commonly used. But it seems particularly inapt with regard to the semantic uses, especially when we move from propositions or sentences to utterances and inscriptions. For of course all such things that are, are, and so they are all true. It is impossible to say anything false.

Now in order to account for the possibility of false inscriptions or utterances, I want to refocus on the causal, physical (and social and psychological) situation in which the u/i comes to be produced. If this situation is "correct" or "appropriate" then the u/i is true; false if the situation is distorted in various ways or by various factors.

First of all, of course, the bits of the inscription have to latch on to bits of the world; they must have some external reference, however we may understand this, in a case where what one is talking about is external. So for example, if the situation is distorted by hallucination, if there's no guy out there with a champagne flute, but merely a figment of my imagination, then what I assert is false (well, I'm not going to tackle negative existentials right here). The sounds and shapes have a context/factual reference primarily external to the body of the person doing the uttering/inscribing, where one is not referring to specific states of oneself, but states internal to the situation in which that body and the referent are located. Naturally, I would avail myself here of a causal theory of names, and in general connect reference with chains of causation of particular kinds, such as perception and ostension and communication. (I should add that, in my view, even a reference to your own dreams, pains, etc., implicates a referring situation that extends beyond the individual human body.) And there are syntactic requirements and communicative conventions of the language that must successfully be enacted or discharged, and which again we conceive as massively large concatenations of things and events.

The situation within which an utterance or inscription is produced are, *a fortiori*, always actual. Semantic falsity arises because of features internal to this situation, or the various strands of relation between the u/i and other bits: the things referred to (perhaps reference fails), the linguistic and ostensive conventions (perhaps you did not say what you meant to say, or accidentally did say what you meant), the moral stance or bearing or condition of the utterer/inscriber. Or perhaps the light was deceptive or you were under the spell of a charlatan. Well, there are myriad ways to end up false, myriad ways things go wrong. But we should conceive them as distortions or internal ruptures among the elements of the truth-bearer: the situation in which the utterance comes to be produced by a person.

Truth on my view is radically nonepistemic: it means reality, which is on my view not a matter of what anyone thinks, or the forms of human consciousness. But semantic entities are produced by human consciousness, that is, in physical systems of which human consciousnesses form a part. The truth conditions for the semantic entities are similar to what a reliabilist or externalist might take to be conditions on knowledge: that the causal situation that produces the u/i be of a truth-preserving sort. What sorts of events/causal juxtapositions/physical situations are truth-preserving events/causal juxtapositions/physical situations? Here we deploy the Department of Redundancy Department: the truth-preserving relationships are those that include saying or writing of some real thing that it is a thing of a certain sort, when it is actually of that sort, or that it displays certain features, when in fact it does display those features, or that it is, when in fact it is. The resulting semantic chunk is "true to life," "true to the facts." And here, of course, we lurch back into straight-up metaphysics.

However, I don't think the details of the truth-preserving causal situation are going to be exotic; they are the familiar decent perceptual situations: having a clear view, for instance, so that you you've got a reasonable relation to the object via the media of light and air. Unobstructed: whatever amounts to undistorted, in a reasonable state of alertness, and so on. There will be more detailed scientific treatments of perception, of course, but insofar as they are true they give details of the decent truth-preserving fusion of external-world fact, medium (light, reflectivity of surface, brain activity), and human body. These are illuminated by the analogy to various terms that are substitutable in some contexts for "true": the accuracy of the observation; the fact that one remains faithful to the experience including its object. Directness helps: clarity, and a dose of the virtues. And then the uses of language need to be authorized by the conventions in the right way: that the person wasn't crazily miseducated about the meaning of words (in a cult, perhaps), or isn't subject to some brain disability that involves constantly randomly interchanging various words, and so on. (It is also worth saying that such conventions are potentially at stake or changing even in the utterance itself, and creative extensions and reversals are always possible.)

12.

With regard to the utterer/inscriber, focusing with particular emphasis on that bit of the situation, this relation is irreducibly moral: it concerns intellectual virtues such as self-reflection, sincerity, honesty, assiduousness. It concerns the resolution to face and say the truth. Then truth as a property or aspect of semantic entities (utterances and inscriptions and pictures, for example) would be treated as derivative and, I suggest, primarily as perceptual and moral: the condition of the relevant segment of the world: the condition of the medium, the condition of the agent. It is interesting that the primary Greek term for truth, *aletheia*, means essentially not forgetting, being in a position to render a full account, not repressing or concealing or misstating anything material.

The content of a situation in which a u/i can be true—that is, in which a person utters or inscribes something true—is partly, but perhaps essentially, moral. Truth is accuracy: hitting the target: and people learn to hit the target by a discipline of archery, though of course almost anyone might get lucky from time to time. Likewise there are standards: sanitary or health-related standards if you like, epistemic/moral standards about facing and speaking and daring to write the truth, about willing to see and willing to be revealed. This is the function of truth as a virtue or of keeping faith with the world and with oneself as a part of and perceiver of the world.

It is possible that when I say "The guy drinking champagne is cheating on his wife" I might be lying, even though it turns out that what I'm saying is true. Let's suppose that Freddie is my professional rival, and we're both interviewing for a job with your firm. I've got no reason at all to suppose that Freddie is cheating on his wife. Quite the reverse, in fact: he's always been (to me) a disgustingly upright type. Plus he's married to a lovely person, who's hopelessly devoted to his every whim. I'm merely trying to discredit Freddie in your eyes by purveying scurrilous trash about him. Unbeknownst to me, however, Freddie, incomprehensibly, is actually cheating on his boo. He's having a passionate affair with a repulsive idiot. This is a variation on what in the theory of knowledge is called the Gettier problem, but there it's a problem about knowledge and here I am pushing it as a problem about truth. If lying is intentionally saying something false, then in one sense in this case I lied, and in another I didn't. If the concept of "truth" here appears within the scope of an epistemic operator like "believes" then I lied. If it doesn't, then I didn't.

Well, one thing we might agree on is that something has gone ethically wrong with me in this situation, even if in some sense "what I said" is true. Whether or not what I said is true, I'm a damn liar. Even vicious inveterate liars get lucky now and then. So the problem, the locus of falsity, in this case, is not the sentence, and it's not even the context or occasion of use, exactly. It's me. The falsity is in my soul, we might say: it's my hypocrisy, or my overweening ambition, that renders me false, even though again in some sense "what I said" was true. "It" was true. But coming out of my lips at that moment, emerging from the complex of character and motivation that infests my head and the real-world context into which my utterance was projected, it was a lie: it was false. Truth, we might say, is not only an epistemic or metaphysical notion, it is an ethical notion, and the locus of truth is not only the utterance and its social context, but also the person of the person who's doing the uttering.

Indeed, "truth" and its brethren in other languages primordially carried a moral flavor, not only because of the centrality and truth-telling to, for example, trade or criminal justice, but in a wide variety of senses. If "true" appears in the Laws of Ethelred relatively early in English in the locution "true man," the phrase is already ancient: you find its correspondents in Plato, for example, who also identified truth as goodness and ignorance of it as the essence of all evil. Ultimately, as Neoplatonists made ever more intense (but it is already intense enough in Plato), the Forms of the True and the Good are identical, and one might as well call this God, precisely as many theologians did.

Rarely has the moral oomph of truth been as elaborately set forth as in Anselm, who could easily have formulated the principle that what is, is true—but did not, quite. But for Anselm in *De Veritate*, "true" means "actual," and then

> [A statement is true] when what is stated, either by affirming or denying, exists . . . Something is true only by participating in the truth, and therefore the truth of the true is in the true itself, but the thing stated is not in the true statement. Hence it should not be called its truth but the cause of its truth. . . . When it signifies that what is is, then truth is in it and it is true.[10]

Here's how I propose to read this: First of all, with regard to truth for semantic items, Anselm holds the "identity theory": what is stated is the fact, or directly what exists. (If so, then we can give this theory a distinguished pedigree.) Second, "truth" is primarily used here to indicate the actual or the existent. Third, the relation of a statement to reality in virtue of which the statement is true, is "participation," which I believe is not being used in a Platonic, but rather in an Aristotelian sense: the statement and the actuality that it affirms or denies are on the same ontological plane, and the relation is causal: the actual thing causes the true statement. But this causation compromises the distinction between the true statement and the true thing, the existence of which it signifies, as I urge that perception compromises the distinction between the perceiver and the thing that is perceived.

But the relation is also essentially normative.

> When [a statement] signifies that what is is, it signifies what it should. And when it signifies what it ought it signifies correctly . . . Therefore when it signifies that what is is, there is correct signification. And again when it signifies that what is is, it is true signification. So it is the same thing for it to be correct and to be true. So for it truth is no different from rectitude.[11]

And Anselm identifies all of these—"truth," "rectitude," and "correctness"—with justice. Now, admittedly, this emerges in part from a theological vision according to which what is actual is—however things appear to us—the best possible. Thus to say that what is is, is (maybe I'll try to land the quad later) also to say that it ought to be. But one thing we should note is that in these very broad identifications of the various value valences as "truth," and ultimately in the wild generosity with which Anselm starts attributing truth and falsity to all sorts of things—statements, persons, actions, the human will, sense experience—he expected to be understood. That is, within the uses of the languages of scripture and of medieval scholarship, "true" and its relatives in Greek (*alatheia*) and Hebrew (*emet*) and Latin (*veritate*) could be applied to all such things, in what Anselm finally treats as a single normative sense.

Indeed, the wide variety of truth bearers that Anselm recognizes is fundamentally motivated by the reading of various scriptural passages that deploy the concept of truth with these different bearers. With regard to truth of the will, Anselm focuses on a description of Satan: "He did not stand in the truth" (John 8:44). The idea of "standing in the truth" connects to Heidegger's views, discussed below. But where Heidegger emphasizes that truth occurs when things find a place in us where they can stand unconcealed, the idea of "standing in the truth"—to which we find many parallels, for example, in the thought of Confucius—indicates that it is not things that come to be unconcealed before us, but we who come to be unconcealed within things. "He who does the truth comes into the light. . . . To bring about rectitude and to do the truth are the same."[12] Truth is both a thing to do or a range of actions and the place in which we stand revealed before God.

Anselm holds that the truth of "signification"—of, for example, what we say or write or believe—does not require formulation into "truths" cast as propositions. So, for example, the truth that can be expressed by a verbal assertion can be expressed or contradicted also by an action.

> If you were in a place where you knew that there were both healthy and poisonous herbs, though you did not know how to distinguish between them, but there was someone else there whom you did not doubt knew how to distinguish them, and when you asked him he told you which were healthy and which poisonous, and he told you that some were healthy yet he himself ate others, which would you believe, his word or his deed?[13]

Now, the usual procedure in such cases would be to try to give an account in which the action was to be interpreted as the expression of a propositional belief: the person does not believe what he's saying; he believes what his actions would allow us to reconstruct as a propositional attitude. But we might experiment with the opposite approach: building a concept of propositional attitudes as expressing the implications of actions, or as an abstract way of interpreting what is revealed in actions or in complex situations. Indeed, often enough in action one realizes what one does in fact believe, or other people realize in your actions what you believe, whether you do or not. Then the primary bearer of truth or falsity would not be a mental state or its object (a proposition), but a course of actions, including perhaps actions of speaking and writing, performed within an unfolding real-world situation.

Fire acts truly, says Anselm, when it does what it ought to—or, perhaps better, when it does what it is—when it consumes and rises.[14] And that is what brings Anselm to the identification of truth with reality, for everything enacts or does what it is. "Everything that is, truly is. . . . Therefore there is truth in the essence of all things, because it is being in the highest truth that they exist. . . . Therefore, whatever is, exists rightly."[15] Secularizing this slightly, we might describe it as an intellectualized but ecstatic affirmation of the world, expressed as and in the midst of truth: an affirmation of world and person and God as connected by virtue of their coreality.

13.

If we wanted to develop various strands of this, we might turn to Heidegger's great and maddening essay "On the Essence of Truth." In some ways, Heidegger's account is obviously similar to the one I've been discussing, and he begins with a very basic insight:

> What do we ordinarily understand by "truth"? This elevated yet at the same time worn and almost dulled word "truth" means what makes a true thing true. What is a true thing? We say, for example, "It is a true joy to cooperate in the accomplishment of this task." We mean that it is purely and actually a joy. The true is the actual. Accordingly, we speak of true gold in distinction from false.[16]

And he points out quite rightly that "the traditional assignment of truth exclusively to statements as the sole essential locus of truth falls away. Truth does not originally reside in the proposition."[17] Heidegger ties truth essentially to Dasein; it is a human artifact, finally. But I also think that he sees that what is truth to us or for us or within our representational systems or languages is only a subset of the actual. His account of what truth is for us retains a normative component, or it requires a certain sort of resolution.

Heidegger urges that the "essence" of truth is a certain "comportment" or, as I would prefer to call it, a certain resolution. Heidegger calls this comportment freedom, and asserts that the accord of intellect with things (truth) can occur

> Only if the pregiving [of beings] has already entered freely into an open region for something opened up which prevails and which binds every presenting. To free oneself for a binding directedness [and hence to have the truth] is possible only by *being free* for what is opened up in an open region. Such being free points to the heretofore uncomprehended essence of freedom. The openness of comportment as the inner condition of the possibility of correctness is grounded in freedom. *The essence of truth is freedom.*[18]

I prefer not to grapple with Heidegger on "essence," a long and difficult project that I would regard as quixotic. "Essence" is alien to my idiom. But I read this passage as saying that truth becomes accessible to us just when and to the extent that we resolve to be open to it, that is, resolve to face what is. Or we resolve to change (for example) what we believe according to what actually comes to be, or with regard to what actually happens. We have the truth insofar as we can keep faith with the world, or insofar as we can respond to it freely, or fail to foreclose on it with a representational schema, or in favor of a representational schema, or merely as an example of a general claim or attitude. This is one way to read the normative oomph of the idea of truth, as spelled out by everyone from Peirce to Brandom, but with less emphasis on the instrumental and social construction of normativity.

> Truth for us is unconcealment of things and hence requires a space of free play in which they can be revealed. Freedom for what is opened up in an open region lets beings be the beings they are. Freedom now reveals itself

as letting things be. . . . [T]he phrase required now—to let things be—does not refer to neglect or indifference but rather the opposite. To let be is to engage oneself with beings.[19]

This is a sort of Taoism or Stoicism, an affirmation that we experience from a different angle in Anselm: a recommendation to make your peace with things as they are that in Taoism proceeds into an exhilaration about what is real or outside your own will, which also yields a kind of aesthetic distance: a place in which to appreciate the things that there are in the world.

Now, however, Heidegger proceeds to the deconstruction, and one would imagine that this text is central to the idea of deconstruction in Derrida, for example. Every means by which we apprehend the truth also occludes it, or every system of ordering it or representing it is relatively impoverished with regard to it; it is selective. Each way of apprehending the world (I am not using "world" as a Heideggerian technical term) affirms the world in some respect, and also flees from it some respects: faces up to some things and represses others. Or, each way of apprehending the world is the product both of our courage or Nietzschean affirmation of some of the questionable aspects of existence and our willful turning away from others.

> Where beings are not very familiar to man and are scarcely and only roughly known by science, the openedness of beings as a whole can prevail more essentially than it can where the familiar and well-known has become boundless, and nothing is any longer able to withstand the business of knowing, since technical mastery over things bears itself without limit. Precisely in the leveling and planing of this omniscience, this mere knowing, the openedness of beings gets flattened out into the apparent nothingness of what is no longer even a matter of indifference but rather is simply forgotten.[20]

I take this as a fairly straightforward "phenomenological" point. We cease to be aware of or open to things insofar as we master them or insofar as they routinely seem to fit into our conceptual structures: our belief system becomes too coherent, too universally applicable, too inevitable, to permit refreshment by the world—the world is "disenchanted."

> As letting things be, freedom is intrinsically the resolutely open bearing that does not close up on itself. All comportment is grounded in this bearing and receives from it directedness toward beings and disclosure of them. Nevertheless, this bearing towards concealing conceals itself in the process, letting a forgetfulness of the mystery take precedence and disappearing in it.[21]

That is, every angle from which or purpose for which we might apprehend something also conceals it, and then itself disappears: it hardens into dogma, we might say, or becomes the set of established assumptions, schemata, a taxonomy or ideological spectrum.

This is what we should expect, I think, given the infinite profusion of things and the relative limitations of human representational systems: that each such system, insofar as it is open to the world and not psychotic or solipsistic, reveals things in certain ways and conceals them in others, and that these two always go together. And then we could consider various representational systems—scientific systems, artistic systems, languages, ontologies, and so on—as distinguishable in terms of what they reveal and what they conceal. A problem is that by definition what is concealed by the representational system you are using can't be detected from within that system. But then again we have many representational systems in different epochs, cultures, disciplines, and there are cases where we can employ one to show the blind spots of another. And representational systems can coalesce or approach one another through partial mutual incorporation, and they are continually being revised and expanded at the insistence of the actual. Now on the other hand, one might unite all the representational resources available to a particular person or a culture as a single representational system, and then point out that what this system conceals is necessarily invisible from within that system, which brings us right back to Rorty, for example.

But I want to say—possibly in disagreement with Heidegger, but certainly with Rorty—that human beings are not primarily semantic engines or only acquainted with representations, and that representational systems themselves bend or collapse in the face of the real all the time. Truth is not only or primordially a property of semantic entities, and it is never a property of semantic entities except on particular occasions and in particular situations. Semantic entities are themselves material situations, and their truth (except in certain peculiar cases) is never a matter of a string of sounds or shapes in isolation from a massive causal and otherwise relational materials.

Mary McCarthy famously said of Lillian Hellman that everything she said was a lie, even "and" and "the." We understand all too well what that means. It not only accuses Hellman of actually lying, it accuses her in some sense of being a lie, of being a deeply false person, of being utterly self-deceived and utterly deceiving of others. Of course now and then I imagine Lillian Hellman said something true, but if McCarthy was right, Hellman was herself false, if you will allow me that form of words. Insofar as you take yourself to understand it, you ought to.

At any rate, in the next chapter, I will avail myself freely of the word *proposition* to mean whatever it is that is a bearer of truth. This is in part so I can engage or contribute to debates in contemporary epistemology. But I want it borne in mind that I collapse truth-bearers into truth-makers, and that ultimately what I mean by *proposition* is an extremely complex situation which includes the material that is referred to, the utterance or inscription (or sentence token in the head, if that's possible), the social practices in which that item gains a meaning, and the resolution of the believer.

14.

The pragmatic conception of truth—that truth is "what works in the way of belief" (James), or that it is a resolution of a problematic situation (Peirce), or that a belief is true when it lets you get into a successful relation to the environment (Dewey)—is false, I believe. First, it makes beliefs the basic truth-bearers. We do speak of beliefs being true of false, of course, or, if we are being more careful, we speak of what is believed as being true or false, but there are all kinds of other truth-bearers as well. Second, whether truths work or help us adjust is relative to specific contexts. Sometimes they do, sometimes not. Facing the truth might drive you insane or to suicide (or it might help you adjust). A correct theory of matter might help you make a better world, or it might help you annihilate life as we know it. People often absolutely need their delusions. But there are many important insights in this theory as well. It puts truth directly in relation to values, or explicitly treats truth as a value, which is basically right. It inculcates intellectual virtues of various kinds. And it explicitly calls into play an unfolding, real-world situation: we see what someone believes by their actions, according to James, and we see whether it's true by how those actions unfold in the world, in society, for example. If nothing else, this is one dimension of truth evaluation, and like any other at all plausible approach it gets outside the head, or gets the head embedded in larger contexts. Dewey has a metaphysics of situation, in which experience is held to be an interaction of organism and environment in which the integrity of each is compromised. Now I would suggest that there can be no other foundation for a theory of truth and for a theory of belief or knowledge: each of these things brings into play a whole situation in which the utterer and utterance are embedded.

Here's a bit from Emerson, which I already quoted:

> A man is a bundle of relations, a knot of roots, whose flowers and fruitage is the world. . . . A mind might ponder its thought for ages, and not gain so much self-knowledge as the passion of love shall teach it in a day. . . . No man can antedate his experience, or guess what faculty or feeling a new object shall unlock, any more than he can draw today the face of a person whom he shall see tomorrow for the first time.[22]

The idea that a human being is a bundle of relations is beautiful and also, I believe, in the strictest sense, as Emerson wrote it, true. Perhaps the deepest and most pervasive betrayal of truth, the deepest falsity, is solipsism. And solipsism is not only a perverse philosophical doctrine, it is a pathology of the self in which the self cannot experience the reality of things beyond itself, or in which it experiences this reality as internal to the self. That is, solipsism is a mental illness, a real one, that consists of loss of faith with the world. But all falsity, we might say, is a little solipsism, all betrayal is an intensification of the self or a detachment from other people and the world in which the reality of other people and of the world is lost. And that in germ is every delusion; every delusion is a loss of contact with the world: that is more or less analytic.

Emerson's idea that the self is intrinsically nothing but in relation everything is one of the most profound and oldest of human thoughts. It is found in the Upanishads, where it is embodied in the great sentence "tat tvam asi": "that is thou." The tree in the forest? That is thou. The stone in the field? That is thou. The lover in your bedroom? That is thou. The world? That is thou. God? That is thou. And to know that you're that and that's you is to come to live in truth, to make the self a zone of traversal of the world, or to acknowledge that the self is always a zone of traversal of the world. It is a thought found repeatedly in the literature of Taoism and Zen in which the self is treated as a mirror, or as clear water: as a flow within and a reflection of the real. The truth emerges in a resolution to remain open to the world in experience, in what might be termed an abandonment of or emergence from the delusion of detached selfhood.

Bradley identifies truth, reality, and knowledge: the idealist trifecta. Provisionally, I can accept the first identification, subject to refinements of use in various contexts. But throwing knowledge into the hopper makes truth and reality epistemic, leaves you wondering how you can believe what is not the case, or indeed what it is you believe at all: I can't see dissolving all semantic entities. So, in one sense every belief is true: that is, it is real, by stipulation, and presumably consists of some physically describable situation. Obviously, some beliefs are false, however, and this is to say they arise in an aberrant, or nonoptimal way within the environment: they do not bear the right set of causal relations and so on.

Kierkegaard famously said that "truth is subjectivity," and I have been saying that truth is the emptying of subjectivity. But I think Kierkegaard's view is deeply in keeping with what I'm saying. Kierkegaard had the idea that all purely objective talk was a kind of empty yammering, an attempt to shuffle off the burden of human existence. That was his criticism of Hegel, for example: that Hegel had managed to account for all of world history, the entire history of "Spirit," without actually saying anything at all about who it is who could know all this or experience it or find meaning in it. What was missing in Hegel was Hegel. Hegel accounted for everything without even mentioning what it might be like to be an actually existing human being living in the world. So, for example, you could know as much as you like objectively about death: could know, for example, that if your heart doesn't beat for a while or you quit breathing for a few days, you're dead as a doornail. But that doesn't help you come to grips with the actual fact that you yourself are going to die, now does it? And in fact the endless piling up of objective truths seems to Kierkegaard to be just a way of evading your own encounter with truth, a way of insulating yourself from the world.

Now "objectively true" sentences can come out of a tape recorder or an MP3 player. Tape recorders, that is, are capable of producing utterances in contexts, and if there is any such thing as a sentence or a proposition, computers are fully as capable of presenting them as are people. But I wonder whether you think tape recorders speak the truth. Well, the problem with a tape recorder is the same problem that Kierkegaard identified in Hegel. And that shows us exactly what truth is and where it is: truth occurs in the human self as it opens itself to the world.

Perhaps the best historical statement of the sort of view I am putting forward is made by Plotinus, a philosopher with whom, overall, I have little sympathy. But he was right about this:

> We [should] not look for the objects of intellect outside of the intellect, treating them as impressions of reality upon it: we cannot strip it of truth and so make its objects unknowable and nonexistent, and in the end annul the intellect itself. We must provide for knowledge and for truth; we must secure reality; being must become knowable essentially and not merely in that knowledge of quality which could give us a mere image or vestige of the reality in lieu of possession, intimate association, absorption.[23]

We might say, in sum, that truth is reality, and that persons are parts of reality. We are traversed and transfixed by other bits, in processes such as perception and communication, as also in movement, ingestion and so on; persons merge into and emerge from situations. We produce true utterances and inscriptions as traces of that situation, calling into play an ethics of truth to situation, or a resolution to remain in it and know it. We can say what's true in virtue of being true, of being situated, entangled, consciously and resolutely, with things.

3

Epistemology

A. Externalism, Realism, and Objectivity

1.

An early expression of the "extended mind thesis" or "externalism with regard to mental content"—and, indeed, a particularly profound one—is provided by the neo-Confucian philosopher Wang Yang-Ming (1472–1529).

Wang Shows that Flowers are Not External to the Mind

> The Teacher was taking recreation at Nanchen. One of his friends pointed to the flowers and trees in a cliff and said: "You say that there is nothing in the world external to the mind. What relation to my mind have these flowers and trees on the high mountains, which blossom and drop of themselves?"
>
> The Teacher said: "When you cease regarding these flowers, they become quiet with [or cease to be in the same relation to] your mind. When you see them, their colors at once become clear. From this you can know that these flowers are not external to your mind."
>
> He further said: "Perception has no structure upon which it depends: it uses the color of all things as its structure. The sense of hearing has no structure upon which it depends: it uses the sounds of things as its structure. The sense of smell has no structure: it uses the odor of things as its structure. The sense of taste has no structure: it uses the taste of things as its structure. The mind has no structure: it uses the sky, the earth, and things as structure."[1]

To say that flowers are not external to the mind could be an expression of idealism, and Wang is often termed an idealist, which in my view is a very bad mistake. Flowers are not external to the mind, according to Wang, because the mind is situated in real-world situations and is of necessity responsive to them and not fully distinguishable from them.

The passage formulates an exquisite contrast to Kant, for example, who precisely asserts that the structure of perception is something we bring a priori to our experience; the world is accessible to human consciousness because it is produced as a spatial/temporal/causal object by that consciousness. For Wang, perception per se has no structure; it is structured by the actual world. He always brings consciousness back to the world as its origin, arena, and outcome. (Also he still awaits a decent translator, and I have worked Henke's old thing over a bit—responsibly, I think.) "If one refers only to the place it occupies, it is called body; if one refers to the matter of control it is called mind; if one refers to the activities of the mind, it is called purpose; if one refers to the intelligence of the purpose, it is called understanding; if one refers to the relations of the purpose, it is called things. Yet it is all one. The purpose is not suspended in empty space, but is placed in some thing."[2] "If all things are put into the class of external things, there will be nothing left in the mind."[3] "Man's mind is a unity with the world, for its contents follow the movements of world."[4]

We might trace a related series of thoughts to Ch'an/Zen or to ancient Taoism (both of which were influences on Wang Yang-Ming, leading to the broad accusation that he corrupted pure Confucianism). The Japanese Zen master Bankei (1622–1693) gives this:

> You didn't come here in order to hear a dog bark, a crow caw, or any of the other sounds which might come from outside the temple during my talk. Yet while you're here, you'd hear those sounds. . . . You could have had no way of knowing beforehand of any of the sights, sounds, or smells you might encounter, yet you're able nevertheless to recognize these unforeseen sights and sounds as you encounter them, without premeditation. That's because you're seeing and hearing in the Unborn. When a dog howls, even if ten million people said in chorus that it was the sound of a crow crying, I doubt if you'd be convinced. It's highly unlikely that there would be any way they could delude you into believing what they say. That's owing to the marvelous awareness and unbornness of your buddha-mind.[5]

Unfortunately, I don't think he's necessarily right that people wouldn't agree with the ten million in such a case. However, it is always possible not to, and of course in this case you should not because then you'll be believing something false. Bankei's Unborn is merely awareness, contact with reality, openness to what is, spontaneous responsiveness. Then Zen discipline consists in maintaining this, in not getting lost in the labyrinth of the self, which really is an illusion. It's an illusion, for one thing, to the extent it loses responsiveness to its world; it is an illusion insofar as it is a monad or a substance. And we might say the same about "the social" or "artificial" when it loses responsiveness, or tries to, with more-than-human reality.

At least since Kant, Western philosophy has concentrated on the way structures of consciousness or practices of representation articulate a world for us by, for example, deploying a series of expectations, schemata, and so on. One might consult the philosophy of art/perception of E. H. Gombrich and Nelson Goodman, for example. In the twentieth century, this has often, as in Rorty, for example, taken the form of the doctrine that we construct reality by social/linguistic consensus or practice. But obviously we often experience things we're not expecting to. Obviously, sometimes someone who keeps faith with the world and herself as an experiencer of it is right, and the ten million are wrong. Obviously you can't have any perception at all without a fundamental receptivity, a willingness or ability to experience what's actually there, an openness to the world that is literal, because the mind is not distinct from its ordinary physical surround. One might interpret various moments in "Asian anti-Kantianism" as expressions of joy and affirmation of being a real thing opening itself to its environment. Or as the great Lin-chi puts it,

> Followers of the Way, the Dharma of the Buddhas calls for no special undertakings. Just act ordinary, without trying to do anything particular. Move your bowels, piss, get dressed, eat your rice, and if you get tired, then lie down. Fools may laugh at me, but wise men will know what I mean.[6]

2.

Ordinary sensation is an actual penetration of bodies by one another. For you to sense something, it must, in some way, or through some intermediaries, actually pass into your body. The sense organs are holes, places where the integrity of the body is compromised, where it is permeable to the world. Or, sensation is to be understood on the model of respiration or ingestion. The light that bathes the environment is reflected from an object in the medium of air and into the pupil, which begins a series of transformations, a causal change in the organism, in virtue of which it sees something. The body participates both as cause and effect, and what we sense depends on in what way and in what direction our attention is directed or seized: the whole body is implicated: you sense a motorcycle rolling by as you turn toward its sound and reorient your attention, by reorienting your whole body. Then, that you are having this sensation directs and articulates further acts of attention and orientation. And a sensation implicates a whole environment: an "object" or event, a context of objects and events, a personal history, mediating factors such as the atmosphere, the time of day or night, the noisy or quiet world. As you retrain your attention, your body is moving in interchange with its whole environment, from which it is not fully distinct. Every sensation is a site at which the integrity of the body is compromised, at which what is in the world leaks into it, and what is in it leaks back out into the world.

There are no single or isolable percepts or sense data or sensations, except as something like theoretical fictions produced out of shifting environing conditions in which we're embedded, in which we're included, or which we form a permeable part. We're not cameras or mirrors, or on the other hand, artists creating our own sensible experience: we're volatile organisms moving through a volatile environment as it moves through us. And the self which is made in the accumulation of these events has elements of stability and elements of flux: it is always being compromised, but there is always something there to be compromised, until there isn't anymore. The idea of experiences, or theories, as being subjective or objective is strangely impoverished, as though we could remove ourselves from the world or the world from ourselves. There is no place from which to see things except where we are; there is no where we are except in and as a segment of the whole world.

The picture of sensation in which, say, we watch little scenes unfold before us as on a screen, and then infer that they come to us from outside sources which they resemble, or which they do not, leading us into mistakes, is profoundly unfortunate for many reasons, but one of these is that it is false precisely to our experience. It's on this that most varieties of philosophical skepticism rest, as in the dream argument, for example. This separates sensation into external causes and internal phenomena which are the only things to which we have access: sense data, brain events, or what have you. But a visual sensation isn't something we see (which, at any rate, introduces an infinite regress): it's a situation in which we are juxtaposed with and in the process of actually merging with, ingesting, an object, or what the object sheds or emits.

The sense data idea gives rise to characterizations of knowledge, wherein we infer from our sense data, or what is immediately given, that, to use an example from J. L. Austin, there's a pig over there. The inference is always supposed to be provisional, and it can go wrong. And yet it underpins the idea of certainty: we are supposed to be actually certain of our own sense data and other mental states; they're "incorrigible," or as Roderick Chisholm puts it, for example, "self-presenting," self-evident: it is self-evident to me that I seem to see a pig. Of that I am certain, and I infer from that that there's a pig. As it were, we try to peer out into the world from behind our own seemings. But this is radically backasswards, as my sensations originate in the outside world, are its products, or actually are world-chunks infested by pigs. Of course this may seem to leave us no account of things like dreams and hallucinations. I would treat these as attenuated or elongated perceptual situations, or byproducts or derangements of normal processes of perception. It is astonishing that normal perception is treated in our tradition as a kind of dream or hallucination plus an actual external object; the direction of explanation has to be the opposite. We do not know things basically by virtue of any inference, and knowledge does not require justification; it requires only actual relations between object and body in which they cease to be wholly distinct from one another.

The contents of our minds consist in part of actual, real-world situations and their constituents. We think with the world, by use of the world, as well by use of events internal to us (which are also, of course, situations in the world). How to ride a bike or what it's like to be whatever you may be, of course, but also extensions of the mind through a library or Google or a notebook or a calendar on your iPhone, intellectual prostheses. Memory makes use of things, as spurs and as contents persisting from the past into now.[7] But also, there are birds in our sensorium; there are other people and other people's utterances and attitudes; there are social conventions; there are languages, only little slices of which we can actually contain at a given moment, and which are constantly leaking into and out of us, and which are building up a massive accretion of history all around us all the time. And the content of the language we use is only partly fixed by what we know or what we mean or intend. It is also fixed by the history of uses and the conventions that give rise to meaning; it is fixed by the actual objects, states of affairs, situations to which words refer or hook up and which are the context of their use.

In Putnam's famous thought experiment, again, there are two planets, identical as to surface appearance, with identical histories and so on. But on twin earth, what we call water is in fact XYZ, a clear, potable liquid, essential to twin earth life. Though the "phenomenological" experience (permitting ourselves this locution momentarily) of my twin earth twin is identical to mine, when he uses the sound or inscription "water," he refers to XYZ, whereas when I do, I refer to H_2O. The meaning of the word is different, though the phenomenological content is the same. What we say when we say "water" or "God" or "light" or "solid" depends on how and what the world actually is. We're always finding out more about what we meant all along: we cannot yet know what we mean, exactly. Perhaps we can never fully know what we mean, for a wide variety of reasons. What "here" means depends on where you are. What "I" means depends on who I actually am.

3.

As I say, I think that modern philosophy, or philosophy since Descartes, has gone down a very wrong road, by thinking about the human mind as essentially a representational system. However, the idea idea is no doubt ancient, though it is rather difficult to assign its precise origin. Dreams and optical illusions and mistakes (the straight stick appearing bent in water, etc.) are early themes in a variety of settings. But one should be cautious about assuming that early mentions of such matters deploy a systematic representational theory of perception. Even the use of "images" and so on should be approached with caution; as we've seen, the Epicureans thought of visual experience in terms of images, but they conceived images as physically emanating in a sheet or film of atoms from the objects that give rise to them. (For similar reasons, apparently obvious mind-body dualism in ancient Greece is often not so obvious after all, as the soul is often conceived as material, though gassy.) One possible origin of the idea idea is in the radical dislocation of reality and appearance that occurs in the magnificently perverse Eleatics. If the universe is indeed a perfectly full spherical plenum in which motion is impossible, all of our experience, more or less, is an hallucination; it definitely does not emanate from the world. But that is, to some extent, an inference from the fragments (drawn by Plato, for example), not a declaration in them.

At any rate, the Greek *phantasia* is the imagination, or the images it delivers; *phainomai* is the verb "to appear," and, for example, Kant's "phenomena" are appearances. But again, to presuppose that the use of such terms in, for example, Aristotle's *De Anima* (at 3.3, for example), refers primarily to the train of imagery allegedly passing before the mind in sensation is anachronistic, and Aristotle carefully distinguishes perception from imagination; *phantasia* is by definition not based in the same way as perception on reality, which is just how we use the cognate terms. Nevertheless, *phantasiai* is often translated as "impressions" or "perceptions." But in the *Categories* Aristotle declares that "body [or matter] itself is a perceptible," and that perceptible things exist before or aside from being perceived.[8] That is, we ("directly") perceive things, not percepts or mere images or phenomena from which we infer things or through which we peer at them.

My provisional view is that the picture of perception in which it is characterized as a train of internal phenomena that might correspond or fail to correspond to the world originates in a clear form in the Sophists—particularly Protagoras—and is taken up by ancient Skepticism in some of its Academic (as opposed to Pyrrhonistic) varieties. In the *Theaetetus*, Socrates speaks in the voice of Protagoras, to state the opinion he will attempt to demolish: "Prove, if you can, that we have not, each one of us, his peculiar perceptions or that, granting them to be peculiar, it would not follow that what appears to each becomes—or is, if we may use the word "is"—for him alone to whom it appears."[9] Protagoras—if he is being fairly represented—reaches a relativistic conclusion, but obviously external-world and other-minds skepticism also looms. Plato himself, of course, broached the idea that the world itself is an image or a deceptive presentation of the Forms, though this does appear to be a metaphor, and I'm not aware of any passage where he clearly constructs a theory of real-world perception that relies on phenomena or phantasms in ordinary vision.

There's no doubt that the Hellenistic philosophers had the idea idea on board, though many rejected it or, at any rate, expressed theories of perception (such as

Lucretius's) that were flatly incompatible with it. So Cicero's *Academica* describes the teachings (or unteachings) of the New Academy, in which full-blown external-world skepticism evolved from an internalist picture of perception, complete with Cartesian-style dream and evil-deceiver scenarios. And Sextus Empiricus attributes a perfectly bifurcated picture of perception and consequent external-world skepticism to the Academic skeptic Carneades:

> When we look at an object we put our sense of sight into a certain condition, and not in the same condition that it was in before we looked; and owing to such an alteration we perceive, in fact, two things, one the alteration itself, which is the impression, and, secondly, that which produced the alteration, which is the visible object. And similarly in the case of the other senses. So then, just as light shows both itself and all things within it, so also the impression, which is the primary factor in the cognition of the living creature, must, like light, both reveal itself and be indicative of the evident object which produced it. But since it does not always indicate the true object, but often deceives and, like bad messengers, misreports those who dispatched it, it has necessarily resulted that we cannot admit every impression as a criterion of truth, but—if any—only that which is true. So then again, since there is no true impression of such a kind that it cannot be false, but a false impression is found to exist exactly resembling every apparently true impression . . . [it is impossible to establish a criterion of truth].[10]

So I speculate that the idea of "impressions," "sense data," "phenomena," originate not as an independent theory of perception, but precisely in the attempt—made for practical reasons (it's going to help you achieve inner peace)—to undermine perception as a or the source of knowledge. Also it perhaps has its origins in rhetorical or polemical exercises, in attempts to show that the Sophist in question can give an argument for absolutely anything, including even the idea that no one knows anything, or that there is no world. But along the way to the eighteenth century, it becomes a theory of perception in itself, even one that seems inevitable or obvious. It is our intuitive view because it is our philosophical legacy, though it is always being called into question as well.

The typical modern form of the idea makes ideas into pictures. One source of this is the Latin translations of Averroes, in turn working on Aristotle. But though this particular construction of the conceptuality is not necessarily present clearly in Aristotle, the translators used *representatio* to express Aristotle's idea of "sensible species," or the contribution of the organism or subject to the perceptual experience. Even Ockham, among many others, takes up such a view.

It is worth connecting these developments in late Medieval philosophy with shifts in actual pictorial practices in the early Renaissance, culminating in the invention or discovery of perspective. As it were, a perspective rendering is a virtual or ideational reality, and it very dramatically suggests that, for example, a basically flat retinal image or image displayed on the screen or panel of the mind could convincingly portray a three-dimensional reality. This, in turn, drives the realist pictorial program of at least portions of the Renaissance, which illustrates or confirms a theory of perception as consisting of accurate pictorial representation. (I will return to such themes in the chapter on aesthetics.) Then one waves vaguely at equivalent readings of the other sense modalities, and one effect of this is to isolate each of the senses: vision can produce *only* images, and we start to generate puzzles about how the impressions of various senses can be coordinated to construct objects that can, for example, be seen, touched, and heard. Before long each object in the world is conceived as a bundle of impressions of the various senses. And not long after that, we have full-blown phenomenalism: a world constructed from percepts.

On my view this set of ideas—which after all amounts to a comprehensive theory of the relation of us to the world—is a kind of millennia-long train wreck. It attenuates our vulnerability in a way; it imposes distance. But it is false. I don't actually believe that anyone has ever sincerely interpreted their own being-in-the-world in the terms demanded by this perspective, even if they could not envision any real alternative. The view runs through empiricists, rationalists, and idealists alike, through neopragmatists and positivists, phenomenalists and phenomenologists. On the other hand, there are always possibilities or tendencies which aim to subvert the "internalist" view or in which you can feel that the philosopher is jammed in, like he knows something's wrong.

4.

The analogy of visual experience to picturing appears to be extremely compelling, but I think it is, among other things, nonexplanatory. So, again, we might think of the function of retinal images, or the idea of mental images, as pictures on a screen, as though we experience the world like a slideshow or film. But even if there are such images, what is it that sees them? A retinal image cannot be seen except by some visual apparatus that can see things, and soon we will be postulating an infinite series of homuncular eyes.[11] There may be ways to stop this regress, but the first thing I want to say is that experiencing the world is not, all in all, much like watching a movie or looking at paintings or photographs (or, for that matter, reading a novel). We create or stipulate a distance between ourselves and our experience that might be thought of by analogy to "aesthetic" distance; we bifurcate ourselves from the world in which we are all the time embedded or entangled; or bits of which we actually are.

One way to state the position I am rejecting is this: veridical empirical experience, experience of the world, is not itself in the world in the way that trees or cars or flies are, but in the head, or the sensorium, or the mind of a person. Experience of the world, on the view in question, has a certain phenomenological character, a certain subjective side which is intrinsic or internal to the experiencer and hence can be considered in isolation from the external-world situations which it may represent or to which it may give us access. In addition, this internal component of veridical experience is epistemically available to the experiencer; indeed, possibly it is the only thing available and the origin of all other mental content (that is Locke, Berkeley, Hume, and Ayer's starting point, for example); it is certainly the exclusive source of beliefs or knowledge about the external world. That this alleged inner aspect or component of veridical empirical experience can be considered in isolation is suggested by cases in which apparently empirical experience fails to give us access to external world situations: dreams, illusions, hallucinations, and so forth. Such cases seem to give us the inner experience without an outer correlate (the world), thus suggesting (or so it is held) that the two can be separated also in the case of veridical experience.

Some versions of internalism with regard to veridical experience refer to the epistemically available inner component of experience as "sense data," "ideas," "impressions," "sensations," "appearances," "representations," "seemings." I will not be concerned with specific characterizations of this component but with the general division of experience on which these views rely. The strongest proponents of a picture like this are what we term in epistemology "foundationalists," such as Descartes. And the motivation for the view, or a motivation for it, is that it appears to make some stuff (that is, our own sensations, or the contents of our own consciousness) matters of certainty. That is, we carve out a place where we can relieve skeptical doubt, or where we can jettison faith or irrational or unjustified belief. The view remains something like the common wisdom in philosophy of mind of many sorts, though of course it has come under criticism in recent decades by "externalists" such as Mark Rowlands and Andy Clark.

5.

We might conceive the idea of direct realism along the lines suggested by Thomas Reid, or the Lu-Wang school of neo-Confucianism, or J. E. Turner, author of the unread *A Theory of Direct Realism*, as "the existential identity between sensed contents and physical entities."[12] Or as Samuel Alexander puts it:

> If I stand in a certain position I see only the corner the table. It is certainly true that I am responsible for seeing only a corner. Yet the corner of the table belongs to the table. . . . The shilling in my pocket owes it to me

that it is mine, but not that it is a piece of silver. In the same way it is the engine-maker who combines iron and steel upon a certain plan of selection, but the steam-engine only depends on him for this selection, and not for its characters or for its existence as a steam-engine. On the contrary, if he is to use it, he must learn its ways and adapt himself to them for fear of disaster. . . . Berkeley saw the truth that there is no idea to act as middleman between the mind and external things, no veil betwixt the mind and reality. He found the reality therefore in the ideas themselves. The other alternative is not to discard the supposed world of reality behind the ideas, but to discard the ideas, regarded as objects dependent on the mind.[13]

Mention of now-obscure figures such as Turner and Alexander is enough to indicate that realism in this sense hasn't exactly been the dominant stream as these things turned out; we have to reconstruct the history of what we might call anti-Kantian philosophy. But my idea is that perception is fusion of perceiver and object in a situation, fusion of persons and world, our oneness with what is. It's mystical, baby, but it is also extremely ordinary: we are having a mystical experience of oneness every time we see something that is actually there.[14]

6.

Now such a view runs afoul of this famous sort of argument.

(1) The experience of hallucinating (dreaming, etc.) a pig may be mistaken for the experience of seeing a pig.

(2) Thus, what is going on in the experiencer during these two experiences is closely similar, or even "qualitatively identical."

(3) Since in both cases one ends up taking oneself to be seeing a pig, in particular the epistemically available aspects of the experience of hallucinating a pig are the same (or very similar) to the epistemically available aspects of seeing a pig.

Therefore,

(4) Internalism with regard to veridical experience is true.

Such an argument has an intuitive appeal, as can be seen from its persistence in the history of philosophy. Indeed, some such argument underlies Cartesian skepticism, and thus, as I will argue, it must to a large extent inform the history of the epistemology of justification in its modern forms, which I reject. But I think it is obviously a very weak argument. It appears to rely on some form of abductive inference, some principle to the effect that if two things have certain similarities, they have other similarities, or even a principle to the effect that if two things have certain similarities, they have some identical component. Obviously, no inference that appeals to such a principle could establish its conclusion with certainty. An android may look for all the world like a human being, yet not be, all things considered, very much like a human being at all; it may have no component which is closely similar to any component of a human being.

Premise (2) is clearly problematic. It seems to appeal to a principle to the effect that we cannot mistake things for one another unless they are closely similar or of the same kind. That principle is obviously false. Furthermore, I can happily admit that hallucinating a pig and seeing a pig are similar in certain respects; similar firings of neurons might take place in both cases for example. It must be established that certain of the similarities are epistemically available. Premise (3) purports to do this, but again, it appears to rely on some extremely tenuous form of abduction.

The argument assumes that internalism is true with regard to veridical experience in order to show that it is. To repeat, it is argued that such experiences as seeming to see a pig may be "qualitatively identical" or "indiscernible" from experiences of seeing a pig. That is, it is possible to seem to see a pig, or have a piggy sense datum, without a pig being present. It is then argued that the similarity between seeming to see a pig and seeing a pig suggests that there is some component common to the experiences, that when one sees a pig, one also seems to see one (the weirdness or wrongness of this formulation should give advocates of internalism pause here).

But we can admit all the facts mustered for this conclusion and deny the conclusion. One rather weak argument to the effect that "qualitative indiscernibility" provides grounds for the conclusion derives from Ockham's Razor. That is, since we can give a more or less univocal account of the two sorts of experience on the internalist view, it might be held that this fact counts in its favor. About this I would merely like to say that although we should not needlessly multiply entities, we ought to acknowledge all the entities there are that need explanation, and that we all recognize a deep and important distinction between veridical experiences and hallucinations.

The argument could perhaps be recast to avoid some of these problems. But, I claim, any way of recasting the argument will be question-begging, because any such recasting of the argument is going to have to appeal at some stage to "qualitative identity" or to an internalistic sense of indiscernibility. These notions smuggle seemings or appearances into the argument in a way that assumes that internalism is true. For qualitative identity and indiscernibility (as used in the argument) are notions of apparent similarity. If two things are qualitatively identical, this is just to say that they seem identical; if two things are indiscernible in the sense required in the argument, this is just to say that they appear the same. Certainly, it cannot be claimed that, all in all, the experience of hallucinating a pig is indiscernible from the experience of seeing a pig. This is because seeing a pig requires the presence of a pig, and a situation in which there is a pig present is not indiscernible from a situation in which there is not a pig present.

The illegitimate move is from the possibility of seeming to see a pig when no pig is present to the claim that seeming to see a pig is an epistemically available aspect of actually seeing a pig, and further, to the claim that seeing a pig causes me to seem to see a pig, and to the claim that I infer that I see a pig from the "fact" that I seem to see a pig. The experience of seeing a pig is then analyzed as (a) seeming to see a pig, and (b) a pig being where I seem to see it (along with some causal and inferential conditions). But why should it be analyzed this way? Why not allow dreams, hallucinations, (as well as pains) and so forth, to be isolated as fundamentally different sorts of experiences than experiences of veridical seeing? In the case where there is a pig under my nose I do not infer from the "fact" that I seem to see a pig that there's a pig. I simply see a pig. It is the pig itself under some of its aspects, which is epistemically available; nothing internal to me is epistemically available.

Again, we can admit all the data involved in hallucinations, dreams, and so on, and we can admit that hallucinations are sometimes mistaken for realities and even that certain aspects of hallucinations may be self-evident or incorrigible (though I doubt it). But what we need to know is, why should these facts be taken as a starting-point for an account of what happens when I am not hallucinating? Why should we start from a position internal to the cognizer? Now surely the answer to this is going to be something like the following: if a person is going to be justified in her beliefs about the external world, it is going to have to be in virtue of facts to which she has access (this is the classic objection to epistemological externalism). And since from her point of view the experience of hallucinating a pig may not be distinguished from seeing a pig, we cannot start with a description of the situation from an external point of view if we are to get an account of the cognizer's own justification going. But even if knowledge does require justification, we can point out that this account of justification presupposes exactly what I am claiming it needs to show, that is, that in a case of seeing something under our noses, there is an internal, epistemically available aspect of the experience that can be isolated; it presupposes that we can usefully describe the experience at all from a "purely internal" point of view; it presupposes that we can bifurcate veridical experience into something like an hallucination plus a state of affairs in the world. It is incumbent on the internalist to show that the appeal to seemings, appearances, and so forth is even possible, that is, to show that, for example, I am experiencing seemings, sense data or whatever, in any way at all when I see a pig, before arguing that empirical beliefs must be justified "internally." There are, after all, competing pictures of how such claims could be justified.

In typical cases of empirical experience, there are no "phenomena" to isolate and study. My experiences do not have any epistemically available aspects which are properties of me considered in isolation from my environment; they are, rather, properties of a situation in which I am a component. To consider how it is "with me," inside me, as I experience a pig, is, as an epistemological strategy, false not only to what is actually happening (I am in interchange with my environment, am situated with respect to it, am in spatial juxtaposition with a pig, literally in contact with it by means of my sense organs), but also to what I take to be happening (I take it that I am spatially juxtaposed with a pig, and so forth). Of course, I can have "phenomenological" experiences; I can have pains, delusions, hallucinations, deceptive dreams. But the extraordinarily odd claim is that I should try to describe cases of actually seeing a pig by appeal to cases of hallucinating a pig, rather than vice versa.

That is why an internalist of the kind we are considering cannot be engaged in a reconstruction of what we actually do. We do not, as a matter of fact, start off with "phenomena" and infer features of reality. Rather, we start with reality, situations in which we find ourselves, and, if we are philosophers of a certain kind, infer (erroneously for the most part), features of phenomena. And if the epistemically available aspects of a veridical experience are aspects under which the experiential relation is fused to the object or situation that is experienced—fully engaged in the situation, we might say—we could not possibly start with "phenomena," because there are no phenomena, if the experience is veridical.[15]

7.

I take this view of experience to make somewhat more precise the view of Dewey, for example. As Dewey saw, experience is an interchange between organism and environment. He writes:

> "Experience" denotes the planted field, the sowed seeds, the reaped harvests, the changes of night and day, spring and autumn, wet and dry, heat and cold, that are observed, feared, longed for; it also denotes the one who plants and reaps, who works and rejoices, hopes, fears, plans, invokes magic or chemistry to aid him, who is downcast or triumphant. It is "double barreled" in that it recognizes in its primary integrity no division between act and material, subject and object, but contains them both.[16]

Or we might consider various moments in Merleau-Ponty—for example, this:

> Just as the sacrament not only symbolizes, in sensible species, an operation of Grace, but is also the real presence of God, which it causes to occupy a

fragment of space and communicates to those who eat of the consecrated bread, provided that they are inwardly prepared, in the same way the sensible has not only a motor and vital significance, but is nothing other than a certain way of being in the world suggested to us from some point in space, and seized and acted upon by our body, provided that it is capable of doing so, so that sensation is literally a form of communion.[17]

The epistemology of sense data and justification, I suggest, requires a bifurcation of the epistemic agent from the world. But if Dewey and Merleau are right, this bifurcation is invidious; we are, as epistemic and embodied agents, already part of the world.

In a certain sense, and as I think Dewey would argue, we can get misled by starting with visual experience, for here it is at least not baldly absurd to separate inner and outer components; it is at least understandable how someone might think that such a separation makes sense in typical cases of seeing an object. But consider other kinds of experience: for example the experience of breathing or of eating, to which I have already paralleled perception. Here the bifurcation of experience into inner and outer components is obviously out of place. Breathing and eating involve actually incorporating bits of the world into one's body; you simply cannot describe a process of eating by restricting your attention to what is internal to the person who is eating. Eating involves appropriating something from the environment and incorporating it into one's body; it is an interchange between organism and environment. Visual experience is a situation of an organism in an environment in which elements of the environment are appropriated by the organism. There is no accurate description of an actual visual experience which is a description of states of the organism in isolation from that environment.

8.

Another very old argument (stretching back at least to Berkeley) is frequently brought to bear in the project of showing that we infer the properties of external things from appearances. The argument, of which we've seen the edge in the quote from Samuel Alexander, above, goes roughly like this: a square table does not in fact appear to be square from any angle except from at a certain orientation directly above or below. From different angles, the table "projects" the appearance of various distorted parallelograms. We infer, it is held, that the table is square as a simplifying hypothesis, as a way of bringing its many geometrical appearances into some sort of unity. But my reply here will be familiar. Nothing constrains us to admit that the table appears to be different shapes from different angles. Now of course, and again, we can make mistakes about the shape of things. But such mistakes do not have to be construed as arising from appearances of any sort; in fact, they are most naturally construed as just what they seem to be: mistakes about the shape of some external thing, mistakes about what data are given in experience.

We should pause for a moment to appreciate how deeply counterintuitive the account in terms of a variety of geometrical appearances is here. If we are in the presence of a square table, staring at it in good conditions from an oblique angle, and we are asked what shape the table looks to have, we answer straightaway: "square." It is anything but evident, that is, that the table does project distorted parallelograms, and so forth. If we were to respond that the table looks to be shaped as a distorted parallelogram, eyebrows would certainly be raised. We can see that it is square. Ordinary language carries with it not a demonstration of the falsity of the position, but a burden of proof. The advocate of appearances is appealing to "facts" which are anything but evident, and needs an argument to show that there are such facts. Perhaps the answer here will be: the hypothesis is a simplifying one; it has explanatory power. But what does it explain? How we get from appearances to reality? That is a question that is manufactured by the view in question; the view scores no points for solving a problem that does not arise except on the condition that the view is true. And as an explanation, it does not have the virtue of simplicity; indeed, it is rather baroque. For the view with which it competes is that under decent conditions the table looks square from any angle (though again, mistakes are not ruled out).

Again, we might tell a story of how this view gets going by considering the fact that in classical empiricism, visual experience is often thought of by analogy to depiction. It is not hard to see how, if this analogy is carried far enough, it will suggest that visually discernible items "project" different shapes onto our visual apparatus from different angles. The analogy here is, again, to perspective rendering. If you want to draw a table from a certain angle, you had better foreshorten it in a certain systematic way; what will appear on the paper will be a distorted parallelogram, and this parallelogram will then be interpreted as, will be inferred to be, a depiction of a square table. One way to understand the present objection to internalism is that this analogy of vision to depiction is illegitimate.

Of course, believing and knowing are in this respect exactly like seeing, perceiving, experiencing. That is, knowing and believing are not to be individuated as internal states of the epistemic agent. I take the present point to have been decisively established by Putnam-style "twin earth" cases. Again, what one believes when one believes, say, that Lake Michigan is a body of water depends, in part, on the nature of the natural kind picked out by our term "water." My double on twin earth has a different belief than mine when tokens of the symbols "Lake Michigan is a body of water" run through his head. The truth of his belief entails that Lake Michigan consists of XYZ, while the truth of my belief entails that it consists of H_2O. Or consider knowledge. If knowing were an "internal" psychological state, there would be no distinction between knowing p and being extremely confident that p. But of course there is a difference: if I know that p, I can't be wrong. Obviously this has nothing to do with my infallibility. But we are liable to make the same kind of mistake with knowing that we make with seeing and so forth; we are liable to think that knowing contains an internal psychological component (belief) and an external, real-world component. That is, I know when I believe that p and it is true that p (with perhaps some added conditions). The problem is not with this general characterization; I certainly need to believe that p in order to know that p. The problem is, rather, with the characterization of belief as an internal state. Belief is something that, as it were, wraps its tentacles around the world, that reaches out and grasps the state of affairs with which it is concerned.

9.

I've been arguing that human beings are not representational systems, or that we do not primarily experience the world in or as pictures. However, there are pictures. It makes sense in some contexts to talk about impressions: for example, in a discussion of wax seals. A photograph is a sort of impression in this sense: something that light, reflecting from things, impresses on a silver or digital surface. Now we also need to hold on to the idea that a wax seal or a photograph is itself a physical thing, event, and situation, and that otherwise it could not be a representation of anything. And to say of it that it is an accurate representation would be to describe how it emerged in a situation, encompassing various strands of resemblance and causation.

The classical attempts to undermine the reliability of the senses include observations like this, which are pre-Socratic: a straight stick appears bent in water; a square tower appears round at distance; things look yellow to those with jaundice, and so on. Now, this approach contrasts the deliverances of some particular person's senses with the objective truth: it suggests that no one's sensible experiences can be shown to match "objective reality." But really, a skeptical conclusion with regard to the external world or the reliability of sensation does not follow at all. If there were a material world embedding material perceivers, we would expect exactly what we have: every point of view is some point of view; every sense experience engages the perceiver's sensory equipment and associated nervous system capacities, including its idiosyncrasies; every perceiver's body is located in space and culture and experiences the world from that location. But a sense experience responds also to the object perceived and the environing conditions: in short, it is a feature of the entire situation embedding object, perceiver, social situation, and environment: the shape of the thing, for example, the play of light in a variety of atmospheric conditions and mediums (humid air, muddy water, fluorescent light), possibly a vocabulary, the perceptual equipment of the perceiver.

There is no objective standpoint: that is, there is no standpoint that is not a particular standpoint or which is all standpoints at once. But there are massive unfolding perceptual situations, none of which is the exclusively true situation, but all of which are, if actual, actual. Any might yield true or false beliefs or reveal real aspects of real things; any might miss its mark. There could be standpoints that are warped, insane, delusional, and so on. But there are certainly standpoints that yield knowledge, or in which you stand in truth. There are standpoints that might be more accurate or useful than others relative to particular tasks or dimensions of assessment. But there cannot be the one right standpoint. Neither looking with a telescope nor looking with a microscope produces the one objective vision of how something is; both can provide good information about how it is.

The opposition between "objective" as against "subjective" or "intersubjective" or "relative" truth and so on seems to me ill-formulated, or at least premature. You have people squaring off on whether "science," for example, is "objectively true" (or seeks or approaches objective truth), or whether, for example, it shifts through a sequence of incommensurable paradigms, none of which is any more objective than the others, or across which the question of which is true does not properly arise, because truth is only a sensible notion within a particular conceptual scheme, vocabulary, or system of representation. Now, first of all, as I have indicated and will develop at greater length, representations are themselves physical situations, in various relations to the physical things they represent. For example, a picture may be to the left of the thing it is a picture of. It's sometimes said (Rorty always said this, for example) that we can't hold up a picture or a sentence next to a real world apart from all sentences and pictures and judge its accuracy. But that seems basically false to me: one can sometimes hold up a portrait and compare it to the person who sat for it, for example. It's only when we get into the shadow world of mental representations and the account by which we only experience the world in representation that we run into a problem: then what we'd be doing is comparing our idea of the picture to our idea of the sitter; there would be no unmediated access to the objects that would permit us to render an unmediated judgment, or indeed enter into any judgment at all without landing in a regress. Or the screen might be linguistic, so that we'd be comparing the description of the one to the description of the other. "Objectivity" would then pick out a situation in which, impossibly, we leave aside our own point of view or structures of comprehension and see the world as it really is apart from that point of view or structure of comprehension.

At any rate, the question of objectivity arises primarily for representational or semantic entities. The kinds of things for which the question of objectivity arises are things like sentences, theories, pictures, and pictorial systems. Objectivity is also a moral concept or demand—an epistemic virtue—as when we demand impartiality from a judge or a legislator or an interlocutor in the context of a debate. Here it means that one's point of view is not distorted by idiosyncratic or self-seeking interests, or that one makes an effort to screen out the stakes one has in the outcome or verdict, or one's prejudices, or even just one's emotions. Provisionally, I think it makes sense to talk about a person as being more or less objective in this moral sense. But I do not think it's particularly helpful to talk about objectivity with regard to theories or pictorial systems. I would prefer to talk about the accuracy or truth of such things instead. Indeed, there is no difference between saying that something is objectively true and saying that it's true. The concept is gratuitous, or is mere chest thumping: you might as well say it's superduper true or whatever it may be.

The contrast between objectivity and subjectivity presupposes a bifurcation of person and world, or of reality and representation. I would trace this contrast to the philosophy of Plato, and I would note that it presupposes a Platonic ordering of "levels" of reality. Plato in the *Republic* held that pictures occupy a different ontological plane than the things they are pictures of, as worldly objects occupy a different ontological plane than do the Forms. In one direction copies and copies of copies, in the other, motifs or originals with regard to the next level down, though I do not think that Plato develops this per se as a theory of human perception. One of the great mysteries of Platonic translation and scholarship is to formulate the relation between the furniture of this plane of reality and the Forms. A table is a table, for example, because it "participates" in the table located at the higher ontological level. But we might more clearly say (as is often said) that it refers to or represents the higher level table, as a picture of a this-plane table refers to or represents the table. Arthur Danto, in a more recent formulation of a similar position, contrasts works of art and mere real things, and distinguishes artworks from mere real things precisely by this semantic or aboutness relation.

My view, of course, tries to array the artist or maker of representations, the experiencer of the representation, the representation itself, and the represented thing on the same ontological plane and to characterize them as elements of a situation. The seal, the wax, and the impression of the seal in the wax are not different sorts of things in the sense that one is more actual, or actual in a different way, than the other. Now it would make sense to say of some wax impressions that they are distorted or damaged or faint, or to say that we can't accurately reconstruct the configuration of the seal from this particular impression of it. But it would not make sense to treat some of the impressions as objective and others not, or to say of one such impression that it was, to the exclusion of the rest, the "objective" impression. We might look at the quest for objectivity as seeking the one true representation, or the one perfect standpoint. Only there is never just one true representation or any perfect standpoint.

10.

Putnam characterizes "metaphysical realism" as the position that "The world consists of some fixed totality of mind-independent objects. There is exactly one true and complete description of 'the way the world is.'"[18] But these are surely two separable theses. That there is a mind-independent world is one thing. That there is in principle one objectively true description is another. Well, it depends on what you mean by *a* description: the description given in principle by our ultimate physics? But this wouldn't make, say, an aesthetic description, or descriptions at various levels of macro-objects false, would it? Would we individuate descriptions by—I don't know—academic fields or fields of endeavor?: the geographer has the objective description, or the carpenter, or the neurologist, or the string theorist, or the banker. We can't know what the world would be like without us in it, or what it would be like seen from no point of view, or seen from all points of view. However, we are in it, and our points of view are in it too, and representations and systems of representation are just as real, and real in the same sense, as the things they represent.

11.

Ernst Gombrich gives a thoughtful account of the history of realistic depiction in *Art and Illusion*, in which he describes it as a "rhythm of schema and correction."[19] One brings visual expectations to the world, or tries to fit things in the world into an existing taxonomy, or to adjust pre-existing images and styles of imagery to deal with new materials: new scenes and new tastes and recently-discovered animals, for example. An example is Dürer's inaccurate depiction of a rhinoceros—featuring armor plates—of which Dürer said "know well that it was painted from life."[20] Dürer's picture formed the basis for almost all European pictures of the rhinoceros for the next three centuries. This suggests that we construct what we see, or see what we expect to see, and to some extent that is certainly true. Nelson Goodman appropriated Gombrich's account in the service of a philosophy according to which we make our visual world by expectation, or structure it according to schemata that antedate the particular experience we are having: a modified Kantianism with a social element (our schemata are cultural). But for Gombrich the way we make pictures is a rhythm of schema *and correction*, and eventually even Dürer's rhino bent before the ways rhinos really look, which is a portion of the way they really are. This process is never complete or perfect, and no representation reflects simply a passive reception by an innocent eye. But neither are our expectations invariably confirmed, and part of being alive in reality is being surprised, and adjusting our expectations through actual sensitivity to what's there, as Bankei might suggest. And I will say again: the expectation is in the world, and the previous images and experiences on which it is based are in the world, and the images produced are in the world, and the thing depicted is in the world. None of these—and certainly not the expectations—make a world: they are derived from it, generated within it; they bend before it and issue into it.

Representational accuracy or realism is only one artistic project, and it is not the dominant project of Medieval art or of art since Impressionism. But it was at least one of the projects of the arts of the pre-to-post-Renaissance period. Elucidating this history, Heinrich Wölfflin, in *Principles of Art History*, describes different ways of representing reality. One pair is "linear and painterly": think Raphael vs. Rembrandt. In Raphael, all the emphasis is on clarity of outline in a well-ordered composition on a receding series of perspective planes. Rembrandt breaks the symmetries and planes and builds figures from within rather than tracing definite outlines. Raphael effaces the brushstroke: you don't see the traces of the manual work; Rembrandt is just the opposite. Rembrandt disperses the light, yet makes clear that it emanates from a definite source; Raphael bathes the scene in a relatively uniform, unsourced light; and so on. Wölfflin writes: "They are two conceptions of the world, differently orientated in taste and in their interest in the world, and yet each capable of giving a perfect picture of visible things."[21] There is not a way to adjudicate between them wherein one would be "objective": there is not one objective system of representation.

12.

Now science is part of the world, but it's also a series of systems for representing the world. At any given moment, like art even where it is concerned with accurate depiction, it also responds to all sorts of factors: cultural moods, funding mechanisms, academic hierarchies, mood. And it responds constantly to aesthetic factors: simplicity vs. complexity, clarity vs. richness, and so on. But this is not to say that science is "nothing but" these factors or that it is not concerned with accurate representation. There can be more than one accurate representation of the same thing. But there can be inaccurate representations. Giotto really is truer to the world and our experience of it than is a medieval altarpiece (not surprising because the medieval painter wasn't trying for accuracy) and Masaccio really is more accurate than Giotto. Perspective really was an advance in truth, even though it was also a set of representational conventions and had its limits. People really did find out more about what the human body was and how it looked by dissecting corpses, and that was reflected in much more accurate and realistic representations and styles of representation. You could hold up the picture next to the real thing and compare them, of course, and I assume that that is precisely what the painters did with the corpses and sketches.

Let us consider Wölfflin's linear and painterly as examples of what Kuhn calls "paradigms." On this parallel, there could be different paradigms neither of which was more accurate than the other, or which highlighted different aspects or approached from a different angle, or had different contexts, purposes, and so on. However, it certainly does not follow that any paradigm is acceptable, and it would take a lot to make me think that two paradigms were in any sense "incommensurable," certainly not if they're consecutive in the very same culture or science. There is a world that science is trying to represent (as well as change, and the representation is itself a change in the world), as there is a world that Raphael and Rembrandt are trying to represent. And the representations and representational systems are massively constrained by that world in myriad ways, including the available materials to make images.

They and we are also liberated by the world and into it: in its infinite richness, it is the source even of imagination. It's what breaks or reconfigures our schemata, what refreshes our seeing. The artists and scientists are massively constrained as real things in the world, and the representations are constrained as well: you can't paint with nothing, and you can't paint on nothing, and both science and painting involve administering actual materials. But the world's externality is what makes it compelling: what we don't know, what we can only find out, what we could never have thought to put there, what is recalcitrant to will and hence promises real adventure.

Certainly linear and painterly are very different. But the painterly style arose in response to the linear style, from a feeling for what it omitted, glossed over, or was incapable of depicting or displaying or expressing, including the trace of the hand of the artist. The paradigms are historically connected—in fact Wölfflin suggested that they more or less had to have the sequence they did—and they are certainly not globally or entirely different in the way they represent the world. What Wölfflin underemphasizes, and what Kuhn underemphasizes, is the massive overlap of alternative paradigms. Rembrandt understood Raphael; he (like us, in fact) could recognize the objects depicted even as he worked through the linear paradigm into a different but equally comprehensible representational schema. Raphael and Rembrandt are very different, but not alien to one another, and there is a story to tell about how you get from one to the other, retold by Wölfflin and many others, that would include the name "Caravaggio." And they are both, among other things, trying to "imitate" or accurately represent the very same world. As different as the styles are, they are not entirely different, and each is comprehensible from within the other—in fact, each is more comprehensible in contrast and other relation to the other—for the reason that they are embedded in the same world and emerge in overlapping histories.

13.

I agree with Paul Feyerabend in many ways. We both account ourselves anarchists, about both politics and inquiry. Like him, I would restrict inquiry to no particular method. Often the most rigorous applications of the canons of logic or the methods of science are the best available techniques in particular situations. But I also think (as I try to defend with some systematicity) that there is no telling in advance where knowledge might come from or how it might be elaborated. Now obviously Kuhn-and-Feyerabend has become a sort of shorthand for a kind of post-Kantian relativism about representation and scientific truth, though in both cases I would say the positions are complex and equivocal in this regard. Feyerabend writes,

> On closer analysis we even find that science knows no "bare facts" at all but that the "facts" that enter our knowledge are already viewed in a certain way and are, therefore, essentially ideational. This being the case, the history of science will be as complex, chaotic, full of mistakes, and entertaining as the ideas it contains, and those ideas in turn will be as complex, chaotic, full of mistakes, and entertaining as are the minds of those who invented them.[22]

What I want to say about this is not that it's wrong, exactly, but that it has a misleading emphasis. For ideas and the people who have them occur within a world, or are situations in the world. And the world is itself complex, chaotic, full of mistakes, and entertaining. It is infinitely rich and complex and difficult and equivocal and recalcitrant. We are too, and this is a symptom of our realness, or our wildness, or our excess to ourselves. Science is "ideational" in that it deploys systems of representation. But systems of representation are porous to the world in myriad ways. Science is a history of projections or representations, and it is a social institution or a series of social institutions, or an array of social institutions, in which scientists are embedded and in which each is also a creative force. And these social practices are themselves embedded in an extremely rich physical surround, which they are dedicated to investigating, elucidating, representing, and transforming, though it exceeds all the possibilities of any single representation. This repleteness is precisely why multiple systems of representation are appropriate, or indeed are required.

How we see and how a dog sees are different; our visual apparatuses are configured to detect somewhat different aspects of the world. But we can tell in our interactions that we experience the same world in somewhat different ways. When the dog wants out, she barks at the door; she doesn't pass through the wall. Well you might point to the similarities of the visual apparatus (we both have two eyes, retinas, visual cortices, etc.). But you might also point out that we inhabit in somewhat different ways the same environments, and that if we weren't capable of detecting real features of those environments, neither of us could survive. That's why we have overwhelmingly similar visual systems even though there are differences. Reading Aristotle's *Physics*, you can see that Aristotle's experience overlaps massively with our own—that the world he's trying to account for is our world (albeit different in the ordinary ways; he didn't have cable)—though he produces such a different representational schema than does Feynman, say.

It is important to try to enter into the Aristotelian paradigm, and you can't evaluate its capacities for truth unless you enter into it as far as you can in its own situation or on its own terms, from—of course—within your own situation: cultural, linguistic, subjective, biological, environmental. Then to some extent it reveals its truths, or its role in a history that does in some ways to some extent make progress.

If you were trying to narrate physics Aristotle to Feynman as a series of paradigms, you'd have to trace all sorts of transformations: smooth shifts between closely related paradigms, relatively radical displacements (such as ancient to Medieval, Medieval to Renaissance), revolutionary developments reexplaining experimental results developed within the previous paradigm, and so on. Certainly it cannot appear as a series of discrete paradigms each occupying its own world, or else it ceases to be a history at all. The Renaissance paradigm (obviously these are simplifications) arises from the Medieval partially by rejection, partially by adumbration, and so on; they form a more or less continuous history even if they amount finally also to a radical break.

Now, on the other hand, I'm not denying that Feynman's physics is nearer true than Aristotle's. Orbits are elliptical and the earth isn't flat and people do believe all kinds of crap. But we need to treat Feynman's physics, or any system of physics, as a system of representation responding to all sorts of factors too: no scientific theory is "objective" in the sense that it does not deploy representational schemata which are alterable, and to which there are alternatives. But representational schemata are not all equal truthwise, even though there could be equally true representations in some two systems of the same thing, as Wölfflin's account of linear and painterly suggests. Some representational systems are sensitive to different kinds of truths or different features of real things than others; no human schema is entirely adequate to an infinitely profuse reality; or, reality is always in radical excess to its representations. That is one thing it means to say it's real.

It is worthwhile really to immerse yourself in different historical moments, different cultures, different groups' experiences, different languages, insofar as that is possible, so that you don't just think your moment or group must have the truth or the only true schema, and so that you don't stop being critical of all sorts of factors in your own representational structure, or so that you can become sensitive to features of the world that were occluded by that structure. For if linear and painterly both reveal real aspects of the real world, they both conceal other aspects, as Heidegger would suggest, which is one reason we need both rather than to decide between them. It's hard to be aware of your own era's/culture's representational resources or their limits and you can't become completely aware. But you need always to try to see the compelling qualities of other schemata, know the present structure is optional, not the last word, because it will certainly be replaced: under aesthetic demands and sociological shifts, but also, relatedly, in a quest for representational accuracy.

And what the history of science shows among other things is that the world will keep blasting through every representational schema, that each is impoverished and vulnerable; none is exhaustive and none is fully adequate and none is objective; but some are true and some are false. That's one reason why you keep observing and experimenting instead of just repeating the commonplaces of your present science or the present syntax of your community's language.

B. The Nature of Knowledge and Proof of the External World

1.

One goal of the internalist account of perception is certainty. I think this is a goal also of related or adumbrated developments such as full-bore transcendental and absolute idealism, and social or linguistic constructionism as well. There is a sense that a real external physical world is too opaque, too obscure, too unpredictable, too outside or distant from ourselves, really to be known. In some ways this is definitely true. The world is threatening, infinitely rich, and it is strange. It resists our mastery. Of course this is not surprising if we are, in fact, little creatures operating within it: highly localized zones of it. But nonomniscience is frustrating, especially to philosophers. The inexhaustibility of reality to a finite intelligence is in many ways an unsatisfactory situation, and an actually dangerous one. You never know what might happen next; as Kierkegaard once said, you might, as you're trying to figure out what death is or what it means that you yourself are going to die, get hit by a tile falling from a building and croak. I think Kierkegaard himself took some comfort in the comedy inherent in this predicament, and I think we should too. At any rate, one motivation for slicing off the human subject from its environment, or the account of human perception in terms of "ideas" or "phenomena" and even "language," is that it reduces knowledge of the world to a kind of introspection. It brings things closer to us, like a telescope. It gives us access to reality through the aid of things we actually can know, supposedly: our human selves, the "immediate contents of our consciousness" and perhaps one another, since we are together human.

That is certainly completely explicit in Descartes, for example, and also in Kant. The things we can know with certainty are the things in closest proximity to ourselves, the things open to our immediate and full inspection. Space and time would be knowable if they were the necessary structures of our own consciousness. Things would be knowable if they reduced for us to us or at any rate swam nearer our ken. Science is possible for the positivists in that it has its ultimate source and justification in our own sensible contents. And I think that this strategy is carried forward, though also compromised, in the linguistic/cultural approaches of the last century or so. It may not be possible to know what things are in themselves, but it is possible, under good circumstances, to know what we ourselves mean or what we are saying; but then that breaks down as well in deconstruction, for example. Admittedly, this last form introduces new and even more acute complexities and difficulties, and even our own linguistic and cultural practices are difficult fully to explicate or to bring to our own awareness. It may be that lumping this approach into Cartesianism or empiricism or positivism—to all of which it also stands in marked contrast—might be premature or unfair. At any rate it expands the real environment to other persons, which is a step in the right direction.

For we are more obscure to ourselves, for example, than our immediate environments are to us. We are subjects, but also objects, with at least all the opacity and complexity of other objects. It is sad and false to reduce an exploration of reality to a journey of introspection, but it also does not in fact get us closer to certainty. The incorrigibility, self-presentation, immediacy, and so on, of our own inner states is highly overrated. As Austin has pointed out (many have written in a similar vein: Timothy Williamson, for one), with regard to one of our own impressions or sensations we are often "not quite sure or certain what it is, what to say, how to describe it: what our feelings really are, whether the tickling is painful exactly, whether I'm really what you'd call angry with him or only something rather like it."[23] Obviously, we are often at a loss to know what our social and linguistic practices are, exactly, or what they prescribe in a case like this, or whether there are multiple practices, terms, dimensions in play and, if so, which.

It is a familiar irony that the quest for certainty, to be achieved by collapsing the world into ourselves, leaves us finally in skepticism, or actually manufactures the skeptical conundrum. But it is also a betrayal of the very experiences it is meant to account for or open to full inspection in its bifurcation of subject and object, or of culture and environment. On the other hand, if we leave this project behind, or to the extent we do, we also leave behind the possibility of certainty. I think the idea that there is a world and that we are in it and of it doesn't require a knockdown demonstration—we all believe it anyway—but I also see that it is a limitation of our finitude that it admits of no demonstration. This is a highly unsatisfactory condition—at least it is experienced that way in certain moods, or by people with certain sorts of identities or engaged in certain projects—but it is also rather a relief. Knowledge, I think, rests on faith, and this condition is irremediable and humbling. But it's also funny.

2.

To believe is to enter into an entanglement or situation qua truth-value bearer; it is to commit yourself to its reality. Or we might say that it is enter into the tangle in a certain way, or to entangle oneself in a certain situation through emotional commitment. Even on the driest propositional-attitude accounts of belief, it seems to me, the emotional element or the element of will is not absent: the attitude of belief is an attitude of commitment: the particular endorsement of a particular thing or fact as true or real in a particular situation by a particular person (or perhaps a group, or whatever sorts of thing can believe). To believe is to take to be true, real; and because truth is an entanglement, to believe is to commit yourself to the reality of a certain situation, to engage it or to enter into it with a kind of force, to dis-detach yourself from it.

Belief is conceptually connected to truth as, on certain accounts, action is to rightness. On such accounts, to intentionally perform an action, one must think that it is best, or best for some purpose. Now that seems false to me, but belief is oriented toward truth in this manner. It is perfectly possible to believe something and take it to be pragmatically disastrous, for example. That is not to say that we don't believe some things (including some false things) because they are useful to believe, but, in order to do that, we need to enter into a process by which we come to regard such things as true (sometimes this process might be called "rationalization"). It is not quite a bald contradiction to say that I believe something and it's false ("Moore's paradox"), yet to believe something and also believe it to be false is to hold contradictory beliefs. Or to resort to proposition-talk: "I believe that p, and p is false" is obviously not contradictory, though it certainly sounds odd and irrational. But "I believe that p and I take p to be false" expresses what we might think of as contradictory propositional attitudes, or it means the same as "I believe that p and I do not believe that p." One might believe it one moment and not the next. One might not know what to believe. One might express a belief one does not hold. One might have a set of beliefs that is profoundly inconsistent (or be in a state of "doxastic dissonance"), but to believe something is to take it to be true.

3.

On my account, the fundamental questions of epistemology are whether we should believe anything at all, and if so, under what circumstances, or how. One way to formulate this would be to ask what, if anything, it would be a good thing to believe, or in what manner it would be good to generate beliefs. Or, we might ask, what ought we to commit ourselves to? Or, under what circumstances should we indeed commit ourselves? So the first question seems to be whether it is an (epistemically) good thing to believe anything at all. I take this to be the problem of universal skepticism. In fact, skepticism about the external world, which I will take as a representative and particularly thorough example of skepticism in general, is usually framed as the question of whether we (can) have knowledge of external objects, not as whether it is a good thing epistemically to believe that there are such things (putting it one traditional way). This alleged distinction is fundamental to Hume's treatment of the question, for example. That is, the question seems to be what justifies us in believing that there are objects "external to the mind" (or that induction is a good inference strategy, or that there are other intelligent beings, etc.)?

However, in my view these are not different questions. Knowledge, I urge, is the epistemic *telos*; it is the purpose of believing. If knowledge were justified true belief, it would be an epistemically good thing for me to believe just those true propositions that I would be justified in believing. So the question of whether I know that there are objects external to the mind is precisely the question of whether it is an epistemically good thing for me to believe that there are or is. (But see Wang Yang-Ming on flowers. I, of course, do not like the formula "external to the mind"; I'd rather ask whether there is a real world with me in it.) I take it, therefore, that the question raised by skepticism about the external world can be formulated alternately as the question of whether I know that there is and whether it is an epistemically good thing to believe that there is. Thus, on my account, the question raised by skepticism about the external world is whether it is an epistemically good thing to take the proposition that there are objects external to the mind to be true. (I am working, toward Moore, with this traditional formulation. Minds and objects are entangled and nondistinct, in my view. But everything that does exist in the world besides minds is also mind-independent. That tree does not depend on me, even though it enters into infinitely many relations with me as well.)

Now as I have said, I can't really have propositions in my ontology, as the "abstract" objects of propositional attitudes. But I am going to permit myself the locution, in order to engage with the tradition I am trying to destroy. Then I will send you back and forward to various attempts to treat "propositions" as a shorthand, promising some sort of nominalistic account in terms of specific utterances and inscriptions, which in any case, as I argued, is required on independent grounds within the theory of meaning and truth.

I am going to take external world skepticism as representative of skepticism about various matters. I think at least some of the conclusions I reach about it can be generalized to skepticism about induction, other minds, the past, and whatnot. And I am going to take Descartes's familiar dream argument as representative of hypotheses designed to show that in fact we do (can) not know anything about the external world. Most of what I shall have to say could be generalized to a discussion of the evil deceiver, the hypothesis that I am a brain in a vat, trapped in the Matrix, and so on.

4.

In the first of the *Meditations*, Descartes asserts that, since he realizes that in the past he has harbored some false opinions, in order to "establish anything firm and lasting in the sciences," he has to "raze everything in my life, down to the very bottom, so as to begin again from the first foundations." He notices that "Whatever I had admitted until now as most true I took in either from the senses or through the senses." And he points out that though his senses have occasionally deceived him about things that are "very small and distant," his sensible experience leads him to believe that he is "sitting here before the fireplace wearing my dressing gown, that I feel this sheet of paper in my hands and so on."

It seems that he would need some special reason to doubt that his senses inform him truly about such facts. And then he introduces the dream argument to undermine the claim that he knows what he has (seemed to) come to know from or through the senses.

> How often has my evening slumber persuaded me of such customary things as these: that I am here, clothed in my dressing gown, seated at the fireplace, when in fact I am lying undressed between the blankets! But right now I certainly am gazing upon piece of paper with eyes wide awake. This head which I am moving is not heavy with sleep. I extend this hand consciously and deliberately and I feel it. These things would not be so distinct for one who is asleep. But this all seems as if I do not recall having been deceived by similar thoughts on other occasions in my dreams. As I consider these cases more intently I see so plainly that there are no definite signs to distinguish being awake from being asleep that I am quite astonished, and this astonishment almost convinces me that I am sleeping.[24]

The case is meant to be generalized. It is as clear a case of apparently waking experience as any could be, and it is typical. If one cannot establish in such a case that one is not dreaming, then it is hard to see in what sort of case such a thing could be established. And the argument is that if one cannot establish that one is not dreaming, if one cannot justify the belief that one is not dreaming, one has no empirical knowledge whatever. That is, we are challenged by Descartes to show that we know something about the external world, or indeed to come to know something about the external world, by justifying our empirical beliefs as a whole from the ground up.

Here are some famous examples of what I take to be the right sort of reply to this sort of argument, by Diogenes the Cynic, Samuel Johnson, and G. E. Moore:

> [W]hen someone declared that there is no such thing as motion, [Diogenes] got up and walked about.[25]

According to Boswell, Dr. Johnson "refuted" idealism by kicking a stone:

> [W]e stood talking for some time together of Bishop Berkeley's ingenious sophistry to prove the nonexistence of matter, and that everything in the universe is merely ideal. I observed, that though we are satisfied his doctrine is not true, it is impossible to refute it. I shall never forget the alacrity with which Johnson answered, striking his foot with mighty force against a large stone, till he rebounded from it, "I refute it thus." This was a stout exemplification of the first truths of Père Bouffier, or the original principles

of Reid and Beattie; without admitting which, we can no more argue in metaphysicks, than we can argue in mathematicks without axioms. To me it is not conceivable how Berkeley can be answered by pure reasoning.[26]

Moore proved that there are things external to the mind by holding out his hands:

> I can now give a large number of different proofs [of the existence of things outside us], each of which is a perfectly rigorous proof. . . . I can prove now, for instance, that two human hands exist. How? By holding up my two hands, and saying, as I make a certain gesture with my right hand, "Here is one hand," and adding, as I make a certain gesture with the left, "and here is another."[27]

Now few moments in the history of philosophy are as charming as Moore's proof of the external world. Indeed, I think it is a masterful work of literature, a satire on the level of "A Modest Proposal" or "On Murder Considered as One of the Fine Arts." However, the structure of the satire is different; it's a burlesque of idealism, a work of extreme academic punctiliousness designed to ridicule, from the (ironically assumed) standpoint of the common man (the man of good plain sense), the funny professors who believe themselves to be the creators of space and time. Moore certainly was ridiculing his own idealist professors: good-naturedly, yet really very viciously. If Moore is right, of course, philosophy had pursued a disastrous—indeed, a ridiculous—line of thought at least since Kant (that is, for a century and more). Moore starts with a quotation from Kant: "It still remains a scandal to philosophy that the existence of things outside of us . . . must be accepted merely on *faith*."[28] He tries to sort through a welter of Kantian locutions, such as "outside us," "external to the mind," "presented in space," and "to be met with in space," discussing along the way after-images, hallucinations, reflections, shadows, and so on.

It is a key point that Moore had developed an ordinary language philosophy by this time (1939), though the basic ideas were traversed much earlier in Moore's authorship; I think it's fair to say with regard to Wittgenstein and Moore that the influence is mutual. Semisystematically, Moore insists that words mean what they are ordinarily used to mean, accusing his opponents of meaning something else or nothing. ("It should, I think, be noted, first of all, that the use of the word "mind" which is being adopted when it is said that bodily pains which I feel are "in my mind," is one which is not quite in accordance with any usage in ordinary speech."[29] Rather, the pain is in my foot, for example.) At any rate, Moore insists that when philosophers use "outside the mind," "to be met with in space" and the like, they mean by "outside" and "space" what people would ordinarily mean by such terms. This ends up being the wedge that Wittgenstein and others will use to answer Moore: well people just do not ordinarily say things like "There are things outside my mind."

After winding up for a while, Moore unleashes the havoc of reality.

> Consider any kind of thing, such that anything of that kind, if there is anything of it, must be "to be met with in space": e.g., consider the kind "soap-bubble." If I say of anything which I am perceiving, "That is a soap-bubble," I am, it seems to me, certainly implying that there would be no contradiction in asserting that it existed before I perceived it and that it will continue to exist, even if I cease to perceive it. This seems to me to be part of what is meant by saying that it is a real soap-bubble, as distinguished, for instance, from an hallucination of a soap-bubble. Of course, it by no means follows, that if it really is a soap-bubble, it did in fact exist before I perceived it or will continue to exist after I perceive it: soap-bubbles are an example of a kind of "physical object" and "thing to be met with in space," in the case of which it is notorious that particular specimens of the kind often do exist only so long as they are perceived by a particular person. But a thing which I perceive would not be a soap-bubble unless its existence at any given time were *logically independent* of my perception of it at that time; unless, that is to say, from the proposition, with regard to a particular time, that it existed at that time, it *never* follows that I perceived it at that time. . . . That is to say, from the proposition with regard to anything which I am perceiving that it is a soap-bubble, there *follows* the proposition that it is external to *my* mind. But if, when I say that anything which I perceive is a soap-bubble, I am implying that it is external to *my* mind, I am, I think, certainly also implying that it is also external to all other minds. . . . I think, therefore, that from any proposition of the form "There's a soap-bubble!" there really does *follow* the proposition "There's an external object!" "There's an object external to *all* our minds!"[30]

In other words, the proof that there are things external to the mind, after all the modal-logic rigmarole, is "Look, there's one now!" But Moore is certainly arguing that being met-withable in space or being outside the mind are built into the very concept of "soap bubble," as being H_2O is built into the concept of water: a fictional soap bubble is not a soap bubble; a hallucinated soap bubble is not a soap bubble; an imagined soap bubble is not a soap bubble, and so on. There are as many proofs of the external world as there are real soap bubbles, and surely there are many real soap bubbles at any given moment.

The proof appears analogous to the ontological argument: well, occupying space and time, or even actually existing, is built into the very concept of being a soap bubble. But Moore, of course, does not conclude from this that soap bubbles exist; he concludes from the fact that soap bubbles exist that there are things that occupy space and time. That is a perfectly good argument, I believe. Or we could phrase it as a rational entailment: if you think there are soap bubbles (and who doesn't?), then you are rationally obliged to believe that there are things that occupy space and time (that are "external to the mind," etc.). The use of bubbles is felicitous. They are evanescent, ephemeral, but they are part of the real world, both extremely ordinary and astonishing. But bubbles are the froth of an infinitely rich universe. You managed to talk yourself out of it in philosophy, though you believed or perhaps knew it all along as well; you availed yourself of it even in philosophy as you also denied or deflected or attenuated it systematically.

5.

A Moore-sentence (m-sentence), let us say, is any sentence (in Moore's parlance, a sentence that expresses a proposition) from which it follows that there exists something "outside the mind" or "external to us." If any m-sentence is true, then there is something "outside the mind" or "external to us." Then Moore tries to select out sentences of the sort that just aren't controversial, which express the most obvious things in the world. "But I do know that I held up two hands above this desk not very long ago. As a matter of fact, you all know it too."[31] Examples of m-sentences are things like "Here is a hand and here is another," "I held up my hands above this desk just now," "There's a soap bubble," "I have never been far from the surface of the earth," "I'm standing closer to the mantelpiece than to the bookcase," "I live north of here." For that matter, many of Descartes' sentences are m-sentences: "I am here, clothed in my dressing gown" or "I extend this hand consciously and deliberately and I feel it."

In his "proof of the external world" and "defense of common sense," Moore takes himself to be trying to demonstrate conclusively that there are things external to the mind. That is, Moore puts forward his argument as a direct refutation of skepticism. If Moore knows that here is a hand and here is another, then it follows that Moore, if he reflects on the entailments of that claim, knows that he is not dreaming that he sees two hands. Thus he will have established that he is not dreaming. But whether Moore knows the former—that here are two hands—is precisely what is at issue. The skeptic holds that because he could in fact be dreaming that he is seeing two hands, he cannot establish that he knows that here are two hands. So in the absence of further argument it does not follow that Moore knows he is not dreaming. And if he can't know that, he can't have any empirical knowledge.

Moore's challenge, however, might be read in another way. By holding up two hands, we might say, Moore is dramatizing to his audience (the paper was delivered as a lecture) that they, in fact, do believe that here are two hands. Moore asserts that this sort of belief is more firmly held by these particular persons (and we may take ourselves to be part of Moore's extended audience) than any belief that could be produced to attack it.[32] If you can declare with this kind of confidence that you know that here is one hand and here is another, and if you see that the assertion that here is one hand and here is another entails that there are things external to the mind, then you ought not to be concerned any longer with skepticism about the external world. We approach actual people, even sceptics, as sincere believers and doubters in actual situations; we present them with a contradiction in their own belief set and invite them to reconcile it, insisting that they do so sincerely, that they say what they really believe.

If I am dreaming that here are two hands, I do not thereby know that here are two hands. But if I believe that here are two hands, and I follow out the implications of that claim, I am rationally committed to affirm that I am not dreaming. And I do believe that here is one hand and here is another; that is to say, I take it to be true. This is also the way I want to read Diogenes and Johnson: as showing us or reminding what we do believe, where our genuine commitments do already lie. They are accusing their opponents, among other things, of being profoundly insincere.

6.

Though I often avail myself of ordinary-language methods, and have been known to disqualify some philosopher's locution on the grounds that "there's just no such use of the word," I think that we ought to reject some sort of hard-and-fast distinction between philosophical and ordinary language, a distinction on which so much of philosophy's self-destructive impulse has depended. Wittgenstein reared an edifice of thought on this foundation, and even if he withdrew the flat claim that philosophical talk was nonsense, he insisted up until the end, in *On Certainty*, that it was nonempirical; he gave it the status of "grammatical" or "logical": philosophical claims might set the rules within which the language game unfolded, but for that reason could not themselves be established to be true or false or testable or at stake within that language game.

> 58. If "I know etc" is conceived as a grammatical proposition, of course the "I" cannot be important. And it properly means "There is no such thing as a doubt in this case" or "The expression "I do not know" makes no sense in this case." And of course it follows from this that "I know" makes no sense either.

> 59. "I know" is here a logical insight. Only realism can't be proved by means of it.[33]

This seems wrong to me on various grounds, beyond not knowing what "grammatical proposition" and "logical insight" mean, exactly. But does "I know that here is a hand" *mean the same as* "There is no such thing as a doubt in this case?" Even roughly? Hardly. Indeed, I don't care whether you and René Descartes doubt it; I will still insist that I know it. Wittgenstein experiments with the idea that it is these sorts of sentences which give sense to the meaning of "I know," but I think that is precisely because m-sentences provide paradigmatic cases of knowledge.

Marie McGinn, in her book *Sense and Certainty*, writes: "Moore is using the fact that skepticism is simply beyond belief, and the fact that it is in conflict with what we are all absolutely convinced of, in an attempt to rout the sceptic."[34] Nevertheless, McGinn attacks Moore's proof as follows:

> [I]t seems to me that Moore's dogmatism is, by the principles of the practice he means to defend, an unacceptable response to a demonstration that one lacks the requisite justification to sustain a knowledge claim. It is impossible to use our conviction that the sceptic's conclusion is false as a legitimate ground for dismissing scepticism, for it is clearly part of our ordinary grasp of the concept of knowledge that personal conviction is never sufficient to warrant the affirmation of a knowledge claim exposed as doubtful. Possessing an adequate justification for believing a given proposition, p, is part of our normal ground for asserting a claim to know.[35]

Now, this argument is beside the point if part of what Moore is doing is precisely trying to show that, in the most run-of-the-mill cases, justification is irrelevant to knowledge claims, which is how I want to read him. I think, in other words, that McGinn is far too credulous in identifying ordinary practice with a particular, optional philosophical orientation. And I also want to remark that McGinn's own solution is unsatisfactory. Following Wittgenstein, she treats m-sentences as part of the "framework," as logical rather than empirical: the ground rather than the result of empirical investigation. I point out, first, that "here is a hand" is empirical; it is about the world, not about language. And second, this view represents an invidious verificationism; it will automatically exempt from the realm of the empirical any claim which cannot or need not be empirically justified. This verificationist orientation is both unsatisfactory in its own right and question-begging in this context, themes I will explore shortly.

Moore took his sort of examples to show not only that there were external things, but that knowledge did not always require justification, or at any rate proof. He insists that he does know such things as that here is a hand.

> I certainly did at the moment *know* that which I expressed by the combination of certain gestures with saying the words "There is one hand and

here is another." ... How absurd it would be to suggest that I did not know it, but only believed it, and that perhaps it was not the case! You might as well suggest that I do not know that I am not standing up and talking—that perhaps I'm not, and that it's not quite certain that I am![36]

He admits that he can't prove that here is a hand, but denies that he needs to, since we all know it perfectly well.

This view that, if I cannot prove such things as these, I do not know them, is, I think, the view Kant was expressing ... when he implies that so long as we have no proof of the existence of external things, their existence must be accepted merely on *faith*. He means to say, I think, that if I really cannot prove that there is a hand here, I must accept it merely as a matter of faith—I cannot know it.[37]

In other words, what Moore is proposing is to reject justification as a necessary condition for knowledge, based in part on the way *know* and its cognates are used in ordinary language. But for Wittgenstein, it's the lack of justification (warrant, reasons, proof, etc.), that drives the back-and-forthing and the promotion of the most humble and widely shared empirical knowledge to the level of the grammatical, the metalinguistic, and possibly the unsayable. I personally think that what went wrong in epistemology went wrong in the *Theaetetus*, or on the first day of your epistemology class: well, but of course if you can't give reasons then you don't know, and so on. Now in some circumstances the demand makes sense; it is precisely an attempt to see whether the target proposition is true. But in others it's silly or wrongheaded. And as in many a Socratic dialogue, once you make that first concession, you're screwed.

At any rate, "I doubt that there's a hand there at all" makes perfectly good sense. You could of course dream up a context, but surely that is precisely the sort of thing Descartes said was doubtful, and Hume thought so too, "in his capacity as a philosopher." At any rate, one will be moving all m-sentences into the realm of rules or logical principles, precisely if the circumstances make them excruciatingly obvious. And there are infinitely many m-sentences, including many things that people say every day, such as "This is my cat, Thistle" or "It's raining" or "I live in south-central Pennsylvania"; sentences like that are supposed to be incapable of being true or false, or of having any sense, or of being known or not. Like a thistle, the language bristles with rules, as many as there are commonplaces, or thereabouts. This position is ridiculous, and it is, ironically enough, completely incompatible with taking ordinary language seriously or regarding use as the source of meaning.

There's no doubt that the language depends on many commonly agreed-upon cases. But one reason the cases are so commonly agreed upon is because we're all operating in the same environment. When Peirce formulates the principle of conversational charity he does it just in terms of beliefs; we've got to believe that most of what our conversational partners believe is true, and the same of ourselves; the possibility of a common language massively depends on that. Wittgenstein can't even frame it in terms of beliefs; for him, insofar as they are embodied in m-sentences, they are not the sorts of things that could be believed or not. But we could explain the commonality alternately in terms of the sheer fact that we share a physical surround with things like human hands in it. It's not just that we've got to believe that; we know it to be true insofar as we can be said to know anything. We're all roughly in the same predicament, we might say. Now, is there any reason Wittgenstein shouldn't avail himself of the real world?

7.

What Moore took himself to be proving was not that he or we know that there are things external to the mind, but that *there are things external to the mind*. That is, he was at least not only concerned with epistemology but with ontology. And I think we need to sort these strands out a bit, because the Wittgenstein dust cloud emerges from the concept of knowledge: that is, Wittgenstein gets befuddled by the question of what the necessary conditions of knowledge are, which he doesn't think Moore meets, precisely because Moore refuses to produce a demonstration, which here means an argument, that here is a hand. I have to remark that the structure of *On Certainty* is hemming and hawing, going back and forth: it's empirical/it's not, we know/it's not the kind of thing that could be known, and so on. Or Wittgenstein deflects all direct answers with more questions: "Can I believe for one moment that I have ever been in the stratosphere? No. So do I know the contrary, like Moore?"[38] You're the philosopher; you tell me. But if you agree that here is a hand, you've agreed that there are things external to the mind. And . . . there really are things out there, as both of us know very well. Also you've never been to the stratosphere, bro, and that's not about grammar; it's about you and the sky.

Even such an apparently innocent worldly claim as "here is a hand" took on for Wittgenstein the status of being part of the grammar of the language in which it is expressed. Though it looks like an empirical claim, and though Moore presented it precisely as an arbitrary example and adduced many similar propositions, it has the status of a rule precisely because, though it is certainly not false, there is no sense in or no possibility of showing it to be true or of justifying it and hence vindicating it as empirical knowledge. Now even in the lecture hall, G. E. Moore was a flesh-and-blood human being, and he was gesticulating with a pair of human hands. It seems to me that perfectly clear empirical observations are going to get automatically promoted willy-nilly to the status of grammatical rules as it is found that they are known without justification. That is, *by definition* there can be no counterexamples to the view; you can't know an empirical claim to be true without being able to produce a justification, so *here is a hand* cannot be an empirical claim. ("Has he . . . got the right ground for his conviction? For if not, then after all he doesn't know."[39]) But it *is* an empirical claim, whatever its bedrock status. For example, empirical evidence could show it was false: it turns out to be a prosthesis, or really we should call that thing a paw.

Wittgenstein asserts that the status of *here is a hand* oscillates: "the same proposition may get treated at one time as something to test by experience, at another as a rule for testing."[40] And when Moore uses it, it's a rule, and no matter what he does he can't bring it back to the status of an empirical assertion: everything he says turns into metagrammar. "When Moore says he knows such and such, he is really enumerating a lot of empirical propositions which we affirm without special testing; propositions, that is, which have a peculiar logical role in the system of our empirical propositions."[41] If one doesn't think that justification is necessary to knowledge, this cannot be regarded as anything but question-begging: just defining the problem away. And what is supposed to be "peculiar"? These are the most typical assertions in the world.

Indeed, Moore tried heroically to make m-sentences into plain empirical claims. In "A Defence of Common Sense," he tries the sentence "The earth has existed for many years past."

> In what I have just said, I have assumed that there is some meaning which is *the* ordinary or popular meaning of such as expressions as "The earth has existed for many years past." And this, I am afraid, which some philosophers are capable of disputing. They seem to think that the question "Do you believe the earth has existed for many years past?" is not a plain question, such as should be met with a plain "Yes" or "No," or by a plain "I can't make up my mind." . . . "The earth has existed for many years past" is the very type of an unambiguous expression, the meaning of which we all understand.[42]

But nothing that Moore can say, at least in this context, is going to suffice for Wittgenstein to make it the case that he means what we might mean by such a sentence on "ordinary" occasions; everything Moore touches turns to the transcendent dross of super-empirical rules or tautological implications of the meanings of terms. He literally cannot articulate his examples, on Wittgenstein's account.

We could take the approach of saying, rather than that most ordinary apparent assertions are not assertions at all, or are grammatical or logical, that there are different ways of coming to know different sorts of things; some might require justification or argument; some might require perceptual situations of certain kinds. Some might even involve, say, coming to know what something looks like by seeing a picture. I don't think that, with regard to actual empirical knowledge of one's environment at a given moment, one comes to know by having certain percepts, sense data, and so on, though in some cases mental imagery of some sort might be involved. You got to the sense data initially precisely because you were looking for a justification of m-type-sentences, for example, "I am sitting by the fire." But not only can't we provide such justifications, they are not needed because no justification is needed; one only needs to be embedded in a certain perceptual situation, that is, to display certain sorts of permeability to the environment and a basic mastery of a language in which the claim can be expressed.

As Wittgenstein points out, there could be cases where it makes sense within a conversational context to say "here is a hand," like when you awaken from your anesthesia to find that they didn't have to amputate after all. But it is worth pointing out that Moore did utter the sentence "here is a hand" in a context. And I must say, it was rather an ordinary context. I myself have listened to hundreds of lectures in philosophy, and I have delivered hundreds. Indeed, I've absorbed or delivered them in bars and coffee shops, in the car, over dinner with the wife and kids, and so on. In all such cases I seemed to myself to be inhabiting a physical space with other bodies, emitting and absorbing sound in the usual way. If I floated free into a metalanguage or articulated a structure of rules for talking—which I did sometimes—I like to think I was aware of it. The hands with which I gesticulated seemed to be the same old hands. Philosophy talk seems to me, as I said in the introduction, to be not all that extraordinary.

Indeed, the program of "ordinary language philosophy" in the hands of later Wittgenstein or Austin or Moore himself would itself seem inclined to fix the meaning of terms used in philosophy by appeal to their ordinary meanings, and I endorse that. Without at least a close connection to ordinary language, we couldn't say anything about what many terms mean in philosophy. What did Moore, qua fly in the fly bottle, or lecturer in the lecture hall, mean by the word "hand"? I am tempted to say: just the sort of thing we more or less always mean by it. There might be distinctive features of "philosophical" uses of the word "hand"; well, there might be distinctive features of the medical or literary or card-playing uses of the word. In none of these cases is a homonymous technical or logical or grammatical term invented with a stipulated meaning; they are all only explicable in terms of the ordinary use of the term, of which they are all also examples. It seems to me the counsel of desperation, or the counsel of thrall to an antecedent theory, to insist that Moore cannot in that context use the word "hand" or the word "here" at all, or that he cannot use them to mean what people ordinarily mean by them.

The confusion, I think, actually arises from the quite mistaken assumption that justification is required for knowledge, but also from the theory of perception that goes with it, according to which perception is pictorial and the justification of empirical claims (and hence their meaning), is construed in terms of pictorial accuracy or match between percept and object. (Also, the confusion arises from Wittgenstein's loathing for philosophy, which is a self-loathing.) Moore at a stroke formulates a direct realism and a theory of knowledge deleting the justification condition; these things need to be paired. No justification for *here is a hand*, in the context in which Moore produces it, or Austin's *lo, a pig,* is possible or appropriate; no self-presenting data undergird them, producing reasons or arguments or demonstrations of such things would usually be ridiculous. But we all know them perfectly well, because there's a reality out there we're all experiencing. "Immediately." "Directly." Or at any rate without screen or systematic intermediary.

And when Moore formulates it, he does it in the most compelling way possible: out of your ordinary experience right now. What I love about "here is a hand" is its pretension-puncturing power: its feet-on-the-ground sensibleness. That's precisely what we try to remove from it by reinterpreting philosophy talk as sub- or supra-sensible. Finally, someone said in philosophy what we all already believe; he just flat said it. It's the power of that which Wittgenstein and many others have tried to remove by making "here is a hand" unsayable. But it's not unsayable: look he just said it! He just really showed you the really real, and it was not a transcendental miracle but the most ordinary thing . . . in the world. *That* is the sort of person that you're disqualifying on the grounds that he's a metaphysician?

8.

Let's return to the initial claim that I can and should give evidence for m-sentences or simple empirical beliefs. The internalist about justification obviously cannot rest content with the mere assertion that I move from appearances to reality; he must also assert that this move confers justification on certain of my empirical claims. Justification, at least in part, and on an internalist conception, is a matter of being in a position to give reasons for a belief. Thus, the internalist is obliged to hold that, if I am reflective, I can give reasons to think that an empirical claim that I know to be true is true by an appeal to appearances (or seemings, sense data, phenomena). It is this claim that will be the subject of discussion: the claim not merely that I do move in some way from appearance to reality, but that, in order to be said to know some simple empirical proposition, I can and must be able to give reasons, and specifically reasons that are framed in terms of appearances and so forth.

Austin gives a famous battery of arguments in *Sense and Sensibilia* against the claim that I need to, or indeed can, give evidence or reasons for certain claims which I know to be true. He considers the very Moorish example, already introduced above, of a case wherein I claim "that is a pig" when a pig is in full view before me:

> The situation in which I could properly be said to have evidence for the statement that some animal is a pig is that, for example, in which the beast itself is not actually on view, but I can see plenty of pig-like marks on the ground outside its retreat. . . . But if the animal then emerges and stands there plainly in view, there is no longer any question of collecting evidence; its coming into view doesn't provide me with more evidence that it's a pig, I can now just see that it is; the question is settled.[43]

I do not give evidence, or have evidence, or have to provide evidence for what, in Austin's phrase "is going on under my nose." That I am certain about what is going on under my nose, that I know it, is the sort of situation that gives the terms "certainty" and "knowledge" their meaning; perhaps this is what Wittgenstein thinks as well, only it seems natural to draw the conclusion not that these aren't cases of knowledge, or that they're super-empirical or are not even beliefs, or are grammatical or logical propositions, but that they are paradigmatic cases of knowledge.

As it stands, we do not justify the claim that that's a pig by appeal to appearances in the described case. That is, the internalist account of justification in cases like this bears no relation to our actual practices: we do not, usually, provide justifications in such cases, and certainly we do not, as a rule, provide justifications by appeal to the contents of our own consciousness. If someone presses me on how I know that that's a pig, she will be merely flummoxed if I respond with "I am being appeared to pigly," or "I am having a pink patch in the upper left quadrant of my visual field." And if you think something like that makes anyone more certain of or more justified in believing anything about the world, I just say, "?"

The problem, I believe, infests every account that makes justification (warrant, reasons, indefeasibility, epistemic virtue, etc.) a necessary condition on knowledge. The advocate of a justification condition on knowledge is obliged to show either that we do or can or ought to justify such claims, or renounce the claim to be giving a reconstruction of practice. If he does renounce the claim to be giving a reconstruction of practice, then he is obliged to say what is wrong with our current practices with regard to knowledge: why we should, and how we could, institute a new practice. In addition, the justificationist program will now be profoundly revisionist about the current scope of human knowledge. That is, when people simply wave off the demand for a justification for "here is a hand" and the like, when they are both unable and unwilling to produce a justification in the envisaged style, the justificationist is going to have to hold that they do not know any of the simple empirical propositions they believe.

But to begin to see what has gone wrong with this view, consider how we would actually respond to the demand to justify the claim that "here is a pig" when there is a pig under our noses. To begin with, the demand is eccentric; it sounds like an aspersion on my sanity; I would probably respond with a raised eyebrow or an expression of exasperation or verbal abuse. But of course, these aren't justifications (at least not in the epistemological sense of "justification"). If for one reason or another I decided that a serious response was in order, I might simply gesture at the pig, or say "look!," just reiterating that this is a pig, which is to reject rather than satisfy the demand for a justification. But also that does show something about our actual practices of justification, when we do justify: my hand actually moves through space toward the external-world pig. Really, I have no idea why Western epistemology retreated inward like this; it's ridiculous. At any rate, in our practices, we do reject the demand for a justification in such cases, or to be more accurate, in such cases the demand for a justification simply does not arise.

Austin considers another, similar (m-sentence-type) case:

> If, for instance, someone remarks in casual conversation, "As a matter of fact I live in Oxford," the other party to the conversation may, if he finds it worth doing, verify the assertion; but the speaker, of course, has no need to do this—he knows it to be true (or, if he is lying, false). Strictly speaking, indeed, it is not that he has no need to verify his statement; the case is rather that, since he already knows it to be true, nothing whatever could count as his verifying it. Nor need it be true that he is in this position in virtue of having verified his assertion at some previous stage, for of how many people really, who know quite well where they live, could it be said that they have at any time verified that they live there? When would they be supposed to have done this? In what way? And why?[44]

One need not agree with Austin's "ordinary language" view about such terms as "verification" and "evidence" to take his point. That point is usually said to be that it only makes sense to talk about "verification" and "evidence" where there is an open question, a genuine doubt. In Ayer's reply to *Sense and Sensibilia*, I think he gets the better of this debate when he says "If I think I know that *p*, I am underplaying my hand, and so misleading my audience, if I say no more than that I have good evidence for *p*. It would, however, be rash to lay any weight upon this in the present context, since my knowing that *p* is certainly not inconsistent with my having good evidence for it."[45] This seems right. But even if we allow that I could have evidence about where I live and could verify where I live, the point is that I do not know where I live in virtue of any particular body of evidence, and certainly not in virtue of having entertained some particular appearances. In some ways, this is a better and more typical case of empirical knowledge than "here is a hand (pig)." In the case of "here is a hand" one can (sort of) understand the temptation to try to justify the claim in terms of appearances. "Here is a hand" is neatly indexed to a time and place; it reflects a momentary state of affairs. If there were any appearances bouncing around in this case, there would be a neat little sense datum bundled up with the claim.

But in virtue of what appearances, subjective experiences, or neurological events might I know where I live? In virtue of the whole series I had as I approached the place, negotiated with the landlord, moved in, and then failed to move out? If there were relevant appearances here, they would include more or less the entirety of the appearances I have had over the last x years. I might say that these appearances justify my claim. But certainly if you demand that I produce my justification, if you ask me how I know I live at . . . I simply cannot respond. Or if I respond by saying it has to do with all the appearances that have appeared to me over the last x years, doesn't this seem useless and doesn't the whole exercise begin to look bizarre, completely unrelated to how anyone actually does justify anything?

Of course, if I have to justify the claim that I live at . . . in virtue of all the appearances that have appeared to me over the last x years, then I am no longer appealing to anything that can plausibly be held to be self-justified, incorrigible, or self-presenting. Obviously I am now subject to mistakes about how things appeared to me years ago, and I am perfectly aware of this fact. (And consider some other examples from Moore, e.g., "I have never been to the moon.")

9.

Even if an appeal to appearances is precluded as bearing no relation to practice, I could produce propositions from which I could infer, for example, that here is a pig, and it is worth taking a moment to explore the question of whether these could be construed as justifications for the claim. (Here we momentarily leave behind the classical internalist program.) For example, I could infer that here is a pig from such claims as "there is a pig in that pen," "I am now looking at a pig," "the pig is oinking," and so on. I don't have to make "here is a pig" my epistemological bedrock. The point is that, when I decide to stop justifying in this way, rather than by a retreat to appearances, I am going to end up with a proposition with the same general status: a contingent, corrigible, empirical claim. As Wittgenstein puts it in On Certainty, I must "begin to trust somewhere."[46] If I am willing to start justifying at all I am going to have to stop somewhere. And if I stop without appealing to appearances, sensibilia, or whatever it may be, I will have an eminently corrigible empirical claim.

Again, one test of whether I know such an assertion as "I have never been to the moon," and whether it is part of my epistemological bedrock, is not that I can produce a justification (say, recite my itinerary for the last sixty years). The test is rather that I reject the demand for justification out of hand, that the demand is absurd. Only someone truly in the toils of a very bad theory would take such a rejection to show, on the one hand, that I must be justified after all, or on the other, that the proposition in question is one that cannot be known because it is a logical principle or a grammatical rule. Of course, in some cases where I do not produce a justification, I could, if pressed. And in some such cases, the justification of my belief might also describe its source. For example, I might know that the car is out of gas because the gauge points to "E," and I might look at you funny if you demanded a justification. But the point here is that the demand is appropriate epistemically; the claim is of a kind for which people normally do have and are willing to produce evidence. That is not the case with the claims I am now considering. I am not saying, when you ask me how I know that I have never been to the moon, that I am so obviously justified that I don't feel like producing my justification; I am saying that justification is not necessary, that the demand is inappropriate. I am rejecting meeting the demand as a requirement to show that I do know.

10.

The argument of the next several sections is a generalized attack on the epistemology of justification, which is historically associated with "methodological doubt." This is because the assumption that methodological doubt is legitimate leads to a picture in which we need, in order to have any knowledge at all, to start justifying our beliefs from the ground up. However, the notion of a purely methodological doubt is not a notion of doubt at all. That is, to doubt some proposition is either to believe it to be false, or to entertain it and fail to believe it. Thus, all doubts are somebody's doubts; all doubts are attitudes somebody really has. I would like to press the question of who is in fact capable of doubting what.

I use the term *faith* in what follows as synonymous with *unjustified belief*. This will annoy some specialists on the subject, and certainly some who use "faith" as a fine-grained theological notion. I think that even in the theological discussion, the notion of faith often includes the unjustifiedness of the articles of faith (though it does not always include that, e.g., in Aquinas). But I do not offer the notion of unjustified belief as an exegetical tool for any particular discussion of faith; if the reader prefers, she can regard my use of the term as a sheer stipulation. My argument, however, will be that faith in the present sense on certain matters is extremely difficult and not desirable to avoid. It will follow that, if what is ultimately desirable in the way of belief is knowledge (as I will argue later), faith can rise to the level of knowledge. If faith in that sense can rise to the level of knowledge, then justification is not logically necessary for knowledge.

The notion of faith as I make use of it here was developed most elaborately by Kierkegaard, James, and Santayana. Kierkegaard characterized faith as an objective uncertainty held fast in passionate inwardness.[47] I suggest that this is roughly what

James meant when he described faith as a believing attitude that is taken up in spite of the fact that our "merely logical intellects may not have been coerced" into the attitude in question.⁴⁸ James, too, centralizes the "emotional" or "passionate" in the matter of believing. At any rate, to have faith in the present sense is, roughly, to believe in the absence of justification, or much in excess to or independently of rational or empirical reasons.

The epistemology of justification holds that we ought to believe just what it is rational for us to believe, and that all assumptions should be subjected to rational scrutiny. Such a view informs the writings both of the rationalists and of the empiricists. Rationalists and empiricists converged on a search for indubitable and objective knowledge, and the former thus took a detour through skepticism (Descartes), while the latter sometimes remained there (Hume). Epistemology conceived as an abrogation of skepticism was rejected by both Kierkegaard and Santayana for roughly the same reasons. And these reasons turn on the notion of faith. To Kierkegaard, who had a supernatural view of man and the cosmos, the epistemology of justification seemed a betrayal of our nature as spiritual individuals, of the ultimacy of subjective experience, and of the emotional core of human belief. To Santayana, on his own account a naturalist and materialist, it appeared to be a misguided and finally impossible attempt to escape our own animality. But both men found hypocrisy at its heart; this style of epistemology insists that its proponent believes what he in fact fails to believe and fails to believe what he in fact believes. It tries to lop the rational from the emotive aspects of human experience. Both Santayana and Kierkegaard found in the epistemology of justification an attempt to leave behind what no person can leave behind and remain a person. If Moore or Diogenes or Johnson try to show us where our real commitments already lie, Kierkegaard and Santayana try to give us an account of why, as persons, our real commitments do lie there. And they try to show why we need not and should not violate those commitments in philosophy, just as we need not and perhaps even cannot violate them in our everyday lives. Well, as I say, philosophy *is* a sort of everyday life.

In an early work, Kierkegaard terms faith the opposite of doubt.⁴⁹ By this he does not mean simply that faith overcomes doubt (though, of course, in certain circumstances it does), nor that faith is a form of certainty while doubt is a form of uncertainty (though, of course, that may be true, if certainty is construed as a subjective state). Rather, in *Johannes Climacus or, De Omnibus Dubitandum Est*, Kierkegaard is concerned with the question of whether a philosopher can begin with doubt, and, if so, whether and how she proceeds after she has doubted.

We could, in other words, come to see what knowledge (if any) we possess, by this technique: doubt everything, or at least everything that we can find a reason to doubt or a strategy for doubting, and see to what extent rational justificatory activities can remove our doubts. Where such activities indeed remove doubt, there we have knowledge. Though one rarely, these days, finds philosophers engaged in the task of doubting everything that can be doubted, epistemology is still dominated by this picture of its project. When philosophers argue over whether a belief is justified in virtue of its coherence within an explanatory structure or rather in virtue of its relation to indubitable or prima facie justified basic beliefs or by social factors such as what the experts say, or by the epistemic virtues of the believer, they are not only arguing about justification. They are arguing about what it would be a good thing to believe and how it would be good to come to believe it. What connects them to the tradition that Kierkegaard and Santayana reject is the assumption (it is very rarely more than that) that these are precisely the same thing, that it is a good thing to believe *p* if and only if one is justified in believing *p* or is in a position objectively to remove doubt about it.

11.

In *Fear and Trembling*, Kierkegaard expresses himself on the matter with characteristic tartness:

> Every speculative price-fixer who conscientiously directs attention to the significant march of modern philosophy, every Privatdocent, tutor, and student, every crofter and cottar in philosophy, is not content with doubting everything but goes further. Perhaps it would be untimely and ill-timed to ask them where they are going, but surely it is courteous and unobtrusive to regard it as certain that they have doubted everything, since otherwise it would be a queer thing for them to be going further. This preliminary movement they have therefore all of them made, and presumably with such ease that they do not find it necessary to let drop a word about the how; for not even he who anxiously and with deep concern sought a little enlightenment was able to find any such thing, any guiding sign, any little dietetic prescription, as to how one was to comport oneself in supporting this prodigious task.[50]

As he does in many places in his writings where this issue surfaces, Kierkegaard goes on to describe universal doubt as something that could be achieved only by a lifetime's exertion, and perhaps not even then. And were one to make this exertion, to spend a life in pursuit of doubt, one would have no time or energy or ability left for the equally prodigious task of extricating oneself.

Now as we have seen, the proponent of justificationism might reply that it is not as an individual human being that he doubts everything or demands that everything be subjected to rational scrutiny (otherwise he could hardly also continue to live and philosophize), but that as a philosopher he finds it necessary to clarify just what it is he does know. Hume, raising doubts about the supposed necessary connection of cause and effect, wrote as follows: "My practice, you say, refutes my doubts. But you mistake the purport of my question. As an agent I am quite satisfied in the point; but as a philosopher, who has some share of curiosity, I will not say scepticism, I want to learn the foundation of this inference."[51]

Now this distinction between agents and philosophers is just what Kierkegaard is puzzled about. When one acts qua philosopher has one ceased to act qua agent? Has one, in Kierkegaard's terms, ceased to be a human being and become, say, philosophy itself? Even supposing that such a metamorphosis were possible, it would divide a person against herself; it would introduce systematically a deep doxastic dissonance—believing and disbelieving the very same things at the same time, or waffling back and forth—with regard to a whole series of things, insofar it is the very same candidates for belief which we approach as agents and philosophers. And it would divide one's cognitive from one's affective faculties. As a philosopher, Hume doubts the necessary relation of cause and effect; he doubts it from the "external" point of view. But as an agent he all the time believes it, because he needs to. The claims in question simply contradict one another. So Hume is in the business of cultivating quite consciously his own dissonant state, of denying what he believes and believing what he denies.

It is Kierkegaard's point that, if one enters deeply and earnestly into doubt, one will find it impossible to begin to philosophize one's way out of doubt. If one were to genuinely doubt the existence of the external world, according to Kierkegaard, one could not in fact establish that it exists. It is plausible to view Descartes's own attempts to extricate himself from doubt as either abject failures or as more or less wholly disingenuous. His "deduction" of God's existence from his own ideas is notoriously fallacious. And it is a rather odd coincidence that Descartes ends up more or less exactly where he began: believing he is sitting by the fire, believing that the Christian God exists, and so forth. Here it is possible to see a dance of rationalization rather than of rationality. Descartes winds up generating arguments, more or less unconvincing, for positions to which he never ceased to be passionately committed. But it is in the passionate commitment that the belief is contained; to believe something is precisely to commit oneself to its truth; the arguments designed to abrogate skepticism only reinforce belief after the fact. What Kierkegaard is claiming is that we need to be honest with ourselves about the sources of our beliefs, that the epistemology of justification "rationally reconstructs" a fundamentally irrational process.

12.

In *Scepticism and Animal Faith*, Santayana goes so far as to assert that all knowledge is faith precisely because we are never in a position decisively to refute skepticism, that is, to remove objective uncertainty. Santayana sets out the familiar skeptical arguments elaborately, and in fact endorses their conclusions. That is, he affirms that we are in a position, as far as the exercise of reason with no assumptions is concerned, of radical and unrelievable doubt as to the existence of the external world, the deliverances of memory, even as to the existence or at least the nature of our selves. Or rather, if we were in fact creatures that generated beliefs by the exercise of reason with no assumptions, our doubts would be radical and unrelievable. But as agents, as passionate, creatures entangled in an actual world, we happen in fact to be under no serious doubt about these things. Santayana says: "the scepticism I am defending is not meant to be merely provisional; its just conclusions will remain fixed, to remind me perpetually that all alleged knowledge of matters of fact is faith only."[52] "Faith only" might be too strong here; but all knowledge of matters of fact rests finally on assumptions that cannot be justified; or rather, it rests on experiences of connection or the reality of nondistinctness from the world.

Every belief is someone's belief; every enduring belief consists of a relation (a relation of passionate commitment) of a particular agent to a situation, even in the case of a philosopher. For Kierkegaard even the philosopher retains an irremediable inwardness, the subjectivity of a spirit. For Santayana, all of us, even philosophers, remain individual organisms, permeated with animal needs and endowed with specific faculties for their satisfaction. I certainly am more in sympathy with Santayana's naturalistic picture of doxastic agents. But what the views have in common epistemologically is equally clear: human beings are not the sort of things by or for whom "objective" certainty can be achieved employing no assumptions, or even the sorts of things that could hope to believe only what we are justified in believing; human belief is at base the emotional commitment of an animal in an environment.

One way to view the faith on which methodological doubt and, in general, the epistemology of justification, rests is that it is faith in the truth: faith that we can find the truth and that we ought to try. I share this faith, but I simply deny that the procedures laid out in various theories of justification provide the only means by which the truth can legitimately be arrived at. It is faith in the truth on which science, on a certain picture of science, depends. The imperative to believe only what we are justified in believing only makes sense if we can find the truth by the exercise of reason and if the truth thus found is of paramount importance. This is a point that was made forcibly by Nietzsche:

> In science convictions have no rights of citizenship, as one says with good reason. Only when they decide to descend to the modesty of hypotheses, of a provisional experimental point of view, of a regulative fiction, they may be granted admission and even a certain value in the realm of knowl-

edge—though always with the restriction that they remain under police supervision, under the police of mistrust.—But does this not mean, if you consider it more precisely, that a conviction may obtain admission to science only when it ceases to be a conviction? Would it not be the first step in the discipline of the scientific spirit that one would not permit oneself any more convictions?

Probably this is so; only we still have to ask: To make it possible for this discipline to begin, must there not be some prior conviction—even one that is so commanding and unconditional that it sacrifices all other convictions to itself? We see that science also rests on faith; there is simply no science "without presuppositions." The question whether truth is needed must not only have been affirmed in advance, but affirmed to such a degree that the principle, the faith, the conviction finds expression: "Nothing is needed more than truth, and in relation to it everything else has only second-rate value."[53]

And James makes exactly the same point:

Our belief in truth itself, for instance, that there is a truth, and that our minds and it are made for each other—what is it but passionate affirmation of desire, in which our social system backs us up? We want to have the truth; we want to believe that our experiments and studies and discussions must put us in a continually better and better position towards it; and on this line we agree to fight out our thinking lives. But if a Pyrrhonistic sceptic asks us how we know all this, can our logic find a reply? No! certainly it cannot. It is just one volition against another—we willing to go in for life upon a trust or assumption which he, for his part, does not care to make.[54]

Now when science sets up hypotheses, the scientist withholds his assent and maintains a healthy doubt. At least, that is the ideal within a certain vision of the scientific project. (As James says, it is far more likely that the scientist sets out to confirm a claim to which he is already passionately committed.) But what James and Nietzsche assert, and I should think this could hardly be denied, is that underlying this doubt, or the exquisite suspension between belief and disbelief which turns a claim into an hypothesis, there is a deeper faith, a faith that there is a truth of the matter, that it is possible and also desirable to reach it. To put it in my terms, it is the faith that we are embedded in a world to which we are connected by many strands, that it and we are not fully distinct, and that we are built to know it. I am simply arguing that we ought to acknowledge that we do have this faith. And the situation is irremediable; we could not leave this faith behind or endorse it without begging the question; it is a presupposition of any argument. Thus, there is, in Nietzsche's terms, no science without presuppositions, without passionate commitments.

Nietzsche asserts that even if we were to accept the scientist as a model of how we ought to conduct ourselves as believing beings, we would still not be able to expunge faith. The faith of the scientist consists of precisely those assumptions which allow science to arise and which keep it in operation. It should be no surprise that the continuing success of science seems to "confirm" that fundamental faith.

On this matter, James's distinction between two epistemological imperatives is relevant. He distinguishes between the desire to know the truth and the desire to avoid error. These, as he points out, are by no means two ways of stating the same goal; the former might invite us to believe what we cannot demonstrate to be the truth, in order to give ourselves some chance at arriving at the truth, while the latter would have us suspend judgement until good enough reason can be produced. James sets out this point in one of the most disarming and characteristic passages in all his writings:

> We must remember that these feelings of our duty about either truth or error are in any case only expressions of our passional life. Biologically considered, our minds are as ready to grind out falsehood as veracity, and he who says, "Better go without belief forever than believe a lie!" merely shows his own preponderant horror of becoming a dupe. . . . For my own part, I have also a horror of being duped; but I can believe that worse things than being duped may happen to a man in this world. . . . Our errors are surely not such awfully solemn things. In a world where we are so certain to incur them in spite of all our caution, a certain lightness of heart seems healthier than excessive nervousness on their behalf.[55]

To avoid error, the skeptic withholds assent. But the epistemological imperative remains in the background as an unstated but obviously important assumption. Nor can this assumption stand aloofly off as the skeptic's only faith. For the very notions of truth and error presuppose the whole fundamental machinery of logic, of the principle of noncontradiction and its elaborations and kindred principles.

13.

For both James and Nietzsche, the claim that we ought to believe all and only what we are justified in believing, or all and only what it would be rational to believe, is a moral claim. I think this is plausible. The epistemology of justification, in both its traditional and its contemporary guises, depends on a certain moral injunction concerning honesty. Here is a passage James quotes from Thomas Huxley: "My only consolation lies in the reflection that, however bad our posterity may become, so far as they hold by the plain rule of not pretending to believe what they have no reason to believe, because it may be to their advantage so to pretend, they will not have reached the lowest depth of immorality."[56] Now as I hope we have seen, it is perhaps less easy than Huxley imagined to believe only what we have good reason to believe, and to eliminate the element of desire from belief. Indeed, desire is a way situations get reconfigured, by which we launch ourselves outward toward what we desire: it is prehensile, we might say; it directs understanding or drags it into the world. But what is relevant here is Huxley's moral outrage, the feeling that faith is not, or is not only, an intellectual failing, but an ethical one.

James quotes William Clifford to similar effect: "If a belief has been accepted on insufficient evidence [even if it is true] the pleasure is a stolen one. . . . It is sinful because it is stolen in defiance of our duty to mankind." James offers the following reply:

> Science herself consults the heart when she lays it down that the infinite ascertainment of fact and correction of false belief are the supreme goods for man. Challenge that statement, and science can only repeat it oracularly, or else prove it by showing that such ascertainment and correction brings man all sorts of other goods which man's heart in turn declares. . . . If your heart does not want a world of moral reality, your head will surely never make you believe in one. . . . Moral scepticism can no more be refuted or proved by logic than intellectual scepticism can. When we stick to it that there is truth (be it of either kind), we do so with our whole nature, and resolve to stand or fall by the results.[57]

To believe without reasoned justification is supposed by those whom James refers to as "logicians," and to whom I have been referring as proponents of justification, to be "sinful."

This is a particularly apt turn of phrase with regard to Nietzsche's formulation of the problem, wherein the faith of the epistemology of justification is a particular faith, namely, and surprisingly enough, Christian faith. Now James proposes that science can only justify its insistence on justification by pointing to its utility. Nietzsche, on the other hand, claims that the justification of belief and the quest for certainty (in Dewey's famous phrase) do not have the sort of utility that is often claimed for them. And indeed this is the case, as perhaps someone like Clifford would admit. It can be useful to believe a truth, on occasion, and just as useful on other occasions to believe a falsehood.

> What do you know in advance of the character of existence to be able to decide whether the greater advantage is on the side of the unconditionally

mistrustful or of the unconditionally trusting? But if both should be required, much trust as well as much mistrust, from where would science then be permitted to take its unconditional faith or conviction on which it rests, that truth is more important than any other thing, including every other conviction? Precisely this conviction could never have come into being if both truth and untruth constantly proved to be useful, which is the case. Thus—the faith in science, which after all exists undeniably, cannot owe its origin to such a calculus of utility; it must have arisen in spite of the fact that the disutility and dangerousness of "the will to truth," of "truth at any price" is proved to it constantly.... Consequently, "will to truth" does not mean "I will not allow myself to be deceived" but—there is no alternative—"I will not deceive, not even myself"; and with that we stand on moral ground.[58]

Thus, the fundamental faith of "science," or "the logician" is not epistemological at all, but moral. And further, according to Nietzsche, it is Christian morality (which he also describes as the faith of Plato), the morality of an otherworldly realm, the morality the source of which declares "I am the way, the truth," that informs the epistemology of mistrust or the quest for certainty.

But conceived as the injunction that one should not deceive oneself, the epistemology of justification is in one sense an abject failure. That is, it can easily lead precisely to systematic self-deception; it can lead to the view that one believes only what it is reasonable to believe and not at all what one would like to believe. To Kierkegaard the whole thing appears to be rather bathetic. He says: "All scepticism is a kind of idealism.... There is no special difficulty connected with being an idealist in imagination; but to exist as an idealist is an extremely strenuous task, because existence itself constitutes a hindrance and an objection.... to understand everything except one's own self is very comical."[59]

14.

Hence, I propose the following analysis of "S knows that p":

(1) It is true that p.

(2) S believes that p.

Each of the two conditions is necessary; together, they are sufficient.

Now, it is sometimes blithely claimed at the outset of a consideration of knowledge that our practices or our intuitions or our preanalytic commitments show that we are already committed to a distinction between knowledge and true belief. Whatever may be the fact of the conceptual matter, I will argue that we are not preanalytically committed to any such thing. I think, I must say, that philosophy professors often come by their intuitions in the intro course they took when they were 18, that is, from other philosophy professors. Now, people have often felt it unnecessary to justify the justification condition on knowledge; they usually appeal in a perfunctory way to our alleged intuitions, along these lines: we do not count a lucky guess as knowledge, so something besides truth and belief is required. I will attempt to show that our practices are, at best, equivocal in this regard. Then I will move beyond an appeal to intuition to mount a conceptual case for the view that propositional knowledge is mere true belief. But for the present, I will often appeal to "what we would say" in certain cases.

To believe, again, is to commit oneself to the truth of some truth-value-bearer. On this and related pictures of belief, it is clear what strategy will be used to generate counterexamples to the claim that knowledge is merely true belief. Such examples arise in circumstances in which the connection between the belief or the believer and the truth of the believed proposition is not of the right kind. Consider, then, the following counterexamples to the claim that knowledge is merely true belief:

(1) I dream that there is an odd number of hydrogen atoms in the universe. On that basis, and for no other reason, I come to believe that it is true. (It is true.)

(2) I close my eyes, put my finger on the name of a horse on the racing form, and then bet the baby that the horse to whose name I have pointed to will win the fifth race. (The horse does, indeed, win the race.)

(3) While I sleep, I am anesthetized and whisked away to an operating room, where a mad scientist performs a surgical procedure on my brain. I am returned to my bed, and I awake to find myself disposed to assent to an unproven mathematical conjecture, such as the Quillen-Lichtenbaum conjecture. (It is destined to be proven correct in a century or two.)

(4) I come to believe on the basis of reading some tea leaves that the swallows have returned to Capistrano. Or take a case of an omen or a divination or an astrological forecast to the same effect. On the present account, such "occult" phenomena are, in principle, as capable of yielding knowledge as is the most careful observation. It need only be the case that the palm or the crystal ball or the tea leaves lead their interpreter to believe something that happens to be true.

In case (3) as described we have, I agree, a deep-seated tendency to deny that the subject knows that the Quillen-Lichtenbaum conjecture is true, whatever the subject himself ("I") might claim. Nevertheless, the case itself is severely underdescribed. For example, am I supposed to know other propositions about mathematics, which I bring to bear on my claim about the conjecture? Do I, for example, know what a spectral sequence, or even a prime number, is? The strongest way to frame the counterexample, one which makes it clear that the belief is not justified on any account of justification, is to isolate the belief completely, to suppose that I am a mathematical naïf. But a problem arises here, namely: is this a case of belief?

In the case as described, I wind up, I know not how, with a disposition to assent, say to nod or produce some conventional sign of agreement, when someone utters the sentence "the Quillen-Lichtenbaum conjecture is true." But if this is to be a case of belief, that cannot be the whole story. Such a disposition could be produced, for example, in someone—or perhaps some animal—who spoke no English and had no knowledge of mathematics, by a schedule of reinforcement. (We starve the subject and then begin to feed him whenever he produces the desired response.) In such a case, it is surely misleading to say that the subject believes that the Quillen-Lichtenbaum conjecture is true. And in a case where I just started saying "the Quillen-Lichtenbaum conjecture is true" out of the blue, and I could not state the conjecture, or say what its terms mean, the proper response would be "you said it, but you didn't even know what it meant: you don't believe any such thing."

And consider also example (2). Here we might think about whether I have a sufficient degree of commitment to the proposition that the horse will win the race to be said correctly to believe it. Now, it is perfectly possible for me to act as though I believe something (say, by betting the baby on it) when, in fact, I do not believe it. (Every characterization of belief, for example, some pragmatist and behaviorist accounts, which is not compatible with this insight is false.) If I am a compulsive gambler, I may look for some technique to pick horses without having any pronounced confidence that the technique is a good way to pick winners, or that any particular application of the technique will lead to the desired result. I may bet in despair, as it were; indeed, I suppose that is fairly typical of the veteran bettor or compulsive gambler. In such a case, I may act as though the proposition is true without believing it. Nor is it enough to believe that it is probable that the horse will win; that is not to believe that the horse will win. I have got to commit myself to the truth of that claim. It is fair, I think, to say that people rarely do that on the basis of their own guesses, at least in cases where they are aware that they are guessing.

So we need, on any account of knowledge, to have a sufficiently rich notion of belief to capture what is missing in cases such as these. That is, to formulate the case described in (3) in such a way that it counts as a counterexample to the view that knowledge is merely true belief, we must give a more substantive sense to belief than mere disposition to assent, and in case (2) we must give a more substantive sense to belief than a disposition to act in other ways as though a proposition is true. However, I need a sufficiently impoverished notion of belief to keep my view from collapsing into triviality, as it would do if I claimed that anything that counted as a belief was ipso facto justified. Counting (2) and (3) as cases of knowledge will seem somewhat (though only somewhat) less implausible if they are framed in terms of belief rather than mere disposition to assent or to act as though committed to the truth of some proposition.

15.

I would like briefly to offer some counterexamples to the claim that knowledge is justified true belief. They are cases where it seems legitimate to reject the demand for a justification, cases where the demand seems inappropriate.

(a) Again, many typical cases of knowledge about empirical states of affairs, such as those expressed by m-sentences, are counterexamples here. That is, it is quite within the bounds of practical propriety to laugh off a demand to say how you know where you live or that there's a pig under your nose. But "Here is a hand," "There is a pig," "I live in Pennsylvania," "I have never been to the moon" show, I think, that various strategies to finesse the unusual examples will not issue in a satisfactory theory of knowledge.

(b) We often reject the last in a sequence of demands for a justification—pressed by a young child, for example, with a series of "whys"—by claiming that no further justification is needed.

(c) Some problems in a variety of disciplines have been solved in what is sometimes termed "a flash of insight," as when a mathematician who has been struggling with a problem suddenly "sees" the solution. Kepler describes himself as having "guessed" the laws of nature, and many of Einstein's ideas were experimentally justified only long after they had been intuited.[60]

(d) Here is another interesting case: that of properly religious faith. Let's consider religious faith to be belief that God exists that is indifferent to any argument or objective evidence on either side of the question. Then if we countenance the claim that religious faith could constitute knowledge if indeed God exists, we at once admit that not all knowledge is justified belief. And again, it is hard to see what makes this a case of knowledge (if it is) except that it is a case of true belief. I said at the beginning that no philosopher has explicitly held that knowledge is merely true belief.[61] But any philosopher who holds that religious faith in this sense can rise to the level of knowledge is obliged to hold that not all knowledge is justified belief. (James may be a case in point, though Kierkegaard is not.) Or think of more mundane cases of faith, such as the faith we occasionally repose in persons. A father whose son is accused of murder might believe, in the face of overwhelming evidence, that his son is innocent. Asked how he knows, he responds impatiently that he just does. Let us stipulate that his son is, indeed, innocent. If this is a case of knowledge (as the father most assuredly believes) then not all knowledge is justified belief.

(e) Here is another sort of case in which we might recognize that someone has knowledge without justification. Consider circumstances in which it is appropriate to produce the utterance "I knew it all along." On some occasions, this means that though I believed something during a certain segment of time t (say, that Nixon was involved in the Watergate coverup), a justification of it was not available to me at t. At $t + 1$ I come to a justification for my belief, perhaps by reading the *Washington Post*. Then I might say that I knew it all along. In this case, though my belief comes at $t + 1$ to be justified, it is perfectly natural to say I knew it at t. This seems to me to mean that at t I believed it, and at t it was true.

Even in cases such as these, we don't simply find ourselves believing something without any history or cause of our coming to believe it. For example, in the case of the flash of insight there is a process of inquiry in the context of which the belief is generated, though we are supposing that nothing in that inquiry entails the solution one proposes. In the case of religious faith, the belief is created and sustained by an emotional commitment to the truth of the believed claim, and by a community of believers. But if these sorts of processes count as justifications on the view of a proponent of the justificationism, it is hard to see what beliefs are not justified. If the father can be justified in believing his son innocent in the face of overwhelming evidence, then the notion of justification has been weakened to such a great extent that its continuing relevance to the theory of knowledge is questionable

And notice that if we admit the case of faith in a person, it will cut equally against internalist and externalist pictures of justification. For example, suppose that we are reliabilists; we hold that a belief is known if it is true and reached by a belief-forming mechanism that yields true beliefs most of the time. Surely, we cannot account for this case, because believing in the teeth of the evidence could not be a reliable belief-forming mechanism. (Of course, the reliabilist can simply deny that this is a case of knowledge, or that faith ever constitutes knowledge.) Indeed, I suppose that an externalist could be fairly sanguine about the whole of the preceding discussion (and I harbor no illusions that the externalist will cease to be sanguine after seeing the examples). A reliabilist can account for the intuitive scientist or mathematician (as long as her guesses are right more often than not, or if some particular answer is the result of a mechanism with a reliable propensity). And the reliabilist is probably in far better shape than the internalist with regard to simple judgements of perception. But the cases of faith are far more difficult. Consider religious faith, for example. Here we are dealing with cosmological beliefs, beliefs about what the universe as a whole is like. As Hume might have remarked, it is awfully hard to see which processes for generating beliefs about what universes as a whole are like could possibly be reliable, since we have only one universe to observe. That goes for materialism, or for any cosmology. If reliabilism is right, then I think no one does know any general proposition about the nature of the universe as a whole to be true, whether the cosmology is theistic or atheistic, spiritualist or materialist. Of course, that might be the right result.

16.

It may well be asked, however, how the present account is going to deal with cases such as those with which I started. Now I suspect that the proponent of the view that knowledge is at least justified true belief is simply going to deny that cases like (a) to (e) are cases of knowledge. Likewise, I am simply going to affirm that cases like (1) to (4) are cases of knowledge, if they are described so that they are cases of belief. Notice, however, that, if someone claims to know something that I do not believe to be true, or about which I have no opinion, it may be perfectly legitimate for me to deny the knowledge-claim when the claimant cannot produce good reasons. That is, it may be perfectly legitimate to deny that the claim is true, or at any rate to suspend belief about it, until good reasons to suppose that it is true have been produced. And in other cases it may be legitimate for me to deny that the claim is believed.

One way to put my point is that justification is a criterion, though not a logically necessary condition, of knowledge. Perhaps different theories of justification provide different such criteria, and, if so, they are not necessarily incompatible with one another. Let us take a criterion, roughly, to be a test of whether an item has some property, a test that we can apply if we are in doubt as to whether the item has that property or not. For example, it is a criterion for something to be gold that it yields a certain characteristic taste when bitten. In cases where we are in doubt about whether something is gold or not, we may employ this criterion in deciding the matter. But it is hardly a logically necessary condition of something's being gold that it yields this taste when bitten. To see this, notice that, in a possible world in which the taste apparatus of persons is differently configured, gold would not yield the taste it does yield in this world. By contrast, the fact that an item has the atomic number 79 is a necessary condition for it to count as gold. Again, I claim that justification is a criterion for knowledge in the sense that, if the case is doubtful, the request for a justification acts as a test of whether S knows that p because it describes the process by which S might test p for truth, and hence by which I might test it as well. But justification is not a logically necessary condition of knowledge.

Nevertheless the position that (1) to (4) count as cases of knowledge if they count as cases of belief sounds like rank irrationalism, like an argument for claiming to know anything you please on any grounds whatever, or on no grounds at all. It sounds like a defense of mysticism and obscurantism, of irresponsibility in inquiry, of charlatanry and quackery of all kinds. It seems that, on the present account, there is nothing wrong with coming to believe something on the basis of dreams, guesses, divinations. In fact, however, this charge is misplaced. There is sometimes something wrong with such belief-generating strategies on the present account: they yield beliefs that are not justified.

We should ask just what the activity of justification is. The practice of justification, I think, fundamentally consists in the attempt to ascertain or confirm whether some proposition is true. Now there is wide agreement among proponents of foundationalist, reliabilist, and even coherentist and virtue-oriented accounts of justification that justification must be truth conducive, that is, that there must be reason to think that beliefs that are justified on any adequate account must be likely to be true. This indicates, though it hardly proves, that justification is subordinate to truth, that our epistemic goal is true belief, while justification is a means by which we reach this goal and a means by which we confirm that this goal has been reached.

My opponents and I would agree that knowledge is a valuable thing. To my way of thinking, that means that *in every matter with which we are epistemically concerned, we ought to believe all and only what is true.* On the present account, any process by which we come to believe the truth is a process by which we gain knowledge. Now to the extent that careful argumentation and empirical observation are superior to dreams, guesses, or divinations in this regard, on the present account there is every reason in the world to pursue the former and neglect the latter. Hence, the claim that knowledge is merely true belief is hardly a prescription for epistemological chaos. (Rather, it is a plea for epistemological pluralism.)

Think of the circumstances in which it is in fact appropriate to press the question of how someone knows something. First of all, such a query is not usually made in circumstances in which the belief is not controversial or obscure. If someone claims to know that 2 + 2 = 4 or that the sky is blue on a sunny day, it would be odd, to say the least, in typical circumstances, to ask how she knows it. But if she claims to know that the Quillen-Lichtenbaum conjecture is true, or that there are hippopotami in Madagascar, or that Fred will be the next president, then it may be appropriate to ask how she knows; that is, the criterion of justification comes into play. Notice that in the usual case, if I already believe that there are hippopotami in Madagascar, I will not press the query. This indicates that, in the usual case, I am trying to ascertain whether the claim is true by asking for a justification. But if I do not know whether the claim is true, I may well ask "How do you *know*?" or, with a shift in emphasis, "How do *you* know?" "Professor Ersatz gave a proof in his recent article"; "Hippopotami are indigenous to tropical climes"; "The Democrats have no viable contenders." These are replies to the first sort of question. The second asks more specifically about the claimant's access to the truth of the matter. "Ersatz demonstrated it to me in the most convincing way"; "I just read an article in National Geographic"; "None of the touted candidates looks very formidable to me." In either case, the process of giving a justification can be plausibly construed as giving reasons to believe the claim is true. On the present view, then, such responses are indeed attempts to establish knowledge-claims. But the demand for a justification operates as a pragmatic rather than as a conceptual restraint. That is, justification is a practice or group of practices, or series or array or thicket of practices, that have as their goal to show that one of the conceptual conditions of knowledge (truth) is met.

When someone claims to know something, and we ask how she knows it, when we demand a justification, we may be doing one of two things. First, we may be attempting to establish whether she does know it, or rather only believes it. That is to say that we may be trying to establish whether the believed proposition is true. Second, we may be trying to assess whether she believes what she has good reasons to believe. This will in turn affect our assessment of her further claims to know, which may be evaluated in the same way, and so forth.

The advantage of the present over the traditional view is that it can allow that there is knowledge that is not constructed with the use of and cannot be manipulated with the tools provided by theories of rational justification. This point, I think, follows from the discussions of skepticism and of veridical experience in the last two chapters. Problems are solved in a variety of ways, ranging from the reliable and rational to the perfectly inexplicable. We should not falsify our own intellectual lives in a philosophical reconstruction of how those lives are conducted by pretending that knowledge always proceeds along some orderly path of justification. We need no belief police.

17.

So we might think of a theory of epistemic justification as doing two things: (a) giving general procedures for inquiry, and (b) evaluating the productions of inquiry, that is, particular beliefs. A belief, then, is justified if it is produced by a correct procedure for inquiry, and to say that a belief is justified is to evaluate it positively along epistemic lines. I regard both projects as worthwhile, though I also think the ways they have been pursued in the tradition are . . . stunted and unreal. My claim here is that an account of justification is not strictly part of the theory of knowledge. Also, once these things are detached, there is no pressure to provide a univocal account of justification: a belief is justified or not by *whatever* considerations bear on its truth.

It is widely held that our epistemic goal with regard to particular propositions is achieving true beliefs and avoiding false ones about propositions with which we are epistemically concerned. And it is widely admitted that on any good account of justification, there must be reason to think that the beliefs justified on the account are likely to be true. Indeed, proponents of all the major conceptions of justification hold this position. For example, the foundationalist Paul Moser writes:

> [E]pistemic justification is essentially related to the so-called cognitive goal of truth, insofar as an individual belief is epistemically justified only if it is appropriately directed toward the goal of truth. More specifically, on the present conception, one is epistemically justified in believing a proposition only if one has good reason to believe it is true.[62]

And the coherentist Laurence BonJour puts it even more strongly:

> If epistemic justification were not conducive to truth in this way, if finding epistemically justified beliefs did not substantially increase the likelihood of finding true ones, epistemic justification would be irrelevant to our main cognitive goal and of dubious worth. It is only if we have some reason to think that epistemic justification constitutes a path to truth that we as cognitive human beings have any motive for preferring epistemically justified beliefs to epistemically unjustified ones. Epistemic justification is therefore in the final analysis only an instrumental value, not an intrinsic one.[63]

In fact, it is often enough taken to be the distinguishing mark of the fact that we are epistemically concerned with a proposition that we are concerned with its truth or falsity. That is what, on the view of many philosophers, distinguishes epistemic from moral or prudential constraints on belief, what distinguishes inquiry from other belief-generating procedures. (My view is that there are no nonepistemic belief-generating procedures in this sense. That fact merely underscores the present point.) The function of the concept of "knowledge," I believe, is to pick out the epistemic goal with regard to particular claims. It would follow that, if a philosopher holds that the epistemic *telos* is true belief, that philosopher implicitly commits himself, his own asseverations to the contrary, to the view that knowledge is merely true belief.

Another way of putting the matter is like this. If we describe justification as of merely instrumental value with regard to arriving at truth, as BonJour does explicitly, we can no longer maintain both that knowledge is the *telos* of inquiry and that justification is a necessary condition of knowledge. So if justification is demanded because it is instrumental to true belief, it should not also be maintained that knowledge is justified true belief. This has become known as the "swamping problem," which is usually framed as the question of what *value* justification adds to true belief, to which I answer: none at all. Our epistemic goal with regard to any proposition/belief/sentence and so on has been met if we believe it and it is true. We might have other goals, for example, continuing to believe truly, or being rational agents (that goal would be highly overrated, or self-deluded). But notice, if knowledge is merely true belief, we have every reason to want to continue to believe true things, and to use whatever sorts of procedures would help that happen. We are perfectly reliable, and our beliefs continue to track reality, and we are good epistemic agents, to the extent this continues. What it means to have an epistemic virtue or a good argument: both are explicable only in that our goal in every case is to believe truly.[64] This goal is built into the very nature of belief, which is taking-to-be-true.

The swamping problem helped drive the rise of virtue epistemology. But virtue epistemology could only return a third condition to knowledge by making knowledge reached from a virtuous (fair minded, for example) disposition a condition independent of truth, or not defined in terms of truth. This is implausible. We would like to have the intellectual virtues, and we ought to have the intellectual virtues, just to the extent that the virtues are better than the epistemic vices for generating true beliefs. If it were the case that self-deception led to truth more often than not, for example, then we should go ahead and deceive ourselves. (Well, then we wouldn't be deceiving ourselves after all.) If listening to people with expertise led you wrong most of the time, there'd be no virtue in it; indeed, we'd have to rethink who is an expert. It's only because or insofar as expertise is truth-conducive that we should listen to experts. And so for anything we might conceive as an epistemic virtue or good social procedures for knowledge.

Knowledge, in short, is the overarching purpose of inquiry, and hence is identical to believing the truth. If we want to withhold the term "knowledge" from mere true belief, but also want to hold that mere true belief is the purpose of inquiry, then I suggest that what remains is a mere verbal dispute. That is, if we treat mere true belief as the purpose of inquiry, but do not equate it with knowledge, then I do not think that knowledge is any longer central to normative epistemology. And I would insist that we are not going to understand what "knowledge" means in the tradition, in Plato and Descartes, for example, if we do not regard them as holding knowledge to be the goal of inquiry. In fact, if it is allowed that mere true belief is the *telos* of inquiry, but asserted that we should still reserve the term "knowledge" for justified true belief (and perhaps something more), I think that "knowledge" will now merely be a technical term with a stipulated definition. And I do not think it will be central to epistemology, since it no longer represents our epistemic goal. And the stipulated definition will either be redundant (if justification is held to be truth conducive) or, as I will argue, incoherent (if it is not).

18.

As you might imagine by now, I regard externalism with some sympathy as an approach to theory of justification. I believe that an agent can be justified in believing p in virtue of facts of which the agent is not aware. In particular, I think some version of reliabilism of the sort endorsed by Goldman is very compelling. I think that internalist pictures of justification cannot count most very simple empirical beliefs of the sort captured in m-sentences as justified. But such beliefs are, I think, when true, paradigm cases of knowledge. Various kinds of epistemological internalism presuppose that there is an internal component of veridical experience which is necessary in order to have the experience in question and which is epistemically available to the doxastic agent. But, as I have argued, there are no good reasons to accept this claim, and many good reasons to reject it. So I regard the reliabilist program as compelling, particularly with regard to propositions such as "Here is a hand," and "I live in Oxford," since one could be a reliabilist and not accept internalism with regard to veridical experience.

For example, Goldman's view about justification is roughly this: a system of justificatory rules is right just if it permits certain psychological processes that result in the generation of true beliefs in some high ratio of circumstances.[65] At a minimum, such a ratio must be more than .5. But I think we have already seen reasons to believe that reliabilism could not possibly yield a necessary condition for knowledge. That is because reliabilism stakes everything on truth-conduciveness. If true belief is not our epistemic *telos*, then reliabilism would lose its raison d'être. For on Goldman's view, reliability of a process is construed precisely as consisting in the fact that the process yields a high ratio of true over false beliefs. Evidently, any technique which yields a high ratio of true over false beliefs is capable of figuring in some system of correct justificatory rules. This is absolutely as it should be. That is, if reading tea leaves is, in fact, highly reliable, then it makes sense to consult tea leaves. (It is precisely because reading tea leaves is not reliable that "the tea leaves say so" is a very bad justification for any belief.)

Now, we are in a position to see that reliabilism construed as part of the theory of knowledge falls victim very directly to the sort of objection I have been pushing, to the swamping problem, as Linda Zagzebski and others (following me) point out. If a belief-generating technique needs itself to be justified by its truth-conduciveness, then the epistemic goal in which it is in service is mere true belief. Reliabilism builds a specification of the mere means of reaching a goal into the description of the goal itself. The goal can be specified independently of those means. And since knowledge is our goal with regard to the generation of particular propositional beliefs, it actually follows from reliabilism that knowledge is merely true belief. The very same argument, with slight variations, can be shown to apply to nomological externalism of the sort put forward by Armstrong, and to causal versions of externalism of the sort endorsed by Goldman in an earlier incarnation.

I would like to consider an analogy that has been repeatedly made in refutation of the treatment I have suggested. Justification, the analogy goes, is like a race, and true belief is its finish line. Winning the race is achieving knowledge. But you do not win simply in virtue of crossing the finish line; you must run the required distance along the required route. That is, to win the race (achieve knowledge), you must reach the finish line (true belief) in the right way (the way of justification). You may recall the case of Rosie Ruiz, who "won" the Boston Marathon by jumping in with a couple of miles to go. To identify knowledge with true belief is to say that Rosie should have been declared the winner, that any way to reach the finish line is acceptable. However, consider the relation of means to ends in that case. If we ask, "why must one run the required distance along the required route?" the answer is simply that one must. Those are the rules of the race. We have reached the level of brute fact (albeit socially fixed), the level of the external conditions that make the race the race it is. To participate in the race is to agree to abide by the rules, and the exact length of a marathon does not itself admit of any justification.

Now if we ask, "why must we reach true belief in the right way?" the analogy suggests an answer: we just must, those are the rules. The account makes justification arbitrary; it simply prescribes justification as the rules of the race. But justification is not arbitrary in this way. First, we could, for convenience, simply stipulate whatever rules we found fun, or convenient, or entertaining. But the thinkers in question do not think we can stipulate any rules we like, or whatever may be the whim or fad of our social circle. Second, it would be a bizarre exercise at this point to engage in a debate about justification; that would be like debating the general question "How long should a race be?" That question obviously has no correct answer: a race can be whatever length we stipulate it to be (though it would be senseless for creatures like we are now to run a one-inch race or a race through interstellar space). A fifty-yard dash is not more correct than a marathon. This would make the entire debate about epistemic justification random or merely arbitrary.

I would like to suggest another analogy, which I owe to Arthur Skidmore. Inquiry is like a journey, and true belief is its destination. Justification is a map. Now using the map may help us arrive at our destination. But the point is to arrive. If we misread the map and get there anyway, everything has turned out fine. If we take a route not marked on the map and still get there pretty directly, we have still done as well as could do on this particular journey. If we do that all the time, we are competent navigators.

19.

I used Moore, Diogenes, Johnson, Kierkegaard, Nietzsche, James, Austin, and Santayana to argue that the claim that justification is logically necessary for knowledge is false to our commitments and practices as believing agents. Now the ultimate reason why I think that knowledge is merely true belief is simply this: it is far truer than the epistemology of justification to our lives as believers in or skeptics about this and that. In my view, all of the doxastic agents we know about are organisms scurrying around on the surface of a planet. We have the commitments necessary to that situation; the world constrains us for the most part to the truth. We are connected to the world by a thousand thousand strands, and the ways we come into a "knowing" relation with it are diverse. The idea that there is only one or only a narrow range of ways of coming to know is wildly false to the ways people actually do come to know, and to the wildly diverse things they come to know. There is no reason to think that all knowledge is rationally justifiable, especially if our relations to the world are fundamentally nonepistemic: not a matter of inference, for example, from an internal component of experience. The doxastic agents with whom we are acquainted are full-fledged organisms, not the bits of those organisms that reason.

20.

Now, so far in this chapter, I have casually treated epistemic agents as sealed-up individuals, and propositions, claims, and so on as sempiternal abstract objects. This may strike you as incompatible with my ontology and account of truth, and it ought to. To try to shatter the epistemology of justification, or—let's say—an overweening scientism or unreal treatment of human beings as rational and an unreal and self-congratulatory emphasis on reason, variously construed, as the source of knowledge, I casually accepted the structure of S's and p's (esses and peas) which informed twentieth-century analytic epistemology.[66]

I think, however, that the picture I am trying to draw of human knowledge can be made much more compelling by being put into relation to the conception of truth I gave in the second chapter, and also, eventually, with the conceptions of agency I give in the next chapter. Now, what is a piece of knowledge? It can only be a situation, a claim which is partly motivated, and partly elucidated, by externalism about "mental content." To know is to be connected in the right way to reality, and "propositional knowledge" is parasitic on the fact that we are creatures embedded in environments, which we have to know, or die. Animals know many truths, as Santayana reminds us, once we drop propositions as the primary truth bearers, or identify truth and reality. Indeed, we are animals. Nor is the knower distinct from the known, to use an expression that one might find anywhere from the Upanishads to Emerson. The knower is not distinct from the known in the sense that the knower is not an ontologically distinct sort of thing: we are physical things in a physical environment and not, primarily, representational systems. And the knower is not distinct from the known in that the physical thing that is me is constantly incorporating and extruding parts of this world in, for example, respiration, but also in perception.

Recall that I identify truth and reality, and try to embed the epistemic agent in that reality. The notion of truth for sentences, propositions, claims, and so on is parasitic on this far larger realm of truth: all that actually is. And recall that I argued that, if we narrow the thing down tendentiously to linguistic items (e.g., sentences) or items represented in language (e.g., propositions), we are going to have to regard as the primary truth bearers in this sense particular inscriptions or utterances, not the abstract entities that I take to be theoretical/pragmatic postulates or ways of arraying inscriptions and utterances. "Propositions" are convenient fictions, as it were, though convenient fictions can become very inconvenient indeed when you start to try to insert them seriously into your ontology. In mine, there are truths that no one knows, because the universe is what is true; everything real is true; to most of it, humans have no epistemic access at any given moment. But "knowledge" is what I called an "experiential situation"; it picks out relations of human individuals or groups within that reality (of which they form portions). In the case of propositional knowledge, this implicates social representational or semantic systems.

The way "propositional" or linguistic truths function when treated this way is "double-barreled": on the one hand, the true u/i (utterance/inscription) is turned outward as a representation of reality. But it does not face this reality as an enduring or abstract object: what it represents and how it represents it is specific to the occasion/place/agent of utterance. To repeat a simple example: a sarcastic and a sincere utterance of "the same sentence" represent reality entirely differently: you could express a contradiction with something that sounds like a tautology (or would sound like that if you didn't understand sarcasm), for example, repeating "the same" sentence once seriously or straightforwardly, once sarcastically. The linguistic truth bearer is itself a physical object/event in the physical world it also represents.

But the question of truth for such items (which, to repeat, I do not regard as the only or fundamental bearers of truth) turns also inward, as I argued. Sarcasm is in part a matter of the relation of the person speaking to the utterance, and to speak the truth, or for what you say to be true, you have to be true, or real. Truth, I argued, is also a virtue, and to speak the truth is to be true to that extent or with regard to that matter. It denotes a resolution to face or capture or keep faith with the world and oneself as they are.

Now, this connects what I'm doing to contemporary virtue epistemology, and it sounds tantamount to equating truth and knowledge, which might return us to some version of the epistemology of justification. That is, if to speak or write the truth is to be connected outwardly in the right way, and that right way includes a personal condition of epistemic virtue of some sort (a "resolution"), then justification in the sense in which it is described in virtue epistemology (one is justified if one reaches one's conclusion in the right way, for example, "rationally," and one knows when one is justified and when what one believes is true), then knowledge might be justified true belief after all on my account.

This would require some elaborations and refinements. So, first of all, I am going to have to treat "propositional attitudes" in specific cases where some person has some propositional attitude, as being concerned with "tokens" rather than "types": belief would be an attitude toward some specific utterance or inscription, or toward a set of utterances and inscriptions which one arrays in some sense, for let's say convenience, as a single thing, or as expressing the same thing. For these to be true in the concrete sense, the believer must be in a certain (virtuous, perhaps) state and the u/i must be turned outward into the world in the right sort of way. This might include "mental tokens" or particular syntactically significant firings of neurons or mental activities which could be treated as tokens of propositions. Now, if you give me this picture, you will have little discomfort in agreeing with me that knowledge is merely true belief, but on the other hand you may well also think that the apparent dispute is merely verbal, because I build in what people want from justification into the other conditions. That is, it appears that some sort of justification has been smuggled into the truth condition from the outset, as I also perhaps smuggled some more of it into the belief condition just now, when I argued, for example, that in the usual case a guess does not count as a belief.

I am comfortable with this reconciliation, provisionally, but I want also to drive home how different the big picture now is from what has usually been associated with accounts of knowledge that require justification. One thing I want to emphasize is that there are many sources of knowledge, or, better, many ways people come to know. Much of the Western philosophical tradition suffers from a bizarre and excessive respect for reason as the only possible source of knowledge or as a necessary aspect of knowledge in every case. (I have tried to show some of the great exceptions to this, including Kierkegaard, Santayana, and Moore.) This is what is enshrined in the justification condition on knowledge. But I think that, first off, we are not nearly as reasonable as we think we are; or perhaps I should say that we and they are nowhere near as reasonable as philosophy professors think they themselves are. I regard the informal assertion that most of what anyone believes is rational as very likely to rest on self-congratulatory self-delusion. We believe as the whole creatures we are, not as some little faculty or region of the brain. I think that the purpose of many of these pictures is to disqualify people as knowers: often, let's say, dark or colonized people, women, children, or one's political opponents. However, if they were able to engage in honest self-reflection, these extremely rational people might see that they are disqualifying themselves as well. No one circulates through the world as a reasoning machine, and if you did you would perhaps make all knowledge of the world impossible for yourself.

21.

Of course, all of this, and an ontology of situations, entails that all knowledge is "situated." I take this to be more than compatible with feminist standpoint epistemologies and also with the general outlines of various approaches that emphasize the social aspects of knowledge, as long these approaches are not reductive and do not entirely displace individuals and more-than-human environments into the social. What a person can know depends on things like where he or she is physically located, but it also implicates vocabularies, practices, and so on, which are interpersonal. Sandra Harding, for one, quoting Donna Haraway, has argued that acknowledging differences of standpoint and acknowledging one's own, are in fact roads to "strong objectivity."

> Many feminists, like thinkers in other new social liberation movements, now hold that it is not only desirable but also possible to have that apparent contradiction in terms—socially situated knowledge. In conventional accounts, socially situated beliefs only get to count as opinions. In order to achieve the status of knowledge, beliefs are supposed to break free of—to transcend—their original ties to local, historical interests, values, and agendas. However, as Donna Haraway has put the point, it turns out to be possible "to have *simultaneously* an account of radical historical contingency for all knowledge claims and knowing subjects, a critical practice for recognizing our own 'semiotic technologies' for making meanings, and a no-nonsense commitment to faithful accounts of a real world."[67]

Now as I say, I would rather drop the notion of objectivity altogether; for one thing, I don't think objective truth is any different than truth. But putting it this way is salutary in that it tries to crack open and humanize scientism from within. "Objectivity" has been a name for the impossibly unmarked standpoint of power, and its use in scientistic theory makes it a good target for feminist and postcolonial critiques of the objectification of the other, and ecological critiques of the objectification of animals and environments. To start with, objectivity is distance, separation from the object, and thus on my view supposes something both undesirable and (fortunately) impossible. Flipping the term over as Harding does has the double effect of reversing the flow of objectification and destroying certain pretensions on their own terms. Still, I prefer to ditch the concept entirely; it is irremediably polluted politically, I think, and also epistemologically.

All knowledge is situated and everything known is a situation. No knowledge is not someone's knowledge, the knowledge of an individual or community or institution. No knowledge does not have various social components, among other things in the construction and circulation of vocabularies, representational systems, systems of projection or mapping. This is one thing that has gone wrong with the objectivity of privilege: it presupposes the disingenuous erasure of the contingency of its own representational systems while it disqualifies all the others. But no vocabulary or community exists without being nested in larger nonhuman situations, and our connections to the world as individuals and communities are not bound to the limits of any particular vocabulary or, rather, always exceed and challenge any such system. Whether by distance or proximity, univocal or multivocal practices, we are not going to be able to generate the representational system that is better than all the others, a final system, or which disappears in its identity to the world it describes, the wacky positivist fantasy of a perfect language of science. So though I would oppose the recuperation of "objectivity," I also see why Harding or Haraway might want to reconstruct it. Perhaps Harding thinks that science stands or falls with objectivity, as so much philosophy of science has centralized it. But I think objectivity is a red herring: we can do perfectly well without it in science and everywhere else, and I think we had better, or fail ourselves continuously in our attempts to exit our own standpoints, reflexively or by any other technique.

"Propositional" knowledge may be parasitic on other sorts of interactions with the world (including "knowing how"), but there can be no propositional beliefs without a public language. That is, knowledge of this sort is an "experiential situation" implicating an organism and an environment and a complex set of social resources for representing and describing them. What can be known from any given location is partly a matter of physical place, but also a matter of where and how one is embedded in social systems. And I would agree with many feminists, critical race theorists, and others, that—for example—the truths about oppression are typically erased for the oppressor, known all too vividly by the oppressed person. For example, oppression brings with it massive blind spots in one's self-knowledge; an oppressor often does not know himself to be an oppressor, and does not know the sort of people that his sort of people oppress to be knowers. He may, and in the West he does, attribute rationality routinely to people like himself, and implicitly or explicitly deny it to women, sages, the uneducated, and so on.

Knowledge is bound up with systems of power in extremely complex ways, as Foucault showed so compellingly in *Discipline and Punish*, and yet I will also assert against Foucault that knowledge may require a relinquishing of power or a relinquishing of the delusion of power, or a resolution to openness, a sort of self-effacement that resolves that the rest of the world is more important than the knower's self, or notes that the self and enclosure in the self is the source of self-deception and delusion. That is something that might be meant by "objectivity." Then again, the move into the social is also inadequate, and to know one often has to break with a consensus, or try to undermine the going vocabularies of a group, whether a dominant or dominated group. Enclosure in the social can be—it has typically been—a source of delusions, and delusions run rampant through a social groups, whether of oppressed or nonoppressed people, or Democrats and Republicans, or whatever it may be.

And of course, human groups are small portions of a big universe, no more central to that universe than rocks, and though the ways that we are connected to other persons are somewhat different than the way we are connected to rocks, the rocks are no less real and no less epistemically available to us than the people, else Sam Johnson couldn't have kicked one. We should take the social aspects of knowing (testimony, etc.) seriously, but we should also place them in the broader context of the nonhuman. As Latour has argued, nothing happens socially without nonhumans; even our communication with one another is impossible unless in a physical surround with specific channels and objects and forces.

22.

One thing the epistemology of justification may represent in a given case is scientism run amok. If so, it represents a false picture of what science is and how it has actually reached its results. We have already seen James and Nietzsche, for example, argue that science itself rests on certain sorts of faith. But what I have in mind here is the role of such things as intuition and aesthetics in science. I would say that very typically the truths of science, as those of mathematics (and philosophy, for that matter) are produced intuitively or guessed or reached on the basis of aesthetic and other extrarational procedures, and are justified by experimentation or argumentation only retroactively. Methodological suggestions that seek to foreclose modes of inquiry or sources of truth a priori are always gratuitous mistakes and embody a kind of epistemic totalitarianism that would, if consistently applied, limit and impoverish human knowledge to a shocking extent.

I will conclude by giving an extended example. Edgar Allan Poe described his bizarre and amazing late work *Eureka* (1848) as a "prose poem" and asserted, with multiple layers of irony, typical of Poe at his best, that "it is as a poem only that I wish this work to be judged after I am dead."[68] But he also asserts that *"What I propound here is true,"* and he has a point: it is fair to say, I believe, that *Eureka* yields that best cosmology of the nineteenth century, at least in the sense of saying very clearly what scientific cosmologists thought a century later. Poe, believe it or not, gives an extremely clear statement of the big bang and the expanding/contracting universe, the very first such statement I know of. He says that the universe originates in an infinitesimal, almost infinitely dense point containing all matter. For reasons Poe does not understand, and which I think Stephen Hawing doesn't understand either, the thing explodes. (Poe calls the cause "the will of God," by which I think he means little except that explanations run out right there.) Matter, and space itself, expand spherically until the force of gravity outweighs the force of the initial explosion, at which point it begins to contract, because the strongest gravitational pull on each particle on the periphery of the sphere is back toward the center: more matter lies in that direction for each particle than in any other direction. (Poe, however, thought the universe was in its contracting, rather than expanding phase. That is perhaps characteristic of Poe's pessimism, though he portrays the final merger of all things into unity as an ecstasy in which each thing ceases to be distinct from every other.) Then perhaps it explodes again: a heart-like systole and diastole. He speculates, in terms remarkably like those of the contemporary physicist Brian Greene, for example, that there may be many such universes, so distant from one another that light from one cannot reach the other even in the whole period that the universes coexist, and so are sealed off from one another (the "multiverse hypothesis"). And he formulates quite clearly what has come to be known as the "cosmological principle": locally, the distribution of matter is radically uneven; at a large enough scale it appears uniform; this, says Poe, enables us to describe it mathematically.

It is a remarkable achievement, and Poe thought it would make him immortal. Instead it seems to have had almost no effect on anyone, and it was eighty years before the Belgian priest and astronomer Georges Lemaître generated very much the same hypothesis in strikingly similar terms. For example, where Lemaître describes the initial condition as the "primeval atom," Poe calls it the "primordial particle," and they both use the term "cosmic egg." (It is just possible that the influence was direct; Baudelaire translated *Eureka* into French in the 1860s.)

Eureka begins with a methodological essay in the form of a letter from the year 2848 found in a bottle (previously published by Poe under the title "Mellonta Tauta"). It ridicules the notion that there is only one road to the truth—the inductive or scientific method of observation and experimentation—or that there are only two: that, and an a priori or Aristotelian method, or reasoning deductively from premises to conclusion. Methodological restrictions of this sort "have operated . . . to retard the progress of true Science, which makes its most important advances—as all History will show—by seemingly intuitive *leaps*."[69] He continues,

> In especial, would it not have given these bigots some trouble to determine by which of their two roads was reached the most momentous and sublime

of *all* their truths—the truth—the fact of *gravitation*? Newton deduced it from the laws of Kepler. Kepler admitted that these laws he *guessed*—these laws whose investigations disclosed to the greatest of British astronomers that principle, the basis of all (existing) physical principle, in going behind which we enter at once the nebulous kingdom of Metaphysics. Yes!—these vital laws Kepler *guessed*—that is to say, he *imagined* them.[70]

It matters, though, says Poe, *who* guesses. He calls his own intuitive method "poetic"; we might call it more widely "aesthetic." One of its aesthetic aspects is that the picture yielded is of a *beautiful* universe: a universe with a fundamental unity, but also "of the utmost possible relation."[71] Poe holds that in such a universe, every particle is related to every other in an infinity of relations, and by sheer natural forces: every particle exerts a gravitational pull on every other.

Nor is this universe cursed by its unity, as Parmenides', for example. Of the atoms composing the universe, Poe writes, "*Difference* is their character—their essentiality—just as *no-difference* was the essentiality of their source. . . . All existing bodies, of course, are composed of atoms in proximate contact, and are therefore to be considered as mere assemblages of more or fewer differences."[72]

> That each atom attracts—sympathizes with the most delicate movements of every other atom, and with each and with all at the same time, and forever, and according to a determinate law of which the complexity, even considered by itself solely, is utterly beyond the grasp of the imagination. If I propose to ascertain the influence of one mote in a sunbeam on its neighboring mote, I cannot accomplish my purpose without first counting and weighing all the atoms in the Universe and defining the precise positions of all at one particular moment. If I venture to displace, by even the billionth part of an inch, the microscopical speck of dust which lies now on the point of my finger, what is the character of that act upon which I have adventured? I have done a deed which shakes the Moon in her path, which causes the Sun to be no longer the Sun, and which alters forever the destiny of the multitudinous myriads and stars that roll and glow in the majestic presence of their Creator.[73]

Now the "poetical" or "intuitive" method by which Poe reaches all these remarkable conclusions is not antirational. Poe himself, to say nothing of Kepler, mastered the scientific literature of his day before he launched his intuitions. But he also trusted in his own connections to the universe to lead him aright. That they did by and large lead him aright, as they did Kepler, or Einstein, constitutes their beliefs as knowledge, and the attempt to shackle such people to an imposed method would make it impossible to know much of what we do know, even in the realm of science. Indeed it is quite possible to come to know, without knowing how you have come to know.

The distinction of rational inquiry from aesthetic arrangement or sudden intuition cannot be maintained in the face of the way science or philosophy or other areas of human knowledge have actually been prosecuted. Most of our ordinary knowledge, as well as our extraordinary knowledge, eventuates from our positions as tiny creatures in a big world: connected to it, part of it, sharing its nature, ourselves swarms of atoms being operated on gravitationally and by whatever other forces operate on things. Rationality takes up its place within this situation but should not be privileged as our only means of connection to it. That is why the picture yielded by the epistemology of justification is itself irrationally constricted and constricting, and underlying it lurks a terrible self-deception about the sorts of things we are.

PART II

Axiology: Goodness, Beauty, and Liberty

Introduction

Values as Situations

1.

Every situation is dense with value, or is potentially the site of many values complexly intertwined. We could start with the paramount dimensions of value that are traditional within Western philosophy: epistemic (truth), ethical (the good, or rightness in action), aesthetic (beauty, etc.), political (justice). My idea is that these always arise in relation to one another or as a system that might have one or another emphasis or weight; each of these values as it appears in a particular situation is always infested or deflected by the rest in a kind of combinatorial pattern. This sounds awfully vague; I tried to describe many specific cases or applications in *Political Aesthetics*. But some general observations might help make the basic position plausible, or at least somewhat clearer. My idea also is that each of these values is itself irreparably plural, that the formulation of each dimension of value as a single ultimate value is misleading. Beauty is only one among many aesthetic values. The tradition immediately produces sublimity, for example, and dozens of aesthetic values have been explored through art history: accuracy, for instance, or extreme complexity or extreme simplicity; harmonious unity or explosive conflagration. But it is worth noting that all of these could be, for example, relevant to questions of epistemic or political value. If truth or reality is a value, it is a value in art and in ethics. Truthfulness might be an important dimension of aesthetic assessment, but also "authenticity" or "truth" is itself the name of a virtue, as I have mentioned: it means something like unaffected and frank and loyal. Of course, the idea of truth is connected to any assertion in ethics: the question of whether it's true, what makes it true, can always be raised; there is an epistemic question for every question about value; there's no keeping ethical apart from epistemic value, obviously.

On the other hand, I pit my view against that of Plato and, in particular, Neoplatonists such as Plotinus or Shelley, for whom beauty, truth, and goodness are one and unchanging. On the contrary, they're plural and shifting, though perhaps not as easily or as quickly as one might like. They bend or shift or transform, and not by anyone's will, though wills might be a factor. They are situations. And the ultimate values are closely related or elaborately tangled; you find among them a kind of rat's nest of conceptual interconnections, and as they develop or fragment historically their relations mutate. Let me put it to you that what music you like matters morally and what end of the political spectrum you occupy is partly a matter of taste and that a work of injustice or an act that is unjust is aesthetically compromised.

Nevertheless, sometimes we have to try to tease the questions apart, and as I have said elsewhere, a famine with a really good view isn't any better than a famine in a pit. It might be morally admirable to believe something false. You can be seduced by beauty—even the beauty of a theorem or a theory—into falsehood. The relation of the values to one another is complex but compositional; each value takes shape as a system of coherences with and distinctions from the others. Or, the dimensions of value emerge as a system; a single value can never be instantiated purely, nor need it be.

Going the other way round, aesthetic considerations inform or infest epistemic assessments: we're looking for unified or economical or bewildering or baroque explanations. We're trying to see how the thing hangs together: an aesthetic question concerning composition, clarity, and comprehension. All representational schemata, including those of science, come with an aesthetic overlay: there is no image or description that is not in some particular system or systems of picturing or poetics. Or, the aesthetic is the faculty of picking out connections or organizing stuff into individuals and individuals into situations: the discipline of form. The connections and ruptures between things as they are organized into wholes or splintered into multiplicities—their forms, that is, their material arrangements—these are the contours of the real world. Likewise, I think the aesthetic implications or sources of political values and concepts—justice, representation, order, or harmony, for example—are far too little appreciated.

For such reasons, I propose to try to articulate a sense of value by waffling back and forth between these dimensions even as in different chapters I emphasize one or another. I try to display them as a tangle by focusing on their connections, or by constructing parallels, or by applying one in elucidation of another. This is a remarkably traditional activity, and one could think of Socrates's constant use of analogies between values: those of a physician or a shoemaker and those of a philosopher or a ruler, for example. When Hutcheson and the young Kant wanted to elucidate the virtues or to move toward ethics, they entered through aesthetics: they praised the virtuous life as a beautiful or a well-ordered life. To make use of the aesthetic in ethics, as to say of some hero's soul that it is sublime, is to flourish a conventional honorific. Even if so, our constant resort to aesthetic categories to describe ethical, political, and epistemic activity is revealing. There may be more of one than another in a particular situation: always where one is in play, the others could be brought into play, or are potentially relevant if one seeks for them.

It would also be worthwhile to show each value as a plurality. I have already sort of said that truth is one thing (though, of course, also infinitely many), which presents some problems of consistency, but the methods of gaining knowledge, that is, coming to believe the truth—that is, to come into contact with the real—are intractably plural, and the world itself is plural as well as one. As there are many aesthetic values, there are many political values, and insofar as "justice" is not just a variable meaning whatever is ultimately politically right, it is one among many values that we are trying to realize through political activity at any given moment: caring, or order, or unity, or plurality, or autonomy, or responsiveness. Ethically we would like to prevent suffering, or to be happy and help others be happy, but we would also like to be treated fairly and treat others fairly, be truthful or sincere and live among truthful and sincere people, be self-controlled or giving, to be free (whatever that means, exactly), and so on.

2.

I use the terms "nature," "world," "universe," "reality" to mean the whole of the skein or, in short, everything, whatever in turn that might mean: the skein as it really is under all dimensions of experience and analysis, but also in itself in all its internal relations. It has no external relations, of course, on my conception, or by that definition. So what are these dimensions? If I were trying to issue a description of the skein, where would I begin? If I were trying to issue an ideally replete description, what would I have to include? And I am, of course, again speaking from within the world—I am included in what I am describing—and my speaking in it of it is itself a deformation of or a tug on it, a material event.

If I said, for example, that this skein or tangle displayed aesthetic properties such as (for example) beauty, what would I be saying? I might point or mark out certain passages—knotscapes, as it were. Maybe I like it when they fall into a regular or predictable repeating pattern, or maybe I like fantastic concatenations of string. Maybe I reach up and make adjustments, in illustration of some point, or just as a matter of more or less arbitrary preference. So if I were trying to give a description of the skein I might resort to aesthetic qualities as holistic sensible qualities of particulars, regions, or the skein as a whole. As significantly, aesthetic values may be guides for interventions in the knotscape: ways of tying, and so on.

If I said of any such thing or array that it was "beautiful," you could take this to denote approval, but typically there is also more that I could say, and there is certainly more that I could say if I'm a professional: picking out qualities or aspects in virtue of which it is beautiful, talking about what makes the pebble or the painting or interstellar space beautiful. Well, essentially we are in this position with regard to all the qualities or things we have names for; they are qualities, as it were, of the ontological object that consists of a culturally embedded perceiver/speaker/body in juxtaposition with the thing being experienced or described, suspended in juxtaposition in an atmosphere or tangle of air and light and language.

G. E. Moore writes:

> It has been . . . commonly supposed that the beautiful may be defined as that which produces certain effects upon our feelings; and the conclusion that follows from this—namely, that judgments of taste are merely subjective—that precisely the same thing may, according to circumstances, be both beautiful and not beautiful—has very frequently been drawn. . . . [But] to assert that a thing is beautiful is to assert that the cognition of it is an essential element in one of the intrinsically valuable wholes we have been discussing [= external object + cognition + emotional response]; so that the question, whether it is truly beautiful or not depends upon the objective question whether the whole in question is or is not truly good, and does not depend upon the question whether it would or would not excite particular feelings in particular persons.[1]

Moore's insight is radical but right: the value is not in the subject, not in the object, but in the whole that contains them both; I propose this is obviously true once it's articulated. William Godwin said that "Justice is a rule of conduct originating in the connection of one percipient being with another."[2]

There are—let us say, provisionally or apparently—four salient moments or zones or aspects of the act of asserting of something that it is beautiful (good, just). This is an application of my general ontology. There is the object/event/situation as it exists outside the interpreter in a context. There is the perceiver or interpreter of whatever sort. There is a set of vocabularies and, more widely, social practices that have to do with beauty (justice): though, note, these are always in flux and up for grabs. (Another language might have another word with a different inflection, and, of course, other peoples or people might have different standards of taste in whatever dimension, perhaps an elaborate system within a system of elaborate systems different from one's own, and these systems are always both mutating and interacting.) And there is the environment or spatiotemporal material context in which all this occurs. Now I start by distinguishing these four dimensions or aspects—the objective, the subjective, the social, and the contextual—because that reflects our way of scientifically, social-scientifically, philosophically accounting for these things. But the idea that "physical reality," "social practices," and "subjectivities" can actually be distinguished in a principled way is the very notion I want to destroy.

Twentieth-century philosophy took it upon itself to collapse the distinction between the individual and the social: you see this in the work, for example, of Mead, Wittgenstein, and Foucault. And you saw it in Rousseau, Hegel, German nationalism, and Marx, for example. Now I think that this collapse took a distorted form; it just reduced the individual to the social, whereas the collapse should have been mutual and simultaneous. But at any rate, having collapsed the social/individual distinction, we should proceed to destroy the distinctions between the material surround—that is, nature, the real—and the social, and between nature and the individual. Bruno Latour's work should be exemplary here, and his view that each object that sociologists could study is a "lash-up" of (what have been considered) social, individual, and material factors finally motivates a desire to completely forego/destroy all the concepts involved, particularly "nature" and "the social."

"The social" is a version of what is also called "the artificial," the fabricated or man-made, and, of course, artifice is the proper complement to nature, so that finally the term *nature* only registers our own hallucinated apartness from the world; nature is itself an artifact of this artifice, "nature." This is why in some ways the whole environmental problem is wrapped up in the concept. Whether nature is the garden from which we have fallen or the merely material over which we. as spirits. have dominion, the human and the rest of the material world are bifurcated in a way that is false but potentially conceptually and practically fatal. In particular, the social is opposed to the merely or the rawly material; "social" explanations of race, gender, and so on resist precisely the naturalization of various socially determined vocabularies or taxonomies. Obviously, however, the social proceeds by a million interventions in and acquiescences to the real world. All our media, for one thing. Sound waves. Gestures. Architectural styles and breaking dishes.

Latour argues that we should replace the social in the surround of the physical: there are no people, practices, institutions, conventions, truths without nonhuman things. Without nonhuman things, he points out, "the social" is an entirely inert mysterious powerless essence that doesn't do or explain anything. (In this it is like "consciousness.") Social science, he says, is a "tracing of associations." "The social," he continues, "does not designate a thing among other things, like a black sheep among white sheep, but a type of connection, between things that are not themselves social."

> At first, this definition seems absurd since it risks diluting "the social" to mean any type of aggregate, from chemical bonds to legal ties, from atomic forces to corporate bodies, from physiological to political assemblages. But this is precisely the point, as all those heterogeneous elements might be

assembled anew in some given state of affairs. Far from being a mind-boggling hypothesis, this is on the contrary the most common experience we have in encountering the puzzling face of the social. A new vaccine is being marketed, a new job description is offered, a new political movement is being created, a new planetary system is discovered, a new law is voted, a new catastrophe occurs. In each instance we have to reshuffle our conceptions of what was associated together because the previous definition has been made somewhat irrelevant. We are no longer sure what "we" means. But in any case, none of these happen merely in the language or in the sensory field; they all presuppose myriad worldly things and events and relations.[3]

There are many admirable things about this conception of the social as fluid and extending well beyond the human, and one of them is that human beings conduct their relationships among one another by administering and working around things: the social is a lash-up of all sorts of different factors and entities, but in it we are also in community with nonhuman things of all kinds. We live together, let's say; then the actual shapes of our lives are massively determined by the parameters and configuration of the shared space. It's no good going out to do mass communications without physical objects. The combinations or assemblages or networks are endless and continually mutating, but there ought to be no denying the embeddedness and dependence on and entwinedness of people in their groups with nonhuman creatures and things.

3.

My idea is that the values are ways of organizing or collecting things—including social conditions and states of individuals and nonhuman things—into situations. I have been calling this process "arraying." Then justice or goodness are modes of arraying, or ways in which things are arrayed. This does not indicate that an array of things is a purely arbitrary or stipulated entity; here as elsewhere, our intelligence bends before what is, so that it makes sense to think of values as actually being inherent in the world. Of course, this is not to say we cannot be wrong on such matters; indeed, the struggle toward becoming right requires many errors, and the fact that we are ourselves only bits of these larger situations or values means that they are in myriad respects recalcitrant to our wills: each of our wills individually or all of our wills together.

The idea of an array immediately seems to implicate aesthetic values, but the aesthetic is only one dimension in which things are arrayed, and it bleeds off irretrievably into the other dimensions of value. One way of arraying is making a collection—of knick-knacks, thingamajigs, the novels of Mark Twain, dachshund-themed statuettes—literally gathering up and redistributing objects in space, which of course is a very typical human activity. Another is to gather up a series of cases on a moral question: Grab the Nazis; or What about a psychopath? or Who's worse, Assad or Mobutu? A beautiful thing is always an array; taste yields principles of arraying. Gathering up objects like this is socially constructing them, we might say, but the things they gather and the situations they yield are as real as any other objects, and they are objects of the same nature. Again, we should think perhaps of collecting or making a museum: there is nothing unreal about your collection of dachshund-themed statuettes; nothing unreal about the mantelpiece on which they're displayed; nothing unreal about their infinitely complex spatial relationships to one another; nothing unreal about your own juxtaposition with them in space—topologies of insane complexity unfolding over time; nothing unreal about the light in which they're bathed, rippling in waves back into your body; nothing unreal about your hand, which reaches to rearrange; nothing unreal about the rearrangement thus produced, and so on.

When we think of the aesthetic properties of an object, we may think of its form or qualities of its form. If form were to be understood, or could be thought or experienced, apart from matter, that would indicate that, in some sense, the aesthetic properties of a thing are not, as it were, real properties of it or capable of appearing at particular locations; not, for example, "objective" or scientifically ascertainable or studiable properties. But, on the contrary, the form of something is precisely its material arrangement. (Here, I think we are close, in some ways, to the dispute between Plato and Aristotle on "form.") The Parthenon, we might say, is that very material under that very configuration. At each actual situation, form and the arrangement of material are identical. Every actual object is a site at which matter and form coincide: they coincide at that site, and neither ever appears independently at any site, that is, in any situation. Skein analysis describes possible knot configurations in an "abstract" way, but the description is a concrete array of inscriptions or image-tokens.

Formalism in aesthetics—Clive Bell's, say—was a sad mistake; it made of art an arid moonscape of abstraction. That formalism derives from Kant. But Kant conceived every aspect of his philosophy as a formalism, as giving the abstract or "purely rational" schemata of values. The terms "formalism," "form," and so on mean many things, of course, in the history of Western philosophy, but often they do seem to inscribe an abstract realm or to appear precisely contrasted to matter, content, and so on. One decisive moment in this conceptuality is Euclid: geometrical form is explicitly defined incompatibly with the possibility of its physical manifestation: lines with no width, and so on. And yet, of course, geometrical formalism derives from empirical experience of space—the activity of surveying, for example—and also feeds back into such practices or rearticulates and reorients them. This is how Kant also conceived moral philosophy: providing the purely rational, abstract principles that might rearticulate reality, or that must be allowed to articulate reality. Their rigor and universality are proportionate to their abstraction from the material.

Form must be reconceived. It is not the intersection of abstract and concrete realities: it is the actual configuration of material. I am not trying to undermine Euclid, and Hutcheson was on to something when (roughly) he held the *Elements* to be the world's most beautiful thing. Only any form with which we are actually acquainted is a material thing in a situation. Matter appears in various arrangements, believe it or not. However we may sort out the amazing intersection of the abstract and physical planes, we might also focus on the ways bodies are juxtaposed in space, unfolding over time: the physical shape of the universe. If an art historian describes the form of the Parthenon, she had better be attentive to the actual proportions and so on of the actual material. Also, the texts of Euclid are instantiated as physical objects, his ideas in figures, the papyrus, vellum, and ink, or for that matter, photons and pixels.

If, at a minimum, to describe the form of something is to describe that very thing, which is a material object, then insofar as the aesthetic aspects are the formal aspects, the aesthetic aspects are germane, and material. So, for example, the question whether the skein is as a whole well or comprehensibly ordered: is that a scientific question or an aesthetic question? Well, I think that is precisely the sort of thing you hope to find out, detect, or even adore in the practice of science. What would it mean for a system to be well-ordered? Various dimensions of fact-value suggest themselves; one is surely aesthetic. We might say that the epistemic standards of science are aesthetic through and through, that the practice demands a standard of rationality that we might call an aspiration to or a reflection of an experience of beauty, its trace. But then, perhaps the aesthetic standards are moral: a chastity of the intellect, a demand for rigorous honesty.

For example, we might think of an ordering principle like Ockham's razor: a nice way to cut cognitive costs, perhaps, but above all a standard of beauty in explanation and virtue of the intellect. Indeed, the standard is identical to Hutcheson's theory of beauty, which he also moralized, or what is really the classical conception: the compound ratio of variety to uniformity: individuals comprehended under the single category in taxonomy. Ockham's razor gave us both materialism and idealism, opposed to the death, *aufhebunged* in Hegel and so on, but both committed to the ultimate singleness of the universe, the coherence of all in a single ontological plane. That is, though the materialists and idealists of the modern period disagreed about ontology, they agreed about an aesthetics opposed to dualism, and that is precisely why even Berkeley at times threw up his hands and said the dispute was verbal: as long as you give me these things—this world, ordered under this aesthetic—I don't really care whether you call it material or mental. He certainly believed that once one no longer believed in the material world one would just keep doing science the same way as always: an extraordinary idea considering the usual association of science with materialism through the nineteenth century.

4.

Attributions of value are true only under conditions which implicate "the natural," "the social," and "the subjective" in every case. What makes truth possible in the matter of value is that these aspects are not insular but strands of the skein all snarled up together. If we said beauty is in the eye of the beholder as opposed to being in the objective world, we would be entirely confused. The eye of the beholder is itself in the objective world. If you don't believe me, pluck out your left eye and look at it. There it is! This is true of your "mental images," true of every aspect of human consciousness.

We might think of color: surely a fundamental dimension of aesthetic experience and a fundamental locus of beauty and ugliness. Locke and many others famously treated colors as "secondary" and, roughly, as subjective properties, which was supported by the fact that that we can't take our color impressions out of our heads and compare them, and even if we could that wouldn't help. Of course, there are some actual differences in the ways different people see colors, or the way the color of something shifts with environing conditions. But I suggest that we should think of colors as things that emerge in situations, in which an object, a light source, an atmosphere or medium, a vocabulary or taxonomy, and a permeable, perceptive body are in relation. One does wrong to think of a color as a wavelength of reflected light in itself, but one certainly does wrong to think of it as a phantasm or presentiment or phenomenon, but one does wrong to think of it as only a vocabulary or set of conventions. It sort of makes sense to say that it is not an objective fact that the sky is blue; if there were no perceivers there'd be no color-experiences; but that is the situation in all our transactions with the world, and though, again, I'd prefer to ditch "objectivity" altogether, that the sky is blue is as objective as any fact can be. It's not true just in my head, or the reality it refers to is a feature of a whole situation; that situation, however, is a real situation in a real world and the sentence is true. It is wrong to think of the blueness of the sky as a phantasm or an impression: there'd be no colors without light and reflective capacities of objects. It is not a merely conventional fact that something is blue: you could alter the conventions and not change the colors. Colors can only be characterized in terms of full-scale real-world, perceptual situations. And, of course, color properties are central to many sorts of aesthetic experiences, assessments, creations. Aesthetic values "supervene" on properties such as color and also participate in their holism: they emerge in and as whole environments. And we might consider also the political or economic uses and meaning of color; color is a locus of moral as well as aesthetic significance. The aesthetic and the political are lashed to the weight properties, color properties, size properties, shape properties and with the ways all of these interact with each other and with an entire physical/social/individual world. That is my model for the ontological status of all real values.

So let us entertain this idea: aesthetic properties are exactly as real as any other properties, which is to say that they are features of a situation implicating many layers of and possibilities for connection: again, a physical object in a physical context, a set of social practices, a set of personal experiences. Delete the personal experience and you have deleted the beauty, not because beauty is subjective, but because subjectivity is one strand in this knot; it ceases to be the particular knot it is when this strand is disentangled. Alright, perhaps there are no ethical values without conscious beings. Perhaps there are no ethical values without social practices and vocabularies about value. But there also are no ethical values without physical bodies and things. That a genocide in process is an ethically bad situation isn't not a matter of vocabularies and subjective judgments and subjective pain, but it is also extremely importantly a matter of bodies being violated, being penetrated by projectiles, infiltrated by poisons, cut off from the air.

4

Ethics

A. Freedom of the Will and Moral Agency

1.

I am afraid I am going to have to take a rather hard determinist line, little missy. One thing that might help remove the sting is that the extraordinary complexity of our situation and of ourselves is insufficiently appreciated. Indeed, the relations in which each thing stands are continuously multiplying, even from their infinities of infinities. Each new thing that emerges, and each moment in a continuously unfolding time, multiplies the relations in which each thing stands. A corollary of this is that, at each moment, each thing that persists through that moment is increasingly individuated or rendered more unique. We might call this the paradox of essence: the more pure a thing is, the more self-enclosed, the less fully itself it is: the less individuated by its unique relations. This is why individuals of the insanely rich sort we find in reality depend for their massive individuality precisely on the ways they are compromised. The richer the world, the more incomparable each thing is within that world. Attempts to purify things or ourselves, to simplify them by abstraction or simplify ourselves into rational calculators or singular souls are brutal falsifications of the real situations that are ourselves and the real situations those situations find themselves in.

  The sort of physicalist or naturalist ontologies that we scouted in the first chapter, with their illusion-puncturing style, are going to have problems with free will, probably as much as anything the source of the repugnance that such standpoints have caused. The thing appears to yield an empty, mechanical world and empty mechanical people inhabiting it, because people are themselves only animals or, even worse, just wadded up particles. Now, various materialists have dealt with freedom one way or another;

the atomists appealed to random or unpredictable swerves, for example, and later to quantum indeterminacy. Some have been hard determinists, from which they drew various moral conclusions, either trying to make the thing seem relatively harmless, à la compatibilism of various sorts, or squaring up to their own slavery to and lack of responsibility in the physical world. Dennett has taught us to beware of effortlessly turning the world into a malevolent agent or slave master, but you have to admit that the physical world is pretty directive. If you thought for a minute about the ways the immediate physical environment articulates your movements and positions or even your thoughts and choices on a given day, you'd have to say that it's thorough.

It is often said that the "scientific" or physicalist or mechanical picture of causation, as well as particular applications in neuroscience or genomics, contradict our phenomenological certainty that we are making free decisions. Then we have to explain the alleged phenomenology. I am going to admit here that this rather puzzles me. It is not at all evident to me by self-reflection that I am free in any respect. This in part may reflect my idiosyncratic subjectivity; to begin with, I am a (recovering) addict. (*That* much, of course, isn't really idiosyncratic.) But at least I would say this: I don't think you are entitled to take our subjective certainty that we are free as a starting point, or to deploy it as the datum that needs explanation, because I don't actually share this certainty. Also, of course, I am not quite clear about what it is that people who are subjectively certain they are free are subjectively certain about, or what sort of freedom such a person commits herself to by her subjective certainty. Well, of course, my puzzlement about this might just reflect the absence in me of the sorts of experiences and intuitions that other people inevitably or automatically have.

2.

Returning to a theme from the chapter on ontology, I want to begin by emphasizing the sort of half-conceptualized identification in a variety of "materialist" texts between necessity and spontaneity. Nietzsche puts the point like this:

> No one gives a man his qualities, neither God, nor society, nor his parents and ancestors, nor *he himself* (the latter absurd idea has been taught as "intelligible freedom" by Kant, perhaps also by Plato). *No one* is responsible for existing at all, for being formed so and so, for being placed under those circumstances and in this environment. His own destiny cannot be disentangled from the destiny of all else in past and future.[1]

One thing I think that this picture—which is my picture, too, of course—leaves you to think is that the ideas of free will and responsibility are actually either too simple to bear, or are so complex as to be interminable, and where in material reality we are free is really a much more vexed question than often appears. Maybe it is not the best question; certainly it is not the only question. But I would like to start with what it might really be like, under the myriad pressures, articulations, causal impingements, compositional relations that we display in reality, to experience freedom. I do think that centralizing the moral dilemma, as in "should I, or should I not, pull the trigger?" or (so much worse), "should I let the trolley smack the fat man?" imposes a raw schematism on our actual situation. That situation, sadly and so beautifully too, bristles with ambiguities.

Derrida says that "the concept of *play* remains beyond this opposition, it designates the unity of chance and necessity in an endless calculus."[2] Perhaps we are most free when we are *improvising*, as in a musical group: you might feel freest when you yourself don't know exactly what you're going to do next or even exactly what you just did. Part of the feeling of being necessitated, that is, comes from being able to predict your own actions before they happen: precisely, for example, one function of ethical principles or one use of self-consciousness. This might account, for example, for the fact that many people have experienced determinism as a kind of personal crisis or internal drama, and why people might rebel against their own expectations for themselves. A great jazz improvisation, however, is not precisely poised opposite this. It also seems to emerge by a kind of necessity; things just fit together right without anyone trying to make sure they are going to.

This is the amazed feeling people got when they first heard Louis Armstrong's recordings: the first time through, you've got no idea what he might do. The third time, each bit has to be exactly what it is, even the mistakes; there are no mistakes (that is more or less the first principle of improvisation), even when there are. Louis might never have played the same solo twice, but he played what he was; even with all the imitators, there is only one Louis, hyperintensely himself even in his abandonment of himself to the music, or because of it. The famous cadenza that introduces "West End Blues" is a compatibilist scripture: perfectly free and entirely necessitated, in the same respects. Or maybe that it is perfectly free and that it is perfectly necessitated are two ways of saying the same thing. It's odd, but if that stuff just comes out of Louis's horn without his conscious direction—that is, if he does not deliberate—he is in some senses freer than if he does. Really, you'd have to say that in a given solo Armstrong does both.

This is what Wang Ch'ung or the Caravaka tradition meant when they said that things emerge "spontaneously": spontaneously and also by an inner necessity, freely and as they must. Indeed, the idea, I believe, is that when someone or something acts spontaneously or by *wu wei*, it is most intensely itself. And the universe as a whole is always itself; there is no place for it to be anything else. So it is spontaneous. The whole cannot be adequately explained, or the principle of sufficient reason runs out here. So the universe is at least in a certain sense perfectly free or improvised. It is not teleologically or narratively ordered. That is a beautiful lesson of materialism: the universe is an improvisation.

I think we had better enrich both the linguistic interpretation and the phenomenology. The idea of human freedom is a rich, multiple, equivocal, and ambiguous notion: the word is used in a variety of ways on a variety of occasions. And then I think this is also true in relation to conceptions of human agency and decision making: it is such a richer terrain than in particular the analytic tradition in the philosophy of action would have it. One thing I will say, we should not approach this question in what we might think of as a posture of defensive egomania; many a philosopher has found the claim that we, and in particular he, is not free to be an intolerable affront. But that a position is insulting to human dignity does not show that it's false, putting it mildly, especially given the rather extreme dignity which has been attributed to us by us: as little gods, spirits in material world, something outside and higher than the order of nature. Squirrels would say that about themselves if they could; perhaps, indeed, they are at present chattering it in squirrel.

The movement toward the Enlightenment was characterized by the rejection of a teleological universe. Now, maybe we have to get away at least provisionally from a teleological conception of ourselves. This might mean, first of all, becoming critics of our own pretensions to agency, of staying aware of how we are connected to the order of the world, through our spontaneity and its, as well as its mechanism and ours, our connections to the causal order as well as our distinction in it from other things.

3.

It's not that Louis Armstrong *wants to* play that next figure: he doesn't himself know what's coming next. He's deliberating in the frame; he knows what song he's playing, for example, and that helps determine the possible improvisations. Indeed, he has engaged in a long discipline by which he learned to play the cornet and in which, even, he learned how to improvise, both as a craft and as a way to cultivate the psychological moments of release from practical rationality. But he's not only deliberating, and no particular note is the result of deliberation. It wouldn't be quite right to say that what he does is unintentional, but it wouldn't be quite right to say that it is intentional. The chain of causation definitely runs through him but not exactly through his agency, as that is usually conceived. He does, we might say, what he is, and he becomes what he is as he does it; the action has some especially intimate relation to his identity but also entirely to his world: you can't have Armstrong without trumpets and cornets and jazz groups and jazz and jazz audiences and jazz venues and New Orleans and Chicago and Harlem and race and poverty and so on. But all of these things, many or even all of which are constraints, create a context in which Louis and his horn are free, and in which the ownership of the action by Louis is particularly intense.

In some ways, it is the structure of rules and established practices in which Louis plays that makes his freedom possible. You can't improvise out of nothing, in no context; it is the mastery of the forms of jazz as he acquired and invented them that liberates Louis into a place where he can simultaneously ramify and violate those structures. The last thing you want to do is free Louis by insisting he play something other than jazz or by deleting the rhythm section over which he riffs and which he draws along with him and undermines. Really we should think of this in terms of the quite strict form of the blues, which jazz foundationally explores and displaces; one of Armstrong's first moves was to play through or over the turnaround, tearing up the twelve-bar structure into something more flexible or fluid, as in his primordial cornet solo on "Chimes Blues." That is the kind of human liberation that might actually be possible: an extension and violation of constraints of various kinds. In such constraints and relatively to such constraints, we might usefully be described as free in certain respects. Freedom simpliciter, freedom as exemption from the order of physical causation, is something very else.

Perhaps we should indeed start with the phenomenology of freedom. Don't defend your dignity by insisting that you are free in some abstract sense, notoriously hard to clarify, but think about under what circumstances you have actually felt free. Travel sometimes yields such a sensation: when you don't know the place you are, you don't know where you might go next. It might be anywhere! Or perhaps after you quit your job, or after the school year's over, or after you've processed the divorce: the sense of possibilities opening up that didn't exist before. A primordial experience or fantasy of liberation is enshrined in the David Allen Coe/Johnny Paycheck chestnut "Take this Job and Shove It": I am emerging suddenly from the constraints that distorted my person. That doesn't mean that I mutate into the unmoved mover of what happens next, but perhaps that I do not yet know myself what factors will move me into the future. Action that is extremely routinized or ritualistic in a negative sense can be experienced as unfree: the more times you drive north on 83, the less free you are to exit. The autistic lifestyle might reduce agency. But that I myself do not know what factors may move me in the future means that I am improvising right now, or the world opens up as a realm of improvisation when the routines explode or dissipate.

But the connections of observations like this to the sense of freedom that is allegedly required for moral agency are vague or strained. The experiences of freedom I've just described are related tangentially to the ascription of moral agency; it's not like Louis is more responsible for his solo when he's improvising than he is if he just plays it through correctly. Or is it? Perhaps it depends on what "he" means here. That he is doing what he does neither purely intentionally nor purely by accident: perhaps that is at least one center of freedom in art and in play.

It makes some sense to say that a child is more responsible for her actions after the school year is over. These facts to some extent shape the debate about compatibilism; Hume liked to point out that if your actions were actually random or not connected with your character and history, you would not be responsible for them after all. The same is true where your action is directed by others, where you rise from your desk when someone rings a bell, or fill in little bubbles on a standardized test at some bureaucrat's behest. These, like actions taken from the "moral law," are cases where you yourself know, precisely from your own acquaintance with your own character and history and those of the authorities, what you will do. That is the feeling of being compelled, though Kant, bizarrely, calls it freedom. Now, how would that bear on moral responsibility? Often enough the idea of freedom or even of personhood is accounted for in terms of holding yourself responsible to certain standards or principles or the deliverances of certain faculties such as rationality. But the phenomenology of freedom centers on the transgression of the rules as much as on the rules themselves, self-imposed or not.

In criminal law, of course, if the murder is purely improvisational rather than premeditated—a jazz murder, so to speak—it is less culpable; you are less responsible for it. But perhaps there are other contexts for explicating freedom than criminal law, and perhaps practical attributions of freedom or unfreedom, even there, are weirder than they appear in theory. In fact, I think that a lot of the urgency of "the free will problem" comes from questions about assigning criminal culpability, and perhaps we should wonder just a bit at the obsession about this question among metaphysicians. The practical question of responsibility as it is assessed at any given moment within any given legal framework is not the same as the problem of human free will: what it's like to have it, if we do, and what it's like to lose it, and how it is related to attributions of responsibility in a variety of dimensions or practices. Admittedly, the criminal justice system stands in desperate need of philosophical underpinnings, but that is not the only task with regard to the issue of free will that might be performed by the philosopher; I myself would not assay it without a substantial retainer. Our project can be more than just figuring out whom to punish or send to rehab.

4.

If free will requires any sort of causal disconnection from a deterministic system of physical reality, then we ought just to admit that it is impossible. But whether that is what it requires, and whether the system of nature is indeed deterministic (well, it's not, if we are free!): we might find such matters difficult to elucidate. I would like, rather, to see what sort of freedom we can have or do have in our full connection and irremediable distinction. Now, first of all, as I've argued or urged, individuality or the mystery of autonomous identity arises precisely out of the accumulation of unique relations; each individual is massively distinguished from all others in virtue precisely of its relations to them. Certainly, we're not going to get anywhere with

Louis's freedom by beginning to locate him in a sphere where we consider only his own consciousness or even his own body: again, Louis needs orphanages and cornets or nothing is going to happen at all. Louis needs to practice and jam all the time; the way he plays is a craft and accomplishment, though it also, of course, contains that apparently unaccountable flash of inimitable genius. But at any rate, we've got to focus on the meanings and forms of freedom that are actually available in a relational universe or the forms of connection in which we experience it, to the extent that, on reflection, we do.

This approach seems in tension with my supposedly basic antihumanism or overweening externalism. Maybe we need to find the possibility of freedom *out there*; maybe I should be looking for the freedom of dogs, dishes, or neutrinos. I would not want to eliminate offhand the notion that some such things could be free in a variety of interesting senses. But there is no doubt that the free will problem arises—or at least is presented as arising—on the phenomenological level: fundamentally, we are trying account for our own sense of our ability to deliberate, and so on. Now, on the other hand, perhaps it arises basically socially, and the question is, under what conditions can we hold someone responsible (for a crime, for a debt, for a car accident, etc.)? And we may be rethinking such things slowly, under the pressure of MRIs and psychiatric medicine. We may eventually or even now be able to get away socially with various quite reconfigured senses of the human self, and I am suggesting that we may be able to get away with it psychologically, too, though I also want to suggest that we don't need to gather up a new conception of agency but simply take more seriously the actual conceptions we do possess in the ordinary experience of the ordinary world and one another.

One of the definitions with which Spinoza begins the *Ethics* is this: "That thing is called free, which exists solely by the necessity of its own nature." Unfortunately, he adds: "and of which the action is determined by itself alone."[3] This is one of the first of many paradoxical characterizations of freedom in modernity, in Rousseau and Hegel, for example, defining it in terms of some variety of necessity. It leads in Spinoza to a version of determinism for human beings, of course, and reserves freedom to God, or . . . nature. Now, within the flow, there is perhaps a sufficient causal explanation of any given thing/event. But as to the whole, it appears to be a kind of spontaneous upwelling within the nothingness.

Now, if the whole is a sort of spontaneous blossoming or arbitrary play or sheer emergence or brute fact or if it arises out of itself or by the necessity of its own nature or by improvisation or however we may grope to express this, we emerge in some sense spontaneously within it: not disconnected from the flow of causation, but arising within a system which is as a whole a spontaneous or improvisational development. "Determined by itself alone" sounds wrong even for Louis's playing, which emerges in collaboration as well as autonomy. Then we might seek human freedom not in autonomy within the flow of events, as an agent among patients, or a prime mover in the order of cause, but in connection with the world in its uncontrollable or arbitrary or inhuman or beautiful flow. No doubt this sounds cosmic, but I envision a sort of freedom that is a collaboration with things, an identity with and emergence from them, a freedom characterized by ways of being in the actual world skillfully instead of standing apart from it in imagination. This could be very mundane; maybe this is precisely the sort of freedom we do routinely enjoy.

At any rate, we might begin by talking about how someone's action, let's say, is caused: outside the influence of various constricting or coercive factors: you're not being blackmailed, for example. You're not *not* doing it just because you fear you'll get caught and executed. But also there are various forms of routinization in which one's unfreedom is basically imposed by oneself on oneself; you behave mechanically because you just can't figure out how to loosen up or how to want to loosen up. An extreme version might be something like agoraphobia; it's as though one imposes on oneself the rule that one isn't to leave the house. In a sense the decision is perfectly autonomous: no person is forcing you, and no physical circumstances preclude going out. You are the Kantian or Rousseauvian lawgiver of yourself, but precisely a relation like that can destroy one's experience of one's freedom from within, even as in other cases, one experiences freedom precisely as the ability to force oneself to obey the rules that one recognizes as legitimate. And, of course, again, any such rule is an extremely complex matter; perhaps it derives from social (e.g., religious) strictures; "don't leave home" presupposes a certain vision of the home and what it means and where it is; it presupposes that one has a home of some sort; you need a world of things and a vocabulary.

Perhaps freedom requires feeling or playing with the strands of connection in a different or refreshed way. Perhaps freedom indicates a certain poise or posture in the world, a certain simultaneous relief from constriction and feeling forward to new forms of constriction. Louis is not relieved of all rules when he plays a perfect improvisation; indeed, he has internalized the structures of jazz thoroughly. But then again, he does not hold himself to these structures: he knows them and observes them and deflects them or puts them in play. He recognizes and optionalizes them. His playing is detached from his conscious deliberation, but it is not released from his self, from what he is feeling or expressing; he is released from certain mechanical forms of agency precisely by making them identical to himself or "internalizing" them: he gains a certain reciprocal mastery that it might not be too strong to say amounts to a kind of love, or reflects both commitment and liberty, connection and autonomy, fixedness and freedom, extreme skill and something beyond skill to which skill is devoted. Perhaps this is only one model or source of freedom, however.

Now, is he *responsible* for what he plays? In some ways, obviously so, and his playing is attributable to him as intimately as anything can be attributed to anyone.

In another way not, and his playing makes one feel the power of the old idea of the arts as coming from the Muses: from we know not where, from something else or more, something outside the self that releases the artist into a kind of self-transcendence. I don't think we can be free if we are not in connection: or, freedom is a certain sort of connection. But I don't think we can be free if we are not also real individuals or capable of acting with more or less (though never perfect) autonomy. There is no expression of the self which is not also the expression of the situations of that self. And the question should be how does a free-ish self emerge, or in what situations can it emerge?

5.

One thing I want to say is that I do not believe that it is anything like an adequate starting point to assert that we are free and/or morally responsible in virtue of our rationality, or free when we can deliberate rationally, or responsible because we act from reasons, or when we act for reasons or for good reasons, and so on. This seems to me like a hangover from dualism, from the point of view that we literally consist of two different and distinct sorts of objects. The art critic Dave Hickey, comparing the films of Stan Brakhage and Andy Warhol, says that "Brakhage told us what we already knew as children of the Cold War, that no matter how hard we tried, we could not be free—thus inviting us, paradoxically, into the rigors of utopian political orthodoxy. Warhol's film, on the other hand, told us what we needed to know, that, no matter how hard we tried, we could not be ordered—that insofar as we were tiny, raggedy, damaged and disorganized human beings, we probably *were* free, in some small degree, whether we liked it or not."[4] At a minimum, if we are free, we are free as tiny, raggedy, damaged, and disorganized human beings, not as rational subjects. Well, the rationality is folded in there somewhere along with the rest, but hardly as the exclusive site of freedom.

The Aristotelian and Kantian pictures associate action (understood, let's say, through the practical syllogism) with moral agency or personhood, and passion with, we might say, moral victimhood, or at least with being a victim of the universe or even of oneself. (By passion, here, I do not mean emotion; I mean stuff that happens to you that cannot be accounted for by your own ends or result from your own practical syllogisms.) But this is not, I believe, how we actually think about freedom. One might have the experience of deciding freely in particular when one is in a position to "follow one's heart," or (in certain circumstances), precisely when one does what one's passions direct rather than, for example, what one "ought to do." One might have the experience of being free (which is what we're trying to account for, at least at this stage) precisely when one does what one ought not to do. The Kantian imposition of universal law upon oneself can decrease one's sense of one's own freedom, like agoraphobia, in which the point is obvious because the rules are irrational. But holding yourself to rational deliberation and sensible decisions continuously can be experientially just as a stunted or dwarfed or miniaturized as being driven pillar to post by wacky desires; you might feel, or be, just as canalized and distorted by rational deliberation as by impulsive or improvisational action. Self control is, by definition, slavery as well as mastery, of course. Or if that's too pejorative, in self control, rational or otherwise, there is the bit that controls and the bit that is controlled. Which is free when, even on the accounts that centralize rational self control as the essence of freedom?

It may seem a dark thought, but transgression of the rules, whether these are the rules of an institution or a theory or of a religion or of a moral theory or orientation that one accepts oneself, is as often experienced as liberating or as much an authentic expression of the self as is holding oneself to obedience. I have to say that I've never felt any real clash of intuitions on weakness of the will: of course, people sometimes do things that they believe are wrong; sometimes people do things precisely *because* they *know* them to be wrong. Nor is this a form of slavery; certainly, it may be experienced as a release from slavery. Consider Huck Finn; he knows that helping a slave escape is wrong, and yet he does so anyway, directed by an unaccountable irrational emotion, or mere sentimentality. Perhaps the lawyers for a murderer try to paint a picture of him in court as driven, internally or externally. And the fact that someone does something that—at a minimum—most other people believe to be wrong, seems itself to count as a kind of provisional evidence that he did not do it freely, that something is bent or ill: compelled. But certainly people who hold themselves to rules all day also appear compelled.

The dark fact is that transgression can be experienced as a release. And the light fact is that transgression of one sort or another is often salutary or requisite. Transgressing certain teachings of the Catholic Church or the Communist Party—even when one has also deeply internalized them—can be an element and emblem in the political, scientific, sexual, artistic, or intellectual liberation of people other than oneself. Simply *not being able to bring yourself into alignment* with the rules you yourself want to want to obey, or being recalcitrant to the workings of your own will, can be experienced as a liberation: people resist because they have to as well as because they want to. If the self is divided into will and recalcitrant body or action and passion or deliberation and impulse, then the conquest of the will by impulse is as much a liberation (and as much an enslavement) as the conquest of the impulse by will. Many self-imposed rules may need to be pressed or tested, or violated and abandoned, in order for us to be free. Sometimes you need to release yourself from yourself. Sometimes you need to relinquish the picture of yourself as the tyrant or technocrat of yourself. This makes it sound like transgression itself is a result of a deliberation that could be rational, but just as often you are liberated suddenly, unaccountably, for better or worse, without knowing quite how or why; you act, as we say, on impulse. But an impulsive action is often experienced as more free in a variety of dimensions than a deliberated one.

6.

We cannot be released from nature, or the order of causation, in virtue of any particular actual faculty we may possess; we cannot stand above it or outside it, though we engage it in different ways. It is a familiar point, perhaps, that the conception of moral agency that one gets in Kant, for example, presupposes a principled bifurcation—perhaps a distinction of ontological planes—between person and, let's say, the ordinary world. In Kant, the free moral agent is a transcendental subject. Freedom in this sense means independence from the order of mundane reality, the deterministic sphere of nature. How freedom arises in a natural order is the great ur-question of German Idealism, and it is not too much to think of Schiller, Fichte, Schelling, Hegel, and even Kierkegaard as obsessed with it. It is a version of the Platonic or Pythagorean crisis: what the hell am I doing *here*? The naturalistic conception of the universe in its revival from classical sources such as Lucretius as well as canons of empirical science articulated by Bacon, for example, was interpreted as a threat to human freedom, as were various forms of deterministic Protestantism that preceded full scientific naturalism by perhaps a century. The Idealists and those connected with them (Goethe, Novalis, the Schlegels, Coleridge) read this as also putting into play reason as against faith, rationality as against passion, and so on into the Romantic dualisms, so centrally embodied by Schelling, who also tried to fend off Idealism as a threat to reality, or to think his way back to reality out of Idealism. Everyone responded to Jacobi's formulation: "It is impossible that everything is nature and not freedom, because it is impossible that everything which elevates and ennobles man—the true, the good, and the beautiful—are only illusion, deception, and lies."[5] On the other hand, if you believed with Jacobi (and dare I say it, Kant and Plato) that nature itself was incompatible with truth, goodness, and beauty, you might have a motivation to believe that there must be something more, even if there is not. But there is no use arguing with Jacobi, who explicitly (and plausibly) denies the jurisdiction of all rational argument on this sort of question.

The thinkers who made this issue central in these terms—as nature vs. freedom—took a variety of positions on the relation. Some thought that freedom could be achieved by a reduction of nature to self or Spirit, locating reason at the world's heart, as in Fichte or Hegel. Or it could be sought by an integration of the spiritual and the natural (Schiller and Schelling), or by an act of spiritual self-realization (Kierkegaard) or in an emptying or annihilation of the tortured self (Schopenhauer). But these figures shared this form of the crisis of modernity: trying to figure out *who we could possibly be* in what seemed more and more like a physical universe in which everything that happens can in principle be fully explained by what happened before and the laws of nature. They are fighting a rear-guard action on behalf of their exalted assessment of themselves, and few human beings in the history of our paltry species have ever had a more exalted assessment of themselves (I am exempting Kierkegaard from that accusation, however). Really, this is the main source of the extreme tension between a scientific standpoint and German Idealism: whatever they said they were doing, the Idealists were defending the spiritual realm from the scientific worldview, which is part of the essence of Romanticism.

7.

What is remarkable and disconcerting is that philosophers still find themselves ensnared just here. Christine Korsgaard, for example, begins *Self-Constitution* by observing that "Both human beings and the other animals act, but human actions can be morally right or wrong, while the actions of the other animals cannot."[6] Parfit starts more or less the same way. Now, I bring this up not to thrash Korsgaard for not taking animals seriously enough, but to point out that moral agency of the sort we supposedly exercise is still basically being conceived as an anomaly in the order of nature; or we're still, at this late date, fending off challenges from the animal kingdom to our moral agency, which in the familiar fashion keeps receding to a single point of light. After that, Korsgaard constructs a conception of agency that, though it brings Kantian noumenal agency down to earth in various ways, is its descendent. Its essence is still rationality as the wise apportionment of means to ends and its freedom is still obedience to the moral law, insofar as a person, in her self-construction, imposes this law on herself in an act of identification. This is precisely as well the Kant/Habermas strategy for constructing the legitimacy of the state: you owe obedience to the law you impose on yourself, and this imposition of law is itself the construction of that very self or its essence.

It is no argument, but it is nevertheless true, when I say that the following passage exquisitely expresses everything I reject on this constellation of issues: personal identity, freedom, and the nature of ethics.

> Both human beings and the other animals act, but human actions can be morally right or wrong, while the actions of the other animals cannot. This must be because of something distinctive about the nature of human action, about the way in which we make choices. . . . The name I give to the distinctive feature is the traditional one—rationality. As I understand it, reason is a power we have in virtue of a certain type of self-consciousness—consciousness of the ground of our beliefs and actions. This form of self-consciousness gives us a capacity to control our beliefs and actions that

the other animals lack, and makes us active in a way they are not. To put the point another way, this form of self-consciousness makes it necessary to *take control* of our beliefs and actions, but we must then work out how to do that: we must find normative principles, laws, to govern what we believe and do. The distinctive feature of human beings, reason, is therefore the capacity for normative self-government.[7]

And then, rationality is conceived teleologically, so that the self is essentially administering bits of the world and possibly itself in order to achieve ends. Any twitch that is not purposive is not an action, and hence not a reflection on or an expression of one's personhood. You are constituted as a person by a series of actions or choices-for-ends; you are a person insofar as you can bring these to order under principles such as those provided by your social roles. You have taken on such roles—supervisor or underling, for example, parent or child, sibling or friend—voluntarily, and in this sense you are the lawgiver of yourself as you come by action to inhabit these roles adequately or well. Well, this is Korsgaard's particular synthesis of Kant and Aristotle. Of course, those names also indicate the centrality of such conceptions to the western tradition.

Here I would just like to remark that this conception of personhood is—if I myself am anything like a person, and not to put too fine a point on it—just false. It is, we might say, bizarrely arid, extremely and arbitrarily attenuated. If it describes what it is to be a moral person, I do not believe there are any, and I am grateful for that. Its conception of freedom detaches human agency from the order of causation in an extremely disconcerting—or I might say personally insulting—way. And it is profoundly distasteful in that (1) it deploys a political model of selfhood (Korsgaard takes Plato's analogy of self to *polis* with great seriousness); (2) the model is authoritarian. It's all very well to say that it is the entire person that acts, divided up in some tripartite manner as in reason, spirit, and desire, but the "constitution" described by Plato or Korsgaard, of course, orders these in a hierarchical fashion, and ultimately rests your very selfhood on whether you can bring your desires under the thumb of universal law. The freedom it describes is not a freedom worth wanting: even Schiller as a critic of Kant understood this. And it is not a freedom creatures such as ourselves—embedded utterly in the order of the world, mysterious to ourselves and imperfectly self-conscious—can possibly possess.

More relevant than these polemics is that this conception of agency is forged in order for a conception of freedom to fall out necessarily; it is built on the alleged insight that we are responsible only for what we freely choose: we are responsible for our actions insofar as we choose them, and we are responsible for the character of our selfhood or moral agency to the extent that we choose that. If this is what it means to be a moral agent, then we had better be desperate for freedom; we need it at every moment even to be ourselves, elusive as it is. But if we take Korsgaard and her ilk to be arguing from our agency to our freedom, we might just say that the argument begs the question. And if the argument is from our freedom to our agency, then I deny the premise. I hold that in many cases we are not free, but we are responsible; hence, freedom is not necessary for responsibility.

8.

For one thing, the conception of agency as activity in the sense of transforming conditions for ends is at best half the story, if creatures such as ourselves are moral agents. We ought to characterize personhood at least as much in terms of modes of receptivity as in terms of activity. Harry Frankfurt, in his classic paper "Freedom of the Will," gives what I think is certainly one of the more plausible conceptions of freedom in the analytic tradition. First of all, he does not postulate a rational subject or sovereign will directing the body and emotions: the old Kantian saw that just keeps turning up in the darnedest places. But not, or at least not exactly, in Frankfurt. "The statement that a person enjoys freedom of the will," writes Frankfurt, "means (also roughly) that he is free to want what he wants to want."[8] Moral personhood is characterized in part by having "second-order desires" or "volitions," desires to desire or not to desire some of the things one more or less immediately desires or fails to. This requires self-consciousness, of course; one must become aware of one's desires. And with self-consciousness, as in Korsgaard, comes the possibility of self-control. "It is in securing conformity of his will to his second-order volitions, then, that a person exercises freedom of the will. . . . The unwilling addict's will is not free. This is shown by the fact that it is not the will he wants."[9] It is no coincidence that addiction comes up over and over again as a puzzle and paradigm of unfreedom in this literature, and I will make it central. But one thing I want to do that I think is rarely done in this context: I also want to make it personal; I want to describe it from inside.

The clarity of Frankfurt's prose, I must say, is entirely refreshing, in particular after one has been reading a bunch of Schelling. But I do not think that he himself sufficiently appreciates the complexity of the sort of psychology that he is deploying. I am free when I can do what I want to want to do, as we might casually put it; but the layers are already piling up: you have basic or grunt or gopher desires and as it were administrative desires or volitions. The administrative desires, in a good situation, control the grunt desires. Then you are free. But then what does "you" refer to here? What is it that has the second-order desires? Perhaps it is—you are—a "will." But that doesn't appear to be the position. *You have* a will, and you can want to have it or not want to have it, or its deliverances. You want it to respond to your volitions: already the self is a sort of bureaucracy of rather hierarchically ordered items. Animals have a will in Frankfurt's sense. It is a faculty of decision at the first level. Then in humans desires of the second level direct the will to constrain or sort out the desires at the which our nature is constrained neither physically nor morally and yet is active in both ways, preeminently deserves to be called a free disposition; and if we call the condition of the sensuous determination the physical, and that of the rational determination the logical, we must call this condition of real and active determinacy the *aesthetic*.[11]

The whole structure is Kantian, but Schiller makes what we might call the Romantic turn by beginning to feel the oppressiveness of reason, which is a self-oppression. Acting according to the moral law because it is the moral law is acting under constraint. For Kant, reason liberates us from Nature. For Schiller (at moments; the *Letters* are notoriously eclectic) reason potentially reenslaves us. But between these forms of necessity, precisely in the gap which separates them or in the contradiction and confusion that erupts between them, we are free to *play*. He uses "play," "beauty," "art," "the aesthetic," "freedom" indiscriminately as the name of this gap. "Beauty," he writes, "can be inferred simply from the possibility of a nature that is both sensuous and rational."[12]

In the Kantian moral realm of pure rational agency, we are determined: our will is determined by the moral law, which is no less external to ourselves than the chain of physical causation, or is much more external, as Kierkegaard, for example, emphasized in volume two of *Either/Or*. (Of course, this is not the way Kant would put it, and Habermas, for example, has more and more rested his political philosophy on a conception of freedom in which to be free is to be the lawgiver to oneself. The anti-Enlightenment and early Romantic figures, I am saying, attacked this aspect of Kant vociferously.) Then the realm of freedom is found between Nature and Reason, or on the way from one to another, in a realm of the free play of the faculties, or the arts, which display the moral law in the sensual realm and make us free in the disco bohemia between them. This would also be a reintegration of a bifurcated self, or of Kant's phenomenal and noumenal subjects. That is certainly the way that Hegel, but also, for example, Fichte and Schelling, conceived their basic project: finding a place for Spirit in the universe, and vice versa, and conceiving the dilemma precisely in terms of the possibility of freedom in a natural world and a reconciliation of a split human subject: animal body and allegedly divine spirit. Kierkegaard is also negotiating this terrain. And in Kierkegaard, there is freedom before and beyond reason, but reason itself is a form of constraint (well, sometimes constraint is necessary or appropriate; Kierkegaard calls that "the ethical," which is certainly conceived in Kantian terms). Indeed, in a vast panoply of versions we might represent this as the great problem of the West, from the Eleatics and Pythagoreans even unto the present, in the form of the question of consciousness: are we, or where are we, in the order of nature? "The free will problem" is surely still engaged in the supposed mystery of human entanglement in the physical, causal order, still worrying at what worried Fichte, Descartes, Augustine, Plato.

Of course, a metaphysics looms behind Schiller that I wouldn't even know how to start to regard as plausible. But one of the many things I like about this account is that it makes freedom a kind of wriggle room in a reality *and a psychology* in which we are hedged about by necessities. The drama of constraint and liberation is a constant complex mercurial negotiation made on the fly, not some sort of primordial condition or faculty of the soul. Now, on the other hand, all these figures certainly had on board the outlines of Hobbes's and Hume's compatibilism, which conceived freedom in a far more mundane way as absence of physical constraint. Freedom, says Kant, is obedience to the moral law. Freedom, says Hegel, is obedience to the political state. These disinformation campaigns must be torn to shreds, if nothing else because rebellion against the moral or juridical law is at least equally, or on at least some occasions, also a locus of freedom. Not to recognize that is to flirt with totalitarianism. And surely this is a more natural way to use the term: freedom is a breaking of constraints no matter whether they originate within oneself or outside. Freedom as obedience to anything is always going to have the ring and the allure of paradox, one of the reasons people keep formulating it that way. Of course, that is also simplistic, and freedom comes if it ever comes at all in a sort of negotiation with the constraints, in imposing them and bending them or moving them, for example in what Kierkegaard called the teleological suspension of the ethical.

I want to keep driving home a point so obvious as to need continual emphasis: that we are all always extremely physically constrained. Compared to the range of actions that might be possible to someone who was not so constrained—whatever in the world that could mean—the range of our own possible actions is infinitesimal. Test this perhaps by considering the range of actions open to a being or "dude" who possessed all the superpowers of all the members of the X-Men and the Justice League of America insofar as they are compatible with one another: someone who can leap tall buildings, turn invisible, levitate objects, control the power of gravity, and so on. We're all always tied up, though the bonds may be looser or tighter. If there is freedom even in the physicalist, compatibilist sense, it too relies on a relatively tiny and evanescent space for movement in the context of an overwhelming physical reality that saturates and articulates our every action. And even if you achieve something intentionally by doing something, you achieve infinitely many things unintentionally by doing it as well. Or if we do achieve anything intentionally we achieve infinitely many things unintentionally simultaneously: we are only extremely sketchily aware of the sources and outcomes of any event including our own actions.

10.

Now, in the compatibilist sense—or a simplistic compatibilist sense on which to be free is to have room to move—animals and all sorts of objects can be free: they might have scope for movement within an environment, or enough void to proceed or material of insufficient density to block their progress: they have play. A sapling takes advantage of access to a spot of open sky to survive, and reaches toward it. Water makes downward unless hindered, and so on. Well, I am not denying that this is a form of freedom, and you are free if you can seek your own level, if you are not dammed up. Only what is "you"? Like everything else: a material object embedded in myriads of situations, and like everything else a situation consisting of objects. And this is true if we consider the matter "psychologically" as well as physiologically, always with the caveat that each token psychological state is also a physical state (though not a brain state): each aspect or faculty a spatiotemporal situation.

Of the Stoic conception of freedom, Dennett writes:

> Each of us is assigned a role to play in the tragedy of life, they suggested, and there is nothing for us to do but say our prescribed lines as best we can . . . Or consider a dog on a leash being pulled behind a wagon; it can trot along peacefully, or it can resist. Either way it will end up at the same destination, but if it resigns itself to the destination and makes the most of the journey, it will enjoy a certain kind of freedom. Being led through life with a rope around one's neck—some freedom![13]

But first of all, I think this wildly underestimates the affirmative possibilities lodged with Stoicism, and even more clearly in Taoism and other philosophies that recommend world affirmation and then proceed to a kind of ecstasy of identification.

> Confucius was viewing Lu-Liang Falls, where the water cascades down nearly three hundred feet into billowing rapids nearly forty *li* long. Not even fish, turtles, or other water creatures could swim there, so when he saw a man swimming, he immediately assumed it was an attempt to end a bitter life. He sent his disciples downstream to try to rescue him, but before they'd gone more than a few hundred paces, the man emerged from the flow, hair streaming behind him, singing as he swam up to the bank.
> Confucius caught up with him and inquired, "I took you for a sprite. But now I see that you're a man. May I ask, is there a Tao to how you go along in the water?"
> "Lost," he said, I possess no Tao. I was born to it. I follow the Tao of water, doing nothing of my own."[14]

That is, there is joy and also competence in knowing and going along with the way things are, or even in an abandonment of the self. It's not the only conceivable sort of freedom, but perhaps Dennett sneezes at it too quickly.

He himself reserves an important place in his account of freedom for various sorts of physical or deterministic constraints. In trying to adumbrate the concept of "control," he deploys the example of a radio-controlled model airplane.

> When you control your plane perfectly, you don't do it by controlling all the causes that influence it. The weather, the density of the air, and the force of gravity, for instance, are all beyond your control, and they are the largest forces to act on your plane. The fact that your plane is constantly under the influence of gravity does not prevent you from controlling—in fact in some regards gravity helps you, just so long as you *know* its effects on the plane.[15]

Dennett connects this to the role of foreknowledge in deliberation. He gives this example: "That Boston is more than 3,000 miles from Oxford is a circumstance quite beyond my control, but knowing it, I was able to take appropriate steps to arrive in Oxford in time for my lectures. I could not change that circumstance, but I could accommodate myself to it."[16] I should think that these are the sorts of facts that ought to be recognized by even the most rabid advocate of first-cause free will: we are everywhere severely constrained. These constraints are necessary to freedom, or at any rate they constitute the sort of environment in which freedom does emerge, if it does: the only such environment we know until we meet with or achieve omnipotence. It's not just that gravity helps you in some respects control the plane: the whole of the activity is impossible or incomprehensible without it. And then, of course, aside from these very general circumstances, each situation teems with particular constraints: if you're flying the plane, you've got the lay of the land, the trees or obstacles, the light and atmospheric conditions right there right then, the features of the controller and of the human hand, and so on. The journey from Boston to Oxford is marked by myriad such accommodations, or indeed consists of them. These are simultaneously constraints and devices: they are both why this isn't much, much easier and why it is possible at all.

We might think of the Stoic conception of freedom as articulating one of the possibilities for freedom in its strongest sense. Frankfurt, though I don't think he has Stoicism in mind, points out in "Alternate Possibilities and Moral Responsibility" that "there may be circumstances that constitute sufficient conditions for a certain action to be performed by someone and that therefore make it impossible for him to do otherwise, but that do not actually impel the person to act."[17] One way to achieve this state of freedom would be that your will actually comes to conform to the way things are, which is exactly the sort of case that Frankfurt imagines. And though we may negate, hate, erase in imagination many aspects of the world, we all also do still will it in many ways as well, I hope. Or we will it as we breathe: autonomically. At any rate, you would have perfect freedom of the will if you could break the world to your will: in that sense, only God or superhero collages are free. But you would also, it seems to me, have perfect freedom of the will if you could will whatever happens: if you could want everything to be exactly what it actually is. Nietzsche calls that "the hardest task." Indeed, I roughly reckon it to be impossible and also necessary, and it is very much recommended not only by Nietzsche and the Stoics, but by the Taoists and Zen masters and the author of *Obscenity, Anarchy, Reality*.

We're always oscillating between poles: accepting and transforming what is, trapped as in Schiller between Nature and Reason, and we require the moment of receptivity at least as much as the moment of activity. Here is Epictetus:

> We should go to receive instruction, not in order to change the constitution of things,—for this is neither vouchsafed us nor is it better that it should be,—but in order that, things about us being as they are and as their nature is, we may for our own part, keep our wills in harmony with what happens. For, look you, can we escape from men? And how is it possible? But can we, if they associate with us, change them? And who vouchsafes us that power? What alternative remains, then, or what method can we find for living with them? . . . But you are impatient and peevish, and if you are alone, you call it loneliness, but if you are in the company of men you call them schemers and brigands, and you find fault, even with your own parents and children and brothers and neighbors. . . .
>
> What, then, is the punishment of those who do not accept? To be just as they are. Is he peevish because he is alone? Let him be in solitude! Is he peevish with his parents? Let him be an evil son and grieve! Is he peevish with his children? Let him be a bad father! Just as Socrates was not in prison, for he was there willingly. "Alas, that I should be lame in my leg!" Slave, do you, then, because of one paltry leg blame the universe? Will you not make a free gift of it to the whole?[18]

Notice that Epictetus always draws near the direct human consequences of radical acceptance: it constitutes a refusal to judge or even a resolution to affirm, other persons: an attitude which, if more universally held, would certainly yield a diminution of cruelty and persecution. What Epictetus finds tragic yet amusing is the predicament of a person who spends an entire life on earth dissatisfied, condemned by his own perversity to permanent peevishness. There is only one possible path to serenity or even to union and ecstasy, for creatures such as ourselves: love of the world.

And I am saying that this, unlike "obedience to the moral law," is indeed a conception of human freedom. But however, I also believe it to be humanly impossible. Even Epictetus and in particular Marcus Aurelius keep showing symptoms of this sad fact throughout their texts. Marcus is continually admonishing himself to accept the completely unacceptable behavior of people associated with the Roman imperial court: all the betrayals, the factions, the intrigues, the murders. He sort of seems to want to keep these vague in the text; they are rather amorphous challenges that keep suddenly coming into focus or manifesting as symptoms. Insofar as we know the details, they are harrowing, including the adultery and treason of his wife, achieved simultaneously. *The Meditations* is kind of a self-siege; it's like Marcus spends all day every day berating himself for not accepting the way things are. "Do not act unwillingly, or selfishly, or impulsively, or tentatively. . . . Let the god who dwells within you command a man, a seasoned veteran, a statesman, a Roman," and so on.[19] The whole book enacts in the most vivid way an heroic attempt to quell or subdue or unify a divided self; Marcus writes a philosophy according to which the self is characterized fundamentally in terms of its divisions, and in which in the familiar fashion the real self keeps receding behind ever-new layers of mere phenomena, false beliefs and unsatisfiable desires, wills and the will that wills. This is the self that, as Epictetus and Marcus always insist, cannot be harmed at all, come what may. But it is also the self in identity with nature and reason; and the struggle is always to explain how we can be so very mediocre, so riven, so mortal, so confused. The answer is traditionally: we are not, really. We might have to face up eventually, though.

But then it is hard also to deny the real stillness, the sense of harmony and identity, to which Marcus arrives in his moments of actual (for one thing, literal) peace:

> We should also pause to consider how charming and graceful are the unexpected effects of nature's work. When bread is baking, for example, cracks appear in the crust. Although this would seem to confound the baker's design, they attract our attention and help to arouse our appetite. Figs too burst open just when they are best to eat, and olives left on the tree to rot achieve a most exquisite beauty. Similarly, the golden grain's drooping head, the lion's furrowed brow, the boar's foaming snout, and so many other details, if taken out of context, are not all that attractive, but when seen in their natural setting, they complete a picture and please the eye.
>
> In this way, the perceptive man, profoundly curious about the workings of nature, will take a peculiar pleasure in everything, even the humble or ungainly parts that contribute to the making of the whole. The actual jaws of living beasts will delight him as much as their representations by artists and sculptors. With a discerning eye, he will warm to an old man's strength or an old woman's beauty while admiring with cool detachment the seductive charms of youth. The world is full of wonders like these that will appeal only to those who study nature closely and develop a real affinity for her works.[20]

This is a remarkably decent stance of appreciation of the world, but also of absorption in it, and a kind of scientific stance of empirical interest in its details. If a Spinoza or Walking Stewart or a Lucretius goes mystical at the heart of matter, Marcus at his best moments just matter-of-factly enjoys the world or takes "a peculiar pleasure in everything," in spite of everything. Or we might say that it is a realist's wisdom, an immanent enlightenment, à la Thoreau or Ruisdael. One thing to notice about this vision is that it integrates the human and the nonhuman: nature for the Stoics is something we are all embedded in all the time; the point is to understand this—moment by moment, in detail—and not to detach ourselves from it in fantasy and find it wanting. And then, right then, Marcus is also admonishing himself to look on the vices of other people and even himself as he would look at a fascinating beast: as remarkable and interesting expressions of nature's profusion.

11.

Human beings may be nature's most amazing production, but whether or not, we are certainly nature's most self-congratulatory production. We have a sort of species patriotism wherein to denigrate the human as not created in God's image or not anomalous free agents in a deterministic order or not the crowning achievement by which evolution finally walked upright seems intolerable. However, that a philosophical position makes you feel defensive is not a demonstration that it is false. I would just like to point out that we do not know right now whether, for example, we will take life to the stars, or annihilate it entirely here on earth, and perhaps the ultimate end of evolution is universal extinction under our aegis; that wouldn't surprise me in the least: it's just the sort of trick evolution has already pulled on most of the species that have ever existed. But now I would like to explore a series of thoughts that arise from the speculation that the miracle of the human is not necessarily very impressive. I say we have no idea whether we are very impressive or not. Moralists of almost all stripes—certainly of the Korsgaard variety, for instance, or take Hegel—are extremely impressed with the distinctively human capacity for self-consciousness. This is what grounds the possibility of freedom and of morality, for much of the tradition. Indeed, this is also an informal or simply hackneyed way in which many of us pay tribute to ourselves: isn't it astounding that evolution ends up producing a creature capable of understanding it? Or there are many variations: as a kind of climax, nature produces creatures capable of telling stories, or understanding nature itself through science. Struggling up from the slime, evolution finally gives rise to language, and so on.

I would like to register an objection. First of all, we don't know how incredible or distinctive consciousness is. The kind of reasoning that surveys and values all of the universe in this way is rather problematic. Perhaps there are possible places to climb after consciousness that are to consciousness as consciousness is to a lump of mud.

Well, hard to know from here, fellow mudlumps. How amazing and great consciousness is, even if it is the sort of thing its enthusiasts think it is: an incomprehensible question. And really, if every species were self-conscious enough to speak good English, each might attribute cosmic amazingness to its own distinctive adaptations: a snakehead fish, say, might be pretty impressed with its breathing apparatus. Second, I don't think we really know much about whether and how different species of animals or plants might, in fact, be conscious. And third, certainly we can at least say this: we are conscious of our world and of ourselves in a severely curtailed way. We have made, and we continue to make, the most incredible errors even in figuring out what sorts of things we are (of course, I've figured all that out in this book, so you really don't have to worry about it anymore). Our awareness within the scope of all of reality is miniscule, just as we can't see most of the light. Even if self-consciousness is as good as locomotion, we are still clawing our way like pathetic trilobites out of the primordial soup onto the beach of awareness.

Nietzsche, in a moment that shows all that is best about him as a philosopher, speculates that consciousness, rather than being miraculous or even adaptive, is a derangement or an affliction. Let me just say that that idea itself emerges from a certain sort of consciousness, one tortured by its own excess. I speculate that Nietzsche experienced his own consciousness as a disease. Everybody is familiar with the experience of being morbidly self-conscious, or too intensely aware of one's own train of thought, bodily postures, expressions, and so on. This condition can become chronic. And there is also the experience of being too open to, too aware of, the world: the feeling that you're being bombarded and you can't stop thinking, sorting, resorting, interpreting and reinterpreting. Deliberation, Nietzsche points out, is slow and often disables a creature from acting.

This argument has a structure that could be used over and over again to demolish arguments based on evolution, particularly those that assert that the fact that a certain trait is widely shared shows that it was selected for. If this could be false of consciousness—and it could be—it could be false of any given faculty or feature. For example, people like Denis Dutton have argued that since art is so pervasive it must be adaptive on an evolutionary scale; this seems vaguely plausible but it isn't. Consciousness might be more like an allergy than it is like an opposable thumb. Consciousness could be, for example, a mere side effect of other, as it were, computational developments in the brain, an "unintended" epiphenomenon of a prodigious capacity for autonomic induction or something. And it could certainly be counteradaptational: the jury is still out on whether it brings species prosperity or total destruction.

> The problem of consciousness . . . first confronts us when we begin to realize how much we can do without it. . . . For we could think, feel, will, remember, and also "act" in every sense of the term, and yet none of all

this would have to "enter our consciousness" (as one says figuratively). All of life would be possible without, as it were, seeing itself in the mirror; and still today, the predominant part of our lives actually unfolds without this mirroring—of course also our thinking, feeling, and willing lives, as insulting as it may sound to an older philosopher. . . . All becoming conscious involves a vast and thorough corruption, falsification, superficialization, and generalization. In the end, growing consciousness is a danger, and he who lives among the most conscious Europeans even knows it is a sickness.[21]

This series of thoughts is, as I say, Nietzsche at his very best. That a particular belief or whole intellectual structure would, if true, enhance the self-image of the person believing it should be a reason to suspect that it is held for bad or no reasons, or that the reasons are just developed retroactively to beef up the ego of the believer. Nietzsche is an artist of this sort of suspicion: he sees the massive insecurity seething under the calm declaration of rational agency and free will in a Kant. This is one of those moments when Nietzsche gives the impression of *standing outside* what everyone else is too in the middle of even to see as an issue. This is the function of the "overman" as a sort of thought experiment, or something with which Nietzsche would like to identify himself or his voice as a philosopher. Really, I have to say that in many ways it is a despicable notion, and as soon as Nietzsche starts developing political hints from it, he adumbrates a nightmare. But it also functions something like Rawls's original position: it is an imaginary place to stand to see about *homo sapiens* what we have such difficulty seeing, or such motivation not to see.

When I wrote *Obscenity, Anarchy, Reality*—urging an ecstatic affirmation of all that is—I think I said that I was the person very furthest from being able to take my own advice. I was urging myself into a stance of affirmation as a response to an annihilating or engulfing negation to which I have been tempted (by the deaths of my brothers, for example). I would also say that writing that book was somewhat successful in this regard: along with many actual experiences both of pleasure and suffering, it gave me a measure of acceptance. But I have probably never had a moment of actually perfect acceptance, and I'm not sure, finally, that I want one. At any rate, this style of self-therapy or consolation by writing books is evident in the whole history of this idea, or even is an element in almost every system of ideas: the part that turns toward the world. Nietzsche, we must see, is tortured by his resentment or hatred of the world. That is what he calls decadence and he associates it with illness: his own, I suggest, above all. He wants to annihilate the world and in particular other people. But above all he is propelled by self-loathing, by the futile desire to become something more than he is by killing the sickness that infests him. In his own eyes he becomes precisely that when he discovers the recurrence, his grail. He *overcomes* his negation, and the achievement is measured precisely by the size of that yawning abyss. He achieves what the Stoics regarded as an antecedently existing coherent self.

Now, to characterize a set of motivations and ideas like these as stupid passivity or as a mere capitulation to being enslaved by reality is an intolerable simplification, and every system of thought at a minimum had better have a moment of loving the world or it had better not be. But I also think that, as has so often been remarked, in its Nietzschean or its Stoic or its Taoist forms radical acceptance is just not a sustainable attitude for creatures such as we, who are built to need. It would be all too easy to represent the madness of Nietzsche precisely as an index of this impossibility; at any rate it was a demonstration of his inability to eradicate his own sickness or even to diagnose it very well. And indeed, to cease to need is not something one would necessarily wish for, nor would it be only liberating to be freed of sexual desire or hunger, for example: here one would be free for one thing of whole arenas of or contexts of choice. The Buddha taught that suffering is caused by desire, and that one could cease to desire. But that is not clearly desirable, and if we lost desire, we would lose pleasure and love and even certain bittersweet varieties of pain or longing that open up entire dimensions of experience. As well as suffering, of course.

A good model here of free action that is left open to creatures such as we are is handcraft. The crafter, of course, does not impose his will on the material in a mere or sheer way: there are certain forms clay or wood or glass will not assume; these parameters are the very conditions of possibility for the craft or skill in question or they constitute it: the tools of the craft and the movements of the body of the crafter are articulated or formed in dialogue with the materials, or in order to nudge or deflect them toward a desired form, selected from among materially and socially determined possibilities. And then, of course, as the crafts have proceeded they have also developed new materials and then shaped them with reference to their own odd stubbornnesses and various ranges of use. At no point is any one thing or stuff the agent or the patient: stuff and person are mutually articulating one another, with tools as a means of communication between them. In my old age, though I am myself without any handcraft per se, I think the freedom made available in such situations—which will include moments of improvisation—is the most freedom we can actually hope for. But, on the other hand, it is very satisfactory.

13.

There are many other ways to conceive the undoubtedly multiple and complex self in all its singleness, and it is, indeed, quite disheartening to conceive it exclusively in terms of the master/slave dialectic. I would very much like to find a self that is more than just a transaction of power, in which bits of me are trying to subdue other bits. It is an awfully Augustinian self: too intrinsically pure and also too polluted by the world. At any rate, if there is a conflict between intention and impulse, it has to be a negotiation in every case if you are to be free: you have to come to intend to do what your impulses drive you to do, or do spontaneously what you also will, like Louis. Another way to put this is that you have to get the individuation/relation ratio right. It has to be you, sufficiently autonomous to act, sufficiently distinguishable within the flow of material to constitute a thing, sufficiently psychologically independent to count as a self. But this self/object must be sufficiently or in the right way connected within a nest of embedded situations; the self is in interchange, of course, or is constituted by its relations. And as itself a situation, the self/object's parts must be internally related in the relevant sorts of ways.

There is no human freedom, or freedom of any finite creature or thing, without a particular configuration among the constituents of that being and a full world in which it is embedded; or, nature makes freedom possible by imposing constraints and hence connections on all things, opening gaps between them. But the gaps also loom within; your singleness as an identifiable being is always provisional and at stake, and also always shifting within its various continuities. You are free: that *means* that you negotiate, merge with, and emerge from the world in certain ways and likewise and in connection that you are "internally" configured and reconfigured in certain ways. I don't think this way is distinctive to human beings or that it is extremely amazing, as opposed to grindingly mundane. Well, of course, it's both.

"Could have done otherwise," I want to say, is an awfully crude instrument for assessing free agency: like using a fireplace poker for the brain surgery. As Frankfurt argues, sometimes you are responsible for something when you couldn't have done otherwise. But the Frankfurt-type cases are the least of it, and the question of whether one could have done otherwise in a given situation, so seemingly clear, is far too clear: every situation in which it might apply is a chaotic tangle. You'd have to build it up out of billions of counterfactuals: turn back to instant t, adjust character trait or momentary mental set x, move the furniture around, and so on. And then also I don't think the question of whether you could have done otherwise bears any very close connection to moral responsibility in any case; I think the intuition that it does is rather manufactured by the philosophical/theological tradition than emergent organically in the actual discourse and practice of responsibility.

One place I might locate this is in the discourse around mental illness. One of the primary purposes of "medicalizing" this range of conditions is to relieve the patient of responsibility for certain actions performed because of or in the thrall or clutches of the mental illness or irrational impulse, for example an addiction. This is often pictured, as again Dennett points out, as an evil agent who seizes control of your innocent self. This can be important in treatment, or useful in the criminal law or psychiatric institutions, but I don't think it corresponds that well to the experience of an addict, who's identified both ways round with the addiction and with the resistance to the addiction. At any rate, the whole exercise by which the admittedly crushing burden of responsibility is relieved or released rests on what I am characterizing as a rather unsubtle conception of freedom and its relation to responsibility. If you have ever lived with a mentally ill person or an addict, I think perhaps you will admit that the question of responsibility is at least . . . vexed. And the cure, too, may require the patient to take as well as foreswear responsibility in various dimensions.

Perhaps Kant and Fichte thought of themselves as pure noumenal transcendent subjects who could will to do the good and hence do it. I have to admit, that doesn't seem to be the way I experience myself, which is one of the things Schelling was trying to say, or a thought in the service of which he "invented" the unconscious. Only that doesn't seem quite right or complete either. Usually the first thing that a recovering addict understands is that she can't *not* do whatever it is that she's addicted to. And this compulsion emerges from something in herself, so that when, in the twelve-step parlance, she admits she's powerless, she's admitting to powerlessness not only over what she's addicted to, but over her addiction itself, or over herself or part of herself, or something in her self that is also external to her self. Now, if we are framing free will in terms of control, then in one sense I am free when I drink: the impulse, no doubt, originates in myself, or if you're still holding out for the will-o-the-wisp, it originates internally to the complex of subjectivity in which the self is concealed. But what addicts are powerless over, finally, is precisely themselves. In some sense many people *are* free over the very things to which others addicted. They're free in at least the tried-and-true Humean manner: if they decide not to drink, they don't drink. But alcoholics know what it's like to decide not to drink and then to drink anyway, to decide to stop and then continue, to decide to quit and then go on a binge. Non-addicts sometimes still want to understand this as a sheer matter of choice; they can't or don't want to understand compulsion, can't or won't understand the experience of acting under almost total constraint, where that constraint originates internally.

This is why addiction is such a fundamental challenge or at least puzzle to Western ethics, always coming up as the proposed counterexample, as a thing that needs accounting for: in many ways, the action of the addict comports with the Kantian self that gives itself the law; the puzzle is precisely the internality of the compulsion, which is analogous to obedience to the moral law: a kind of leering semblance of freedom as it is conceived in that tradition: the rule one gives oneself. Addiction also makes a hash of Stoicism, which rests on a distinction between outer reality, over which we are powerless, and inner reality, over which we allegedly exercise great or even perfect control. Obsession and compulsion are very much the same thing, as it turns out, and the addict is no more in control of his thoughts than of the vodka. And one thing about vodka: it is an external object now, an internal substance later: part of our very brain chemistry.

It strikes me that I have often in my life, when in the thrall of addiction, held myself to be compelled (though it is not at all like being controlled by an outside agent in my experience, no matter what your psychological professional might say). But I also hold myself to be responsible: for the addictive or compelled action itself, and for the bad things that I may do under the influence of the substance or activity to which I'm addicted, and even for the sheer fact that I am an addict. I would find people responsible in many cases in which they were operating under a condition of mental illness because of the way mental illness may, at least sometimes, be correctly described as emerging in or from or as the self. There are two ways to be free of or in addiction: to have a limitless supply of your drug of choice or to go cold turkey. Freedom as always wells from below as well as from above, and the sheer imposition of will or reason is no vision of liberation or even of recovery.

As I say, I personally do not really believe in free will as that is commonly construed, so I don't think that this position that addicts get into where we can't do otherwise—where, for example, the arm simply must raise the bottle to the lips—is unusual. A reflective addict knows he is not free precisely because what drives him is something in his own body, in his own head. We used to call that "jonesing." But the average non-addict could conceive herself to be free insofar as she isn't divided within herself in precisely the same way, or does not know herself to be so divided. I do think in some ways the notion of a free self is parasitic or secondary: the free self is invented as the non-addicted self. I desperately wanted to quit alcohol and drugs for many years. And I could continue to want to quit even as I was lifting the bottle to my mouth. What is going on inside someone who is having that experience is very hard to describe to people who don't have it, but if you take me seriously, I suppose it will be obvious to you that the self is divided or perhaps fragmented in that experience. And there are transactions of power among the fragments. It's just that they're nothing like those described in the tradition that connects freedom with rationality.

Putting it that way is not at all satisfactory because it makes it sound as though there is some unitary self that has been shattered, or a normative single self which the addict falls away from or loses, whereas we need to conceive the self always as an object among other objects and a situation among situations; it is both a single thing and an environment, neither primordially one nor primordially multiple. I have never experienced a clearly free or univocal self. There was no self prior to or external to my addiction. I have experienced a variety of proto-addictive internal divisions from the times of my earliest memories. I don't think that I had a free self and that that self was enchained by addiction; I think I had an addicted self that eventually found something to which to be addicted. Compulsion was my destiny and before I had it I was groping toward it. Nor do I think that I could have lived without becoming addicted; the cycle of addiction and of recovery was as it were bundled up inside me from the beginning and simply unfolded. This makes it sound like an external force. I am saying that I experience it as intrinsic.

On the other hand, no one can be an alcoholic in a world without alcohol. Brain imaging might show certain differences between addicts' and non-addicts' ductwork, but addiction is defined by ingestion or, at any rate, real-worldly action. Indeed, substance abuse might be defined in terms of the effects of incorporation on, among other things, the brain. Addiction, we might say, is a configuration of the self or a family of related configurations, but it is also only comprehensible as a worldly situation in which the self is itself embedded and in which the body is infiltrated or does achieve literal identity with something that was once external. And, of course, addiction is culturally articulated in the most concrete and abstract ways: how the culture categorizes substances, or which substances it makes available; the vocabularies that are used with more or less effectiveness in self-understanding, as in treating addiction as a moral test or as a disease.

14.

I have been characterizing addiction in terms of various forms of self-division and internal power relations. But, of course, even the sheer notion of freedom as control, or even the basic idea of the will as a force or faculty of decision that directs other forces or faculties or the body, also presupposes profound forms of self-division, as we have seen; it is an internal struggle in which some parts command and some are recalcitrant, some judge and others resist, some pitch and others catch, as it were. Korsgaard wants an integrated subject; like Plato, she wants it integrated by subduing parts of it. The idea that *I* am in control of myself: one needs to work out what parts and what relations between the parts of the self this pre-supposes; it certainly is a puzzling locution in a number of respects. In some ways, the structure of addiction is inscribed in the concept of free will itself; the parts of the divided self may be in a different relation in addicts than in non-addicts, but the structure of the division is the same: or, freedom and addiction are conceived together in the same conceptual space of internal power relations. The concept of free will has as part of its content its contrast with addiction.

The notion of control, as we have seen, is central to contemporary versions of compatibilism, and to the free will debate as it stands today. People often say "control yourself," for example, to children, assholes, and addicts. When we train children that way, we are not only teaching them, say, "impulse control," we are also teaching them an ontology or ecology or politics of the human self; we are showing them who they are, or rather we are making them into selves we recognize as human (now, within our current practices, etc.), by inculcating the particular sorts of configurations of the potentially opposed parts of the self that we recognize as comprehensible, in contrast, for example, to the ways animal or machine selves are constructed, at least in our imaginations. Perhaps this is the insight that Fischer is pointing to when he says that the possibility of this sort of self-control is essential to personhood. Only he needs to replace this within wider social power relations.

When you tell me, as I dance around and scream or start barking like a poodle, to "get ahold of myself," you mean something like this: my will should get ahold of my body: I should be telling myself what to do: there's some kind of inner voice that should be hectoring my dancing legs or shutting my barking mouth. This picture would, of course, also entail that there is a corresponding capacity in my legs or in my mouth to listen to what this voice is saying and respond. The will, or reason, or self-consciousness (whatever word we may throw out as indicating the true self) is conceived as the dictator or the police of the self: it's supposed to seize the unruly populace of impulses and body parts and transform or execute them.

Without this vision of the self, Western culture would be unrecognizable politically and psychologically. But the vision is optional in the sense that there are cultures that get along without it and the disciplines of the self that it engenders. One might say that power as it operates within the self and power as it operates in the public sphere are mutually simultaneously caused. Power, to use the Foucault move, circulates through situations; some of these situations are human selves, which are embedded in turn in cultures, political systems, hierarchies of surveillance, and so on. We perhaps imagine a free self, and we construe freedom as subordination (of what, precisely?) to will or reason or whatever term we may use to designate the leader within. That is indeed one of the fundamental attractions of addictive substances: one loses the hectoring will in one's head and yields to one's impulses more easily: intoxication in that sense is a liberation of subordinated aspects of the self, and it is in part this liberation or revolution that the addict seeks again and again in what finally becomes a slavery to one's own impulse.

It is well worth thinking about where in the self the freedom lies—in self-control or precisely in the release of desire from self-control—and the idea that philosophers would effortlessly identify it with the former seems wildly out of keeping with the phenomenology. Sometimes, imposition of the will yields an experience of freedom. Sometimes, release from the demands of the will yields an experience of freedom, and one effect of taking an adequate dose of a substance to which you are addicted is the sensation precisely of a release from self-control, which is liberating. As again Schiller saw, we can feel determined or enslaved at both ends: to impulse, or to "reason"; otherwise there would have been no counter-Enlightenment seeking to free us from the slavery of reason and science: Hamann, Jacobi, Kierkegaard. Self-control also, in some conditions, reflects social—for example, economic, political, institutional—control; it is experienced as an inner version of the parent, authority figure, institution. Then the rebellion of the impulses or passions is a directly political liberation, an insurrection of the subalterns.

"The passions" are supposed to be things that happen to us; passion traditionally and etymologically is the opposite of action. But a creature who unerringly followed the dictates of reason—whatever that might mean, exactly—or who always only acted in the Aristotelian manner, would not be human and would certainly not be a free human being. It is possible, of course, to be carried away by anger and do something in the heat of the moment that one would not do if one were able to deliberate rationally. Then again, a person who does not or cannot express or release anger, even violently, is not free either. The idea of freedom as the restraint of passion has very little to do with the ways in and occasions on which people do feel free, and, of course, passions themselves can be intentionally cultivated or intensified. One thing is sure: if we are free, we are free in a way that takes account of or moves among the passions: no one is free as a rational agent, because no one actually is (merely) a rational agent. Things like us are free, insofar as we are, only in a complex ever-transforming negotiation.

I suppose desire, some of it anyway, comes from the body (well, in relation to desired things, of course!). It articulates the will but it is involuntary. I have little control over what I desire. If I want some kind of kinky sex with the wrong partner or something, I can't make myself not want that: indeed, if I try to make myself not want that I convert the desire into an obsession and myself into an addict; this is the kind of thing that someone who thinks that their reason is going to subdue their desires just does not understand, or does not until he realizes that he is himself addicted, or in possession of uncontrollable desires. So I suppose that on this view, the will or perhaps rational agent sifts these desires and prescribes a series of bodily actions or inactions to realize or fail to realize these desires. For that is also certainly what it means to "control yourself": your will should be doing a better or more emphatic job of sifting your desires and holding you back. So maybe we get a feedback loop: bodily desires or impulses get sifted by the will which moves the body, which produces desire out of its particular situation. Even the commonplace or supposedly common-sense self is a profuse multiplicity of faculties and functions, a chaotic welter of power relations that is constantly articulated and reconfigured in internal transactions of power between shadowy pseudo-entities.

Now, let me focus on one part of this: the will. "Get ahold of yourself" or "control yourself," I think, means something like this: tell yourself what to do, and listen. The will in this little structure is conceived to be linguistic: the little Napoleon in your skull makes you do things by issuing orders in a language; the body is supposed to become a mirror or reflection of those orders. The practical syllogism is fundamentally linguistic, and the theorists who focus so relentlessly on acting from reasons or from rational agency, make all human action fundamentally linguistic or inconceivable without language. It is like the *Tractatus* in reverse: the body is a representation, a reflection, of the will: the body assumes the posture or performs the movements prescribed in the propositions formed in the will. Then we can, as it were, read off your identity from your body; we can infer from your bodily actions what your self is, how it is arranged, which parts are privileged and which subordinated. And then we perform a moral assessment on your self from that point of view. If you are criminal or reprehensible, that is an inference we draw from what your behavior shows about your self: you fail to manifest certain prescribed forms of self-control. As the Foucault folk say, the body is a site of inscription. But for one thing here I think we are confusing self and social control; we actually do infer in many cases in which someone acts in a way that is out of "our" control or the usual range of social norms that that person is out of his own control in something like the same sense. (I think that, other things being equal, the criminal is just as likely, or much more likely, to be controlling his own actions than the noncriminal.)

But the will does not operate in a vacuum and these little propositions of which it makes the body a mirror are developed in the public language and themselves arise or are articulated within institutional power contexts. On this picture, the will is trying to impose a comprehensible form on the body, trying to convert the body from a random or meaningless set of gesticulations into a story or into some appropriate repertoire of behaviors, appropriate by the standards of, say, a school, a prison, a coffee shop, a marriage. And really our individual histories are like this. Babies start off twitching randomly and more or less incomprehensibly; with great struggle we teach them to twitch meaningfully; we subject them to language and incorporate them into institutions—the family, the daycare center, whatever—until their twitchings are semiotic and their bodies are subject to their wills, which we measure by their loose conformity to social norms. The will is itself a reflection of the institution and vice versa. Christine Korsgaard's philosophy takes the administrative structure of Harvard University as the very essence of the human self.

Now, it is actually a hopeful thing, I guess, that the body cannot always be effectively inscribed. Sometimes you still twitch incomprehensibly. Sometimes you act on your desires even when your little will is telling you not to. Sometimes you can't bring your body into the appropriate configuration: it resists, like when you're dieting or something and your will is trying explicitly to reconfigure your body and perhaps is unable to do so. Or when you're engaging compulsively in any behavior. Here, in a way, what we think of as the "appropriate" power relation of will and body are reversed. The apparently chthonic, prelinguistic animal thing is resisting the blandishments of its trainer: it's like the lion devouring the lion tamer. In fact, you might notice that it's possible for the will to get rearticulated by the bodily compulsion in such cases: that's what I did, so that must be what I wanted. Compulsion is a useful, at times liberating, experience because it reverses the power relations within the self or makes them dialectical, which is exactly why compulsive behavior is also aberrant, scary, in need of treatment, and so on. We conceive of it as the invasion of the animal or machine into the pristine world of the pure linguistic self and its efficacious syntax.

Perhaps in order to be free, you need to negotiate a way to gain scope for movement; you are constrained by the external world, by a variety of impulses, rules, a cacophony of your own willings and reasonings, and by other people's too. Then perhaps there are routes or ways of movement in which one expresses oneself clearly, or fulfills one's intentions to a degree, or in which one can as it were attribute an action to oneself. Power, even or particularly power as it operates within a single self, is always dialectical or rather chaotic. Will is never perfectly and instantly obeyed. The will orders the body forward, or reconfigures it, but except in cases of deep insanity, the possibilities of what can be willed are articulated within the bounds of bodily possibility. I'm not out here willing myself to lift up the earth like Atlas; I'm not able to will that except in a moment of deep aberration. Power, specifically the power of the will (if any) in this sense, is never transparent and is never originary: power and its object are mutually simultaneously constituted. Power is a craft or skill: it works with, and not only against, the stuff over which it is empowered, or it is at best completely irresponsible or at worst utterly delusory and demented. So even if we were to characterize free will in terms of control or self-control, the thing is complicated, and the forms of the will take shape in relation to what is possible for the willing body in a world.

15.

Now, let me say this: I hate my will. (I picture Schopenhauer bellowing this at Kant, for example.) My will is extremely powerful and I experience myself as its slave. I experience my *self* not as the will that linguistically articulates my body, but at least also as the body that resists that articulation and delineates the limits of its possible forms. Addiction is often conceived of as a failure of will. Now, if that were so—and perhaps in one mode or moment it is so—addiction would be an act of revolution, an act of liberation whereby the body frees itself, in at least one mode or moment, from its linguistic articulation. But in fact, and not necessarily incompatibly, addicts often suffer from an excess of will. Ask yourself what it takes to pour vodka down your throat until you puke or pass out. Ask yourself what it takes to do that, say, every day. I'll tell you what it takes: it takes willpower. You have absolutely got to stop listening to your body; you've got to overcome a thousand bodily recalcitrances and make yourself keep pouring. Ask yourself what it takes to keep doing this even while everyone around you is telling you that you need to stop, even while you pay the price in a thousand practical ways. It takes a masterful individual will.

One thing that motivates the use of drugs is an extreme desire for self-control. Being an alcoholic requires iron self-discipline. Addiction is an attempt to control how you feel. A typical addict wants to wake up instantly with cocaine or caffeine, wants to feel ecstasy on demand, wants to go to sleep by knocking himself unconscious; he wants perfect control over his brain chemistry. The things he puts into his body are toxic: he is damaging his body, but he is seeking a transcendence of the mundane limits of his biology: he is seeking to make himself safe and independent of the world by perfect control and transformation of his body. He has turned against his own body or pitted one desire against another until the inner conflict begins to rip him apart or collapse him into permanent coma.

For in my opinion, what is sought through this intensification of will, finally, is a place where the will is annihilated; this is one actual form of freedom, as I have urged. One seeks through a kind of absolute self-command, a perfect discipline of ingestion, to bring body and will into the sort of flawless alignment which collapses them into identity. One seeks to make correspondence of will and body perfect, to create a body that is perfectly inscribed or which cannot be inscribed, wherein the dialectic of will and body is terminated because the will finally conforms to the body instead of vice versa: a reversed semiotic in which the reality effects an inscription, in which body writes will, in which the inscription is composed by what it is about. I don't see a person in this position as being by that fact itself either more or less free than a hypothetical someone who directed every single action by rational will. What this amounts to, finally, is a complete erasure of inscription, or a collapse of the self out of the linguistic order: the desire for the end that is the desire to be seduced, to tumble into the abyss of pure desire or even the erasure of desire, an edenic dream of man before or outside of language, where I escape finally into and from my will, a dream of nondifferentiation where I desire whatever I get, or desire nothing at all, a letting go into a will that is not mine or a perfect seduction where there is no will operational, just a door into absence from myself, a relief from myself, a place where all the chattering stops, where I let go completely.

Addicts suffer from an excess of will, and through a deep prolonged intensification of will they seek an annihilation of the distance between will and body: they seek to collapse into a single thing or to find a nonfragmented or nondifferentiated or nonalienated or free identity. Or perhaps we should conceive this as an animal identity, or a machine identity, or an identity of stone: an identity that can no longer be conceived fundamentally in terms of language and self-division, an identity that is no longer a "self," because the "self" as we conceive it is always a site of power. Understand: it takes will power to inject heroin into your bloodstream: obviously. But where you get when you do this is a place at which the will is less importunate: at which you experience a surcease or extinguishment of will, which for a person suffering from an excess of will is the deepest relief and release, the only real vacation: freedom. To be in a heroin nod is to finally feel cured of the self, defragmented. What lurks out there as the end of the high, the end of highs, is the extinction of consciousness, the extinction of the fiction of the self: death as a sifting back to presence.

It is certainly right to say that none of us fully chose our own bodies, or fully chose to be who we are. In that sense we are our own victims or the victims of fate:

for the most part we all have to play the hand we are dealt. But we also all engage in an attempt to expand the operations of our own wills in the arena of our selves, to get some kind of rudimentary command over something about ourselves. Now, I suggest that many of the things we do, and indeed many of the things we think of as pathological, are attempts of this sort to make ourselves the objects of our own will and hence to transform ourselves into things that are free in something like the Kantian sense. We're trying to make ourselves free by treating our own bodies as material that is subject to the operation of our wills—as in piercing and tattooing and bodybuilding and anorexia, for example—trying to make ourselves free by enslaving ourselves, by taking command of ourselves. We're trying to carve out a zone of control in the uncontrollable crushing chaos of the universe, even if this zone extends no further than our own skins.

One lesson I want to draw from all this is that the idea of self-control is extremely complex and cuts both ways. Perfect self-control would be a form of slavery as well as a form of freedom; perfect lack of self-control likewise. At any rate neither is possible for us, even if we fantasize about both, or even as these stand as opposed but equally charismatic teloi, ways of figuring our desiring lives which have taken many names. Talk of "persons" is not my idiom, but anything that is recognizably a person is negotiating between self-control and self-abandonment; their intersection is the only place human freedom, if any, could be located. Whatever freedom really is, it is not perfect self-control, or else freedom and slavery are the same thing. We are the authors and the victims of ourselves; if we are moral agents, moral agency has to arise in that snarl. This is what we should expect given basic compositional facts: that we are both distinct within and connected throughout to our environments, and are both ourselves environments and individuals. It is no good recommending one or the other, or associating human freedom with self-control or with self-abandonment, especially as the portions of the self doing the controlling and the releasing are always shifting or reversing, and always in many other relations than power relations (really, my reason loves or at least tolerates my desires), and always passing into and out of one another.

16.

It is commonly held that moral responsibility is connected to free will, though, of course, what is meant by "free will" is still anything but settled. I suggest that we experiment with detaching the two notions, or exploring views according to which it is not the case that free will in any sense—from agent causation à la Chisholm to a control condition à la John Martin Fischer—is necessary for moral responsibility. Since almost all philosophers working on responsibility connect it to freedom or to allegedly related notions such as rational agency, they have not felt it necessary to defend elaborately the general thesis that freedom is necessary for responsibility. Rather, like the notion that truth and belief are not sufficient for knowledge, the matter is usually consigned to the ground-clearing phase before the argument—whatever it may be in a particular text—gets going. These ground-clearing maneuvers fall in this case into three broad categories: an appeal to intuition, a series of distinctions among different senses of such terms as "responsibility," and a treatment of excuses. I will sketch a response to each of these. What I want to accomplish is to get to the point at which the burden of proof is shared, or at which the question could be regarded as open.

That freedom is necessary for responsibility is held to be intuitively obvious, for example, in cases where we do not treat someone as responsible who is insane or acting under coercion. Within the discourse of free will and responsibility, these alleged intuitions are deployed almost perfunctorily, and that is legitimate insofar as they represent assumptions on which the debate rests, and which all the participants acknowledge. However, these alleged intuitions are, in my opinion, extremely theoretically laden. They are not nearly as widely or clearly shared as the philosophers who begin with them appear to believe. And, of course, if such claims were seriously challenged, or if reasons could be given to doubt that they did have an intuitive status, insisting that they are intuitive could not be an adequate justification of them. On the other hand, the fact that philosophers have not felt it necessary to defend these intuitions does not, of course, entail that they could not do so.

In typical preliminary ground-clearing, Susan Wolf writes,

> It makes sense that we should take agents who can control their behavior in intelligent ways more seriously than other agents; it makes sense that we should regard the features of the world that fall within the sphere of their intelligent control as being more deeply attributable to them; and it makes sense that we should regard these features as saying more about them, as being more significant indications of these agents' selves. . . . A kleptomaniac who steals a piece of jewelry from a store intentionally performs an action she knows to be criminal and wrong. Indeed, the fact that her action has these properties is essential to her motivation to perform it. Yet she is not responsible for stealing—the action is not deeply attributable to her.[22]

Here, Wolf registers that there is no particular argument for these intuitions, and evidently feels little pressure to defend them; "it makes sense" is surely an appeal to what we supposedly already obviously believe rather than being itself any sort of reason to believe it.

However, our intuitions on such matters are very mixed. When I ask people what they think about a case like this, some of them think the kleptomaniac is not responsible; others think that is ridiculous. Some think she is still culpable but less culpable than she would be if she were not ill; some people think she is all the more culpable as a chronic offender. Indeed, people often react with mere puzzlement or bemusement to the practices that eventuate from the connection of freedom and responsibility. When murderers "get off" because they are insane, there is often widespread outrage, but also puzzlement: that he's sick in a way that makes him do evil is all the more reason to imprison or execute him, according to my barber, and I don't think such an intuition is any less plausible or fundamental than its rival.

Consider two serial killers, Smith and MacGillicuddy. Smith kills impulsively, unpredictably; even he doesn't know when or whom he might kill next. He is subject, as it were, to sudden psychopathic episodes, or he simply becomes hysterical and doesn't have any impulse control. MacGillicuddy, on the other hand, is a master of Aristotelian practical rationality; he's the most concerted, intentional, well-organized person you could ever imagine. He meticulously plots his heinous deeds years in advance, pursues his nefarious intentions with consummate self-control, and always takes as means the most directly useful available items: he doesn't floridly garrote you, requiring a trip to the piano store; he simply and directly bludgeons you to death with his own club. Stipulate that Smith and MacGillicuddy dispatch the same number of victims with similarly devastating effects. According to most of the familiar accounts of responsibility in relation to practical rationality—and hence, on many views, to freedom—Smith will be regarded as less culpable than MacGillicuddy. The justification of this conclusion appeals to the alleged fact that we share a set of intuitions about cases like this. But we do not share a set of intuitions about this. I do not think most people would draw any moral distinction at all between Smith and MacGillicuddy on this basis; at any rate I certainly would not, and so I think an argument is required that is not an appeal to intuition.

Our practices of holding responsible, it seems to me, are no less equivocal than our intuitions. In the Jerry Sandusky sex abuse case, for example, the question of whether Sandusky acted compulsively essentially never arose. If it had, and if evidence had been given that Sandusky had indeed acted compulsively, that might have had the legal effect of mitigating his responsibility, though in my view it probably should not have that effect. But if the court proceeded in this way, there would have been an outpouring of outrage from victims and the community at large. One could represent such outrage as expressing incomprehension of important philosophical insights, but I do not believe that it could plausibly be said to express incomprehension of intuitions we all share.

Our actual practices, even in the legal context which is informed by the history of Western speculation about free will and responsibility, are much more equivocal than they may appear. Indeed, the kleptomaniac is very likely to be criminally charged and convicted. Even in a case where we determine that the perpetrator is insane and hence send him to a treatment facility rather than a prison, I do not think that it is perfectly clear that we are not holding him responsible and punishing him, and one might note many similarities between the prison and the mental hospital. Perhaps the idea that John Hinckley is not guilty and is not being held responsible or punished is as much a verbal maneuver as a self-reflective account of our actual practices. The fact that one is an alcoholic, even where this is supposedly exclusively conceived on a disease model, is not considered a defense against a charge of drunk driving. Now, perhaps this is just meant to have a utilitarian deterrent effect, but that does not show that it is not also in keeping with our actual practices of holding people responsible. If it profoundly outraged our moral sense, it would never have been instituted. We do frequently blame drunk drivers, without reference to whether they were free.

17.

I would like, in addition, to draw attention to one assumption behind the kleptomaniac example and similar cases of mental illnesses or behavioral compulsion: that the illness is external to the self of the person who has it, that it is an alien influence. Even if this is a presumption of contemporary psychology, it is surely optional. I want to say it is certainly false. Perhaps we ought to reconceive psychological afflictions, such as addictions or even certain forms of psychosis as, at least often, intrinsic to the person who possesses them, even in cases where they eventuate in "compulsive" action. In some such cases, it seems to me, a person should be deemed responsible. Indeed, it is precisely the association of human selfhood with freedom that leads to the basic psychological picture we possess—one to which there are certainly alternatives—of a rational or a free or a pure self that is riddled with illnesses and dysfunctions that are alien to it, and which infest it like parasites or beset it like a besieging army or are encrusted on it like barnacles. Your self in this scheme is something like a pure rational faculty of decision (and hence, among other things, indistinguishable from any other self), but it may be under coercion from an illness or many illnesses, or be covered up or disguised, muffled, disfigured, or asphyxiated. This does not appear to me to be plausible, and in any case it is only one among possible pictures. It instantiates all the sorts of fantastic political self-divisions we examined earlier, and it sets the self again on its journey to a single extensionless yet glowing point: a complete mystery that has no relation to anyone's actual inhabiting of a self.

18.

Another move on which the connection of free will to responsibility often depends is sorting out a variety of "senses" of the term *responsibility*. Many attributions of responsibility obviously do not raise questions of free will at all, such as when I say that the housing bubble is responsible for the financial collapse of 2008, or that my old windows are responsible for the draft, or that it's not my fault I didn't get the paper in on time; it's my computer's fault. At any rate, let us consider some examples of attributions of responsibility to which free will does not seem to be in play. One kind of apparent counterexample to the thesis that freedom is required for responsibility is provided by the Frankfurt cases.[23] Imagine in the now-familiar fashion a demon who will force you to do what it wants you to do if you do not do it anyway on your own. However, as it happens, you want to do what the demon wants you to do, and you do it because you want to. Then, Frankfurt argues, you are responsible for your action, despite the fact that you could not have done otherwise. The Frankfurt cases, at any rate, tend to show that free will is not required for responsibility on certain construals of free will: those that centralize the idea that a free agent could have done otherwise, whatever in turn that might mean, exactly. Frankfurt's cases threw the conception of freedom into something of a crisis in philosophy, and various philosophers have in response articulated accounts of freedom that do not rely on the principle of alternate possibilities.

I would like to consider several other possible counterexamples. I'll start with an extreme one:

(1) *attributions of responsibility to inanimate objects.* I often blame information-processing devices and hold them responsible for delaying, distracting, or disabling me. I hold plumbing fixtures or cabinetry responsible for various balky or malfunctioning episodes, and sometimes in such circumstances I smack or bang them or ridicule them. I blame the drawer for being what it is: old, shoddy, flimsy, and so on. I resent it for that, and though you might not think of the frustrated hammer blow that smashes the thing as a punishment, I may. Truly, I would have been on time. The weather, the traffic, the GPS is responsible.

In the patronizing tone that persons often take toward inanimate objects, John Martin Fischer writes that "I might say I'm grateful for the many years of service given by my Hoover vacuum cleaner, but this feeling is fundamentally different from the kind of gratitude I feel toward a friend who remembers my birthday with a telephone call."[24] Fischer, like many other philosophers, begins by distinguishing moral persons from inanimate objects (and animals). Nevertheless, we often regard inanimate objects with a very wide range of affective and evaluational attitudes, and we attribute responsibility to them in a variety of dimensions. Often our discourse in this matter very closely resembles the language of moral responsibility: obviously, it is possible to resent or blame or coddle or appreciate or praise an inanimate object.

(2) *attributions of responsibility to nonhuman animate objects.* When I bought a house in a rural location in 2012, I realized I had a rather serious

poison ivy problem: there were vines growing up into the trees and up the walls of the house, vines crawling out of the underbrush into the yard with their glossy green leaves. I came to think of the thing as one huge organism or a single monstrous vine that had my house in its clutches like a hand. I fought back with herbicides, but the accursed poison ivy was responsible for many rashes.

Again, though philosophers often simply assert, for example, that you would not hold your dog responsible for eating the Thanksgiving turkey, the response of a dog owner or, at any rate, the turkey preparer in that situation is very likely to include a whole moral vocabulary and very direct attributions of responsibility as well as punishment. You know better than that. What did you think you were doing? Bad dog! In response, the dog may well whimper. Now, if this is not moral discourse that engages questions of responsibility, I would like to know what it is.

(3) *attributions of responsibility to events, policies, institutions, abstract objects groups, and so on.* What is responsible for the debt crisis? The tax cuts, declines in tax collections due to a recession, stimulus spending, and so on. And of course the fact that the tax cuts are responsible for the deficit might give us reason to condemn the tax cuts or regard them as . . . immoral. The United States invaded Iraq. Who would you hold responsible? Perhaps some of the individuals involved. But we do treat nations or states as agents at least in conversation; even the sentence "the United States invaded Iraq" registers this usage. Colin Powell asserted that because of the U.S. role in the destruction of the Iraq, the United States was responsible for the rebuilding effort. "Break it, you bought it." Many held that the United States was blameworthy. But did the United States act freely? Or how did it act at all?

(4) *ascriptions to one person of responsibility for the actions of another.* Sometimes, people can be responsible, including morally responsible, for other people and things. For example, a superior officer might be in some sense or to some degree responsible for the misbehavior of one of his subordinates, or a parent for a child, or a dog owner for a dog, and so on. Obviously, of course, even if my child does something that is frowned upon, and does it freely, I do not do that action freely or at all; I may even have been working to change my child's behavior and through no fault of my own have been unable to, and perhaps I could not reasonably have been expected to prevent it in this situation. When a baby cries on take-off, perhaps it is due to the changing

pressure in her ears; it is not her choice to cry, nor is that her parents' preference. People still look daggers at the parents, as I know only too well. They hold the parents responsible. Perhaps there is nothing that the superior officer should have done to prevent a crime committed by his subordinate. Still he may be called on to "accept responsibility" and even to make reparations, or to see to it that the institution does. Indeed we think of institutions as responsible for the actions of the people embedded in them under certain circumstances, at least to the extent of having to make reparations for their misdeeds, for example. I suppose we could try to account for such a case by examining the decision-making procedures of the institution to see whether it is analogous to the decision making of an individual moral agent: free or rational or controlled. But, in fact, I do not think that these procedures would be terribly relevant to questions of institutional responsibility.

By way, again, of ground clearing, Michael McKenna distinguishes a number of different kinds of responsibility, including causal responsibility, legal responsibility, personal responsibility ("between intimates"), professional responsibility, aesthetic responsibility, and responsibilities with regard to etiquette. All of these, McKenna argues, are distinct from moral responsibility. Some such approach will underlie many of the possible treatments of the sorts of examples enumerated above: a silverware drawer or a Weimaraner or the administration may be responsible in some sense, but not in the moral sense. I think we have already seen some reason to doubt this, at least to the extent that we do use various apparently ethical terms of evaluation and manifest various reactive attitudes in these sorts of cases.

Nevertheless, the various kinds of responsibility or senses of the term "responsibility" are certainly closely related. "Responsible" is not a massive homonym. Then we are faced with various questions about how these various sorts of responsibility are related to one another, or whether they are to be distinguished from one another, and if so how. These are interesting questions, of course, but what concerns me here is the efficacy of such distinctions in refuting the sort of view I am putting forward. My assertion is that the claim that Manson is responsible for the murders is much more like the claim that the tax cuts are responsible for the deficit, or that the dog is responsible for eating the turkey, than various philosophical theories make them appear. And for the purposes of this argument, moral responsibility cannot be distinguished from other sorts of responsibility by the sheer alleged fact that the former requires freedom, or self-control, or rational agency, while the others, or some of the others, do not. That would be to legislate the problem away a priori or by a series of stipulated definitions. Or it would be merely to assume the preferred answer to the question at issue, namely, whether freedom (self-control, rational agency) is necessary for moral responsibility.

But there are also cases in which it is entirely implausible to deny that the sense of responsibility in question is a moral sense:

(5) *attributions of responsibility for good actions to "naturally" good people.* Various philosophers—Chisholm, for example—have argued that people who are "naturally" good, generous without effort, and so on, are less praiseworthy than those for whom generosity is a terrible struggle. I do not think that lines up with our practices, and a naturally good person is more liable than any sort of person to be widely admired and credited with her good works. The idea that the moral quality of each of her actions is undermined by her personal excellence seems odd, and it is not normally relevant, as we assign such a person responsibility for her actions, exactly how those qualities of character emerged. Chisholm quotes Thomas Reid quoting the Roman historian Velleius Paterculus on Cato the Younger: "He never did a right action solely for the sake of seeming to do the right, but because he could not do otherwise." Chisholm approves Reid's remark that this "strictly, is not the praise of Cato, but of his constitution, which was no more the work of Cato than his existence."[25] Obviously, however, Velleius Paterculus intends this as the highest praise imaginable. And we may be somewhat puzzled as to Reid's distinction between persons and their constitutions. Indeed, I would think that the idea that Cato is not morally praiseworthy, because his character is not his own doing, is something that would only occur to someone laboring under a theory; it surely does not correspond at all to our natural reactions or our practice with regard actually to dealing out praise, as the actual reception of Cato makes clear. Indeed, if the view that freedom is necessary to responsibility entails that naturally good people are not responsible for their good actions, that would be in my view be enough to suggest that the debate about moral responsibility should never have gone in this direction at all.

Perhaps (5) is a specific example of a much wider ethical dimension:

(6) *attributions of responsibility for states of mind and dimensions of character.*

Robert Merrihew Adams argues as follows.

Many involuntary states of mind are objects of ethical appraisal and censure in their own right. . . . It matters morally what we are for and what we are against, even if we do not have the power to do much for it or against it, and even if it was not by trying that we came to be for it or against it. . . . In truth there is something odd about the search for voluntary faults to explain our responsibility for wrong states of mind. If someone says to me that I am incapable of feeling gratitude, or that I do not sincerely care about my moral character, or that although I act rightly I do so only because I think it the most effective way to get what I want from other people, this claim about my feelings or motives is already an ethical indictment; and if it is true, I stand condemned. There is no need to search for guilty actions or omissions of which I may be accused. . . . In the second place, the struggle against a wrong state of mind in oneself is normally a form of repentance, which involves self-reproach. At the center of such a process is one's taking responsibility for one's state of mind. Your ingratitude (to return to a previous example) is not a voluntary action; but if you take responsibility for it you also do not see it as something that just happens to you, like a toothache or a leak in your roof. You see it as an opposition that you yourself are making, not voluntarily but none the less really, to the generosity of the other person and to your own position as a recipient of love and assistance. In repentance you repudiate this opposition, not as an evil existing outside the inner circle of your selfhood, but as your own; and you reproach yourself for it.[26]

It is even less plausible to distinguish the self from its emotional and appetitive faculties than to distinguish it from its constitution or dysfunctions, if indeed anything can be less plausible than that. What we have to see is how central the sorts of practices that Adams describes are to our moral lives. "It matters morally what we are for and against": hardly anyone acts as though that is false. Now, one might in the familiar fashion argue that we implicitly take people's opinions to be freely chosen, and that opinions or whole structures of thought *can* be freely chosen, perhaps indirectly, by cultivating certain sources of information and ignoring others, for example. I am not arguing that such things are obviously impossible; I am saying, with Adams, that they are largely irrelevant to our actual practices of assigning responsibility in this regard.

As a matter of fact, I know that people's political opinions tend to vary with things like region, income group, race, gender; I know that most people's politics is likely to be similar to their parents' and that of others perhaps express a rebellion against them by negation, and so on. I don't really think opinions are usually freely chosen, even indirectly. But whether they are or not is, I believe, in most cases just irrelevant to whether they are culpable.

Adams as well begins to show what could be salutary or important or even useful about the detachment of responsibility from freedom with regard to states of mind or qualities of character. There might be therapeutic value in some cases in regarding your illness or your moral defects as things external to yourself that could be jettisoned. But a deeper reflection that could lead to certain sorts of "repentance" or other forms of remediation requires one to acknowledge that one has oneself been at fault or even that one's self is irremediably flawed. Twelve-step treatment programs for addiction are based in part on a separation of freedom from responsibility, and the cultural currency of such programs begin to indicate that people simply do not share any very simple intuition about the relation of between the two. Alcoholics Anonymous is the origin of the disease model of addiction. But, according to it, recovery requires taking responsibility. Step eight, for example, directs one to "make a list of all persons one has harmed, and [become] willing to make amends to them all." One is always supposed to be reflecting on how one's actions emerged from one's own (diseased, compulsive) self and taking responsibility for them on precisely that basis.

19.

One sort of argument that freedom is necessary to responsibility emerges in the discussion of excuses. Some excuses seem to relieve one from responsibility on the grounds of absent or diminished freedom. So for example, if one is being blackmailed or otherwise coerced by another person, we think in some situations this can reduce responsibility. Of course, this is a complex matter, and there is a spectrum of possible degrees of interpersonal coercion. That someone is threatening to reveal your adultery is not a terribly good excuse for committing murder, no matter how constrained you might feel to do so. But consider the extreme case: (a) *Andre the Giant and his posse are operating your body like a marionette* as they roll about on their crime spree. Then surely you are not responsible, and it may be rather hard for someone who does not connect freedom and responsibility to say just why. I have already suggested in a variety of ways that I am not going simply to accept the going range of excuses. I pointed out that our intuitions are at most divided on the responsibilities of the insane, for example. I think it is perfectly legitimate to call for some legislation about excuses for principled reasons. But I don't think I can legislate away the case of Andre's marionette.

Or consider the excuse that it was a sheer accident and perhaps of a sort that no one could have been expected to foresee, really; (b) *I tripped over your completely unexpected chihuahua.* Then it appears that I did not attack you intentionally, or deliberately, or even at all. This sort of case apparently has the effect of bringing back into play the whole machinery of rational agency, or it could be read that way; I did not do it *on purpose*, we might say, or I did not form the intention to do it, or I didn't want to do it, in the sense that I did not choose it from a menu of possible next courses of action. Or we might say that I was unable to control the situation, or indeed, once it was precipitated in your direction, my own body's course.

This appears similar in some respects to at least some cases in which ignorance could be regarded as an excuse; (c) *I didn't even know you were here, asleep in the next room, when I launched into my version of 'Land of 1000 Dances.'* " However, if unfreedom is in play here, it has to be a very different sort of unfreedom that bears in a very different way on the event than in the case of Andre's marionette; my Wilson Pickett imitation was not involuntary glossolalia. Perhaps I could have sung some Al Green instead, or lapsed into a soulful silence. But though I certainly did wake you up, this might be excusable. And perhaps we would say that is because, since I did not know the real situation, I did not deliberate about whether to wake you up; I did not decide or choose to wake you up. This again connects agency, if not necessarily to freedom, at least to rational deliberation or reason-responsive control. (I did not know that there was a good reason not to sing.)

Perhaps we have arrived at a bit of a standoff, in that I have presented a variety of counter-examples to the notion that responsibility requires freedom. But these excuses appear to lean on the attenuation of freedom, at least in some broad sense of "freedom." However, consider the conceptual situation even if these excuses do entirely rest on attenuated freedom: in some cases, it appears, if someone is responsible, then, necessarily, she is free. In other cases (take Adams' qualities of character and states of mind, for example), not. If that is the way the matter stands, then after all freedom is not a necessary condition for moral responsibility *simpliciter*. The argument might be that in the excuse cases, the lack of responsibility is *explained by* the underlying lack of freedom, or even that the latter is a sufficient condition of the former. But even were that true in some cases, it hardly shows that freedom is a necessary condition for moral responsibility, given that there are counterexamples to this thesis.

However, we might also see to what extent we could give an account of these excuses that does not appeal to the notion of freedom. One strategy, which really has been tried, is to proceed piecemeal: it's a kind of brute social fact that we recognize excuses of these sorts, and there is no particular coherent account underlying this practice; we just treat sheer accidents involving no negligence differently than we do things about which the agent deliberates. Austin could almost be construed this way, though something deeper underlies his strategy, I believe. And I remark again that the range of excuses that should be recognized is always up for grabs or is always potentially a matter of controversy.

What might we say about you, Andre the Giant's marionette? Well it would be natural to proceed by describing the causal roles played by your body and his respectively, but in fact both bodies are embroiled in a complex causal conflagration and it is difficult to sort this out plausibly or systematically without directly appealing to, say, Andre's body as the locus of decision or guidance or control. Now, as Dennett famously argued, it is important to distinguish cases where I am being determined to act by another agent from those in which I am being determined to act, for example, by the general flow of things, or by my own feelings. The case of Andre's marionette has the quality of collapsing metaphysical determination and agency into political unfreedom or oppression by other agents. No one would not feel resentful and constrained as Andre's marionette, doing entirely as he directs. But we might not have the same feeling were we being driven by various impersonal forces, as in fact very frequently or always we are. It is no more legitimate for Andre to force me to do what he wants me to do, all other things being equal, than vice versa, and the event fills me with outrage about human equality and my political/natural/social rights. I might get angry at a mountain that is in my way, but I do not think it is violating my rights or my autonomy in anything like the sense Andre is. When I get in my car, I have to basically assume the posture directed by the seat. I do not regard this as violating my personhood in the same way I might if a policeman forced me to "assume the position."

So I suggest that one of the ways this provides an excusing condition is that in the event one's rights or autonomy have been violated by an agent who has no legitimate reason to do so; our excusing is in part an expression of our outrage at the indignity suffered specifically at the hands of another, who has no legitimate legal or ethical claim. We excuse such a person on the grounds, as it were, of slavery, we being abolitionists, and we may extend and qualify this excuse across a range of cases as the spectrum of force and coercion being applied grows milder. And we excuse in this case, too, because we have someone else to blame, so that we will be able to discharge our outrage/sense of justice at someone's expense. We've got someone to hang, and we have good reasons to hang him. The fact that someone else is responsible might be a convincing excuse, even without any direct appeal, for example, to the ability to do otherwise. This is one reason that various coercive strategies to shape people's choice situation, even in cases of relatively mild coercion where they are very much in control of their own actions by many standards, may function as more effective excuses than situations in which one's choices are comparatively very constrained by other sorts of factors. The excuse calls into play a complex set of judgments about legal and political values, interpersonal relations and structures of power, interpersonal freedom and crime.

In the case of the unexpected chihuahua, the idea that I am not responsible because I am not free is only one way to frame the excuse. If I held your dog responsible, or said it was your dog's fault—if that thing *is* a dog—you would understand me, I believe. Or if I thought you were responsible for not restraining your chihuahua, I might get into an excuse-and-responsibility assessment involving all sorts of objects, people, and circumstances. Indeed, we all had our role. We are, however, imagining an unforeseeable accident, a relatively alert, agile me, and so on. If I am just unbelievably clumsy all the time—even if, as seems likely, that is not my doing—it's quite likely my fault after all. That is, I may be blameworthy specifically in virtue of my chronic lack of control.

But the problem here is the situation, we might say, not the subjectivity, and the responsibility or the excuse emerges in the context of the whole. The responsibility is distributed among the objects in the situation: me, you, Julio, the ground, and so on. This possibility is open to us once we have opened the concept of responsibility itself beyond things that are obviously persons or agents. Many of my own choices might be involved in getting me to trip; I decided to come to the park today, for example. The way we're going to distribute it this time is going to rest minimal responsibility on my shoulders; perhaps if I had been completely alert, but realistically. . . . Responsibility, we might say, gathers around or in things in situations in which they are juxtaposed; if we do not presuppose that it requires free or rational agency, we see that it is a very complex transaction among the objects embedded in a given moral situation. Then some excuses might involve distributions of responsibility or assessments of how it ought to be distributed, which I believe is just how we would proceed in a case like this if we were motivated to examine it in detail.

The idea of taking responsibility for another is relevant here, because there the responsibility seems obviously to be distributed among the things which are juxtaposed in a situation: me, the baby, your unbabyproofed house and hysterical overreaction. We take responsibility for whole regions to various extents and degrees: for our yards, our trash, our kids, our neighborhood. In every case, partial responsibility is distributed among the elements, and excuses often consist of reassessing or weighing the relative responsibility of the various elements involved. Such procedures are of the essence of tort law, for example. What was the role of the faulty product, the negligent user, the careless manufacturer, the incorrect installation, the fact that it was used for the wrong task or in the wrong situation? It may be the case that all of these are to some extent responsible.

Focusing a bit, one way to read a number of excuses that have been considered failures of freedom or control is as calling into question the attribution of the action or event to the person. Nor is this incompatible with the idea of working out responsibility as distributed through the elements of a situation. I might say, in defending myself from the assault charges, that I didn't assault you at all, since "assault" brings in a legal context where intentions are relevant. It doesn't, for example, serve as an accurate representation of my moral character. This is an insight of Hume, again, who argued that if an action did not proceed in some comprehensible way from your existing character, it was excusable; it would be a random event, or certainly would not support a moral assessment of you and hence, perhaps, also not an ascription of responsibility. Indeed, this is what "responsibility" seems primordially to mean: *ownership* of the action, which is what supports the idea that one is properly to be held to account for it. And again, the question of whether one's character is the result of one's free choice appears in most cases to be irrelevant to the ascription of responsibility.

Now to the Wilson Pickett alarm clock. I am here, of course, the direct cause of your waking up, and in virtue of an action I freely perform (let us suppose), singing "Land of 1000 Dances." Here the usual reading would be that I am not responsible because I did not intend to wake you, and could not reasonably have foreseen that my action would have that effect. Nevertheless, I did wake you, and my opponent might challenge me to generate an account of the content of the excuse that does not appeal to freedom, control, or practical rationality and the fact that they fail here through no fault of the agent. Of course, I did not sing "Land of 1000 Dances" reflexively or compulsively or under coercion, though I may have been barely conscious that I was singing at all, knowing me. Where the practical rationality broke down is that I lacked an adequate acquaintance with the situation. So I suppose we might say that I couldn't control the situation in certain important ways because I didn't know about the situation in those respects. Certainly, it might be right to say that my waking you was inadvertent; it is definitely not right to say that it was involuntary or compelled. And I think, in general, to say that we are determined with regard to things which we do inadvertently is a very odd way of talking. I voluntarily, more or less, let's say, sang "Land of 100 Dances." I did not voluntarily wake you up, I suppose, but neither did I wake you up involuntarily, say by literally being seized or made a marionette by the spirit of Pickett.

One thing to notice about even this small selection of excuses is that even on traditional accounts, the ways they apparently put attenuated freedom into play is extremely various, and that, even if freedom is in play, many other things are in play too in every sort of case. If we were really concerned to evaluate an excuse in a complicated situation where we are trying to assess responsibility, "his action (or he) was unfree" does not help very much; we need even on the most sympathetic construal of the connection of freedom and excuses to say in any given case how exactly freedom, and what sort of freedom, is compromised, and by what. We will want to work out a distribution of responsibility among the elements of the situation.

This discussion will have done what I intended it to do if it opens or re-opens the question of whether freedom in any plausible sense (or allegedly connected notions such as practical rationality or control), is a necessary condition of moral responsibility. In some ways, the present position would be a version of compatibilism, depending on what it is one thinks the compatibilist is trying to save. My position is that *whether or not* determinism is compatible with free will, it is compatible with moral responsibility. A compatibilist whose fundamental project is to save a vision or version of human freedom in a deterministic universe may find the present version of what Fischer has called "semi-compatibilism" disturbing or ridiculous. But a compatibilist whose fundamental project is to preserve the possibility and importance of moral responsibility in the face of a quite possibly deterministic universe of which persons are wholly a part, might find it wholesome.

20.

One of the sharpest discussions of free will in the tradition is Jonathan Edwards' *A Careful and Strict Inquiry into the Modern Prevailing Notions of Freedom of the Will, Which Is Supposed to Be Essential to Moral Agency, Virtue and Vice, Reward and Punishment, Praise and Blame*. It is just possible that Edwards had read Hume's *A Treatise of Human Nature*, though he doesn't display this explicitly. His discussion follows Locke's pioneering treatment of all these issues, but like Hume's, is much more clear as a statement of compatibilism, while then going further than either. In the first set of definitions and arguments, he simply states the compatibilist conclusion: we are free when we can do what we want or will, though our will may be, or according to Edwards as to Hume, certainly is, determined.

Of course, Edwards was a Puritan divine and held to the uplifting doctrine of the total depravity of human beings. He frames the matter in terms of "Calvinism" and "Arminianism," and the usual interpretation of Calvin suggests a total denial of free will, both because of our fallen estate and because of God's perfect foreknowledge. Then the initial set of compatibilist moves might be taken as attempts to reduce the sting of these devastating doctrines: well, we are free after all, when we use the term in the "ordinary sense": we are free when we can do what we want to do. So God's foreknowledge and our depravity leave us free after all, when the word *freedom* is not abused. (Like many others, Edwards uses addiction as a puzzle and as an argument: the drunkard does what he wills, though he cannot will otherwise, and so he is responsible. Edwards, like most contemporary philosophers, has no idea what he's talking about when he talks about addiction.)

Edwards goes on to deny that we are free in the stronger senses demanded by "Arminianism," which he characterizes as (1) that we have or could have a "self-determining power of the will" or that the will has a certain "sovereignty over itself"; (2) that we act freely from a point of "indifference" in which the will is suspended between two courses of action with nothing determining which one it is to take; (3) the action taken is "contingent" or not necessitated by external factors, whether that's the order of nature, or God's omniscience.[27] Of course, he denies that any human being can be free in this sense.

He then gives a battery of arguments to the effect that we can be responsible when we are not free in the Arminian way. But what puzzles me about the discussion is that it would also tend to show that freedom even in the compatibilist sense is not necessary to moral responsibility, which I also think would be more in keeping with Calvinist theology. Be that as it may, I would like to annex some of these examples to the stronger thesis that moral responsibility can be detached entirely from freedom of the will. His first example is "the infinitely holy God," who always used to be esteemed by God's people, not only virtuous, but a being in whom all possible virtue, and every virtue in the most absolute purity and perfection, and in infinitely greater brightness and amiableness than in any creature; the most perfect pattern of virtue, and the fountain from whom all others' virtue is but as beams from the sun; and who has been supposed to be, on account of his virtue and holiness, infinitely more worthy to be esteemed, loved, honored, admired, commended, extolled and praised, than any creature . . . this Being [according to the Arminians] has no virtue at all . . . and he is deserving of no commendation, or praise; because he is under necessity, he can't avoid being holy and good as he is.[28]

That Edwards flatly states that God is not free—not free to do evil—is really a somewhat remarkable and radical moment in Christian theology; people had many ways around this puzzle, but rarely took the position that God was himself necessitated because perfectly and necessarily good. But, I suppose, he is free in the compatibilist sense: he has the power to do what he wills to do, though his will is itself necessitated.

What I would ask Edwards if we were hanging out, however, would be whether the praiseworthiness of God arises from freedom in this compatibilist sense, or, putting it another way, whether His praiseworthiness arises from His sheer power to do what he wills, or presupposes it. I don't think Edwards thinks that. So, imagine a God who faces a devil of equal power in a Manichean universe. And suppose that (as in our world) Satan has won a slow but inexorable victory, so that God's power to do good becomes ever-more circumscribed over time, until he sits there helplessly, a perfectly good and powerless being. In such a case, the prudential course of action would be to spend all day praising Satan, though disingenuously. But a perfectly good being with no freedom to do what He wills is, all in all, still worthy of praise. For God to be worthy of praise, he does not need to be free in the Arminian or in the compatibilist sense. And we praise Him for His goodness, not His freedom.

And then Edwards traverses the sorts of considerations that I touched on earlier: that "naturally" virtuous people would not be praiseworthy, if free will is required for responsibility; and "naturally" vice-ridden people would not be blameworthy. He throws out some pretty provocative examples.

A woman of great honor and chastity may have a moral inability to prostitute herself to her slave. A child of great love and duty to his parents, may be unable to be willing to kill his father. A very lascivious man, in case of certain opportunities and temptations, and in the absence of such and such restraints, may be unable to forbear gratifying his lust. A drunkard, under such and such circumstances, may be unable to forbear taking of strong drink.[29]

I think compatibilism was being invented by such figures as Hobbes, Locke, Hume, and Edwards precisely to try to save the intuition or teaching that free will is required for moral responsibility. They do this by narrowing the idea of liberty extremely, insisting the whole time that that's all most people ever meant by it. But I think the right conclusion after a while is that assessments of responsibility simply do not, or do not necessarily, depend on or deploy freedom of the will in any sense. Had the woman of great honesty and chastity not had adequate opportunities to prostitute herself to her slave (e.g., if she didn't have any slaves), still her honesty and chastity, and the acts which flow from it, are worthy of praise. Whether God could have done evil had he willed it is neither here nor there.

21.

In my view, the human self is a real thing that has real causal effects. I think it is a material thing, if it is anything, and I think that it is volatile, and I think that it is composed of other things. Now, I do think that whatever the human self is doing at any given time is whatever all the pieces of that self are doing at that time, but the reduction of the self to particles or faculties or whatever is no more or less justified than the construction of the self out of particles, and the particles are no more real causal agents than is the whole self/situation. So I think in some cases human selves are real causal factors in events, and if they are the right sort of factors, then those selves can be held responsible. There may be no entirely clear or systematic way of characterizing the circumstances under which a self is in the right sort of configuration and relations, or there may be a wide variety of configurations and relations that could support a reasonable attribution of the act to that self, or any particular degree of responsibility for it.

But I want emphatically to distinguish the sort of self I am countenancing or declaring myself to be from Chisholm's or Korsgaard's or Kant's or Fischer's, which has the problem we see arise again and again: the self is always receding, is an extensionless point: in short, is a soul, monad, and so on. This requires, as we have seen, a distinction of the self even from its beliefs and desires, much less its diseases. Now, I would certainly accept various fragmented views of the self. My self, I believe, is a congeries, no more or less a single real thing than a table or possibly a heap. And obviously I am not going to trace any causal chain in some ultimate sense to an origin in a self, conceived thinly or thickly; the self I am saying I am is fully, entirely embedded in the ongoing flood of physical causation. The question isn't whether the causal chain originates in the agent; the question is whether it runs through the agent in the right ways, whether the action was indeed in that sense *something you did*.

In other words, more or less accepting some form of determinism or at least declaring it to be obscure how freedom actually does or could emerge in a natural universe, it is open to us what approach to take. We could start to suggest that our attributions of responsibility should be attenuated or even eliminated. They are not necessary, for example, to a utilitarian justification of punishment, and in any case toning down the blame might be a good thing. This actually does seem to be proceeding in many arenas including the criminal law, which is in a slow transformation to what we might think of as a medical model or the self as beset by illnesses and treatable by pharmaceuticals, for example. Or one could take the compatibilist approach of continuing to regard responsibility as important and even as underlain by freedom, but a freedom compatible with physical causation. Or one could take the approach of decoupling responsibility from freedom, as I am suggesting.

This reflects, as I have said, for one thing, a desire to take responsibility even for actions in which I did feel compelled; I think that even if certain sorts of compulsion, or certain situations in which a person is compelled, constitute legitimate excuses, others do not. In the familiar way (familiar at least since Austin's "Plea for Excuses") we need to carefully distinguish different sorts of cases. Perhaps doing something because you're being blackmailed, doing it because you tripped, and doing it because you're addicted have in common that you could not have done otherwise, sort of, but that doesn't mean they are the same sort of case or that any of them should be expanded willy-nilly into a model of all "involuntary" acts, or that it might not be the case that you are in some such cases responsible after all, partly or even fully responsible, and so on. As the Frankfurt cases tend to show, the question turns on whether the agent has the right sort of relation to the act, not on whether various counterfactuals obtain.

Now, you might ask why I am so concerned to preserve the notion of moral responsibility, since I'm trying to destroy much of the superstructure meant to keep it standing. Some of the answers to this are more or less what you'd expect, I hope. Have you ever dealt with someone who fails to take responsibility for what they do or what happens because of what they do? Well it could be a child, but it might not be. Ever dealt with a bureaucracy, in which no one is capable of making a decision and everyone is deferring to some amorphous authority or rulebook somewhere? Collective consciousness is a kind of universal excuse: I was just following orders is one famous form of the nightmare in which conscience is moved in imagination into a collective agent but in fact is simply jettisoned: the whole idea of the state, I believe, is that no one is responsible for anything. People live their whole lives in devotion to a single proposition: it's not my fault.

Ultimately, what I want is not happiness or pleasure, but what I deserve. At least, I want that on what I think of as my good days. The point is not to achieve happiness, but to deserve happiness. But I am talking about what *I* deserve: I with my illnesses and my stubborn desires, not the true I that's supposedly always getting overwhelmed by these things.

B. Moral Values

1.

I do recognize certain moral principles as binding. I think cruelty is wrong, for example. I place a great deal of value on honesty, or I might say I feel the moral power of truth: I try to resolve not to deceive myself and I try to resolve not to deceive others, and to show them to whatever degree is appropriate to our interaction and one degree more, who I actually am. I am congenitally opposed to placing adherence to the rules over consideration of the real human situation at hand, and so on. Of course, I fail by my own standards all the time, which is a source of pain. I am glad about this pain, for it is almost the only thing that motivates me actually to improve. Now, I ask myself, why do I believe such things? Vague as they are, I have felt in certain situations even that I would willingly die rather than violate them: my commitment is serious; perhaps these are my most serious commitments. But why have I committed myself to these things and not others, and why do I feel such power emanating from these notions, power to move me or to force me to move, to make me act or cease acting, speak or fall silent?

I have spent years pondering the is/ought problem, or perhaps the problem that underlies the is/ought problem: the problem of the sources and nature of normativity. Of course, this problem is held to be particularly acute within a naturalistic worldview of the sort I have been articulating. Well, let me acknowledge that this is a mystery; indeed, it is difficult even to come to an adequate formulation of the problem: one might ask, for example, whether there are moral properties and, if so, what sort of properties they are and in what they can inhere. Or one might frame the matter in terms of the force of moral claims, as a challenge to show the force of obligation or prohibition on each person. It's a familiar problem, of course, that you can't get obligation in a beaker or watch it fire up an MRI, so that properties such as "goodness" have been termed "nonnatural," and so on. I am not sure, I must admit, where to find ground to stand on in this rather too quickly abstracted set of difficulties.

Again, there are moral principles that I regard as more or less absolutely binding, or as absolutely binding with suitable refinements. There are decisions I have made that I regarded as morally obligatory to make, and cases where I disappointed myself by failing to do what I regarded it as morally obligatory to do. And when I ponder the question of where the force of these constraints originates, I have to say (rather unfortunately for an anti-Kantian such as myself) that I impose them on myself, or that my sense of their power comes from my own commitment to them. But then this just appears circular: I commit because I feel the power. At any rate, I think, taking all in all, that the status of moral principles has to be as commitments, more or less personal. Or I might say I take a somewhat existentialist approach to the source of normativity in decision. Obviously, social situations play into such commitments, but they cannot be dispositive: of course, one is right in many situations in attacking a social consensus or questioning it or violating it pointedly. But there is no doubt that at a minimum personal resolutions take place within social configurations and in relation to the commitments of others.

There is, indeed, something arbitrary about such commitments, and I believe that there is no moral principle—including such anodyne formulations as the golden rule, which I endorse—which could not be thrown directly into doubt in, for example, an enumeration of counter-examples. Or at a minimum they can all be thrown into meta-doubt: what is the source of their binding power? Why should I do what such a principle tells me, if I do not myself feel its force or prefer some other rule? No moral principle is immune from doubt, and yet some such principles function in one's mental economy (well, mine, I should say) as absolute requirements: their binding force is far out of proportion to any rational defense that might be given for them, which is one reason people like Kant have taken such elaborate measures to try make them stick. This binding force can be recognized or actually felt even as the requirement is violated. The Kantian and post-Kantian project of finding ethics in reason strikes me as perverse, and I think that a commitment to a moral principle is a fundamentally rationally arbitrary commitment. I have argued, indeed, that every belief involves an element of emotional commitment in excess to evidence: you could regard something as both extremely probable according to the evidence and false; you do not believe anything until you commit yourself emotionally to its truth. This is more obvious in the case of moral commitments than in the case of many other sorts of commitments, or the element in excess to rationality is necessarily larger in this case than in many others.

No merely external force is enough to make you moral or make you into a being with moral content. No merely external force is enough to move you to act from moral principle. It makes sense to ask why you should do what God demands, what reason demands, what your fellow creatures demand, what evolution demands, what the law demands. The history of ethics is partly a history of trying to find a way to assure ourselves of the external validity of the standards to which we try to hold ourselves and (in particular) one another, to attribute their force to something external, to assure ourselves thus of their legitimacy, especially of their legitimacy for other people. It's a way we try to make a claim that other people should abide by the principles we have committed ourselves to, or at any rate the principles we think they ought to abide by. We want moral principles to have the status of legislation, of law, and then we've got to show or at any rate assert that the force of our principles is binding on others; this is heart of Kant's ethics and aesthetics, for example, and despite his heroic efforts, it is fundamentally rationally indefensible. Or perhaps the idea is to assure ourselves that some moral principles are binding on us, that we are not merely making a contingent and yet, as it were, infinite decision.

Indeed, to be honest I don't think the appeal to reason, even if it worked in other respects, would account for the binding force of moral principles. The analogy is to things that appear to exert a cognitive binding force; there are moves that are rationally forced, for example, in a logically valid argument or a mathematical demonstration or a chess problem. You are rationally obliged to accept the conclusions if you accept the premises, since the argument is valid. The source of even this sort of obligation is mysterious, however, or it is difficult to formulate the principle precisely: of course, one may understand the premises perfectly well, accept them, and see how the conclusion follows, and reject the conclusion anyway. Perhaps one just has an irrational episode, or cultivates the conviction that something has gone wrong somewhere, even if one can't say exactly where. To be rationally obliged to agree is not, as it turns out, to be actually constrained or bound or even obligated. One is not necessarily, all things considered, obligated to believe what one is rationally obligated to believe. This fact, I think, leaves the sense of "rationally obligated" mysterious, or perhaps it and its like are figurative expressions or counterfactuals: were you rational, you would agree.

However, what the sort of view I am struggling to articulate has in common with Kantianism is that I am saying that each person is the lawgiver of herself, or is the author or appropriator of the principles by which she lives or in relation to which she lives. (That might be only one dimension of the moral life, however.) Where I agree with the anti-Kantian backlash represented by existentialism is that I think that the choice of such principle is rationally arbitrary or far in excess of the possibility of rational defense. If a moral principle is anything, it is a way of actually being, or something in relation to which one actually is, not an argument or an equation, and it has the uncertainty of all our worldly commitments and then some.

There is no way ultimately to be assured of the truth of any moral principle and hence there is no way to be assured of the moral rightness of any given action, the moral goodness of any particular goal, and so on. If you are going to commit, you are going to have to commit without knowing even whether such things can be known, which ought to be obvious in a way. The extremity of some people's moral certainty, to which they might be faithful unto death, is in obvious disproportion to the certainty of the theoretical justifications of such principles, if any; in overflowing excess. You don't have to read the *Critique of Practical Reason* to commit yourself to certain moral principles, and I don't think that very many people have emerged from reading that book as better people, or committed to principles that they were not before, though they may have sharpened their sense of the content and application of principles they sort of already held. Well, if an argument helps, that's good. But that's not where we live, and that's not what gets us out the door to help someone, say.

Now, however, where I disagree with the existentialists, and begin to temper the individualism, is that while we may face radical choices and while moral principles must have the status of personal commitments insofar as they have real outcomes, I do not think that we make such choices or undertake such commitments in a condition of anything like radical freedom. I think we make such choices under myriad restraints: we are restrained by the people around us and by the available linguistic possibilities, by other aspects of the environment in which we are embedded and from which we are not fully distinct, by various recalcitrant aspects of ourselves. Values are things we make—in what will now be a familiar structure—in collaboration with each other and with a world of creatures and things. They have centrally to do, of course, with the way we treat one another, but this is something you learn: you learn how you want to be treated and you learn how other people want to be treated, which might not even be that similar. You learn what a person is by actually dealing with persons; you learn to respect persons, if you ever do, in actual transactions in which, for example, another person demands or expects respect, and in which you feel the force or appropriateness of that demand.

2.

In her book *Normativity*, Judith Jarvis Thompson argues that there is no reason to suppose that normative claims are any less empirical than any other claims, or that they have truth conditions that take us outside the realm of normal experience and discourse about it. She quotes Simon Blackburn's formulation of the is/ought problem: "The natural world is the world revealed by the senses and described by the sciences: physics, chemistry, and notably biology, including evolutionary theory. However we think of it, ethics seems to fit badly into that world. Neither the senses nor the sciences seem to be good detectors of obligations, duties, or the order of value of things."[30] Now, I would agree that science is just not going to get you any ethics. So, for example, many people have tried to get ethics out of evolution, which I think is a nonstarter. Evolution cannot account for normative force of moral claims. Suppose it was counterevolutionary of me to take your stuff. Is that a *reason* not to take your stuff? You might have many good arguments that it's wrong to take your stuff, but the idea that I am swimming against the tide of evolution might legitimately be met with a mere shrug. Evolution has no claim on me, and it expends organisms and species willy-nilly. I do not at all doubt that certain forms of cooperation are adaptive in certain situations, Kropotkin's *Mutual Aid* being the *locus classicus* of that argument. On the other hand, that doesn't show or even suggest that if I do not cooperate with you right now I am acting counter to evolution. But even if I were, so what? What do I owe to evolution? And the idea that anyone can act counter to evolution is silly or incompatible with the basic theory of evolution: everything I do is, obviously, compatible with evolution insofar as evolution is responsible for me being the kind of thing I am. What if it turned out that some forms of violence or crime were adaptive?

(I would say that they certainly are under some conditions.) Would that show that they were right? Natural selection makes use of greed or violence as of anything else: everything that happens is compatible with evolution, if the theory of evolution is true. Evolution makes use of counteradaptive behavior as much as adaptive behavior.

The basic inference has to be from actuality to etiology: arguments from evolution start by presuming that we are what evolution made us. So look: staring squarely at the data, we ought to speculate that both what we would think of as good behavior and bad have been selected for, insofar as we so stubbornly display both. Insofar as evolution has selected us, it has, obviously, selected both cooperation and competition, good and evil, happiness and pain, and so on. It appears, like the rest of nature, to be morally indifferent. If it were really selecting against theft or capitalist economics or something, it should have done better than it has so far in weeding out thieves and capitalists.

And one thing I would resist is the identification of "the empirical" or a naturalistic metaphysics with science. Right, I don't think you'll find a justification of ethical values in brain scans, beakers, or fossil records. But it does not at all follow that values are not in the world. I admire science and regard it as often the source of genuine knowledge. I do not regard it as the exclusive source of all knowledge about the world, however, or I wouldn't write a book like this one, which is not an experiment. That science can't seem to, or even in principle necessarily cannot, account for values does not, without a scientistic premise, entail that values are not in the world or even that they have some mysterious ontological status.

Now, Thompson's strategy is to start out with ascriptions of value that do not appear to put in play moral considerations, such as "that is a good umbrella," and she says of Blackburn,

> He must have in mind by "ethics" something narrower than I refer to by that word: he must have been thinking of it as standing for something concerned with morality in particular. I say that partly because he thinks of ethics as concerned with obligations and duties, but also because what he says about it is so very implausible if taken to be about evaluation in general. For surely it might be precisely by the senses—with the help of some elementary science—that I discover that DRY is a good umbrella. ["DRY" is the name of a particular umbrella.][31]

By "elementary science" Thompson is referring to things like looking at the umbrella, opening it and closing it, and taking it out in a rainstorm. In that sense we're all scientists all the time.

Thompson, as she indicates, has a very wide conception of ethics as concerned with the entire realm of normativity, though it is not perfectly clear whether she would include, for example, aesthetic values. And she demands that people of Blackburn's ilk, if they believe that moral values have a profoundly different status than other sorts of attributions of goodness or rightness, produce an argument to show why they must, in principle, be distinguished. She starts with what we might think of as ordinary or humble ascriptors of value, such as being good at doing crossword puzzles, being good for England, being good to look at, being good in *Hamlet*, and being good with children. It seems eccentric to say that the fact that Jimmy is good with children is a transcendent or mysterious fact, something that no one could detect with their senses. Well, you need more than your senses: you need a structure of thought, a vocabulary, a set of cultural norms, and so on. And the idea of testing whether someone is good with children by a scientific procedure is silly and irrelevant, as though someone you just observed having a useful blast as a pre-school teacher could be discredited as not good with kids after all by scientific experiment. All you'd do in a case like that is assume that something has gone terribly wrong with the science, and start picking holes in the methodology, and in particular in the set of assumptions with which the scientist began.

With regard to "responsibility," I argued that its uses in various contexts including the moral does not at all support the idea that the word is being used in different senses when it is used to ascribe moral responsibility and supposedly other sorts of responsibility. A similar move to the one I was arguing against there is made by Thompson's opponents here: they will assert that there are various senses of the term *good*, for example, and that while some uses do not raise the is/ought problem, or are perfectly ordinary observations about the world, others transcend the empirical or have some other sort of ontological status, or at any rate present serious ontological challenges.

> It cannot be too strongly stressed that "good" does not mean something different in moral and nonmoral linguistic contexts. The adjective "good" is not ambiguous. It means the same in "good government" as it does in "good umbrella." (Just as the word "big" means the same in "big camel" and "big mouse.") It means the same in "morally good plan" as it does in "strategically good plan." "Morally good plan" means something different from "strategically good plan," of course, but that is not because "good" means something different in these two expressions; the difference is entirely due to the difference in what modifies "good" in them.[32]

Thompson asserts, or rather demonstrates, that there is no quality of goodness *simpliciter*, and she goes further, showing that there's no such thing as a good action or event without further specifications of particular dimensions, any more than there is any such thing as a good pebble *simpliciter*, though there might be pebbles that are good to look at, or good for smashing a window, or good for gravelling your driveway, or well received among the fishes. And certainly, some of the weight of the is/ought problem, some of the mysteries of value, turn on wild overgeneralizations or account for realities that don't exist. Perhaps "goodness" is not more mysterious than "redness." Once you start getting into the weeds of what properties are being ascribed on specific occasions, the mystery derived from looking for goodness through a telescope or trying to precipitate it into a flask is partly caused by the fact that one is looking for a dimension or property that no real thing can instantiate. But it would be highly eccentric to hold that the fact that something is a good umbrella is a mysterious matter that opens up a different plane of reality or a different sort of truth.

3.

To take other persons seriously as real physical things and as subjects, to take them as analogous to oneself and as genuinely different than oneself and as genuinely in relation to oneself: this is what I want to think of as the essence of ethics. Indeed, there is no reason to restrict the scope of ethics to persons: ethics proposes to understand things and situations as real or to take them seriously insofar as they are real, to understand the similarities of things to oneself and the differences of things from oneself, to understand the relations of things to oneself and the excess of things to that relation (these are not definitions). To do good ethics it is necessary to take seriously one's embeddedness in and myriad connections to these things; to note one's constitution out of them and the ways one bleeds off into them, and also one's isolations from them: the gaps, the detachments. An ethics in which only subjective states—pleasures and pains, for instance, or desire and satisfaction—count, is wacky. But an ethics in which subjective states do not count at all is also wacky. An ethics that is a sheer social construction or vocabulary is impossible if the social world is embedded in a physical world of objects and bodies, air and water, light and mountains, highways and soup, guns and bandages. But an ethical world is social nevertheless.

There is no reason to choose an exclusive location for ethical facts in general and stick them into heads or vocabularies or cultures. Here as everywhere, we might as well avail ourselves of the real world we have and avail ourselves of ourselves and of one another in that world, as though we had any choice in the matter. The fundamental problem is not how a world or nature is possible or how it might be inferred from our impressions or our words; it is how we are possible as distinct things in a web of connection. The fundamental inference is not from our subjective or collective experiences to a flow of reality or a universe, but to a separation or the constitution within this flow of a thing that can be differentiated out of it, even momentarily or provisionally. The problem isn't how persons or cultures create time and space, it's how time and space permit the composition of relatively stable or differentiated nodes such as we and the things around us actually seem to be. Ironically enough, that's also the basic subjective question, and the basic cultural question. It's not: how do words refer to things? but, how do words arise in an environment of things, or as things? It is the failures of relationship—the hallucinations, the fictions, the lies, the dreams, the cruelty as an imposition of selfhood—that stand in need of explanation. Not: how do we create worlds, but how do worlds create us? Our distinctness is always a *problem* or an achievement, and always a matter of degree; a great error of philosophical modernism, for example, is to take the distinctness of the self as a fundamental datum; at latest by Schelling, but also in Hume, for example, it seems to be disintegrating.

Though autonomy, individuality, and personal virtue are obviously important in ethics, it is equally obvious that ethical questions are primarily relational, and that relations among human beings are a or the central site at which ethical questions arise. This maybe stands in some need of fixing, and other relations may require some emphasis. Nevertheless, I think we do well, perhaps even in many of the nonhuman cases, to think in terms of communication, and to conceive communication as a situation of mutual permeation or penetration or merging: perception is obviously a necessary condition for communication, and every act of communication is, among other things, an act of shared perception. We might say, in fact, that communication is a particularly intense or entwined or mutual mode of perception: a form, dimension, or content of perception: a mutual production and reception of "percepts" (things like sounds and books) that compromises individuality and depends on it.

Let's first off insist that communication is not limited to semantic transactions between representational entities. A perhaps absurdly representational standpoint might indicate that I have experiences, which I represent internally, and then I create representations of those representations in communications of various kinds, which are then represented in your idiolect, completing the circuit. (The kinds are things like words, pictures, expressions, gestures, etc.) One thing we might say is that representation at this level of iteration is like a game of phone call, and by the time you were communicating with someone, you'd be pretty worried about the content in its translation through several levels of representation, each characterized by a style as well as a semantics. At any rate, we'd do better to start by thinking about bodies in juxtaposition, responding to one another in an unfolding collaborative causal event or reconfiguration in a shared environment of objects. The interaction supposes environing conditions, so that you can reach for my hand, create soundwaves in which we're both bathed, or give a kiss. Kisses are impossible in a universe without space and time and floors and ceilings that are external to the kissers as well as around and inside them. Then we might describe various modes of communication precisely in terms of the situations in which it takes place: mass media, or social network, or e-mail, or voice, or Skype: the persons embedded and the ways the connections between them are configured in a shared environment.

There is a myriad of ethical dimensions in any possible situation, but the primary ethical site is at the communicative connection, the place where the voices, glances, words, pictures, projectiles, bodily fluids are transmitted, broadcast, whispered, launched in barrage, insinuated. Your communication with your dog as you pet her is a real physical communicative situation, and one with various ethical valences; same with your electronic connection to Doctors Without Borders or the Internal Revenue Service; your physical proximity to the people in the same store or town; your coreligionists, scattered compound- or worldwide; your children; everyone. Ethics is about persons in relation; the way we compose a whole, or fail to, degrees of intimacy and distance rippling out from you across the fabric. Perhaps it's wrong to use persons as mere means. But then, in your ken, what counts as a person and what are the ends? and so on: even if we try to simplify the terrain with a few swift principles (as well we should, considering the ever-multiplying complexity of the data), they live ethically in the application, in actual interventions in actual situations; they are tropes in the Keith Campbell sense, here spread over a whole situation, arraying it into a value. We might think that the material underdetermines the principles, but in fact it always exceeds them or exposes their presuppositions; the evolving situation is always tossing up new practical puzzles, predicaments, conflicts of intuition, and every principle is radically inadequate to deal with the massive particularities of any given situation.

Derek Parfit, as many before him, have written against "subjectivism" in ethics, and I think the matter is just as clear and even more urgent here than in aesthetics. Subjectivism is wrong, but not primarily for the sorts of reasons Parfit gives (though—what the hell—for those, too), but because ethics deals with actual transactions among or between things; if you lose the sense of the other as an agent in the same sense as yourself, or if you lose the sense of the situation in which you're embedded with that person, or if you lose your sense of why you shouldn't hit people with baseball bats—taking "people" and "baseball bats" in the most literal concrete sense—you lose the ethical.

The ethical correlate to the idea that I know the world because I represent it accurately in my sense impressions is that I figure out what you are like by examining myself; I treat you by analogy to myself, or come to regard myself as a representation of you or as a heuristic for understanding what it's like to be you. Well, it's like being me. I might be motivated to seek your welfare because it strikes me that you are something sort of like me, or I infer this from your gesticulations, or I infer it from my sense impressions that seem to be images of your gesticulations, if any, so your pain sort of hurts me by analogy: "empathy." I get a faint echo of your pain, which quasi-hurts. Now, on the other hand, we might proceed on the assumption—which I suggest that the nonpsychotic among us all make anyway—that we're in an environment that includes actual other human beings. Perhaps we understand ourselves by analogy to them as much as the other way round. Once we give up on the idea that we are, for example or as it were, transparent to our own percepts, we have to see that we are anything but evident to our own introspection, and that we come to understand ourselves in ways parallel to our understanding of others, as well as vice versa. And being in communicative relations with one another, we are not fully distinct from one another, which I mean literally: communication as mutual perception compromises our distinctness from one another, just as perception compromises our distinction from the environment; I have called this "fusion" in the theory of perception. We might term this sort of orientation "ethical externalism": maybe I actually care about you, not as an analogue to me (though perhaps as that as well) but as something genuinely external to me and joined to me by actual procedures of communication between two distinct things. Obviously the picture on which I am acquainted with you only by the mediation of my own internal states is optional. That's good because it's false.

If I thought I was primarily engaged in transactions with my own sense data or pleasure receptors, I would not take yours with sufficient seriousness. Now, admittedly, finding real subjectivists about ethics is difficult; the position is hence a good place to unload. But what I want to emphasize is that the place of ethics is not just in your head, not just in the social practices, but there also in relation to real other things; in an encompassing situation, with some people closer than others, some truths more urgent, some resistances more difficult

5.

So now I am going to try to grapple with the question of ethics. There is a reason I've never gone straight at ethics, except to attack the whole idea. First of all, even buried under jargon, ethics itself is fundamentally preachy or puritanical. Even though I am preachy and puritanical, I don't want to convey the impression that I am. As well, I would say that my basic ethical intuitions are hard to regiment, and that—perhaps oddly, given my proclivities in other areas—I do not feel any great need to regiment them. Indeed, I might say that ethics is too close to us to admit of neat theorizing by us; it's a question of what I should believe, endorse, do, or be right now, and now, and now, and in a way we'd expect it to be about as messy as we are. I have teleological intuitions, virtue-ethic intuitions, and deontological intuitions, though I might say that the least powerful of these for me are the teleological; if I have the impulse to do something I think is right, or to admit that I've done something I think is wrong, it usually comes with an abandonment of the hedonic calculus; I'm usually thinking "consequences be damned." Sometimes I think that suffering, my own or someone else's, is deserved and is right. On the other hand, I try with mixed success not to inflict suffering needlessly, and if I were trying to account for what was evil about, say, the Killing Fields, or trying to say why poverty should be ameliorated, I would not try to avoid doing so in terms of suffering and the costs to human happiness or its possibility.

Perhaps as we muddle through we're deploying various notions or principles that don't fall neatly into any of these categories. I have argued for a kind of epistemological pluralism: that there is no single right way to come to believe, and no small set of right ways to come to believe, and even though I gave a crisp definition of knowledge (true belief), its purpose was to open up many roads to knowledge, or to try to acknowledge all the open roads there are. I will not provide a similarly crisp definition of the right or the good, and I want to emphasize the plurality of factors that might be relevant in ethical deliberations about different sorts of things (e.g., persons, actions, policies). Bringing everything to the tribunal of a single principle seems to me to be a falsification of our ethical lives, which more or less coincide in their complexity with our lives taken as wholes. And though I have become more explicitly a moralist since *Obscenity, Anarchy, Reality*, I also want to preserve the dangerous notion that there can be value in a lapse or transgression of ethical values, which was the obsession of that book. Incessantly bringing everything to the tribunal of ought has its own drawbacks for creatures who cannot always do what they ought to do, in a world that is so relentlessly not what it ought to be.

Because we live in such a world—a world that fails all the time by any particular ethical standard, or that is too rich and equivocal to be reduced to principles—a world that definitely wasn't made by Leibniz's God, and so on—the ethical point of view, applied too rigidly or too continuously, will falsify or despise the world. It will make an affirmation impossible, as we have already seen reasons to believe. But on the other hand, as I now think and as I have said, a perfect, permanent affirmation is not, in fact, possible, and a real response to reality is a response of hatred as well as love. Indeed, we can't and we needn't face up to everything all the time, and insofar as we are intelligent or even conscious, we have preferences, directions, taxonomies of excellence and its opposite. And in my heart I do believe that some things and some people are just wrong, bad, evil, and I would like to be able to say, however haltingly or unsystematically, something about why I believe that and what I believe about it.

Parfit has argued that the teleological and deontological approaches are not as opposed as they seem to be, and that at a minimum they yield the same result in most sorts of cases. For the most part, I would try provisionally to reconcile the approaches by holding them roughly to range over different material, or to provide the right way to measure ethical rightness in different sorts of cases. We do not have to reduce what it is to be a good person, what it is to be a good policy, and what it is to be a right action to a single principle. And for the most part, I conceive a good person in terms of virtue, a good policy in terms of its effects, and a right action in terms of the principle which gives rise to it or which it instantiates.

I take it to be obvious that any of these require that the "agent" be a real thing in a real world. We might think of the virtues as intrinsic properties of character or personality, but virtues are not in the head any more than are meanings or experiences. You can't be generous or miserly in an interaction with your own sensibilia, no matter how you hoard your sense data or keep them to yourself. In a universe consisting of sense impressions I could do nothing wrong: there's no wrong way to treat your own mental images or conduct your own internal linguistic activity. Indeed, we might say that something like the metaphysical orientation of this book is required to do anything in ethics: I have to acknowledge the reality of other people and things, and I have to experience it, and I have to deal with it. I have to acknowledge the externality of other persons to myself, and their complete reality on the same plane of reality as myself, and our ontological equality and real connections. I would connect the problematic way we treat other animals and environmental features or ecosystems with a failure to experience their reality fully, a failure to place ourselves and them on the same level of reality. The idea that there is something profoundly different—differentially real, ontologically different—between persons and pigs, or persons and mountains, is an error from which evil flows. And the idea that I am acquainted with myself in a way I am not with anything else, that I am real to myself in a way that other people and animals and things and environments are not, lurks at the heart of a great many bad things that people do.

Supposedly, I know myself immediately, but you only mediately, through my knowledge of myself. That is, you are, for me, a bundle of impressions. You are like my dream, or like a movie character, and then that you are real turns out to be an inference, and perhaps a shaky one. Now, what happens to representations of people in a dream or in a film is morally attenuated: there is all the difference in the world between shooting an image of a person with an image of a gun in a video game and shooting a real person with a real gun in reality. We are not responsible in fantasies in the same way we are responsible in relation to actual other people: a rape fantasy is not as culpable as a rape, putting it mildly. The distance inserted between subject and object, or between subject and subject, by a representational theory of mind, constantly opens the possibility of a moral distance or attenuation or even a full-fledged universal excuse.

A psychotic person—a person whose mentality is a barrier or a screen between himself and the world—is not fully responsible for his actions. Obviously, I don't think that's necessarily because he's not free. It's because he is not sufficiently responsive to reality, or has lost a sense of the externality of things and persons to himself. He can't tell what is real and what is a representation, what is happening and what he's merely fantasizing. And I would say that every theory of mind that opens this distance is an invitation not to account for ourselves as full-fledged agents in that we cease to operate in a world of things, which is a necessary condition for the possibility of agency. Descartes wondered how he could know whether that person he seemed to see from his window was not a cleverly disguised automaton. Well if he really didn't know this, then he really didn't know whether that thing counted morally. He didn't know whether it would be bad thing to empty his chamber pot on the supposed thing below his supposed window. The doubts about everything opened by methodological skepticism and the accompanying account of mind as a representational system: these are universal moral and well as epistemic doubts.

Such doubts lurk near the heart of some ways of conceptualizing means-ends rationality, for example. In ascribing a sort of reality or countingness to myself for myself that other things lack, I hint that there is no wrong way for them to be used. I open a distance between myself and mere inanimate objects or even mere other people. My commitment to myself cannot be the same as my commitment to someone else or to a thing or to a world, as my knowledge of myself is not the same as my knowledge of them (which arises through my knowledge of myself), my contact with myself is not the same as my contact with them; their reality is not the same for me as my reality is for myself. What I owe them is, hence, not what I owe myself. Heidegger thought that by this means we had lost or concealed Being, and I am saying in other words that that seems right to me.

6.

Certainly, for example, the idea that we all seek to maximize our own pleasure—much less that we ought to—is analogous in ethics to the idea that we only experience the world in and as our own representation. It is a kind of moral-methodological solipsism, a way to cut off the interaction or to snip the relations. Nothing can motivate me except my own pleasures and pains; an unimaginably counterintuitive claim in a world where I am pushed and pulled by and where I push and pull all sorts of different things in different ways on different occasions for different reasons or no reasons at all. The world becomes in this impoverished account something to serve my needs or desires, or a thing that is only of use, or is only a means. It is no wonder that tortured arguments or psychological speculations are then needed about why I should take the suffering of others into account; I can experience that suffering only from behind the screen of my own pleasure-pain. What if that just isn't right? Certainly at a minimum I think I can be motivated by the real pains and pleasures of others.

I would like briefly to address the concept of "happiness," which is, at this writing, in a renaissance in "positive psychology." "Happiness," I think, is a variable or blank indicating the sum total of everything people want (insofar as the things people want are compatible with one another: no one can have everything he wants, probably by definition, thank god). In that sense it doesn't really mean anything particularly, and you get to fill up the empty vessel with any vision of wonderfulness you prefer. Indeed, "wonderfulness" is a word like "happiness." What if I constructed a moral system according to which anything is of value insofar only as it contributed to wonderfulness, because wonderfulness is what we're really after; we want everything else for the sake of wonderfulness, but we don't want wonderfulness for the sake of anything else. It's sort of obviously true, but also empty and ridiculous. No, I strongly disagree: the goal of human life is total phatness. Total phatness is totally amazing. Obviously, we live for one purpose: to avoid suckiness. Every human being always chooses wonderfulness over suckiness. If you don't choose wonderfulness over suckiness, you are irrational; in fact that's the very essence of rationality.

"Happiness" (like "well-being," "amazingness," "grooviness," etc.) is just a positive-valence blank, or it is not the purpose of human life. That is, once you give it any particular sense, then some people want it and some people don't, sometimes it's good and sometimes it's bad. You could define it hedonically: balance of pleasure over pain. But people seek pain all the time, and not just for the sake of more pleasure later on. Sometimes pleasure is good; sometimes it's bad, and the actual things people want are irreducibly multiple.

I guess I could raise the philosophical-type objections: what if you could hook yourself to a machine that made you happy, and so on? People want truth, or contact with reality, or some do sometimes, I hope. And they want all sorts of other things too, for their own sake: we do not want beauty or justice for the sake of happiness any more than vice versa, and likewise for a million other things. We want music for the sake of music, not as an instrument of happiness, or not only as that. Listening to Billie just makes me melancholy, but here I am, pressing play on "Am I Blue?" again. Suppose people are happier when they are politically unfree (I'd say history is incomprehensible without the idea that many people at least think that being subordinated is an element of happiness). Still they should be free. Still they should free themselves. Still they should want to be free.

Aristotle first supposes that there must be some one goal of human life: there is no argument for that, and in my opinion it is obviously false. He calls it *eudaimonia*, which, again, functions initially as a blank or a name for whatever the alleged ultimate goal is. When he then describes what happiness is, it takes him a whole long book: it is all the virtues, it is learning, it is friendship, it is not a state but a process of a whole life, it happens in relation to a *polis* or even is primarily a condition of a *polis* rather than an individual, and so on. That is what gives his *eudaimonia* content, and the content is actually more or less the whole of human moral life: a hundred different values, virtues, desires, events, a plurality reduced to unity only by gathering them up and tacking a word on them.

Ask yourself: do you want sex in order to be happy, or only insofar as it is conducive to happiness? What kind of sex do you want? Only ever happy sex? Or is it possible that you want sex for its own sake? Ever had sex in a situation wherein you knew it was unlikely to increase your happiness quotient? I no more want to write good books in order to be happy than I want to be happy in order to write good books. Even if writing books made me miserable, and insofar as it has, I still want to write good books.

Now, Aristotle is one thing: the account is extremely subtle, elaborate, and implicitly addresses many of the apparent implausibilities of the claim that all we want intrinsically and ultimately is happiness. He's wrong, but still. Positive psychologists are something else again. Perhaps they mean whatever anyone takes the word to mean when they fill out the questionnaire, maybe they have some sketchy hedonism or whatever it may be in the background. With regard to any specific content we may give to the concept, it is not plausible that we should devote our society to or measure it exclusively by, happiness. On the other hand, if you fail to give it any specific content, you are not studying anything, any more than you would be by measuring wonderfulness. We're not doing anything but whirling around in empty non-concepts of our own invention, grappling only with an intolerable meaningless simplification.

So, we're going to measure policies or the quality of societies by self-reports of happiness. But there is nothing that psychologists are asking their subjects to self-report on except the analytical implications of their own quasi-concepts. It sounds like the goal of human life: self-evidently the goal, and none of these researchers question that status at all. But it's just trivially the goal in that it means whatever the goal is. Each respondent just fills in the blank herself with a picture of whatever she wants: shoes, chardonnay, and George Clooney, say. And with each actual content, whether Aristotle's or shoes, chardonnay, and Clooney, it is not the only goal and not everyone's goal. It's the very air of tautology that draws you in or makes it all seem inevitable: happiness is the goal of human life. That doesn't tell you any more about actual humans in an actual world than does the observation that no bachelor is married. Studying happiness like this isn't any more helpful or any better a use of resources than going out and trying to find the married bachelors empirically.

7.

One of the most difficult things about teaching the *Nicomachean Ethics* is trying to convey to students what Aristotle can possible mean by *eudaimonia*. Of course, the translation of the term as *happiness* is often said to be inadequate, for particularly good reasons since the modern turn in philosophy and culture. We think that happiness just has to be an internal state. My students have no trouble understanding Bentham's or Mill's characterization of happiness as much pleasure and little pain, which is an essentially subjectivist notion, and one that my students and most of the people I know, when pressed, seem to agree nonproblematically is the goal of human life. But then it is a struggle—as Mill acknowledged very elaborately, and such as even contemporary utilitarians such as Parfit and Singer find themselves in—to moralize this notion, or to make it match up with acknowledged moral strictures on how to treat people and other things. The basic move here is to count the happiness of all things that are capable of being happy, or of experiencing pleasure or pain, provisionally, as the same. Of course, utilitarianism is not egoism or moral solipsism. It is a collective solipsism: the goal is the best possible set of subjective pleasure states distributed through a population.

But when Aristotle defines happiness, he does it in terms of a life of virtue, and the virtues are relentlessly placed in a social/political context: there is no properly human life at all, and no proper exercise of the virtues, outside a *polis*. The happy life is the blessed or fortunate life, but it is also essentially a social life and life of friendship: no one is happy in virtue merely of having a lot of pleasure and little pain. Happiness is essentially relational, for Aristotle. He does not face the sort of problems that are faced by hedonistic utilitarians, for whom happiness is essentially subjective: for example, what if someone takes a great deal of pleasure in the pain of others? Well, perhaps as a matter of fact the pleasure that someone gets from harming someone never outweighs the pain of the victim. Then again, we have a tendency to say that a situation in which someone gets pleasure out of inflicting pain is worse, not better, than a situation in which she does not. There are plenty of moves to try to finesse these problems, but they arise essentially from regarding the happiness of all as a sum of the subjective states of each.

I have always had a puritanical streak, and I think in some ways it is philosophically defensible. I think it is relatively obvious that some pleasures are good and some pleasures are bad. Fundamentally, I think that pleasure is not morally significant; roughly, its presence or its reverse in itself does not constitute moral value, though that is somewhat too strong. This is perhaps not true at the margins; certainly torture is wrong, when it's wrong, in part because of the pain inflicted, though there are other features of a torture situation that are also relevant to its moral evaluation: whether the pain is unjust or undeserved; the profound violation of the autonomy of the victim. That violation is the same whatever the pain or pleasure of the torturer, and does not really correspond in detail to, or track, the pain of the victim. But at any rate, let's drink heavily, snort some cocaine, and have indiscriminate sex with whomever. Now, admittedly, I think the pleasure of such an experience is liable to be overrated by the person proposing it, but the whole thing is worse or better without regard to whether it's painful or pleasurable. As Aristotle says, you should want to take pleasure in the right things, at the right times, with the right companions.

I would reject the doctrine of Mill, Sidgwick, and others that the alleged fact that we all seek pleasure and avoid pain entails, or just as good as entails, that we ought to seek it. "Happiness," to repeat, is a blank or variable meaning the human *telos*, which is precisely why philosophers think it's absurd to say you want to be happy in order to play like Hendrix, but trivial to say that you want to play like Hendrix in order to be happy. (However, these could each be perfectly sensible things to say in a particular conversation.) So you get people nodding along; yes, I want to be happy. Then you attach a very specific meaning to it: a great deal of pleasure and very little pain. Well who's not for that? But if you ponder all the things you might do or think or accomplish, you'll see that it's wrong to think we do all of what we do for sake of pleasure or to avoid pain: there are many sorts of situations that we regard as good in themselves, good for their own sake. That is a dimension of the richness of our connections; we seek out many sorts of situations, some of them painful or difficult, some of them pleasurable. Difficult manual or intellectual labor—painful labor—can be, as it were, intrinsically valuable: not merely as a means but for itself.

I am attracted by the rigid ascetic moralism of the Stoics, for instance, in which the moral questions centered on self-control. Well, as they did not acknowledge, that's only one sort of question, but it's important. For one thing, it displays the fact that, as against Leibniz, selves are not monads: they are internally complex and divided. But then self-control in this sense is precisely an art of living, a skill or craft, not a sheer faculty; it is nothing if it does not manifest itself in a world.

Or we might briefly consider what passes for a kind of moral system in popular culture: Oprah-style self-esteem as a kind of intrinsic goal and also as a means to realize all other goals. This shares the subjectivist twist of the pleasure/pain continuum. But I think the point, as again Aristotle might have said, is to deserve self-esteem, to have it, if at all, to just the extent you deserve it. The point is not to possess great self-esteem; the point is to live so as to deserve your own esteem. Or at least, that's my opinion. The moral point of view, I think, encompasses situations in which other people, and also tribal/linguistic resources are engaged, and also other things: guns, buckets, cars, chipmunks. Each agent is a zone or network; the ones we are most concerned with center on a human body such as yourself; you face moral situations: breaking an institutional rule, applying Round-Up™ to the poison ivy, whether to buy some new shoes, just saying no when some particular person waves the coke under your nose; the situation depends on a myriad of details about the stuff in that bag, where and when you are and why; what happened the day before.

We might even try to reconstrue pleasure itself along these lines. It is a subjective state if anything is. But first off, "pleasure" is an awfully general notion, and one might point out that the pleasure of eating a good meal is not necessarily much like the pleasure of winning the World Cup or the Nobel, which is not much like the pleasure of sex, which is not much like the pleasure of lying down after a long day, which is not much like the pleasure of appreciating a Gauguin, and so on. So different are these, indeed, that one might wonder how profitable it is to call them all by the same name. Be that as it may, it is going to be hard to characterize any particular pleasure without characterizing the sorts of situations in which it arises, the sorts of persons or objects with whom or with which one is juxtaposed or merging.

For that matter, the pleasure of lying down after a long day is itself indefinitely rich: the actual experience depends on what you did that day, where and on what you're lying down, what happened yesterday and what you're anticipating tomorrow.

There are very many kinds of long days, from long days in the factory to long days taking care of the kids to long days laying bricks to long days lecturing on Aristotle to long days drinking tequila. There are many places to lie down: on your front lawn, in Polynesia, in your supersoft or superfirm bed, under the bridge, at the hotel, and so on.

And indeed, for certain very intense experiences, "pleasure" is definitely the wrong term altogether. We'd usually use "pleasure" to describe, say, a day at the spa, or soaking in a bubble bath, or eating a nice dessert: small indulgences, little glows. In the hedonistic version of utilitarianism—in Hutcheson, Hume, Bentham, Mill, Sidgwick—far too much weight is placed on the idea of pleasure as the essence of all human motivation, or as the only human motivation. The notion can't bear that weight. But no pleasure can even be picked out without referring to the situation in which it arises, or at any rate few can be: What is it like to soak in the bath? Or to listen to Mozart? Or to eat a piece of chocolate? Why, it's just like, quite as though you were in the bathtub, listening to Mozart, eating chocolate: the pleasure is in our very consciousnesses as encompassing external relations to and among objects. That could be phenomenology, but then again there really are things in these situations, including oneself.

So impoverished is the hedonistic tradition that pleasure is used to account for the effect of beauty as well as the good. This stuckness is due to trying to keep values in the head; these positions are jammed into a bad picture that produces the problem. Now, you cannot describe the pleasure only as it is internally or intrinsically, without its relations; no adjectives cling to it, exactly (except maybe extremely abstract ones such as "aesthetic" or extremely general, such as "sexual"). At any rate pretty soon you are running myriads of myriads of things into one category willy-nilly and losing what is distinctive about each one. Bentham's formulation at the beginning of *Principles of Morals and Legislation* is justly famous:

> Nature has placed mankind under the governance of two sovereign masters, pain and pleasure. It is for them alone to point out what we ought to do, as well as determine what we shall do. On the one hand the standard of right and wrong, on the other the chain of causes and effects, are fastened to their throne. They govern us in all we do, in all we say, in all we think: every effort we can make to throw off our subjection, will serve but to demonstrate and confirm it. In words a man may pretend to abjure their empire: but in reality he will remain subject to it all the while.[33]

Well, now I ask you seriously, is that true? Do you do everything you do for the sake of pleasure? And then how widely are you willing to apply "pleasure"? Don't you do things out of all sorts of motivations, causes, reasons: duty, whim, a perverse desire to undergo an ordeal or challenge, a perverse desire for transgression? The idea that there is only one sort of or dimension of motivation is just false on the ground, and there is rarely any argument for it. For whatever reason, it sounds relatively harmless or trivial; really it is luridly false. And neither, or much less, does the question of what one ought to do turn on pleasure and pain. Now, there are various more plausible formulations: well-being, or the realization of interests, welfare, and so on; with regard to all such invasive, imperialistic dimensions of decision-making, one should just point to the richness, complexity, ambiguity of actual human motivation.

8.

One advantage of a physicalist ontology or a mechanistic universe is that it allows us to escape from a teleological conception of history; even the ancient atomists saw this, or at least Aristotle, who was obsessed with teleology, understood Leucippus and Democritus as providing a challenge to it. One might point out, however, that teleological conceptions of history are remarkably persistent, often creeping in even within systems of thought that begin by repudiating them. It's quite easy to inflect the idea of natural selection with a teleology that has nothing to do with the empirical evidence for the theory: we are on the road to an adaptation to the environment and vice versa, or we are the successful, the "dominant" species. Or we try to derive a normative orientation: we *ought to* do as natural selection demands, as though we could know such a thing. That's why we ought to compete, or why we ought to cooperate, or even why we should have the sort of political system you think we should, you dork.

At any rate, surely the idea of encompassing all of history in a comprehensible intellectual structure or a few swift principles—Hegelianism, in brief, as expressed by everyone from Croce to Riegl and Wölfflin, Marx and Comte—is over. A univocal account of history as (in the favored trope) the realization of freedom is just ridiculous: it's chaos down here, as microbes bloom and blow hither and yon, typhoons and earthquakes arrive unexpectedly and spoil your plans, and people act like inanimate objects, or apes, or disembodied souls, and appear recalcitrant to all your good efforts. Or: the closer we come to realizing our dream the more thoroughly is that realization infected with the fatal flaws of the persons who designed them: their inability to know the future, their self-delusion. The power you need to achieve justice turns you into a monster. The exquisite adaptation that makes you a beautiful segment of an environment becomes a fatal mistake as the environment shifts. Your technological mastery of the environment entails the end of life as we know it.

This is not to say that people don't have any goals, or even that more or less every member of the species might have some of the same: usually we'd prefer to live than to die—which is probably "adaptive"—and so increases in life expectancy represent progress in this sense. You might see poverty rates or rates of illness go down somewhere for some time. It's just that even progress like that is locally defined, multivalent, always liable to be reversed. Indeed, all the concepts—life, death, member of our species, and so on—are culturally inflected at any given point or could be absent or at stake in a given conflict. Looking at history as a triumphant march to somewhere—perhaps interrupted here, now—is a formula for disappointment and for believing all sorts of fatuous hoohah.

I have no time for the retroactive past, and it will surprise me if time travel is possible. Phenomenologically, we might say, to start with, what makes the past the past is exactly its hard-and-fastness, even in the face of its loss or continual absence. The past is that about which regret is always possible because, as we say, it's too late to fix it now. Now, I strongly reject Aristotle's teleological conception of ethics and indeed of more or less everything: Aristotle regards the universe as a goal-directed system, or as caused to be by its end. Here is the first sentence of the *Nicomachean Ethics*: "Every art and every inquiry, and similarly every action and pursuit, is thought to aim at some good; and for this reason the good has rightly been declared to be that at which all things aim."[34] This notion reappears in fits and starts through the tradition, and has a particularly fraught relation to Christianity. But in Adam Smith's economics and in utilitarian ethics, as well as in the economic and political orders they reflect, they reassert their dominance. And in pragmatism, teleology becomes a theory of all value, and in particular a theory of truth.

The West, however, also suffers from teleology, or from (in the current phases) "excellence" or a "purpose-driven life." And it is possible for the planet to suffer from our enthusiasm for its technological transformation. Within the Western tradition, the Eastern tradition is read as a cure for teleology, as a place where ends are annihilated into being, or into immediacy, in which one lets go of purpose and finds peace. But even Aristotle, and even the pragmatists, felt an urgency to collapse ends into means, to find meaning in the process as well as the products of living. They found it, I propose, and perhaps they found the zone where the West meets the West's East, in the concept of art, particularly as set out in Dewey's great work of aesthetics, *Art as Experience*.

Let's ask some basic questions about human action, truth, art, and the relation of means and ends. Is all, or for that matter any, human action comprehensible within a teleological structure? That is, is each, or any, human action undertaken for the sake of some goal or purpose? For example, should we consider Aristotle's practical syllogism a reasonable global account? Considering beliefs as actions, are beliefs held, or propositions entertained, or commitments undertaken, for the sake of some goal? Let me just baldly state my position on these questions: It's not the case that all human action is oriented toward goals, and no human action is fully comprehended by a specification of its purpose and a description of how it conduces to that purpose. Whether a belief effectively conduces to some goal (leaving aside truth itself) never has anything to do with the truth of that belief. Beliefs that are extremely or maximally effective in achieving any goal (other than truth, of course) may be false, and beliefs that form a barrier to the achievement of any other goal may be true. Of course, I take this to be an entailment of my realism, but it has ethical implications as well.

Here is one formulation of the point of view I reject, Dewey's in *Reconstruction in Philosophy*:

> If ideas, meanings, conceptions, notions, theories, systems are instrumental to an active reorganization of the given environment, to a removal of some specific trouble and perplexity, then the test of their validity and value lies in accomplishing this work. If they succeed in their office, they are reliable, valid, good, true. If they fail to clear up confusion, to eliminate defects, if they increase confusion, uncertainty and evil when they are acted upon, then they are false. Confirmation, corroboration, verification lie in works, consequences. Handsome is that handsome does. By their fruits shall ye know them. That which guides us truly is true—demonstrated capacity for such guidance is precisely what is meant by truth.[35]

One way to state the pragmatist position is in Peircian terms of problematic situations—practical confusions, for example, or mathematical quandaries, artistic puzzles—where truth, art, science, cookery, teaching, and so on would consist of resolutions to these problems. Human action on this account consists of attempted resolutions to a series of problems, and the solution is true where it yields a sort of satisfaction that accompanies such solutions; a place of rest or surcease preparatory to addressing the next problem. Every truth would, hence, be provisional: the problem might arise again in a related way, and the human condition consists in the fact that there are always new problematic situations calling for resolution.

Obviously, there is a variety of cases in which this is more or less a proper phenomenological description. You're trying to decide whether to accept a marriage proposal. You contemplate your long-term happiness in relation to this proposal, deciding whether the marriage is likely to conduce to that end. Then you accept, or not. Someone assigns you a math problem and you solve it, thus helping you get a diploma and, down the line, income. You're trying to figure out how to provide energy to a certain region, so you design, fund, and build a power station. Democrat or Republican? Depends on the future you envision and your understanding of the means to achieve it. You're bewildered and confused, then things become clear and you experience a sensation of peace.

But the basic situation of me the schlumph trying to make it through another day is just not usually like this. I'm exhaustedly staring at the television, let us say. Do I think this will push ahead my purposes? Well, it might occur to me that I stand in need of rest and refreshment in order to return to my problematical situations. Or

I might just be staring. As I allow myself to drift off to sleep, I'm letting go of the problematical situations, and I'm no more sleeping so I can solve problems than I am solving problems so I can sleep. Or perhaps I am letting myself drift off to sleep because my sleepiness itself represents a problematical situation which I resolve by sleeping. If you think this is how people think or act, you should perhaps introspect, and sleep is, of course, a letting-go of thinking and acting and introspection. In that sense it is an end, or at least a surcease from problematical situations. In fact, that is usually the only real resolution of our problems: allowing our consciousness to disintegrate around them, or learning the slow hard important lesson of apathy and cynicism: make yourself cease caring. Or, slightly more optimistically, giving up and yielding to the problem, living within it, or playing around with it, or reveling in it, or something. Indeed, since our basic problematical situation is massively unresolvable, cynicism and play are fundamental.

To take an example, American politics represents a series of situations that are radically problematical. The way to resolve these problems is through the experimental democratic process, in which Dewey placed such faith. All I can do is wish you good luck, and tell you that my own approach is mere verbal abuse, restricted to my tiny irrelevant circle. I gave up a long time ago, and I suggest that you do likewise. Life without giving up is truly useless and, from an external view, hopeless. If I told Dewey that it is breathtakingly obvious that I can't do shit, I wonder whether he'd regard that as compatible with his pragmatism. No? Then pragmatism is false. You've got to intelligently administer means to ends, intelligently adjust organism to environment, to live a decent human life. And you've got to surrender, to let things be, whether they're groovy, happy, beautiful things or worldwide intractable disasters. With the worldwide intractable disasters, I suggest, you've got no real choice but to let them be.

When I have myself gotten married now and then, I have been well aware that I had no idea what my life would be like afterward: that sort of alteration introduces uncontrollable variables, chaos. If one stopped to make a calculation, one would be frozen in inaction. Indeed, the beautiful thing about being overwhelmed by love is that it is indifferent to goals, or that it explicitly introduces chaos. I might say that I knew marriage to Marion Winik was a formula for disaster, and I got married anyway. Should I have gotten married? Answering that question in terms of means and ends—much less making the answer's truth depend on its resolution of problems—is just a sad misunderstanding of human motivation and of truth. Marriage, we might say, is an act of expression, not experiment. You're committing yourself to a risk, not a solution. And if it was no solution, if your spouse turned out to be terminally ill or terminally annoying, it would not follow that you made the wrong decision. Indeed, even if you knew this about your betrothed, and knew that marriage would simply exacerbate your problems or make them unresolvable forever, it still would not follow that you shouldn't get married.

Now, on the other hand, we could merely assert that sleep, marriage, cynicism, or play are themselves always attempted resolutions to problematical situations. Obviously, or else we wouldn't do stuff like that. Here we sink into the merest apriorism. I suggest that if you think about most of your actions or for that matter most of your thoughts, you'll see that resolving problematical situations is an occasional activity, from which, thankfully, we continually lapse. Indeed, allowing oneself to lapse is, on the pragmatist account itself, itself the goal: one resolves the problematical situation in order to release it and gain release from it, to experience the perhaps ecstatic moment of letting go. If you're a pragmatist, you'd better keep this lapse short, because the new problematical situation (i.e., the human condition itself) beckons. Your goal is a realization and a release; that is, your goal is a lapsing of goals, of thinking in terms of means and ends. Pragmatism seeks resolutions—albeit local, temporary, provisional. Its goal is the constant disintegration or letting go of goals. The truth is pursued for the sake of holding it and being in a position to let it go. Or, there is no goal. Either the resolution is merely instrumental to the next goal, and is hence no resolution, or it is a lapse in which it is itself erased: realization of the goal is a release from the means-ends rationality which supposedly describes human action. Or, means-ends rationality is at its very heart paradoxical, is itself a problematic situation from which we need periodic release.

9.

Ethics is not primarily a set of principles or virtues: it is a set of communications between and among persons, animals, and things; a relation, situation, juxtaposition of (among other things) human bodies. Of course, insofar as a virtue is real, let's say, it is something you carry around in your head; it is a set of relations to other people or the world; it is a bunch of words; it is a history; it is the virtue of a human being, massively constrained by and articulating a world. Perhaps, for example, there is a set of environmental virtues: one recycles, tries not participate in the abuse of animals, drives a hybrid, all because of a culturally received set of meanings and practices, but also, of course, because of (other) real-world situations: actual carbon in the actual atmosphere, for example, actual animal species and bodies and their actual pain.

Communication makes use of our holes: it is, we may say, at its most intense in sex, when bodies actually merge. (And sex, we might say with unutterable blandness, is an important ethical site.) But in all communication, bodies cease to be separate: one's body produces actual sounds or visible marks which then proceed into the bodies of others. Individuality is asserted and compromised in communication, in an immensely complex nexus of facts. Indeed, human beings are produced as individuals in situations which centrally include communicative aspects of the environment: human individuals originate within the bodies of other human individuals, and are constantly reembedding themselves in other bodies through communication.

If we think of human beings as an unfolding sets of experiences, histories of experiences each of which produces an alteration of the person and its environment, then every human individual is massively incomparable as well as massively in communion and conflict with others. I want an ethics of situated individualism. Each human individual is of incomparable value as an accreted history of the world and of communities, a locus within which the whole exists in some particular hyperelaborate set of particular relations. Above all, ethics has to actually consist of communication, of ways we join together or merge while also maintaining individuality, in which individuality is formed and put at stake *on particular occasions*. And, of course, we do wrong to focus only on the principles and not on the particular connections, or we would do wrong to focus on principles as anything but registers or histories of particular connections. A universal principle of ethics is an attempt to capture and extend and array these connections, or it is merely an hallucination.

10.

A primary function of Eastern thought for Westerners is that it represents for us a release from teleology. I don't think we, or at least I, can understand "Eastern philosophy" except as a cure for the teleological illness, a cure that Aristotle and Dewey, entrapped in the strangling coils of goals, had perforce to seek in their own places, in their own philosophical crafts. For example, Eastern philosophy might be provided as a cure for the nightmares and even the pleasures of technology, which is always conceived as the means to some end. (Though this is a mere conception: technology presents means which can be intrinsically absorbing, and always acts in excess to, and often in opposition to, its goal; technologies are always also arts.) I say we need rest, surcease, from the practical syllogism, from the rational contractor of Hobbes or Smith, from the diplomas and policy successes, and all the flimsy ends (i.e., disasters) that we might achieve or that we have achieved.

The *Bhagavad Gita*, for instance, is devoted to the "art" of war: Krishna tells Arjuna that he should fight because he is a fighter; fighting is his craft. What you end up doing by fighting will be wrong; the outcome once you start is in doubt (you're in doubt, though the outcome is determined already, or in other words your action is useless, purposeless, except as action); even if you achieve by means of fighting the goals for which you fight—which is not possible—the result is liable to be misery. So stop focusing out there on the realization of your purposes, and let go into the fighting you must do right now. Your goal is to be who you are in this moment; that is, the goal is the means is your identity.

Taoism, in my reading, approaches this matter from every possible angle all the time. There is a reason for the Western obsession with the *Tao Te Ching*, and there is a reason that the hundreds of translations of it into Western languages take on the shape and emphasis they possess. The cardinal message of the *Tao Te Ching* as we, or I, read it, is that we should not seize control and transform, but accept and affirm. The West's *Tao Te Ching* is the antiteleological, antipragmatist, antitechnological scripture. We present it to one another as the cure for . . . ourselves. Here are some passages, in my translation.

29
Do you intend to seize the world
and make it better?
I hope you will not succeed,
and I don't think you will.
The world is sacred.
It cannot be improved.
If you try to transform it
you will only damage it.
If you try to control it
you will only lose it.
Just let it happen, and yourself within it.

32
The emptiness at the heart of real power
renders it impossible or pointless to resist.
Reside in this central stillness
and all things begin to shape themselves
and come to exist with ease in your experience.
The sky unites with the earth in a gentle rain.
People find unity without constraint.
Names dissolve and namelessness with them,
until each thing is precisely itself;
each thing stands as itself in your awareness,
names itself, depicts itself, contains itself.

38
Reality does not represent itself as real:
that is its reality.
Reality abandons itself into reality:
that is its presence.
It cannot judge this to be high or that to be low:
that is its exaltation.
It has no purpose:

that is its fulfillment.
It is without compassion:
that is its mercy.
The man of rectitude tries to make things turn out right,
and when that fails he rolls up his sleeves and redoubles his efforts.
Can you remain in the center and allow things to be?
Either way, you always return.

One message of the text as I need to read it is political, and here it responds to the Western ideal of the state as the form and agent of human transformation, a vision shared by Hobbes, Hegel, Marx, Dewey, and Rawls, for example. The state for these thinkers is the (fantastic) agent of collective teleology, the only thing capable of transforming our lives among one another in accordance with our goals, the technology of the social.

The *Chuang Tzu* is a very funny and deeply cynical text as well as a work of art.

> Once, when Chuang Tzu was fishing in the P'u River, the King of Chu sent two officials to go and announce to him: "I would like to trouble you with the administration of my realm."
>
> Chuang Tzu held on to the fishing pole and, without turning his head, said, "I have heard that there is a sacred tortoise in Ch'u that has been dead for three thousand years. The king keeps it wrapped in cloth and boxed, and stores it in the ancestral temple. Now would this tortoise rather be dead and have its bones left behind and honored? Or would it rather be alive and dragging its tail in the mud?"
>
> "It would rather be alive and dragging its tail in the mud," said the two officials.
>
> Chuang Tzu said, "Go away! I'll drag my tail in the mud!"[36]

Well, exactly. Anyway, once you rule the realm, you'll still be sitting there with your butt in the mud, only now you will be doing so while being deeply impressive to yourself and others: your impotence, ignorance, and incompetence will now spread across the globe like a poisonous gas. Kuo Hsiang, in his great commentary on the *Chuang Tzu*, makes such fundamental remarks as the following: "Everything happens precisely as it happens." "Each thing has its spontaneity, and in the spontaneity of each thing what it is emerges necessarily. Follow things and come into accord with them. Keep silent." "Try to do whatever happens."[37]

Nietzsche regarded the Eastern religions as nihilistic, and he was right in at least a Nietzschean sense: rather than inventing values and imposing them on the world, the Eastern religions in the eyes of a Westerner counsel surrender, yielding, letting go. They recommend the collapse of ends and values by a total immersion in means. But such tendencies, as Taoism and Ch'an, are the opposite of nihilistic, also in a Nietzschean sense; they do not replace the world with something else; they offer you again the real choice: immersion or extinction: or the nonchoice: immersion and extinction. They refuse your fantasies: of a God, of a realization of human purposes, of a transformation of the human condition. In brief, they constitute life as an art, as Dewey and Aristotle also finally had to do: as labor and craft in which purpose becomes chaotic, by which we participate as makers and victims of the chaos in the chaotic world. And at the end of effort, always, extinction beckons: the realization of our purposes, our peace, surcease. Kuo Hsiang says, "some people try incredibly hard to be great artists. But great artists become artists without even knowing how. Some people try hard to be wise. But wise people become wise without trying. We can't even become fools or dogs by trying."[38]

If you're getting the feeling that, all in all, this means-ends thing is complex or confusing, that means and ends are constantly oscillating or disintegrating or coalescing and detaching, you're on the right track. Dewey actually recuperated from the sort of instrumentalism he was pushing early in the century; *Art as Experience*, I want to say, is his recantation of pragmatism.

> There are two kinds of means. One is external to what is accomplished; the other kind is taken up into the consequences produced and remains immanent in them. There are ends which are merely welcome cessations and there are ends that are fulfillments of what went before. The toil of a laborer is too often only the antecedent to the wage he receives, as consumption of gasoline is merely a means to transportation. The means cease to act when the "end" is reached; one would be glad, as a rule, to get the result without having to employ the means. . . . But the moment we say "media" we refer to means that are incorporated into the outcome. . . . Colors are the painting; tones are the music. . . . The difference between external and intrinsic operations runs through all the affairs of life. One student studies to pass an examination, to get a promotion. To another, the means, the activity of learning, is completely one with the results of it. . . . Means and ends coalesce. If we run over in mind a number of such cases, we quickly see that all cases in which means and ends are external to one another are non-esthetic. This externality may even be regarded as a definition of the non-esthetic.[39]

This is strikingly reminiscent of Aristotle's definition of happiness, which is also an attempt to resolve the oppressive implications of his own teleological orientation: happiness is virtuous activity over the course of a life. The only decent characterization of the *telos* of human life is that it consists of the means of its own realization: a life of virtue or moderation. And the only way to help realize the *telos* of the *polis* is to participate as a citizen in the realization of that *telos*. That is, the purpose of human life or human political organization is the *technē*, the art or craft, of human life and political organization. Aristotle, in other words, moves through teleology well beyond teleology. He builds the means into the end, and characterizes *eudaimonia* in terms of whole lives, not a moment of goal realization.

You might say that this is itself the deepest resolution to any problematical situation: to live within and as the problem. Or you might say that with regard (at least) to such activities, the vocabulary of problematic situation and resolution is inadequate or has already collapsed. That's why I say that Dewey's aesthetics is the culmination of pragmatism and its end; that's how Dewey resolved his problematic situation, where at a culminating intellectual moment West met West's East: by coming to regard means as ends, by joining them in an indissoluble whole, or by understanding that the process is both the problem and its resolution, or that there is no problem, only work and play, which are the same.

11.

I won't pretend not be a bit flummoxed about the status of "abstract" or comprehensive ethical principles, such as the categorical imperative or the principle of utility. Putting it mildly, I think that we need to start someplace else and build toward principles in the end, if possible. And it won't surprise you at this point that I think the fundamental data have to be creatures such as people and other things in specific juxtapositions in a situation. An ontology of relations, we might hope, is a pretty promising as a way to describe the real-world status of ethical values.

Now, one purpose of principles is precisely to simplify the bewildering profusion of specific situations. That shows one reason why principles are an invitation to falsity as well as truth. Indeed, we might say that to pick out a certain situation as a situation is always to reveal some aspects of some things and to occlude others: or, truth builds on a massive bed of falsehood. This is a problem in picking out properties, for example, or in ascribing properties to things: if we fix the color of something, say, aren't we also foreclosing other color-taxonomies or various uniquenesses of the color of the very thing in question? The difficulty is introduced by the infinite multiplication or the flourishing of reality: it's always in excess to whatever refers to it. This problem is at its most acute when the principles reached are most general: even if the in-some-sense maximal object is revealed, an infinity of realities is preempted, short-circuited, or concealed. A principle which encompasses or encapsulates a whole domain of inquiry is always formulated at a cost. This is as true in physics as it is in ethics. On the other hand, as I've been saying, this is also an appropriate zone for a certain insouciance, and precisely because principles are such brutal simplifications of such bewilderingly large situations, a certain swashbuckling attitude seems appropriate; the distance to an actual juxtaposition of medium-sized things is like a layer of ethical baffling: a bad generalization is relatively harmless as long as people keep dealing particularly with particulars.

I am an intensely moralistic person, and, of course, also a failure by my own moral standards. This is why I understand the Augustinian notion of original sin only too well: my own judgment feels inevitable and inexorable, and so does my failure and that of others in respect to it. And such a standpoint indeed brings with it danger of a detachment from the situations over which it ranges: not only an attempt to fix the situation or mount a tendentious, persistent representation of it, but to stand outside it—and even outside oneself, or hence outside oneself—at an ethical distance that might be compared to aesthetic distance. Ethics in this sense is dangerous, or is itself original sin or its site: principled ethics always operates at a distance from our lives and has the comforting and concealing functions of distance.

There is pleasure and power in distance, and in the generalization or comprehension or subsumption of many specific situations under general principles. Ethics, necessarily, is a falsification of the world, but it is also an engagement with the world or a way of drawing all sorts of apparently unconnected strands together. An ethics dedicated to holding other people to account had better be dedicated to holding oneself to account. If it's not, it really is a mode of disconnection rather than connection, or a mode of falsehood rather than truth. An ethics has to be a way that you connect yourself to people and things, even if that connection supposes various distinctions, and even if any form of connection that is represented in a principle also precludes various other connections.

Perhaps the most depressing concept ever enunciated—and it appears to be "scientifically" supported—is "depressive realism": depressed people have a truer set of beliefs about the world and themselves than nondepressed people. Whether they're depressed because they face reality or face reality because they are depressed is a difficult question. But my apparently depressing view is: face up: look at the damn thing squarely; actually live as actually yourself in the actual world. I might take a moment to rag on the self-esteem industry: remember that you are a beautiful and good person! Well, you are precisely as good and beautiful as you actually are, not as beautiful and good as you can tell yourself you are. And it's worth saying that self-delusion is not likely to be a long-term road to happiness, precisely because you'll be constantly confronted by the truth in some form, by the indefatigable realities. Delusory self-esteem is a remarkably fragile item. I've known people who just kept telling everyone how amazing they were: cock an eyebrow at them funny and they shift into rage or collapse in a heap on the floor.

One cannot behave ethically unless one sees how things actually are: morality requires knowledge; it is a form of responsiveness or it is pathological. My ethical commitments center around the conception of truth: an awareness of webs of connection and my place therein. Real ethics requires facing up, squaring up. Without the initial affirmation of reality, it loses the material over which it operates. Even apparently abstract principles—the golden rule, the categorical imperative, the principle of utility—have to be conceived fundamentally as dimensions or modes of connection, and they all explicitly take that form: you've got to experience other agents as real; you have to not let their suffering or flourishing become an abstraction. This is the paradox at the heart of ethics: it formulates connection as abstraction or generalization. Or what is characteristic of ethics is that it wields abstraction as connection. It prescribes specific connections in a general way; the principle bends or breaks on the situation, and any principle is inadequate to the infinity of situations in which we're embedded. On the other hand, the situation bends too or is altered by the principle; one might say that they elaborate one another. A principle is a strategy or a rule for arraying, and is limited or interpreted under the aegis of the real arrays.

One thing this means is that ethics is not an entirely human affair. It may be that human beings are the only things we know that formulate ethical principles, though maybe not. But ethical situations embed all sorts of agencies: animals, trees, crops, inanimate objects. There are right or wrong ways of treating all sorts of things, and though ethics demands that we regard different agencies as having differences, though human beings are different from squirrels and different from bookcases and from mountains, we are caught up in myriad situations that call out ethical responses to such things as well as to one another. This can be made clear with various mundane examples: property rights, for instance: I can't just smash your bookcase. But there's something wrong with someone who lives in an extremely destructive relation to inanimate objects even where they are his own property or no one's property in particular. Ethics is not only about human relations to one another, but about situations in which all sorts of things are embedded.

12.

I have been relentlessly emphasizing connection, in ethics and in everything else. But now I also want to emphasize integrity, singleness, individuality, distinctness. One challenge for human beings in a vast system of connections is to forge an identity or to make oneself a thing. No thing is alone; every thing is the thing it is because of its connections. But on the other hand, there are knots and nodes, and the connections not only provide many dimensions of fascination, intimacy, and pleasure, but also a continuous existential threat. We will all be untied eventually, or released into a new configuration. But to assert that all things are constituted in connection is not to assert that individual things do not exist, or are illusory. For things like us, fighting to survive or to expand our effects, existence as an individual thing is an achievement, always provisional and a matter of degree and endangered. I would say that this is one of the defining features of anything that is a real thing: it fights to hang together, we might say. If a rock has no resistance to dissolution, it's not a rock. The knot is as real as the whole skein. Or each thing has a little gravity, forces that hold it together, always provisionally and always under pressures of transformation.

One thing we are fighting for is to be ourselves in our relations to other things: to stay alive, but also to forge and hold to an identity or a coherent personality. This is where I think the idea of virtue ethics has some purchase. Saying what you mean and meaning what you say, and changing relatively slowly—that is, for example, believing today most of what you believed yesterday, or displaying many of the same preferences or commitments—these are marks of someone or something that actually does exist. Kierkegaard once ridiculed the idea that a person who had not stayed the same for a fortnight could wonder whether he was immortal: if you want to be the same for all eternity, concentrate first on being the same for the next ten minutes. Being something, or being an immortal soul, was something to be achieved, not an underlying necessary fact. And the task of becoming and being something is a task, as Kierkegaard said, to last a whole lifetime.

> Of course, people can combine for many things; thus several families can combine for a box at the theater, and three single gentlemen can combine for a riding horse, so that each of them rides every third day. But it is not so with immortality. . . . The question is raised, how immortality practically transforms his life; in what sense he must have the consciousness of it always present to him, or whether perhaps it is enough to think this thought once and for all, whether it is not true that, if the answer is to this effect, the answer shows that the problem has not been stated, inasmuch as to such consciousness of immortality once for all there would correspond the notion of being a subject as it were in general, whereby the question about immortality is made fantastically ludicrous, just as the converse is ludicrous, when people who have fantastically made a mess of everything and have been every possible sort of thing, one day ask the clergyman with deep concern whether in the beyond they will really be the same—after never having been able in their lifetime to be the same for a fortnight.[40]

This is not only about the question of immortality, of course, and I am not worried that we may be immortal. It is a question about personal identity as an achievement rather than as an underlying metaphysical truth, or about the extent that some sort of coherence can be achieved in the course of an actual human life.

Now, the locus of consciousness is the individual body, even if, as I have elaborately insisted, it encompasses parts of the actual environment. This is not really up for grabs, though people are always denying it or inventing fantastic dimensions of collective consciousness. Usually, this is a political program that drives an ontological theory, rather than vice versa, but if your claim is actually that classes are consciousnesses, or nations, or races, or humanity in general, I do not believe you are entirely sincere. There is an easy way to demonstrate this beyond all quibble: drop a bowling ball on your foot and see whether someone across town—your fellow whatever-it-is—screams in pain. We spend a lot of time wishing to cease being distinct from one another, but it's not something that can be achieved except by actually working with particular other bodies, actually having sex with them or something, and even there, of course, the deindividuation is provisional and ephemeral and very partial. Collectivism is both a fantasy and a nightmare, and its advocates hold both that it is an ontological fact and that it must be enforced under coercion.

Our mergers with other people are no more or less real than our mergers with other sorts of things, and social coalitions cannot exist without all sorts of physical objects and communicative media. Part of our separation from each other, our real distinctness, is just the space between our bodies. This can, of course, be literally compromised, for example in a case where I cut you open, pull out your bleeding heart, and devour it in a blood ecstasy. Well, these are the mundane ways we merge with all sorts of things all the time, and the ways we are actually distinct from one another are no less real than the ways we are actually distinct from the trees, for example, and can only actually be offloaded by physical procedures of incorporation or blending, like when we become blood brothers. But, for just such reasons among others, we are lonely. To deal with this, I'd suggest joining the Loyal Order of Elk rather than inventing fantastic metaphysical or psychological systems (e.g., Jung's) in which we're a priori not lonely after all. Either of those, of course, is preferable to an attempt to make everyone simulate connection or collective identity under threat of internment or whatever it may be.

Ethics is just one of many sites at which we express our urge to merge, which probably is sexual at its heart or something. We want to be food-processed together into a kind of human soup. The only way to do this for real is to do it to corpses, as collectivists operating on real bodies in the real world have often done. In particular, in ethics, we are simply not going to be rid of our personal agency, much as we would like to be. We're not going to be able to ameliorate the condition in which we are particular human beings trying to muddle through an infinitely complex world. We're not going to be able to offload the dilemma in which we confront the question of what to do by dumping it on God (that is one of Kierkegaard's points), or on Reason à la Kant or Korsgaard, or on a single principle by which everything suddenly becomes clear or decisions become obvious or are coerced by abstractions. We're not going to get into a situation where we can't make fatal mistakes; no principle can indemnify us against that. We're not going to be able to simplify actual interactions with actual other people and things into something clear or in which we know ourselves to be doing the right thing. That's just not the sort of thing we are. For such reasons, I have plenty of sympathy for, for example, Jonathan Dancy's particularism: the idea that we don't have any valid universal principles and don't need any, and that the seductive power of such principle often leads us to make terrible mistakes.

A perfect integrity, if it meant losing one's connections or becoming a kind of monad or an ontologically independent spiritual substance, would be impossible. And it is possible to have too much integrity: to configure an identity around the wrong factors, for instance, or to be insufficiently responsive to your environment and other people, a kind of moral psychosis. But it also possible to lose your existence as a coherent subject in connection, to be too flexible, to be too different in different contexts or with different people. This, I think, is the region in which the moral dilemmas of individuality play out, where the virtues gain meaning, where we realize or lose ourselves. We need to lose ourselves; we need to experience our non-distinctness from people and things of all sorts; we need to see that we are not alone: these are moral facts. But we need also to be or become something in these relations, to persist even as we shift and everything shifts all around us. Experiencing one's relations entails experiencing oneself in excess to any particular relation. Persistence of a person through time is not a given (obviously, else there'd be no death), but the notion is also rich and more than a metaphor in terms of our day-to-day comportment. I would take seriously the idea, for example, that an Alzheimer's patient could lose herself, or that many different circumstances might be so profoundly transformative or damaging that it might make sense to say that someone has ceased to be, or ceased to be the person they were. Or even that, really, there is nothing there, only a set of responses or random reactions rather than a full-fledged personality.

Obviously, these factors are in dialogue, and if we could define each thing by its relations, perhaps we could also define each relation by its relata, or at any rate, certainly we cannot in their absence. You can't have relations between things without the things, just as you can't have things without their relations. The skein is not smooth, and though there is only one ontological plane, it's bumpy, variegated, full of differentiations. The ethical is constantly in play in this situation, in how you connect and in how you hold together, how you are compromised and how you are integral, how you change or even disintegrate and merge, and how you persist and fight for consistency.

As I say, I share Dancy's sense of the radical inadequacy of any principle to any particular situation. Dancy calls the alternative he develops "holism," which he describes as the position that "a feature that is a reason in favour of action in one case may be no reason at all in another, or even a reason against."[41] Dancy makes the case for this very compelling, and a "situationist" orientation in ontology gives reasons to think it is plausible, looking suspiciously on attempts to bundle situations under general principles, much less to bundle all human situations under one or a few principles. Any particular situation is bristlingly complex, and no principle can be or even should be refined to deal with all even of the particular situations it is meant to encompass. Our ethical responses are going to have to start with a rich sense of the actual situation, and I do think that even beautiful principles are going to have to be suspended, or refined out of their own spirit, or supplemented by others that come from different orientations, in order to constitute a good person in a real environment. Nevertheless, perhaps ethical principles such as the categorical imperative have a role to play, even if it not quite the role that they attribute to themselves, as providing reliable ethical guidance in every situation.

I'd like to consider the idea of eternal ethical principles—or of a single eternal ethical principle like the categorical imperative, which appears completely incompatible with a one-level ontology or a universe in constant change—as a resolution to hold together, what we might call an existential resolution, following vaguely the ideas about selfhood we get in Kierkegaard or Sartre, for example. Indeed, it is a resolution of the most pointed kind: it hints at a pure integrity even as it defines this integrity in connection. It is a kind of fantasy: its ontological status cannot be elucidated; it is an impossible object.

The question for an ethical principle is not exactly: where does it come from and how can it be real or true? But: what kind of resolution does it inscribe, or what kind of integrity and what sort of relations does it help us aspire to? It's not a thing, it's a decision, or a relation of the self to the self that articulates its relations to other selves and other things. No more than any other sentence or belief or object can it stand outside the ravages of time: it accretes and erodes, snarls and comes undone, like anything else. So it is not what it appears or claims to be. But it is an aspirational principle of identity over time, a guideline for becoming or, alternatively, self-realization, self-actualization within the web of relation. It also inscribes the threat that time and ambiguity presents to persistence: in a way it is a desperate expedient, and the desperation is a measure of how threatened we are by our own continual disintegration into the environment; certainly it is an extreme expedient, apparently floating from particularities into total generality. But one of its purposes is to help create an existing or coherent subject. Such resolutions have social causes and social roles, and the human individual self is indeed constituted and experienced somewhat differently in different cultures and moments, or even in different families or sub-cultural groups.

If that is the status of moral principles—as resolutions, or strategies for imposing coherence on ourselves—then, of course, we run into various problems. For example, on what grounds might we distinguish correct from incorrect moral principles? There could be disastrous principles, or selfish principles, or even, it seems, morally wrong principles and morally wrong selves that are (to an extent) unified by means of those principles. I myself am uncomfortable with the claim that any principle which helps create a coherent self is as good as any other. But I think that meta-ethics on this level may not be fully resolvable, that we may face irremediable, and certainly not fully rational, controversies about what constitutes a good self or even what constitutes a coherent self. They are always possible sources of contestation, refinement, criticism, abandonment; they are always subject to clashes of wills or coercive attempts to remake or re-educate individuals; but they can be deployed the other way round, as a technique for individuals and groups to criticize dominant notions or even to spur a rebellion. I wouldn't think it likely that such matters can be resolved once and for all, and this is one place where we come up against the limits of our knowledge and experience, and into a spiraling self-referentiality and self-consciousness that make the question interminable. On the other hand, perhaps we also can't stop trying; of that I am not certain.

It's easy to say "a universe in constant change." It's much harder to live in one, or actually to be something in what often enough seems a chaos. We are constantly leaking out of ourselves, fraying, not really making sense, being invaded or infected. Perhaps nothing ceases to exist in the sense that matter is never perfectly annihilated, but knots come undone all the time, and you have to gather your resolve, you have to be willing to fight to be. There are persons about whom it is only a courtesy or convenience to say that they persist through time, or people that shift through a myriad of personalities. (That, for example, is what is wrong with politicians.) On the other hand, we should not underestimate the involuntariness of persistence, or the factors that are not under our control with regard to whether we exist, and just as often as people find themselves compromising their integrity, they appear again as themselves even in an effort to cease to be themselves, as Emerson keeps hinting or presenting as a sort of clinching argument. And we long not only to persist but to disintegrate. As far as the world is concerned, one is as good as another, and we enact these dramas, in a way, alone. We may be condemned to be ourselves, or condemned to respond again and again the same way in similar circumstances though we'd rather not. We are not the creators of ourselves, or not our only creators. Integrity can be annoying or misplaced or wrong or excessive. There are people who simply cannot be persuaded or cannot change their minds no matter what shocks or problems they undergo. It is a difficult thing to be something in a world of relations, or to be something that is also situated. How to be integral and responsive, a knot and a string, is a hard question that we all face all the time.

5

Aesthetics

1.

The centrality of aesthetics in my picture of the world will long ago have struck my readers, if any. Where other people have science or culture, where they have reason or epistemes or information or bosons or *différance*—where, in short, other people have whatever categories of discourse they tend to find or intend to find fundamental—I have aesthetic categories. I think of these as picking out real material aspects of the world, of course; otherwise, they wouldn't be eligible for reality in my ontology. But they are features of the way the world is organized or its shapes, its forms, contours, its topology, and also the ways it appears to the senses in a culture. The ways the world appears to the senses are, as I have somewhat relentlessly emphasized, themselves material aspects of the world.

Ideas emerging from the discipline of philosophical aesthetics inform, more or less, every aspect of this system I'm constructing. Thinking about both the concept of beauty and the concept of art, as well as dealing with various beautiful songs, helped me build, first, an ontology of individuals in connection and then to think about the nature of those connections in epistemology and ethics. The concept of craft, which I make essentially synonymous with art, is probably central to my ethics, such as it is. I'm constantly resorting to aesthetic categories, parallels, and structures. When I have thought through political theory, I have centralized aesthetics or asserted flatly that all politics is aesthetic (though not merely or only aesthetic). In some ways I recognize this as a tic or a preoccupation, and one could take another of these dimensions as fundamental and perhaps account for the aesthetic in its terms. True, and yet it's my tic, and it's my tic because I think, over and over, that it helps. In some ways, this whole book might best be conceived as an essay in aesthetics. Anyway, it's an essay from aesthetics.

In my time, I've had a crack, or taken a stab, at both "art" and "beauty." Let me say how I think about my attempts to "define" such terms or develop "theories" of the concepts at issue. I think they are historically unfolding family resemblance terms or open concepts. This is glib because the devil is in the details; concepts like that unfold thickly, with myriad relations to other ideas with which they are constellated and in process and the concrete activities and objects these concepts crystallize or conflate. You're not going to be able to give the all and only definition, not really. But that doesn't mean you don't feel your way toward a center, toward what you think is the most important or consistent thing the term holds, like a vessel.

Take soul as a genre of music. Now, what counted as soul music, or what made something a soul song, was not the same in 1964 as it was in 1973. To try to elucidate the concept, think about what you would say to a sophisticated person who doesn't know what soul music is. The first thing you'd do is proceed historically, but not only historically. First of all, *soul* was the term for the dominant African American pop music form in that period. I'd start with the origin of soul as a secularized version of African American gospel music (of course, one would have to work on "gospel" as well). The career of Sam Cooke is emblematic, as he made precisely the transition from singing about the love of God to singing about sexual and romantic love. But soul music after it begins has a quasi-autonomous history, and it develops in directions not already present in the gospel tradition, even as it feeds back into that tradition. Also, it was a term used in promoting certain sorts of music in the commercial marketplace. The vocal styles originate in the black church: often hoarse, rough, impassioned, unpredictable, with improvisational elements. After you've heard where Aretha takes "Think," it seems inevitable, but the first time through it was very surprising, like a Louis Armstrong solo. The instrumentation as it developed was a basic rock unit (electric guitar, bass, drums, keyboard), with a horn section and back-up singers, often engaged in very intricate vocal and horn arrangements. Now, let's play some paradigmatic examples: Otis Redding, Wilson Pickett, Betty Wright, Al Green. There, hear that? Soul music is not some eternal form or essence; it was a volatile, developing pop style, different at each moment than it was before, but also subject to a certain continuity. Where soul leaves off and, say, funk begins—really, a very difficult question, and if you were completely serious you'd have to work through dozens of examples and criteria. Reasonable music critics might disagree. It does have to do with departures from the original defining conditions of soul music, and it doesn't follow from its continuity with funk that "soul music" is an empty phrase, or that people don't know what you're talking about, or that you don't yourself know what you're talking about. In fact, the richness and ambiguity of a reasonably good account show that you do know what you're talking about, for they are inherent in the material.

This is more or less the sort of procedure I would try to apply, say, to "art" and "beauty" or, for that matter, to "justice" or many other notions. If I started by boiling soul down to "secularized gospel music," that would be simplistic, and there would be many cases left obscure and much, much more to say. But it wouldn't follow that that isn't a useful generalization or doesn't get at something historically criterial. I also try to convey in quasi-definitional form *why these things matter*, as one would in calling soul the dominant black pop style, 1964–1973. But even more, as I play the paradigm examples of soul music for you, I am going to swoon, maybe with a slight exaggeration, to try to convey how great this stuff is, because I don't think you quite get it. Now, let's play it again.

Say you were listening to Ann Peebles' "I'm Gonna Tear Your Playhouse Down" or Shirley Caesar's "Don't Be Afraid," and you managed to achieve "aesthetic disinterestedness" or "distance": you took it *qua* pure form and appreciated the arrangement of its formal elements. Well, form is important. Nevertheless, you would be misunderstanding such things completely. They are incredibly excellent and intense personal expressions (of a whole collaborative group of creators, actually, including writers, producers, band members), but they have definite cultural locations that make them comprehensible: they emerge out of histories and you must engage those histories to some extent if these things are to be understood. And they have definite purposes: to get you up dancing and yelling and celebrating and worshiping or connecting to a dance partner or a sexual partner or to God. Also, Ann Peebles and the Hi Records team were trying to make a living and were partly making what they thought they could sell; the art was certainly made in relation to or for an audience. However, that is also true of, say, Rembrandt or Michelangelo. These songs are socially unifying and socially distinguishing. They issue from the body—pointedly, in this case: there are few more rough, more sheerly physical, more insistently embodied, singers in the history of music than Wilson Pickett, for example—and they directly engage the bodies of the audience in myriad dimensions. They connect embodiedness to spirituality: really, Shirley Caesar does that as well as anyone has, and she does it right there. And they are, in my opinion, paradigmatically excellent works of art, for precisely these reasons. The further you are from Kant, as an artist or appreciator, other things being equal, the better the art, though the union of body and spirit plays variously across the tradition, as we have already seen in Schiller.

2.

In *Against the State*, I described the arguments for the moral legitimacy of state power—social contract theory, for example—as embarrassments to the human intellect. I'd like to propose another: the concept of "art" as it has been elucidated by philosophers since perhaps Shaftesbury. This is art in the "aesthetic" sense, or "the fine arts" in Kant's acceptation: the concept of the arts as an autonomous exalted cultural sphere, what distinguishes Picasso from a potter, or Schoenberg from Benny Goodman, or whatever it may be. Or, the concept that Danto or Dickie attempted to describe by means of "the institution of the art world": art as what is in museums, symphony halls, poetry books. This is art as opposed to craft, art as opposed to popular culture, art opposed to industrial labor, and so on.

Kant, of course, gives the first systematic treatment, and he does it in terms of the disinterested attitude that is appropriate before the exalted objects of the fine arts, as opposed the engagement of the crafts or popular prints with our animal needs and emotions.

> By right it is only production through freedom, i.e., through an act of will that places reason at the basis of its action, that should be termed art. . . . But where anything is called absolutely a work of art, to distinguish it from a natural product, then some work of man is always understood. . . . Art is further distinguished from handicraft. The first is called free, the other may be called industrial art. We look on the former as something which could only prove final (be a success) as play, i.e., an occupation which is agreeable on its own account; but on the second as labor, i.e., a business, which on its own account is disagreeable (drudgery), and is only attractive by means of what it results in (e.g., the pay), and which is consequently capable of being a compulsory imposition.[1]

People have been trying to define this notion for close to three centuries now, and what I think the whole unwholesome history shows is that there just is no such concept, by which I mean that there is no definite meaning attached to the term "art" in the fine or high art sense at any moment of its history. No coherent or even sort of plausible account can be given that distinguishes fine art in this sense form all its lowborn opposites: no plausible historical elucidation, no way to coherently organize the paradigmatic cases and (in particular) the exclusions.

If I were trying to define or characterize the concept of fine art (as opposed to craft, etc.), I would proceed as sketched above with regard to soul: here's more or less how it starts and here's how it unfolds; here are some of the objects it encompasses at a given stage of its development; here are some of the central conceptual strands that run through this history in various ways; here are some reasons why this is important. I would be happy to do this for "art" as a general term in English: start by struggling with *technē* and *ars* and run through possibly similar conceptions in non-Western languages, such as *silpa* in Sanskrit. But I do not believe that such procedures can be performed with regard to the concept of fine art since the eighteenth century. I do not believe there is a conceptual core at any stage of its development, or a sensible way to specify the extension of the term "work of art" in this alleged sense. I do not believe that good reasons can be given to regard it as important, though I can see many reasons to try to puncture it, compromise its edges, show its internal incoherences or, in short, destroy it once and for all by showing that it never existed in the first place.

So, Morris Weitz and perhaps Wittgenstein took the view that "art" is a "family resemblance" or "open-textured" term, that is, one that couldn't be defined in terms of necessary and sufficient conditions. This was supposed to be true by and large of general terms in ordinary language, perhaps, but "art" was a particularly good example, because it was obvious to Weitz, looking at Duchamp's *Fountain*, for example, that it had gotten to the point where every new season or movement refuted the theory of the season before. By the time Weitz wrote in the late 1950s, there were counterexamples everywhere to everything: there were works of art that didn't express emotions, that didn't imitate the real world, that weren't beautiful or formally super-excellent, that couldn't be distinguished from ordinary plumbing fixtures. Soon after, with pop and all the rest, it got much worse. Dickie saved the day with the institutional theory: what characterized works of fine art was their social position, we might say: very much what distinguishes a lord from a peasant, for example: not anything by way of intrinsic difference or excellence, but precisely that he's sitting there in a manor house, wearing the insignia of office, treated with deference, and so on.

One's worst suspicions about the situation are confirmed nicely in the work of Pierre Bourdieu, for example: you can track people's aesthetic affiliations extremely closely by their class position, and fine art in precisely the institutional theory sense is—whatever else it might be—a zone in which the bourgeoisie express their dedication to social climbing. "Fine art" turns out to mean the art of white middle- and upper-class people, and the mere crafts and popular arts and technical arts are just the arts of unprivileged people. Well, the political critique doesn't exactly nail the conceptual problem, but it should start to make us a bit queasy about the concept, especially as we are not able, as it has so elaborately turned out, plausibly to elucidate its content in any other terms. Coming out of this history, I want to state flatly that the concept of "fine art" is ideological, something invented rather than discovered, and that it is impossible to spell out its content even as relativized to a particular moment in its development. There is no such thing as art.

3.

I am going to try not to merely recapitulate *The Art of Living* (in which I give a "theory" of art) and *Six Names of Beauty* (in which I do the same for beauty). And yet I might as well avail myself. So, in the former, I characterize art in the general sense in terms of process; roughly, *a work of art is a thing that eventuates from a process that is engaged in for its own sake, as well as for the sake of the finished product and possible other purposes.* In addition, *it is of a kind which is suited to play a role in such processes.* Or, art is devotion to process, and works of art enhancements of the processes of living. I think of "art" and "craft" as synonyms, or at any rate as closely connected. This is certainly true etymologically, and the Greek *technē*, Latin *ars*, the Sanskrit *silpa*, and the Chinese *yi*, for example, primordially denote skilled making in all material disciplines.

Among the Greeks, even great sculptors and painters were regarded as crafters, and though the products were sometimes venerated, the makers were regarded as manual laborers, albeit highly skilled. In an autobiographical essay, Lucian has the spirit of Culture speak as follows:

> The advantages that the profession of being a sculptor will bring with it . . . amount to no more than being a worker with your hands. . . . You may turn out to be a Phidias or a Polyclitus, to be sure, and create a number of wonderful works; but even so, though your art will be generally commended, no sensible observer will be found to wish himself like you; whatever your real qualities, you will always rank as a common craftsman who makes his living with his hands.[2]

Of course, Socrates himself was a stonecutter, but Plato has him condemn the arts partly on, among others, the grounds that they embed you ever more thoroughly in the merely sensible or material. Sculptors and painters in medieval Europe were part of the craft guild system, often folded in with masons or joiners. The closest things one gets in the Greeks to our conception of works of fine art are the products of *mimetic technē*, which Plato groups together—for the first time, as far as we know—in order to condemn them. It is not clear what exactly is and what is not representational skill in this sense, but Plato and Aristotle certainly include painting, sculpture, music, poetry, and drama.

The social status accorded to manual laborers has been a problem for those who would exalt the arts, throughout the history of the West. Indeed, I think this has a lot to do with the conception of art as it has developed in modernity. It is ever more spiritual or intellectual or nonphysical or conceptual; these are partly ways to try to associate it with the things the West—ancient, medieval, and modern—values: spirit and mind, and with them a conception of human beings as not merely physical or even as not essentially physical at all. The struggle to exalt the arts but not the material world in which they arise and in which only they could arise is perfectly apparent in different ways in Kant and Hegel, for example, following Shaftesbury or Plotinus. The idea that art is not primarily a matter of physical bodies making physical things is, first, the product of dualist metaphysics, and second, of class structures that privilege intellectual over manual work. But that is a terrible betrayal of the history and nature of the arts, as well as a ridiculous and perhaps evil conception of human beings. It is evil in this sense: it severs important connections in imagination, while leaving them intact in fact, leaving one careless of or unconsciously malevolent toward the erased entities.

Plato and Aristotle's account of *mimetic technē* serves to demarcate roughly what came to be regarded, starting in the late Renaissance at earliest, as the realm of the fine arts, as distinguished from the crafts. And yet skill continued not only to be highly valued in the fine arts, but to be part of the concept of "art" and its cognates and correspondents in different European and Asian languages. The detachment was finalized—I want to say, both ideologically and provisionally, or locally in certain cultural zones—in Modernism. As art came in Impressionism to value immediacy of sense experience, and in Expressionism to value the intense outpouring of emotion, and in postmodernism to value irony or political commentary, the concept of art was detached conceptually from skill, at least provisionally within "the art world." It is worth remarking, as well, that these and other agendas turned the arts simultaneously away from the concept of beauty, which was mostly ignored as a project in high-end twentieth-century fine art.

4.

And yet, skill has never ceased to be cherished in many other walks of life, nor has the term "art" in English ceased to be used in precisely the sense that the Greeks used *technē*. "The art of the cupcake," "the art of war," "the art of love," "the art of the deal": these are perfectly good locutions of contemporary English. There is no reason, in approaching the concept of art, to regard such uses as extensions or metaphors: they are far older than and just as central to contemporary usage as the specialized use of the term in the upper end of the fine arts. At any rate, I would like the recentralize skill as at least historically pivotal to the arts, and I would like to characterize skill as emerging in an intense, prolonged engagement with tools and materials. The arts in this sense are ways that we cease to be distinct from stuff, and it's appropriate that many an artist has been poisoned or severely injured by the material he worked with: literally ceased to be distinct from it. When people say they "live and breathe" their beat building, pottery, gardening, or writing, they are speaking the literal truth. The crafts are systematic ways of cultivating nondistinction with things, and what you learn is that our relation to things is never a sheer imposition of will. Even though craft is a certain sort of power over materials, it is a power drawn from the capacities of the materials as well as of oneself and limited by those capacities; you become one situation with an object by collaboration, not sheer effortless incorporation or command. This is an image of a decent way to be in the world: we no more impose our will on it than it operates us like sheer puppets; we emerge in it with it. Craft skills are precisely ways of addressing the recalcitrance of materials, not by annihilating them, but by connecting with them and respecting them; crafts are "ethical" in that sense.

But there are, of course, other ways to be invested in or devoted to materials that do not amount to skill or craft. When Pollock threw his paint around, it was hard to tell whether he was rejecting the centrality of skill in the arts altogether, or whether he was himself channeling an almost supernatural skill, a Zen skill beyond skill, a moment at which craft and improvisation merge. Well I'd rather centralize Pollock's contemporaries, various jazz musicians, but the point is that one approaches materials in all sorts of ways for all sorts of intense interchanges. It does matter that Pollock used paint, I believe, or even that he overcame the imperative to display skill precisely with paint, a medium in which wizardly displays of skill had become almost commonplace. Now, of course, there are arts that seem to dispense with materials entirely, though I think you'll find that they can't, actually, and still communicate; at any rate, there are certainly art practices in which skill and materials are both deemphasized, even if process is not.

Now, art as engagement with materials of various kinds also ramifies outward; it is in general anything but solitary; rather it is a kind of ecstasy of communication, taking "communication" at a very broad sweep. Materials are found, produced, and taken up in an interchange with the maker in which both or all are transformed. The act and product of making then takes up a place in an interpersonal world of communications within a situation encompassing human beings and materials; well, that was inscribed on the activity from the beginning as part of its character, and what form the materials can possibly assume is partly driven by those materials, partly by vocabularies and technologies of craft and atmospheres of meaning (then again, these technologies and vocabularies are themselves developed in collaboration with the materials), partly by gravity, or myriad aspects of the physical situation. You are making a pot, a novel, a dance, an outfit; these are extremely rich cultural formations which you've internalized, or practices in which you're participating from the outset, even if you are also rejecting them in various ways. Then there is a body of specific meanings and a penumbra of associations that the work makes available to the viewer or receiver.

This is what Tolstoy thought art was, in an intense and reactionary aesthetic/ethical vision: real communication leading finally to nondistinction between persons, through shared experiences and emotions.

> Art begins when one person, with the object of joining another or others to himself in one and the same feeling, expresses that feeling by certain external indications. To take the simplest example: a boy, having experienced, let us say, fear on encountering a wolf, relates that encounter; and, in order to evoke in others the feeling he has experienced, describes himself, his condition before the encounter, the surroundings, the woods, his own lightheartedness, and then the wolf's appearance, its movements, the distance between himself and the wolf, etc. All this, if only the boy, when telling the story, again experiences the feelings he had lived through and infects

the hearers and compels them to feel what the narrator had experienced, is art. If even the boy had not seen a wolf but had frequently been afraid of one, and if, wishing to evoke in others the fear he had felt, he invented an encounter with a wolf and recounted it so as to make his hearers share the feelings he experienced when he feared the world, that also would be art. And just in the same way it is art if a man, having experienced either the fear of suffering or the attraction of enjoyment (whether in reality or in imagination) expresses these feelings on canvas or in marble so that others are infected by them.[3]

Of course, I do not limit art to the realm of emotional communication, but Tolstoy's view is compelling because—unlike formalism, for example—it shows a dimension in which art is central to human life. And it also does give examples—as do Tolstoy's novels—of the intensity of communicative interaction in the arts. But we should consider art not only as communication—that is, compromise of distinction—among human beings (though that, too) but of human beings with potentially all the world's things, materials, and creatures.

5.

The very worst theories of art in intellectual history were the "idealist" theories of people like Croce and Collingwood, which even had their influence on Dewey, for example. This began with the claim that the work of art was an internal mental object in the mind of the artist which was then externalized or realized in materials.

> I will say at once, in the simplest manner, that art is *vision* and *intuition*. The artist produces an image or a phantasm; and he who enjoys art turns his gaze upon the point which the artist has indicated, looks through the chink which he has opened, and reproduces that image in himself. "Intuition," "vision," "contemplation," "imagination," "fancy," "figurations," "representations," and so on, are words continually recurring, like synonyms, when discoursing upon art, and they all lead the mind to the same conceptual sphere, which indicates general agreement. . . . And if it be asked, why art cannot be a physical fact, we must reply, in the first place, that physical facts *do not possess reality*, and that art, to which so many devote their whole lives and which fills all with divine joy, is *supremely real*; thus it cannot be a physical fact, which is something unreal. . . . The unreality has . . . been proved in an indisputable manner and is admitted by all philosophers (who are not crass materialists).[4]

I actually don't quite see how anyone ever entertained idealism of this sort, perhaps because I missed the indisputable proof that there is no world, only chumps like us. In its application to aesthetics here, it is in some ways the culmination/nadir of the modern conception of philosophy and the world. First, it wants a series of screens between consciousness and world that ends up moving everything into the mind, or just leaves you lopping off the world as a redundancy or a snare. It grotesquely expresses hatred of the world. It hyperintensifies classical mind/body dualism: the mind is of infinite value, the material world of no moment, or a complete delusion, or an unfortunate source of friction to the mind. It is connected to the ideology of artistic genius, making the entire scene of goddish creativity the artist's mind. Also, I would say, once you swallow idealist metaphysics, there is absolutely no point in denying that works of art, or some of them, are physical objects, and that all involve physical processes. For Croce, a painting—that thing on the wall over there, that panel covered with pigments—is itself not a physical object, but an idea or an intuition, and so on, a mental object. So why get worried if people treat physical objects as though they were works of art? According to Croce, works of art are ideas, and "physical" paintings are also ideas. So there's no ontological reason physical objects can't be works of art, even on Croce's view.

This got to the point, in the 1960s, at which Richard Wollheim could identify what he called the *bricoleur* problem: the problem of why certain artists favored certain materials or media rather than others. Wollheim identifies two problems for the "Ideal theory":

> The first concerns the nature of mental images. For it is hard to believe that mental images could be so articulated as in all respects to anticipate the physical pictures to be realized on wall or canvas. For this would involve not merely foreseeing, but also solving, all the problems that will arise, either necessarily or accidentally, in the working of the medium: and not merely is this implausible, but it is even arguable that the accreditation of certain material processes as the media of art is bound up with their inherent unpredictability: it is just because these materials present difficulties that can be dealt with only in the actual working of them that they are so suitable as expressive processes. . . . A second difficulty is this: . . . it is because the artifact is of such and such a material that the image is in such and such a conceived medium. The problem of why certain apparently arbitrarily identified stuffs or processes should be the vehicles of art—what I shall call the *bricoleur* problem, from the striking comparison made by Lévi-Strauss of human culture to a *bricoleur* or handyman, who improvises only partly useful objects out of old junk—is a very real one: but the answer to it cannot be that these are just the stuffs or processes that artists happen

to think about or conceive in the mind. It is more plausible to believe that the painter thinks in images of paint or the sculptor in images of metal just because these, independently, are the media of art: his thinking presupposes that certain activities in the external world such as charging canvas with paint or welding have already become accredited processes of art. In other words, there could not be Crocean "intuitions" unless there were, first, physical works of art.[5]

The question of why certain materials are accredited vehicles for art could not possibly have arisen much before the nineteenth century, and it is as the transformation of a particular set of materials that each art originates. One direction in which Wollheim's insight presses is toward forms of externalism: mental images derive their content from physical things, and if they don't maintain a constant dialogue with the external world, they dissolve at best into sketchy schemata. The mental life that Croce privileges is given content by the world. Indeed, one should throw versions of the private language argument at Croce and company with regard to images or melodies; in a sheer internal gallery, there are no right or wrong answers to questions about content or meaning. Human creative processes cannot possibly take place in the mind alone.

The arts and crafts create webs of connection stretching outward indefinitely: to materials and hence to nature and technologies, to other human beings, and to God (if any). The characteristic stance of the crafter is *devotion*, and art might be defined as devoted making. Not all artists and crafters have conceived this devotion in religious or spiritual terms, but many or perhaps most have. The devotion of the Shaker craftsman is to the perfection of the utilitarian objects he produces as an expression of his devotion to the maker of this world: craft as prayer. Or it is a participation as creator with God's creation, a way we are made in God's image—are ourselves crafted by God—and a way we are assigned to help make the world, our apprenticeship.

Wollheim's answer was obviously right, once you gave him the notion that there was actually a material world that we lived in: the painter conceived his work in terms of paint from the outset: the mental activity was a trace of the physical engagement; the mental activity was continuous with the physical manipulation of the material. There was not, Wollheim said, a primordial "artistic" or "creative" impulse which could be expressed in different media, though there might be an impulse connecting one medium to another. The impulse was to create by working a particular material.

Art has to be conceived in terms of intensity and extensivity of connection, or as a demonstration that connectedness is the mode of our being. The devotion to materials of a master craftsman is at once an emptying of the self and a realization of it in materials, both a reduction of the self's inwardness and an expansion of it into the world, into actual physical stuff. I think it is a central crystallization of human life and activity and experience, in that it has value both intrinsically and instrumentally. I don't think our lives are stories, but our lives might be apprenticeships that entail an ever-deepening set of skills. Probably there are many possible shapes for lives, but craft is one I could want. It is the condition of all of us at all times: none of us is not connected to everything, shaping it and being shaped by it. But the arts and crafts explore these connections explicitly, consciously, and extremely elaborately; and the arts and crafts communicate such explorations, which is also a way to rearticulate connections, environments, and hence consciousness, too.

6.

One way that the arts have been mislocated is in terms of the account of "aesthetic properties" as formal properties, and, again, the contrast of form with matter. We would associate this doctrine with Kant, of course, though it was articulated earlier by Shaftesbury and could be said to be implicit or nascent in aesthetic discourse throughout the eighteenth century. Formal properties would be shape, line, mass, possibly color: the arrangement as presented to sense in contrast of the sort of interpretation that would treat it as "meaningful," as telling a story or conveying a character, narrating a history or portraying a fact, for example: "content," in short. Now, in Shaftesbury, working from a long neo-Platonic tradition particularly centering on the Italian Renaissance, form is centralized precisely in contrast to matter, and unformed matter is treated as the very essence of the ugly, which was also Plotinus's position. Art, for Shaftesbury in *The Moralists*, is the application of the power or force of spirit to the material world, embodied above all in *disegno* or drawing, very much the sort of position rationalized by Kant later in the century.

"In painting, sculpture, and in fact in all the formative arts," Kant writes, "in architecture and horticulture insofar as fine arts, the *design* is what is essential. Here it is not what gratifies in sensation, but merely what pleases by its form, that is the fundamental prerequisite for taste."[6] Kant distinguishes "free" and "dependent" beauty and says, "In the estimate of a free beauty (according to mere form) we have the pure judgement of taste."[7] The Kantian program, to some extent, drives the arts for almost two centuries after he wrote and particularly sets painting and sculpture on the road to pure abstraction. And what drives Kant, as he makes plain many times, is the idea that aesthetic experience is a way to overcome our grubby engagement in the material world, to liberate us from nature or to show that we are more than animals.

That is, formalism emerges historically from idealism with its attack on the body and the physical world. But the arts and crafts are, again, in their essences, modes of engagement with the material. In defending the arts as an exalted or important activity, the art theorists of high Modernism betrayed the arts in their entirety. And much art was actually produced in service of this program; for example, formalism helped drive the invention of abstract painting and sculpture in the West. I want to remark, however, that no painting, whether abstract or figurative, is not the result of a process with materials, and even the works that were produced from formalism were counterexamples to it. Also, the form of any object is the arrangement of its material. Perhaps in the intellect, form and matter can be distinguished. In the real world, there is never either without the other. Form is where the matter is, the structure and distribution of matter.

The value of sheer form, of "the arrangement of lines and colors," in Clive Bell's terms, is rather mysterious, and in exalting the value of Significant Form and identifying it with art, Bell resorts to many a sublime metaphor or quasi-mystical gesture: "the snow-white peaks of art," and so on.

> Let no one imagine that a representation is bad in itself: a realistic form may be as significant, in its place as part of the design, as an abstract. But if a representative form has value, it is as form, not as representation. The representative element may or may not be harmful; always it is irrelevant. For, to appreciate a work of art we need bring with us nothing from life, no knowledge of its ideas or affairs, no familiarity with its emotions. Art transports us from the world of man's activities to a world of aesthetic exaltation.[8]

In exalting the arts, Kant and Bell make them by definition irrelevant to human life, which I think is a bizarre betrayal of their actual role, and an extreme impoverishment of their interpretation. I am more interested in following the arts toward immanence, which is where I think they naturally lead: toward particular objects and particular processes of devoted making or participation in the world's becoming. And the value of skilled making cannot be doubted; it is entirely characteristic of our species, and we would be extinct without it. (On the other hand, certain kinds of skilled making may end up extinguishing our species entirely.) We value skills as virtues of character, and they require many of the virtues: patience, fortitude, even love. And we value the product of skill as making our practical activities more effective and more intrinsically satisfying, and for making many practical activities possible in the first place.

7.

The idea that beauty must either be located in the subject or in the object (it is almost always then said to be located in the subject) is a false and crushing dilemma. If we treat beauty as a property of objects apart from subjects, we seem to omit the transport of soul, or at any rate the pleasure, with which we associate beauty. That seems to leave us without an account of the wide variations in the appreciations of various persons, eras, times, cultures; or at least it seems to suggest that some of these appreciations ought to be disqualified. And then it would be incumbent upon us to produce criteria by which we could make this disqualification, and there appear to be no standards by which we could establish some such criteria to be better than others. Indeed, the idea that anyone is called upon to disqualify other people's appreciations, or to function as the taste police, appears arrogant, oppressive, and arbitrary.

Then again, the idea that beauty is a subjective state—a variety of pleasure, for example—is entirely out of keeping with the way the term is normally used, and with the actual experiences it picks out. It would be odd to gaze upon the Pacific Ocean at sunset and then to find your own response beautiful, or to attribute the beauty to your pleasure;[9] the pleasure is not beautiful and is certainly not beauty itself or its source; the pleasure is a response to a beautiful thing, or rather situation. Beauty calls us out of ourselves into the beautiful thing; that's exactly why it produces pleasure, and locating the beauty in your subjective state, or taking the pleasure to be the beauty, is a sad solipsistic falsification of the experience that loses all that is important about it, loses what we take pleasure in; it's a sense-data theory for beauty. Indeed, the idea that beauty is subjective misplaces beauty entirely. Beauty cherishes its object: the experience of beauty is turned outward: it is an emptying or a dedication of the self to something outside itself. There are myriad beauties, not because human beings are capable of myriad pleasures (we're not, really), but because of the profusion of things. Experiencing the beauty of a rose is not like experiencing the beauty of the night sky which is not like experiencing the beauty of a movie star. The beauty of any beautiful meal is different than the beauty of any other beautiful meal. What I appreciate when I appreciate a beautiful thing is not my own transport of soul, or else I lose even the transport of soul and sink into an egocentric or narcissistic delectation of my own mental states.

Beauty is a form of connection to a particular thing or event, and it is of all experiences most attentive to the details of things, the differences among things, the real externality and the real connection and the real profuse character of real things. It can only be accounted for as an entanglement: a situation in which person and thing are embedded, as a connection between them that encompasses environing conditions, and also vocabularies and other social practices. And I would like to treat beauty as in that respect exemplary of the traditional material of axiology, or what are usually conceived to be values, such as moral goodness, the rightness of actions, and justice in social systems. None of these can be considered subjective, and none of them do not implicate consciousnesses and practices. Beauty, goodness, rightness, justice are—like knowledge, like experience, like truth for semantic entities—entanglements. They are situations or emerge in situations in which individual human beings and human groups are entangled; they are certain sorts of connections, of people with one another, and of people with other sorts of animals and other living things, and of people with inanimate objects. Each situation which is good or just or beautiful is a site at which the autonomy of a person and the autonomy of other things is compromised or in which things and persons enter into real connections with one another.

Now, on the other hand, beauty holds the distinctness of its objects precious, as I've said. The externality of the object is venerated: beauty does not merely put things to use; it cherishes connections, but also autonomies; it is a mode of respect. And to respect connections, we must also hold dear the things that are connected. A situation is a juxtaposition of distinct, though vague, things, not a single undifferentiated blob. One must be in relation to what one experiences as beautiful, but that entails that it must not be oneself. The beautiful thing must be juxtaposed with the subject in a situation that preserves and constitutes both their connection and their separation. Connection is impossible without compromising the identities of the things that are connected, but it is also impossible without those identities; things must be compromised in their integrity, but they must be cherished in their integrity. Nothing can merge with itself.

Another way to frame the question is by analogy to truth for semantic entities: the truth of an utterance is a complex situation involving the character of the utterer, the occasion or moment of the utterance, the linguistic practices within which the utterance occurs, the real-world things that are indicated in the utterance, and the situations in which they are all embedded together. Values, in this sense, are semantic entities or meanings: situations in which subject and object are embedded and in which their distinctness is compromised and emphasized.

So "the tree is beautiful" implicates the social in, for example, a romantic celebration of nature (behind it lurks Joyce Kilmer or Muir or Thoreau or Wordsworth, etc.: a whole history and vocabulary of appreciation characteristic of big swathes of culture). It implicates the social for that matter in that "beautiful" is a word and there are no private languages. "Tree" is a word too, believe it or not. That it picks out what it does and fails to pick out what it doesn't isn't any individual's decision. Perhaps it implicates the social in that in emitting the utterance I am trying to do something with you or to you: impress you, agree with you, attack you, distract you. But at any rate, entirely delete the "individual" or "subjective" dimension of the experience and it is senseless to talk about beauty. But I also insist on this—and here I call on the shades of Muir, Thoreau, and Wordsworth to testify—when I say "the tree is beautiful," I am talking about the tree, not about myself. "The tree is beautiful" does not mean "I feel funny."

Beauty, rather, is a feature of a situation in which the beholder and the thing beheld are both embedded. Or, beauty is an entanglement. Indeed, it is also not contained in the sheer pair beholder/object, but in a complete situation, including an environment in which object and beholder are both embedded: an atmosphere, an outpouring of light or sound through the air. And it implicates also the history of each element: beauty is not a formal property but a fully contextual one. It matters when and where soul music emerged, and in order to assess the beauty of "All Your Kissin (Sho Don't Make Good Lovin)" by Betty Wright you are going to need to ramify it out through a series of histories: of black popular music, of race relations, of commercial music concerns, and so on. Every situation is infinitely complicated because each thing in it is infinitely related to elements internal and external to it. But people who are in the situation can make such judgments or have such already richly interpreted experiences, often effortlessly.

In this sense, beauty is quite characteristic of our concepts; it is no more subjective than most, and it is a feature of the real world because, of course, the whole situation—including the social practices and the "inner" response of the beholder—is part of the real world. But it is a particularly intense and . . . positive mode of entanglement for a "subject": an affirmation of this world. Seeking beauty is explicitly seeking intensity of relation and pleasure in and transformation by it. Sometimes I am tempted, with Moore, to think it's the point of this whole kaboodle, or one of the few points. But I am more concerned to regard beauty as continuous with and as an element of all sorts of experiences: in the crafts, as I say, for example, where the beauty might be everywhere; in the object; in the process of making and the process of using; in the hand and heart of the master; in the materials; in the users or the audience; in the home in which the object takes up a place, for example. Or also, beauty is a mode or a multiplicity of modes of immersion in the world; it requires openness, sensitivity, permeability; and it is connected to love in all dimensions: we love what we find beautiful, or find beautiful what we love. Beauty is erotic, among other things, and the erotic impulse is an impulse to allow one's emotional carapace, or indeed one's actual skin, to be compromised. The experience of beauty, I want to say, is the best example of what this book says everything is.

8.

In *Six Names of Beauty* I defined "beauty" as "the object of longing." There were political objections to that, especially as I immediately went on to women. My bad! Also the whole thing was a bit misleading and overly general. But to me it got the essential thing, I suppose. I meant "object" to register that what was beautiful wasn't the alleged pleasure chemicals going off like fireworks in your brain, but that apple tree. Then "longing" was supposed to contribute the subjective element, culminating not in an argument but an observation to the effect that you shouldn't get caught in the false dilemma between yourself and the things around you. I'll say this: the last thing you want to do is go killing or exhausting beauty with a theory: leave the thing vague, and then enjoy. Then I riffed on "longing": unfulfillable desire, the condition of a human being or even of a finite creature in time, the condition of mortality, the aching experience of finitude, or of a heterosexual man among lovely women or whatever it may be. It's cosmic!

Plato's *Symposium* is among the most astonishing and influential documents in intellectual history. I would wonder briefly about the provenance of the text; it hints at an apocryphal scriptural tradition around Socrates, although it is hard to tell which is really the apocrypha, *Symposium* or *Republic*. In my view the text has fueled an incredibly rich and problematic esoteric tradition: one might mention Ficino and Strauss. Well, it is certainly a cult of what we would call gay sex, in a particular configuration, as it were: where the sex is part of the beautiful youth's education. So, that's pretty funky. I have a feeling that this idea was elaborately incorporated into the Catholic Church, though not usually in its exoteric teachings except insofar as it is related to misogyny or perhaps gynophobia. But I think the *Symposium* first of all frames Idealism in a completely different way than much of the Platonic corpus: it makes the whole thing fundamentally erotic rather than rational (though, of course, it points to an integration of these), and connects it to becoming as well as being, with finitude aspiring to infinity by yearning. But also, it is full of jokes, even at the expense of its own vision, embodied above all in the figure of Alcibiades. It certainly hints that underneath the relatively dry exercises in dialectic or tributes to sheer reason, there is a rich, complicated, and problematic erotic world of philosophical longing.

The author of the *Symposium* affirms one thing above all: erotic longing is what draws us toward the truth. *Eros* is affirmed emphatically, even as it is, of course, also to be constrained in certain ways, or to the expression of certain sort of aspirations. Often in Plato, Socrates just seems baldly to condemn the world and the body as unreal and the source of evil and ignorance; here the author affirms it conditionally as the only place from which finite embodied creatures can start on a road to transcendence. But it's awfully easy only to quote the ladder of transcendence and its destination, leaving out the whole flirtatious drinking party. The *Symposium* hints at Socrates moving to an affirmation, even a hearty affirmation, of the world, a figure fully concealed in the *Phaedo*, for example.

The accounts of beauty that go with "disinterested pleasure" or "a compound ratio of uniformity to variety," for example, are just pitifully dry. They leave out the whole bizarre, rich, erotic lives of human beings among one another in a world: all the twists. I have to say that the *Symposium* affirms the twists. Of course, Sappho connected beauty to love before Socrates, and that connection is the basis of Edmund Burke's profoundly hetero theory of beauty.

> Man, who is a creature adapted to a greater variety and intricacy of relation, connects with the general passion the idea of some *social* qualities, which direct and heighten the appetite which he has in common with all

other animals. . . . The object therefore of this mixed passion, which we call love, is the *beauty* of the *sex*. Men are carried to the sex in general, as it is the sex, and by the common law of nature; but they are attached to particulars by personal *beauty*. I call beauty a social quality: for where women and men, and not only they, but when other animals give us a sense of joy and pleasure in beholding them, (and there are many that do so,) they inspire us with sentiments of tenderness and affection toward their persons; we like to have them near us, and we enter willingly into a kind of relation with them, unless we have strong reasons not to.[10]

This is exemplary in its connection of beauty with *eros*, and exemplary too in its relentless emphasis on relation, on the social broadly construed, in its naturalism and good sense too. Sorry about the sexism, which could be redacted. But perhaps what's more important for the theory of beauty is that you have the erotic, rather than what erotic you have. I think any philosophical treatment of the topic which doesn't place it in the realm of desire is impoverished and basically misleading. But beauty, engaged by longing or as longing, is always a longing for another; our yearnings that yield beauty and reflect it are ways we are drawn or driven outward. I do think probably the human erotic has a basis in the evolutionary imperative to propagate, as Socrates more or less says. Mating takes two mammals, traditionally; it takes actual bodies in juxtaposition and merger. Then the experience of beauty is one way we get drawn out of ourselves and into another, or in which we become permeable or vulnerable; this is why the experience of beauty is exemplary of situation.

Now, when Socrates starts climbing the erotic ladder through institutions to generalizations to numbers or whatever it may be, he thinks he's climbing toward truth. I'd locate truth as the bodies all around us. But in either case, the erotic is certainly one dimension of intense connection, an image perhaps of all mergers. If I were writing the *Symposium*, the particular erotic configurations celebrated would be different, and the final destination would be elsewhere. But the structure or rather process of wanting and loving and merging and separating and yearning and knowing might be the same.

9.

Along with formalism I will attack hedonism; they have been connected in some philosophies. So, first, though the experience of beauty may be pleasurable, it isn't, always. Or "pleasure" might just be too impoverished, or too mild, or too subjective a term to be of much help here, as in ethics. Certainly I've already had a crack at the idea that only pleasure and pain motivate people to do things, which is ridiculous. But a hedonistic (and hence subjectivist) account of human motivation and value in terms of pleasure and pain no doubt lies at the heart of accounts of beauty in terms of pleasure (of whatever sort: e.g., "disinterested"): if it's good it has to reduce to pleasure. I think there are disturbing beauties, or evil beauties, or questionable beauties. If beauty is connected to *eros*, well then it participates in the incredible multivalence of the erotic, which is always drawing people into new constellations: it might be a seduction into evil; or it might be a ladder to the stars. "So beautiful it hurts" is a relatively commonplace expression. Longing is not merely pleasurable.

Moore, in *Principia Ethica*, tries to clinch what we might call a certain sort of externalism with regard to ethical and aesthetic values simply by contrasting as situations those in which a good or beautiful thing exists from those in which it does not. "The question I am putting is this: Whether the *whole* constituted by the fact that there is an emotional contemplation of a beautiful object, which both is believed to be and is *real*, does not derive some of its value from the fact that the object *is* real?"[11] The way I'd like to read this question is: "Are not values situations? Do they not encompass things as well as feelings, or the two in juxtaposition?" At every stage, Moore is fighting the idealist undertow of his moment, but I don't think that philosophers have sufficiently availed themselves of Moore's treatment of value. The view is—surely consciously—poised precisely opposite Kant, who argued that insofar as you really found something beautiful or had an experience of disinterested pleasure in regard to it, you were indifferent as to whether it existed or not; you were to regard it as a pure sensual appearance, not as meaning or indeed being anything.

Earlier I quoted parts of this:

> It has been . . . commonly supposed that the beautiful may be defined as that which produces certain effects upon our feelings; and the conclusion that follows from this—namely, that judgments of taste are merely subjective—that precisely the same thing may, according to circumstances, be both beautiful and not beautiful—has very frequently been drawn. . . . [But] to assert that a thing is beautiful is to assert that the cognition of it is an essential element in one of the intrinsically valuable wholes we have been discussing; so that the question, whether it is truly beautiful or not depends upon the objective question whether the whole in question is or is not truly good, and does not depend upon the question whether it would or would not excite particular feelings in particular persons.[12]

Again, I take this to be a classical statement of the idea that a value can be an entanglement, that it might or must have a location across subject and object. This passage is, as a number of commentators have remarked, somewhat obscure. But the point is precisely that Moore is refusing to get caught in the objective/subjective dilemma. His ethics might be read along these lines too, and the idea of values as situations encompassing subject and object is also made available precisely by Moore's realism: Moore's ontology, bizarrely enough for its era, includes a real external world, the existence of which he had proven to his own satisfaction, and mine.

Indeed, Moore's famous idea that it is beauty and sociality that make life worth living (more or less the credo of the Bloomsbury Group) has a nice flat as well as exalted ring, characteristic of Moore: "By far the most valuable things we know or can imagine, are certain states of consciousness, which may roughly be described as the pleasures of human intercourse and the enjoyment of beautiful objects."[13] Here he sounds like a subjectivist, and then he keeps making preconcessions. "I have myself urged in Chap III that the mere existence of what is beautiful has *some* intrinsic value; but I regard it as indubitable that Prof. Sidgwick was so far right, in the view there discussed, that such mere existence of what is beautiful has value, so small as to be negligible, in comparison with that which attaches to the *consciousness* of beauty."[14] Moore could be extremely elaborate in his irony, and what interests him in the rest of the chapter, as in his epistemology and his ethics, is the existence of real and beautiful, or real and good things "externally to the mind" and the contribution of that existence to the whole that includes the consciousness of them. "But then," he seems to say, "there is the trivial matter of whether beautiful things exist or not . . . well, it matters a bit; it's not as important as consciousness of course." But it is precisely in his insistence on the importance of beautiful things coming actually to exist in the world that this becomes an inspirational program for the Woolfs and Stephens, and even the Bells and Frys, though they take the matter in a directly idealizing formalist direction. I imagine Clive Bell and G. E. Moore at the opening. Moore nods along as Bell asserts that to appreciate art we need bring with us nothing from life and then strolls over to one of the postimpressionist paintings, raps on it with his knuckle, and grins, doing again his analytic Diogenes.

In "the pleasures of human intercourse," too, we are moving outward rather than inward, or both, but the point is to enter into relations with real other persons; quietly, Moore's ethics and his aesthetics keep bringing you back to a sort of humble wonderment at the real, a conviviality with everything. It is very much in the spirit of Burke. True, says Moore, what really matters are the pleasures. However, these certainly seem rather general and unspecifiable if we restrict our attention to what's going on in the subject. Well, it does vaguely matter that these other people with whom you are, as it were, having intercourse, are actually real people. Just a little, you know. To show this, he goes Matrix.

> We can imagine the case of a single person, enjoying throughout eternity the contemplation of scenery as beautiful, and intercourse with persons as admirable, as can be imagined; while yet the whole of the objects of his cognition are absolutely unreal. I think we should definitely pronounce the

existence of a universe, which consisted solely of such a person, to be *greatly* inferior in value to one in which the objects, in the existence of which he believes, did really exist just as he believes them to do.[15]

Whatever his fully considered view, Moore is certainly attacking subjectivism in both ethics and aesthetics; some of our feelings are good, but their goodness also depends in part on their engaging the right objects in the right ways: the value is a configuration or array.

What if you thought seriously about a thing you think is beautiful in this wise? What sort of thing it is and where it comes from and of what and by what or by whom it was made; how it is connected to you, that is, what conditions of the environment make it possible to experience the thing at all and to experience it in the way you are experiencing it; what alterations this experience is making in your sensory organs and emotions; how you would describe it or what features or dimensions of it struck you: what vocabularies or concepts are relevant and what are their histories; how it appears in the experience of other people, and what conditions make that possible; how people communicate about it and what sort of discourses or communities arise among its appreciators/critics; what it sets moving into the future; and so on.

Consider a storm; a hummingbird; the Bill Monroe song "When the Golden Leaves Begin to Fall" and all its cover versions (particularly the Johnson Mountain Boys'); the woods at night; a Broadway musical; that perfect glass of whatever it may be; a Vermeer; a starlet; your mother; a feather; an elegant solution to a chess problem; a quiet moment; a deafening concert; dancing, dancing, dancing.

All right? Start with the right thing and its relations to you and to other things and your relations to it as well: if it's beautiful, some of these relations are intense and accessible in experience. Now, perceive that there is no limit to the situation you are in, even as you isolate something or someone for delectation or use or collaboration. That is a revelation of the truth of our condition, which is more or less what Plato and Iris Murdoch think beauty is, only it is not the sort of thing they think it is. It was right here, all the time.

Where Moore does not go, but where his basic insights could easily draw him, is into a series of wider characterizations of relevant situations for the purposes of understanding value. For one feature of the sociality that he identifies as a fundamental value is that it can be configured around experiences and objects of beauty or aesthetic objects more broadly construed. This is what Moore and Bell and Woolf and Keynes and Strachey would do of an evening. The aesthetic object is constituted partly in its social context as well, of course, and partly by environmental conditions of all sorts, and by all sorts of conditions of the embedded subjects and objects: the lighting, the temperature, what booze we're serving, but also the aesthetic vocabularies and practices of Bloomsbury and the histories that lead up to them and the ways they encroach on or contradict various aesthetic practices around them: after all, we're dealing with a rebel avant-garde of sorts.

10.

It might seem that the sort of realism I am pushing throughout this book is incompatible with what might be termed "social constructionism." Well, yes and no. I do not think anyone's going to be constructing anything without nonhuman creatures and objects, and identities of various sorts have to be constructed as bodies and around bodies. But on the other hand, we are certainly entangled with one another, and I think it is very important to hold on to the fluidity of identities; people are constantly forgetting how volatile the spectrums of race or sexual orientation are; they are always trying to freeze your gayness or straightness, for example, into your genes or brain chemistry. I think this is rather silly, because if you look at the variety of ways that sexual identities have been distributed across various cultures and subcultures over periods that are infinitesimal on an evolutionary scale, you see very broad shifts and global reconfigurations. Even if orientation, gender, and race bear various complex relations at a given time to biological differences and similarities, it is worthwhile considering all of them in relation to social practices and socially articulated subjectivities, or to see them as in part explicable within a social context, or as social constructions, as vocabularies or repertoires shifting over time (and also in relation to economic practices, or education, or other fundamentally human areas: areas inside history, we might say). This might also shed some light, however, on what a "social construction" is.

Speaking of the erotic as the source of beauty, I suggest, for example, that gender and sexual identities, for example the male/female and gay/straight dyads, whatever else they may be, are aesthetic repertoires. They are, we might say, fundamentally systems of the arts. However, it is important to take "arts" or "the aesthetic" in their broadest possible scope. I want to include, for example, bodily comportment or movement styles, including dance and sport but also styles of walking or laying down; manners of articulation or communication; slangs, informal or formal poetries and polemics, verbal and written styles; personal adornment including clothing and hairstyles and body alteration of various sorts, plastic surgery or piercing; distributions of the environment as in interior design or landscaping, the design and arrangement of artifacts and styles of shelter, architecture and design arts at their broadest sweep; crafts or ways of making or manufacturing; sound design including music; scents and cookery; film and video and social media; and so on.

This list is generated by starting with what are commonly accepted as "the fine arts" and then taking on board the insight that there are no defensible distinctions between fine and popular art, between art and craft, between art and technological making. So, poetry is an art, but people use words in felicitous or euphonious or intentionally surprising or cacophonous ways all the time. Dance is art, but it opens up the ways bodies move, quite in general, to aesthetic consideration, as dancers such as Yvonne Rainer have done quite intentionally. Paintings dangle on walls, but that's only one of myriad ways people compose their environments.

Now, one thing to notice about all these things is that they make use of other things. There's no use calling your outfit merely social code or vocabulary; you'd better have the fabric and then the fabric's making in mind, too. One good thing about centralizing the arts conceptually is that they are social practices that always obviously make use of things and transform things. But of course your outfit does also function as a social vocabulary, and you are conveying all sorts of things about your identity by the way you dress, while even what's possibly available emerges from a set of social practices around clothing, even in cases where one intentionally defies or teases the going conventions.

So, for example, it's not necessary to agree quite with Judith Butler that the man/woman split is a matter of performance rather than biology to note that it is at least in part a matter of performance. The ways we experience the gendering of others and the way we express our own gendering to others is largely contained in things like styles of movement and clothing, hair growth and removal, scents and grooming procedures, and preferences in the arts. For example, there is media (cable networks, Internet zones) generally aimed at women and media generally aimed at men. But then as well as the apparently normative cases we've got to keep in mind all the crossings, betrayals, and emigrations, all the tiny bits of gender dysphoria: pretty much all media are available to anyone.

David Halperin holds out for a meaning of "gay," a perfectly good historical use, that refers to more than what sort of body one wants to have sex with.

> I'm going to argue that the transformation of homosexuality from a sexual perversion into a social identity, and the political requirements of gay pride, have tended to militate against any serious gay inquiry into the inner life of homosexuality—especially those *nonsexual* dimensions of it that gay people are still unsure or nervous about. Gay subjectivity, and the distinctive cultural practices that manifest it, may now have become just as disreputable, just as taboo, as queer sex. . . . My basic problem with the political functioning of gay identity nowadays is that in the course of claiming public recognition and acceptance of the fact of homosexual *desire* (sometimes at the expense of gay sex, to be sure), the official gay and lesbian movement has effectively foreclosed inquiry into the queer sensibility, style, emotion, or any specific, nonsexual form of queer *subjectivity* or *affect* or *pleasure*.[16]

Halperin is referring, perhaps somewhat nostalgically, to the world of the gay bar, the drag queen, diva culture, opera saturation, cross-dressing or cross-cross-dressing, and so on, and he's focusing on the "subjectivities" from which these things emerge and the pleasures they make available. This is sensible, but I would prefer, rather than to start with subjectivities and pleasures, to start with the incredibly elaborate aesthetic practices, mutating over time, that are associated with "gay culture." The subjectivities, it seems to me, have to articulate themselves by and large from these elements, even while they also reinforce them or create subversive zones within them. And it is all very well to refer to such things as "nonsexual," but they are pervasively erotic, as the very emphasis on pleasure attests. *Desires* are being communicated in aesthetic vocabularies, often ironically or with a twist, and beauty emerges from these desires; the whole of the aesthetic interchange within gay culture is erotically charged and volatile, but so are the relations of that culture to the other subcultures, and they to it.

Let's begin by exploring one simplistic set of relations, or grid of four boxes: female and male, gay and straight. First you get the disclaimer: everything is at an absurdly general level: I'm trying to describe an entangled cultural imaginary; no person occupies any point in the taxonomy with perfect centrality—and that goes for male and female as well as gay and straight and the various clusters of taste. Also every interstice is occupied.

My idea is that each of these things is centrally an aesthetic vocabulary. I suppose one could sum it up like this: a celebration of artifice, an apotheosis of appearance, an orientation toward spectacle. Go watch Katy Perry perform "California Gurls" in her film *Part of Me* and you'll see the sort of thing I mean. (When I wrote this, I had a twelve-year-old daughter.) Now, the appearance/reality split itself needs all sorts of examination; it is ideology as well as a metaphysics. But one way it needs examination is precisely as a gendered and orientated aesthetic pair. It's a complementary system, a yin/yang. You can't have one without the other. But I might just sketch: You're rococo, we're neoclassical. You're impressionist, we're cubist. You're pop, we're minimalist.

As styles, gender and sexual identities annex material from everywhere; so for example they absorb the appearance/reality distinction, now translated into a series of aesthetic expressions. Femininity, we might say, involves a composition of appearances, whereas masculinity deploys an aesthetics of reality. What is interesting about this is that it is not exactly metaphysics but not exactly not; femininity/masculinity translates appearance/reality into a series of tropes or symbols or narratives; it is definitely not a revelation of the very nature of reality, nor is it, I believe, its source; rather, it is at play with reality, showing its liquidity as well as its stubbornness. Nor should we regard femininity as the creation alone of straight women or of straight women under pressure by straight men. Gay men have rearticulated femininity profoundly, but then and hence masculinity as well, but then gay women have constant input to the meaning of masculinity, and femininity too: all of these things are in constant interchange, and what is reality at one moment or for one purpose is appearance at the next, or is deployed consciously as an aesthetic repertoire. All poles are being constantly naturalized and then appropriated in self-conscious or ironic aesthetic articulations. But this naturalization is redoubled or erased and reinscribed in masculinity.

So, we might think of ornament, cosmetics, scent as the witchcraft of femininity: a play with appearance that also signifies frivolity, pleasure, or an autoerotic enjoyment of the appearance of oneself one creates, as well as a seduction of the masculine or a disempowerment of it, an act both of acquiescence and resistance. But then, in relation to the structure of femininity, the aesthetic repertoire of masculinity comes to a certain consciousness, and one learns an ethics of simplicity or straightforward naturalness precisely as an aesthetic repertoire: one learns to move like a man, whether one is a man or not. One learns to move like a man within gay communities, or within lesbian communities, or within heterosexual male communities, or within mixed communities—in all of which masculinities are deployed—which is emphatically not to say that masculinity is a primordial character which gets reinterpreted in these contexts. For one thing, it is at stake in each context and always mutating, and what signifies truth or nature or reality at one time and place will not at another.

These roles or identities or aesthetic systems arise in a system of complements, but they are in action in time, like art movements, which they also literally are; they merge and diverge, divide within and coalesce across; the situation at a given time is complex and it's in the middle of reconfiguration. Without touching the biology or genetics at all, the way male and female and straight and gay and masculine and feminine function makes them, I think obviously, interdependent and unstable. Ultimately, the destabilizing element is desire, which constantly pushes and pulls each particle in different directions. The center or eye consists of all the sexual and erotic and aesthetic pairings and triangulations, all the ways people in different groups are drawn to each other and repelled by each other, all the places and ways they merge and segregate themselves from each other, and each other from themselves: psychologically, linguistically, musically, visually, sexually.

11.

The distinction between straight women and straight men—the immense Venus/Mars differences that supposedly make us incomprehensible to each other—are, of course, also the center of heterosexual erotics. We want to be incomprehensible to each other and hence be ourselves. This is actually symbolized in the yin/yang, for example: it's a fucking cosmology of difference. Within heterosexuality, the differences become more and more intense because they are the center of the erotic lives of both sorts of people. But what it means to be a heterosexual man is to emphasize the differentiation and want precisely people who drink creamy lattes and have closets full of incomprehensible grooming products and phones full of the worst music ever. We are conniving to make ourselves so different that we can't communicate, and so different that we can't not want, can't not be for one another what the other lacks.

Then again, precisely because of wanting, we are drawn into proximity. We get to know each other. We want to be friends. We're frustrated that we can't communicate. We try. We oscillate toward similarity, and, of course, we are massively the same as embodied human beings and as part of the same culture or system of identities, even if our bodies and cultures are a bit different too. We try to approach our heterosexual relationships homosocially. But and so, I don't think there's any objective normative weight in the eroticization of difference: sameness can also be eroticized (and every nuance in between). So we might call that homonormativity or yin/yin or yang/yang. But heterosexual men and women are the same—we are allied, affianced—in that we are heterosexuals, and gay men and women are both gay. So this dimension is not just in play within gay and lesbian groups. In every combination and in every point in between given nodes, there is both sameness and difference, and either might be used erotically or conceived as repulsive. Now, as, say, lesbians emerge into a kind of erotic solidarity, straight men are migrating to similar symbol systems and erotic configurations, and vice versa: or as the hets push out they enter into an erotics of identification with the homos of the other gender, scattering outliers throughout the journey. One thing I'm trying not to do here is make the het categories fundamental; or to define the homo categories as parasitic on the het categories: I do think in their contemporary configuration they are mutually simultaneously caused, and inconceivable except as a whole system.

We might consider the aesthetic of "cool," which I propose at least originates as a straight male category: classic examples are Humphrey Bogart and Miles Davis. Coolness suggests simplicity, stillness, dignity, a withdrawal in some sense from the social, or it suggests that one is not dependent emotionally on others. One of its opposites might be the fabulous: an aesthetic of over-the-top display that is a constant reaching out or the opposite of cool self-containment. The history of fabulousness might be as old as the aesthetic coalition of gay men and straight women, something coeval with it in the late nineteenth century or something. In a way it's a feedback loop in which people are egging each other on, for example in the whole of the way that Katy Perry is styled by a committee of gay men and straight women, as portrayed in *Part of Me*.

Again, one way into the aesthetics of gender/sexual identity is in terms of natural against artificial, which is part of the way the male/female yin/yang is set up. But in this context naturalness is, first, an ideology, and second, it is an aesthetic repertoire or set of conventions, and depends conceptually on the artificial. So, for one thing, heterosexuality itself has been conceived ideologically/aesthetically as natural, by virtue in part of its reproductive function, so that one conceived heterosexuality as an evolutionary imperative, and homosexuality as a twisted misexpression of the natural process of human reproduction. Whatever. Even in the straight man/straight woman pair, the construction is complementary, and straight men try to distinguish themselves from straight women, or to express masculinity, by contrast and by rejection and by finding straight women's aesthetic practices, especially self-ornamentation of certain kinds, incomprehensible. I think the coolness of a Miles or Humphrey is specifically constructed to contrast with a specific stage of femininity, which is why the Bogart/Bacall pair is perfect: a quite complex gendered array. Straight maleness *is*, precisely, a set of styles of self-ornamentation, of movement, speech cadence and so on that is no less stylized than its complement, but which by its own ideology must suppress this fact. And it is constantly mutating, partly by contrast to whatever constitutes the feminine or artificial at a given moment; or rather they mutate mutually, season by season. If you did the history of cool het men, the looks and mannerisms would be revealed as quite volatile period by period. The naturally masculine is a sequence of historical styles.

Let's start with "laconic"; we straight guys tend to think of other groups as chattering too much. Thus Eastwood's Man with No Name in the spaghetti Westerns: so withdrawn is he from language that there is no word for him at all, or his name is the fact that he has no name. Or as Miles said, "I always listen for what I can leave out"—precisely the opposite of, say, a Liberace or operatic style of excessive expression. Guys are always wanting you to bottom line the thing, cut to the essence, just recite the plain facts, and the way gay men or straight women chatter and emote fills us with boredom and, possibly, loathing. We want words and other things to be of use: they and everything else ought to be restricted to their utilitarian function. Now, this may appear to be an anti-aesthetic mode of comportment, precisely a rejection of ornament, or whimsy, or excess, or appearance. But it is, I am asserting, just as much an aesthetic as its complement, and, if you will pardon my saying so, just as conscious of itself as an aesthetic, and just as important and excellent as part of the world's aesthetics. It's a Catholic/Protestant split, a Baroque/Classical split, abstract expressionist/minimalist. Both sides are equally aesthetic; both sides, provisionally, are equally valid as aesthetics.

So one thing we need to understand is how volatile the aesthetic expressions are over time and how subject they are to many inputs. So, for example, having hippie-length hair or New-Wavish earrings might, at some times, have offended normative masculinity or even got you kind of gay bashed, whatever your sexuality. By the 1980s at latest, though, younger redneck guys had adopted long hair (David Allen Coe circa 1980: "My long hair just can't cover up my red neck"), and now a country star like Brantley Gilbert or Jason Aldean manages to signal masculinity with jewelry, though it really matters in detail exactly what the jewelry is like: Gilbert favors black and silver, and his rings would be pretty functional weapons, while the bracelets have the quality of gauntlets. Indeed, one sort of has to infer what Brantley Gilbert looks like under all the decoration, just as Dwight Yoakam or Clint Eastwood hid behind a hat in a way that almost made them each into a logo or symbol. I think that in the case of country music you see an aesthetic coalition of straight men and straight women, and one thing to look at is the way men get done up in this context; as I say, the affiliations are complex, the crossings continual. For one thing, people consume in pairs and groups, so that if a straight woman and a straight man are coupled up, they have to negotiate about the music, find things they can both stand or stations they can listen to when all else fails, ways to look that keep the others' interest.

The volatile swirl of sexual/aesthetic identities is an erotic vortex or tornado, in which people are pulled in all sorts of directions by identifications and by misidentifications or disavowals. So the fact that I'm not female, and that I signal that with an entire repertoire—the way I move, the way I dress or groom, the way I adorn my environment, and so on—just is also the fact that I'm male: a complete aesthetic arsenal, but one that only makes sense in relation to its complements. And then the fact that I'm straight, well, that makes use of the same stuff. And so does the fact that you're not a straight woman. And then, with a tilde, that you're not a lesbian; then, that you're a gay man; then, with a tilde, that I'm a straight man, and so on, on each whirl picking up more debris, the whole thing changing shape as it spins. And in this storm, each individual is altered or damaged or consolidated or compromised, changed internally by the aesthetic storm in which it is caught: each individual as well as the whole is in flux in its identity. It gets exponentially more complex because you've got all sorts of other social/aesthetic categories involved: race, for example. And each vocabulary can be used ironically, even from within: each is subject to parody. Each group is always welcoming a new young cohort with different cultural icons, outfits, slangs, and so on, which is one way it evolves over time. And even if Katy Perry is demonstrably inspiring young gay men, their elders have their own icons or their more mature taste, which also ranges up and down class identities, so there's highbrow gay aesthetics and rowdy lowbrow celebration, and those are themselves in interaction.

What tugs or attracts or magnetizes in the experience of beauty is the force of unsatisfied or even unsatisfiable desire: and every identity expresses a different dimension or vocabulary of longing by embodying its vision of beauty. This is what drives the cyclone round and round, as people reaffiliate and reexpress, catch up or hold on. We might consider the cult of the diva, with all its doubly complex longings for the same and for the different. One thing a diva is likely to be is a sex symbol among heterosexual men: the diva manifests various flavors of extreme femininity. Gay and straight men end up appreciating Beyoncé from different angles, but certainly erotically both ways round, or in different registers of the erotic: yearning to identify or yearning to possess, which are not entirely separable ideas. But then these pairs might also put the eroticization of differences at an ironic distance, might put them in play, might be too conscious of them to regard them as natural, might see them as erotic resources rather than unbridgeable gaps.

There are many oppressions in this unfolding situation, long histories of oppression that are also eroticized, as dominance and submission, for example. Also these patterns are complex. For example, if gay men are oppressed as gay in patriarchy, they are also privileged as male in the same system, and there is also a history of gay misogyny: even in the simplest square each identity is doubled or multiplied. But even with all its weight, we don't want to be without the system of identities, because then we'd stop wanting, and also become incomprehensible to ourselves. There are also many liberations, many zones of liberation, many Stonewalls in this configuration or process. All sorts of loves and all sorts of beauties are opened up as possibilities in the midst of the storm; it's the longings opening up within and across that make the beauty possible or give rise to it or even are it.

What I think we should want to do with these identities is not destroy or overcome them: no one really has that power even if they are sheer or mere cultural constructions. (However, they are also material constructions, and among other things would have to be literally disassembled.) What we should do is play with them. We need to try to lighten the weight, or some of the power of these systems to configure hatreds—hatreds of the same and hatreds of the different—even as we try to hold on to the ways they configure loves. For these are also systems of exclusion, of course, or that's just to say the same thing again. What you want to try to do is increase the pleasure of them and decrease the pain, and I say the best place to focus and celebrate is the art, taking art at its broadest possible sweep, from body presentation to food to music to scent to interior design to cityscape. This is where the play of differences is relatively harmless, but profound. You can't have the identities without exclusions or at least judgments of taste that more or less condemn what is in contrast. But the question is: to what extent can you have these judgments without contemplating destruction?

In short, we should really love each other. Secretly or not, we do. We certainly need each other and depend on each other and want each other. We should stay different and we should yearn and try to appreciate. We should slum in each other's bars from time to time, and smile. I think if you let these things play with you and play with them, the system might become more liquid or improvisational or multidimensional. But it might even get more extremely differentiated or simplified, which could be interesting too if it doesn't freeze. But you want to start thinking of the gender/sexuality square as an immense set of aesthetic resources, which are also ways to be.

12.

Here I would like to emphasize something which we have had plenty of opportunity to see already: that the self is also a swarm. This is as much true of the human self as it is of the universe as a whole as it is of a water molecule. As we have seen, the self is a site of power relations. But it is also an aesthetic site, partly in virtue precisely of those power relations, and any organization of the self raises aesthetic questions or has aesthetic aspects. You can see this, for example, in the structures of the self described by Plato or Freud: the tripartite classical constructions. We are still embroiled in these structures, now being converted into brain scans: your executive region should be subduing your amygdala. To say that these structures are simplistic and excruciatingly problematic is to state the obvious.

First of all, the system of social identities is marked on each self, and the flow of these identities over time tracks various flows within the self. The self is partially cobbled together out of gender roles or racial and class taxonomies, as well as specific representations of these in the media, for example, and specific instantiations of them in one's social milieu. This is an extraordinarily complex matter with regard to any particular person, and any particular person's racial and gender history—including the history of representations that a particular person has absorbed, for example, or what region a person is located in or what spot within that region, and so on—is just massively incomparable and hence individual. And then there are all the features, including the social, that are also more than social, all the material relations, of course, but the whole "internal" or "intrinsic" environment: all the internal negotiations, aspects of one's personality or personalities, all the self-loathings and self-delusions, all the ways we are turned into or against ourselves. I don't think you get much of anywhere dividing up the self into three or seven aspects or faculties or functions, as traditional as this project is (cf. Descartes, Spinoza, Hobbes): the self is quite the chaotic entanglement, really, and our attempts to pin it down and clear it up are, by and large, merely false.

If the way I have been describing gender and social identities is anything like right, however, one thing we can say is that whatever socially articulated identities we have, they are haunted by their others or articulated in their terms. There's no manifesting masculinity without engaging femininity in real detail by repudiation or by incorporation, or always both. This in itself marks the self as a complex, volatile multiplicity, as these categories are mutating externally to the self season by season, and then getting more or less internalized in a particular interpretation or manifestation. And to the extent that these identities are aesthetic repertoires, aesthetic vocabularies or the aesthetic administrations of the material world, they are also technologies of the self, and the self is an aesthetic environment. The incorporation of social identities is only one dimension that makes this obvious. One might think of the attempts of the self to be a self, or the extent and style to which and in which we cobble together something coherent or allow ourselves to lapse from coherence, as aesthetic modes of arraying. What "coherence" means in this context can only be addressed aesthetically, I believe.

One symptom or even cause of oppression is the conception of a self that is too coherent, too transparent to itself, too full of monadic quiddity. This is a sort of immortal, single soul, or the white man's identity: too pure not to be in constant danger of corruption; too insular even to experience the ways it is always being compromised. A self which is not experiencing its permeability to the external world also struggles to experience itself as an ambiguous or contradictory multiplicity, which only intensifies the contradiction, or adds terrifying layers of self-misunderstanding. One thing that is good about Freudianism, as opposed to many of its precursors, is that it really begins to make the self a very labyrinthine space, reflecting all sorts of incorporated and extruded aesthetic materials.

One thinker who I think registers the volatility and mutual interdependence of identities, as well as the ways they articulate the self as a multiplicity, is Julia Kristeva. And what she wants is not to seize and transform the representations in which such identities may (always provisionally, problematically, and ambiguously) be crystallized, but to appreciate their liquidity over time, and to use them as resources in transforming or compromising selves: the other as essential to the self, present all the more intensely in its exclusions, but distorted in the relation. "Let us not seek to solidify, to turn the otherness of the foreigner into a thing," she writes. "Let us merely touch it, brush by it, without giving it a permanent structure. Simply sketching out its perpetual motion through some of its variegated aspects spread out before our eyes today, through some of its former, changing representations scattered throughout history."[17] If we are to reduce the pain and increase the fun of our volatile, entangled social identities, we have to ditch out of various kinds of universalism, especially enforced universalism, where we are all considered the same on some fundamental level, and where, hence, we are constrained to be the same and constrain others to be the same. And, first, you have to celebrate hybrids and be a hybrid; we each need to acknowledge our actual location by depurifying ourselves or creolizing ourselves. Even the pure or most-insulated identities—those emerging from colonialism or black nationalism, say, or lesbian separatism—yield aesthetic and other resources by which the miscegenation can occur.

Whereas most portions of the tradition that acknowledge the soul's multiplicity prescribe an integration, or seek to achieve or recover a coherent self therapeutically or philosophically or spiritually, Kristeva, in suggesting that we refuse to "reify" or even offer an interpretation of the foreigner, suggests also that we might also by the same act refuse to reify or even offer an interpretation of ourselves, that we might acknowledge our own elusiveness and lostness to ourselves, merely brushing by it and letting it be.

She recommends acknowledging the alien within, or allowing the subject to disintegrate as well, or even affirm the fissures and confusions, the oppositions and incoherences, the tangledness of the self. The self, we might say, is also a social system. You could think of these partially as connected to social identities: the woman in the man, the gay in the straight, the black in the white, and vice versa and vice versa and vice versa. This is partly where we open and close ourselves to one another, or define what we can welcome and what we need to try to push away. But also that's not so simple, and complements can receive or exclude complements, and similars can receive or exclude similars. Gay and straight or black and white or male and female go together, of course, and repel one another, of course, as do gay and gay or black and black or female and female, as I've been arguing. And then though we try to simplify these things into pairs, or I do, they are infinitely divisible spectra in flowing relation, in nondenumerable conflagrations and intersections. Nor should we conceive of tangled selves internally as exhausted by being mirrors of the social; of course, the social reflects everyone's internal divisions and coherences as well, and we can read the social as a mirror of selves as well as the other way round. The social is also complexly embedded in all sorts of more-than-social situations, and no individual can be completely specified in terms of social relations or identities. Each of us is a swarm of genetic materials, hormones, impulses, molecules, loves, bacteria, in relation together as a body, in relation to the world.

What the aesthetics of identity shows, as well, is that these cannot be conceived as psychodramas or communions between minds or even as discourses; they are constantly in operation within and on the physical surround. To some extent, male and female, foreigner and native, and so on, are mutating aesthetic repertoires that involve actual fabrics, buildings, meals, knick-knacks: they both emerge from and ramify into nonhuman material things all the time: obviously, these things are no more or less real than human selves or social configurations, which are inconceivable without them. The aesthetic repertoires express or externalize the selves and the social situations, but constitute them as well; to a large extent racial or sexual identities, for example, just are aesthetic repertoires, but of course they are also economic situations or interchanges. They are also literal couplings or entanglements of bodies, or places of fucking and being fucked, or beating and being beaten, or nurturing and being nurtured, all of which compromise bodies and expand them, and all of which are configured by and configure natural or artifactual environments. And they are snarls within the self. When Kristeva moves from the story of immigration to the psychodrama of immigration or the self and the other within, she is moving from apparently physical situations to apparently psychological, but either is both, of course, and they are, as well, physical juxtapositions and aesthetic repertoires and located identities, configuring objects and configuring selves and making them real in the world.

13.

"Realism" in metaphysics is not the same thing as "realism" in painting, but they are connected. Let me try to say, first of all, how I intend to use the term "realism" in the context of the arts. The term certainly is used in a variety of senses in this sphere. "Realism," for example, picks out a nineteenth-century literary movement, associated with figures such as Balzac and Flaubert, which often focused on the quotidian lives of what we might term ordinary people. A connected movement in the arts, associated above all with the name Courbet, criticized academic history painting, for example, by exhibiting rough-hewn depictions of peasants painted on a heroic scale. Among other things, realism in this sense is highly political, and it turns to human reality—the truth of impoverished or stunted lives—in part as a motivation for a democratic or anarchist or communist transformation.

Courbet's realism is related to the sort of realism I want to talk about, but they aren't identical. I mean to pick out a recurring tendency in the history of Western visual arts, and in the arts of some other cultures, toward accuracy or verisimilitude, a devotion to the way things really look and, since the way things really look is a feature or aspect of the way they really are, a devotion to the way things are. In order to get a sense of what sort of things I'm going to be talking about, let's look at examples. So, compare a Madonna by Raphael to one from Metsys. One thing to notice about the Metsys (1529) is that it is composed of elements or details that would later be separated into landscape, still life, portraiture, and genre.

Now, I admit that the distinction between realism and all its opposites and relatives—idealism, impressionism, abstraction—is an extremely elusive one. Whether Ingres or Manet or Velázquez is a realist, or to what extent or in what dimensions their work is realistic: these are difficult questions. Certainly it's a matter of context and degree, and every intermediate point in occupied; a painting is relatively or extremely or sort of realistic, but it's never perfectly realistic, I believe; or else it would be a replica of what it depicts in every aspect. Now, the very idea that a painting can look more or less like what it's a painting of, or be more or less accurate, has been called into question by a number of philosophers and art theorists. All in all, no painting is much like a bowl of fruit; try taking a bite, if you don't believe me. But here, I am gesturing at certain works as realistic and others as unrealistic, or defining "realism" by ostension: paintings *like that* are realistic. I will leave it open right now whether "realism" marks out a family of conventions or practices, or whether in some direct sense realistic pictures are more like the things they depict than are unrealistic pictures.

One of the traditional opposites of realism in all its manifestations is idealism, a concept which is at least as multivalent and ambiguous as its antagonist. But at any rate realism and idealism are not only metaphysical or epistemological theories and styles of art; they are theories of representation. We might term these accounts of representation *mimetic* and *eidetic*. On a mimetic theory of representation, a picture is a picture of what it is a picture of in virtue of "imitating" it or reproducing certain aspects of it. This is a very ancient theory of representation and, more or less, of art, put forward in both Plato and Aristotle, for example. It becomes a theory of perception in the moderns. But developing in the Greeks at the same time, and also to a large measure attributable to Plato as a philosophical idea is the familiar notion that a picture might generalize from the particular, or might present something better or less contingent than everyday physical reality. Aristotle asserts that poetry is more philosophical than history, on the ground that poetry shows general truths, history particulars. From this point of view the great artist occupies a hallowed station as giving us a vision of a better or truer or more beautiful world, or as providing general truths that are unavailable elsewhere.

Plato, in *Republic* Book X, compares a painting or a poem to a mirror that shows the appearance of the world, and he condemns the representational arts on that ground. Leon Battista Alberti, in perhaps the most important treatise on art theory of the early Renaissance, says that painters and sculptors "strive, though by different skills, at the same goal, namely that as nearly as possible the work they have undertaken shall appear to be similar to the real objects of nature."[18] "That painting is most praiseworthy which conforms most to the object portrayed," Leonardo insisted, though one may wonder how well this account applies to Leonardo's own paintings.[19] Vasari, in his life of Masaccio, says that "painting is simply the imitation of all the living things of nature with their colors and designs just as they are in nature."[20] The mimetic view was the common wisdom from around 1400 until around 1700 in Europe, and it was more or less the official line of the Renaissance and early Baroque periods, both in southern and northern Europe.

The mimetic tradition runs in parallel with what I'm calling eidetic or idealistic views, which hold that the artist does not merely imitate real objects, but improves them: idealizes, makes more beautiful, or reveals the essences of things. In the *Symposium*, again, Socrates describes the allure of beauty as a seduction into the realm of the Forms: loving a particular beautiful person draws you to try to understand what beauty itself is. He does not explicitly tie this thought to the representational arts, but many followers for a couple of thousand years did just that. This is "Neoplatonism" as applied to the arts: they are a route from the particular to the general, from the physical to the spiritual, and they accomplish this by an idealization of everyday reality made possible by the imagination. Cicero, in a typical formulation, says this of the sculptor Phidias: "When he produced his Zeus or Athena, [he] did not look at a human being whom he could imitate, but in his own mind there lived a sublime notion of beauty; this he beheld, on this he fixed his attention, and according to its likeness he directed his art and his hand."[21] I term the underlying view of representation *eidetic* after the Platonic Ideas.

The great Neoplatonist Plotinus argued that the most beautiful things are the most abstract things, the least material things: the Forms, and in particular the Form of Beauty itself, which was also identical to goodness, truth, and God. He and like-minded figures in the Renaissance such as Marsilio Ficino conceived art as a transformation of sheer ugly matter by spirit into a semblance or image of what is unsullied by the material realm. Within this tradition, a kind of realism could be incorporated. Art is a bridge between the real and ideal, and so the real is indeed represented, but as idealized: for example in painting an ideal of female beauty, one was to study many beautiful women and assemble, as it were, the best bits of each into a semblance of the very Idea of Woman; this is one of the most ancient conceptions of the artist's task. The initial activity is mimetic, but the final product approaches the ideal of womanhood. Then the sexuality of the nude itself was supposed to have a spiritual dimension, and the relation to the ideal that transcends the mundane is an erotic relation that is first called forth by particular bodies.

I think this Neoplatonic orientation, which was cultivated by many humanist philosophers, literary figures, architects, and visual artists from let us say 1420 to 1600, accounts for the basic way that works of art tend to look in particular in the Italian High Renaissance. Raphael provides perhaps the very clearest examples. Looking at his paintings, you are in no doubt about their representational content and the disposition of the objects in space: the perspective rendering is perfect, and the people and things more or less familiar. That is, there are obviously many mimetic elements. But they are arranged with consummate consciousness into a geometrical or almost abstract array; they are extremely composed. Each person and each thing is a sort of emblem, more or less a perfect example of its kind. One does not dwell on wrinkles or imperfections or idiosyncracies, except insofar as these themselves are emblematic, as in the depiction of a wise old Plato in "The School of Athens." And we might remark that this style of painting relentlessly emphasizes the divinity of Jesus and the holy family, their transcendence of embodiment into a realm of celestial light.

Idealism of this sort, if I may be so bold, is perhaps an inspiring vision, but as regards the visual arts it is something of a dead end. I do not think that it's a coincidence that Raphael's Madonnas are, as has often been remarked, emotionally blank: in her divinity they transcend any particular personality. Beautiful as they are, they are just a little inhuman, a little too perfect for viewers as flawed as we are; they are disconnected from reality, quite intentionally. We still narrate the High Renaissance as embodied by Leonardo, Raphael, and Michelangelo as a culmination, and though there could be and have been other neo-Platonic arts, I'm not sure there have been or can be better neo-Platonic arts. Idealism is designed to be teleological; when art comes as close as possible to realizing the ideal in reality, then it has performed its task and, as Hegel hinted, it might could end. Indeed, the High Renaissance is often represented in sketches of art history as an almost instantaneous or infinitesimal moment of perfect equipoise. The stretch between where Leonardo emerges from the Early Renaissance and Michelangelo falls off into Mannerism is pretty short, and shrinks up shorter the harder you look. Have you ever jumped off a swing? First you rise, then you fall and land or crash. But there's that instant in the air where you at least have the illusion that you are quite still and weightless: that's the High Renaissance. Well, it's been quite the tumble since that momentary culmination. Hardly had art reached perfection than people grew weary of perfection and started pulling it apart or distorting it quite intentionally: a mannerist and baroque distortion and excess and whimsicality breaks out in your pristine ideal universe, almost at the moment you've finally got it cleaned up.

I think we have lost a sense of what is valuable about realism in the arts. This has to do with the turn in Romanticism and Modernism to the genius of the artist and the intensity of his expression as distinguishing features of art. And in complement, we now actually have devices that are capable of producing images instantaneously that might make Kalf or Chardin gasp or give up: mere mimesis is now something that can be done mechanically or digitally. My idea is that in recovering the tensions and connections between mimetic and eidetic representations, we can recover some of our sense of the value of realism, and hence reconnect more fully to important aspects of our visual traditions, not to speak of the world.

Before a series of disciplinary reconfigurations that took place in the late seventeenth and early eighteenth century, art was not necessarily clearly distinguished from science: both could be accounted for in part as ways of showing us how things really are, including the conditions under which they are perceived. In Renaissance humanism, the visual arts and the texts of antiquity are equally treated as sources of empirical knowledge, and careful observation in the sciences has always been reflected in careful illustration. Alberti and Dürer, indeed, argue that art is what we would term an empirical science, and they and other Renaissance figures pursued it as such, accompanying it with scientific accounts of light, color, and vision that relied heavily on the theory of perspective. Many, of course, dissected corpses in order to depict the human body accurately, and brought various sorts of items into the studio to render them as accurately as possible. Svetlana Alpers has documented the persistence of this vision of the arts in the use of lenses and instruments such as the camera obscura in seventeenth-century Dutch art and science, and in the connections between the artists and the scientists of the period. In an era before photography, even paintings and drawings by great masters could serve as both historical documents and instruments for the development and dissemination of empirical or scientific knowledge. Of course, pictures in general, and graphic representations of many sorts, have been central in the development of the sciences, which is usually recovered historically as a series of textually expressed theories, but which is also a history of depiction.

Another feature of the post-Renaissance reconfiguration of disciplines was the emergence of the fine arts as a sphere of activity in distinction from craft skills. The paintings of Gysbrechts or even Zurbaran are virtuoso displays of skill, something like conjuring tricks. When you go to see a stage magician, you know very well that you are not seeing a display of supernatural powers, but that the illusion is, finally, due to the skill and ingenuity of the performer and staff. This skill is itself necessarily hidden or concealed, which is itself a display of skill. At least some realist paintings are extremely impressive displays of hand skills in this sense, and they conceal the skill from the audience, which makes it all the more evident; you don't see the brushstrokes at all, and yet you know it's a painted surface and yet you can't not see it as a bowl or a tree or a letter rack. Now, in Romanticism, and certainly by the time of High Modernism, art is associated with intense emotional expression or the expression of genius. Van Gogh is certainly not as good as craftsman as Gysbrechts, but that's not the point, and there was a moment—say 1955—where one might have asserted, without great fear of disagreement, that van Gogh was an artist and Gysbrechts not. I think they are certainly both artists.

It is traditional that the Renaissance in Northern Europe hewed closely to the mimetic program, whereas the Italian Renaissance always proceeded with a greater admixture of idealism, though, of course, the matter is immensely complex. Roughly, however, I accept the traditional way of formulating the distinction. As we gaze astonished at the unimaginable skill of a Van Eyck, all of it devoted to getting every detail of the world as exactly right as possible, we see, I believe, the development, which lasted centuries, of a very conscious refusal of the ideal. Taking it the other way round, Northern European realism is a pointed affirmation of the actual. It is above all a this-worldly art. Among other things, this has theological implications; especially as applied to religious paintings, it suggests that God is found in the ordinary as well as the extraordinary. It emphasizes the embodiment, rather than the divinity, of Jesus. Raphael paints Mary as a Platonic Form. In Rembrandt's view, Mary is a perfectly ordinary young Dutch woman raising a baby in an artisan's household, though she is visited by angels. (It's hard to tell if her illumination is a manifestation of God or of Caravaggio.)

As an artistic orientation, realism has one considerable advantage over idealism: the world is visually and in many other aspects inexhaustible. In the service of this program, artists, we might say, broke pieces off Metsys or zoomed in on the details. They invented pure landscape and pure still life painting, for example, and also the genre scene. These became artistic specialties, and a Ruysdael or Heda or Saenredam or Steen could never have emerged in an eidetic tradition. They reached the point of specialization at which an artist could spend a whole career on flowers, or food, or dogs. And I believe that seventeenth-century Dutch artists, and many of their northern predecessors, consciously, pointedly rejected the Italian idealizing style (though, of course, many also emulated it). In particular, they rejected its grandiosity, even as Italian idealism was being criticized from within by artists such as Caravaggio. Well, imagine what the history of Western art would be without still life or landscape. Look, they are saying, there are other things out there besides the idealized nude, and even the human body is more or less an ordinary physical object. As far as the visual resources that the world affords, there is no need to stop there, and one might focus a career on a single kind of flower—the rose, say—or even on painting with perfect truth a single flower glimpsed decades before. One could look ever more deeply into the world—more and more deeply, apparently without limit—by microscope or telescope; the seventeenth-century Dutch saw a world of inexhaustible visual riches opening before them.

14.

Alpers argues that seventeenth-century Dutch artists and scientific illustrators turned to the camera obscura and all sorts of other visual devices in part because these things yielded an event in which "it is as if visual phenomena are captured and made present without the intervention of a human maker."[22] We might think of one sort of tradition in the arts and in philosophy, for example, as turning inward or as trying to explicate the world by means of explicating the human. Even the greatest realist moments in Italian art, for example, center on the human figure. On the other hand, we might first of all represent the thrust of Baconian experimental, empirical science as trying to understand nature on its own terms, or "objectively," which might mean so far as possible taking ourselves out of the equation: trying to erase our own subjectivity in certain respects, in order to allow what is before us to reveal itself. Its proponents thought of this at times as an attitude of self-deflation or humility.

I have said that I don't think that we can make any sense of objectivity as a standpoint from which to generate the one accurate representational schema, whether in scientific or other contexts. But objectivity in the sense which Bacon deploys it here is what we might term an epistemic virtue: an attempt to hold one's own ego or tendency toward self-serving distortion in abeyance, insofar as that is possible, and find out about the world outside one's own skull: a resolution to let it be as real as oneself. This virtue is typical of science at its best, I would say, and whether it describes a procedure for coming to experience what is really there or not, it is admirable in many respects and, if we are going to experience the truth about the world, as I have been arguing, we are going to have to try to apply disciplines like this: disciplines that display both attenuation or deflation of the self and courage in the face of the real—attitudes which, I believe, go together.

The realism in seventeenth-century Dutch art arises in part from a scientific orientation. But the way that the sciences themselves were understood and the way they were pursued in the Netherlands and other parts of northern Europe (notably England) also drew on a history of realistic depiction that was already centuries old; it extends back beyond van Eyck. There are many names one might give this and many connections one might make in the economics, politics, and religion of the region and era. By the seventeenth century, the art is intertwined with capitalism, Protestantism, and republicanism, for example. Articulating the opposition at its broadest sweep, we might narrate Western art history and intellectual history beginning in the Renaissance as a competition and dialogue between transcendence and immanence, or Plato and Bacon, or humanism and experimental science, or even God and the material world.

So I provisionally want to identify a sensibility of love for this world that pervaded seventeenth-century culture of northern Europe and Great Britain. This shows itself in many ways: in a delectation of luxury merchandise and exotic stuffs, in observations of the natural and artifactual environment of unprecedented exactitude, in masterful craft in dialogue with materials, in what might be termed a cult of the mundane. If Plato rejected completely the idea of getting to the truth by mirroring reality or picturing it accurately, for Bacon and others who articulated the empirical method, the mirror and the lens were metaphors for truth and also practical instruments for developing or investigating it.

In the Netherlands, for example, the father and son pair of Constantijn and Christiaan Huygens systematically prosecuted the Baconian scientific program, using optical instruments including the telescope, microscope, and camera obscura, all of them recent innovations in the intensification and broadening of the faculty of vision, for seeing more and seeing more accurately, precisely the project of Northern art. Christiaan, in the preface of his *Treatise on Light*, expressing his hopes for the book, wrote that "I would believe then that those who love to know the Causes of things, and who are able to admire the marvels of Light, will find some satisfaction in these various speculations regarding it. . . . [The properties of light are] the main foundation of the construction of our eyes and of those great inventions which extend so vastly the use of them."[23] One interesting feature of this formulation is that it attributes the structure of the eye and of the microscope and telescope to the properties of light itself; or, generalizing, that the structure of our artifacts and even our biology is a reflection or a result of the qualities of the external world. (This is a view we saw in the third chapter expressed by Wang Yang-Ming.) Obviously, light is a or even the great theme of seventeenth-century Dutch art: famously in Vermeer, of course, but also in many different ways in many different painters: no less in Rembrandt than in Vermeer, for example, though to almost opposite effect.

Spinoza was connected to the Huygens circle; he certainly knew the illustrious Christiaan, the inventor of the pendulum clock and discoverer of the rings of Saturn. Spinoza "polished lenses" for a living, and it is likely that he prepared lenses for Christiaan's telescopes and microscopes; Christiaan expressed his admiration for Spinoza's lenses in letters. The right lens in the right condition was absolutely essential for the new sciences being developed and for the new general conception of science, its abandonment of its humanistic origins, which one can see happening very vividly in the writings of Constantijn and Christiaan Huygens. The right lens made it possible to see what was really there. The creation and use of lenses was connected to the theory of optics under development in philosophy, science, and the arts since the discovery of perspective. The great innovator of the microscope, van Leeuwenhoek, who also knew the Huygenses, possibly supplied a camera obscura to Vermeer, who possibly depicted him in "The Astronomer." Well that's a lot of possibilities, but what I think should be beyond dispute is that the empirical and realist orientation in the art is connected to the realist or "post-humanist" orientation of the science and of the philosophy. I want, however, to take the participation of Spinoza in this circle with some seriousness.

It would be usual to oppose the empirical, this-worldly orientation of the Northern Renaissance and Baroque to various more spiritual or profound or poetic styles of thinking and rendering. But I would like to consider the Northern empirical orientation as itself a deep and perhaps even spiritual orientation that underlies together the science and the art (as well as much of the theology and philosophy). I would not explain the pictorial styles by the science, nor the science by the pictorial styles, but speculate that they arise together from something that runs even deeper. The Northern tradition turns away from transcendence and even from subjectivity toward an immersion in and celebration of the things of this world. This is evident from the writings of scientists, which often rapturously and poetically pay tribute to the beauty of real things: the stars, for example. But it is certainly evident from the art. The still lifes of Kalf, the landscapes of Brueghel or Patinir, the portraits of Hals or Rembrandt: these are just enraptured by the real. They are beautifully crafted celebrations of its amazing stuffs and our amazing artifacts. And in realist portraiture—in which we might provisionally range Holbein, Hals, and Rembrandt—we have a reintegration of the human in the material world. Holbein loves stuffs as much as countenances; Hals and Rembrandt tried to reproduce through the external appearance the whole range of human experience, a la Shakespeare, for example. In Vermeer, but also in a thousand other places, this orientation produces objects of an intense, devotional beauty; you don't get that by coincidence; you find it in love.

Spinoza was obsessed with collapsing the dualisms between mind and body, spirit and matter, freedom and necessity. But despite his overweeningly rationalist method, Spinoza was at heart both a mystic and a materialist: a fascinating and apparently transgressive combination that I explored in the first chapter. He wanted to identify God with nature because he wanted to *adore* nature or to find in the real world a worthy object of his love and his inquiry. During the period in which Spinoza was the most notorious thinker in Europe, he was regarded as a materialist and an atheist. The pantheism and so on were often taken to be insincere, or as, like deism, a way to say that we don't need God to do science. I would like to read him, or at least suggest that he can be as plausibly read, as trying to institute a religion of this world, an adoration of Nature. Schelling says of Spinoza,

> Instead of descending into the depths of his self-consciousness and from there attending to the creation of two worlds in us—the ideal and the

real—he surpassed himself: instead of explaining out of our nature how the finite and the infinite, originally united in us, arise out of one another, he at once abandoned himself to the idea of an infinite outside us.[24]

Schelling thought that this was Spinoza's great mistake, but I am suggesting that it arises from an adorational stance toward the real, a love of the world that rises into mystical identity. The notion that Spinoza both "surpassed" and "abandoned" himself seems exactly right to me, and what Schelling doesn't quite see is that Spinoza recovers himself into identity with God and nature. But Spinoza wants to start with "an infinite outside us" and not from within himself. Spinoza defines "God or nature" as "a being with infinite attributes": God is all that is, and the world is an inexhaustible, infinitely infinite object of inquiry from which we ourselves are not, in the end, distinct.

So I am arguing that in seventeenth-century Dutch realism, a hard-nosed dedication to accurate empirical observation coexists with, and beautifully comports with, a sort of religion of reality. These paintings and Spinoza's philosophy, it seems to me, arise out of a deeper philosophical/spiritual/economic/scientific/aesthetic orientation. This consciousness turns away from Christian themes to dwell in fastidious detail on the qualities of glass or the appearance of a particular insect, but perhaps these are a sort of religious expressions nevertheless, and not only because one can often find religious symbols in them. One way to understand Dutch realism is as pantheist prayer: in landscape, still life, portraiture, you get a celebration of the natural and artifactual environment, an attempt to attenuate consciousness or to release oneself from subjectivity and to see clearly what really is.

In the centuries that followed, this tradition was to a large extent left behind in the arts; its value became harder and harder to discern, despite outbreaks such as the one around Philadelphia in the late nineteenth century associated with Thomas Eakins and William Harnett. In philosophy, various forms of idealism emerged which sought to lodge reality in consciousness. And in the arts, Romanticism and Modernism turned ever more intensely to subjectivity, and perhaps finally lost the world. The arts and sciences go their separate ways by the late eighteenth century at latest.

I don't know how much there is left to explore in the inner terrain, particularly when it is separated in imagination from the external world. Actually, I might say that I'm bored with my consciousness: sick of my four emotions or whatever; tired of my own stories. But I think we're still only beginning to explore and understand the external world and show how it also creates and shapes consciousness. Perhaps even if the goal is the exploration of human consciousness, we can do it through an exploration of the world in which it emerges and with which it is engaged; by itself, consciousness is not much of anything. But whether or not moving outward is the best way to move inward, the world itself is a helluva deal: in the world, we have constant access to an endless source of beauty and ugliness and sublimity, as well as the materials of knowledge and craft and wonder, a being with infinite attributes.

We live now in a world in which realist images appear everywhere all the time: as I say, anyone with an iPhone can make images that would be wonderful to a seventeenth-century Dutch artist or lens polisher. The introduction of photography indeed contributed to the decline of realism in painting: the reproduction of reality was not a worthy project for a genius when it could be performed mechanically. But I do want to remark that realist painting continues, both among weekend hobbyists and avant-garde artists: the project has never been fully abandoned. And in a situation in which you can just snap a shot, to spend weeks carefully crafting a realistic image is a more intense expression of devotion to the real world even than it was four hundred years ago. To apply great craft to the production of a realistic image today is to express a love of the actual that is perverse, but needed. The real is always disappearing behind a screen of images, as many modern and postmodern theorists have insisted. But the character of devotion in some of those images continues to express the eruption of the more-than-human into the human world.

15.

Alpers' idea that the artists and scientists were trying to figure out what the world is like without us in it, which is quite like Schelling's idea that Spinoza abandoned himself to an infinite outside us, could be applied personally as well as collectively and aesthetically. Returning for a moment to a theme from the ethics chapter: one thing that Bill W. taught was that an addict is caught in the toils of self. We might put this by saying that an addict is in danger of descending into solipsism, that the inner life is so tortured and repetitive and conflicted that there seems to be no way out into the actuality of other people or other things. They become markers or representations within oneself; their reality for you is your internalization of them as emblems or aspects of bits of your own consciousness.

A most beautiful expression of the opposite point of view—not that you aren't caught in yourself, but that you oughtn't to be—is the ethics of Iris Murdoch. She represents a central ethical experience, a central existential commitment, as the experience of feeling the reality of persons and things (and God) in genuine externality to oneself. Or, taking the thing the other way round, she represents it as an emptying or even an abandonment or loss of the self: "selflessness."

> It is difficult to be exact here. One might start from the assertion that morality, goodness, is a form of realism. The idea of a really good man living in a private dream world seems unacceptable. Of course a good man may be infinitely eccentric, but he must know certain things about his surroundings, most obviously the existence of other people and their claims. The chief enemy of excellence in morality (and also in art) is personal fantasy: the

tissue of self-aggrandising and consoling wishes and dreams which prevents one from seeing what is there outside one. Rilke said of Cezanne that he did not paint "I like it," he painted "There it is." This is not easy, and requires, in art or morals, a discipline. One might say here that art is an excellent analogy of morals, or indeed that it is in this respect a case of morals. We cease to be in order to attend to the existence of something else, a natural object, a person in need. We can see in mediocre art, where perhaps it is even more clearly seen than in mediocre conduct, the intrusion of fantasy, the assertion of self, the dimming of any reflection of the real world.[25]

Murdoch resorts casually to the most extreme formulation, or calmly to the most ecstatic. I admit when I first came across that "we cease to be," I read it several times in order to be sure that it said what I thought it said. Or I thought there must be an adjective missing after "be": we cease to be self-concerned, or something. But no, Murdoch means that we cease to be. In remarkably rational prose, Murdoch is marking off what might be thought of as a mystical experience, and she's of course going to go on to God and the Form of the Good. But the basic insight makes me want to try to follow her even to those destinations, though I find that I cannot.

One way to cease to be, or at any rate to stop suffering so much from too much selfhood, is to feel the connections; I mean really experience them as fully as possible. In this sense your excess being is something that traps you in a delusion: you cease to experience the connections to things that are really there; losing the world and losing other people through intensification of the self is also losing the real self: you lose the tangle because you lost the cords. That connects Murdoch's mysticism to realist art, which she also, as I have, treats as a kind of pantheist prayer. And she connects this as well to what we could term "objectivity," in the sciences and elsewhere, which in her account is not some sort of rational procedure—though it might undergird such procedures—but rather begins in an erasure of selfhood: a profoundly "religious" or "spiritual" orientation. Murdoch makes the loving mistake that Schelling attributes to Spinoza: the mistake of loving things other than herself more than herself or of longing toward reality.

And we could also approach this from within, as Murdoch also does, and Kristeva: you've got to start getting skeptical of the integrity of the self or its singleness, start feeling all the complexities and conflicts: find and face the incoherences. Not because you want to resolve them by producing an integral self, but because you want to see accurately the self that really is. If you are going to dissolve or dissipate outwards, you are going to dissolve within; you are going to lose yourself into the world, but you are going to lose yourself. You are going to lose yourself into respect for other people or for things, but you are also going to have to lose some of your self-respect. You'll have to face up not only to the world but yourself as the sort of thing that does exist in this world: a multiple, complex thing: a real thing, entangled.

And one thing about Murdoch's mysticism: she makes it also sensible; it's a mysticism of the mundane. It's the mysticism of craft: in the visual arts, in her fiction, in everyday ways we treat or intertwine with other people. "Beauty," she writes, "is that which attracts this particular sort of unselfish attention."

> It is obvious here what is the role, for the artist or the spectator, of exactness and good vision: unsentimental, detached, unselfish, objective attention. It is also clear that in moral situations a similar exactness is called for. I would suggest that the authority of the Good seems to us something necessary because the realism (ability to perceive reality) required for goodness is a kind of intellectual ability to perceive what is true, which is automatically at the same time a suppression of self. *The necessity of the good is then an aspect of the kind of necessity involved in any technique for exhibiting fact.* In thus treating realism, whether of the artist or of the agent, as a moral achievement, there is of course a further assumption to be made in the fields of morals: the true vision occasions right conduct. This could be seen simply as an enlightening tautology: but I think it can in fact be supported by appeals to experience. The more the separateness and differentness of other people is realised, and the fact seen that another man has needs and wishes as demanding as one's own, the harder it becomes to treat a person as a thing. That it is realism that makes great art great remains too as a kind of proof. . . .
>
> If, still led by the clue of art, we ask further questions about the faculty which is supposed to relate us to what is real and thus bring us to what is good, the idea of compassion or love will be naturally suggested. It is not simply that suppression of the self is required before accurate vision can be obtained. The great artist sees his objects (and this is true whether they are sad, absurd, repulsive or even evil) in a light of justice and mercy.[26]

At this point, it may not surprise you that I think Murdoch's program is very right and, of course, connected with the accounts of realist art, ethics, and knowledge that I have been giving. But it may also not surprise you that I think she does cast over this material a somewhat too roseate hue. To see something as it really is might require a certain sort of love, or a pouring outward of the self. But what you find when you get there: I think that's as likely to bring hatred and disgust as anything else, and then the question becomes whether you can continue to look unflinchingly at what is really there. Perhaps Murdoch did not, quite, and that's where the move into transcendence, whether Plato's or Christ's, is lurking from the outset. She's also, of course, trying to redeploy what might be the most fundamental and characteristic teaching of Socrates: goodness is knowledge: to know the real is to do the good.

Well I'd be much happier with a notion like that if the real in question were more immanent. But on the other hand either way I don't think that to know the real is to do the good. *Look at* the damn real!

Right, but there is so much here that's true or that shows even Murdoch's optimism not to be entirely misplaced: so, consider something like Goya's "Horrors of War." There is, everywhere all the time, a resolution to face the horror, and to communicate it. Though Goya is often noted, say, as a transition between Velazquez and Van Gogh because the handling is loose, there is an intense objectivity there, as well as an intense moral repudiation: these things, fellow scientists, are not rivals. The emotions are all over objectivity, if we're going to formulate it in those terms: to see what Goya saw and resolve to communicate it without flinching requires moral fierceness; it's a test of your courage, as Murdoch would lead you to expect. But did Goya *love* what he saw? It might be true to say that Goya loved the world; I think that is a place to start with the art. But he didn't love the war, and he didn't love war, and he was not necessarily on a quest for the grail or the Form of the Good. Maybe God loves the world, the whole world: everything, everyone. If so, he does love war; he loves your dismemberment. But stepping off to the being of all beings or whatever it may be, or trying to take up its ethical or epistemic viewpoint, is not the only, and not the best possibility, because it is falsifying: it precisely refuses to face up at the moment of truth, and perhaps you see that also in Murdoch's novels.

Or from the other side again: I feel the impulse not to be very strongly, in both ways: to cease to exist or to efface myself before the real or even the divine. I want to be released from the burden of self. But though I know from elaborate experience that this burden can be eased, I don't think that offloading it entirely is one of the options without a bullet to the head. If I'm experiencing the connections, I am experiencing myself as composed of these connections; that is not the same thing as ceasing to be a center of experiences, as little like an integral nucleus as I am. I want something to take away my self-involvement, but I want to be present to experience the release as well.

6

Political Philosophy

A. Squishy Totalitarianism and the Left-Right Spectrum

1.

Political philosophy has to start in concrete situations, with infinitely individual and infinitely relational persons. It has to start from taking persons seriously as making a moral claim, that is, from a resolution toward real relations with real things. The characteristic derangements of political philosophy begin to treat persons in abstraction as representations or texts: in terms of general will, for example, or nations—epistemological or aesthetic markers that desituate real organisms. Indeed, textualism is at the heart of the modern nation-state: its cult of law, its demographic surveillances, its modes of control. The state fantasizes a global transformation of persons by texts, pledges, anthems, standardized tests, and spreadsheets of bureaucratic functions that one person can fulfill as well as another. Abstractions disavow their own origins and result in concrete oppressions of actual bodies. Hegel's "state"—spirit working in history—disavows its origin and its issue in breaking real bodies, the better to break bodies, literally destroy their reality.

The only answer to this is to make politics what it is: human bodies in communication, an erotic site of mergings into and emergings out of one another. Always particularize; always emphasize the real relations that make even the formulation of principles and the generation of collective agencies possible. Always keep in mind that although collective decision is possible and central, individual divergence from such decision is also possible and frequently necessary.

2.

I have described philosophy as being concerned to elucidate (or, for that matter, throw into doubt) the "ultimate values," and I have had a go at elucidating several of them. However, I am a lot less happy with justice as a concept than with truth or beauty, for example, and I find that I cannot really make clear to myself what it is or even what it is about, exactly. I seem to have had a similar problem with happiness, if I am recalling chapter 4 correctly. William Godwin, in his *Enquiry Concerning Political Justice*, uses the word in the very general sense in which it often appears: "we use the term justice as a general appellation for all moral duty."[1] Others use it much more specifically to refer to a structural feature of societies, for example, in "distributions." There is criminal justice and income justice and tit-for-tat personal justice, and so on. Perhaps these uses boil down to one concept—fairness, or something—but that is very not clear to me. And I do think that in many uses, the idea of justice—particularly "distributive" justice—is question-begging with regard to statism, as Nozick and others have pointed out. If you want to redistribute the resources of your society, then you've got to constitute a mechanism that is capable of doing that. This mechanism is going to have to operate by coercion, of course. Nozick's own concept of justice boils it down to noninterference in people's liberty, which I think is overall a good thing. But it's hard to tell whether that's a theory of justice or not, because in ordinary language the terms *liberty* and *justice* are very far apart; they just do not mean anything like the same thing. However, that's also yet another symptom of the fact that *justice* is a Humpty Dumpty term: you could mean anything you like by it, pretty nearly. To put that another way, the question of whether the term means anything at all is a real question. At any rate, I think most people should have enough stuff, or perhaps I think every person should get what they deserve, but I think we need to be extremely leery of a coercive power that would allegedly make something like that happen. That's my theory of justice, I guess.

But I do want to try to confront Rawls's theory of justice and argue that, if rational (hence, nonhuman) agents were to gather in the original position, they would actually be constrained to choose not to constitute a state. In my view, enough and much, much more has been written about *A Theory of Justice*. Indeed, it has been attacked, refuted, and revived so many times from so many different angles that it would be, so to speak, rational to replace the volume on the shelf and not pull it down until some decades or perhaps millennia have passed.

However, I regard the criticism that follows as fundamental, both as exposing a contradiction or at least an extreme tension in Rawls's account and as showing something important in political philosophy: namely, the problematic nature of state power with regard to the matter of justice and the conceptual tendency of state power to produce injustice in precisely Rawls's sense. The objection can be stated briefly as follows. Political power is, by Rawls's definition of the good, a good for every person. Indeed, it is a fundamental good in the sense that it is a presupposition of other goods, because some political power is required to be secure in other goods, such as material welfare and self-respect. But the political power that is constituted in Rawls's account in order to achieve justice also entails that his contractors constitute an inequality of power so severe as to compromise utterly the security of the other goods that they rationally want to preserve.

Another way to put this is that there is a tension within the principles of justice concerning equality: the power constituted to achieve a just degree of equality (qualified by the Difference Principle) is conceptually and practically incompatible with that very equality. Rawls writes,

> For the present, it should be observed that the two principles [of justice] (and this holds for all formulations) are a special case of a more general conception of justice that can be expressed as follows.
>
> All social values—liberty and opportunity, income and wealth, and the bases of self-respect—are to be distributed equally unless an unequal distribution of any, or all, of these values is to everyone's advantage.
>
> As a first step, suppose that the basic structure of society distributes certain primary goods, that is, things that every rational man is presumed to want. These goods normally have a use whatever a person's rational plan of life. For simplicity, assume that the chief primary goods at the disposition of society are rights and liberties, powers and opportunities, income and wealth. (Later on in Part Three the primary good of self-respect has a central place.) These are the primary social goods. Other primary goods such as health and vigor, intelligence and imagination, are natural goods. . . . Imagine, then, a hypothetical initial arrangement in which all the social primary goods are equally distributed. This state of affairs provides a benchmark for judging improvements. If certain inequalities of wealth and organizational powers would make everyone better off than in this hypothetical starting situation, then they accord with the general conception.[2]

The serial or "lexical" ordering of Rawls's principles of justice does not allow an exchange of rights and liberties for other social goods, such as "economic or social gains."[3]

Rawls in this passage includes "powers" among the primary goods, a theme to which he rarely returns. But surely, given both the general characterization of goods he gives above, and the more specific formulation he gives later,[4] powers, or at any rate certain powers, are primary goods. Indeed, like liberty and opportunity, power may be said to be a primary primary good, in the sense that it stands as an empirical precondition for the pursuit of various other primary goods. Notice, for example, that wealth, security, opportunity, and self-respect are historically connected to political power. I can think of no society, for example, wherein the group that exercises primary political power is impoverished, even in cases wherein the society as a whole is impoverished. I will eventually deploy this as the "Principle of Hierarchical Coincidence."

It is a familiar point, as well, that exclusion from political power is incompatible with self-respect or with educational equality, for example. This sort of criticism, for example, was fundamental to the civil rights movement, as regards voting rights. Martin Luther King, Jr. and many others argued that without the minimal political power exercised through equal access to the electoral process, black people in America could not make themselves secure in any dimension. Exclusion from political participation, they also argued, compromised the self-respect and dignity of black people, just as did the system of apartheid in schools, for example. African Americans came to achieve legal equality in such respects partly through the exercise of political power.

Thus by Rawls's own account, political power is a primary social good. That is, political power is obviously something that a rational person would want (no rational person, finding himself inside or subject to a political hierarchy, could want to be stripped of such power entirely), and it is subject to procedures of social distribution, which will require a state. Rawls, I would say, is not perfectly clear on this; yet it is, indeed, perfectly clear. As Nozick argued elaborately in his libertarian critique of Rawls, Rawls must constitute a set of institutions with the power to make an initial distribution of goods, and to oversee future exchanges in order to keep them roughly in line with the principles of justice. This will require, at a minimum, that the institutions thus constituted have the power to take certain goods from some persons and give them to others, in order to enforce equality and opportunity, and to ensure that private exchanges redound to the benefit of all.

In Rawls, the political institutions or institutions of the state appear to be, as we might put it, impersonal. They are portrayed as forces or procedures (in particular, structures of rules) rather than as consisting (in part) of a group of persons. However, surely the state consists in part of actual human individuals, individuals who are themselves part of the population to whom rights, liberties, wealth, opportunities, powers, and other goods are to be distributed (in this case by themselves) according to the principles of justice. If powers are indeed goods, and if political power in particular is a primary social good, then the assignment of political power is itself a distribution of goods which is subject to the principles of justice. But to the extent that the individuals who operate state power are by definition empowered politically to a degree that others cannot be, the distribution of a political power is necessarily unequal. Then the question of whether it is just or not would appear to turn on whether this unequal distribution redounds to the benefit of all.

The situation appears offhand to be extremely unpromising. The distribution of political power in a situation where a group of individuals constitutes the state is unequal. But political power is itself the power to distribute other goods. To the extent that people tend to pursue their self-interest—that is, to the extent that they seek the greatest possible quantity of goods, even if this desire often observes certain limits—we should expect that the resulting distribution of all goods will favor those who exercise political power. Indeed, Rawls's own view is precisely that rationality consists in the effective pursuit of the good. I think that is certainly false, or at a minimum incredibly simplistic, but if it is anything like true, then we should expect that among rational agents an asymmetrical distribution of political power will be followed by an unjust distribution of all other social goods.

Furthermore, the situation is fundamentally irremediable. Since the distribution of goods is made by those who have already received an unequal share of the power to make such distributions, there is no recourse short of continuous insurrection. Indeed, the power to distribute will increase as it is put into the hands of the distributors, and the more unequal the distribution becomes, the more unequal it becomes, unto eternity.

This is, I believe, a conceptual incoherence at the heart of *A Theory of Justice*. But it is, of course, anything but an academic problem. It could not be more obvious that the ruling elite—class, race, gender, religion, caste, and so on—of any given society assigns itself an inordinate share of the menu of goods. And even if one distributed political power, not according to any of these arbitrary categories, but according to desert, or by lot, for example, the people thus assigned would quickly constitute an elite, a class, a caste, and so on. That is, according to Rawls, the persons in the original position have, by doing what he recommends or what he claims rationality demands, constituted a profoundly hierarchical society, and one which, other things being equal, will become ever more hierarchical in the fullness of time.

Yet another way to put this is that the original contractors cannot constitute a polity that realizes the principles of justice without constituting a polity that massively violates them. Now, on the other hand, there may be no recourse. That is, the asymmetrical assignment of power and resulting hierarchical distribution of all goods—as a matter of fact typical of all state-ridden societies—may be the best we can do. That is, it may be to the benefit of everyone. This leaves us in a position in which no social situation can be expected to produce anything but profoundly unequal distributions of goods. That may, of course, be the case, and perhaps we ought merely to face up. Or for that matter, give up.

It is truly remarkable that, with regard to this massive work of political philosophy, neither *power* nor *state* appear in the index. Indeed, any general arguments that Rawls gives for the legitimacy of state power are, we might say, superficial, and

A *Theory of Justice* deploys itself within the presumption of the legitimacy of state power, rather than, as in traditional social contract theory, devoting itself to the task of trying to establish it. Nevertheless, Rawls's contractors constitute a coercive state. This entails that among other things they are distributing political power, or at any rate setting out principles or procedures according to which it will be distributed. Rawls defines "institutions," including state institutions, in terms of rules and behavior in accordance with these rules rather than in terms of powers of some persons over others. That is all very well, but these rules themselves concern among other things the conditions under which some people can legitimately coerce others.

That is, though at least in ideal circumstances the group of people who operate political power do so according to a set of rules and procedures, they do so through coercion; they possess political power that rests on force, force to which the people not part of the institutional apparatus have no access.

> It is reasonable to assume that even in a well-ordered society [wherein principles of justice are universally agreed on] the coercive powers of government are to some degree necessary for the stability of social cooperation. . . . [E]ven under reasonably ideal conditions, it is hard to imagine, for example, a successful income tax scheme on a voluntary basis. Such an arrangement is unstable. The role of an authorized public interpretation or rules supported by collective sanctions is precisely to overcome this instability. By enforcing a public system of penalties government removes the grounds for thinking others are not complying with the rules. For this reason alone, a coercive sovereignty is presumably always necessary.[5]

Rawls, indeed, argues that the original contractors will want to constitute a "paternalistic" power, that being rational they will want to hedge against the possibility of their becoming irrational through mental illness or addiction, for example: "the parties adopt principles stipulating when others are authorized to act in their behalf and to override their present wishes if necessary; and this they do recognizing that sometimes their capacity to act rationally for their good may fail, or be lacking altogether."[6]

In doing these things, the parties constitute other persons as political authorities, not only to enforce rationality on themselves, but to determine whether or not they are, in fact, rational. They constitute other people, as well, as authorities over their goods, for example, their incomes. Such authority is to be exercised according to the rule of law, which makes the persons thus authorized subject to the rules they enforce. This, I submit, is impossible, in that in being constituted as the authorities who, for example, determine the extent of rationality of other citizens, these authorities are by definition exempted from judgments concerning their own rationality. (Rather, there may be a hierarchy of such paternalistic authorities, each level of which answers as regards their rationality to those who operate at the higher levels; one level must be exempt from anyone's judgment as to its rationality.) And in non-ideal circumstances, the parties are simply placing all their social goods at the mercy of other parties, no likelier to be rational than they are themselves. And the power to coerce, along with the means to do that, are things that the authorities exercise, while they are illegal for the rest of the population. In that sense, those operating sovereign power are not subject to its laws.

But my argument here does not rest on such observations, richly confirmed though they are in history. What concerns us here is that because the segment of the population that wields political authority has access to coercive power that is sufficient to redistribute social goods and to strip them entirely from those it judges irrational, this coercive power is sufficient to be practically irresistible; the distribution effectively distributes all political power to one segment of the population while stripping it entirely from another. In order to assure a just and rational distribution, Rawls's just institutions presuppose a radically unequal distribution of a particularly fundamental social good. That is, the distribution of social goods in accordance with Rawls's principles of justice is practically impossible; the nature of the distributive mechanism or institution is incompatible with the principles on which it is itself supposed to make that distribution.

If, indeed, the original contractors were making a distribution of political power, they could not, compatibly with the principles of justice, constitute some of their number as political authorities with access to coercive power. As I argued in *Against the State*, and as widely agreed, coercive power is criterial for statehood. Thus I assert that the contractors would have no choice, in the original position, but to choose anarchy, or more precisely they could not rationally choose to constitute a state. This is evident if we keep in mind that political power is the mechanism by which other goods are distributed. Once they have distributed political power in a radically unequal fashion—investing some with it entirely and stripping others of it completely—they would expect that the distribution of other goods would come to mirror the distribution of coercive power. That it does, I propose, is empirically typical, as I will argue below.

3.

There are no good arguments for the moral legitimacy of state power. Here I will compress *Against the State*. The state consists of a group of people that claims, and with some effectiveness operates, a monopoly of coercive violence over a given region. There are three traditional strategies for justifying something like that.

Social contract theory rests the legitimacy of state power on the consent of those over whom it operates. Not only is there not any such consent, but the monopoly of coercive force itself compromises the very possibility of consent.

Utilitarian theories rest the legitimacy of state power on the happiness it achieves and the misery it avoids. All the major wars and genocides of the twentieth century—millions upon millions of deaths—were delivered by the state. The state was a necessary condition for the Holocaust, the Killing Fields, and so on. The state developed the nuclear weapons that may kill everything yet.

Finally, there are "justicial" arguments that rest the legitimacy of the state on the supposed fact that it is necessary to justice. The argument just given against Rawls shows the sort of reason this argument is not convincing, as do, for example, the racial effects of the criminal justice system in the United States over the last several decades.

4.

The arrangement of positions along the left-right axis—progressive to reactionary, or conservative to liberal, or socialist to capitalist, or for that matter Democrat to Republican—is conceptually confused, ideologically tendentious, historically contingent, and disconnected from reality. Any position that is comfortably located anywhere on the left-right spectrum is beset by contradictions. We need at this point to think *about* the left-right spectrum rather than *from* it. The thing can seem permanent and inevitable. But the left-right terminology arose in revolutionary France in 1789, where it referred to the seating of royalists and antiroyalists in the Assembly. It is plausible to think of an early version of the conceptuality, though not the terminology, as emerging in Europe in the run-up to the Revolution, in figures such as Rousseau and Burke. The first use of *left* and *right* in something like its current political sense in English is attributed in the *Oxford English Dictionary* to Thomas Carlyle's *French Revolution* in 1837. The spectrum only crystallized fully with the emergence of and under the aegis of Marxism, in the middle of the nineteenth century, and was not fully current in English-speaking countries until early in the twentieth century. Before that, and elsewhere than in the West, there have been many intellectual structures for defining and arranging political positions, as I will show in some concrete cases as we go on.

One way people talk about left and right is in terms of time: progressives want time to continue to move forward or even want to accelerate it, taking us into a future bright with promise, while conservatives want time to stand still or even to run it backward to a golden age. Either approach appears to depend on a conception of time on which it is extremely malleable, its pace and direction depending on the outcome of the next election. Well, that's what you get if you move from Kantianism to the social or linguistic or political construction of reality: a nice turn of phrase and time is running backwards or accelerating so fast that you can't keep up. I think such a picture is incompatible with any plausible conception of time in metaphysics or in ordinary experience. No one needs to help make sure that time keeps moving forward and, proverbially, no one can stand in its way. Ted Cruz and Rafael Correa, the Taliban and Beyoncé, the "stone age" Suruwaha people of the Amazon and the prime-time hosts of MSNBC: they coincide in time, all moving temporally in the same direction at the same rate, contemporaneously. Among other times, they all exist precisely now, as I write.

Perhaps progressives (and real reactionaries, if there are any) would say that the idea of hastening or retarding time is a sort of shorthand or metaphor. But I think the matter is much more complicated than this. Both sides of the American political spectrum are continuously appealing to American traditions, principles, bromides, and so on. And one typically "makes progress," to whatever extent one does, by revivifying or reinterpreting existing traditions: Barack Obama engages in this rhetoric no less than Rand Paul. It's never a matter of simply starting afresh employing no assumptions; both sides are engaged in interpreting and reapplying existing traditions, and both sides are doing that under constantly mutating conditions, so that each reapplication is a new and potentially controversial interpretation. Time is relentless in that sense, too.

Another way that the left-right spectrum is conceived is as state against capital, and that conceptuality is what I focus on here. It is central to contemporary American politics, as Democrats urge that government makes many positive contributions to our lives, while Republicans argue that it is a barrier to the prosperity created by free markets. The basic set of distinctions on both sides and in the middle rests on the idea that state and corporation, or political and economic power, can be pulled apart and set against each other.

The left-right spectrum is an arrangement of practical politics, and most political parties in most parts of the world perhaps understand themselves as falling along that spectrum somewhere. But as a framework or taxonomy of political positions, or for the purposes of, say, research in political science, it has got to be optional. You've got to keep open the possibility that it is a flawed paradigm or could be replaced qua explanatory framework. If not, then you are yourself embroiled in the ideologies that you're supposed to be accounting for or categorizing. The left-right spectrum is an historical artifact, like any other taxonomy of political systems. Now, it may be that at this point many of us cannot think about politics without it. The spectrum widely shapes behaviors, affiliations, passionate commitments the world over. But it may also be that many assertions involving it—including characterizations of one's own position, and attacks on the positions of one's opponents—have far less meaning or practical upshot than one feels that they do as one is making them. It may be that what sounds clear under almost infinite repetition is in fact garbled nonsense, a kind of inarticulate noise taking the form of a familiar syntax. It may be that even as we, say, conduct party politics, we are engaged in a series of contradictions or have wandered into a limbo of pseudo-sense.

At any rate, if we are conceiving left vs. right as state vs. capital, then on the outer ends we might pit Chairman Mao against Ayn Rand in a cage match: state communism against laissez-faire capitalism. The basic set of distinctions on both sides and in the middle rests on the idea that state and corporation, or political and economic power, can be pulled apart and set against each other. This brings us to the following:

> Principle of Hierarchical Coincidence (PHC): *hierarchies tend to coincide*.
>
> Corollary: *resources flow toward political power, and political power flows toward resources; or, the power of state and of capital typically appear in conjunction*.

As a practical matter, if you legitimize any hierarchy, whether of experts, races, capital, the Party, and so on, you are, in reality, recommending hierarchy in every dimension. So, if a hierarchy of education or expertise is important in your society, then resources and political power will flow toward experts. Same with a hierarchy of beauty or athletic prowess or race or gender, or whatever it may be. But the fundamental dimensions I want to pick out are economic and political.

I'd say it's obvious that PHC is roughly true, and everyone knows it to be true. A white supremacist polity in which black people were wealthier than white people, for example, would be extremely surprising. It would be no less surprising if regulatory capture were not pervasive, for example. You could keep trying to institute reforms to pull economic and political power apart: I wonder what it would take empirically to show you that this was counterproductive. It's counterproductive because when you beef up the state to control capital, you typically only succeed in making capital more monolithic, more concentrated, and more able to exercise a wider variety of powers. (Consider the relation of Goldman Sachs to the Treasury Department over the last several decades, or Haliburton and Defense, or Google and NSA. The distinction between "public" and "private" is rather abstract in relation to the on-the-ground overlap.)

5.

Thus it is time to deploy the second of my stunning principles, which is a description or definition of the form of government we labor under today over much of the world.

> *squishy totalitarianism*: the political/economic/aesthetic/psychological system or syndrome shared in common, for instance, by contemporary China, the European Union, Russia, Iran, and the United States. It is characterized by a complex so-called technocratic merger of state and capital; large-scale mechanisms of subject-formation such as compulsory state education and regulation/monopoly ownership of the media; welfare state or "safety net"

programs that stabilize consumption and render populations (within limits) secure and dependent; a relative tolerance for some forms of diffuse dissent and scope for individual choice, particularly in consumption, combined with pervasive state and corporate surveillance; overwhelming police and military force and sprawling systems of incarceration; entrenched extreme hierarchies of wealth and expertise; regulation of the economy by monetary policy and central banks in conjunction with banking concerns; an international regime of national sovereignties combined with international state/corporate mechanisms for the circulation of wealth.

State and economy have merged in different permutations in Iran and Egypt, in China and Japan, in the United States and the EU. Once they have, everyone is over the barrel, and you might even be able to let them tweet their little opinions. You want them fundamentally to conceive themselves as consumers and receivers of benefits from the state, and you want them to think of their freedom as primarily a freedom to choose between different things to buy or benefits to receive (which are, however, real freedoms). Then your economy will be a self-stimulating spiral of growth, your tax coffers will fill, and your elites will grow in wealth, prestige, knowledge, and power.

The familiar picture is that, to the degree that you reduce the power of the state, you increase the power of capital, and vice versa. Putting it mildly, this claim is nonempirical. The rise of capital, its consolidation into a few hands, and the enduring structures of monopoly or gigantism to which it gives rise are inconceivable without the state, as I will argue with many examples below. Even Marx saw this, in a limited way: he regarded the modern state as the agent of the bourgeoisie. Putting it gently, that was more or less true. But then Marx recommends placing communications, banking, education, agriculture, transportation, and so on in the hands of the dictatorship of the proletariat. You might as well hand them all to Cornelius Vanderbilt, because the people who actually make the decisions with regard to these things are the people who will actually become the dominant class or group. No dictator is a proletarian.

Anarchists such as Kropotkin also saw the connection and almost uniquely did not present an alternative that just made the nightmare worse. Here he is in 1901, stating the obvious: "The State (state-justice, state-church, state-army) and capitalism are, in our opinion, inseparable concepts. In history these institutions developed side by side, mutually supporting and reinforcing each other. They are bound together not by a mere coincidence of contemporaneous development, but by the bond of cause and effect, effect and cause."[7]

We might say that the current Chinese state combines the best features of Maoism and corporate capitalism: it's all devoted to generating maximum cash and putting it on a barge. Destination: the very top of the hierarchy. And yet it also attempts to bestride the earth, stomping that ass with the iron boot of collectivist totalitarianism.

Now, your basic taxonomy of political and economic systems or ideologies would regard this as an incoherent merger. A conventional political scientist associates capitalism with John Locke and Adam Smith and democracy: "liberalism," I suppose. On the other hand, if socialists reject free enterprise and engage in grand redistributivist schemes, then, of course, they require a big, extremely powerful state. (Once you're done with the redistribution, the state either withers away, or deposits your entire country in their leaders' Swiss accounts and absconds; I forget which.) So for a long time people thought of the Chinese system as combining opposed or contradictory elements. At a minimum, I'd say no one is so sure anymore.

We should think instead of the contemporary Chinese state as a provisional culmination of both state socialism and corporate capitalism. In ideology, they are opposites. But we don't live in the textbook for a course on political ideologies. We live in a world where, *from the outset, corporate capitalism depended on state power, and the basic practical thrust of left statism was annexation of the economy.* The Soviet Union was a variety of monopoly capitalism, and modern America is a variety of state socialism.

What went wrong in our thinking is that we believed the account these ideologies gave of themselves. But the scrim of philosophy, theory, ideology, rhetoric was always thin. There are capitalist theoreticians who have fantasized and recommended stateless free markets, and there are communist theorists who have fantasized no markets at all, always slightly glossing over the fact that what they actually meant was an entire permeation of every aspect of life, including markets, by the state. But these were, indeed, fantasies. What these people wanted appeared to be entirely opposed. But they were each devoted to their own sort of hierarchy, and hierarchies tend to coincide. They were designed to rationalize or moralize what is really a single indefensible system, or to enhance the self-esteem of ideologues while pursuing the hard work of subduing populations and gathering up all the resources.

The Cold War disguised the fact that the systems were, in playing out their real essences, converging toward a situation in which state and economy are fully integrated and held in very few hands: a truly permanent, systemic, chronic, sclerotic hierarchy with the world's worst rhetoric. One of the meanings of "globalization" and the various "international mechanisms" that go with it, may be that it is a premonition of a world system of this variety, which is already emerging. (One name is *technocracy*. If you insist, you could call it "late capitalism" or "neoliberalism," with the proviso that it is enthusiastically statist and really has very little do with classical liberalism.) But there are many barriers to overcome, from nationalism and tribalism to religious chauvinism and individualism/tribalism of the "I/we dissent/withdraw/slack off/sabotage/hack" variety.

Consider the Soviet system. What nationalizing industry, imposing five-year plans, and so on accomplished was not to make the society more equal; they just made the Communist Party a committee of capitalists. State and economy merged, but sadly the state turns out to be actual people, as opposed to whatever the left thinks it is. What people faced in communist totalitarianism was a particular and particularly extreme form of the merger of state and capital, which is one good meaning of the term *totalitarianism*. And what you have created when you're finished is an overwhelming power that confronts you now as a sheer alien force while also trying to work on everybody's mind and everybody's family through propaganda and secret police procedures. Just to put it squarely: if you supported the communist revolution or helped spearhead it, you richly deserved your show trial and execution: you helped create the force that killed you.

6.

The main historical point I want to make is this: the rise of capitalism is not explicable without state power, which has increased throughout the capitalist period. The modern nation-state and capitalism have the same origins, or arose together, or really—simplifying slightly—are one thing in different dimensions or aspects, as Kropotkin says. It will be important to try to deal from the outset with the interlocked state/capital formations arising in the early modern period rather than exclusively with later theorizations of these developments, with the history of political economy rather than the history of political-economic theory and ideology.

Economists who undertake as broad a project as "defining" capitalism or tracing its origins and history invariably connect it to the emergence of the modern state. Michel Beaud in his *History of Capitalism* finds the state connection criterial:

> What one in any case should remember is the importance of the state in the birth, the first beginnings of capitalism; this is linked, too, to the national character of the formation of capitalism: there is no capitalism without the bourgeoisie, which developed within the framework of the nation-state at the same time as the rise of *nations* occurred. . . . Within Europe itself, the primary transforming factor is the state. National unity, currency standardization, juridical coherence, military strength and the beginnings of a national economy: all these were created and developed by the state, or with the state as organizing principle.[8]

There is extreme ambiguity, I must remark, around the term *state*. Perhaps we've had states since ancient Egypt and China, proceeding to religious states like the caliphate and imperial states such as the Romans, or Mongol horde states, feudal states, and tribal states. Or perhaps these are all different sorts of nonstate configurations and there have only been states since the peace of Westphalia in 1648, and perhaps in a few other places and periods historical epochs such as the Spring and Autumn and Warring States periods in China. In some ways I think the term is irremediably ambiguous. Indeed, all the terms in this vicinity are irremediably ambiguous and are constantly being hijacked or annexed for someone's ideological project.

Proceeding with these items as rough and ready notions, the sorts of events that economic historians focus on in the development of capitalism are, for example, the rise of the city-state of Venice and the great banking families of Europe, such as the Medici; the sixteenth-century influx of South American gold into the economy of Spain and into this same financial system; the development of securities, futures and other "abstract" instruments and markets for them in Holland and Great Britain; enclosure of internal commons and the establishment of international tariffs and free-trade zones; war both internal and external to establish and police boundaries and territorialize and commodify and garrison entire regions and continents;[9] manufacturing, trade, and technological development, in part to equip belligerents in civil and international strife; and so on. In no case can we imagine what these developments in the history of capitalism would have been like without simultaneous developments in the crystallizing and internationalizing state. Even right-wing historians tell a similar tale, and the sort of figures who later came to be considered conservative icons, such as Smith, Hume, and Ricardo—both in their historical and prescriptive moments—centralized in their accounts the necessary role of state action in regulation of internal markets and conducting international trade.

One way to read this history, as Marxists do, is as showing that liberal democracy/constitutional monarchy were bourgeois forms. Another is simply to read it as showing that state and economic power are indissoluble, hence that attacking capital by beefing up the state or adding capital flatly to the state portfolio is not promising as a road to justice. Leftists got into this pickle in part because under Marx's influence they came to perceive only economy as reality, and hence to hold that political hierarchies are not real hierarchies at all. This delusion reached a literally psychotic state, so that Stalinist Russia or Maoist China—two of the most rigidly and murderously hierarchical societies in world history—could be justified on egalitarian grounds.

However, Marxism also yields plenty of insights that could be used to float the other way. Indeed, strands of leftist economic thought are currently being used to clarify this situation even as other strands are dedicated to obscuring it. An example is Leo Panitch and Sam Gindin's book *The Making of Global Capitalism: The Political Economy of American Empire*. They write:

> One of capitalism's defining characteristics, compared with pre-capitalist societies, is the legal and organizational differentiation between state and economy. This is not to say there was ever anything like an actual separation between the political and economic spheres of capitalism. The distinction between *differentiation* and *separation* is so important because as capitalism

developed states in fact became more involved in life than ever, especially in the establishment and administration of the juridical, regulatory, and infrastructural framework in which private property, competition, and contracts came to operate. Capitalist states were also increasingly major actors in trying to contain capitalist crises, including as lenders of last resort. Capitalism could not have developed unless states came to do these things. Conversely, states became increasingly dependent on the success of capital accumulation for tax revenue and popular legitimacy.[10]

The political and economic institutions are completely interdependent and mutually entwined, for Panitch and Gindin. Yet the distinction of the spheres is important. Partly, it is important to the right-left ideology on both sides; neither could be justified without the distinction. But I, too, endorse the differentiation of spheres in this sense: I do not believe that political power can be reduced to economic power, as in classical Marxism. They are distinct and mutually interdependent. The President is not the wealthiest American. The danger in collapsing them is that if one reduces either to the other, one ends up justifying and intensifying both. If political hierarchy is epiphenomenal while economic hierarchies are real, then one can institute a totalitarian political regime without even noticing that one is in fact advocating inequalities of the most extreme variety. On the other hand, if only political oppressions are real and economic inequalities merely natural and salutary, you get in the name of liberty varieties of "free market" capitalism deranged in their practical oppression. For example, if you are starving you are not free, especially if others have more than they can imagine consuming.

Panitch and Gindin concentrate on the international effects of the projection of American capital and markets on the world by the American state, culminating in an account of "neoliberalism," or in their preferred terminology "informal empire," by which they mean very much what I mean by "squishy totalitarianism." "Despite the Reaganite rhetoric in which neoliberal politics were enveloped ("government is not the solution, government is the problem"), it was the state that was the key actor. . . . Neoliberal *practices* did not entail institutional retreat so much as the expansion and consolidation of the networks of institutional linkages to an already globalizing capitalism."[11]

Both left and right accepted an ideological framework in which state and capital were opposed; indeed, to a large extent, the left-right spectrum just is this idea. And yet, as soon as this opposition is prodded empirically with regard to any particular fundamental development in practical political economy, it disintegrates. Panitch and Gindin adduce also the world financial crisis of 2007–2008, which was created, in part, by the American government's support for home ownership and the development of financial instruments based on it. Of course, the American government and those of other nations, as well as international coalitions of bankers and officials, massively infused specific private financial concerns with cash in response to the crisis. The United States government purchased and then resold domestic car manufacturers and both it and European governments circulated trillions of dollars through "private" banking and insurance firms in response to the crisis.

The interlocked histories of the corporation and state war machines, for example Krupp in Germany or Halliburton in the United States, must on any account be regarded as fundamental to the nature and growth of both the modern state and the modern corporation. Adam Smith approvingly and accurately describes the origin and basic function of the modern state as a military machine, and he connects national military establishments to the rise and nature of capitalism fundamentally. The military establishment and the capitalist economy are seen to be mutually reinforcing. This is true internally and externally, because organizing a nation on a military basis requires imposing on it a systematic system of taxation and conscription, while the industry configured around the production of military equipment such as uniforms and artillery pieces transforms the economy and drives technological innovation and advances in productivity.

> As it is only by means of a well-regulated standing army that a civilized country can be defended; so it is only by means of it, that a barbarous country can be suddenly and tolerably civilized. A standing army establishes with an irresistible force, the law of the sovereign through the remotest provinces of the empire, and maintains some degree of regular government in countries which could not otherwise admit of any. . . .
>
> The first duty of the sovereign, therefore, that of defending the society from the violence and injustice of other independent societies, grows gradually more and more expensive, as the society advances in civilization. . . . The great change introduced into the art of war by the invention of firearms, has enhanced still further both the expence of exercising and disciplining any particular number of soldiers in time of peace, and that of employing them in time of war. Both their arms and their ammunition are become more expensive. A musquet is a more expensive machine than a javelin or a bow and arrows; a cannon or a mortar, than a balista or a catapulta. . . . . The canon and the mortar are, not only much dearer, but much heavier machines than the balista or catapulta, and require a greater expence, not only to prepare them for the field, but to carry them to it. As the superiority of the modern artillery too, over that of the antients, is very great; it has become much more difficult, and consequently much more expensive, to fortify a town so as to resist even for a few weeks the attack of that superior artillery. In modern times many different causes contribute

to render the defence of the society more expensive. The unavoidable effects of the natural progress of improvement have, in this respect, been a good deal enhanced by a great revolution in the art of war, to which a mere accident, the invention of gun-powder, seems to have given occasion.

In modern war the great expence of fire-arms gives an evident advantage to the nation which can best afford that expence; and consequently, to an opulent and civilized, over a poor and barbarous nation. In antient times the opulent and civilized found it difficult to defend themselves against the poor and barbarous nations. In modern times the poor and barbarous find it difficult to defend themselves against the opulent and civilized. The invention of fire-arms, an invention which at first sight appears to be so pernicious, is certainly favourable both to the permanency and to the extension of civilization.[12]

The force projected internally and externally is continuous, and is continuous with the economy; for Smith, it is above all *as war machine* that the state and capital are interlocked. This is one moment among many in Smith of direct descriptive realism rather than mere ideology, and yet he reads it ideologically as well, and pens tributes to the wonders of gunpowder for civilizing all sorts of persons for all sorts of reasons. One wants to be rich in order to defend oneself and expand one's force abroad so that one can become richer so that, and so on. At least Smith doesn't pretend that the whole thing doesn't rest on killing.

Smith's basic account of mercantilism in *Wealth of Nations* (vol. 1) could certainly describe today's interlocked state/capital military machine. An early model of squishy totalitarianism was provided by the European East India and West India Companies, state/capitalist hybrids or state-enforced and regulated private monopolies fielding public/private armies here and there but by their own lights engaged primarily in maximization of profits for shareholders, who in turn were often government officials of one sort or another. The profits reaped were presented as being at once of patriotic service to the home countries and of humanitarian service to the persons with whom the companies were trading or whom they were conquering. Similar state/private hybrids have been central to the construction of all large capitalist economies, and would include entities such as Fannie Mae and American utility companies in cooperation with government bodies. "Infrastructure" is constructed or repaired in the current American economy through state contracting, and the entire economy of the DC region is dominated by Federal contractors.

Smith justifies such entities on various grounds. Parliament or the King could grant an exclusive monopoly to a group of merchants and stockholders over the trade in some region, constituting the East India Company, the Africa Company, the South Sea Company, and so on.

> Some particular branches of commerce, which are carried on with barbarous and uncivilized nations, require extraordinary protection. An ordinary store or counting house could give little security to the goods of the merchants who trade to the western coast of Africa. To defend them from the barbarous natives, it is necessary that the place where they are deposited, should be, in some measure, fortified. . . . [I]t was under pretence of securing their persons and property from violence, that both the English and French East India Companies were allowed to erect the first forts which they possessed in that country. . . . The interests of commerce have frequently made it necessary to maintain ministers in foreign countries, where the purposes either of war or of alliance, would not have required any. The commerce of the Turkey Company first occasioned the establishment of an ordinary ambassador at Constantinople. The first English embassies to Russia arose together from commercial interests. The constant interference which those interests necessarily occasioned between the subjects of the different states of Europe, has probably introduced the custom of keeping, in all neighbouring countries, ambassadors or ministers constantly resident even in the time of peace. This custom, unknown to antient times, seems not to be older than the end of the fifteenth or the beginning of the sixteenth century; that is, than the time when commerce first began to extend itself to the greater part of the nations of Europe.[13]

Many historians have emphasized that the conception of the nation-state emerges in this period because—or insofar as—an international system emerges in Europe. Certainly the military square-off and the fortification of various borders within the continent were central to this consolidation of the modern conception and reality of the state. But just as certainly the interaction across borders in trade was also central, as was the cooperation or merging of "state" military force and "private" capital in the colonial project of globalizing Europe and putting the rest of the world to tribute or the gun. In either case, the nation state and the international system of modern Europe emerge with various state/capital configurations, from fantastic fortunes accumulated and squandered by Spanish lords to the rise and fall of centuries-long state/capital enterprises such as the great British or American banks.

Both state and company fleets defended various companies' monopolies, others plying the trade routes being considered pirates. This is the origin of the very idea of monopoly capitalism. The companies were responsible for fortifying or securing land access from the sea, establishing a chain of forts around the world, defended by both company and state forces, between which there was little distinction in many cases, as Walking Stewart among others itemized. The investors stood to earn huge profits if all went well, and the capital of these companies would be invested in turn in government bonds, enabling a permanent military establishment, particularly an unprecedented construction of naval forces. These bonds would pay an extremely reliable return, funding yet more company expansion. Military needs would be fed by private textile and steel mills which would employ millions of people. Labor would have to be organized on a quasi-military basis, but wages would establish a reliable pattern of domestic consumption. Certainly such policies were disastrous for many people all over the world and were a mixed bag in terms of their success at home. This squishy colonialism proved a successful alternative to the Spanish and Portuguese strategy of annexing continents and subduing/converting whole populations directly from Madrid or Lisbon. It also led to one of the most entrenched and unjust domestic and international hierarchies ever devised, or the first really global hierarchy, in which the immiseration of the Third World was interlocked with the prosperity of the First.

8.

One way to frame the debate between Democrats and Federalists, or Jeffersonians and Hamiltonians, in the early American republic is as a debate between an agrarian, or quasi-feudal (and, of course, slave) interest and an emerging market and financialized economy centered in New York. It was the capitalist interest that demanded an activist state, in particular in economic matters. Hamilton's primary concerns were securing a tax base (he particularly favored taxing spirits), paying the national debt, establishing a national bank that could stabilize currency values and facilitate credit markets, and closely regulating and taxing foreign trade in both directions. Such steps ended up being taken by every emerging capitalist economy and required larger and larger structures of state surveillance and control of various sorts of transactions. It was primarily with regard to the development of such economies and the shift from an agrarian to a manufacturing to a service model, for example, that education was made compulsory and has come more and more to be regulated at national and even international levels. In general, procedures of subject formation have become ever more elaborate in both state and private sectors, even as such techniques are constantly revealing their limitations. The way state and capital institutions mutually reflect one another in bureaucratic structures and procedures and in aesthetic preferences is remarkable, and every change in management style, from the cubicle to institution-wide commitment to "teamwork" and "excellence" is a shared legacy.

State repression of striking workers, for example the severe outbreak in the United States in the 1890s, or the less violent outbreaks in Thatcher's Great Britain or Reagan's United States, is a tried and true tradition. Obviously, capital massively wields state police power to protect itself. State regulation of business concerns increases barriers to entry into the market and hence helps consolidate markets in established hands. This effect increases exponentially when the regulators are themselves essentially representatives of those very concerns, who after all are the only ones who understand their segment of the market, the health of which depends on their activity. The way the FCC has actually imposed corporate oligarchy on communications is entirely typical; in the public interest it auctioned off and licensed first radio and then television frequencies, and now cellular bandwidth. This made the great broadcast networks possible, and for some time most Americans had perhaps four sources of information, all basically purveying the same interpretation of the world. Or again, the state enforced copyright laws in such a way as to limit publishing or the dissemination of recorded music to a few large corporations. But it did the same with the railroads and mineral rights in the nineteenth century, for example, leading directly to the great American personal fortunes of that period.

The state has been a key force in territorialization of many dimensions of the world and human experience. The consolidation of the European nation-state took place in complement to the annexation of whole continents, and as many a Marxist has well asserted, one central function of the rule of law is the establishment of private property. Ownership of intellectual property—like the ownership of land—cannot possibly be maintained without exhaustive bodies of records and archives of various kinds, a central function of the state from time immemorial, necessary to taxation and to trade. Of course, ownership of land also requires police power in some form. It has gotten to the point where state and corporation mutually enforce ownership of sequences of tones, strings of symbols and other abstract pseudo-objects. By the 1890s the American economy was being bailed out by J.P. Morgan, a gesture which it has repaid to the financial sector many times, and in response to which the idea of a central or national bank was expanded to include uniform regulation of currency under the Federal Reserve. These mechanisms for mutual stabilization of state and capital were refined and internationalized throughout the twentieth century, though they still have their little glitches.

One effect of a state which presents itself to the population primarily as a distributor of benefits—welfare benefits, healthcare benefits, retirement and disability pensions, food assistance, and unemployment insurance, for example—is that it stabilizes supply and demand, or manufacturing, sales, and consumption by, for example, giving many people a certain amount to spend every week or month. Consumption can be increased by increasing such benefits, for example in a slump with regard to unemployment benefits; this assures retailers, for example, of a certain minimal level of sales. To look at state and corporate interests as opposed in these dimensions is, as everywhere, distorting.

The mutual reinforcement of economic and political hierarchies that has occurred in its capitalist permutations at least since the seventeenth century is a kind of apparently infinite spiral, in which we might say the right and left have colluded since there have been a right and left. In oscillating between liberal and conservative or Democrat and Republican, we oscillate between beefing up one segment of the hierarchy or another, and if I had to identify a direction of history, it would be simply be in terms of ever-increasing inequality of both varieties.

This has reached the point of the worst outbreaks of violence in human history, of great annihilating wars and genocides. It might well lead to human extinction, and our collusion in allowing squishy totalitarian systems to emerge entails that our extinction will be well-deserved. But even if it led to a relatively mellow world democratic state, I would be completely opposed to it. I think it ignores a fundamental moral fact about us: we're mostly more or less the same. You are not that much smarter or more industrious or more right in your ethics or more likely to abide by it than anyone else. The sorts of hierarchies to which people on both sides offer their prayers and their lives cannot be morally justified on any plausible grounds. They rest essentially on the self-delusion of superiority of some groups over others. You should always suspect yourself when you effortlessly assume that you, or people more or less like you, or also people you admire for one reason or another, have a clear idea about how other people or people *like them* should live, particularly when the people you are proposing to transform seem to disagree.

9.

The idea that free markets are historically distinguished from large, powerful states is, in brief, a completely ahistorical ideology, shared by the capitalist right and the communist left and even by almost everyone in between. In this regard and in a number of others, we might think of the left-right spectrum as a single ideology rather than as a taxonomy of opposites. Thus, the left-right split, which defines politics in a hyper-repetitive, mechanical set of partisan bromides about free markets and positive government programs with egalitarian results, depends on a historical mistake.

Insofar as they embody anything definite, both the left and the right are incoherent positions. One place the left runs aground is on its central value of equality: defining it exclusively in economic terms, the left proposes to achieve it by the imposition of extreme political hierarchy; we have seen a mild case of this in Rawls. One place the right runs aground is on its central value of liberty: people who are essentially being forced to labor at a grinding pace for very little in order to enhance the wealth of the people exploiting them are not free. A realization of the vision of either annihilates in the world the ideals that drove it, and that has actually happened over and over to both positions.

The left-right spectrum, since it is linear and not infinite, can be characterized in terms of two extreme poles. One way to see that the thing is incoherent is that these poles can be defined in a number of mutually incompatible ways. So, for example, in the 1930s it was Marxist communism against fascism. It is odd that the left could define the right pole as fascist one minute, laissez-faire the next. The left pole could be a stateless society of barter and localism; or a world of equality in which people are not subordinated by race, gender, and sexuality; or a giant Pentagon-style welfare state; or a Khmer Rouge reeducation-by-execution regime. The Nazi Party, the Catholic Church, hereditary aristocracy, Ayn Rand go-go capitalists, and redneck gun enthusiasts are *all on the same side* in the left-right conceptuality. So are hacktivists, food stamp officials, antiglobalization activists, anarcho-primitivists, and advocates of a world government.

In my suggested bipolar replacement, there are two political philosophies: hierarchical and antihierarchical, statist and anarchist, totalitarian/squishy totalitarian and resistant. But whereas the squishy-totalitarian side funnels into a single situation—a frozen economic and political and knowledge hierarchy—the anarchist side is thousands upon thousands of possibilities, as many as there are possible voluntary arrangements: a million mutant communities. Don't think of it as single thing, think of it as all the possibilities but one. On the up/down spectrum, hereditary aristocracy, monopoly capitalism, the Communist Party, military juntas, and American liberals are on the same side, some more extremely or mildly than others. I am a lot more comfortable with that, and I think it's more plausible. But, of course, any linear account is awfully simplistic.

Ayn Rand and Vlad Lenin, Kim Il Song and Barry Goldwater, Barack Obama and Rand Paul, Francois Mitterrand and Margaret Thatcher, Ronald Reagan and Fidel Castro, Friedrich von Hayek and Leo Trotsky, Slavoj Žižek, and Augusto Pinochet, for all I know, disagreed on several matters. But they agreed on this, or said they did: the state was a force that was historically pitted against private capital. To reduce one was to increase the other and to increase one was to reduce the other. They vary inversely and the balance between them that you recommend constitutes the fundamental way of characterizing your political position. From an antiauthoritarian point of view, this spectrum stretches from authoritarianism on the one end to authoritarianism on the other, with authoritarianism in between. It makes anything that is not that incomprehensible. It narrows all alternatives to variations on hierarchy, structures of inequality, or profoundly unjust distributions of power/wealth. And also as a single ideology, it is merely false. Quite obviously false; throughout the last five centuries, economic and political hierarchies have been massively mutually reinforcing. This is not to say that in some local moment the balance could really shift according to some left or right political program; it is meant to point out that the choice is extremely constructed and incoherent.

B. The Anarchist Utopia that Beckons Like a Babe

1.

I will try to set out my version of anarchism historically, by describing a sequence of developments and figures. The goal is an individualism that is not an ideology of egoism, self-seeking, or rapacious capitalism. Likewise, I want to acknowledge and explore connections between persons without idealizing these connections, simulating them by coercion, or taking them to be more real than the individuals embedded in them.

Anarchism, and in particular my anarchism, is subject to the criticism that it does not sketch out a detailed future, so that one can't reassure people about how it's going to be. They can comfort themselves, I think, with the thought that it's not going to *be* at all. One reason for this is because people have two great political and psychosexual impulses: the desire to subordinate others and the desire to be subordinated. I think of statist politics as basically an S&M drama, in other words, and I don't think the existence of the state arises from our desire for collective identity, but rather from our sexual twistedness. Here I may be doing a little *tu quoque* on all those people who diagnose rather than argue against my political orientation.

2.

The prehistory—or stray bits that might be incorporated—would be the spirit of individual dissent and insistence on independent thought of such ancient figures as Diogenes the Cynic and Chuang Tzu the Taoist. But the direct line begins in radical elements of the Protestant Reformation. The most basic teaching of the Reformation as a whole, I believe, is that no one can administer anyone else's relation to God. Luther's famous formulation is "the priesthood of all believers," that is, the priesthood of each believer. Luther and Calvin continuously asserted this teaching, but also very much retreated from the radical consequences and really could not imagine religion without institutions and the enforcement of dogmas.

I'd like to centralize various political options that emerged before the dawn of the left-right spectrum, and I become alert whenever anyone articulates a position that falls outside it. In particular, I associate my politics with a strand of American radicalism—both religious and secular—that arises in the early nineteenth century, though it has much older origins. It is a radically individualist tradition centering around the abolition of slavery. But to my mind it also solves the individual/collective problem in politics in an inspiring way, or even in the only possible way. This is the central "metaphysical" problem in political theory: the problem of political ontology and the individuation of agents. Occasionally, groups of human beings are very seriously asserted to be the primary objects of politics and are contrasted in this respect to individuals. But at a minimum, collectivities are made up of individuals as, say, a rock is composed of molecules: you can't pick up that rock and throw it but not throw the molecules that comprise it.

The leaders of various elements of the radical Reformation—a movement that lasted well through the nineteenth century and continues in various forms—took many of the teachings of Luther more seriously than he did himself. The priesthood of each believer is an explicit commitment to independence of thought and conscience. This had myriad implications, including eventually the rise of scientistic secularism and the Enlightenment. But it also had very many radical political implications and extreme expressions of egalitarianism as well as religious pacifism and antistatism arose in pockets wherever the Reformation extended. Figures such as Thomas Müntzer, Andreas Karlstadt, and Hans Denck began to build a theology around the radical independence of the individual human conscience, intellect, and relation to God. Even as Luther, Calvin, or the British monarchy attempted to reimpose an institutional and state Church on various regions, these figures began to develop the sort of theology that led to Diggers and Ranters, Shakers and Quakers, abolitionist saints, feminist ass kickers, and anarchist freaks.

Denck, an Anabaptist, was one of many figures—later including Anne Hutcheson, Søren Kierkegaard and Theodore Parker, for example—who pursued the "antinomian" implications of the Reformation.

> All commandments, customs, and laws, insofar as they are written in the Old and New Testaments, have been abolished for a true follower of Christ (I Timothy 1:9). That is, the true follower has the word written on his heart; he loves God alone. . . . God sets aside his divinity, and the person should set aside his humanity, so that the sacrifice may be perfect and the love become one, as happened in Jesus Christ, the only-begotten son of god—and as should still happen to the elect. Insofar as one is united with God, he is free of all time and space, and released from all human laws. But he is no longer able to enjoy such freedom. For to the same extent he gladly wants to be subject to all laws. . . . To the degree that one possesses the law, the written law has been abolished.[14]

What it meant to "have the law in one's heart" or to possess "the inner light" or "the voice of conscience" was the subject of centuries of extremely heated debate featuring many conversions and excommunications, rebellions and executions. But on the radical edge, this was not something upon which we were called upon to pronounce; God alone would bring people to judgment. Anne Hutchinson appealed away from the religious and legal strictures of the Massachusetts Bay Company on the grounds alone of "the voice of his own spirit to my soul."

The specifically political split between radicals of the Reformation and representatives of established churches continued in many guises for some centuries. There is a more genteel Protestant tradition—though at times quite radical itself, and with remarkable effects—that centralizes individual rights; educational attainment, scientific research, and meritocracy; various forms of republicanism and constitutional monarchy; political and social reform; and mercantilist capitalism. Here we might range Harrington, Hobbes, Locke, Hume, Montesquieu, Voltaire, Adams, Mill. Simultaneously, there is a wave of much more egalitarian and utopian and millinerian visions: the peasant rebellions that demanded economic equality or that attacked enclosures of the commons; utopian communities all over the world, but specifically all over the United States (I draw your attention to Nashoba, Oneida, Modern Times, Mormons, the Amish, Brook Farm, Fourierist Phalanxes: practicing various forms of communal economy and nonstandard gender relations). This history has been marked throughout by the emergence of radical movements for the amelioration of poverty, war, slavery, and gender oppression.

One expression of this conflict between the genteel and ecstatic forms of Protestant individualism is what came to be called the Enlightenment and Counter-Enlightenment in Europe of the eighteenth century: the skepticism and emphasis on reasoned argumentation in Hume or Voltaire as against the religious ecstasy of a Hamann or Jacobi. An extraordinary literary and philosophical expression of the radical, "irrationalist," ecstatic side of Protestantism is the authorship of Kierkegaard, and one might locate the American transcendentalists in the gap between genteel and ecstatic Protestantism. Rousseau, I think, became an important and radical figure as he worked this gap—and also the gap between individual and collective—from his own cultural and idiosyncratic angle.

This would be a very complex assertion pay off on historically, but I don't think you end up even with the radicalism of Rousseau, the French Revolution, and Marx without the Reformation and specifically without the radically egalitarian elements. That strand of political theory—roughly, "leftism"—specifically abandons the individualism that drove many of these figures and movements, and it deploys various forms of collective consciousness and agency, "general will," or nation, class, race, gender, or whatever it may be. In a way, not to be too cute about it, leftism of this sort re-Catholicizes or tries to institutionalize or collectivize the individualism of the Reformation, while holding on to the egalitarianism.

3.

In the period roughly between 1820 and 1850, an astonishing group of American radicals were active—astonishing for their purity, for their extremism, for their eccentricity, and for their profundity: William Lloyd Garrison, Josiah Warren, Adin Ballou,

Lucretia Mott, Nathaniel Peabody Rogers, Sarah and Angelina Grimké, Maria Weston Chapman, Theodore Dwight Weld, Samuel J. May, and many others. The names of some of their positions give a sense of how radical they were: "ultraism," "come-outerism," "perfectionism," "immediatism," "no-governmentism," and—going beyond even that—"no-organizationism."

One thing these figures have in common, and that binds their reform movements together, and binds them also with the transcendentalists—with whom they were intertwined—is a pervasive antiauthoritarianism. We might trace the hostility of such figures towards power—the power of the state, but also of the church, of the white race, of men, of the military, and of capital—to three fundamental and connected sources.

The first of these is the individualism of radical Protestantism, and in particular three strands: Unitarianism (of which, for example, May and Emerson were ministers), Hicksite Quakerism (Lucretia Mott was a preacher), and the revivalism of Charles Grandison Finney (Weld was one of his assistant pastors). These taught that each person was ultimately answerable only to God, that all persons were equal before God, and that God expressed himself in and as the conscience of each individual. The doctrines originate, as I have sketched, in the sixteenth and seventeenth centuries, in radical elements of the Reformation, such as various Anabaptist groups and the Diggers of the English Civil War, some of whom made their way to the New World. All of the strands of Protestantism that eventuated in the radicalism of the early nineteenth century were, as well, anti-Calvinist: they rejected the idea that human beings are intrinsically depraved, affirmed free will, and often taught that all people would be saved and could live even now without sin. This "universalism" and "perfectionism" is expressed, for example, in Emerson's premonitions of a transformed humanity. Indeed, eventually Emerson withdrew from the pulpit and the Grimkés from their adopted Quakerism in large measure because even these compromised individual responsibility for the conduct of one's relation to God and one's fellow human beings.

A second impetus for or element of the basic convictions of this group of reformers was Christian nonresistance or pacifism as articulated in exemplary ways by many Quakers including Lucretia Mott and the Grimkés, and by Samuel J. May, William Lloyd Garrison and Adin Ballou, whose works directly influenced Tolstoy, Gandhi, and King. From absolute pacifism, these figures drew the direct conclusion that government that rests on force (a category that includes all the world's states) is entirely morally repugnant, even as their position precluded any forcible resistance to it. These figures were anarchists, in the sense that they opposed all state power as morally illegitimate.

The most important and immediate source of their antiauthoritarianism, however, was antislavery, which was the fundamental moral driver of the entire enterprise. The American abolitionist movement in its immediatist varieties came to see ownership of persons as a violation of nature and nature's God. And it came to understand human evil quite in general as the attempt to enslave or to claim ownership in persons. Finally, these figures condemned capitalism, war, marriage, and government as it existed in their time on precisely the same grounds: all of them rested on coercion, and coercion amounted to a claim to own other people, to be able to annex their time and energy and their very lives to purposes not their own. Abolitionism is the structure by which these figures thought through all political and economic questions. It is what took Protestant spiritual individualism and brought it out of the church community and into a movement to reform society in every aspect. One place to see this emerging is John Woolman's *Journal* (1774), in which the structure is traversed in diary form.

I will briefly explore some of the connections between these figures' various radical positions, especially abolitionism, pacifism, antistatism, and women's rights. Theodore Dwight Weld, writing to his wife, the great abolitionist and feminist Angelina Grimké, summed up the ethos:

> No condition of birth, no shade of color, no mere misfortune of circumstances, can annul that birth-right charter, which God has bequeathed to every being upon whom he has stamped his own image, by making him a *free moral agent*, and . . . he who robs his fellow man of this tramples upon right, subverts justice, outrages humanity, unsettles the foundation of human safety, and sacrilegiously assumes the prerogative of God.[15]

Weld gave the following definition of slavery as the essence and acme of human evil: slavery is "Holding & treating persons as things." Lucretia Mott formulated the general principle in a particularly clear and interesting way: "Every man has a right to his own body."[16] Maria Weston Chapman wrote that "the antislavery cause [is] one, with regard to which *all human beings*, whether men or women, citizens or foreigners, white or colored, [have] *the same duties and the same rights*."[17] Antislavery, in short, became an entire political orientation: the meaning of the term *slavery* was extended, to some extent metaphorically but to some extent literally, to refer to any coercive authority, and hence *antislavery* came to mean antiauthoritarianism quite in general. "It is always unsafe to invest man with power over his fellow being," Mott told a woman's rights convention in 1853. "*Call no man master*—that is the true doctrine."[18]

Many of these figures took antistatism to follow directly from nonresistance. Exemplary in this are Garrison, his associate Henry Wright, Sarah Grimké, Nathaniel Peabody Rogers, Adin Ballou, Bronson Alcott, and Lucretia Mott. Here is a bit of Garrison's extraordinary "Declaration of Sentiments Adopted by the Peace Convention," expressing the consensus of the first great interdenominational meeting of American nonresistants in 1838.

> We cannot acknowledge allegiance to any human government; neither can we oppose any such government by a resort to physical force. We recognize

but one King and Lawgiver, one Judge and Ruler of mankind. We are bound by the laws of a kingdom which is not of this world; the subjects of which are forbidden to fight; . . . which has no state lines, no national partitions, no geographical boundaries; in which there is no distinction of rank, or division of caste, or inequality of sex. . . .

As every human government is upheld by physical strength, and its laws are enforced virtually at the point of the bayonet, we cannot hold any office which imposes upon its incumbent the obligation to compel men to do right, on pain of imprisonment or death. We therefore voluntarily exclude ourselves from every legislative and judicial body, and repudiate all human politics, worldly honors, and stations of authority.[19]

Tolstoy quoted the Declaration of Sentiments in its entirety in his fundamental statement of modern pacifism, *The Kingdom of God is Within You*, which was an important text for Gandhi and King.

Sarah Grimké, in a letter to Gerrit Smith in 1837, drew what she took to be the obvious global antiauthoritarian and individualist conclusions from nonresistance. One way to understand the doctrine she espouses is as an extension to the political state of the Reformation attack on ecclesiastical institutions; but she makes this extension universal, to economic exploitation, sexual subordination, and every form of force and coercion by one person against another.

Dear brother the more I contemplate this sublime doctrine of acknowledging no government but Gods, of loosing myself from all dominion of man both civil and ecclesiastical, the more I am persuaded it is the only doctrine that can bring us into that liberty wherewith Christ has made us free; until we receive and believe this doctrine we have not the faith which over cometh the world, and without faith it is impossible to please God.[20]

These figures, including Garrison, came to their pacifism, in turn, at least in part through abolitionism: slavery to them was a festival of violence, torture, and coercion. All of these positions, we might say, were mutually entailed, or were held as a single interlocking system. Lucretia Mott was as anarchistic as Garrison: "We see many giving up their undue attachment to political parties and governments, giving up their constitutional veneration and refusing to have any lot or part in a government and constitution which are based upon the sword, the ultimate resort of which is the destroying weapon."[21]

The women of this circle were remarkable as the first American women who insisted on full public participation in the debates of the day and as the first American feminists. And the men of this circle, notably Weld and Garrison, were remarkable for their antisexism. Lucretia Mott struggled to make her anarchism compatible with advocacy of women's suffrage:

> Far be it from me to encourage woman to vote, or to take an active part in politics, in the present state of our government. Her right to the elective franchise however, is the same, and should be yielded to her, whether she exercise that right or not. Would that man too, would have no participation in a government based upon the life-taking principle—upon retaliation and the sword. It is unworthy a Christian nation. But when, in the diffusion of light and intelligence, a convention shall be called to make regulations for self-government on Christian, non-resistant principles, I can see no good reason, why woman should not participate in such an assemblage, taking part equally with man.[22]

All these figures also drew anticapitalist conclusions. For example, they all extended the idea of slavery to the buying and selling of labor in emerging industrial capitalism. Nathaniel Peabody Rogers, the New Hampshire publisher of the abolitionist paper *Herald of Freedom*, wrote this in 1845:

> The Institutions make Slavery, and therefore cannot overthrow it. And they cannot allow us to overthrow it. The overthrow of Slavery must involve the doing away [also] of the oppressions practiced by these institutions on the white poor. White Labor is all but enslaved among us. It is the slave of Capital. Capital buys it at auction. The capitalist bids off the bones and sinews of Labor. . . . It is impossible for Labor to get rich or free. I mean Labor generally. The institutions of capital will exhaust Labor's means, and keep it down. The black laborer it enslaves outright in this country. The means of abolishing slavery must be employed in opening the eyes of the people to these tyrant Institutions. Anti-Slavery tells the truth about them.[23]

And by "these tyrant Institutions," Rogers meant government, capital, and the subordination of women and even of animals, as well as chattel slavery.

4.

Now, these figures, at one time lionized by America's and even the world's subversives, have essentially been dropped from the canon of dissent or of American thought in general. I think there are several reasons for this, which might be summed up by saying that the left-right political spectrum makes their thought incomprehensible: it has no place for them at all, and that goes for Emerson and Thoreau as much as any of the others. They obviously cannot be read as conservatives, but neither do they translate sensibly as leftist by the standards of the now-dominant statist left. I think there are two factors that contributed to all these figures being more or less jettisoned from the history of "progressivism" or "socialism" or what came to be known as "leftism": their religiosity and their individualism. Many of them are extremely, indeed ecstatically, religious, all in one vein or another of evangelical Protestantism. One way to frame the anarchism of these figures is—as they often put it—that they recognized no human government because they recognized only the government of God: antinomianism. Later European and European-influenced anarchism was atheistic and took up Bakunin's slogan "No Gods, No Masters," and, of course, Marxist communism was also explicitly atheistic.

But as a program of reform on this plane of reality, I must say, it amounts to much the same thing: opposition to government conducted by coercion by some people of others. The religious and the nonreligious antistatists all regard human government as operating by imprisonment, conscription and other forms of slavery, and by wide-scale application of warlike violence and the threat of warlike violence. That the Quakers, for example, located God in and as each person's conscience, made the actual question of God's existence otiose, as Thoreau, who held all the political positions—with the possible exception of nonresistance—but without the Christianity, saw clearly. All the views of May or Mott or Garrison were quickly secularized, or appeared contemporaneously in secularized versions. So, for example, Josiah Warren took on in the 1820s and 1830s all the individualism of the most radical Protestants, and drew their antistatist conclusions without appealing at all to God or scripture. And he extended these insights as well to anticapitalism: he detested the profit motive and tried to set up working economies that deleted it. By the 1860s he was an important figure in early attempts to organize labor in the context of industrial capitalism.

Warren's basic political concept was "self-sovereignty," or as Aristotle might put it, the rule of each, which he opposed precisely to slavery: no one can own another because each person is the owner of herself. This discourse derives from the religious antislavery of the era. So for example Sarah Grimké described a slave's attempted escape as a resolution to "take possession of himself."[24] And Angelina wrote: "The great fundamental principle of Abolitionism is, that man cannot rightfully hold his fellow man as property. Therefore, we affirm, that *every slave holder is a man stealer*. We do so, for the following reason: to steal a man is to rob him of himself."[25]

In the extension of antislavery thought that became the common coin of American feminism, Sarah Grimké condemns patriarchy on the grounds of slavery in her pioneering feminist text *Letters on the Equality of the Sexes*: "The cupidity of man soon led him to regard woman as property, and hence we find them sold to those who wished to marry them, as far as appears, without any regard to those sacred rights which belong to woman, as well as to man in the choice of a companion. . . . I am persuaded that the rights of woman, like the rights of slaves, need only be examined to be understood and asserted."²⁶ Though Mott's and the Grimkés' feminism had a strongly religious flavor, they easily made common cause with more secularized feminists such as Elizabeth Cady Stanton, who also made use of their work. Margaret Fuller took Mott's or the Grimkés' abolitionist feminism and secularized and transcendentalized it but retained entire the individualism, and her position was precisely that contemporary marriage and other forms of hierarchical gender relations were violations of individual self-sovereignty, which demanded to be respected in each woman as in each man.

Emerson and Thoreau are exemplary figures in the secularization of these ideas. Emerson's evolution from Unitarian minister to beloved universal sage brought versions of all these ideas before the American public—perhaps not always under their most radical construals, though Emerson's individualism is as extreme as anyone's. I don't think it will do simply to call Emerson and Thoreau "atheists," however, and they maintained various stances that we might think of as spiritual: they were interested in Eastern religions, and, of course, manifested many moments of pantheism. They connected free individuality to Nature and to God, and the positions are, to say the least, no less compelling in that "post-Christian" context than in the other figures' Christianity. They retained from their post-Calvinist Protestantism a premonition of the perfection of every person. And Emerson and Thoreau knew these other figures well, in person and by their writings, and supported them more or less entirely. Emerson intermittently and Thoreau consistently took on their antistatism as well.

5.

If I had to choose a text to epitomize the movement as a political philosophy, or indeed my own political philosophy, I would certainly choose "Civil Disobedience," which also has the considerable advantage that it was written by the best American prose stylist of the period. In this passage, for example, he endorses both Garrison's "immediatism" and his "disunionism": the most radical varieties of abolitionism in the 1830s and 1840s.

> I do not hesitate to say, that those who call themselves Abolitionists should at once effectively withdraw their support, both in person and property, from the government of Massachusetts, and not wait till they constitute a majority of one, before they suffer the right to prevail through them. I think that it is enough if they have God on their side, without waiting for that other one. Moreover, any man more right than his neighbors constitutes a majority of one already.²⁷

Both Garrison's immediatism and his secessionism constituted a spiritual stance: withdraw from sin; stop sinning immediately; you and the world can be transformed in a twinkling; all you have to do is actually want it. Thoreau pursued the same series of thoughts but without the directly Christian motivating force.

Thoreau took whatever practical steps he could to secede. But the passage above is verbatim what Lucretia Mott had been preaching for decades. Indeed, the influence was direct. Thoreau saw Lucretia Mott preach in 1843, and wrote to his sister about it.

> I believe I have not told you about Lucretia Mott. It was a good while ago I heard her at the Quaker Church in Hester St. She is a preacher, and it was advertised that she would be present on that day. I liked all the proceedings very well . . . At length, after a long silence, waiting for the spirit, Mrs. Mott rose, took off her bonnet, and began to utter very deliberately what the spirit suggested. Her self-possession was something to say [remark on], if all else failed—but it did not. Her subject was the abuse of the Bible—and thence she straightaway digressed to slavery and the degradation of woman. It was a good speech—transcendentalism in its mildest form.[28]

"Mildest" here I believe is used in a somewhat Christian, lamb-of-God sense because there is no doubt that Mott's preaching was fierce; we have a fair example of what Thoreau heard in her sermon of the same year, "Righteousness Gives Strength to Its Possessor."[29] But it is certainly significant that he regards her as preaching transcendentalism, throughout. Indeed, according to one of Mott's letters from 1858, she talked to Emerson after he gave the lecture "The Law of Success." He told her, "I got some leaves out of yr. book."[30]

In "Civil Disobedience," Thoreau writes,

> It is not a man's duty, as a matter of course, to devote himself to the eradication of any, even the most enormous wrong; he may still properly have other concerns to engage him; but it is his duty, at least, to wash his hands of it, and, if he gives it no thought longer, not to give it practically his support. If I devote myself to other pursuits and contemplations, I must first see, at least, that I do not pursue them sitting upon another man's shoulders. I must get off him first, that he may pursue his contemplations too.[31]

One source of this notion of an obligation not to participate in evil is the conscientious objection of Anabaptists and other religious groups, but also the Free Produce movement launched by Quakers starting in the time of John Woolman, in which Mott was active: the idea of not selling or purchasing goods made by slave labor, at once a consumer boycott and a secession/divestment from the slave economy that deploys a particular individualist vision of human moral obligation common to Mott and Thoreau.

Emerson and Thoreau were fundamentally non-joiners and maintained some philosophical distance from practical reform movements, while also participating, for example, in the underground railroad. Yet they were also inspired by these movements and emerged in the same atmosphere, and their politics was informed by them. Emerson expresses his admiration for Garrison in a number of journal entries and describes meeting him in his "dingy office." "I cannot speak of that gentleman without respect."[32] Of "the principle of nonresistance," he says "Trust it. Give up the Government without too solicitously inquiring whether roads can be still built, letters carried, & title deeds secured when the government of force is at an end."[33] That is, he immediately associates nonresistance with antistatism, a connection that appeared obvious to many of these figures. Emerson, too, saw Mott preach. He praises her courage and says "she makes every bully ashamed."[34]

6.

So I don't think the sheer religiosity should eliminate these figures from the radical canon. The individualism, on the other hand, is a more stubborn problem, as the left, since its domination by Marxism, has conceived itself even in mild versions as essentially collectivist and statist. Yet individualism, like collectivism, has its liberatory and its oppressive versions or applications. Josiah Warren developed a metaphysics of radical individualism and wrote that the first principle of his thought, "or rather, the foundation of the whole subject, is the study of individuality, or the practice of mentally discriminating, dividing, separating, disconnecting persons, things, and events, according to their individual peculiarities."[35] To contend against individuality, Warren wrote, "is to contend against our nature's constant production. Such is the subtle and inherent nature of this individuality, that it accompanies every one in every thing he does, and any attempt to conquer it is like undertaking to walk away from his mode of walking, or to run away from his breath—the very effort calls it more decidedly into play. Out of the indestructibility or inalienability of this individuality grows the absolute right of its exercise, or the absolute sovereignty of every individual."[36]

Adin Ballou, among many others, made the spiritual/political connection.

> With us, at present, perfect individuality is a fundamental idea of the true man. We believe that by setting the individual right with his Creator, we shall set social relationships right. We therefore go for unabridged independence of mind, conscience, duty, and responsibility; for direct divine government over the human soul; and, of course, for as little human government as

possible. We wish to know whether there is any such thing as man's being and doing right from the law of God written on his heart, without the aid of external bonds and restraints.[37]

Ballou started as a Universalist minister and eventually founded a community of eccentric Christians at Hopedale, MA. Warren was a deist or perhaps an atheist, and took no justification from anywhere but here on earth. Thoreau was a naturalist in both a scientific and a spiritual sense. But all were radical individualists and advocated radical reforms of various sorts on that basis. I am suggesting that though the background religion or metaphysics was extremely important to each of these people, those things are of little political moment; all these figures were massively agreed on the nature of human beings and the sorts of social arrangements that were morally legitimate: namely, noncoercive arrangements.

Emerson, in his essay "New England Reformers" and in his later reminiscences, always connected all the reforms and the character of the reformers to individualism; he thought the whole thing followed from that.

> In politics, for example, it is easy to see the progress of dissent. The country is full of rebellion; the country is full of kings. Hands off! let there be no control and no interference in the administration of the affairs of this kingdom of me. . . . I confess, the motto of the Globe newspaper is so attractive to me, that I can seldom find much appetite to read what is below it in its columns, "The world is governed too much." So the country is frequently affording solitary examples of resistance to the government, solitary nullifiers [Thoreau and Alcott, for example, who refused to pay taxes during the Mexican War], who throw themselves on their reserved rights; nay, who have reserved all their rights; who reply to the assessor, and to the clerk of court, that they do not know the State; and embarrass the courts of law, by non-juring, and the commander-in-chief of the militia, by non-resistance.[38]

But these figures also, like Emerson, viewed individualism as essential to a real social harmony.

> Each man, if he attempts to join himself to others, is on all sides cramped and diminished of his proportion; and the stricter the union, the smaller and the more pitiful he is. But leave him alone, to recognize in every hour and place the secret soul, he will go up and down doing the works of a true member, and, to the astonishment of all, the work will be done by concert, though no man spoke. Government will be adamantine without any governor. The union must be ideal in actual individualism. . . . And

as a man is equal to the church, and equal to the state, so he is equal to every other man.[39]

That is also Warren's political philosophy in a nutshell. All these figures associated individualism with egalitarianism, which unfortunately appears incoherent to the post-Marx left. But the connection is obvious, and a demand for the equality of black people or poor people or women or industrial workers or American Indians is naturally framed in terms of the equal freedom or autonomy of each individual; that is what equality meant to all these figures. There are forms of inequality other than economic inequality, and a statist left that is intent on redressing inequalities of wealth is also at the same time constituting in the most obvious way a hierarchy of political power.

Emerson was often completely explicit in his anarchism, for example in "Speech on Affairs in Kansas," delivered as Kansas descended into slaughter around slavery, partly due to the work of John Brown and his sons.

> I am glad to see that the terror at disunion and anarchy is disappearing. Massachusetts, in its heroic day, had no government—was an anarchy. Every man stood on his own feet, was his own governor; and there was no breach of peace from Cape Cod to Mount Hoosac. California, a few years ago, by the testimony of all people at that time in the country, had the best government that ever existed. Pans of gold lay drying outside of every man's tent, in perfect security. The land was measured into little strips of a few feet wide, all side by side. A bit of ground that your hand could cover was worth one or two hundred dollars, on the edge of your strip; and there was no dispute. Every man throughout the country was armed with knife and revolver, and it was known that instant justice would be administered to each offence, and perfect peace reigned. For the Saxon man, when he is well awake, is not a pirate but a citizen, all made of hooks and eyes, and links himself naturally to his brothers, as bees hook themselves to one another and to their queen in a loyal swarm.[40]

As we think of the beloved, mild sage of Concord, we should remind ourselves of passages like that, and perhaps each American needs to be reminded of these sort of values from time to time, whether that American is a Saxon or not. Sometimes when people have noted my enthusiasm for Emerson and Thoreau, they have said things like, but you're not a *rugged* individualist, are you? I don't know; why not? Many have been the attempts to tone Emerson down, annex him to the pragmatists or American progressivism of later periods. Good heavens, no.

So, one suggestion I am making is that we need to recover various forms of radicalism that preceded or stand outside the left-right political spectrum. There just have to be alternatives to both the statist left and the capitalist right, which are not as distinct from each other as they conceive themselves to be. As it happens, the sort of radicals I am describing developed one: it is individualist but completely opposed to greed; it is profoundly egalitarian but it associates equality with liberty for each person. That these positions sound incoherent only shows that the way we conceive our politics is itself incoherent.

7.

If I could create a canon for the more or less secular expression of the political orientation I am describing—American antiauthoritarianism—I would start with Garrison's "Declaration of Sentiments of the Peace Society," Emerson's "Politics," Thoreau's "Civil Disobedience," Warren's *Equitable Commerce*, and Voltairine de Cleyre's "Crime and Punishment." One thing I think is immediately apparent: this particular line of discourse takes its conceptual structure and its moral urgency from antislavery.

> The fact of two poles, of two forces, centripetal and centrifugal, is universal, and each force by its own activity develops the other. Wild liberty develops iron conscience. Want of liberty, by strengthening law and decorum, stupefies conscience. . . .
>
> Whilst I do what is fit for me, and abstain from what is unfit, my neighbor and I shall often agree in our means, and work together for a time to one end. But whenever I find my dominion over myself not sufficient for me, and undertake the direction of him also, I overstep the truth, and come into false relations to him. I may have so much more skill or strength than he, that he cannot express adequately his sense of wrong, but it is a lie, and hurts like a lie both him and me. Love and nature cannot maintain the assumption: it must be executed by a practical lie, namely, by force. This undertaking for another is the blunder which stands in colossal ugliness in the governments of the world. It is the same thing in numbers, as in a pair, only not quite so intelligible. I can see well enough the great difference between my setting myself down to a self-control, and my going to make somebody else act after my views: but when a quarter of the human race assume to tell me what I must do, I may be too much disturbed by the circumstances to see so clearly the absurdity of their command. . . .
>
> The tendencies of the times favor the idea of self-government, and leave the individual . . . to the rewards and penalties of his own constitution, which work with more energy than we believe, whilst we depend on artificial restraints. The movement in this direction has been very marked in modern history. . . . It promises a recognition of higher rights than those of personal freedom, or the security of property. A man has a right to be

employed, to be trusted, to be loved, to be revered. The power of love, as the basis of a State, has never been tried.[41]

That Emerson was influenced at this period by Garrison's nonresistance and antistatism is evident from his journals as from his essays, and this is certainly as radical as Emerson's public politics ever became, with the possible exception of the defense of John Brown. But one thing I would like to remark on and that Emerson shares in the same hyperintense form as Mott: the individualism does not end in selfishness; individuation is a realization of one's real place in a real whole. Your individuality is potentially your contribution to the whole; your difference is more necessary than your sameness, precisely in order to connect intensely across lines of identity, in order to ameliorate oppressions. As I quoted Emerson all those pages ago as saying, a person is a "knot of roots," constituted in relation, individuated by its relations.

This is why force is a lie, which is quite a striking formulation: it is an interruption of the self-development of another infinitely valuable human individuality. Unanimity of belief or action, conformity, demands and enforces falsehood. But ultimately—and this is entirely characteristic of the Protestant tradition from which it emerges—the individual is developing precisely toward and ultimately as part of, a greater whole: for Emerson, the human community, but also Nature, the Oversoul. And he is not just reciting automatically when he leans on the word *love* here, just as Garrison and Mott had before him; love is the mode of the connection that is forged in the flourishing together of individualities. It is the political expression of Emerson's entangled ontology and phenomenology: one must feel one's reality as an individual, and one must help genuine connections to emerge: all governments really have is scissors.

At any rate, the nature of American radicalism mutated and fragmented from the 1840s. The abolitionist movement split first over the role of women, then again over political participation, and finally, by the 1850s, over militancy. By then even clergymen such as Thomas Wentworth Higginson and Theodore Parker supported John Brown's various projects and other violent actions to end slavery, and Thoreau was moving in that direction as well. Twenty years of nonresistance might convince you that the slave's condition is more urgent than the purity of your principles. By the time of the Civil War, which was one of many factors that made a pure idealism difficult to maintain, a decadent period of reform had emerged, involving fad medical treatments, free love, and spiritualism, among other ideas; individualism devolved into mere eccentricity, and people such as Stephen Pearl Andrews and Victoria Woodhull seemed to select positions according to which was least plausible.

Even that had a certain anarchic beauty. But the abolitionist saints, feminist ass kickers, and anarchist freaks of the early nineteenth century remained for the reformers of the 1860s and 1870s, and I hope can be recovered now as, a trace of truth and a demonstration of the possibility of personal and social transformation.

8.

I would like to construct some sort of positive vision out of the political tradition I have described, out of figures such as Mott, Thoreau, Garrison, Warren. I'll sketch a utopia in one sense, but not in another. In my Republic, people are extremely jealous of their autonomy, as families, groups, and communities of various sorts as against larger configurations of coercion or force, and of their own individual liberty even within such situations. There is, I believe, a multiplicitous inspiring history of the ways that people have organized themselves outside of state control, on frontiers or what James C. Scott calls "shatter zones," but also in a million interstices within the state/corporate order. This is not mere pie in the sky: people routinely take steps to avoid state surveillance, for example.

When people release themselves from coercive power, I believe, they will find that extreme economic and political hierarchy is not sustainable without it, but they will find it necessary to provide some of the things that these hierarchies previously provided, including perhaps some forms of security as well as provisions for economic activity, technological advancement, and so on. Then the question will be how these can emerge in voluntary configurations. I have explored in other writings some of the ways people have tried to do this, especially Josiah Warren's labor note economy. At Utopia, Ohio; Modern Times, New York; and elsewhere, Warren's conception allowed destitute people to construct their own homes because they controlled their own labor.

But this is just one vague sort of answer; what I want is for all the voluntary possibilities to be explored. Mill or Warren would cast this as a series of experiments; I think probably it's going to be a lot less systematic than that suggests. I do think one useful framework conceives the matter in terms of the relation of individual and collective. And one way I could state my basic political intuition is that the correct balance is achieved wherever you allow it to be achieved, that it is precisely coercion which distorts or destroys many possibilities of a decent collective life (many nightmares, too, I suppose), that severs essential connections and hence compromises individuals. My feeling is that we went terribly wrong in treating polities/economies as things to be shaped under coercion. For example, I far prefer a medieval European city center to a planned-out grid, even with all the disadvantages of the former: something that grew up rather than was planned and implemented. Or, you could say, I prefer improvisation in the arts, at least within certain limits or understood in certain ways: improvisation as requiring consummate craft, as I have been saying, but also improvisation as a collaborative environment in which new connections emerge willy-nilly—radical democracy as jazz.

One obvious way to frame my point would be in terms of natural as against artificial political orders, and I am sympathetic to such an account. The organic/Aristotelian polis and the classical republicanism that embodies it is the least disgusting of political ideologies, and Aristotle's treatment of Plato's *Republic* as absurdly artificial is plausible. I admire the recent revival of this tradition by Philip Pettit and others. On the other hand, I know of no way to make the natural/artificial distinction pay off here any more than anywhere else. It may even be that people are literally incapable of living without coercion. I would like to see an argument—evolutionary, for example—as to why that should be.

Something else I'd like to see while I am utopianizing is the slow development of the idea that much of the world's stuff and various aspects and products of human activity are essentially unownable and hence unsellable. I think the annexation of any aspect of experience as a commodity is something that will tend to spell disaster in that arena. The idea of ownership of everything and the development of each thing—even abstract sequences of words or tones—as a commodity is something that occurred historically, unfolded over centuries. It might fold up again; members of our species have paid a horrendous price for it. And yet I think that ownership or control of objects in one's immediate surroundings and control or even ownership of the space one inhabits is an important human experience and dimension of freedom and autonomy.

I think work is important, and that underlying any economy there is or should be or must be actual skill and actual labor and production: of artifacts, devices, ideas, melodies, and so on. I would emphasize cooperation and mutual aid a bit more than do individualist anarchists such as Warren and Lysander Spooner, but I do note that religious anarchists such as Garrison and Mott emphasized the duty to help others above all things. I am not sure how heroic teachings like that can be motivated fully outside the religious conceptions within which they arose, however, though I am also certain that moral heroism is possible in the absence of belief in God.

Admittedly, this is almost unbelievably half-assed, and I resist the project on which I am now engaged on many levels. I don't think I can predict the future on this global scale, and I definitely don't think I am predicting the future. According to my religion of cynicism, I will not be disappointed because I will not expect things to get better. And in all seriousness, I see the direction of history right now as the consolidation of hierarchical power, so such developments as I am describing would surprise me.

There's one very bewildering mistake that a lot of people make: confusing what they want the future to be like with what it will, in fact, be like. Why in the world should one expect these things to coincide? Rather, the maneuver is rhetorical: the idea is to force you to agree or be on the wrong side of history. But really, the future will not be realizing any particular idea, and articulating ideals would be a lot less dangerous if there was no real tendency to expect their fruition. And, of course, my "anarchism without adjectives" means to me that I am explicitly repudiating the project of telling other people how to live. If one articulates an ideal, one is tempted to try to constitute a power sufficient to its realization or simulation. Nevertheless, I am permitting myself to do some spitballing.

9.

The great American anarchist and feminist Voltairine de Cleyre was exasperated by the economic wars in the anarchism of her times, but she thought they were swamped by the agreement.

> I have now presented the rough skeleton of four different economic schemes entertained by anarchists [socialism, communism, individualism, and mutualism]. Remember that the point of agreement in all is: *no compulsion*. Those who favor one method have no intention of forcing it upon another, so long as equal tolerance is exercised toward themselves. . . . For myself, I believe that all these and many more could be advantageously tried in different localities; I would see the instincts and habits of the people express themselves in a free choice in every community; and I am sure that distinct environments would call out distinct adaptations. Personally, while I recognize that liberty would be greatly extended under any of these economies, none of them satisfies me.[42]

Directly, de Cleyre's voice rises in rhapsodies I have quoted, edited, recited elsewhere—Whitmaniac or Emersonian ecstasies. But I also think the chastened tone was appropriate in 1907 and is triply appropriate now; we know neither very clearly what will happen nor what ought to happen. That would be a dangerous insight to take on board. But maybe the delusion represented by its negation has given rise to some problems.

I do think that the early American anarchists had various excellent ideas in economics. The economy of Warren's communities was based in the Time Store, in which a cooperative labor economy was established by the exchange of labor embodied in "labor notes."

> If a traveler, on a hot day, stop at a farm-house, and ask for a drink of water, he generally gets it without any thought of price. Why? Because it costs nothing, or its cost is immaterial. If the traveler was so thirsty that he would give a dollar for the water, rather than not have it, this would be the value of the water to him; and if the farmer were to charge this price, he would be acting upon the principle that the price of a thing should be what it will bring, which is the motto and spirit of all the principal commerce of the world; and if he were to stop up all the neighboring springs, and cut

off all supplies of water from other sources, and compel travelers to depend solely on him for water, and then should charge them a hundred dollars for a drink, he would be acting precisely upon the principle upon which all the business of the world has been conducted from time immemorial. It is pricing a thing according to what it will bring, or according to its value to the receiver, instead of its cost to the producer. . . .

It will here be seen, that prices are raised in consequence of increased want, and are lowered with its decrease. The most successful speculator is he who can create the most want in the community, and extort the most from it. This is civilized cannibalism.

The value of a loaf of bread to a starving man, is equivalent to the value of his life, and if the price of a thing should be what it will bring, then one might properly demand of a starving man his whole future life in servitude as the price of the loaf. But any one who should make such a demand would be looked upon as insane, a cannibal, and one simultaneous voice would denounce the outrageous injustice, and cry aloud for retribution. If the producers and venders of the bread had bestowed one hour's labor upon its production and in passing it to the starving man, then some other articles which cost its producer and vender an hour's equivalent labor, would be a natural and just compensation for the loaf.[43]

This represents Warren's general theory of exchange, which is at the same time a prescription for a transformed economy. He called it "the cost limit of price": things should be priced according to the cost in labor required to produce them, rather than their "value" as fixed by supply and demand.

He continues:

A watch has a cost and a value. The cost consists of the amount of labor bestowed on the mineral or natural wealth, in converting it into metal, the labor bestowed by the workmen in constructing the watch, the wear of tools, the rent, firewood, insurance, taxes, clerkship and various other contingent expenses of its manufacturer, together with the labor expended in its transmission from him to its vender; and the labor and contingent expenses of the vender in passing it to the one who uses it. In some of these departments the labor is more disagreeable, or more deleterious to health than in others, but all these items, or more, constitute the costs of the watch. The value of a well-made watch depends upon the natural qualities of the metals or minerals employed, upon the natural qualities or principles of its mechanism, upon the uses to which it is applied, and upon the fancy or wants of the purchaser. It would be different with every different watch, with every purchaser, and would change every day in the hands of the same purchaser, and with every different use to which he applied it.

Now, among this multitude of values, which one should be selected to set a price upon? Or, should the price be made to vary and fluctuate according to these fluctuating values, and never be completely sold, but only from hour to hour? Common sense answers "neither," but, that these values, like those of sunshine and air, are of right the equal property of all; no one having a right to set any price whatever upon them. Cost, then, is the only rational ground of price, even in the most complicated transactions. . . .

The doctor demands of the wood-cutter the proceeds of five, ten, or twenty days' labor for a visit of an hour, and asks, in excuse, if the sick man would not prefer this rather than continuous disease or death. This, again, is basing price on an assumed value of his attendance instead of its cost. It is common to plead the difference of talents required: without waiting to prove this idea false, it is, perhaps, sufficient to say that the talents required, either in cutting wood, or in cutting off a leg or an arm, so far as they cost the possessor, are a legitimate ground of estimate and price; but talents which cost nothing, are natural wealth, and, like the water, land, and sunshine, should be accessible to all without price.[44]

This economic vision was elaborated by a number of figures, including Ezra Heywood and William B. Greene. The former tried to show, in such essays as "Hard Cash," how a large-scale labor note economy could emerge. The latter developed a system of "mutual banking" based on the ideas of Warren, the transcendentalists, and Proudhon. These are rudimentary models for relatively large economies organized on a noncoercive and relatively egalitarian basis. I believe Warren's experiments and many others have suggested that such a thing is possible.

10.

We had better rethink our criminal justice system as well, which doesn't seem to work very well. But it should be admitted that anarchists have a difficulty in this area, and the question of how people can be secured from crime without police power is, indeed, a striking conundrum. "Crime," I think, has two actually opposed acceptations: what is actually prohibited by a law enforced by a state, and, on the other hand, what is a violation of another person that suggests or demands redress. Obviously, for me, "crime" in the sense of a violation of the law of a state is neither here nor there; it is never morally relevant in itself that something is against the law. But stealing, murder, and rape, though they have themselves been brought to unprecedented excellence, systematicity, and impunity by governments, are a problem with or without government, and what a statist has that I don't is a police force; at a good moment, let us suppose, such a thing might reduce rather than increase crime in the extralegal as well as the legal sense. But what can an anarchist do?

Garrison and de Cleyre are among the anarchists who have scouted the extraordinary idea that "criminals" should not be constrained or punished in any way.

> Ask yourselves, each of you, whether you are quite sure that you have feeling enough, and *have you suffered enough*, to be able to weigh and measure out another man's life or liberty, no matter what he has done? And if you have not yourself, are you able to delegate to any judge the power which you have not? . . . The vengeance that the great psychologist [Dostoevsky] saw was futile, the violence that the greatest living religious teacher [Tolstoy] and the greatest dead ones advised no man to wreak, that violence is done daily and hourly by every little-hearted prosecutor who prosecutes at so much a day, by every petty judge who buys his way into office with common politicians' tricks, and deals in men's lives and liberties as a trader deals in pins. . . . [Their] respectable bargain-counter maxims of morality have as much effect to stem the great floods and storms that shake the human will as the waving of a lady's kid glove against the tempest. Those who have not suffered cannot understand how to punish; those who have understanding *will* not.
>
> I said at the beginning and I say again, I believe that in every one of us all things are germinal; in judge and prosecutor and prison-keeper too, and even in those small moral souls who cut out one undeviating pattern for all men to fit, even in them there are the germs of passion and crime and sympathy and forgiveness. And some day things will stir in them and accuse them and awaken them. And that awakening will come when suddenly one day there breaks upon them with realizing force the sense of the unison of life, the irrevocable relationship of the saint to the sinner, the judge to the criminal; that all personalities are intertwined and rushing upon doom together.[45]

This does not turn on some sort of theory or metaphysics; it does not purport to be or to emerge from a solution to the free will problem, for example. It is, rather, grounded in intense experiences of darkness, of obsession and suicidal despair (which de Cleyre knew from inside). It is based on trying to understand how people fundamentally like oneself can end up acting even abominably. Such understanding is possible for many of us insofar as we have actually behaved more or less abominably or undergone great real-world and emotional suffering.

Often the sort of positions that de Cleyre takes on heroically radical moral grounds, as Garrison did, are reached on the basis of determinism, as they are in Warren; these figures plead for a reduction of the awful religious sense of individual responsibility, and urge that changing the circumstances that lead to theft, murder, or rape would be more rational than punishing offenders. Now, the twinned hierarchies of political/police and economic power no doubt create crime of all sorts, but I think the idea that crime can be cured by economic justice is wishful thinking. Crime driven by addiction, mental compulsion and delusion of various kinds, the fact that some people enjoy cruelty and others want to be dominated, and suchlike, I believe, are irremediable. Unlike the figures I have been discussing, I do not hold out hope for a transformed humanity. Every technological advance and reform movement is an environment of depravity, for example, because it has things like us in it.

11.

I wish I could serve you with a set of solutions to our dilemmas, as we rush, intertwined, upon doom. The only way out I ever found from anything was deeper in. Start by seeing clearly or by not too quickly generalizing. In the case of suffering and evil and madness, I think you had better start by trying to see what it's like from inside. Connect first, or take people's descriptions of their own experience as seriously as humanly possible; that's the only beginning. At any rate, the way we think about responsibility and punishment is wide open at the moment. I don't, of course, advocate the direct elimination of responsibility by brainiac determinism, which may well be followed by a brainwashing program or other authoritarian adjustments to the environment. But, on the other hand, I have tried to show some of the ways that responsibility melts and generalizes or becomes obscure; that's typical. I don't think the approach of confining millions of people in big buildings and camps is working as well as we might have hoped, and I share at least to some extent the misgivings about punishment expressed by Mott, Emerson, Tolstoy, de Cleyre.

Again, I'm imagining all sorts of communities engaged in all sorts of practices, and I will emphasize the disadvantages of gigantic institutional approaches interning millions of people. Small communities, including some tribal communities and also, for example, many religious ideal communities, practice forms of isolation or exile. These might be effective in some cases, or they might lead to wandering gangs of predators. I doubt we are ever going to stop needing to defend ourselves from one another. The people I am imagining would face such decisions with extreme jealous care of their own prerogatives—as have many tribal cultures (David Graeber mentions the Piaroa, the Tiv, and cultures of highland Madagascar)—but I am not going to pretend that such decisions do not arise.

What I think is worth exploring, here as everywhere else, is to what extent we could live by voluntary rather than coercive arrangements. One way to put the matter is this: suppose we actually did live by a social contract, something to which we each actually did commit ourselves voluntarily, as opposed to the grotesque semblance of choice offered by Hobbes, Locke, and Rousseau? Or, to what extent could we? And in every area, whether it's crime or public works or education, for example, we should be asking ourselves right now: how could we do that while actually treating one another decently, or even with a vague minimum respect? How could we operate in concert without creating oppressive hierarchies by the use and threat of force? If we cannot do better than we are now on that, if all the solutions are statist coercive solutions, we are a species that richly deserves the extinction that lies at the end of this road. And I will say again that if you think arming a portion of the population, giving them uniforms, permitting them to surveil the rest, and putting them in charge of internment facilities is a formula for reducing the violation of some persons by others, you are confused.

12.

There is going to be no utopia, and in my opinion, overall, we are not getting better and are quite unlikely to. I understand or feel the plausibility of the idea of original sin, intrinsic depravity. I'm more Edwardsy than my nineteenth-century heroes. As Pascal obsessively puts it, we are the victims of our own concupiscence, which is essential to things such as ourselves. I think in some ways the very most dangerous people are people who don't feel that about themselves, who think they are free and good, and hence to be trusted with coercive power in the public interest. Such people are just showing that they are terribly self-deluded, and they are the last people you want operating power over you, in their self-righteousness and inability to reflect. One of the most absurd spectacles in human history is rule by "experts" or "meritocracy," wherein we are all deferring to Harvard-trained lawyers and sociologists. These people need to reflect on their unanimity, their inability even to see their own basic assumptions or categories, the extreme arrogance which gives them to think that they should be telling people in some little town in Louisiana, which they know nothing about, how to live. It is a grotesquely elitist and hierarchical orientation: literally a caste system. They need to cultivate a sense of their own ignorance, as Pascal would recommend. In general, manufacturing a better world appears to entail that we need a mechanism powerful enough to transform everybody, in particular those who aren't hopping aboard our inspiring vision of collective uplift: in short, making a better world appears to entail a death machine that can reach anybody.

So I am not going to imagine a transformed humanity in a state of collective unanimous bliss; I actually do not want that, and we can't have it, and all the attempts to force it into being have amounted merely to mass execution. As Pascal formulates the overall result,

> Equality of goods is no doubt just; but, since we are unable to make might obey justice, we have made it just to obey might. Unable to strengthen justice, we have justified might. . . . If it could have been done, we would have put might in the hands of justice. But since we cannot handle might as we like, because it is a palpable quality, whereas justice is a spiritual quality we manipulate at will, we put justice in the hands of might. And so we call just what we are forced to obey.[46]

It is likely that one way or another Pascal had in mind here the positions of his contemporary Hobbes, but he was also pointing out something fundamental to the history of human consciousness. He talks frequently about how we are flummoxed by the signs of authority and the cloud of mumbo-jumbo surrounding it: the banners, the outfits, the symbol systems, all the signs of power. The average person "must not become aware of the usurpation; it was originally introduced without reason and has become reasonable. It must be made to seem authentic and eternal, and its origin must be concealed if we do not want it to end soon."[47] (We have, of course, shifted these signs out of an imperial or monarchical model.) Now, you would think that, as in Hobbes, the irremediable ignorance and moral depravity of human beings, combined with our excessive self-esteem, makes all this more or less inevitable, or makes it the most rational option, which really would be a shocking refutation of rationality in general, which is just how Pascal wants to use the point.

But what Pascal wants, and what he thinks is hardest for us and most admirable, is to let our own depravity, mediocrity, out-of-control desires—our own lostness to ourselves, our own lack of control over ourselves—teach us, by humiliating us, the humility that could constitute an approach to making things better for real human beings like ourselves. "Man's greatness lies in his knowing himself to be wretched."[48]

> If he exalts himself, I humble him.
> If he humbles himself, I exalt him.
> And I continue to contradict him
> Until he comprehends
> That he is an incomprehensible monster.[49]

If you want to imagine the opposite of this humility, consider the works of Karl Marx, for example, who has figured out the very shape of history, the nature of the world and of us, the future, and so on. On the other hand, I have myself had a crack at some of this, so perhaps I better stop writing for a bit and engage in self-reflection.

Having an optimistic view of the nature or potential of human beings—expecting a transformed human reality—leads extremely quickly to actual frustration about our actual suckiness, and hence one quickly decides that if people won't voluntarily change in the way you know they ought to, you'd better start forcing them to. In other words, it leads very quickly to an extremely convincing demonstration of the depravity of all concerned. The thing tumbles completely into the abyss, however, when you have an extremely optimistic view of yourself, real self-confidence, so that you don't lay awake all night wondering whether these transformations you're trying to impose might not be ridiculously or entirely mistaken. Why might they be mistaken? Well, among other things, because they are made by an irremediably depraved and ignorant human being. It's only the people who know such things about themselves who have any business leading anyone in anything, only they who should be trusted with any sort of power. Our practice, as Pascal says again and again, is to invest power in just the opposite sort of people, a sure sign precisely of our own depravity. This is actually the sort of thought that motivates Emerson's and de Cleyre's approach to punishment, for example. The only decent sort of person is a person who really does know and face her own confusion, mediocrity, slavery to her own desires, self-deception. The state is an expression of pride and arrogance on a world-bestriding scale, or as Pascal, I believe, would have it—in agreement with Hobbes, actually—of how terrifyingly and irremediably flawed we are. But a real solution cannot involve us becoming unflawed: it can only come by fully knowing of ourselves that we are, and uniting one to another in virtue of our need, and with real humility.

13.

A more realistic future is one that is more like the past: one in which regions or pockets—Kabul, perhaps—are monopolized by authority, but in which peripheries and interstices harbor all sorts of evasive and resistant elements that are ineradicable. These things are not only opposed; they are also mutually aesthetically and economically dependent, or are mutually constituted, as power takes the shape of the threat to power and vice versa. But also, of course, order and chaos, safety and danger, mind and body, civilization and its malcontents, policeman and criminal: all the many dualisms characteristic of our last few millennia may find their origin here. I'm going to speculate about us not only that we suck but that there is something in us that is just not subduable, not fully amenable, not merely receptive, shall we say. Indeed, part of what is non-subduable in us is precisely our ignorance, concupiscence, depravity: we can't subdue ourselves internally, nor can we fully yield to any external power even if we want to.

Perhaps the good parts of us are not entirely subduable either, and also some people, as one sees throughout the history of our species, are built to resist, and can no more not try to resist than others cannot not try to capitulate. And I think that the drama of human existence is enacted significantly around this dynamic, in which we try to submit to others and make others submit to us and in which we try to subdue ourselves and try to resist being subdued by ourselves. This process never wears us smooth, and among other things we are never simple or pure expressions of the regimes of power in which we are embedded. What revolution means now is primarily the defense and expansion of spaces or resistance and spaces of a solidarity that is not simulated under coercion, and the opening up of new ones everywhere. For coercion falsifies, and you never know whether someone who is capitulating to the "social contract"/police power is capitulating in his heart or inwardly rolling his eyes or seething or plotting a bloody coup.

James C. Scott's *The Art of Not Being Governed* gives an account of the cultures of the highlands of Southeast Asia, "from the Central Highlands of Vietnam to northeastern India and traversing five Southeast Asian nations (Vietnam, Cambodia, Laos, Thailand, and Burma) and four provinces of China."[50] He describes the human history of this region at a general level as characterized by "a settled, state-governed population and a frontier penumbra of less governed or virtually autonomous peoples."[51] Scott calls this "frontier penumbra" a "shatter zone," and describes similar situations in "Amazonia, in highland Latin America, . . . in that corridor of highland Africa safe from slave-raiding, in the Balkans and the Caucasus."[52] One of Scott's points is that shatter zones are, to a large extent, made up of refugees from state societies and the posterity of such refugees.

> Living within the state meant, virtually by definition, taxes, conscription, corvée labor, and, for most, a condition of servitude; these conditions were at the core of the state's strategic and military advantages. When these burdens became overwhelming, subjects moved with alacrity to the periphery or to another state. . . . And finally, the early states were warmaking machines as well, producing hemorrhages of subjects fleeing conscription, invasion, and plunder. Thus the early state extruded populations as readily as it absorbed them, and when, as was often the case, it collapsed altogether as the result of war, drought, epidemic, or civil strife over succession, its populations were disgorged. . . .
>
> This pattern of state-making and state-unmaking produced, over time, a periphery that was composed as much of refugees as of peoples who had never been state subjects. Much of the periphery of states became a zone of refuge or "shatter zone," where human shards of state formation and rivalry accumulated willy-nilly, creating regions of bewildering ethnic and linguistic complexity.[53]

Scott is an "anarchist anthropologist," though he has qualified his own endorsement of anarchism as a political program. But though that sounds like an ideological orientation that would be incompatible with the objectivity a discipline like anthropology demands, here I think this has the effect of removing a set of ideological blinders.

For the first time really since Rousseau, I believe, Scott's approach begins to reconstrue the way peoples might see one another, or the way that civilized peoples such as ourselves might see savage peoples such as you. Under the aegis of the left-right spectrum, we really have developed a very odd sense of time, and we often speak of people all of whom exist right now as being scattered on a timeline: there are "stone age" people somewhere still, perhaps, or Islamists who still inhabit the medieval period. Ever since Europeans became aware or more aware of Africans and Americans, they have seen in them their own living ancestors, the condition they had themselves risen from. What they met, in fact, was an immense diversity of peoples and systems and languages, all of whom were living at precisely the same moment and had developed for precisely as long as themselves.

And what they certainly did not understand was that the character of many of these peoples, especially the ones they thought most primitive and called savage and tribal and so on, arose by forced or conscious rejection of various state and imperial bodies, from the Yoruba to the Inca.

> According to [the usual] tale, a backward, naive, and perhaps barbaric people are gradually incorporated into an advanced, superior, and more prosperous society and culture. If, instead, many of these ungoverned barbarians had, at one time or another, elected, as a political choice, to take their distance from the state, a new element of political agency enters the picture. Many, perhaps most, inhabitants of the ungoverned margins are not remnants of an earlier social formation, left behind, or, as some lowland folk accounts in Southeast Asia have it, "our living ancestors." . . . Their subsistence routines, their social organization, their physical dispersal, and many elements of their culture, far from being the archaic traits of a people left behind, are purposefully crafted both to thwart incorporation into nearby states and to minimize the likelihood that statelike concentrations of power will arise among them[selves].[54]

It may be that, arising along with the state, there have been many nonstate and antistate social configurations, some successful, some not.

The modern era has been haunted by Hobbes's state of nature and obsessed with turning against Nature and our own nature, whatever that may be. Nature is what we rose out of, by spirit or by reason or by consciousness or by means of evolution. And the way we did this, above all, was by coercive political arrangements: that is what is meant by *civilization* and similar terms, and it is mirrored in the picture we get of rational agency in Kant or Korsgaard. The very conception of the modern state as articulated by Hobbes—the state as a collective agent welded together by force—arises together with its origin and other: the savage. And the crisis of state legitimacy to which Hobbes, Locke, Montesquieu, Rousseau, Burke, and so on respond in the world of ideas corresponds to the discovery of tribal cultures: it's a kind of hysterical self-defense. It is really remarkable how much "the savage" and "primitive" is present at the dawn of modern political philosophy and throughout; it is right there as the frame in virtually all the major figures up to the present moment. It is the philosophical imprint of the political nightmare we call colonialism. The conceptuality and the nightmare are born together out of extreme cultural hubris and extreme lack of self-reflection that require incomprehension and terrifying yet absurd condescension toward actual other people. The progenitors of such views have always been confused as between the descriptive and normative contributions of the savage/civilized duality, even if as in Rousseau or Margaret Mead, a revaluation was scouted.

But Scott's work, which builds on that of Clastres and others but in a less problematical vein, lets us begin to narrate a story that is at once more realistic and more potentially liberating. In it, configurations of wealth and political power extend outward from certain centers, proceeding among other things by regularization, mapping, census, measurements, records, linguistic standardization; people are lured or attracted or driven to the center. But then various factors—well enumerated by Scott above—drive them off again. Some people take to the comparative security of state life in times of peace; some resent it. Some peoples arrange their societies hierarchically or acquiesce in such arrangements; others resist them. Some standardize languages or music or land parcels; others splinter, enrich, distort, improvise. All this time, and even now, there are many alternatives to coercive power. But these are rendered invisible by an ideology that teaches, though rarely aloud, that being under coercion is our fate and our redemption, what distinguishes us from them, culture from nature, why we are better and higher. This result seems rather ironic, since as Pascal and Paine point out, the state is a or the most conspicuous demonstration of human depravity.

14.

What I would like to emphasize is that there are existing shatter zones everywhere. As a matter of fact, it's still possible to withdraw into something like rural isolation. The Amish are doing that collectively and publicly still here in Pennsylvania. But every little knot of teenagers, graffiti writers, media remixers, sexual subculturalists, underground music buffs, organic fanatics, witches, isolates, hacktivists, vegans, militia members, strange little freak families, cults, squats, bigamous compounds, crackpots, and so on is itself a little shatter zone. Every white trash heaven up in the holler with rusting Fairlanes in the yard and chickens; every ghetto corner where three old dudes are sitting around with a bottle; every situationist coffee shop in Brooklyn. Maybe these aren't everything you're looking for in a shatter zone, but you could go pretty far offline if you really were intent on doing so. Or you could find your messed up corners of the Internet. The important thing is that there continue to be relatively free spaces, whether physical or virtual, or free aspects of community and connection to which it is possible to escape for some time or more or less permanently. I emphasize every bit of us each and of us all that is not fully colonized or that is resistant to power, consciously or unconsciously, or even just in virtue of being intractable physical objects. But I also want to emphasize that our continued zones of freedom will have to be struggled for, hacked for, and that they will be always swamped or under attack. That is also what makes them meaningful and us brave.

Sadly or happily, that is all the positive political program I actually have to offer. All I believe we can practically do is to try to defend, or shift, and expand the shatter zones. All we can do is try to cultivate in ourselves and one another a humility that recognizes our own internal shatteredness, our elusiveness and excess to ourselves, and learn in that to try to resist the emergence of authority within our shatter zones or the incursion of the authorities into them and into ourselves. I might also recommend that we try to cultivate the ability to love specific other persons; any place where that actually happens is itself a shatter zone. I know that it looks more every day like coercive authority is expanding; it certainly threatens everyone everywhere in the world all the time now. But one reason it will never be implacable is precisely that at its heart sit persons, with all the incoherence, mediocrity, and self-delusion of our kind. People like that, like us, can be resisted because they are going fuck up continuously: oppression is always, among other things, a circus of mistakes that is always undermining itself, even if it often also does more or less subdue whole populations for a time. And creatures such as we are often can't help fighting back or evading or ignoring the whole thing and all its empty nonsense and trying to get on with our lives and real connections. That involuntary resistance is the source of what is most admirable in ourselves, believe it or not: the only redemption that is not a nightmare.

Conclusion

Now I've tied up the universe in a nice, neat bow. I'd rather be wrong about everything than accomplish that task, but I am not worried that I have accomplished it, though I am a bit worried that I might be taken as thinking that I have. It's not that I don't have such impulses, and I have displayed them throughout. But the danger of this project, as I said near the outset, is too much system, too much coherence, too much pretension to omniscience. I also want to leave loose ends, or else, really, the thing would be obviously false. What I hope is that the various strands hang together but not too together. Now, I think that the discussions of free will, for example, and sexual identities, and the left-right political spectrum are compatible with the metaphysics and epistemology, and they are connected by many explicit or hidden strands, but I also think that none directly follows from any of the others. One could develop all sorts of epistemologies compatible with my ontology (though it might be harder to go the other way round). I kept returning to the string to try to assemble things, but the connections have been loose, and I'm going to admit that the formation of string and tangles and knots and snarls is all too easy to connect to any given subject matter. There are social entanglements, aesthetic entanglements, political entanglements, physical entanglements: it's the kind of thing that you can wield anywhere, but just to that extent it also tends to disintegrate or lose content or give an impression of meaning without having much meaning. Well, of course I like the flexibility of the figure and have exploited it, but if I returned gratuitously, or introduced an ersatz or unearned or oppressive unity, I apologize for that. All "systematic" philosophers have faced such temptations and have succumbed to them. Me, too.

Notes

Part I. Introduction

1. George Jean Nathan and H. L. Mencken, *The American Credo* (New York: Knopf, 1920), 3.
2. George Berkeley, *Principles of Human Knowledge* (London: Penguin, 1988), 54.
3. Arthur Schopenhauer, *The World as Will and Representation* (New York: Dover, 1966), 3.
4. Immanuel Kant, *Critique of Pure Reason*, trans. Norman Kemp Smith (New York: Macmillan, 1929), 22.
5. David Hume, *A Treatise of Human Nature* (New York: Penguin, 1969), 52.
6. Rudolf Carnap, *The Logical Structure of the World*, trans. Rolf A. George (Berkeley: University of California Press, 1967), 100ff.
7. Willard van Orman Quine, "Things and Their Place in Theories," in *Theories and Things* (Cambridge, MA: Harvard University Press, 1981), 1.
8. Thomas Reid, *An Inquiry Into the Human Mind on the Principles of Common Sense* (Edinburgh: Bell and Bradfute, 1810), vii.
9. Ralph Waldo Emerson, "History," in *Emerson: Essays and Lectures* (New York: Library of America, 1983), 254–55.
10. Blaise Pascal, *Pensées*, trans. Roger Ariew (Indianapolis, IN: Hackett, 2004), 62.
11. Hans Vaihinger, *The Philosophy of "As If,"* trans. C. K. Ogden (New York: Harcourt, Brace, 1935).
12. John Dewey, *Art as Experience* (New York: Minton, Balch, 1934), 13.

Chapter 1

1. Immanuel Kant, *Prolegomena to Any Future Metaphysics*, 2nd ed., trans. James Ellington (Indianapolis, IN: Hackett, 2001), 56–58.

2. Thomas Kuhn, *The Structure of Scientific Revolutions* (Chicago: Chicago University Press, 1970), 117.

3. Jon Barwise and John Perry, "Situations and Attitudes," in *Semantics: A Reader*, ed. Steven Davis and Brandan S. Gillon (Oxford: Oxford University Press, 2004), 305.

4. Martin Buber, *I and Thou*, trans. Walter Kaufmann (New York: Charles Scribner's Sons, 1970), 69.

5. Benedict de Spinoza, *On the Improvement of the Understanding, the Ethics, Correspondence*, trans. R. H. M. Elwes (New York: Dover, 1955), 290.

6. Henry David Thoreau, "The Maine Woods," in *Thoreau* (New York: Library of America, 1985), 646.

7. Simplicius, quoting Aristotle's possibly apocryphal text "On Democritus," reprinted, e.g., in Richard D. McKirahan, *Philosophy Before Socrates* (Indianapolis, IN: Hackett, 1994), 305.

8. Wilfrid Sellars, "Philosophy and the Scientific Image of Man," in *Frontiers of Science and Philosophy*, ed. Robert Colodny (Pittsburgh, PA: University of Pittsburgh Press, 1962), 35–78.

9. Brad Inwood and L. P. Gerson, eds., *The Epicurus Reader* (Indianapolis, IN: Hackett, 1994), 7–8.

10. Ibid., 9.

11. Democritus, in McKirahan, *Philosophy Before Socrates*, 305, from Aristotle's *On Generation and Corruption*, 1.1 315b6–15.

12. McKirahan, *Philosophy Before Socrates*, 326.

13. Bertrand Bronson, "Walking Stewart," in *Essays and Studies by the Members of the Department of English* (Oakland: University of California Press, 1943), 123–55.

14. William Thomas Brande, *The Life and Adventures of the Celebrated Walking Stewart* (London: R. Wheatley, 1822), 13.

15. Bronson, 13.

16. Brande, 6.

17. Bronson, 130.

18. John Stewart, *The Moral State of Nations, or Travels Over the Most Interesting Parts of the Globe, to Discover the Source of Moral Motion, Communicated to Lead Mankind Through the Conviction of the Senses to Intellectual Existence, and an Enlightened State of Nature* (Middletown, NJ: George H. Evans, 1837), 226.

19. Bronson, 130–31.

20. Thomas De Quincey, "Walking Stewart," in *The Collected Works of Thomas de Quincey: London Reminscences and Confessions of an Opium-eater* (London: A. & C. Black, 1890) 96.

21. Kelly Grovier, "Dream Walker: A Wordsworth Mystery Solved," *Times Literary Supplement*, February 16, 2007, 156.

22. Ibid., 160.

23. De Quincey, 116.

24. Ibid., 107.

25. Ibid., 116.

26. John Stewart, *Opus Maximum, or The Great Essay to Reduce the Moral World From Contingency to System* (London: J. Ginger, 1803).

27. De Quincey, 111.

28. Ibid., 109.

29. John Stewart, *The Philosophy of Sense; or, Book of Nature: Revealing the Laws of the Intellectual World, Founded on the Laws of the Physical World* (London: Printed for the author, 1815), 166.

30. Ibid., 22.

31. Inwood and Gerson, 11.

32. Stewart, *The Philosophy of Sense*, 24–25.

33. Ibid., 28–29.

34. A. J. Pyle, *Atomism and Its Critics: From Democritus to Newton* (Bristol, UK: Thoemmes Press, 1995), 176.

35. Benedict de Spinoza, *Ethics*, in *The Collected Writings of Spinoza*, trans. Edwin Curley (Princeton, NJ: Princeton University Press, 1985), vol. 1.

36. Wing-Tsit Chan, *A Source Book in Chinese Philosophy* (Princeton, NJ: Princeton University Press, 1963), 303. I've worked on the translation a bit; where Chan renders *T'ien* as "Heaven," I make it "nature," which is one of the term's meanings.

37. Ibid., 328.

38. Sarvepalli Radhakrishnan and Charles A. Moore, *A Sourcebook in Indian Philosophy* (Princeton, NJ: Princeton University Press, 1957), 233.

39. Clement Rosset, *Joyful Cruelty*, trans. David Bell (Oxford: Oxford University Press, 1993), 13.

40. Terence Horgan and Matjaz Potrc, *Austere Realism: Contextual Semantics Meets Minimal Onotology* (Cambridge, MA: MIT Press, 2008), ch. 2.

41. Ibid., 19.

42. William James, *A Pluralistic Universe* (New York: Longmans, Green, and Co., 1920), 116.

43. David Lewis, *On the Plurality of Worlds* (Malden, MA: Blackwell, 1986), 211, 213.

44. Peter van Inwagen, *Material Beings* (Ithaca, NY: Cornell University Press, 1990), 74.

45. G. W. Leibniz, *Discourse on Metaphysics and Other Essays*, trans. Daniel Garber and Roger Ariew (Indianapolis, IN: Hackett, 1991), 8.

46. Ibid.

47. G. W. Leibniz, *Monadology*, § 56, in *Leibniz: Discourse on Metaphysics/Correspondence with Arnauld/Monadology*, trans. George Montgomery (La Salle, IL: Open Court, 1979), 263.

48. Graham Harman, *The Quadruple Object* (Alresford, UK: Zero Books, 2011), 47.

49. Spinoza, "Ethics," 49.

50. Paul Levi Bryant, *The Democracy of Objects* (London: Open Humanities Press, 2011), 70.

51. Graham Harman, *Guerilla Metaphysics* (Chicago: Open Court, 2005), 85.

52. Ibid.

53. David Wiggins, *Sameness and Substance* (Cambridge, MA: Harvard University Press, 1980), 2.

54. Alexander Bryan Johnson, *A Treatise on Language* (New York: Dover, 1968), 80–81.

55. Ibid., 115.

56. Keith Campbell, *Abstract Particulars* (Oxford: Basil Blackwell, 1990), 2–3.

57. J. L. Austin, "Unfair to Facts," in *Philosophical Papers* (Oxford: Oxford University Press, 1961), 158–60.

Chapter 2

1. Keith Donellan, "Reference and Definite Descriptions," in *Readings in the Philosophy of Language*, ed. Jay Rosenberg and Charles Travis (Englewood Cliffs, NJ: Prentice-Hall, 1971), 195–211.

2. Hartry Field, "Tarski's Theory of Truth," *Journal of Philosophy* 69, no. 13 (1972): 347–75.

3. Gottlob Frege, *Philosophical and Mathematical Correspondence*, ed. Gottfried Gabriel, Hans Hermes, Friedrich Kambartel, and Albert Veraart (Chicago: University of Chicago Press, 1980). The exchange occurred in 1904.

4. Plato, "Cratylus," in *Plato: Collected Dialogues*, trans. Benjamin Jowett (Princeton, NJ: Princeton University Press, 1961), 423 (385b).

5. Marian David, "Truth and Identity," in *Meaning and Truth: Investigations Into Philisophical Semantics*, ed. J. K. Campbell, M. O'Rourke, and D. Shier (New York: Seven Bridges Press, 2002), 124–41.

6. G. E. Moore, "Truth and Falsity," in *G. E. Moore: Selected Writings*, ed. Thomas Baldwin (London: Routledge, 1993).

7. F. P. Ramsey, "Facts and Propositions," in *Philosophical Papers*, ed. D. H. Mellor (Cambridge, UK: Cambridge University Press, 1990), 39.

8. Edwin Bissell Holt, Walter Taylor Marvin, William Pepperrell Montague, Ralph Barton Perry, Walter Pitkin, and Edward Gleason Spalding, *The New Realism: Cooperative Studies in Philosophy* (New York: Macmillan, 1912), 252, 256.

9. David Lewis, "Scorekeeping in a Language Game," *Journal of Philosophical Logic* 8, no. 3 (1979), 339–59.

10. Anselm of Canterbury, "On Truth," in *The Major Works* (Oxford: Oxford University Press, 1998), 153.

11. Ibid., 153–54.

12. Ibid., 156–57.

13. Ibid., 164.

14. Ibid., 157.

15. Ibid, 160.

16. Martin Heidegger, "On the Essence of Truth," in *Basic Writings*, ed. David Krell (New York: HarperCollins, 1993), part 1.

17. Ibid., § 2.

18. Ibid., § 3.

19. Ibid., 4.

20. Ibid., 5.

21. Ibid., 6.

22. Emerson, "History," 254–55.

23. Plotinus, *The Six Enneads*, trans. Stephen McKenna (Chicago: Encyclopedia Britannica, 1952), 229.

Chapter 3

1. Frederick Goodrich Henke, *The Philosophy of Wang Yang-Ming Translated from the Chinese* (Chicago: Open Court, 1916), 169.
2. Henke, *The Philosophy of Wang Yang-Ming*, 146.
3. Ibid., 147.
4. Ibid., 167.
5. Bankei, "Record of Bankei," trans. Norman Waddell, in *The Roaring Stream: A New Zen Reader*, ed. Nelson Foster and Jack Shoemaker (Hopewell, NJ: Ecco, 1996), 299.
6. Ibid., 108.
7. This point is developed beautifully in Mark Rowlands, *Externalism* (Montreal: McGill-Queen's University Press, 2003).
8. Aristotle, *Categories*, ed. J. L. Ackrill, in *The Complete Works of Aristotle*, ed. Jonathan Barnes (Princeton, NJ: Princeton Uiversity Press, 1984), 1:13 (8a1).
9. Plato, *Theaetetus*, trans. F. M. Cornford, in *Plato: Collected Dialogues*, ed. Edith Hamilton and Huntington Cairns (Princeton, NJ: Princeton University Press, 1963), 872 (166c).
10. Sextus Empiricus, *Against the Mathematicians*, quoted in Leo Groarke, *Greek Scepticism: Anti-Realist Trends in Ancient Thought* (Montreal: McGill-Queen's University Press, 1990), 103.
11. Daniel Dennett, *Elbow Room: The Varieties of Free Will Worth Having* (Cambridge, MA: MIT Press, 1984).
12. J. E. Turner, *A Theory of Direct Realism* (London: George Allen & Unwin, 1925), 23.
13. Samuel Alexander, *Space, Time, and Deity* (New York: Humanities Press, 1920), 15–16.
14. See Crispin Sartwell, "Radical Externalism With Regard to Experience," *Philosophical Studies* 78, no. 1 (1995), 55–70.
15. For a full-dress, logical-notation presentation of my version of externalism and the concept of "fusion" between perceiver and perceived thing, see Ibid.
16. Dewey, *Art as Experience*, 197–98.
17. Maurice Merleau-Ponty, *Phenomenology of Perception*, trans. Colin Smith (1945; London: Routledge, 2002), 247.
18. Hilary Putnam, *Reason, Truth, and History* (Cambridge, UK: Cambridge University Press, 1981), 49.
19. Ernst Gombrich, *Art and Illusion* (Princeton: Bollingen,1960).
20. Roderick Long points out to me that "Gombrich unfairly stacked the deck against poor Dürer by printing Dürer's drawing next to a photograph of an *African* rhinoceros, to which it indeed bears little resemblance. The similarity between Dürer's depiction and an *Indian* rhonoceros is considerably stronger."
21. Heinrich Wölfflin, *Principles of Art History* (New York: Dover, 1950), 18.
22. Paul Feyerabend, *Against Method* (London: Verso, 1975), 19.

23. J. L. Austin, "Other Minds," in *Philosophical Papers*, 3rd ed., ed. J. O. Urmson and G. J. Warnock (Oxford: Oxford University Press, 1979), 93.

24. Rene Descartes, *Meditations on First Philosophy*, trans. Donald Cress (Indianapolis, IN: Hackett, 1979), 13.

25. Diogenes Laertius, *Lives of Eminent Philosophers*, trans. R. D. Hicks (London: William Heinemann, 1925), VI:39.

26. James Boswell, *Life of Johnson* (Oxford: Oxford University Press, 1985), 333. As Boswell suggests, Johnson's refutation is hopeless against Berkeley. I will not consider it as a refutation of idealism but as an answer to skepticism about the external world.

27. G. E. Moore, "Proof of an External World," *Philosophical Papers* (London: George Allen and Unwin, 1959), 145–46.

28. Kant, *Critique of Pure Reason*, 34.

29. Moore, "Proof of an External World," 141.

30. Ibid., 144–45.

31. Ibid., 148.

32. Moore, "Some Judgements of Perception," *Philosophical Studies* (New York: Harcourt, Brace & Co., 1922), 228.

33. Ludwig Wittgenstein, *On Certainty*, ed. G. E. M. Anscombe (New York: HarperPerennial, 1972).

34. Marie McGinn, *Sense and Certainty* (Oxford: Basil Blackwell, 1989), 46.

35. Ibid., 50.

36. Moore, "Proof of an External World," 147.

37. Ibid., 150.

38. Wittgenstein, *On Certainty*, 218.

39. Ibid., 91.

40. Ibid., 98.

41. Ibid., 136.

42. Moore, *Philosophical Studies*, 36–37.

43. Austin, *Sense and Sensibilia*, 115.

44. Ibid., 119.

45. A. J. Ayer, "Has Austin Refuted Sense Data?" in *Metaphysics and Common Sense* (London: Macmillan, 1969), 289. Dude. Austin stomped on sense data with hobnail boots.

46. Wittgenstein, *On Certainty*, 9.

47. See, e.g., Søren Kierkegaard, *Concluding Unscientific Postscript* (CUP), trans. David F. Swenson and Walter Lowrie (Princeton, NJ: Princeton University Press, 1968), 286.

48. William James, "The Will to Believe," in *Essays in Pragmatism* (New York: Hafner, 1948), 88.

49. Søren Kierkegaard, *Johannes Climacus, or De Omnibus Dubitandum Est*, trans. T. H. Croxall (Stanford, CT: Stanford University Press, 1958), 146.

50. Søren Kierkegaard, *Fear and Trembling*, trans. Walter Lowrie (New York: Doubleday, 1954), 22.

51. David Hume, *An Enquiry Concerning Human Understanding* (Indianapolis, IN: Hackett, 1977), 24.

52. George Santayana, *Scepticism and Animal Faith* (New York: Dover, 1955), 49.
53. Friedrich Nietzsche, *The Gay Science*, trans. Walter Kaufmann (New York: Vintage, 1974), 280–81.
54. James, "The Will to Believe," 94.
55. Ibid., 100.
56. Ibid., 93.
57. Ibid., 103–4.
58. Nietzsche, *The Gay Science*, 281–82.
59. Kierkegaard, *Concluding Unscientific Postscript, 315–16.*
60. A mathematician of my acquaintance describes her process for solving problems in just this way. She reports that she knows the solution to the problem (which usually comes to her in the shower) well before she can formulate a proof, and often before she has any story at all to tell about why the solution is right. This is by no means atypical. See Henri Poincaré, "Mathematical Creation," trans. G. Bruce Halstead, in *The Foundations of Science* (New York: The Science Press, 1913); Jaques Hadamard, *The Psychology of Invention in the Mathematical Field* (Princeton, NJ: Princeton University Press, 1945).
61. There are cases, as Roderick Long points out to me. I think Moore and Santayana, but he points to David Martens, and Martens points to McTaggart, Russell, and Schlick. Well, I'm not sure in some of these cases. But I am happy to have progenitors.
62. Paul Moser, *Empirical Justification* (Dordrecht: D. Reidel, 1985), 4.
63. Laurence BonJour, *The Structure of Empirical Knowledge* (Cambridge, MA: Harvard University Press, 1985), 8.
64. The locus classicus of the swamping problem is Linda Zagzebski, "The Search for the Epistemic Good," *Metaphilosophy* 34 (2003): 12–28. However, I am going to assert that I developed this problem, though not its excellent name, in the late 1980s, and that it is clearly stated in my papers "Knowledge is Merely True Belief," *American Philosophical Quarterly*, 28, no. 2 (April 1991) and "Why Knowledge is Merely True Belief," *The Journal of Philosophy*, 89, no. 4 (April 1992).
65. Alvin Goldman, *Epistemology and Cognition* (Cambridge, MA: Harvard University Press, 1986), 106.
66. Here's more like the real story, semi-ingenuously just presented as a strategy: I developed the ideas I have just presented in the 1980s and early 1990s in an engagement with the analytic debates as they stood at that time. I was desperate to pry that sucker open on its own terms. You can't refute something in someone's face if you don't enter, to a certain extent, into the assumptions they deploy. I was trying to create a more open space. One thing I've tried to do in that space is to enrich or make more chaotic (and, of course, I hope, more realistic) the notions of truth bearers and truth and also the nature of the epistemic agent.
67. Sandra Harding, "Rethinking Standpoint Epistemology," in *Feminist Epistemologies*, ed. Linda Alcoff and Elizabeth Potter (New York: Routledge, 1993), 50.
68. Patrick Quinn, ed., *Edgar Allan Poe: Poetry and Tales* (New York: Library of America, 1984), 1259.
69. Ibid., 1264.
70. Ibid., 1269–70.

71. Ibid., 1280.
72. Ibid., 1282.
73. Ibid., 1286.

Part II. Introduction

1. G. E. Moore, *Principia Ethica* (1903; New York: Dover, 2004), 201. One of the best expressions of the ridiculousness of subjective accounts of beauty is given by C. S. Lewis:

> In their second chapter, Gaius and Titius quote the well-known story of Coleridge at the waterfall. You remember that there were two tourists present: that one called it "sublime" and the other "pretty"; and that Coleridge mentally endorsed the first judgement and rejected the second with disgust. Gaius and Titius comment as follows: "When the man said 'This is sublime,' he appeared to be making a remark about the waterfall. . . . Actually . . . he was not making a remark about the waterfall, but a remark about his own feelings. What he was saying was really 'I have feelings associated in my mind with the word *Sublime*,' or shortly, 'I have sublime feelings.'" Here are a good many deep questions settled in a pretty summary fashion. But the authors are not yet finished. They add: "This confusion is continually present in language as we use it. We appear to be saying something very important about something: and actually we are only saying something about our own feelings."
>
> Before considering the issues really raised by this momentous little paragraph (designed, you will remember, for "the upper forms of schools") we must eliminate one mere confusion into which Gaius and Titius have fallen. Even on their own view—on any conceivable view—the man who says "This is sublime" cannot mean "I have sublime feelings." Even if it were granted that such qualities as sublimity were simply and solely projected into things from our own emotions, yet the emotions which prompt the projection are the correlatives, and therefore almost the opposites, of the qualities projected. The feelings which make a man call an object sublime are not sublime feelings but feelings of veneration. If "This is sublime" is to be reduced at all to a statement about the speaker's feelings, the proper translation would be "I have humble feelings." If the view held by Gaius and Titius were consistently applied, it would lead to obvious absurdities. It would force them to maintain [p. 4:] that "You are contemptible" means "I have contemptible feelings": in fact that "Your feelings are contemptible" means "My feelings are contemptible." But we need not delay over this, which is the very *pons asinorum* of our subject. It would be unjust to Gaius and Titius themselves to emphasize what was doubtless a mere inadvertence.

C. S. Lewis, *The Abolition of Man; or Reflections on Education with Special Reference to the Teaching of English in the Upper Forms of Schools* (1943; New York: HarperCollins, 2009), 2–3. Thanks to Roderick Long for this beautiful quotation.

2. William Godwin, *An Enquiry Concerning Political Justice* (London: G. G. and J. Robinson, 1798), 126.

3. Bruno Latour, *Reassembling the Social: An Introduction to Actor-Network Theory* (Oxford: Oxford University Press, 2005), 5–6.

Chapter 4

1. Friedrich Nietzsche, *Twilight of the Idols* (New York: Dover, 2004), 7–8.
2. Jacques Derrida, "Différance," in *From Modernism to Postmodernism: An Anthology*, ed. Lawrence Cahoone (Malden, MA: Blackwell, 2003), 228.
3. Spinoza, *On the Improvement of the Understanding*, 46.
4. Dave Hickey, "The Delicacy of Rock-and-Roll," in *Air Guitar* (Los Angeles: Art Issues Press, 1997), 199.
5. Quoted, e.g., in Dale Snow, *Schelling and the End of Idealism* (Albany: State University of New York Press, 1996), 26.
6. Christine Korsgaard, *Self-Constitution: Agency, Identity, and Integrity* (Oxford: Oxford University Press, 2009), xi.
7. Ibid.
8. Harry Frankfurt, "Freedom of the Will and the Concept of a Person," in *The Importance of What We Care About* (Cambridge, UK: Cambridge University Press, 1998), 20.
9. Ibid., 20–21.
10. John Martin Fisher, *The Metaphysics of Free Will* (Oxford: Blackwell, 1994), 3.
11. Friedrich Schiller, *Letters on the Aesthetic Education of Man*, trans. Reginald Snell (1795, Mineola, NY: Dover, 2004), 98–99.
12. Ibid., 60.
13. Dennett, *Elbow Room*, 2.
14. Sam Hammill and J. P. Seaton, trans., *The Essential Chuang Tzu* (Boston: Shambhala, 1999), 107–8.
15. Dennett, *Elbow Room*, 54.
16. Ibid., 55.
17. Harry Frankfurt, *The Importance of What We Care About* (Cambridge, UK: Cambridge University Press, 1998), 1–2.
18. Epictetus, *The Discourses as Reported to Arrian*, trans. W. A. Oldfather (Cambridge, MA: Harvard University Press, 1985), 93–95.
19. Marcus Aurelius, *The Emperor's Handbook: A New Translation of the Meditiations*, trans. C. Scot Hicks and David V. Hicks (New York: Scribner, 2002), 35 (Meditation 3.5).
20. Ibid., Meditation 3.2.
21. Nietzsche, *The Gay Science*, § 354.
22. Susan Wolf, *Freedom Within Reason* (Oxford: Oxford University Press, 1990), 8–9.
23. Harry Frankfurt, "Alternate Possibilities and Moral Responsibility," in *The Importance of What We Care About* (1969; Cambridge, UK: Cambridge University Press, 1998), 1–10.
24. John Martin Fischer, *The Metaphysics of Free Will* (Oxford: Blackwell, 1994), 2.
25. Velleius Paterculus, *Compendium of Roman History*, trans. Frederick W. Shipley (Boston, MA: Loeb Classical Library, 1924), 126; Thomas Reid, *Essays on the Active Powers of Man*, (Edinburgh: John Bell, 1785), essay iv, ch. 4. Roderick Chisholm, "Human Freedom

and the Self," anthologized, e.g., in Derk Pereboom, ed., *Free Will* (Indianapolis, IN: Hackett, 1997), 45.

26. Robert Merrihew Adams, "Involuntary Sins," *The Philosophical Review* 94, no. 1 (January 1985): 12–16.

27. In *A Jonathan Edwards Reader*, John E. Smith, Harry Stout, and Kenneth Minkema, eds. (Yale University Press: 1995), 205.

28. Ibid., 212–213.

29. Ibid., 203.

30. Quoted by J. J. Thompson in *Normativity* (Peru, IL: Open Court, 2008), 35. See Simon Blackburn, *Ruling Passions* (Oxford: Clarendon Press, 1998), 49.

31. Thompson, *Normativity*, 36.

32. Ibid., 37.

33. Jeremy Bentham, *Principles of Morals and Legislation* (Oxford: Oxford University Press, 1879), 1.

34. Aristotle, *The Complete Works of Aristotle*, 1729 (1094.1).

35. John Dewey, *Reconstruction in Philosophy* (1920; New York: Mentor, 1950), 128.

36. Burton Watson, trans., *The Complete Works of Chuang Tzu* (New York: Columbia University Press, 1968), 188.

37. See Crispin Sartwell, ed., *Waterway: A New Translation of the Tao Te Ching, and Introducing the Wu Wei Ching* (Seattle, WA: Createspace, 2016).

38. Ibid.

39. Dewey, *Art as Experience*, 201.

40. Kierkegaard, *Concluding Unscientific Postscript*, 155–57.

41. Jonathan Dancy, *Ethics Without Principles* (Oxford: Oxford University Press, 2004), 191.

Chapter 5

1. Immanuel Kant, *Kant's Critique of Aesthetic Judgment*, trans. James Meredith (Oxford: Clarendon Press, 1911), § 43.

2. Quoted in Moshe Barasch, *Theories of Art: From Plato to Winckelmann* (New York: Routledge, 2000), 24.

3. Leo Tolstoy, *What is Art?* trans. Aylmer Maude (1899; Indianapolis, IN: Hackett, 1996), 50–51.

4. Bendetto Croce, *The Essence of Aesthetic*, trans. Douglas Ainslie (London: Heinemann, 1921), 8.

5. Richard Wollheim, *Art and Its Objects* (1968; Cambridge: Cambridge University Press, 1980), § 23, 42–43.

6. Kant, *Critique of Aesthetic Judgment*, § 14.

7. Ibid., § 16.

8. Clive Bell, *Art* (London: Chatto and Windus, 1914).

9. Again in Lewis, *The Abolition of Man*: If, when you say, "that is sublime," you mean "I have sublime feelings," then perhaps when you assert that I am contemptible, you mean that you have contemptible feelings.

10. Edmund Burke, "A Philosophical Inquiry Into the Origin of Our Idea of the Sublime and Beautiful," in *Edmund Burke* (New York: Collier, 1937), 38.

11. Moore, *Principia Ethica*, 197.

12. Ibid., 201.

13. Ibid., 188.

14. Ibid., 189.

15. Ibid., 197.

16. David Halperin, *How to Be Gay* (Cambridge, MA: Harvard University Press, 2012), 77.

17. Julia Kristeva, *Strangers to Ourselves*, trans. Leon Roudiez (New York: Columbia University Press, 1994), 3.

18. Leon Battista Alberti, *On Painting*, trans. J. R. Spencer (New Haven, CT: Yale University Press, 1966), 72.

19. Leonardo da Vinci, *Treatise on Painting*, trans. A. Philip McMahon (Princeton, NJ: Princeton University Press, 1956), 161 (¶433).

20. Giorgo Vasari, *Lives of the Artists*, trans. George Bull (London: Allen Lane, 1978), 46.

21. Cicero, *Orator ad Brutum*, II, 7, quoted in Erwin Panofsky, *Idea*, trans. Joseph J. S. Peake (New York: Harper and Row, 1960), 12.

22. Svetlana Alpers, *The Art of Describing: Dutch Art in the Seventeenth Century* (Chicago: Chicago University Press, 1983), 30.

23. Christiaan Huygens, *Treatise on Light*, trans. Silvanus P. Thompson (Chicago: Univeristy of Chicago Press, 1912), vii.

24. Friedrich Schelling, *Ideas for a Philosophy of Nature*, trans. and quoted in Dale Snow, *Schelling and the End of Idealism* (Albany, NY: SUNY Press, 1996), 72.

25. Iris Murdoch, "On 'God' and 'Good,'" in *Existentialists and Mystics: Writings on Philosophy and Literature*, ed. Peter Conradi (1969; New York: Penguin, 1997), 347–48.

26. Ibid., 353–54.

Chapter 6

1. Godwin, *An Enquiry Concerning Political Justice*, 125.

2. John Rawls, *A Theory of Justice*, rev. ed. (Cambridge, MA: Harvard University Press, 1999), 62.

3. Ibid., 63.

4. Ibid., e.g., 399ff.

5. Ibid., 211.

6. Ibid., 219.

7. Emile Capouya and Keitha Tompkins, eds., *The Essential Kropotkin* (New York: Liveright, 1975), 83.

8. Michel Beaud, *A History of Capitalism, 1500–2000*, 2nd ed., trans. Tom Dickman and Anny Lefebvre (New York: Monthly Review, 2001), 42–43.

9. Victoria Tin-bor Hui, *War and State Formation in Ancient China and Early Modern Europe* (New York: Cambridge University Press, 2005).

10. Leo Panitch and Sam Gindin, *The Making of Global Capitalism: The Political Economy of American Empire* (New York: Verso, 2012), 3.

11. Ibid., 15.

12. Adam Smith, *An Inquiry Into the Nature and Causes of the Wealth of Nations* (Indianapolis, IN: Liberty Fund, 1981), 2:706–8.

13. Ibid., 731–32.

14. Hans Denck, "On the Law of God," in *The Radical Reformation*, ed. Michael G. Baylor (New York: Cambridge, 1991), 147–51.

15. Quoted in Lewis Perry, *Radical Abolitionism: Anarchy and the Government of God in Antislavery Thought* (Ithaca, NY: Cornell University Press, 1973), 512.

16. Lucretia Mott, "Law of Progress," in *Lucretia Mott: Complete Sermons and Speeches*, ed. Dana Green (New York: Edward Mellen Press, 1980), 73–74.

17. Maria Weston Chapman, *Right and Wrong in Massachusetts* (Boston: Dow & Jackson's Anti-Slavery Press, 1839), 26.

18. Lucretia Mott, "The Laws in Relation to Women," in *Lucretia Mott: Complete Sermons and Speeches*, ed. Dana Green (New York: Edward Mellen Press, 1980), 218.

19. William Lloyd Garrison, "Declaration of Sentiments Adopted by the Peace Convention," in Crispin Sartwell, ed., *American Defiance: Classic Writings from the Colonial Period Through the 19th Century* (Seattle, WA: Createspace, 2016), 152.

20. Gilbert Barnes and Dwight Dumond, eds., *Letters of Theodore Dwight Weld, Angelina Grimké Weld, and Sarah Grimké* (New York: De Capo, 1970), 1:408.

21. Lucretia Mott, "Sermon Delivered at Cherry Street Meeting (1849)," in *Lucretia Mott: Complete Speeches and Sermons*, ed. Dana Green (New York: Edward Mellen Press, 1980), 139.

22. Ibid., 156.

23. Nathaniel Peabody Rogers, "The Anti-Slavery Movement," in *A Collection from the Newspaper Writings of Nathaniel Peopbody Rogers*, ed. John Pierpont (Concord, NH: J. R. French, 1847), 308.

24. Sarah Grimké, "Narrative and Testimony of Sarah M. Grimké," in *American Anti-Slavery Writings*, ed. James G. Basker (New York: Library of America, 2012), 351.

25. Angelina Grimké, *Letters to Catherine E. Beecher in Reply to an Essay on Slavery and Abolition* (Boston: Isaac Knapp, 1838), 4.

26. Sarah Grimké, *Letters on the Equality of the Sexes and the Condition of Woman Addressed to Mary S. Parker, President of the Boston Female Anti-Slavery Society* (Boston: Isaac Knapp, 1838), 2–3.

27. Henry David Thoreau, "Civil Disobedience," in *Thoreau: Essays and Poems* (New York, NY: Library of America, 2001), 212.

28. Henry David Thoreau, *Familiar Letters*, ed. F. B. Sanborn (Boston, MA: Houghton Mifflin, 1894), 115.

29. Mott, *Lucretia Mott: Complete Speeches and Sermons*, 35–52.

30. Beverly Wilson Palmer, ed., *Selected Letters of Lucretia Coffin Mott* (Champaign: University of Illinois Press, 2002), 283.

31. Thoreau, "Civil Disobedience," 209.

32. Lawrence Rosenwald, ed., *Emerson: Selected Journals 1841–1877* (New York: Library of America, 2010), 237.

33. Ibid., 1: 711.

34. Ibid., 2: 508–9.

35. Crispin Sartwell, ed., *The Practical Anarchist: Writings of Josiah Warren* (New York: Fordham University Press, 2011), 56.

36. Ibid.

37. Quoted in Valarie Ziegler, *The Advocates of Peace in Antebellum America* (Bloomington: Indiana University Press, 1992), 72.

38. Ralph Waldo Emerson, *Essays: Second Series* (New York: Library of America, 1991), 593.

39. Ibid., 599.

40. Ralph Waldo Emerson, "Speech on Affairs in Kansas," *Miscellanies* (New York: Houghton, Mifflin, 1884), 247. Thanks to Roderick Long for this quotation.

41. Ralph Waldo Emerson, "Politics," in *Essays: Second Series* (New York: Library of America, 1991), 565–69.

42. Voltairine de Cleyre, "Anarchism," in *Exquisite Rebel: Writings of Voltairine de Cleyre*, ed. Sharon Presley and Crispin Sartwell (Albany: State University of New York Press, 2005), 79.

43. Sartwell, *The Practical Anarchist*, 67–71.

44. Ibid.

45. de Cleyre, "Crime and Punishment," in *Exquisite Rebel*, 143–44.

46. Pascal, *Penseés*, 25.

47. Ibid., 20.

48. Ibid., 32.

49. Ibid., 34.

50. James C. Scott, *The Art of Not Being Governed: An Anarchist History of Upland Southeast Asia* (New Haven, CT: Yale, 2009), ix.

51. Ibid., 3–4.

52. Ibid., 8.

53. Ibid., 7.

54. Ibid., 8.

Index

abduction, 131
abolitionism, 249, 360, 361–81
   immediate, 362, 367
   See also Garrison, Grimké, Mott
abstraction in art, 302–303, 323
actuality operator, 99–100
Adams, John, 361
Adams, Robert Merrihew, 245–48
addiction, 204, 241, 332, 380
   Edwards on, 252–54
   and freedom, 216, 229–38
aesthetics, 4–5, 25, 139, 193–202, chapter 5
   centrality of, 291–93
   distance or disinterest, 128, 284, 293, 307, 309
   and epistemology, 291
   and ethics, 291, 310
   experience, 302–303
   and gender, 312–19
   and ontology, 291
   pleasure, 273
   and political theory, 291, 295, 383
   properties, 199–200, 291–93, 302–303
   and race, 312
   in science, 140, 187–90, 200
   scope of, 312
   and the self, 219–22
   and sexual orientation, 312–19
   and squishy totalitarianism, 346–47
   and truth, 85
Against the State, 293, 343
agency, 23, 25, 27, 165, 287
   Aristotle on, 212–14
   Louis Armstrong's, 206–207
   collective, 361
   divine, 48
   Edwards on, 252–54
   epistemic, 182
   Kant on, 212–14, 219, 227
   Korsgaard on, 214–16
   moral, 209, 229, 234, 244, 247, 248–50, 285, 287
   political, 367, 386
   and situational ontology, 238
   Walking Stewart on, 55
   in Taoism, 59–60
   See also consciousness, freedom, reason
agoraphobia, 212
Alberti, Leon Battista, 326
Alcibiades, 307
Alcott, Bronson, 363, 370
Aldean, Jason, 317
aletheia (truth), 112
Alexander the Great, 66

Alexander, Samuel, 129–30, 134
Alpers, Svetlana, 326, 328–29, 332
alternative possibilities, principle of, 229–32, 242, 249, 255
Alzheimer's disease, 288
American Idol, 22
Amish, the, 361, 386–87
Anabaptists, 362, 368–69
   See also Amish
anarchism, 25, 28, 217, 323, 347, 359–87
   American 19th century, 361–81
      See also de Cleyre, Emerson, Garrison, Mott, Thoreau, Warren
   anarcho-primitivism, 358
   and anthropology, 374, 384–86
   Emerson on, 371–72
   general characterization of, 358
   and pacifism, 363–65
   and Rawls, 338–43
   without adjectives, 376–78
   See also Godwin, Kropotkin, Scott
Andre the Giant, 247, 248–49
Andrews, Stephen Pearl, 373
animals, 33, 185, 198, 232–33, 235–36, 237, 259, 263, 264, 285, 304–305
   and art, 139, 302
   beauty and, 308
   in Carvaka, 59
   and consciousness, 226
   and ethics, 27, 267, 278
   and freedom, 220–21
   humans as, 29, 183, 203, 302
   and knowledge, 183
   Korsgaard on, 214–15
   and moral responsibility, 213, 216, 217–18, 219, 220–21, 242–43
   Rogers on, 365
   and utilitarianism, 270–71
Anselm of Canterbury, 111–13, 115
anthropology, 6, 23–24, 374, 384–86
antinomianism, 359–61, 366
apeiron, 69

Aquinas, Thomas, 162
architecture, 302, 312
Arcot, Nabob of, 49
Aristotle, 8, 11, 15, 46–47, 57, 58, 60, 105, 112, 142–43, 188, 282
   on action, 211–12, 215, 234, 275–76
   on art, 296–97, 323
   on atomism, 43–45
   on ethics, 269–74, 275–78
   on form, 199
   on perception, 126, 127
   on politics, 366, 374–75
   on teleology, 275
   on truth, 82, 108
Arminianism, 252
Armstrong, David, 181
Armstrong, Louis, 205–11, 217, 229, 292
arraying, 4, 18, 25, 26, 40, 44, 138, 142, 177, 183, 184, 195, 198–200, 264, 284–85, 311
art, 11, 24, 196, 275, 291–97
   definition of, 28, 292–93, 295–97, 301, 312–23
   enumeration of arts, 312
   etymology of, 294–97
   and evolution, 226
   and freedom, 219
   idealist theories, 299–300
   institutional theory of, 295
   no such thing as, 294
   Pop, 295, 314
   and science, 326–32
   of war, 279
Art of Living, 295
Assad, Bashar, 199
atheism, 366, 367
   Spinoza's alleged, 330–32
   See also God
atoms and atomism, 4, 31, 35, 39, 43–48, 54, 58–59, 69, 72, 176
   See also Democritus, Epicurus, Gassendi, Leucippus, Lucretius

Augustine, 219, 284
authoritarianism and anti-authoritarianism, 215, 358–59, 362–64, 372, 380
autumn, 61–62, 64
Austin, J. L., 12, 15, 19, 26
   on excuses, 248, 255
   on facts, 76–77
   on introspection, 145
   on knowledge, 158–62, 182
   on meaning, 93–94, 106, 157
   on sense data, 124, 396
   on truth, 88, 92, 100
   See also ordinary language philosophy
Averroes (Ibn Rushd), 127
axiology, 24, Part II
   See also aesthetics, ethics, political philosophy, values
Ayer, A. J., 19, 129, 160

badminton, 8
Bacall, Lauren, 317
Bacon, Francis, 42, 213, 328
Bakunin, Mikhail, 366
Ballou, Adin, 361–62, 363, 369–70
Balzac, Honoré de, 322–23
Bankei, 122–23, 139
Baroque, 30, 317, 322–32
Barwise, Jon, 35
Beach Boys, 84
Beaud, Michael, 349
beauty, 4, 6–7, 9, 11, 24, 79, 193, 269, 287, 291, 324–25, 331–32, 346
   alleged subjectivity of, 196–97, 201–202, 303–308
   classical conception of, 307
   definition of, 27, 306–308
   and eroticism, 306–308
   free and dependent, 302
   C. S. Lewis on, 398, 400
   Marcus Aurelius on, 224
   Moore on, 196, 308–12
   personal, 284
   Plato on, 306–308
   and pleasure, 273, 308–10
   Sidgwick on, 310
   social dimensions of, 307–308
   and truth, 305
behaviorism, 172
being and non-being
   in Heidegger, 267–68
   in Kuo Hsiang, 59–60
belief, 136, 275–76, 289
   and ethics, 257
   and knowledge 170–90, 266
   definition of, 145–46, 162, 179, 257
   Peirce on, 155
   and skepticism, 136–70
Bell, Clive, 199, 303, 310, 311
belly up to the smorgasbord, 18
Bentham, Jeremy, 270, 273–74
Berkeley, George, 16, 18, 74, 129, 130, 134, 200
   Samuel Johnson on, 148–49, 396
Beyoncé, 318, 345
Bhagavad Gita, 270
Bhaksar, Roy, 70
Bhutan, 48
Bible, 112, 366, 368
big bang, 188
Blackburn, Simon, 259–61
Black Nationalism, 321
blobject, the, 62, 70
Bloomsbury Group, 310–12
   See also Moore
body, human, 35, 136, 140, 212–16, 220, 272, 287, 296, 300, 307, 322
   and addiction, 231, 232–37
   alteration, 238, 312
   Andre the Giant's, 247–48
   and the arts, 228, 293, 302–303, 326–27
   and communication, 263, 319
   and sexual identity, 213
Bogart, Humphrey, 316
BonJour, Laurence, 178, 179

Boswell, James, 148–49, 396
boulders and rocks, 30, 31, 37–38, 41–42, 71, 76, 90, 187, 286, 360
Bourdieu, Pierre, 295
Brackhage, Stan, 211
Bradley, F. H., 99
Brande, Everard, 49–50
Brandom, Robert, 114
Bronson, Bertrand, 49
Brook Farm community, 361
Brown, John, 373
Brueghel, Pieter the Elder, 330
Bryant, Levi, 36, 53, 70–71
Buber, Martin, 35
Buddhism and the Buddha, 122–23, 228
  See also Zen
bureaucracy, 208, 217–18, 255, 337, 355
Burke, Edmund, 310, 344, 386
  on beauty, 307–308
Butler, Judith, 313

Caesar, Shirley, 293
Calvin, John, and Calvinism, 252, 359, 360, 362, 367
Campbell, Keith, 75–76, 264
capitalism, 260, 344, 345–46, 362–63, 365, 366, 371
  history of, 347, 349–59
Caravaggio, Michelangelo Merisi da, 141, 327
Carlyle, Thomas, 344
Carnap, Rudolf, 7, 8, 18
Carneades, 127
Carvaka, 48, 59, 60, 205
Castro, Fidel, 358
categorical imperative, 283, 285, 289
Catholicism, 212, 317, 358
Cato the Younger, 245
causal theory of naming, 109–10
causation, 38, 59, 205, 213, 215, 254
Cezanne, Paul, 333
Ch'an. See Zen
Chapman, Maria Weston, 361–62, 363

Chardin, Jean-Baptiste-Siméon, 326
Chechnya, 73
China, 42, 50, 58, 60, 346, 347, 349–50, 384
Chisholm, Roderick, 124, 238, 245, 254
Chomsky, Noam, 17
Christianity, 41, 42, 59, 165, 169–70, 275, 331, 368
Chuang Tzu, 26, 221, 281, 359
Cicero, 127
civil disobedience, 256–57
civilization, 352–53, 383, 385–86
civil war
  American, 373
  English, 360, 362
Clark, Andy, 129
class, social or economic, 287, 295, 341
classical, neo-classical, classicism, 30, 200, 314, 317
Clastres, Pierre, 386
Clifford, William, 169
Clinton, Bill, 96–97
Clooney, George, 270
clothing and fashion, 312–13
Coe, David Allan, 207, 317
coercion, 239, 241, 247, 287, 290, 338, 342–43, 363, 366, 370, 372–76, 376, 381
Cold War, 348
Coleridge, Samuel, 51, 52, 213
collectivism and collective consciousness, 255, 262, 287, 337, 347–48, 359–61, 381–82
Collingwood, R. G., 299
colonialism, 185, 321, 352–55, 386
color, 62–63, 201–202, 282, 302, 324, 326
comedy, 12–13, 14, 144, 145
communication, 11, 109, 198, 263–65, 278–79, 298–99, 305, 312, 347, 356
communism, 212, 323, 345–46, 349–59, 366, 376
compatibilism, 60, 207–208, 220–21, 232
  semi-compatibilism, 238–54 (defined, 251)
  Edwards's, 252–54
composition, 37–38, 70

Comte, Auguste, 274
concealment, 70
Conewago Creek, 9
Confucius, 3, 9–10, 11, 59, 112, 221
conscience, 255, 366, 369, 372
consciousness and self-consciousness, 7, 14, 21–24, 26–27, 48, 197, 201, 287, 302, 310, 331–32, 385–86
   and addiction, 237
   contents of, 129, 144, 159
   and determinism, 205, 208–209
   and free will, 214–15, 216, 219, 225–27, 233
   Hegel on, 226
   in Idealism, 13, 16–18, 122–23
   Leibniz on, 66–67
   in phenomenology, 18
   and realism, 68–69
   Walking Stewart on, 54, 56–57
   and truth, 109
   Wang Yang-Ming on, 122
   Wiggins on, 71–72
   See also collectivism and collective consciousness
consent, 343
conservativism, 5, 7, 9, 11, 298, 344, 350, 357, 366
constructivism, linguistic or social, 19, 21–24, 144, 199, 344–45
contextualism, 21, 25, 65, 67, 76–77, 111, 124–25, 197, 206–207, 271, 306, 315, 323
   in truth theory, 93–94, 102–104
contract and social contract, 279, 343–44, 381, 384
   Rawls on, 338–43
control. *See* self-control
convention, 4
Cooke, Sam, 292
cool, 316–17
copyright, 356
Correa, Rafael, 344
cosmology and cosmogony, 43, 48, 57, 60, 175, 187–90, 316

Courbet, Gustave, 323
craft, 228, 236, 282, 291, 295–96, 306, 312, 332, 374
   Kant on, 294
   Murdoch on, 334–35
crime, 378–80, 383
   See also justice, criminal
Croce, Benedetto, 274, 299–300
Cruz, Ted, 344
Cubism, 314
cynicism, 277–78, 359

dance, 298, 311, 312–13
Dancy, Jonathan, 288–90
Danto, Arthur, 138, 294
Dao De Jing. *See Tao Te Ching*
Daoism. *See* Taoism
Darwin, Charles, and Darwinism, 17, 59
   See also evolution
David, Marian, 98–99
Davidson, Donald, 26, 88, 95–96
Davis, Miles, 316–17
death, 42–43, 66–67, 73, 78, 144, 227, 237, 258, 275, 287, 288
   and materialism, 57
   de Cleyre on, 379–80
   Kierkegaard on, 118–19
de Cleyre, Voltairine, 372, 373, 383
   on criminal justice, 379–80
deconstruction, 8, 19–20, 115, 144
definitions, general treatment of, 292–93
deism, 58, 330, 370
Delacroix, Eugène, 52
Deleuze, Gilles, 23
democracy, 10, 44, 277, 285, 323, 348, 350, 357, 374
Democritus, 42, 43, 44–45, 48, 57, 58
Denck, Hans, 360–61
Dennett, Daniel, 128, 204, 221–25, 229, 248–49
deontological ethics, 265
   See also Kant, on ethics
De Quincey, Thomas, 50–56, 149

depravity, total, 252
Derrida, Jacques, 7, 19, 23, 26, 115, 205
Descartes, René and Cartesianism, 8, 18, 42, 144, 179, 320
   dream argument, 147–51, 153, 154
   dualism of, 41, 219
   and ethics, 267–68
   foundationalism of, 129
   and representational theory of mind, 16, 19, 125–26, 130–31
   and skepticism, 12, 47, 148, 153, 163, 165
desire, 234, 269, 306–308
determinism, 203–55, 225, 251–52, 255, 279, 380
   Dennett on, 221–22
   internal, 205
   and materialism, 203–204, 208–209, 213
   and Protestantism, 213
   Spinoza on, 209
   See also freedom
Dewey, John, 6, 7, 19, 22, 117, 133–34, 169
   aesthetics of, 275, 282–83, 299
   political philosophy of, 281
   and teleology, 275–78
Dickie, George, 294, 295
Diderot, Denis, 15
difference, 39, 189, 262, 283–84, 291
Diggers, 360, 362
Diogenes of Sinope, 26, 34, 46, 148, 152, 163, 182, 310, 359
disegno, 302
Donellan, Keith, 93–94, 103
Dostoevsky, Fyodor, 379
doxastic dissonance, 146, 165
dualism, 41, 126, 211, 218, 296, 300
   See also Descartes
Duchamp, Marcel, 295
Dürer, Albrecht, 139, 326, 395
Dutton, Denis, 226

Eakins, Thomas, 331
East India Company, British, 48–49, 353–55
Eastwood, Clint, 317–18
economics, 33, 201, 233, 312, 322, 328, 331
   capitalist, 260, 349–55
   economic hierarchy, 345–48
   Rawls on, 339
   Smith's, 275
   and squishy totalitarianism, 345–49
   See also capitalism, communism, Marx
education, 307, 312, 340, 346–47, 355, 358, 361, 381
Edwards, Jonathan, 252–54, 381
egoism, 271
Einstein, Albert, 189
Eleatic philosophy (Parmenides and Zeno), 43, 44, 46, 54–55, 69–70, 126, 219
Elk, Loyal Order of, 287
embezzlement, 93
Emerson, Ralph Waldo, 12, 26, 51, 183, 290, 376, 380, 383
   on human beings as relational, 20, 117–18
   on Lucretia Mott, 368
   on politics, 362, 369–72, 373–74
empathy, 264
empiricism, 16, 18, 128, 135, 144–45, 163
Enlightenment, 19, 52, 206, 219, 233, 360, 361
environmentalism, 278
Epictetus, 26, 223–24
Epicurus and Epicureanism, 42, 43, 44, 45, 54–55, 56, 126
epistemology, 5, 24, 37, chapter 3, 310, 389
   epistemological pluralism, 266
   virtue, 159, 164, 168–70, 179, 184
   standpoint, 10–11, 136–38, 185–87
   See also belief, justification, knowledge, truth
equality and inequality, 339, 351, 357–58, 361, 364, 370–72, 378
   and coercion, 249
   ontological, 267
   Pascal on, 382
   Rawls on, 338–43
essence, 17, 60
   in Heidegger, 113–14
   in Walking Stewart, 53, 55

Ethelred, Laws of, 88
ethics, 5, 6, 7, 25, 27, 55, 60, 73, 137–38, 193, 201, chapter 4
  and aesthetics, 193, 194–95, 310, 332–35
  and freedom, 203–55
  general characterization of, 278
  and knowledge, 163–65, 168–70
  meta-, 257, 290
  moral principles, justification of, 256–59
  particularism in, 288–90
  and truth, 85, 87–88, 109–19, 183–84, 193, 194, 199–200, 284–85, 289
  virtue, 265–67, 269–70, 285–90
Euclid, 199–200
eudaimonia, 269–73, 282, 285
evolution, 225–28
  and aesthetics, 308
  and ethics, 257, 259–60, 274–75
  and politics, 375, 385–86
excuses, 239, 247–51, 267
existentialism, 256–57, 258–59, 289, 332
expression, 295
expressionism, 297
extended mind. *See* externalism
externalism
  and aesthetics, 301, 309–12
  ethical, 265
  about freedom, 209
  about justification, 174–75, 180–82
  about meaning, 106, 125
  about mental content, 27, 121–25, 133–34, 182, 287
  about truth, 117

fabulousness, 316–17
facts, 30, 32–33, 36, 76–77, 98
  Austin on, 76–77
  fact-value distinction, 24, 256–62
  Feyerabend on, 141–42
faith, 11, 12, 123, 184, 213, 364
  definition of, 162–63
  James on, 167–70
  Kierkegaard on, 163–64
  and knowledge, 129, 145–46, 149, 154, 173–75, 187
  Nietzsche on, 166–67
  Santayana on, 165–66
  and truth, 78–79, 84–85, 107, 110, 114, 118
famine, 194
fascism, 358
Federalism, 355
femininity, 314–15
feminism
  early American or 'first wave,' 360, 361, 363–65, 373
  and beauty, 306
  in epistemology, 185–87
Feyerabend, Paul, 141–43
Feynman, Richard, 142–43
Fichte, Johann Gottlieb, 12, 13, 213, 219, 230
Ficino, Marsilio, 307
Field, Hartry, 96
film, 312
Finney, Charles Grandison, 362
Fischer, John Martin, 218, 233, 238, 242, 251, 254
Fish, Stanley, 26
Flaubert, Gustave, 322–23
fleas, educated, 78
Fodor, Jerry, 17
form, 199–200, 291, 293, 302–303, 306
formalism, 299, 302–303, 306, 308
Forms, theory of, 8, 22, 33, 57–58, 138, 292, 327, 332–35
  See also Plato
Foucault, Michel, 6, 10, 12, 22–23, 26, 186–87, 197, 233, 235
foundationalism, 129, 178
Fourier, Charles, 361
Frankfurt, Harry, 216–17, 222–23, 229, 242
Franklin, Aretha, 292
freedom and free will, 27, 60, 203–55, 259, 330, 379, 387, 389
  and beauty, 302

freedom and free will *(continued)*
   and craft, 228, 294
   Heidegger on, 114
   and history, 274
   Kant on, 204, 208, 211–19, 220, 223, 238, 294
   and materialism, 203–204
   political, 269, 339, 340, 347, 360–61, 371, 375, 376, 381
   See also determinism, oppression
Free Produce movement, 368–69
Frege, Gottlob, 12, 76, 92, 97, 99, 102
Freud, Sigmund, 6, 218, 319–21
Fry, Roger, 310
Fuller, Margaret, 367

Gadamer, Hans-Georg, 23
Gandhi, Mahatma, 362, 364
Garrison, William Lloyd, 28, 361–62, 363–65, 366, 367, 372, 374–75, 379, 380
   Emerson on, 369, 373
   See also abolitionism, pacifism
Gassendi, Pierre, 42, 43, 45
Gauguin, Paul, 272
gay. *See* sexuality
gender, 28, 306, 312–19, 320, 341, 346, 361
genealogy, 26
genius, 300
genocide, 265, 344
Gettier, Edmund, and the Gettier problem, 111
Gilbert, Brantley, 317
Gindin, Sam, 350–52
Giotto, 140
globalization, 348, 358
God, 7, 13, 37–38, 47, 72, 79, 105, 118, 125, 206, 225, 282, 359–60, 375
   Anselm on, 112–13
   and art, 300, 301, 327, 329–32, 335
   existence of, 5, 6, 13, 165
   and freedom, 222–23, 252–54, 257, 287
   government of, 362–67
   imminent, 42
   and knowledge, 14, 174–75
   Leibniz on, 66–67, 266
   Marcus Aurelius on, 224
   Merleau on, 133–34
   Murdoch on, 332–34
   and music, 292–93
   and nature, 41, 58
   Nietzsche on, 204
   and Platonism, 111, 324, 332–34
   Poe on, 188
   Spinoza on, 209–10, 330–31
Godwin, William, 51, 196, 338
Goethe, Johann Wolfgang, 213
golden rule, 27, 257, 285
Goldman, Alvin, 180–81
Goldman Sachs, 346
Goldwater, Barry, 358
Gombrich, E.H., 123, 139
Goodman, Benny, 293–84
Goodman, Nelson, 123, 139
Google, 346
gospel music, 292–93
Goya, Francisco, 335
Graeber, David, 380
gravity, 39–40, 47, 187–90, 286
Green, Al, 248, 292
Greene, Brian, 188
Greene, William B., 378
Grimké, Angelina, 361–62, 363
Grimké, Sarah, 361–62, 363, 364, 366–67
Grovier, Kelly, 50
gunpowder, 352–53
Gysbrechts, Cornelis, 326

Habermas, Jürgen, 214, 219
haeccity, 65–67, 70
Haliburton, 346, 352
Halperin, David, 313–14
Hals, Frans, 330
Hamann, Johann Georg, 233, 361
Hamilton, Alexander, 355
happiness, 27, 255, 265, 268–74, 344
   attack on the concept of, 268–70

Haraway, Donna, 185–87
Harding, Sandra, 185–87
Harman, Graham, 53, 68–71
Harnett, William, 331
Harrington, James, 361
Hawking, Stephen, 188
Hayek, Friedrich von, 358
Heda, Willem Claesz, 327
hedonism, 265, 268–74, 308–309
Hegel, G. W. F., 6, 8, 9, 12, 13, 14, 15, 19, 52, 59, 197, 200, 225–26
    on art, 296, 325
    and collective consciousness, 197
    on freedom, 209, 213, 218, 219, 220
    on history, 274
    political philosophy, 281, 336
    and truth, 118–19
    See also idealism
Heidegger, Martin, 7, 8, 12, 14, 15, 19, 26, 70, 143
    on ethics, 268
    on language, 22
    on truth, 85, 88, 112, 113–17
Hellman, Lillian, 116
Henke, Frederick, 122
Heraclitus, 11–12, 43, 46, 78
hermeneutics, 85
heroin, 237
heterosexuality. *See* sexuality
Heywood, Ezra, 378
Hickey, Dave, 211
Hierarchical Coincidence, Principle of, 340, 346, 357
Higginson, Thomas Wentworth, 373
historicity of concepts, 292–93, 317
history, philosophy of, 274–75, 375–76
Hobbes, Thomas, 220, 254, 279, 281, 320, 361, 381, 382, 383, 385–86
Holbein, Hans, 330
Holiday, Billie, 269
holism, 288
Holocaust, the, 344
home, 306

homosexuality. *See* sexuality
Hopi, 10
Horgan, Terry, 62–63, 72
Hubble telescope, 69
humanism and anti-humanism, 58, 59, 209
    Renaissance, 326, 328–29, 330
Hume, David, 8, 12, 74, 129, 146, 163, 250, 252, 254
    clarity of, 15
    on ethics, 6, 250, 273
    on freedom, 207–208, 220, 230, 250
    on knowledge, 17, 129, 154, 175
    on political philosophy, 250, 361
    on the self, 263
    skepticism of, 6, 19, 146, 163, 164–65
humility, 11, 12, 15, 59, 154, 225, 310, 328, 382, 383, 387, 398
Husserl, Edmund, 18, 19, 70
Hutcheson, Francis, 194, 200, 273, 307
Hutchinson, Anne (misspelled in text), 360–61
Huxley, Thomas, 168–69
Huygens, Christiaan, 329–32
Hyder Ali (Dalwai of Mysore), 49

idealism, 99, 128, 144, 149, 200, 323
    and art, 299–300
    and beauty, 207
    Berkeleyan 16
    German, 13–14, 16–17, 18, 24, 213, 302–303
    See also Berkeley, Fichte, Hegel, Kant, Schelling, Schopenhauer
identity, 237–38, 289
    personal, 60
    sexual and gender, 28, 312–19, 389
    See also self
ideology, 116, 314, 345, 348, 351–53, 374–75
immigration, 319–22
immortality, 286–87
Impressionism, 297, 314, 323
improvisation, 60, 205–11, 298, 374
Incas, 385

indexical expressions, 34, 94–97, 102–104
  'quasi-indexicals,' 94
individuals, 3, 4, 26, 30, 35, 56–57, 61–62, 69, 182, 374–81
  and aesthetics, 305
  and ethics, 208–11, 263, 279, 285–90
  vagueness of, 62–64
individualism, 256–59, 279, 337, 359–87
  American 19th century, 361–81
  and egalitarianism, 371
  Kierkegaard's, 285–90
  Josiah Warren's, 369–71
  See also Emerson, Mott, Thoreau, Warren
insanity defense, 239–40, 247
intention and meaning, 102–103
internalism, 129–33, 144, 158
  about justification, 174–75, 180
internet, 387
Inuit, 31
Iraq, 243
irrationalism, 12–13, 78, 165, 176, 190, 361

Jacobi, Friedrich, 213, 233, 361
James, William, 7, 15, 63, 88, 117, 182
  on faith, 162–70, 174
jazz, 205–11, 298
  democracy as, 374
Jefferson, Thomas, 355
Jesus, 325, 334, 360
Johnson, Alexander Bryan, 73–76
Johnson Mountain Boys, 311
Johnson, Samuel, 34, 148–49, 152, 163, 182, 396
Jung, Carl, 287
justice, 4, 6, 9–10, 24, 193, 198, 269, 292
  criminal, 208, 235, 239–40, 255, 378–81, 383
  definition of, 338
  Pascal on, 381–83
  Rawls on, 338–43
justification, 130–31, 132, 146–47, 157–58, 158–90
  coherence theory of, 178

  James on, 163
  Moore on, 154–55
  purposes of, 176–82
  Wittgenstein on, 152–58

Kalf, Willem, 326, 330
Kant, Immanuel, 8, 12, 13, 14, 15, 17, 29, 52, 122, 123, 130, 141, 144, 154, 230, 254, 344
  on aesthetics, 194, 199, 257, 293–94, 294, 296, 302–303, 309
  on ethics, 256, 257, 258, 287, 386
  on freedom, 204, 208, 211–12, 213, 214, 215, 216, 218–19, 220, 223, 238, 294
Kaplan, David, 102
Karlstadt, Andreas, 360
Kepler, Johannes, 189
Keynes, John Maynard, 311
Kierkegaard, Søren, 12, 26, 118–19, 144, 184, 233, 360
  on faith and knowledge, 162–70, 174, 182
  on freedom, 213, 219, 220
  on the self, 286–90
  See also existentialism
Killing Fields, 265, 344, 358
Kilmer, Joyce, 305
Kim Il Song, 358
King, Martin Luther Jr., 340, 362, 364
kiss, 263
kitten, 12
knots and knot theory, 3, 4, 23, 34, 36, 61, 195, 285–90, 389
knowledge, 4, 17, 37, 69, 132, 135–36, chapter 3B, 145, 158–90, 260, 331–32, 334
  Austin on, 158–61
  and beauty, 308
  definition of, 27, 146–47, 170, 266
  and ethics, 258
  Pascal on, 20–21
  Wittgenstein on, 152–58
  See also belief, epistemology, justification, truth

Korsgaard, Christine, 214–16, 217–18, 225, 232, 235, 254, 287, 386
Kristeva, Julia, 321–22, 333
Kropotkin, Peter, 259, 347, 349
Krupp, 352
Kuhn, Thomas, 10, 31, 140–41, 143
Kuo Hsiang, 59–60, 281

Lamb, Charles, 51
language, 6, 11, 17, 21–23, 26, 32–37, 39, 54, 71, 92–95, 99, 125, 143–44, 145, 196–98, 206, 225, 262, 272
  and addiction, 237
  Alexander Johnson on, 73–76
  and ethics, 234–41
  and facts, 76–77
  games, 24, 104, 152
  and gender, 315, 317
  and knowledge, 186–87
  Latour on, 197–98
  and materiality, 34, 36–37
  and meaning, 109–10, 125
  ordinary, 12, 15, 22, 64, 76–77, 83, 135, 149–50, 152, 160, 295, 338
  philosophy of, 32–34
  and power, 186–87, 344–45, 385
  private, 301, 305
  Saussure on, 43–44
  and the self, 235
  and the state, 337, 386
  Walking Stewart on, 53–54
  and truth, 27, 82–83, 85–89, 92–97, 104–106, 107–108, 109, 114, 116, 183, 305
  Wittgenstein on, 153–56, 162
Lao Tzu. See *Tao Te Ching*
Latour, Bruno, 24, 26, 197–98
law, 198, 211–12, 255, 257, 258, 378–81
Lavoisier, Antoine, 31
Leeuwenhoek, Antonie van, 329–30
left-right spectrum, 28, 344–46, 357–61, 365–66, 369–72
Leibniz, Gottfried Wilhelm, 37–38, 56, 63, 65–67, 68, 72, 272

Lemaître, Georges, 188
Lenin, Vladimir, 358
Leonardo da Vinci, 325
lesbian. *See* sexuality
Leucippus, 44–45, 58
Lévi-Strauss, Claude, 300–301
Lewis, C.S., 398, 400
Lewis, David, 64–65, 72–73, 104
Liberace, 317
liberalism, 348
liberty, 339, 357–58
Libya, 33
Lin-chi, 123
lions, 4
Locke, John, 11, 16, 201, 348, 381
  on free will, 252, 254
  political philosophy of, 361, 386
logic, 5, 11, 152–53, 155–56, 159, 162, 169, 258
Long, Roderick, 395, 398
Lotze, Hermann, 78
love, 9, 83–84, 86, 253, 292, 297, 303, 333–35
  and beauty, 306
  and politics, 372
  and sexual identity, 318–19
Lucian, 296
Lucretius, 6, 38–39, 42, 225
  on perception, 46, 126–27
  on personal identity, 60
Luther, Martin, 359, 360
lying, 110–11

Mabutu Sese Seko, 199
Malaysia, 49
Malebranche, Nicolas, 41
Mannerism, 325
Manson, Charles, 244
Mao Zedong, 25, 345–46, 350
Marcus Aurelius, 223–25
marriage, 276–78
Marx, Karl and Marxism, 6, 11, 42, 197, 281, 344, 350–51, 356, 258, 361, 366
  on history, 274, 382

Marx, Karl and Marxism *(continued)*
  on the state, 347
Mary (the Madonna), 327
Masaccio, 140
masculinity, 314–15
materialism, 8, 40–62, 76, 136, 188, 199–200, 204, 220, 225
  and aesthetics, 291, 297–99, 302
  definition of 'material,' 47–48
  and history, 274
  liquid, 54–58
  and the self, 254
  Spinoza's, 330–32
  Walking Stewart's, 53–58
  Thoreau's, 41–42
mathematics, 149, 258, 308, 397
Matrix (film), 310
May, Samuel J., 361–62, 366
Mazis, Glen, 51
McCarthy, Mary, 116
McGinn, Marie, 153
McKenna, Michael, 244
McKirahan, Richard, 48
Mead, George Herbert, 19, 197
Mead, Margaret, 386
media, 263, 313, 346–47, 356
Mencken, H. L., 15
mental illness, 229–38, 240–41, 255, 380
mercantilism, 353
meritocracy, 381
Merleau-Ponty, Maurice, 22, 133–34
metaphysics, 4–5, 8, 25, chapter 1, 70, 77–79, 81, 158, 220, 286, 300, 370
Metsys, Quentin, 323
Mexican-American War, 367–68, 370
Michelangelo, 293, 325
Mill, John Stuart, 270, 271, 273, 361, 374
mimesis, 85, 91, 296, 323–32
mind, 26, 300
Minimalism (art movement), 314
Mitterand, Francois, 358
modernism, 297, 300, 302–303, 326, 327, 331

monads, 35, 254, 272, 288, 320–21
  See also Leibniz
Monroe, Bill, 311
Montague, William Pepperrell, 101–102
Montesquieu, Baron de la, 361, 386
Moore, G. E., 26, 163, 184
  on beauty, 196, 306, 308–12
  and Burke, 310–11
  on knowledge, 158, 182
  'Moore's paradox,' 146
  'Moore-sentences' (m-sentences), 151, 156–57, 158, 160, 173, 180
  proof of the external world, 147, 149–62
  on truth, 98–100
Morgan, J. P., 356
Mormons, 361
Moser, Paul, 178
Mott, Lucretia, 28, 361–62, 363, 364, 366, 367–69, 373, 374, 375, 380
  Emerson on, 368–69
  Thoreau on, 368
Mozart, Wolfgang, 273
mudlumps, fellow, 225–26
Muir, John, 305
multiculturalism, 11
mumbo-jumbo, 48
Munden, Joseph, 50
Müntzer, Thomas, 360
Murdoch, Iris, 311, 332–35
Mussolini, Benito, 25
murder, 149, 174, 208, 212, 224, 240, 244, 381–82
music, 205–11, 282, 291, 296, 356
  country, 317–18
  funk, 292
  and gender, 315–19
  gospel, 292–93
  musicals, 311
  soul, 248, 292–93
mutualism, 376

Napoleon, 234
narrative and narrativism, 18, 205–206, 302

nations and nationalism, 287, 347, 349, 352–55
natural selection. *See* evolution
nature and the natural, 27, 195, 201, 252, 262
  and beauty, 305
  and freedom, 209, 213, 214, 217–20
  in Alexander Johnson, 74–75
  naturalism, 26, 58, 59, 203–204, 213, 255, 260, 308
  and sexual identity, 315–19
  in Spinoza, 41, 330–32
  in Walking Stewart, 50–58
  in Stoicism, 221–25
Nazism, 358
necessity and possibility, 58, 60, 70, 97–100, 199, 204–206, 219
  See also actuality operator
Neo-Confucianism, 121–22, 129
neo-liberalism, 348, 351
Neo-Platonism, 22, 111, 194, 302, 307–308, 323–28
neurology, 37, 161, 184, 204, 209, 260, 306, 320, 380
Newton, Isaac, 42, 188–89
Nietzsche, Friedrich, 6, 7, 14, 15, 115, 166–70, 182, 223
  on consciousness, 226–28
  on Eastern religions, 281–82
  on responsibility, 204–205
nihilism, 282–83
nirvana, 55
Nixon, Richard, 174
nominalism, 36, 73–76, 79, 92, 97, 102, 147
non-resistance. *See* pacifism
nothingness, 36, 47, 54–55, 59, 60, 115, 118, 141, 209, 380
Novalis, 213
Nozick, Robert, 338, 340

Obama, Barack, 345, 358
objectivity, 26, 136–40, 166, 185–87, 201, 328, 335
object-oriented ontology (OOO), 68–71
  See also Bryant, Harman
objects, 29–30, 68–71, 306–308
  See also individuals
obligation, 256–59
Obscenity, Anarchy, Reality, 223, 227, 266
occasionalism, 41
Ockham, William of, and Ockham's razor, 31, 127, 131, 200
Oneida, 361
one-plane principle in ontology, 40–43
ontology, 4, 24, chapter 1, 213, 232
  and art, 299–302
  economy in, 31
  elements of, 37–40
  Emerson's, 373
  and intellectual property, 356
  and politics, 287, 337
  and truth, 91, 100–10
  and value, 196–97, 200, 261–62, 283–90, 309–10
  See also dualism, idealism, materialism, situations
opera, 314, 317
oppression, 25, 186–87, 219, 249, 319
ordinary language philosophy, 12, 15, 22, 64–65, 72–73, 76–77, 99, 106, 135, 152, 157, 160, 171, 295, 338
  Moore's, 149–50
  and truth, 83–88
  See also Austin
Oxford English Dictionary, 37, 83, 88, 344

pacifism, 362–65, 366, 373
Paine, Thomas, 50, 386
painting, 296, 298, 301, 302–303, 313, 322–32
Panitch, Leo, 350–52
panpsychism, 53
pantheism, 48–58, 327–32, 333, 367
Parfit, Derek, 214, 264, 270
Parker, Theodore, 373
Parmenides, 11–12, 44, 46, 54, 56, 60, 78, 89

Parthenon, 199, 200
Pascal, Blaise, 15, 26, 59, 381, 382
　on justice, 382
　relational ontology of, 20–21
Patinir, Joachim, 330
Paul, Rand, 345, 358
Paycheck, Johnny, 207
Pearce, William, 50
Peebles, Ann, 293
Peirce, C.S., 114, 117, 155, 276
perception, 4, 29–30, 35, 109–10, 123–38, 142, 201–202, 263, 291, 326
　in ancient atomism, 45–46
　representational theory of, 16–20, 21–22, 124–36
performance, 313
Perry, John, 35, 102
Perry, Katy, 314, 318
personal identity. *See* self
perspective (in picturing), 128, 135, 140
Pettit, Philip, 375
phainomai (Greek, to appear), 126
phantasia (Greek, imagination), 126
phenomenalism, 74, 128
phenomenology, 18, 19, 22, 128, 133, 207, 273, 276, 373
Phidias (Pheidias), 296
philosophy
　analytic, 64, 81, 93, 182, 206
　end of, 7–9
　general characterization of, 4–7, 78, 338
　methodology of, 11–13
　nadir of, 300
　and ordinary language, 157–58
　as pudding, 12
　sub-disciplines of, 5
　systems of, 13–15
phlogiston, 31
photography, 326, 332
physicalism. *See* materialism
physics, 43, 47, 56, 70, 139, 142–43, 259, 283
Picasso, Pablo, 293–94

Pickett, Wilson, 248, 251, 292
Pinochet, Augusto, 358
Plato, 9–10, 14, 22, 33, 41, 46, 48, 57–58, 78, 126–27, 199, 219, 325, 327, 332–35
　on art, 296–97, 323–28
　on beauty, 306–308, 311
　on justice, 8
　on knowledge, 154, 179, 328–29
　Nietzsche on, 170, 204
　on politics, 217, 374–75
　on representation, 91–92, 138, 323–24
　Rosset on, 61
　on the self, 215, 217, 232, 320
　on truth, 98–99, 111
　on value, 112–13, 194, 213
　as a writer, 11–12
　See also Forms, Neo-platonism
play, 205, 209, 277–78
pleasure and pain, 6, 27, 313–14
　and beauty, 303–10
　and ethics, 255, 256, 262, 264–65, 268–70, 271, 284, 287
　See also utilitarianism
Plotinus, 22, 93, 119, 194, 296, 302
Poe, Edgar Allan, 187–90
poetry, 11–12, 187–90, 296, 312–13
Poincaré, Henri, 397
Pointillism, 54
police power, 249, 347, 356, 380, 383, 384
polis, 269
Political Aesthetics, 193
politics and the political, 5, 6, 22–23, 24, 25, 27, 28, 33, 56, 193, 201, 289, chapter 6
　and aesthetics 291, 295, 323
　and the self, 214–17, 232, 241, 287
　taxonomies of, 344–46
Pollock, Jackson, 298
Polo, Marco, 48
Polykleitos (Polyclitus), 296
positivism, 18, 19, 128, 144–45
possibility. *See* necessity and possibility
postmodernism, 6, 26

poststructuralism, 18
Potrc, Matjaz, 62
poverty, 265, 274–75, 361
power, 6, 25, 70, 185–87, 220, 223, 280, 302
   and craft, 210, 297
   and distance, 284
   and freedom, 214–15
   and knowledge, 185–87
   Rawls on, 338–43
   within the self, 231–38, 319–22
powerlessness, 228, 230
punishment, 240–41, 255
pragmatism and pragmatics, 7, 11, 18, 29, 81, 177, 275–78, 283
   and Emerson, 371
   neo-, 128
price, 376–78
prisons, 240–41, 347, 379, 381
privilege, 185–87
properties, 72–77, 283–84
property, 285, 351, 372–73, 375
   intellectual, 356
propositions, 77, 98, 100–102, 113, 161, 171–72, 175–79, 181–84, 186, 235
   analytic, 96
   Heidegger on, 114
   Moore on, 150, 151, 155–56, 180
   propositional attitudes, 78, 90, 113, 145–46, 162, 172
   as truth-bearers, 27, 65, 83–109, 116–17, 119, 172–73
   and epistemic value, 146–47, 154, 275
   Witgenstein on, 152–53, 159–60
Protagoras, 126
Protestantism, 213, 317, 359, 362, 366, 373
psychiatry, 209, 229
psychology, 56, 97, 108, 135, 136, 180, 206, 209, 216, 220, 233, 284, 287
   and politics, 346–47
   positive, 270
psychosis, 267, 288
punishment, 10, 208, 380, 383
Puritanism, 252–54, 265, 359–61, 362

Putnam, Hilary, 106, 125, 135–36, 138–39
Pyle, A. J., 58
Pyrrho, 59, 126
Pythagoras and Pythagoreanism, 45, 213, 219

Quakerism, 360, 362, 366, 368
quantum mechanics, 47
queer theory, 26
Quillen-Lichtenbaum conjecture, 171–72, 176–77
Quine, W. V. O., 15, 18, 19, 23, 93–94, 96–97

Racanati, Francois, 102–103
race, 10, 26, 32–33, 185, 186, 206, 287, 320–22, 340, 341, 346, 363
   and art, 295, 306, 312, 318
Rainer, Yvonne, 313
Ramsey, F.P., 76, 81, 99, 100, 101
Rand, Ayn, 345, 358
Raphael (painter), 140, 141, 323, 325, 327
rationalism, 16, 128, 163
rationality, 87, 163, 164–65, 176, 177, 179, 182, 199, 278, 382
   definition of, 269
   deliberative or practical, 60, 206, 209, 216, 251
   in ethics, 27, 257
   and freedom, 211–16, 218, 227, 231, 238, 247, 250
   in philosophy, 11–12
   Rawls on, 339–42
Rawls, John, 227, 281, 338–43, 357
Reagan, Ronald, 351, 355, 358
realism, 138–39, 152, 225, 276, 322–32
   depressive, 284
   direct, 21, 24, 27, 126, 159
   in ethics, 332–34
   in literature, 322–23
   Moore's, 99, 159
   'new,' 101–102
   in picturing, 139–40, 303, 322–32
   representative, 26

realism (*continued*)
  Rosset's, 61
  and social construction, 312
  speculative, 53, 68–71
  Walking Stewart's, 53–58
Redding, Otis, 292
reductionism, 26
Reformation, Protestant, 359–62, 364
  See also Calvin, Luther, Catholicism, Protestantism, Puritanism, Quakerism
Reid, Thomas, 19, 129, 148–49, 245
relations and relational ontology, 20–21, 37–40, 57, 61, 208–209
  and aesthetics, 308–12
  and ethics, 263, 267–68, 271, 278, 283–90
  in Alexander Johnson, 74–75
  in OOO, 68–71
  and the self, 228–32
  and the social, 262–66
  See also situations, string, knots
reliabilism, 174–75, 179, 180–82
  See also externalism
Rembrandt van Rijn, 26, 140, 141, 293, 327, 329, 330
Renaissance, 47, 128, 139–40, 143, 302, 322–32, 326–28
representation, 24, 26, 27, 32, 83, 101, 135, 136–38, 183, 264, 280, 283–84
  in art, 299, 303, 322–32
  and communication, 263
  eidetic theory of, 323–28
  and ethics, 267
  in Epicureanism, 45–46, 126
  mimetic theory of, 85, 91, 296, 323–32
  in OOO, 68
  in perception, 16–20, 21–22, 124–40, 157–58
  in political theory, 337
  in science, 140–43, 194
  and the self, 234–35
  systems of, 4, 30–31, 64, 71–72, 116, 142, 184, 196–97
republicanism, 328, 361, 374–75

resemblance, 39, 323–24
  family, 292, 295
resistance, 315, 362, 384–87
responsibility, 25, 27, 203–55, 261, 380
  and addiction, 229–38
  of animals, 242–43
  for another, 243
  criminal, 208, 235, 239–40, 255, 378–80
  Foucault on, 10
  Hume on, 207–208
  and freedom, 215–16
  institutional, 242–43
  for mental states, 244–46
  of non-human agents, 241–42
  and politics, 362, 369, 380
  and the principle of alternative possibilities, 229–32, 241
revolution, 17, 143, 233, 236, 384
  communist, 349
  French, 50, 53, 344, 361
Riegl, Alois, 274
rights, 249, 339, 361, 366–67, 372–73
Rilke, Rainer Maria, 333
Rococo, 314
Rogers, Nathaniel Peabody, 362, 363, 365
Romanticism, 48–58, 219, 305, 326, 327, 331
Rorty, Richard, 7, 8, 14, 19, 23–24, 26, 93–94, 116, 123
Rosset, Clement, 61–62
Rousseau, Jean-Jacques, 197, 209, 344, 361, 381, 386
Rowlands, Mark, 129, 395
Royal Society, 48
Ruisdael, Jacob van, 225, 327
Ruiz, Rosie, 181
Russell, Bertrand, 12, 97–100

sadism and masochism, 359
Saenredam, Pieter Jansz, 327
Sandusky, Jerry, 240
Santayana, George, 162–70, 182, 183, 184
Sapir-Whorf hypothesis, 24

Sappho, 307
sarcasm, 102–103
Sartre, Jean-Paul, 289
Satan, 14, 112
Saussure, Ferdinand de, 43–44
Schelling, Friedrich, 12, 13, 14, 52, 213, 216, 219, 230, 263, 330–31, 332
Schiller, Friedrich, 52, 213, 218–20, 223, 233, 293
Schlegel, Friedrich and August, 213
Schoenberg, Arnold, 293–94
Schopenhauer, Arthur, 13, 16–17, 19, 78, 213
science, 9, 12–13, 27, 47, 52, 63, 74, 115, 137, 175, 225, 284, 360
   and aesthetics, 140, 187–90, 200, 335
   and art, 326–32
   and ethics, 259
   and materialism, 40, 57–58, 63, 204, 260
   Nietzsche on, 166–67
   progress of, 10, 58, 140–43
   and representation, 140–43
   scientism, 52, 185–90
   social, 42, 197, 381
   tension with empiricist philosophy, 18
   tension with idealist philosophy, 19, 213
Scott, James C., 374, 384–86
sculpture, 296, 301, 302–303
self-control, 212, 215, 216, 218, 230–38, 244, 249–50, 251, 272, 372
self-delusion, 116, 179, 185, 190, 217, 284, 320, 381, 387
self-esteem, 284, 382
selfhood, 40, 42, 209, 228–38, 241, 254–55, 387
   abandonment of, 221–22
   Robert Adams on, 245–46
   and art, 206–11, 301–301, 304, 331–35
   and beauty, 304–307
   Emerson on, 118
   as entanglement, 4, 27, 124, 228–38, 288–90
   and ethics, 262–65, 267–68, 285–90
   and freedom, 212–13
   Hegel on, 213–14
   and Kant, 210–12
   Kierkegaard on, 118–19, 171, 289
   Korsgaard on, 214–16
   Kuo Hsiang on, 59–60
   and language, 85
   Leibniz's, 67
   Nietzsche on, 227–28
   and power, 216–17, 219–20, 223–25
   Schopenhauer on, 16–17
   and solipsism, 117–18
   Walking Stewart on, 54–58
   and Stoicism, 223–25
   as swarm, 217, 319–22
   and truth, 109, 110–11, 114–15
   and Zen, 122–23
self-knowledge and self-consciousness, 7, 11, 25, 26, 185, 204–205, 214–15, 216, 264–65, 268, 330–31
   Emerson on, 20, 117–18
   and knowledge, 124–25, 132, 145, 158, 161, 186–87
   Hegel on, 13
self-respect, 333, 341
Sellars, Wilfrid, 26
semiotics, 91, 185, 235, 237, 263
sensation. *See* perception
sense data (sensibilia, impressions, sensations, appearances), 16–19, 124–43, 158, 161
   in Academic skepticism, 127
   and aesthetic properties, 201–202, 299–301, 304
   Austin on, 158–60, 396
   and ethics, 264–65, 266–67
   Alexander Johnson on, 73–74
   Kant on, 126
   and knowledge, 21, 144
   and pictures, 128–29, 139–40
   See representation
Sextus Empiricus, 127
sexuality and sexual orientation, 10, 28, 212, 228, 273, 278, 287, 292, 293, 321–22

sexuality and sexual orientation *(continued)*
   as aesthetic repertoire, 312–19, 389
   and beauty, 307–308, 309
   in politics, 359
shadows, 23
Shaftesbury, Third Earl of (Anthony Ashley Cooper), 293, 296, 302
Shakers (religious sect), 301, 360
Shakespeare, William, 261, 330
shatter zones, 374, 384–87
Shelley, Percy, 51, 194
Sidgwick, Henry, 271, 273, 310
Simplicius, 43
sin, original, 252, 284, 381
Singer, Peter, 270
Situationism, 387
situations and situational ontology, 21, 30, 35–40, 61–62, 78–79, 90, 117
   and art, 297–99
   and beauty, 303–12
   and ethics, 262–65, 267–68, 278–79, 283–90
   and freedom, 221–25
   and knowledge, 136, 182–90
   snd responsibility, 249–50
   and the self, 229–38
   and truth, 98, 116–17
   and value, 193–202, 304–12
   See also knots, individuals, objects, relations, string
Six Names of Beauty, 295, 306
skateboarding, 5
skein, 3, 195, 199, 200
skepticism, 58, 145, 168, 177
   Humean, 6, 19, 146, 163, 164–65
   moral, 267–68
   my solution for, 146–70
   Pyrrhonian, 59, 126
Skidmore, Arthur, 181
skill, 210, 228, 236, 272, 297–99, 326–27
slavery, 249, 361–81
Smith, Adam, 275, 279, 348, 352–55
Smith, Gerrit, 364

soap bubbles, 150–51
social, the, 23–24, 27, 183, 186, 196–98, 201–202, 265, 285–90, 373
   and aesthetics, 293, 295, 305–306, 308, 310
   constructionism, 32–33, 199–200, 262–63
   Latour on, 197–98
   media, 312
   and science, 142
   and the self, 320–22
social contract. *See* contract and state, justifications for
Socrates, 57, 154, 194, 223, 296, 307, 334–35
solidity, 31
solipsism, 18, 117–18
   and aesthetics, 304
   and ethics, 267–71, 332–34
Sophists, 126–27
Southey, Robert, 51
soul music, 248
   definition of, 292–93
sovereignty, 252, 342
   self-, 252, 366–67, 369–72
space, 17, 38–39, 144, 149–50, 196, 199, 262, 263, 287, 383–86
Spinoza, Baruch, 42, 72, 79, 225, 320, 330–32
   on freedom, 209–11
   ontology, 40–41
   on substance, 69–70
   on teleology, 58–59
Spooner, Lysander, 275
sport, 312, 346
squishy totalitarianism. *See* totalitarianism
Stalin, Joseph, 350
Stanton, Elizabeth Cady, 367
state, political, 217, 281, 337, 374, 378–81
   and capital, 347, 349–55
   definition of, 343–44, 349–50
   Emerson on, 370–73
   and the left-right spectrum, 344–46
   legitimacy of, 293, 338–44, 351, 378–81
   Rawls and, 338–43

Steen, Jan, 327
Stephen, Leslie, 310
Stewart, Dugald, 50
Stewart, John "Walking," 42, 46, 48–58, 60, 73, 225, 354
   biographical sketch of 48–52
   service in India, 48–50
   suicide of, 57
   suspended in chicken coop, 49–50
   in Bhutan, India, Persian Gulf, Arabian Peninsula, Ethiopia, Marseille, Sweden, Lapland, Turkey, Russia, North America, Ireland, 48–52
Stoicism, 115, 221–25, 228, 230, 272
Stonewall, 319
Strachey, Lytton, 311
Strauss, Leo, 307
Strawson, P.F., 76–77, 218
string, 3–4, 12, 36, 195–96, 389
subjectivism
   in ethics, 264–65, 267–68
   in aesthetics, 308–12
   See also solipsism
subjectivity, 17, 25, 27, 137–38, 262–63, 303–308, 313–14, 331–32
sublimity, 193, 331–32
substance (*ousia*), 44–46, 62–63, 65–72
suicide, 117, 379
   Walking Stewart's, 57
superheroes, 220, 223
surveillance, 241, 337, 347, 355, 374, 381
swamping problem, 176–82, 397
Swift, Jonathan, 149
Syria, 73
system, general idea of, 13–15, 389

Taliban, 345
Taoism, 58, 115, 118, 221–25, 228, 270–83, 359
Tao Te Ching, 279–83
Tarski, Alfred, 87, 89–90, 92, 96, 107–108
taste, 196, 302
tattooing and piercing, 238, 312

taxation, 347, 352, 355
technē, 294, 295–96, 297
technocracy, 346, 348
technology, 274, 275, 279–83, 312–13, 380
teleology, 27, 58, 177–82, 205–206, 215, 298, 325
   and Asian philosophy, 279–93
   teleological ethics, 265, 268–74, 275–83
   and history, 274
tests, standardized, 6
Thales, 43
Thatcher, Margaret, 355, 358
theology, 162, 327
Thompson, Judith Jarvis, 259–62
Thoreau, Henry David, 20, 26, 41–42, 51, 52, 305, 365, 366, 370
   on personal identity, 60
   politics of, 367–69, 372, 374
Tibet, 48
T'ien, 59, 393
time, 17, 30, 38–39, 144, 196, 262, 263
   and the arts, 303
   and beauty, 306–308
   persistence through, 71–72
   and politics, 344–45
   travel, 275
Tolstoy, Leo, 298–99, 362, 364, 379, 380
tornadoes, ontology of, 64
torture, 271
totalitarianism, 220
   squishy, 28, 346–59
Turner, J. E., 129–30
tragedy, 14, 221
Transcendentalism, American, 361, 367, 368
   See also Alcott, Emerson, Mott, Thoreau
transgression, 208, 212, 273
translation, 8, 9, 31
tropes (Keith Campbell's notion), 69, 75–76, 87, 264
Trotsky, Leon, 358
truth, 4, 7, 9, 11, 12, 13, 24, 26, 30, chapter 2, 137–38, 143, 275, 283, 328
   in aesthetics, 193, 305, 307–308

truth *(continued)*
　and appearance, 46
　bearers, 82, 92, 100–108, 117, 145–46, 171, 183
　　and makers, 116–17
　　pictures as, 83
　　semantic and non-semantic, 83, 86, 90–91, 101, 103–104, 116
　and belief, 145–46
　cataract of diamonds, 15–16
　coherence theory of, 82, 83, 88
　conduciveness, 176–82
　correspondence theory of, 82, 83, 88, 90–91, 98
　definition of, 27, 82, 89–90, 108
　and ethics, 195, 201, 262, 265, 266, 269, 289
　etymology, 83–88
　Foucault on, 10
　identity theory of, 97–102
　and knowledge, 170–90
　makes girlfriend reach for pistol, 6
　Nietzsche on, 167
　pragmatic theory of, 7, 81, 117, 275–78
　recursive theory of, and related, 81–82, 83, 96, 107–108
　in science, 10
　situational account of, 97–100, 107–108
　truth-to, 84–85, 91
　as a virtue, 87–88, 110–19, 183–84, 193, 256, 285
Twain, Mark, 212
twelve-step programs, 230, 247, 332

United States, ontology of, 33, 243
Upanishads, 118, 183
utility and utilitarianism, 169, 241, 255, 265, 270–73, 275
　and art, 301
　utilitarian justifications of state power, 344
　principle of utility, 283, 285
utopia, 25, 28, chapter 6B, 375–78, 381–86

utterance/inscription (u/i), 77–78, 94–95, 100–109, 183, 184

vagueness, 62–65
Vaihinger, Hans, 22
values, 24–25, 27–28, 29, Part 2, 259
　aesthetic, 193–202, 261, 304–12. *See also* beauty, sublimity
　epistemic, 177–82, 193–95
　general treatment of, 193–202, 304–12
　historical development of, 194
　moral, 256–62
　ultimate (goodness, justice, truth, beauty), 4, 6, 11, 24, 193–95, 201–202, 213, 338
　See aesthetics, ethics, political philosophy
Vanderbilt, Cornelius, 347
Van Eyck, Jan, 327
Van Gogh, Vincent, 327, 335
Van Inwagen, Peter, 62, 65
Velazquez, Diego, 335
Velleius Paterculus, 245
Vermeer, Jan, 329, 330
virtue
　Aristotle on, 271
　epistemic, 159, 164, 168–70, 179, 184, 328
　ethics, 265–67, 269–70, 285–90
　and skill, 303
　Tao Te Ching on, 280–81
Voltaire, 361
voting rights, 340, 365

Wang Ch'ung, 58, 59, 60, 205
Wang Yang-Ming, 121–22, 147, 329
war, 279, 334–35, 352–55, 361, 363
Warhol, Andy, 211
Warren, Josiah, 361–62, 366, 369–71, 372, 374, 375, 376–78, 380
Waters, Muddy, 106
weirdness of the real, 13
Weitz, Morris, 295
Weld, Theodore Dwight, 361–62, 363

welfare programs, 346–47, 356
Whitehead, Alfred North, 68
whiteness, 32
Whitman, Walt, 376
Wiggins, David, 71–72
Wildebeests, 69
will, 212, 216–17, 297
Williams, Donald Cary, 76–77
Williams, Timothy, 145
Wilson, Bill (Bill W.), 332
Winfrey, Oprah, 272
Winik, Marion, 277
Wittgenstein, Ludwig, 6, 7, 8, 14, 15, 22, 26, 44, 76, 107, 197, 234
    on art, 295
    on knowledge, 152–58, 159, 161
    on language, 37, 93–94, 301
    and Moore, 149–58
    on propositions, 98
Woodhull, Victoria, 373
Woolf, Virginia, 310–11
Wolf, Susan, 217, 239–40
Wölfflin, Heinrich, 26, 139–41, 143, 274
Wollheim, Richard, 300–302
Woolman, John, 363, 368–69
Wordsworth, William, 50, 51–52, 305
work, 375
Wright, Betty, 292, 306
Wright, Henry Clarke, 363
wu wei (non-doing), 205–11

X-Men, 51

Yoakam, Dwight, 317–18
Yoruba, 385

Zagzebski, Linda, 180–81, 397
Zen, 34, 118, 122–23, 223, 282, 298
Zeno of Elea and Zeno's paradoxes, 54–55
Žižek, Slavoj, 358
Zhuangzi. *See* Chuang Tzu
Zurbaran, Francisco de, 326

www.ingramcontent.com/pod-product-compliance
Lightning Source LLC
Chambersburg PA
CBHW060241240426
43673CB00048B/1936